New Treasury of Bible Doctrine

'THINGS MOST SURELY BELIEVED'

New Treasury of Bible Doctrine

'THINGS MOST SURELY BELIEVED'

Edited by

Ken Totton

PRECIOUS SEED PUBLICATIONS

34 Metcalfe Avenue, Killamarsh, Sheffield, S21 1HW, UK

First published 1977

Revised and updated 2017
ISBN: 978-1-871642-1

Printed in the UK

Preface to 1977 Edition

We record our thankfulness to God for the continuing and developing interest in the publications ministry of *Precious Seed*. Notably, the volume *Church Doctrine and Practice* has established its own usefulness, as is indicated by the several reprints which have been called for since its first appearance in 1970. When that venture into the publication of a sizable book was first embarked on, a companion volume covering a more wide-ranging field of biblical teaching was already envisaged. This book, entitled *Treasury of Bible Doctrine*, marks the realization of that vision.

The wise man builds his house upon the rock by hearing and doing the things which the Lord has said. Christian practice must be based upon Christian principles and precepts. This book aims at presenting the doctrines of the Bible, those major elements of God's truth which may be considered profitably both analytically and synthetically. Hence, it supplements our earlier volume which deals with the doctrine of the church.

The many subjects of the present symposium are grouped under the following 'heads of doctrine': The Doctrine of the scriptures (8 chapters), The Doctrine of God (11 chapters), The Doctrine of Christ (27 chapters), The Doctrine of the Holy Spirit (7 chapters), The Doctrine of the Fall (7 chapters), The Doctrine of the Believer's Blessedness (22 chapters), and The Doctrine of the Last Things (14 chapters). The subdivision of the material into manageable units facilitates the consideration of these very large areas of truth. Further, the two indices, one of scripture references, which contributors have been encouraged to supply liberally, and the other a general index of the subjects and words treated, should prove useful in directing the student to the whole range of information in the book.

Material has been included which previously appeared in *Precious Seed*, though it must be remarked here that a large proportion of the contents have been specially commissioned and written. Here a wise scribe will find treasures, both new and old.

The objective has been to achieve a comprehensive treatment of the whole field of doctrine, along with that balance and variety characteristic of any edited symposium. Some of the chapters are more demanding than others, being written to stimulate personal research and further study, while others would prove more appealing to the general reader. Such variety of style and approach has the advantage of providing help for a wider range of readers. While unnecessary repetition has been eliminated in the coordinating processes, some slight over-lapping has been permitted so that individual contributors might produce a more rounded and complete end-product, and so that each paper may be read more or less independently. Also, the Editors have not imposed on contributors their own judgement on certain subjects or verses of scripture, so that they do not necessarily concur with all the considered opinions of the authors.

While the secret things belong to the Lord, the things that are revealed are for us and for our children. May the Spirit of truth use these handfuls 'profitable for doctrine' to enrich the understanding and deepen the devotion of the Lord's people until the Lord comes, and we shall know even as we are known.

1977

JOHN HEADING
CYRIL HOCKING

Preface to 2017 Edition

It is forty years since the *Treasury of Bible Doctrine* was published. It was warmly received at the time and has proved to be a very useful doctrinal resource for the Lord's people.

The task of scripture exposition continues, however, and during the intervening years much useful material has been published in *Precious Seed International* and its associated publications. Therefore, the Trust felt it was timely to issue a revised edition, retaining the value of the original, but adding important new topics.

Concerned that we live in an increasingly man-centred age, we have included a series of articles on the attributes of God, previously published under the title *Behold your God.* It has also been possible to address some gaps, with contributions on topics such as the unity of the Spirit, the personality and power of Satan, angels, the trial of faith, etc. In cases of overlap a few of the original papers have been removed in order to avoid an unwieldy book. The contents page identifies thirty papers new to this edition. In addition to this book, it should be noted that papers published by the Trust during the past seventy years are readily accessible at the *Precious Seed* website.

In publishing this new edition, we are conscious of its many shortcomings, but we pray that the Lord will graciously use it to establish rising generations of Christians in the timeless truths of scripture, 2 Tim. 2. 2.

2017 KEN TOTTON

Abbreviations

AMP	Amplified Bible
ASVmg	American Standard Version margin reading
ESV	English Standard Version
JND	New Translation – J. N. Darby
KJV	King James Version
LXX	Greek Septuagint version of the Old Testament
Nestle	Eberhard Nestle's Greek New Testament
NIV	New International Version
NKJV	New King James Version
NKJVmg	New King James Version margin reading
NT	New Testament
OT	Old Testament
RSV	Revised Standard Version
RV	Revised Version
RVmg	Revised Version margin reading

Contents

Articles marked with an asterisk are new to this edition

THE DOCTRINE OF THE SCRIPTURES

The Importance of Doctrine - C. E. Hocking

The Bible is the truth of God for all peoples, for there is one God, and for all time, because God is the King of the ages, the unchanging and eternal One. The Bible, however, is not simply a compendium of doctrine, nor are its doctrines arranged systematically. The wonder of God's word is that in it we are faced with an almost unstudied presentation of the loftiest of truths in order to spur us to the lowliest of duties, e.g., Phil. 2. 5-11. In the varying contexts of Israel's history, and amid the changing scenes of the foundation-laying processes in the early church, God unfolded the timeless treasures of divine revelation to those humble souls willing to do His will, cp. John 7. 17. It is still so.

The Meaning and Importance of Doctrine. In the New Testament there are three different words translated 'doctrine' in the King James Version. One of these, the word *logos,* is so translated only once, Heb. 6. 1. The marginal rendering here is 'word', which is adopted as the more usual English equivalent. It refers to the word spoken, as this in turn conveys the inward thought. The other two words, both springing from the same root, refer either to the actual **act of teaching**, or objectively to the subject-matter taught, **the substance of the teaching**. When we read that the word of God is profitable for doctrine, we are to understand that the man of God is to draw upon the subject-matter contained in the divine library if his life and ministry are to be complete, and equipped for every good work, 2 Tim. 3. 16-17. However, when Timothy was exhorted to give attendance to doctrine, we are to understand that he was **to devote himself to the public act of teaching** the believers, 1 Tim. 4. 13. The 'doctrines' considered in this book are an important part of that teaching material which should be understood, and taught among God's people. The range of truth covered here oversteps the boundaries to which the preachers, or heralds of the gospel restricted themselves. The preacher, *kerux*, gave himself to the preaching, *kerugma*, of Jesus Christ, that by the foolishness of preaching he might save some, Rom. 16. 25; 1 Cor. 1. 21. The teacher raised of God, *didaskalos*, was to give himself unreservedly to his teaching, *didaskalia*, Rom. 12. 7, with all longsuffering and teaching, *didachē*, 2 Tim. 4. 2.

The place given to teaching in the Bible indicates something of its importance. In the Old Testament the child was to be instructed regarding those things which God had revealed, Deut. 29. 29, and the parent was to be ready to inform and explain whenever his son questioned a practice.[1] Because the preacher was wise, he still taught the people knowledge, Eccles. 12. 9, while Ezra made capital of that occasion when the people gathered together to hear the word ensuring that they understood the reading, Neh. 8. 8. The priest's lips kept knowledge, and the people were to seek the law at his mouth, Mal. 2. 7. In the New Testament the Lord commissioned the apostles to teach those who had been baptized 'to observe all things whatsoever I have commanded you', Matt. 28. 20. Paul, too, reminds the Ephesian elders that he had taught publicly and from house to house, Acts 20. 20, for it was the word of God which was able to build them up, v. 32. The elder in the assembly was to be the one 'holding to the faithful word which is according to the teaching, that he may be able both to exhort in the sound doctrine, and to convict the gainsayers', Titus 1. 9 RV. The teaching of the Bible is the God-given foundation upon which the good, the godly, and the Christ-like character may be built, while also providing all that is necessary for the development of gift and the complete equipment of the man of God for his God-appointed sphere of service.

The Teaching Material and Method. Paul reminds the Corinthians that, while he had planted the work there, and Apollos had followed up with watering that which had been planted, it was God Himself that had given the increase, 1 Cor. 3. 6. What guarantees does the sovereign disposition of God afford to us! Yet we are not to ignore those ministries through human vessels which were crowned by the increase of God. The assembly having been planted under the good hand of God, now needed to be watered and nurtured by those equipped of God. The single act of planting had to be followed up by the continuous process of watering. The water that was used was the word of God. Line upon line, the faith once-for-all delivered, the truth which is according to godliness, the word, the doctrine according to godliness, as it is variously described, was imparted.

---

[1] Exod. 12. 26, 27; Deut. 6. 20-25.

This included systematic instruction in the Old Testament. While Jewish believers, and even proselytes, could be expected to be familiar with this, the many accretions of their scribes, which were nothing more than the commandments of men,[2] called for the unlearning of much with which they were familiar. Again, the quite revolutionary insight into Old Testament interpretation unveiled by the Lord, Luke 24. 27, 44, 45, demanded a fresh handling of the well-known if there was to be a full understanding of the present phase of God's dealings with men. But then, there were many Gentiles in the assemblies with no knowledge of the Hebrew Bible, converts from idolatry with all the 'hang-over' problems that this could bring. The early church teachers applied themselves to this situation, using the Old Testament. The frequent references to the Old Testament writings in the addresses of Acts, and even in the Epistles addressed to believers who were mainly of Gentile stock, are quite striking.[3] Patently, 'whatsoever things were written aforetime were written for our learning', Rom. 15. 4. Even when the apostles refer to the scriptures as inspired, it is to the Old Testament that they essentially point.[4]

To this firmly established canon, the early teachers added the sayings of Christ Himself during His ministry among men. Clearly, Acts chapter 20 verse 35 and 1 Timothy chapter 5 verse 18 are examples of this, and also that which lies behind 1 Corinthians chapter 11 verses 23. There are other verses which give similar hints, but all of the oral and written tradition which had the lasting approval of God became incorporated permanently in the records of the four Gospels which open our New Testament.

To these must be added the revelations given to apostles and prophets, given as the need arose in the early church. All of these which would be necessary throughout the whole course of church history were ultimately enshrined in the New Testament Epistles. The form of sound words heard from the apostles were committed to other faithful men, 2 Tim. 1. 13; 2. 2. Not only were the words of the holy prophets to be remembered, but God's people were also called to obey 'the

[2] Matt. 15. 9; Mark 7. 7; Col. 2. 22.

[3] See, for example, 1 Cor. 10. 1-11; 2 Cor. 3. 7; Gal. 4. 21-31; Rom. 9-11.

[4] 2 Tim. 3. 16; 2 Pet. 1. 21.

commandment of us the apostles of the Lord and Saviour', 2 Pet. 3. 2. Hence, in the process of time, Paul's Epistles were classified with the 'other scriptures', vv. 15, 16. Now we have in our hands the completed New Testament canon, and the faith once-for-all delivered to the saints has been handed down firm and unalterable, Jude 3.[5]

In New Testament times, they were not only concerned to guard the deposit committed to them, 1 Tim. 6. 20, but they gave themselves unstintingly to the teaching of the whole counsel of God. Barnabas and Saul felt justified in devoting a whole year to the instruction and exhortation of the converts at Antioch, Acts 11. 22-26. Paul, encouraged by the Lord concerning His purpose in blessing for Corinth, taught the word of God among them for some eighteen months, 18. 9-11. He had a more extended ministry at Ephesus, 19. 8, 10; 20. 31, with even greater results, for 'all they which dwelt in Asia heard the word', and not surprisingly we read, 'so mightily grew the word of the Lord and prevailed', 19. 10, 20 RV. Some years later Timothy was exhorted to stay at Ephesus, and was to 'give heed to reading, to exhortation, to teaching', 1 Tim. 4. 13 RV. Nor was such work to be restricted to the visits of those specially equipped of God. In each assembly there were elders who were apt to teach, and these were to 'labour in the word and in teaching', 5. 17 RV.

Apart from such consecutive teaching of the word, assemblies will wane, gifts will not be fully developed, and individual believers will grow cold. The assembly, in one aspect, should function as a school, and the long-term and short-term needs of believers should be prayerfully considered and met by those raised of God to do so. We are not left in doubt as to the curriculum, for that which is profitable for all is the whole counsel of God, Acts. 20. 20, 27. Only this is able to build up, and foster spiritual growth, v. 32; 1 Pet. 2. 2. Of course, a classroom atmosphere is not the ideal, neither is the development of a *merely* academic knowledge of divine truth. The manner in which the writers of the Epistles gave themselves to heart-warming and challenging ministry is an object lesson for all time. Let instruction be inextricably interwoven with exhortation, and doctrine with duty. Along with

[5] See also Luke 1. 1-4; Rom. 6. 17; 1 Cor. 11. 23; 15. 3; 2 Thess. 2. 15; 1 Tim. 4. 6; 2 Tim. 1. 13; 2. 2.

teaching (doctrine), there must also be reproof, correction, and instruction in righteousness, 2 Tim. 3. 16. The work is never finished, we never arrive at the ultimate. The Lord is not concerned that His people merely be taught all things. A somewhat academic syllabus could be devised to meet this need. Rather He defines the objective for His servants as 'teaching them to observe all things whatsoever I have commanded you', Matt. 28. 20. The doctrine of scripture is 'according to godliness', designed not only to inform but to promote a life well-pleasing to God, 1 Tim. 6. 3.

There is much abroad which is 'contrary to sound ['healthful'] doctrine', 1. 10, even 'the doctrines of demons', 4. 1 RVmg. Many of God's people are 'tossed to and fro, and carried about with every wind of doctrine', Eph. 4. 14. There are divisions and occasions of stumbling through teaching that is 'contrary to the doctrine which ye have learned', Rom. 16. 17, and 'the time will come when they will not endure sound doctrine', 2 Tim. 4. 3. We must seek, therefore, to be 'nourished in the words of the faith, and of the good doctrine', 1 Tim. 4. 6 RV, to 'give attendance . . . to doctrine', v. 13, to 'take heed . . . unto the doctrine', 4. 16, to 'labour in the word and doctrine', 5. 17, to speak 'the things which become sound doctrine', Titus 2. 1, taking care so to live 'that the name of God and his doctrine be not blasphemed', 1 Tim. 6. 1, and that we 'may adorn the doctrine of God our Saviour in all things', Titus 2. 10, being examples of good works in all things while 'in doctrine shewing uncorruptness, gravity . . . sound speech, that cannot be condemned', 2. 7, 8. We must continue 'steadfastly in the apostles' doctrine', Acts 2. 42, abiding always in 'the doctrine of Christ', 2 John 9.

The Scriptures of Truth - E. W. Rogers

It is to be feared that in these ever busy days the study of the scriptures is being neglected by young believers. Yet we are enjoined to 'search the scriptures', John 5. 39, to 'give attention to [the public] reading [of the scriptures]', 1 Tim. 4. 13, 'to give the more earnest heed to' them, Heb. 2. 1. We have 'Moses and the prophets' and we should listen to them, Luke 16. 29.

It may, however, be asked, '**Is the Bible reliable?**', to which question an undoubted affirmative may be given. 'For ever, O Lord, thy word is settled in heaven', Ps. 119. 89. 'Heaven and earth shall pass away: but my words shall not pass away', Luke 21. 33. 'The scripture cannot be broken', John 10. 35. A vessel which has been broken into sundry pieces is no longer useful for its original purpose. But this cannot happen to the scriptures of truth: they are a homogeneous whole and are indestructibly held together.

A lawyer, in studying and acting upon a legal document, has to be concerned not with what he supposed the original writer intended but with what he has actually written. It is **the words** that concern him. He must abide by what is written and act accordingly. So, too, in the case of the Bible. It is of the utmost importance that we should observe what it says, not what we think it should say or what we imagine the original writer may have intended. What is written is a rock foundation: all speculations concerning it are dangerous quicksands.

But in reading the scriptures it is necessary that the mind should be properly adjusted. 'The natural man receiveth not the things of the Spirit of God'. Not that we must be inspired in order to understand it, as some have asserted. The inspiration of the writers was unique to themselves, but in order to apprehend the truth of God (as distinct from conviction being brought to the mind by the scripture) we need the indwelling of His Spirit. They are foolishness to the unregenerate man, but to those who are Spirit-taught they become the unequalled exposition of the mind and purpose of God throughout the ages.

The implication of this becomes obvious: to receive the Bible as the authoritative and unerring word of God is to become possessed of all those promises so richly strewn here and there throughout the volume. Not those promises which relate to other parties and other times; we must be careful to discriminate and not to purloin. But there are a vast number of promises made to believers of our present day which, if the scriptures are accepted unreservedly as God's own written utterances, may be enjoyed by faith and realization. Similar remarks may be made, *mutatis mutandis,* concerning their warnings. In a word, the scripture means what it says and says what it means; its promises are open for the enjoyment of the believer and its warnings stand there as a caution to all.

The inspiration of scripture is plainly affirmed therein, but its process will ever remain a mystery. Seeing that the Bible is a living thing, like all other living things, the mystery of the origin of its being must remain unsolved. The inspiration of scripture is far different from that of a great poet or painter. Nor is it mere mechanical dictation. That would destroy the 'human element' which we discern throughout it. Like the living word, the Lord Jesus (who indeed is the very heart of scripture), the Bible is at once divine and human. Divine, in that it came from God. Human, in that it was given through fallible men who, for the time being, became the penmen of the Holy Ghost to write infallible words. The circumstances of the times in which the various writers lived, and their particular relations to individuals or communities, furnished special opportunity for their writings, be they essays, treatises, or letters. Therein may be seen evidences of the feelings of the human penmen: their indignation, sorrows, misgivings, tears, perplexity, and so on. It is utterly impossible to disentangle the divine from the human. It would entail the destruction of the book.

The Scriptures Affirm their own Inspiration. Time and again we read the phrase 'thus saith the Lord' or similar phrases. Daniel claims again and again (see Daniel chapter 2) that God reveals His mind to men. The rationalist cannot accept the doctrine of revelation. He will not concede that the God who has created man does at times reveal Himself to man. But this is a cardinal item in the doctrine of inspiration. It presumes **revelation**. Else one may ask, how did Moses (or his informants) learn of the original creation seeing that no one of the human race was existent in the beginning of things? Many other things, also, are disclosed in scripture which are altogether unascertainable by human investigation. It would take far too long to enumerate all these things: almost every page of the Bible at some point or other touches upon those things which man, by all his searching, could never discover.

God is the Source of Scripture: the writers were the channels. This is significantly stated by Matthew when he constantly used the phrase 'spoken **by** the Lord **through** the prophet'. God is the speaker: the prophets were the medium. It is so both with the old and new covenants. In the upper room discourse the Lord Jesus told His disciples that the Holy Spirit, whom He would send from the Father, would do three things: (a) He would bring all things to their remembrance, thus enabling them to record the deeds, discourses and sufferings of the Lord Jesus without error, or distortion; (b) He would take of the things of Christ and show them to them, thus enabling them to disclose to the early Christians those massive spiritual truths to be found in the Epistles; (c) He would show them things to come, thus enabling them to disclose the future as is done in the book of Revelation.

This is dealt with by Paul in 1 Corinthians chapter 2. His remarks may be summarized under the three words 'revelation', 'communication', and 'explanation'. What Paul wrote was not that which he had seen with his natural eye: nor was it hearsay: nor was it the product of his uncontrolled imagination, but God had **revealed** it by His Spirit.

Paul further claims that the very words he used were a spiritual means of **communicating** these spiritual truths. Such would appear to be the sense of 1 Corinthians chapter 2 verse 13. The scriptures are not the sophisticated writings of clever men: they are the teachings of the Spirit and these teachings, 'spiritual things', are communicated by 'spiritual means'.

Thus Paul elsewhere calls it 'the word of the Lord', 1 Thess. 4. 15. The Thessalonians received his message 'not as the word of men, but as . . . the word of God' as, indeed, it actually was, 2. 13. Paul is so sure of his ground that he ranks his Epistles on a level in authority with the Old Testament scriptures which were read in the synagogue. He enjoins that this and other Epistles of his should be read 'in the churches', 5. 27; Col. 4. 16.

The plural should be noted in John chapter 17 verse 8 and 1 Corinthians chapter 2 verse 13. It is 'words', not 'word' in these passages. Nothing could be plainer in its affirmation of verbal inspiration. It is not sufficient to suggest that the thoughts were inspired and that the writers were left to clothe those thoughts in words which they deemed to be most suitable. Everyone knows that that is a dangerous process. No businessman would leave his secretary to express in her own words the thoughts which he has in his mind unless they be of the simplest and most inconsequential character. And is it to be supposed that God would entrust fallible man to express His thoughts, which are of the highest importance and eternal in their issues?

'All scripture is God-breathed'. What applies to one part applies to the whole. It is sufficient to say that the word 'scripture', whether in the singular or plural, is **always** used in the Bible of the sacred writings and of nothing else. The Revised Version, therefore, 'every scripture', would seem to imply otherwise. We have in our Bible a complete compendium of all the writings of God and in every part it is God's voice to man. It follows, therefore, that it must be 'profitable'. The reader should consult 2 Timothy chapter 3 verses 16, 17 in this connection.

Features of scripture. The Bible is in many respects **unlike all other books**. Men who write books are supposed to understand what they write, but the 'Spirit of Christ' who was in the old-time prophets caused them to write things which, afterwards, they themselves had to search and inquire into, in order to ascertain their meaning and to what times and what parties they related. How odd, it may seem, that this was the case. But they were tools in the Spirit's hand and wrote beyond their time and understanding.

Consequently, **no prophecy of scripture can be interpreted isolated from the bulk of all other scripture**, as Peter later stated, 2 Pet. 1. 20, 21. In the beginning it did not owe its origin to a prophet determining to write a book. It did not become of its or anyone's own unfolding. Rather, men from God, were borne along by the Holy Spirit, as ships are borne along under the force of the wind at sea, and that which they spoke or wrote was the very word of God.

We rightly expect a man nowadays to explain his own writings. But as to the Old Testament scriptures, no writer could claim an exclusive monopoly in the interpretation thereof, if for no other reason than that he was not the author. It is the author who explains and to whom we may appeal for an explanation. Seeing that the Holy Spirit is the author of all scripture, it follows that it is by His power alone that we may interpret them. John puts this thus, 'Ye have an unction from the Holy One and ye know all things', 1 John 2. 20.

The scriptures are **reliable** in their promises; **true** as to their statement of facts; **authoritative** as to their origin; and **inevitable** as to their foreshadowings. They lie **open** to the understanding of the believer;

and are so **complete** that we are forbidden three times either to add to them or to take from them.[6]

The Bible is a **homogeneous whole**. It is impossible at any time to secure absolute agreement between scientific men on one particular subject, and this becomes more marked if we listen to professional men who lived in different times and in different countries. But the Bible touches all kinds of subjects, and was written by men who lived at different times, were of different occupations, resided in different countries, and yet one and all agree, each with the other, without the slightest possibility of collusion or collaboration.

The subject of **fulfilled prophecy** is a vast one but the fact that the New Testament in so many details records the historical fulfilment of Old Testament prophecy shows the unity of scripture and demonstrates that one mastermind was behind each of the various writers. Shepherd, farm labourer, doctor, tax collector, rabbi, fisherman, and others, all had their share in the production, yet had no communication one with the other. Notwithstanding, the production was, in every part, in agreement with the other. The very existence of the Bible is proof of its divine origin, for no one person or no persons together could produce such a book. Its survival, despite all the attempts to destroy it, shows it to be of God. For if this work be of God you cannot destroy it. Its effects upon the lives of individuals and the character of peoples, clearly mark it out as being supernatural. By it inquisitors have been made disciples; the vicious have been made gracious; the wild have been tamed; and the corrupt have been cleansed.

It will bear microscopic investigation as well as a panoramic survey. Its very **tenses** are inspired, as witness John chapter 8 verse 58. Correct grammar would have demanded the words, 'Before Abraham was, I was', but correct doctrine demands the alteration of the tense to the present I AM. The **number** in which a particular word is found is important, as witness Galatians chapter 3 verse 16: not 'seeds' as of many, but 'seed' as relating to one. There were other words available to the Spirit of God such as 'sons' or 'generation', but God selected 'seed'

---

[6] Deut. 12. 32; Prov. 30. 6; Rev. 22. 18, 19.

because it can bear both a singular and plural sense: it is, indeed, a multitude-singular. Again the doctrine of the Trinity is to be found, veiled it is agreed, in the use of a plural noun with a singular verb, Gen. 1. 1, 'God (plural) created (singular)'.

The **omission** of certain facts is not by accident but by design, as witness the teaching elicited by the writer to the Hebrews touching Melchizedek in Hebrews chapter 7. The 'silences of scripture are like the pauses in music: they add to its harmony'. We dare not fill them in without running the risk of spoiling the handiwork of God.

Old Testament quotations are used in the New Testament to a new purpose. There are no misquotations. An author has the right to quote from his first work in a later work to a different purpose, and as he will. All such differences are most instructive though space does not permit of our examining any. But reference may be made to the Greek Septuagint (LXX) of Genesis chapter 5 verse 22 where, instead of 'walked with God' we read 'pleased God'. The one is cause and the other effect. Also in Hebrews 10 where 'a body hast thou prepared me' is substituted for 'mine ears hast thou digged', Heb. 10. 5; Ps. 40. 6-8. Here we have the LXX's paraphrase approved by the Spirit and used in a later writing. Likewise, the omission of the latter part of Psalm 24 verse 1, because that latter part relates to millennial times, but the former – quoted by Paul, 1 Cor. 10. 26 – is as true today as when Paul wrote. Also in Romans chapter 10 verse 15 the pronoun 'him' of Isaiah chapter 5 verses 2-7 is altered by Paul to 'them' to accord with the present missionary charter of the scriptures. And so we might go on.

The Bible is the word of God. But **not all in the scriptures is, in the first instance, a statement made by God**. Sometimes Satan is the speaker: sometimes man in his perversity, such as Balaam; sometimes it is an ass that speaks. But the record of all this is God's word to us. It is not correct to say that the Bible contains the word of God. In all its parts it is the word of God. But it contains also the utterances of men, which utterances in many instances do not represent what is true. The record is true: but the statements may be far from the truth, and in this way God shows the blindness and wickedness of men and others, whilst He demonstrates His own faithfulness.

Much has been made of **alleged errors** in the scripture, but if we possessed all the data we should see that no such errors occur. Because one Gospel says there was one blind man and another Gospel says there were two, it does not follow there is a mistake. Certainly if there were two, there was one! **Copyists' errors** are few and not of such a character or number as to affect any doctrine of our faith. **Numerical inconsistencies** there may appear to be, but do we know all there is to be known of ancient numerology?

The critics have done their utmost to smash the validity of the scriptures, but their critical hammers have been broken on the anvil of the word of God. The impregnable rock of holy scripture still stands, despite all the raging of the furious tempests of hostile criticism. The simplest may read the Bible and derive food for the soul, comfort for the heart, and rest for the dying. Likewise those who have soared high into the realms of the sciences may find the scriptures to be their comfort in sorrow and peace in stormy days, provided they are willing to 'become fools that they may be wise'.

What other book can claim to have had **so many minds engrossed with it** over so many centuries and with such close investigation as the Bible? It is surely the best book of all.

The devoted labours of its **translators** would form a separate volume. Many have laid down their lives in so doing, while before making the supreme sacrifice they have had to flee hither and thither for safety. In their work they deemed accuracy in detail essential. We must, in our times, beware lest we become content with inadequate paraphrases with the consequent forfeiture of accuracy, in order to accommodate our thinking to modern development. God providentially caused His words to be written in what have for long been **dead languages**, so that their meaning has not been subject to the fluctuations of living languages. We can ascertain with precision what He intended by His carefully chosen words. That meaning remains unaltered.

Like the works of creation **holy scripture is infinite**. Psalm 19 speaks of both. But things are attributed to the written word of God that could not be said of the tangible creation around us. The Bible is far **more precious** than the finest gold; let us value it. It is far, far **sweeter** than the choicest honey; let us then enjoy it.

The Inspiration of the Scriptures - E. L. LOVERING

'Inspiration' – a fascinating word and so full of meaning! But what does it mean? Some will say, SHAKESPEARE was 'inspired' to write his plays, BACON his essays, TENNYSON his poetry, HANDEL his music. Though this is true in part, it is not the kind of inspiration with which we are now concerned, for that originated in the mind and emotions of the writers themselves.

What then do we mean when we speak of the scriptures being inspired? We mean the manner in which God communicated His thoughts and words to the writers of the scriptures. Apart from the writing on the wall during Belshazzar's impious feast, we read of only two occasions when deity wrote – (a) upon tables of stone in law, and 'the writing was the writing of God' written with 'the finger of God', Exod. 31. 18; 32. 16, and (b) upon the temple floor in grace when 'Jesus stooped down, and with his finger wrote on the ground', John 8. 6, 8.

How then were the words of holy scripture placed on record? Broadly, the theories of inspiration are three in number:

The Mechanical Theory, by which we mean that the writer, like a recording tape, placed on record a mechanical dictation from God. If, however, we carefully read the books of the Bible we cannot but notice that, whilst they are stamped by the mark of deity, they also reflect the individuality of the writers themselves. In **Luke** we note the careful detail of the doctor; in **John** the sentiments of the apostle of love; and in **the Letters of Paul** the mind of the cultured scholar.

The Liberal Theory interprets this as suggesting a possibility of human error.

It is clear from the scriptures themselves that neither of these theories is the correct one.

The Dynamical Theory, as it is sometimes called, is surely the correct answer, for Peter tells us in his letter that 'no prophecy of scripture is of special interpretation. For no prophecy ever came by the will of man: but men spake from God, being moved [or borne along] by the Holy Spirit', 2 Pet. 1. 20, 21 ASVmg.

Further, let us note that it is not the writers only who were inspired of God, but the writings themselves, for Paul tells us all scripture is inspired of God (or is God-breathed) and is profitable for teaching, for reproof, for correction, for discipline which is in righteousness, 2 Tim. 3. 16.

What then of

Verbal inspiration? Some may say that God inspired not the words of holy scripture but the thoughts, leaving the writers to choose their own words. This is not true, for God always gave the words, though He did not always give the thoughts. The prophets who wrote of Christ did not fully understand what they wrote, but inquired and searched diligently the matter for themselves, 1 Pet. 1. 10, 11.

In Daniel chapter 12 verses 8-9 we read that the prophet 'heard, but understood not' and God commanded him to go his way for 'the words are closed up and sealed till the time of the end'.

Testimonies to inspiration. Four instances of testimony to the inspiration and veracity of the scriptures occur to us:

(1) **The spade** – external evidence. Again and again recent discoveries in exploration have proved the truth of holy scripture, but space will not permit us here to discourse upon them.

(2) **The scriptures** – internal evidence. We have already referred to 2 Pet. 1. 21 and 2 Tim. 3. 16; but here are some others:

- 2 Sam. 23. 2: 'The Spirit of the Lord spake by me and his word was in my tongue';
- Jer. 1. 7, 9: 'Whatsoever I command thee thou shalt speak – behold, I have put my words in thy mouth';
- Ezek. 2. 7: 'Thou shalt speak my words unto them';
- Acts 1. 16: 'The Holy Spirit by the mouth of David spoke concerning Judas'.

Such passages might easily be multiplied, as any concordance will show.

(3) **The Saviour** – eternal evidence. And if no other testimony existed, surely this would be sufficient.

- Matt. 5. 18: 'Verily I say unto you, Till heaven and earth pass, one jot or one tittle shall in no wise pass from the law, till all be fulfilled'.

This asserts that not only are the words from God but even the fractional parts of the letters themselves.

- John 10. 35: 'The scripture cannot be broken'.
- Luke 24. 44: 'All things must be fulfilled, which were written in the **law of Moses**, and in the **prophets**, and in the **psalms**, concerning me'; this takes in the whole range of Old Testament scripture, as expressed by the Jew.

To those on the Emmaus road the Saviour said, 'O foolish ones and slow of heart to believe **all** that the prophets have spoken', and then 'beginning from Moses and **all** the prophets he interpreted to them in **all** the scriptures, the things concerning himself', Luke 24. 25-27 NKJV.

(4) **The Sinner** - practical evidence. To the foregoing undoubted testimonies we may add yet our own; for we who were 'dead in trespasses and sins' have been made alive by the living, life-giving word of God, the 'incorruptible seed, which liveth and abideth for ever', 1 Pet. 1. 23.

Cling to the Bible! – this jewel and treasure
Brings life eternal, and saves fallen man;
Surely its value no mortal can measure:
Seek for its blessing, O soul, while you can!

M. J. SMITH

The Sufficiency and Finality of the Scriptures -

W. E. VINE

All quotations taken from the Revised Version

We meet not infrequently with the opinion that the Bible was not intended to be a complete guide in the matters of doctrine and practice throughout the present era. Some hold that, while the scriptures are of divine origin and authority, they were not a final revelation, and that the authority of the church would be such as to provide for additional doctrines and guidance. Others hold that truths essential for Christians in the early days may not be essential in the changed circumstances of modern times; in other words, that the advance of civilization has rendered much of the apostolic teaching out of date.

Now the Epistle of Jude declares that the faith was 'once for all delivered unto the saints', v. 3; 'once for all' is the correct translation, as in the Revised Version. The King James Version 'once' might mean 'once upon a time'; the word *hapax* in the original will not bear that meaning, which is represented by *pote.* Since the faith has been delivered 'once for all', it is obvious that it was not the divine intention for it to receive addition or modification. The faith is contained in the Bible as we have it handed down to us. To attempt to add to it or readjust it or to issue additional decrees as if they were of divine authority, is to impugn the perfect work of the Holy Spirit and to be guilty of presumptuous impiety. It is doubtless with this in view that a warning against tampering with scripture is given three times in the Book. The first is in the injunction given to Israel. 'Ye shall not add unto the word which I command you, neither shall ye diminish from it', Deut. 4. 2; 12. 32. The second is in Proverbs chapter 30 verses 5, 6, 'Every word of God is tried . . . add thou not unto his words, lest he reprove thee and thou be found a liar'. The third is in the Apocalypse where the warning is given, 'I testify unto every man that heareth the words of the prophecy of this book, if any man shall add unto them, God shall add unto him the plagues which are written in this book: and if any man shall take away from the words of the book of this prophecy, God shall take away his part from the tree of life, and out of the holy city, which are written in this book', Rev. 22. 18-19. This last refers, of course, immediately to the contents of the Apocalypse, but taking the three passages together they constitute a prohibition against any attempt to extend or diminish any of the contents of the word of God.

The Apostle Paul gives clear intimation of the finality and permanency of scripture. He instructs Timothy to give a charge that no other doctrine was to be taught, 1 Tim. 1. 3; he was to guard, through the Holy

Spirit, that which had been committed to him, 2 Tim. 1. 13, 14. The things he had heard from Paul he was to commit to faithful men, that they might be able to teach others also. The duty devolving upon him therefore was to maintain the truth, not to produce more. Again, he predicates in 2 Timothy chapter 3 verses 16 and 17 the absolute sufficiency of scripture. In declaring both that it is God-breathed, and that thereby 'the man of God may be complete, furnished completely unto every good work', he enforces both the divine origin and authority of the scriptures and their finality in doctrine. If a man of God by their means was thus to be complete and completely furnished, no additional doctrine was required, or was expected. The apostles warn believers to abide in the teaching already given them. The Apostle John says, 'Let that therefore abide in you which ye have heard from the beginning', 1 John 2. 24; and Paul, 'Continue thou in the things which thou hast learned', 2 Tim. 3. 14 (see also 1 Tim. 6. 20).

Certain teachings in 1 Corinthians have been regarded by some as applicable merely to the church to which that Epistle was addressed. It was written, however, not only to that church, but to 'all that in every place call upon the name of Jesus Christ our Lord', 1 Cor. 1. 2. Many of its teachings are the foundations of the faith, and what was of local application contains principles essential for churches at all times. As to the injunction in the chapters 11-14 regarding the conduct and arrangements of church meetings, concerning, for instance, oral ministry, the exercise of gift, the silence of women, and the regulation as to their wearing a covering for the head, the apostle says that the things which he was writing were 'the commandments of the Lord'. Again, in chapter 4 verse 17 and chapter 7 verse 17 he says that what he is inculcating is what he teaches in every church.

The Apostle John insists upon adherence to the faith as follows, 'Whosoever goeth onward and abideth not in the teaching of Christ, hath not God . . . if anyone cometh unto you, and bringeth not this teaching, receive him not into your house, and give him no greeting', 2 John 9, 10. It imposes an undue limitation on the phrase 'the teaching of Christ' to make it refer merely to one doctrine concerning Him. From this it will be seen that 'the teaching of Christ' is all the divine revelation concerning Him, and this is 'the truth' of which the apostle says in verses 1 and 2 'shall be with us for ever'. He makes a startling claim for the teaching given by himself and his fellow-apostles, a claim which, were it not valid, would be nothing short of presumption, but which, in point of fact, bears witness both to his divine authority and the completeness of the doctrines of scripture. He says, 'We are of God: he that knoweth God heareth us; he who is not of God heareth us not. By this we know the spirit of truth, and the spirit of error', 1 John 4. 6. From this, obviously, the teachings of the apostles are the standard by which to judge what is true or false in doctrine. Therefore what is not corroborated by the New Testament has not the authority of God.

By the word of God we are to be judged hereafter; for it is given as the standard of our life and for our obedience to the faith. How important therefore it is to see that our ways are directed in adherence to the scriptures, both in private life, and in dealing with our fellow-men! Important too, that in matters relating to the church we should follow not the traditions and tenets of men, but the scriptures of truth! Being the handiwork of the Spirit of God, who Himself has come to guide us into all truth, as our Lord promised, the scriptures are infallible counsellors. Being sufficient and final as the complete word of God, they should be sufficient and final for us in everything in the regulation of all our affairs. Let our appeal be, 'What saith the scripture?' and, having received an answer, be it ours to say, 'I cannot go beyond the word of the Lord my God, to do less or more'. Thus in the fulfilment of His 'good and acceptable and perfect will' shall we be able to say, 'I have kept the faith', and shall look forward with confidence to receive from our Lord His commendation, 'Thou didst keep my word, and didst not deny my name'.

The Inspiration and Authority of the Holy Scriptures* - J. MITCHELL

The purpose of this paper is to provide several positive reasons for believing that the holy scriptures are verbally inspired by God and are therefore of final and binding authority.

The inspiration and authority of the Old Testament. There is much evidence from within the Old Testament itself that it was regarded as having authority. The law, as embodied in the first five books of the Bible, was undoubtedly recognized as authoritative in later books of the

Old Testament.[7] In many of the prophetical books of the Old Testament we often find expressions like 'thus saith the Lord' or 'the word of the Lord came to me saying', showing how the authority of God lay behind the prophet. Observe also how Daniel clearly recognized the authoritative nature of the prophecy of Jeremiah, Dan. 9. 2.

The Lord's Acceptance of the Old Testament. The Lord regarded the Old Testament as having divine and lasting authority over men. He often introduced quotations from the Old Testament with the expression, 'It is written', which has the force, 'It stands written'. In saying this the Lord not only drew attention to the actual quotation but also to its abiding efficacy.[8] In this connection we can note the use of the present tense, Matt. 13. 14 and Luke 20. 42, and the striking words, 'unto you', Matt. 22. 31.

The Lord Jesus did not derive His authority from the Rabbis or from the traditional teaching of the scribes about religion; see Matt. 7. 28, 29. He relied rather on the Old Testament. Indeed on occasions He went so far as to contrast the current teaching of His day with the scriptures, 15. 1-6; Mark 7. 1-13. His constant attitude to the Old Testament can be determined from such passages as Matthew chapter 5 verses 17 and 18 and John chapter 10 verses 34 and 35. In Matthew chapter 19 verses 4 and 5, He attributed the words of Moses, Gen. 2. 24, to God Himself. Compare Romans chapter 9 verse 17, where Paul attributed to 'scripture' the words of God, Exod. 9. 16.

The Lord's resistance to the temptations which He faced in the wilderness, Matt. 4. 1-11, established that He fully accepted the authority of the Old Testament relative to Himself. He would obey God's voice as expressed in scripture, and certainly not the voice of Satan. In this lay His victory, compare 1 John 2. 14b. We can also note His willing submission to scripture at the critical time described in Matthew chapter 26 verses 53 to 56.

The Lord ever stressed the importance of a true understanding of the

---

[7] Josh. 1. 7, 8; 1 Kgs. 2. 3; 2 Kgs. 14. 6; Mal. 4. 4.
[8] See Matt. 11. 10; Luke 22. 37; John 6. 45.

Old Testament.[9] Over against the Pharisees and scribes, who regarded themselves as the sole custodians of the correct interpretation of the Old Testament, He presented Himself as its true expositor, Luke 24. 27, 32, 45.

Beyond doubt the Lord accepted the historicity and reliability of the Old Testament. Observe His references to the union of Adam and Eve, Matt 19. 4-5; Abel, 23. 35; Noah and Lot, Luke 17. 26-32; Abraham, John 8. 56; Moses, 3. 14; Jonah, Matt. 12. 39; Daniel, 24. 15.

The Acceptance of the Old Testament by the Early Church. The early church followed the Lord in accepting the Old Testament as divinely authoritative. To them the Old Testament provided:

(1) Written Authority. They reasoned with the Jews by appealing to the Old Testament scriptures.[10] Tremendous stress is placed in their writings upon the authority of that which was written in the Old Testament.[11]

(2) Present Authority. As in the case of the Lord, the recurring expression 'It is written' stresses the lasting value of the scriptures, as does also the use of the present tense.[12] There are also many passages where it is clearly stated that the Old Testament was written with New Testament times in mind.[13] We can also compare James' appeal to the Old Testament as decisive in the great circumcision controversy, Acts 15. 13-18.

(3) Clear Predictions of Christ.[14] The believers recognized that the Old Testament required careful and spiritual interpretation. This is apparent from the explanation of Isaiah chapter 53 verses 7 to 8 which Philip gave to the Ethiopian eunuch, Acts 8. 30-35. By the help and guidance of the Holy Spirit, he was enabled to point the eunuch to Christ

---

[9] For example, Matt. 9. 13; 12. 3-8; 21. 42; 22. 23-33; 24. 15.

[10] Acts 17. 2, 3, 11; 18. 28; 28. 23.

[11] Mark 1. 2; Rom. 1. 2; 2 Tim. 3. 16; 1 Pet. 2. 6; 2 Pet. 1. 20.

[12] Rom. 4. 3; 9. 25, 27; Gal. 4. 30; Heb. 8. 13.

[13] For example, Acts 7. 38; 13. 47; Rom. 4. 22-24; 15. 4; 1 Cor. 10. 11.

[14] Examples of this can be found in: Acts 2. 25-31; 3. 18, 24; 26. 22, 23; 1 Pet. 1. 10, 11.

through his reading of the Old Testament.

One book which sheds great light on the attitude of the New Testament writers to the Old Testament is the Epistle to the Hebrews. The many references to the Old Testament demonstrate the exceedingly high regard the writer had for it. In fact, the writer quotes freely from the following Old Testament books – Genesis, Exodus, Deuteronomy, Joshua, 2 Samuel, Psalms (which provides the majority of the quotations), Proverbs, Isaiah, Jeremiah, Habakkuk and Haggai. It is not only that the writer made many references to the Old Testament but he also indicated his belief in its inspiration. He often wrote of God, 'He says' when he quoted from the scriptures. He took the scriptures to be the equivalent of God speaking; see 1. 5-8, etc. On occasions he stated that it was the Holy Spirit who was speaking, 3. 7; 9. 8; 10. 15, showing his undoubted acceptance of the divine inspiration of the Old Testament.

Hebrews 4 verses 12 and 13 provide an excellent example of the way the writer viewed the close connection between God and His word. Verse 12 describes the word of God and its unique ability to do something which nothing else can, namely to divide between soul and spirit. But whereas the verse refers to it, the next verse refers to 'him', v. 13. The revelation which the scripture brings is nothing less than the revelation which God Himself gives. God's word is living, active, sharp, discerning and revealing.

The writer clearly accepted the Old Testament as absolutely reliable by way of an historical record: see chapter 4 and chapters 7 to 10. The same can be seen from his many references to scriptural personages, see ch. 11. His familiarity with the Old Testament and ready acceptance of its inspiration, without quoting the exact reference, can be seen, 2. 6; 4. 4, 5; 5. 6. Such is his appreciation of that which was written aforetime, that he regarded even the silence of scripture as a part of the inspiration of God, 1. 5; 2. 16; 7. 3. Note also his emphasis on its verbal accuracy in chapter 8 verse 13. He saw Christ and the new covenant as the complete fulfilment of the Old Testament types, but this only served to emphasize his belief in the inspiration of that which had pointed on to Christ, 1. 1. The meaning and significance of the Old Testament is raised to a higher level in view of the complete revelation of God in Christ. The writer made full use of scripture to show how it found its 'full blossom' only in the Lord. For example, chapter 1 employs a series of quotations to confirm the essential deity of Christ. It is evident that the writer to the Hebrews not only held the Old Testament in high regard, but also held it to be verbally inspired.

The inspiration and authority of the New Testament. The authority of Christ was delegated to the apostles, who held a unique and unrepeatable position in the church.[15] The apostles were sent on their mission with precise terms of reference, Matt. 10. 40; that is, they had a special commission given them personally to represent Christ. This is a most important consideration when we realize that it was to the apostles in the main that the writing of the New Testament was committed.

Sometimes the term 'apostle' is used in a broad sense, 2 Cor. 8. 23, Phil. 2. 25. We need to bear in mind, however, that the appointment of Paul was to apostleship in a unique sense, Gal. 1. 1; 1 Cor. 9. 1. Apostolic tradition is frequently referred to in the New Testament.[16] This deposit of apostolic testimony possessed the authority of Christ behind it, for the apostles were taught by Him; see for example Acts chapter 1 verses 1 and 2. This stands in marked contrast to the Jewish traditions which the Lord opposed, when the accumulated teachings of the Rabbis were placed on a par with the word of God, Mark 7. 1-13. The teaching given to the apostles by the Lord, both before and after His resurrection (by Himself personally or by the Holy Spirit), gave the tradition of the apostles the same authority as in His oral teaching.

The apostle Paul emphasized that his teaching had the authority of Christ underwriting it; that is, he wrote with the authority of his Master.[17] Great emphasis is placed on the written teaching of the apostles.[18] As Christ had commissioned the apostles, and others like Mark and Luke who were evidently in close fellowship with the apostles, so their writings were invested with His authority. Paul regarded his own teaching as being on the same level as that of the Old

---

[15] Matt. 10. 1 - 11. 1; Mark 3. 13-19; Luke 6. 12-16; cp. Eph. 2. 19, 20.
[16] Acts 2. 42; 1 Cor. 11. 2, 23; 15. 1; Gal. 1. 9, 12; 2 Thess. 2. 15; 3. 6.
[17] See: 1 Cor. 11. 23; 1 Thess. 4. 15.
[18] See: 1 Cor. 14. 37; 1 Thess. 5. 27; 2 Thess. 3. 14; Rev. 22. 18, 19.

Testament, 2 Tim. 3. 14, and he commanded Timothy to pass it on to others, 1. 1-14; 2. 2. When writing to the Corinthians, Paul often referred to his responsibility as an apostle of Christ to pass on teaching and spiritual judgements to God's people, in view of his special commission from Christ Himself. For this reason he was concerned (as also in Galatians) to emphasize the genuineness of his apostolic calling. Indeed both Paul and John tell us that all teaching is to be tested by the standard of apostolic doctrine.[19] The authority of the apostles was derived from Christ Himself and their commission was unique.[20] It is therefore only in scripture that we find our final authority, and this can be traced ultimately to the Lord Himself. The apostles were the channels of the communication of the truth of Christ, Eph. 2. 20. This truth related to the person and work of Christ, and was presented to produce faith in Him. This call to belief was related to 'the faith' – the unchanging body of Christian truth,[21] which must be accepted by Christians without modification of any kind.

The teaching of the apostles is now available to us only in the New Testament, with which the authority of Christ is indissolubly linked, as it is also with the Old Testament, 2 Tim. 3. 15-17.

May we then gladly accept, for both doctrine and practice, the Bible for what it is – not the word of men but, in truth, the word of God, 1 Thess. 2. 13.

For further help on this important subject, readers are directed to the following articles in 'The Doctrine of the Scriptures' section of the *New Treasury of Bible Doctrine:* The Scriptures of Truth; The Inspiration of the Scriptures; The Sufficiency and Finality of the Scriptures; and Christ and the Bible

The Unity of the Scriptures - J. Heading

Men love unity, though usually when men unite for a common purpose, their differing outlooks and ideologies rapidly produce disunity. In

[19] See: 1 Thess. 5. 19-22; 1 John 4. 1-6.
[20] See: Heb. 2. 3, 4; Jude 3, 17.
[21] See: 1 Tim. 6. 21; 2 Tim. 4. 7; Titus 1. 13.

wider spheres, disunity is prevalent, particularly in political, international and religious issues. How good, then, to turn to divine things, there to find that God is a God of unity. In His creation, there may be outward diversity, but in things physical throughout the universe and in things biological on earth, the underlying laws and principles demonstrate the creator's love of unity. In spiritual things, too, there is unity. 'How good and how pleasant it is for brethren to dwell together in unity', Ps. 133. 1, said the psalmist. 'That they all may be one; as thou, Father, art in me, and I in thee', John 17. 21, said the Lord Jesus.

This unity also pervades the holy scriptures, embracing both the Old and New Testament. 'The dream is one', Gen. 41. 26, said Joseph of two dreams, 'What therefore God hath joined together, let not man put asunder', Matt. 19. 6, said the Lord Jesus. If men easily break what God has joined, how much more can they treat the books of the Bible (thirty-nine in the Old Testament and twenty-seven in the New) as separate entities, written by men of diverse ages and of diverse social standing and education, with no connection the one with the other, except a historical continuity, with perhaps a development of religious practice over the ages. Such profanity would leave the heart cold, were it not for the believer's conviction in the vital subject of divine inspiration. An editor today may work for a year or more, coordinating the work of many individual writers of the same period, to compile some handbook or encyclopaedia. To have done this over a period of 1,600 years would be miraculous indeed. But Christians must not think of God as a superintending editor! An editor is sometimes disappointed in what his individual writers produce. But God was not disappointed in what Moses, David, Jeremiah, Matthew, Luke, Paul, John and many others wrote or dictated, Jer. 36. 32. Rather, the divine author by His Spirit was working in the minds of many human authors, using their individual styles, languages, research, Luke 1. 2, 3, and personal experiences - human thought being thus moved by the Holy Spirit to produce an exact communication from the divine mind.[22] Consequently we expect unity in the Book, although written by men separated by such vast intervals of both time and space. The consistency of the mind of the one author transcends the diversity of the human authors used by God in His work.

---

[22] See: 2 Pet. 1. 21; 1 Cor. 2. 10-14.

A unity of thought, expressed historically, doctrinally, typically, prophetically and in song, therefore pervades the whole divine composition. Perhaps this is most clearly seen in the manner in which the New Testament makes use of the Old. Direct quotations from specific references and passing allusions to it, occur in their hundreds, even perhaps in ways that we could not properly use ourselves. An Old Testament quotation can be altered to convey a different meaning if such suited the New Testament writer, but such are the ways of divine inspiration. To assist the reader assess and appreciate this, we may discuss briefly various different subjects to bring out the all-pervading unity, leaving it to the readers to fill out each subject for themselves.

Unity of the Doctrine of God. In confrontation with all the multiplicity of the gods and idols of the nations, God has maintained a constant revelation of Himself as unique, eternal, all-powerful, holy, elevated and righteous. He is seen as the Creator in both Old Testament and New Testament.[23] His essential oneness is always stressed throughout.[24] His permanent moral and separated being is seen by the description 'holy' ascribed to Him.[25] His being is unchanging, eternal, independent of creation and of men, yet radiating mercy and love.

Unity on the Subject of Creation. The theories of men relating to how the universe and solar system came into existence, and how they will end, have fluctuated widely in the years of scientific progress. But the scriptures present a consistent account, whenever the subject was mentioned over the 1,600 years of their composition. Genesis chapter 1 verses 1 to 27 shows that the work of creation was solely divine, being the work of One who transcended the works of His hands. John chapter 1 verse 3 shows that the Word was in action in the beginning, the worlds being made of things that did not pre-exist, Heb. 11. 3. He now upholds all things, and ultimately will bring all things to an end, Heb. 1. 3, 10-12, quoted from Psalm 102 verses 25 to 27.

Unity on the Subject of Mankind. The most complex structure in God's creation is man himself, man being the highest objective in God's

---

[23] See: Gen. 1. 1; Ps. 136. 5-9; Acts 14. 15; 17. 24.

[24] See: Exod. 20. 2, 3; 1 Cor. 8. 4-6.

[25] See: Lev. 19. 2; Rev. 4. 8.

creatorial work.[26] Man is never seen as evolving from lower beings; revelation is consistent, man was created and not developed. Evolution is invented to deny God and His transcending miraculous power. Again, the separateness of nations was God's doing, Genesis chapter 10, based on the presumption of men, 11. 1-9. This is also a New Testament doctrine, Acts 17. 26, and today men cannot without trouble bring together into a hoped-for harmony what God has divided.

Unity of the Jews. One nation was singled out by God for the accomplishment of His special purpose amongst mankind. Of Abraham, God would make a great nation, Gen. 12. 2. To this nation belonged the glory, the covenants, the giving of the law, the service of God and the promises, Rom. 9. 4. This nation dominated Old Testament history, and from it Christ came according to the flesh. Now, in unbelief the nation is distinct from the Gentiles and the church of God, 1 Cor. 10. 32, but its future is secure in kingdom millennial blessings, Isa. 62. 1-5; Rom. 11. 25-32.

Unity of Typical History. Not only were the Old Testament historical events moving onwards surely to the coming into the world of the Son of God, but the events themselves were often given a typical or allegorical meaning in the New Testament. Thus the movements of the ark from Sinai to Moriah constitute a pre-history of the movements of the Lord Jesus, the highest point being reached when David took the ark up Zion, used as a representation of the ascension of the Lord, Ps. 68. 18; Eph. 4. 8. Again, the history of Joseph traces the story of the Lord Jesus. Again, the history of Hagar and Sarah reflects upon bondage and liberty, the flesh and the promise, Gal. 4. 22-31.

Unity in Typology. Types were suited to Judaism, but the anti-types are suited to Christianity. The tabernacle and the Aaronic priesthood are seen to be typical in Hebrews of the Lord entering into heaven with His sacrificial work complete. The temple is used in the New Testament to speak of the Lord's body, John 2. 21; the believer's body, 1 Cor. 6. 19; the local assembly, 1 Cor. 3. 16, and the mystical church, Eph. 2. 20-22. The sacrifices speak so eloquently of the sacrifice of Christ, Heb. 10. 12,

---

[26] See: Gen. 1. 26; Matt. 19. 4.

and then of the various aspects of our own offerings acceptable to God.[27]

Unity of the Story of Jesus. Woven throughout the Old Testament is the story of One who would come down to die and to rise again. His birth is found.[28] His mission is found, Isa. 61. 1, 2. The Lord's betrayal is foreseen, Zech. 11. 12, while His crucifixion is spoken of.[29] His resurrection is found,[30] and His ascension.[31] All these verses, together with many others, can be found in the New Testament. The Father's heart was occupied with the future, and the Spirit recorded it through psalmist and prophet – the blessed life of the Son of God who was to come according to God's purpose.

Unity in Doctrine. Doctrine outlined from Genesis to Revelation is completely consistent, not because the various writers collaborated over vast tracts of time, but because there was ultimately one author, thereby making His mind known to believers amongst men, 1 Cor. 2. 10-13. Doctrine is developed, of course, from its beginnings in Genesis to its fullest manifestation in the Lord's teaching and in the Epistles. For example, justification by faith is found in Genesis chapter 15 verse 6 up to its highest pinnacle, Romans chapter 3 verse 21 to chapter 8 verse 39. The demand for holiness is found in Leviticus chapter 11 verse 44, up to 1 Peter chapter 1 verse 16.

Unity of God's Standards. Light is light throughout the scriptures; sin is always sin; God's standards remain unaltered. Men's national laws may be changed to redefine crime and what is legal, but the details around the ten commandments cannot change; only the unalterable standards of heaven are suitable for earth. Consequently the way of salvation draws throughout a scarlet cord relating to blood-sacrifice. Before Christ came, blood-sacrifice could cover sin, but after He came, His own blood enables sin to be removed. Not works but faith, not law but grace, provide salvation from sin and its consequences in judgement.

---

[27] See: Rom. 12. 1; Phil. 4. 18; 1 Pet. 2. 5.
[28] See: Isa. 7. 14; Mic. 5. 2.
[29] See: Pss. 22. 1, 16; 69. 21.
[30] See: Pss. 16. 10; 118. 22.
[31] See: Pss. 68. 18; 110. 1.

Unity on the Subject of the church. It is no strange accident that the church is not found explicitly on the pages of the Old Testament – in type, yes, but not as the subject matter of prophecy. This principle was never broken even though the preciousness of the church was ever before the mind of God. In other ages, this mystery was not made known to men, but later was revealed through the apostles, Eph. 3. 2-9. This is why Daniel, for example, failed to perceive the church period, and why the Roman beast (when the Lord was here on earth) seems to merge with this beast at the coming of the Lord in future glory, Dan. 7. 7-14.

Unity of Prophecy. Scientists over the ages who predict the future are inconsistent with each other. Yet the prophets always spoke of the same events – the first advent of the Messiah and His second advent in kingdom glory.[32] The book of Revelation in particular contains more allusions to the Old Testament than any other book, showing in its futuristic unfoldings its unity with the Old Testament, where the prophets 'inquired and searched diligently', 1 Pet. 1. 10.

Unity in Judgement. Judgement upon sinners is not a subject relegated to the so-called period of lack of enlightenment in the Old Testament, abandoned when the love of Christ was revealed in the New Testament. The examples of judgement in the Old Testament, Jude 7, are but pictures of worse events yet to come when God will judge the world by that Man, Acts 17. 31. The coming kingdom is brought in by judgement not by preaching, and eternity is introduced by the final judgement. God's love does not remove His righteous demands anywhere in scripture: rather, it provides a way of escape through grace.

Christ and the Bible - D. W. Brealey

1. CHRIST'S TESTIMONY TO THE SCRIPTURES

The attitude of the Lord Jesus Christ to the Bible is a matter of first importance, for, seeing that He is our Exemplar, our attitude should be precisely His.

It is one of Confidence in its Inspired Pages. In support of this

---

[32] New Testament passages: Matt. 24; Luke 17. 21-37; 21. 7-33; 2 Thess. 2. 1-12; 2 Pet. 3. 3-13; Jude 5-19. These all tell the same story with fuller revelation.

consider some of His own utterances.

To God – 'I have given them thy word . . . thy word is truth', John 17. 14-17. His ministry on earth completed – part of which, and the power of which, lay in giving His hearers the word of God – He lifts up His heart in prayer to His Father with the satisfaction of a mission fulfilled, 'I have given them thy word', and with the assurance of its value, 'thy word is truth'. There is confidence in this.

To Man – 'the scripture cannot be broken', 10. 35. We must remember that the Bible of the Lord Jesus Christ was the Old Testament, described on one of its pages as 'the scripture of truth', Dan. 10. 21. Such confidence had He in 'the scripture of truth' that He roundly asserts that it cannot be broken. But it is also well to remember that all the utterances of our Lord Jesus Christ, necessary for our enlightenment and, further to be unfolded by His apostles, have been incorporated in the New Testament and concerning these He said, 'Heaven and earth shall pass away, but my words shall not pass away', Matt. 24. 35.

Thus His attitude to both the Old Testament and the New Testament was one of the uttermost confidence; and we need not be surprised, therefore, at its logical outcome.

His Confirmation of its Reliability. The logical outcome of Christ's confidence in the Bible as being the truth was that, to Him, the characters of the Old Testament were real, not mythical; its stories were history, not allegory; its laws were binding, not optional; its prophecies were reliable, not fanciful; and the whole was of deep moral and spiritual value.

He believed in the actual existence of the Old Testament characters. His references to them, and the way He referred to them, rule out any other conclusion, as for example: Abel, Noah, Abraham, David, Solomon, the Queen of Sheba, Isaiah, etc.; and to make assurance doubly sure, He not only believed that they lived once, but that they live now, Matt. 22. 32, quoting Exod. 3. 6.

He believed in the historical accuracy of the Old Testament records. Consider two examples. He believed in the *flood*, 'For as in the days before the flood, they were eating and drinking, marrying and giving in marriage, until the day that Noah entered the ark, and did not know until the flood came and took them all away, so will the coming of the Son of Man be', Matt. 24. 38, 39 NKJV.

He believed in the story of Jonah. 'Jonah was three days and three nights in the belly of the great fish', 12. 40 NKJV.

He believed that the laws of God were binding. 'Think not that I come to destroy the law, or the prophets: I am not come to destroy, but to fulfil. For verily I say unto you, Till heaven and earth pass, one jot or one tittle shall in no wise pass from the law, till all be fulfilled', 5. 17, 18.

He believed in the certain fulfilment of prophecy. Unlike many intellectuals of the present day, He appears to have had not the slightest difficulty about the book of Daniel; He did not try to discredit it, but actually quoted it in support of His own words, 'When ye therefore shall see the abomination of desolation, spoken of by Daniel the prophet, stand in the holy place, (whoso readeth let him understand)', 24. 15. And again, 'All things must be fulfilled, which were written in the law of Moses, and in the prophets, and in the psalms, concerning me', Luke 24. 44.

There may be difficulties which at the moment we are unable to explain; but we may draw vast comfort from Christ's own confidence in, and confirmation of, the scriptures; and, without fear for the Book, quietly await the day when all difficulties will be cleared up and the Bible will be finally vindicated, as to-day, it is being vindicated, as 'the scripture of truth'.

2. CHRIST'S USE OF THE SCRIPTURES

Christ's attitude to the Bible is one of **conviction of its living power**. We gather this from His habit of **using the scriptures** in different circumstances and toward all sorts of different people, and from the effectiveness of such use. This He did with very great skill.

His Skill in the use of Scripture may be seen:

In subduing the tempter: He met each temptation with a quotation from the scriptures, 'It is written . . . It is written . . . It is written . . . Then the devil leaveth him', Matt. 4. 4, 7, 10, 11. It was an effective answer.

In saving the lost. No better example could be found than in the case of Nicodemus, where Christ refers to the account of the brazen serpent in Numbers chapter 21, 'And as Moses lifted up the serpent in the wilderness, even so must the Son of man be lifted up: that whosoever believeth in him should not perish, but have eternal life', John 3. 14, 15.

In silencing His enemies. To their foolish question about the resurrection He replied, 'Ye do err, not knowing the scriptures, nor the power of God . . . have ye not read that which was spoken by God, saying, I am the God of Abraham, and the God of Isaac, and the God of Jacob? God is not the God of the dead, but of the living', Matt. 22. 29-31, 32, quoting Exodus chapter 3 verse 6. So, 'He put the Sadducees to silence', Matt. 22. 34. And in the same chapter His masterly use of Psalm 110 in regard to the Messiah put everyone to silence, 'And no man was able to answer him a word neither durst any man from that day forth, ask him any more questions', v. 46.

In strengthening and reassuring His disciples. When Christ died, some of the disciples thought that that was the end of everything; but on the third day He rose again. To these amazed disciples He did not first of all show Himself so obviously that they would recognize Him at once; rather did He **open their eyes to Him by opening the scriptures to them**, thus giving them the strength and reassurance that they so much needed, 'And beginning at Moses and all the prophets, he expounded unto them in all the scriptures the things concerning himself . . . and their eyes were opened, and they knew him . . . and they rose up the same hour, and returned to Jerusalem, and found the eleven gathered together, and them that were with them, saying, The Lord is risen indeed', Luke 24. 27-34.

So it is clearly seen with what skill and effect the Lord used the scriptures upon different kinds of people and in such varying circumstances. It is, in itself, a testimony to His conviction of the living power of the word.

The Secret – His Knowledge of the Scriptures. We may say, without hesitation, that the secret of Christ's skill in the use of the Old Testament was His knowledge of it. As the Son of God He was, of course, omniscient: yet Isaiah chapter 50 verses 4 to 5 seems to let us into the secret of His profound knowledge of the scriptures as the Son of man.

He is listening, 'He wakeneth mine ear to hear', v. 4.

He is learning, 'The Lord God hath given me the tongue of them that are taught that I should know how to speak a word in season', v. 4 RV.

He is obedient, 'The Lord God hath opened mine ear, and I was not rebellious, neither turned away back', v. 5.

Seclusion with God seems to have been the secret of His knowledge: the open ear; the attentive mind; and, the willing heart. Yet Christ was a reader! His reading of a part of Isaiah chapter 61 in the synagogue at Nazareth must have been arresting indeed, Luke 4. 18, 19.

His knowledge mystified His hearers! 'And the Jews marvelled, saying, How knoweth this man letters, having never learned?', John 7. 15. But He had learned! Not in the schools, perhaps, but in seclusion with God.

If we would share His knowledge, we must follow His example and precept, and 'search the scriptures', 5. 39. That is how the Lord would have us come to His word, how He would have us study it. And if we thus search the scriptures, and listen to the voice of God, we shall learn: and if we follow what we learn, we may expect to use it with skill and effect in our measure, as Christ did without measure.

Every Christian needs this knowledge: children at school; young people at college or in business and in the world; as well as preachers and teachers, need the knowledge of the scriptures as their principal safeguard from the errors that abound, their weapon of offence and defence. And as our knowledge grows, so will our conviction grow that 'the word of God is living, and active, and sharper than any two-edged sword', Heb. 4. 12 RV.

So we may say that the second attitude of the Lord Jesus Christ to the Old Testament was conviction of its living power. He studied it, followed it, taught it, because He was convinced of its effectiveness, and His conviction was borne out by its use.

His Method of Interpreting the Scriptures. In His interpretation of the scriptures, the Lord affirmed two basic principles:

The principle of apprehension: Christ 'in all the scriptures'. Apart from an understanding of this principle the Bible largely becomes a closed book to us. But use it as a key, and it will unlock the rich treasures of its teaching. He Himself has told us, 'the scriptures . . . testify of me', John 5. 39; and it was as He 'expounded . . . in all the scriptures the things concerning himself' to His disciples that He 'opened . . . their understanding, that they might understand the scriptures', Luke 24. 27, 45.

The principle of application: 'not of the letter, but of the spirit', 2 Cor. 3. 6. What is understood from the scriptures must be applied in the life, not just by the keeping of its letter, but by the keeping of its spirit. This is the principle for which Christ contended so clearly in the Sermon on the Mount, where He showed how He had come not 'to destroy . . . but to fulfil' the law, by adding to the letter of its commands and prohibitions His own command to observe the spirit that lay behind them, Matt. 5. 17-48.

May the Lord help us to follow the example of His own attitude to, and use of, the Bible, leading us into a fuller confidence in its truth, into conviction rather than ideas, and to a reverence for its spirit that shall lead us into a holy walk with God.

Faith and the Word of God - T. W. Carron

We live in a day when human knowledge and achievement have increased to a remarkable extent, especially in the realm of science. Much of what was thought and taught in the past has been discarded in the light of fuller knowledge. Moreover the scientific achievements of recent years are truly staggering. But, as the Bible says, 'knowledge puffeth up', and it is not surprising therefore that many educated people feel that they have outgrown Christianity. They are asking for something up-to-date, and there are those in the professing church who are prepared to offer them a revised version of Christianity tailored to fit modern people.

The whole matter turns on the answer to one question: 'Is the Bible the word of God?'. If it is, if God has spoken, as the Bible claims, in times past by the prophets, and finally in His Son and by the Spirit of God Himself through the apostles, to reject the Bible is to reject God: to change it or to modify it is an insult to God, and He will judge those who do so.

Now we have the Lord's own witness to the veracity of the Old Testament. He said, 'The scripture cannot be broken', John 10. 35. Defending the writings of Moses, He said, 'If ye believe not his writings, how shall ye believe my words?' 5. 47. He said, moreover, 'Think not that I am come to destroy the law, or the prophets . . . but to fulfil', Matt. 5. 17.

He upheld the inspiration of the Old Testament from which He frequently quoted. In 2 Timothy chapter 3 verse 16 we read, 'All scripture is given by inspiration of God (God breathed)'. Peter, writing of Paul's Epistles, puts them on the same level as the other scriptures, 2 Pet. 3. 16.

If you were asked, 'How do you know the sun is shining?', you would say, 'What a silly question! I see its light and feel its warmth'. Precisely! Just as we see the light and feel the warmth of the sun on our bodies, so the rays of truth from the Bible shine into our minds and warm our hearts. This has been the experience of millions in all ages. The Bible has transformed the lives of men and women in every generation since Pentecost. In this respect it is unique, and wherever it has been read with willing heart and unbiased mind it has produced the miraculous change we call conversion. Lives have been changed from sin and degradation to honesty, purity and holiness. This miracle has occurred times without number all over the world, among all races, civilized and uncivilized. The most degraded heathen, even cannibals, sunk in sin and debauchery below human level, have been raised and transformed beyond recognition, and given a new life in Christ. Hatred has been replaced by love, drunkenness by sobriety, lying by truthfulness, robbery and theft by kindness and honesty.

The annals of missionary endeavour abound with accounts of such transformations. There is the well-known story of Calvert who went to the Fiji Islands, armed with the Bible alone, and worked among the cannibals who were converted in large numbers. DARWIN, who at one time regarded the natives of Tierra del Fuego as the lowest specimens of humanity, wrote years afterwards, 'The success of the Tierra del Fuego Mission is most wonderful, and shames me, as I always prophesied utter failure'. In his book, *The Bible in World Evangelism*, A. M. CHIRGWIN develops this theme, and shows what the Bible has done throughout the ages. He tells some amazing stories of conversion through the reading of the Bible. Among others, he records the remarkable story of Tokichi Ishii who, in circumstances of fiendish brutality murdered men, women and even children. This man was visited in prison by two Canadian ladies, and though he would not listen to them, he was prevailed upon to accept a Bible.

He read it, and coming to the story of the crucifixion was completely broken down. He believed, his heart was changed. 'Later, when the jailer came to lead the doomed man to the scaffold, he found, not the surly hardened brute he expected, but a smiling, radiant man, for the murderer had been born again'. If such testimonies, corroborated times without number over nineteen centuries, fail to convince a person that the Bible is the word of God, then nothing will convince him. The Lord Himself said, 'If they hear not Moses and the prophets, neither will they be persuaded, though one rose from the dead', Luke 16. 31. There is such a thing as the *will* to disbelieve.

But what produced these wonderful transformations in the lives of men? *Faith*: faith not simply in the Bible, but in the author of the Bible, faith in God Himself. Faith, however, is not mere mental assent. It is a matter of the heart. The Bible says, 'With the heart man believeth unto righteousness', Rom. 10. 10. There lies the crux of the matter. The heart is the core of man's being, the seat of his desires and impulses. Men follow their desires more than their reason, their hearts rather than their heads. If we want something badly enough our heart will often override our reason or our common sense, and the heart will suggest or invent a reason for getting it. On the other hand, we may find ourselves resisting what reason or common sense dictate if it is in conflict with our desires. Little though he may realize it, man has an instinctive bias against God. The Bible tells us that 'the mind [tendency] of the flesh [our fallen nature] is enmity against God', 8. 7 RV. Hence there arises much of the criticism of the Bible. It has been attacked again and again, and the attack has often recoiled on the attackers. Many times archaeology has shown that what the Bible stated was true after all. So many of its prophecies have been fulfilled that the possibility of the events prophesied being coincidences is completely ruled out. A recent complaint, publicised on television, is that it is too difficult to understand. Yet millions of children have been able to grasp its message. The Lord said 'If any man desires to do His will (God's pleasure), he will know whether . . . the teaching is from God', John 7. 17 AMP.

Fear of man is another hindrance to faith, fear to confess faith in Christ because of scorn or ridicule. How many are afraid to believe for this reason, and so find excuses for their unbelief?

We must not forget that there is a being greater than man who is opposed to God, and uses all his devices to prevent faith. He is a spirit. The apostle Paul speaks of him as 'the spirit that now worketh in the children of disobedience', Eph. 2. 2. The Lord called him 'the prince of this world'. The Apostle Paul says he is also the god of it, 'the god of this world hath blinded the minds of them which believe not', 2 Cor. 4. 4. Satan uses two powerful weapons. One is doubt. His first words to the woman in the Garden of Eden were, 'Hath God said?' And he uses that weapon very effectively today. Modernism and higher criticism are his work, instilling doubt into the minds of those who read the Bible. By this means he has largely nullified the reading of the Bible in schools. Doubt is cast on the Bible from Genesis to Revelation, doubt as to its veracity, doubt as to the Lord's words, doubt as to His deity, doubt as to His miracles; this is simply another form of the old question, 'Hath God said?' When the poison dart of doubt has done its initial work, the devil follows it up with a direct lie, as he did in Eden. God said if they ate of the forbidden fruit they would die; the devil said 'Ye shall not surely die'. The Lord said of him, 'He is a liar, and the father of it'. Says the Apostle Paul, take 'the shield of faith . . . and the sword of the Spirit, which is the *word of God*', Eph. 6. 16 (italics mine).

'But without faith it is impossible to please God', Heb. 11. 6. Hence the stress that is laid on it in the New Testament. The word 'faith' and its corresponding verb both occur over 240 times, and the adjective translated 'faithful' or 'believing' nearly seventy times.

Towards the end of his Gospel John writes, 'These (things) are written, that ye might *believe* that Jesus is the Christ, the Son of God; and that believing ye might have life through his name', John 20. 31. This is saving faith, this is the way into eternal life. It is however but the beginning of the Christian path. That path is a path of faith (trust) all the way. The world teaches self-reliance, but faith is reliance on God. The worthies of Hebrews chapter 11 became strong out of weakness through faith. The Christian is like an electric train drawing power from an overhead wire; the power lies in constant contact with the wire which links it with the source of power. 'For we walk by faith, not by sight', says Paul, 2 Cor. 5. 7. The word of God lights the way. The psalmist of old had learnt this, for he wrote, 'Thy word is a lamp unto my feet, and a light unto my path', Ps. 119. 105.

THE DOCTRINE OF GOD

The Doctrine of God* - D. Craig

As we commence this study we must acknowledge the dignity and awesome majesty of the being of God. Truly, the subject is profound and inexhaustible. We can hope only to discuss in brief some of the great issues that flow from a consideration of the One whom we have come to know as 'our Father'.

We must remind ourselves that only sons can speak intimately of a father. So it is with God. While the believer, born into the family of God by the new birth, can claim a unique intimacy with God, He still remains the creator of all things, the Father of eternity, and the God of glory.

THE BEING OF GOD - the basis of Theism

Theism can be defined as the belief in God as a person, a being who is the object of worship. It is, in fact, the belief that this God has revealed Himself in the person of His Son. Scripture does not set out to prove the existence of God, it states, as a matter of fact, that, 'In the beginning God', Gen. 1. 1, and, in the New Testament, 'In the beginning . . . the Word was God', John 1. 1.

Even unregenerate man can be assured of the existence of God, Rom. 1. 19-20. The proof is the creation, the natural and the physical, indicating that behind nature's laws is nature's Lord. However, it is true that the greatest appreciation of God comes through the supernatural, that is, the spiritual. It brings into focus revelation, inspiration, and faith.

It is true that the existence of God cannot be intellectually proved, but we will look at some considerations, which, if taken together, form compelling arguments for God's existence.

Intellectual Arguments

Five such arguments used by scholars deserve a brief mention:

1. Ontological. This means 'perfection' as an ideal. Perfection may mean freedom from all limitations, or total impeccability. If this can be found, then there must be an actual being – the absolute. The being of beings must exist, or else all other existence is impossible, and without meaning;

2. Cosmological. The universe does not exist apart from this being. He is the first cause, and the universe, with its order and organization, demands a first cause. This idea is borne out by the New Testament, in such passages as Colossians chapter 1 verse 16 and Hebrews chapter 1 verse 3;

3. Teleological. This is the argument from design: natural forces; the immensity of space; the marvels of every created thing. These, and much more, present the argument that there is a grand design. There can be no design without a designer! We are considering something far more than a haphazard kaleidoscope;

4. Anthropological. This declares that God is a personality, greater than man or any other intelligent thing. Old-fashioned pantheism, and modern New Age culture, unite to proclaim that God is everything and everything is God! The revelation in the Bible states the very opposite. God produced the man in His image and, ultimately, God revealed Himself in the Word incarnate;

5. Moral Purpose. It is inconceivable that such a being should bring the universe into existence for no reason and without an objective. There has got to be a purpose for it all. The scriptures give support to this. Ephesians chapter 1 verse 10 says that all things are to be summed up in Christ, and Colossians chapter 1 verse 16 tells us that 'all things were created by him, and for him'. Hebrews chapter 2 verse 10 gives us the grand design, seeing the Son of God as 'the captain (pioneer) of . . . salvation', 'bringing many sons unto glory'.

THE NATURE OF GOD

God is infinite. This is a term incomprehensible to man. It is not merely that God has no beginning and no end. It is that He is limitless. It is impossible to measure, weigh, or quantify who, and what God is, but faith allows belief in such a concept. An example of what faith can take in is found in scripture, 'But will God indeed dwell on the earth? behold, the heaven and heaven of heavens cannot contain thee', 1 Kgs. 8. 27.

God is transcendent and immanent. Transcendent means separate from His creatures. It underlines the fact that, although He is distinct from His created ones, He is intimately connected, and involved with them. Again, scripture states that by Him all things hold together, Col. 1. 16, and that He upholds 'all things by the word of his power', Heb. 1. 3. Both of these characteristics, transcendence and immanence, must be equally balanced. T. C. HAMMOND gives a useful comment into the consequences of imbalance: 'Agnosticism stresses only the mystery of God and says, 'I don't know'; Deism stresses apartness (transcendence) and says, 'He is not one of us'; Pantheism emphasizes immanence, and says, 'God is everything and everything is God'; whereas the true revelation of God is a balance of all, a harmonious blend which embraces theism – stressing personality'.

The personality of God is difficult for human minds to grasp. But the Bible details all the elements of personality – mind, emotions, will, reason, speech, action, etc. It is these combined features of personality that give 'flesh' to the bones of the mechanical, and physical, and tell out that God is, and that He can be known. Faith says we believe that 'he is the rewarder of them that diligently seek him', Heb. 11. 6. Isaiah speaks on the same theme, 'Seek ye the Lord while he may be found, call ye upon him while he is near', Isa. 55. 6.

God is immutable. A key scripture reference to this is, 'Now unto the King eternal, immortal (incorruptible), invisible, the only wise God, be honour and glory for ever and ever. Amen', 1 Tim. 1. 17. This means God is unlimited by time and space, that He has no disposition, and that His attributes are constant. 1 John teaches that God not only loves, but *is* love.[1]

THE ATTRIBUTES OF GOD

We will consider these under two headings: general attributes; and moral attributes.

General Attributes

God is omnipotent. This means that God's creative force, or energy, is

---

[1] See also Ps. 102. 27; Mal. 3. 6; Heb. 13. 8.

unsurpassed. It is not dependent on any outside influence. God is all powerful independently. However, it should be remembered that God's power is governed by His own self-imposed laws. For example, in mathematics, seven times one is seven. Omnipotence cannot make it eight! This is not arbitrary or irrational. God will not, and cannot, act outside the boundaries He has laid down in His wisdom for the proper workings of His universe.

However, omnipotence is sometimes manifested in the miraculous, but man is very often unaware of this because He chooses to allow measures which obscure God's hand, e.g., natural healing. The creation and sustaining of animate, and inanimate things, are perhaps the greatest evidences of omnipotence.[2]

God is omniscient. The all-knowing God does not acquire knowledge. It is not attached or built on to His nature. For some, God's foreknowledge raises many difficulties, particularly in the context of freedom of action. Man is said to have a free will, but, although as moral beings we have freedom of choice, we are not perfect moral beings. If we were, we could do only one thing in every situation – i.e., the right thing! The absence of alternatives is the highest form of freedom.[3]

God is omnipresent. There are two principles governing omnipresence. In the first place, God is so great that He cannot be separated from His own works. Secondly, as first cause and creator, He is actively involved in every part of His creation. We must try to grasp the concept that God is everywhere, in the same way that God is love. He is not partly present, or sometimes present, e.g., Thomas, after the resurrection. He is totally, wholly present to every person in every place. In many circumstances, the believer perceives a special sense of God's presence, e.g. Matt. 18. 20; Exod. 33. 15.[4]

---

[2] Some useful references: Job 42. 2; Pss. 95. 3; 135. 5-7; Jer. 32. 17, 18; Matt. 19. 26; Mark 14. 36.

[3] Some key references: Pss. 33. 13-15; 139. 1-6; 147. 3-5; Ezek. 11. 9; Acts 15. 18; 1 John 3. 20.

[4] Other references: Ps. 139. 7-10; Jer. 23. 24; Acts 17. 24-28; Isa. 66. 1.

Moral Attributes

I emphasize that these are examples of the moral characteristics of God.

God is good. God seeks the welfare of His creation continually. He gave to man the best, and man spoiled it! The Old Testament has the recurring theme of God's goodness. 'And God saw . . . that . . . it was very good', Gen. 1. 31, is the formula of creation. And, as time passed, and crises followed crises, man demonstrated repeated failure. The creator intervened in new beginnings: e.g., post-flood; the call of Abram; the approach of God in tabernacle and temple; the granting of a monarchy; the restoration after captivity. Psalms 106 and 107 are testimonies to this principle.

God is holy. The often-recurring phrase 'the Holy One of Israel' implies separation from all that is impure. It also implies the concept of loftiness. It is that awesomeness that puts the creator on a totally different level from His created ones. Without this, holiness would have little meaning, and man would conceive of a God made in his (man's) own image. The word 'holy' appears 170 times in the first five books of the Bible. In the Psalms it occurs thirty times and about the same number in Isaiah. Such is the importance attached to this attribute of God.

God is righteous. This is the attribute which upholds the moral order in the world, and establishes the principle of right and wrong, good and evil. The message of Romans chapters 1 to 8 is that the righteousness of God revealed in the law shows man for what he is – unrighteous! It follows, therefore, that there are connected attributes, such as justice, truth, anger, etc. Some find it difficult to reconcile justice with the injustices, inequalities, and calamities which happen to people in the normal course of living. The scriptural answer must be that such happenings emerge as the result of man's departure from God. The creator gave man freedom, and he used it to his own destruction. The mercy and grace of God are continuously available to secure righteous acts, even though such acts are often done without the knowledge of the sovereignty of God.[5]

---

[5] Some helpful references: Ezra 9. 15; Pss. 11. 7; 103. 6; John 17. 25; Rom. 2. 2; 3. 4-6.

God is wise. The heart is the seat of wisdom, hence, 'He is wise in heart', Job 9. 4. God, alone, possesses all wisdom. He is called 'the only wise God', 1 Tim. 1. 17. All the treasures of wisdom are vested in Him, and are seen working in His intelligence, and precision. As to His workings, we have only to think of His creatorial and redemptive powers.

In relation to His creatorial powers, the relationship of the earth to the sun, and the appointment of the seasons of the year are examples, Ps. 74. 17. Equally, the division of day and night, light and darkness, and the division of the earth into land and sea. 'O Lord how manifold are thy works', 104. 24.

What can excel the wisdom of God in redemption? That God, Himself, should be the redeemer, become incarnate, and yet know no sin! And that He should devise a righteous way to condemn the sin, but save the sinner. This is wisdom indeed! But more, that God should take the redeemed sinner and place the treasure of the gospel in him, and send him into the world to preach it, is marvellous wisdom indeed!

God is just. Concerning God's justice the psalmist wrote, 'Justice and judgement are the habitation of thy throne', 89. 14. Justice gives to everyone his due. God is an impartial judge. It cannot be otherwise, because of equal weight given to attributes of holiness, righteousness, mercy, and grace. It is not only that God acts justly, but that He is just, Rom. 11. 33.

The justice of God is evident in two ways: in rewarding the righteous, Ps. 58. 11, and in punishing the offender by law, Rom. 4. 15. We may not see justice done in this life, but eternity is to follow, and then it will surely be done. The Lord never afflicts His people without a cause. The trials and afflictions of the godly are to purify and refine them.[6]

God is merciful and gracious. Simply, mercy is that attribute of God which holds back God's judgement deserved by man. Grace, on the other hand, gives to man what he does not deserve.

---

[6] Other references: Job 8. 3; Ps. 119. 75, 76; Rom. 9. 14.

It is true that the righteousness, holiness, and justice of God demand that sin be punished, and the guilty brought to justice. Exodus chapter 34 verse 7 says explicitly, God 'will by no means clear the guilty'. But, against this one statement, there are five statements of mercy and grace! This is the kind of God we have! So the grace of God is seen in longsuffering, and an abundance of goodness, the greatest of which is salvation, eternal life.

Psalm 57 verse 10 tells us that God's mercy is far above the heavens. Acts of severity are forced from God, 'He doth not afflict willingly nor grieve the children of men', Lam. 3. 33. The human caricature of God as a sadistic creator, who delights in administering pain, is contradicted by scripture, 'He is slow to anger', Ps. 103. 8. He is called the 'Father of mercies, and the God of all comfort', 2 Cor. 1. 3.

We might describe God's grace and mercy as like an intertwined garland: the one is impossible without the other. Titus chapter 3 verse 5 says, 'According to his mercy he saved us'. Ephesians chapter 2 verse 8 says, 'By grace are ye saved through faith'. It was mercy that met the prodigal when his father welcomed him home; it was grace that put the ring on his finger and shoes on his feet! It was mercy that stopped the stoning of the adulteress in John chapter 8; it was grace that said, 'Go and sin no more'.

God is love. One brief word must suffice where volumes of books have expounded this highest of all attributes. The Hebrew word for love signifies love 'out of the bowels'. In Old Testament language, 'bowels' were used to describe the centre, or seat, of the affections. In the New Testament, there are three different words used for love. The one that is most often used for the love of God is the Greek *agape*, a love whose main characteristic is sacrificial giving.

The Gospels and Epistles say all that needs to be said about love, and all are beautifully summed up by the apostle John, 'Herein is love, not that we loved God, but that he loved us, and sent his Son to be the propitiation for our sins', 1 John 4. 10.

THE PROVIDENCE OF GOD

Providence, in the scriptural sense, points to the inscrutable acts of God which are seen throughout the world in the course of its history. It is the ordering of events after the counsel of His will, for His own glory. THOMAS WATSON says, 'It is the eye that sees and the hand that turns all the wheels in the universe. God is not like a builder who builds a building then leaves it. He is actively working in His creation'. Jesus said, 'My Father worketh hitherto, and I work', John 5. 17.

Scripture teaches that providence is complete and all embracing.[7] Not only does it include all persons, but all actions, and events. The Bible, however, opposes the ideas of 'chance', and 'fatalism', which both reject the truth of a controlling deity. The raven, a bird which scarcely feeds its young, providentially sustained the prophet Elijah, 1 Kgs. 17. 6. In the example of Esther, among all the young women brought before the king, she found favour. This was due to God's special providence. It was God's way of saving His people, a fact hidden from the king.

It is often objected that there are many things happening in the world which are disastrous, disorderly, and irregular. How can God's providence be in such things? Has not history shown that even in events like these God has turned misery and suffering to man's benefit? He has often made the wrath of man to praise Him, Ps. 76. 10. The prophet Habakkuk asked God to do something about Israel's gross sin. When God did it through the Babylonian invasion, the prophet complained about the method! In using evil to correct good, is God condoning sin? This cannot be! God is not the author of sin, but in His providence He allows men to engage in sin without apparent intervention. However, Acts chapter 14 verse 16 tells us, 'He suffered all nations to walk in their own ways'. Had God not permitted sin, we would never have known justice in punishing it, and mercy in pardoning it.

Providence manifests itself in many 'accidental' ways. An example is in 1 Kings chapter 22 verse 34. The archer drew his bow and shot his arrow without a target, a 'chance' shot. But that arrow was guided by God right between the joints in King Ahab's armour, 'so the king died', fulfilling the prediction of the prophet, and the purpose of God. Things that seem to happen by chance, or coincidence, are really demonstrations of God's providence, and the interpretation of His will.

---

[7] Ps. 135. 6; Acts 4. 28.

It was HENRY LAW, the Puritan, who said, 'Great doors swing on small hinges'. A 'chance' remark by a fellow-prisoner to Joseph, 'Wherefore look ye so sadly today?' Gen. 40. 7, was the turning point in Joseph's life. God had providentially ordained that the question be asked!

We must accept and submit to God's providence. Job, who wrestled for a good part of his life with the providence of God, ended up saying, 'I uttered that I understood not; things too wonderful for me, which I knew not', Job 42. 3.

DIVINE GOVERNMENT

Scripture reveals that God governs the intelligence of those He has created, both humans and angels, according to fixed moral laws. For example, it is clear from scripture, and spiritual experience, that God has ordained redemption as a cure for sin and fallen mankind. In this, He has ordered a process for man's recovery which results in a spiritual rule, and authority in the life that changes aims, goals, and habits.

The Bible supports the view that God is able to, and does, use every means for the moral government of the world. We could think of Isaiah's challenge to the gods, and his prediction that Cyrus should perform God's will, Isa. 44. 28; 45. 1.

At His temptation, Matt. 4, we should note the Lord's rebuttal of Satan, when Satan offered to give Him all the kingdoms of the world, and their glory. The truth was they were not his to give! Satan, like all others, even in his unfallen state, is a created being, and subject to the authority of the creator. It is true that Satan is called 'the god of this world . . . the prince of the power of the air', 2 Cor. 4. 4; Eph. 2. 2. But this was granted to him by God to fulfil His sovereign purposes, and that for the lives of individuals in this 'present age' and not extending to the rule of the nations.[8] In any event, this earth (world) is a tiny orb in the vast creation of God, and His government is observed in its maintenance and movement.[9]

---

[8] See Dan. 2. 2-21; Ps. 76. 8.

[9] Other scriptures for further study are: Pss. 33. 13-17; 66. 1-7; 72. 11; 75. 6-8; Dan. 4. 25; Rom. 13. 1; 1 Tim. 1. 15.

CONCLUSION

While intellectual arguments can bring us some way towards an understanding and belief in the existence of God, only revelation through the Holy Spirit in the word of God can really tell us all that we need to know about Him. The inspired authors do not suggest it can be questioned. May our reading and consideration of the scriptures direct our hearts, and stimulate our meditation, on this God who is our God.[10]

[The author acknowledges the significant help he received from T. C. HAMMOND's book *In Understanding Be Men* in the writing of this paper.[11]]

The Unity of the Godhead - J. HEADING

The scriptures cannot define the Holy Trinity, yet they reveal many different phases of the unity of manifestation of the three persons of the Godhead. The wide variety of this manifestation is shown by the following co-ordination of purpose and action.

The Lord's Baptism. This is the first time that the Trinity is implied in the New Testament, Matt. 3. 16, 17. The Spirit descended upon the man Jesus Christ, and the voice of the Father commended His Son chiefly to John the Baptist, so that he might know for the first time that Jesus was the Son of God, John 1. 32-34.

The Lord's Death. When the Son of God gave Himself, Gal. 2. 20, He was in prayerful contact with the Father prior to and after the hours of darkness, Luke 23. 34, 46, but during these hours, as One made sin, He could address God as Judge, Matt. 27. 46. At the same time, it was through the eternal Spirit that He offered Himself to God, Heb. 9. 14, for a sweet-smelling savour, Eph. 5. 2.

Believers' Baptism. In Matthew chapter 28 verses 19-20, after His

---

[10] For further reading see, Ps. 90; Isa. 40. 12-26; Jer. 10. 10-16.

[11] T. C. HAMMOND, *In Understanding be Men*, Inter-Varsity Fellowship, 1965, particularly pp. 41-52.

resurrection, the Lord instituted a new thing, believers' baptism replacing John's baptism. Now disciples out of all nations were to be baptized in the name (singular) of the triune God, such disciples showing themselves willing to observe all things commanded by the Lord.

Believers' Benediction, 2 Cor. 13. 14. The grace of the Lord Jesus reflects back to chapter 8 verse 9; the love of God to chapter 13 verse 11, and the communion of the Holy Spirit also to verse 11, 'be of one mind'. The boards of the tabernacle show similar thoughts; the silver sockets correspond to the grace of the Lord Jesus, the bars to the communion of the Holy Spirit and the overlaid gold to the love of God.

Giving of the Spirit. In John chapter 14 verses 16 and 26, it is the Father who would send the Holy Spirit, but in chapter 15 verse 26, the Lord sends the Spirit proceeding from the Father. These two thoughts are explained, Acts 2. 33, where the Father provided, but the Lord Jesus, being in contact both with His Father and with His own on earth, transmitted the gift of the Spirit.

Dwelling in the Saints. The fact that the body of a saved soul is a vessel for divine occupation is humbling, yet precious. The Spirit dwells within.[12] The Lord Jesus dwells in our hearts.[13] And the Father Himself dwells within. Note the word 'we' in John chapter 14 verse 23; see Eph. 2. 22.

In Worship. The Spirit speaks by us, 2 Sam. 23. 2, the Spirit of His Son having been sent into our hearts to cry 'Abba, Father', Gal. 4. 6. Such are spiritual sacrifices, acceptable to God by Jesus Christ, 1 Pet. 2. 5.

Giving of Spiritual Gifts. Notice that these are distributed according to the divine will to **all** saints. God deals to **every man** the measure of faith for these gifts, Rom. 12. 3; to **every one** the grace of gift is given according to the measure of the gift of Christ, Eph. 4. 7; it is the Spirit who divides the gifts to **every man** severally as He will, 1 Cor. 12. 11.

---

[12] See: John 14. 17; 1 John 2. 27; 1 Cor. 6. 19; Eph. 3. 16.

[13] See: John 14. 20; 17. 23; Eph. 3. 17.

Divine Interest in Service. In 1 Corinthians chapter 12 verses 4-6, the three persons of the Godhead are occupied with service. In verse 4 the Spirit is occupied with **ability freely bestowed** for service; in verse 5 the Lord directs **when, what, and how** service is taken up ('putting me into the ministry', 1 Tim. 1. 12,); in verse 6 God is seen as **producing results** through service (see 1 Corinthians chapter 3 verse 7, where it is 'God that giveth the increase').

Sending Forth into Service. From Antioch, Paul was sent forth by the Spirit, Acts 13. 2, 4. The Lord would send forth His servants.[14] Such movements were according to the will of God, Acts 18. 21.

Divine Intervention in Hard Hearts. The phrase, often quoted in the New Testament, 'Make the heart of this people fat', Isa. 6. 10, is remarkable. In Isaiah chapter 6 it is the voice of God, the King, Jehovah of hosts. In John chapter 12 verses 39-41 the glory is that of the Lord Jesus, while in Acts chapter 28 verse 25 it is the voice of the Holy Spirit.

Anointing of the Lord. Three times in Isaiah we find the anointing of the Lord for commission as Man to public service. In Isaiah chapter 61 verses 1 to 3 it is the voice of the Son; this corresponds to Luke's Gospel, 4. 16-22. In Isaiah chapter 42 verses 1 to 4 it is the voice of God concerning the anointing of His servant; this corresponds to Mark's Gospel. In Isaiah chapter 11 verses 1 to 9, it is the voice of the Spirit of prophecy, corresponding to the kingdom in Matthew's Gospel.

The Holy Trinity* - M. Horlock

Scripture quotations are from the New King James Version unless otherwise stated.

'In no other subject is error more dangerous, or inquiry more laborious, or the discovery of truth more profitable', Augustine, *On the Trinity, Book* 1, Chapter 3, Paragraph 5.

1. What we mean when we speak of the Holy Trinity

The expression 'the Holy Trinity' does not occur in the Bible. But this

[14] See: John 17. 18; 20. 21; Acts 22. 21; 26. 17; 1 Cor. 1. 17.

does not mean that the doctrine is in any way unscriptural; neither do such words as 'substitution', 'sovereignty', 'providence' or 'incarnation'. What matters is whether or not the doctrines conveyed by these words are scriptural. We begin therefore by asking, 'What do we mean when we say that we believe in the Holy Trinity?' We then need to satisfy ourselves that this meaning is in full accord with God's word.

Basically, we mean three things. We believe:
(a) In the unity of the Godhead. That is, that there is one God, and not three;
(b) In the deity of the Father and of the Son and of the Spirit. That is, that each of the three can be properly described as 'God' in the fullest sense of the word;
(c) That the Father, the Son and the Spirit are personally distinct. That is, that the Father is neither the Son nor the Spirit, and that the Son is not the Spirit.

2. Matthew 28. 19-20
The closing verses of Matthew's Gospel provide a good starting point because the concise statement of verse 19 furnishes us with our Lord's own authority for each of the three statements made in paragraph 1.

When commissioning His disciples, the Lord Jesus spoke both of the authority that was His ('All authority has been given to me') and of the task that was theirs ('Go therefore, and . . .'). Happily for them He links these two statements with the promise that '**I** [the One who has the authority] am with **you** [who have the task]'. The Lord spoke clearly of their duty to baptize all disciples 'in ['into', literally] the name of the Father and of the Son and of the Holy Spirit'. In effect this meant that converts were enlisted into the service of the triune God. The Jews circumcised their children and proselytes 'in the name of the covenant . . . denoting both entry into the covenant and commitment to it'.[15] That is, by circumcision Jews were brought under the authority and control of the covenant. When Paul wrote of the children of Israel who came out

---

[15] *Theological Dictionary of the New Testament* (abridged in one volume), pp. 697-698.

of Egypt that 'all were baptized into Moses in the cloud and in the sea',[16] he was saying that they had identified themselves with Moses and had submitted themselves to his authority and leadership.[17] In a similar way, when baptized in the name of the triune God, Christian converts identified themselves with, and expressed their allegiance to, the Holy Trinity.

First, we must understand what Jesus meant by, 'the name'. A Hebrew did not regard a name as a mere label or means of identification. A name said something about the person who carried it. To the Jews a person's name expressed what the person was. We might think for instance of the words of Abigail concerning her husband Nabal, 'as his name is, so is he: Nabal [meaning 'folly'] is his name, and folly is with him'.[18] For this reason the Old Testament frequently draws attention to the significance of names.[19] A name, then, often signified not so much **who** a person was as **what** he was. The being of God likewise found expression in His name. Pre-eminently, in the Old Testament, 'the Name' signified 'Jehovah': 'this glorious and awesome name, the Lord your God'.[20] In the period between the Testaments (when Jews ceased to use the word 'Jehovah', out of a curious mixture of reverence and superstition) 'the Name' became one of the popular substitutes for 'Jehovah'. When in John 17 verse 6, our Lord said, 'I have manifested Your name',[21] He meant much the same as that which John had said of Him in chapter 1, 'He has declared Him ["He has made Him known"]'.[22]

There is no mistaking the implication of His words in Matthew chapter 28 verse 19, 'baptizing them in the name of the Father and of the Son and of the Holy Spirit'. We should note the exact words He used.

---

[16] 1 Cor. 10. 2.

[17] 'He turned the sea into dry land; they went through the river on foot', Ps. 66. 6. 'The children of Israel are the only people of whom I know who were properly baptized without even getting their feet wet!' (My comments on 1 Corinthians 10. 1-4 in *Precious Seed* Volume 61, Number 3, August 2006.)

[18] 1 Sam. 25. 25.

[19] See, for example, Gen. 3. 20 (Eve means 'living'); 4. 1 (Cain means 'gotten'); 5. 29 (Noah means 'rest' or 'comfort'), 17. 17-19 (Isaac means 'laughter').

[20] Deut. 28. 58.

[21] John 17. 6.

[22] John 1. 18.

(a) 'The name'. The Saviour does not say, 'the names of the Father' etc. Nor does He say, 'the name of the Father, the name of the Son' etc. The single name embraces the three persons. And by speaking as He does the Lord Jesus emphasizes the divine unity. There are not three separate beings.[23]

(b) 'Of the Father and of the Son and of the Holy Spirit'. The three are united in the single name. The three together can be correctly described by the one 'name', which to Jews was the equivalent of 'Jehovah', the only true God.

(c) The repeated article 'the' emphasizes the distinction of the persons. The three are not passing phases or modes of one person. There are three distinct persons.[24]

These truths are well illustrated by an ancient diagram.

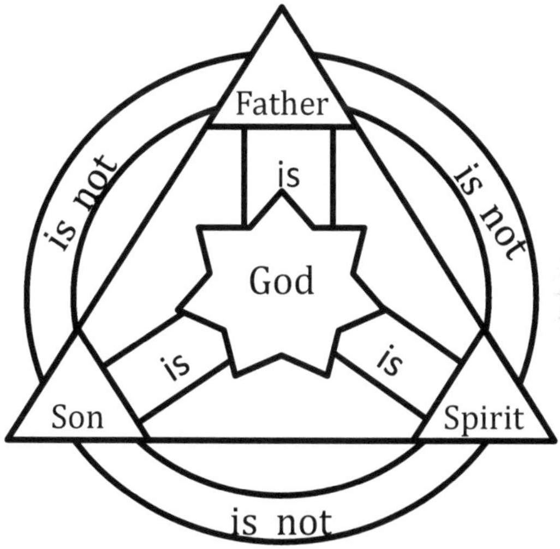

---

[23] 'The common name . . . expresses the unity of being', *Theological Dictionary of the New Testament*, Volume V, pg. 274.

[24] We read therefore of the three persons of the Godhead speaking to one another; e.g., Mark 1. 11; Heb. 1. 8; Matt. 11. 25-26; Rom. 8. 26; and acting towards each other – e.g., in sending or being sent, Gal. 4. 4, 6, or in glorifying one another, John 16. 14; 17. 1.

The Lord should be understood therefore as enlarging the name 'Jehovah' into that of 'the Father and of the Son and of the Holy Spirit'. He identified the Lord God of Israel with the Father and the Son and the Holy Spirit, and, in so doing, ascribed a threefold personality to Jehovah.

And so, a Gospel which more or less commences with the record of **a manifestation of the persons** of the Trinity (at the banks of Jordan, when the Son is baptized, the Spirit descends, and the Father speaks[25]) closes with **an affirmation of the doctrine** of the Trinity.

3. The New Testament evidence

The New Testament contains no carefully formulated statement of the doctrine of the Holy Trinity such as we find later in the creeds of the established church.[26] Indeed, I know of no reference to the word 'Trinity' until late in the second century, when Theophilus of Antioch used the Greek word *trias*. A little later, Tertullian used its Latin equivalent *trinitas*. We should not draw wrong conclusions from this. The fact that the New Testament contains no precise definition or systematic treatment of the subject does not mean that the subject had not been carefully thought about in apostolic days. And we possess in its various books more than enough data for us to establish clearly what the early church believed.

To substantiate the truth of the doctrine of the Holy Trinity biblically, we will need to firmly establish each of the three propositions in paragraph 1 above; namely, (a) that there is one God, (b) that the Father, Son and Spirit is each properly described as God, and (c) that the Father, Son and Spirit are each personally distinct from one another.

---

[25] Matt. 3. 16, 17. Compare the mention of the three persons of the Trinity in connection with the coming of the Holy Spirit on the day of Pentecost, Acts 2. 33.

[26] The Athanasian Creed, for example, commences, 'We worship God in Trinity and Trinity in unity, neither confounding the persons nor dividing the substance. For there is one person of the Father, another of the Son and another of the Holy Spirit. But the Godhead of the Father, of the Son and of the Holy Spirit is all one, the glory equal and the majesty coequal'.

A. There is one God
This is the fundamental article of faith of both the Jewish nation and the Old Testament, 'Hear, O Israel, Jehovah our God is one Jehovah', Deut. 6. 4 JND.[27] These words have been repeated twice every day for many centuries as part of the Jewish liturgy. The ideal attitude for a Jew was represented in the conduct of Rabbi Akiba of the first century, who, in the hour of his execution, continued to repeat the single word 'One'. The Lord Himself reiterated the words of Deuteronomy chapter 6 verse 4 when He summarized the law: 'The first of all the commandments is: "Hear, O Israel, the Lord our God, the Lord is one"'.[28]

The unity of the Godhead lay at the foundation of all Paul's teaching. For example, '**there is one God**, who will justify the circumcised by faith and the uncircumcised through faith', and '**there is one God**, and one mediator'.[29] Nor was Paul alone of course. We note the words of James, 'you believe that there is one God. You do well. Even the demons believe – and tremble'.[30]

That there is one God is a belief therefore that Christians shared with both Jews and demons. The 'fool' says, 'There is **no** God', Ps. 14. 1. Idolaters say, 'There are **many** gods', 1 Cor. 8. 6. But Christians say, 'There is **one** God'!

'Thus says the Lord, the King of Israel, and his Redeemer, the Lord of hosts: "I am the First and I am the Last; besides Me there is no God"', Isa. 44. 6.[31] We emphasize that we do **not** worship **three** gods; the Father, Son and Spirit are not three separate beings.

---

[27] Literally, 'Jehovah our God Jehovah one'. 'The significance of this paragraph is reflected in the fact that it became the centrepiece of Jewish daily worship, the Keri'at Shema' ("Recitation of the Shema"), named for its first word', *The Jewish Publication Torah Commentary*. For the fact that Jehovah alone is God see also Deut. 4. 35, 39.
[28] Mark 12. 29.
[29] Rom. 3. 30; 1 Tim. 2. 5. See also 1 Cor. 8. 4; Gal. 3. 20.
[30] Jas. 2. 19.
[31] See also Isa. 43. 10; 44. 8; 45. 5, 14, 18, 21, 22; 46. 9; 47. 8; 55. 5.

B. The Father, Son and Spirit is each properly described as God

B. 1. The Father is God

We do not need to adduce a great deal of evidence for this. It should be sufficient to refer to the many occurrences of the expression 'God the Father'.[32]

B. 2. The Son is God

Ever since New Testament days this statement has been attacked and challenged. Yet the evidence is overwhelming. We will briefly examine a sevenfold proof:

(1) ***Passages which directly assert the Godhead of the Son***. (a) Both the commencement and the climax of John's Gospel assert the full deity of our Lord: (i) 'In the beginning was the Word, and the Word was with God, and the Word was God', John 1. 1,[33] and (ii) 'Thomas answered and said to Him, "My Lord and my God!"', 20. 28.[34] (b) 'Who are Israelites . . . of whom, as according to flesh, is the Christ, who is over all, God blessed for ever', Rom. 9. 5 JND. (c) 'The blessed hope and glorious appearing of our great God and Saviour Jesus Christ', Titus 2. 13.[35] According to Acts chapter 19 verse 27, the Ephesians had a 'great goddess' (Artemis/Diana), but, according to Titus chapter 2 verse 13, the Christian has a 'great God' – Jesus Christ. (d) 'The righteousness of

---

[32] For example, Gal. 1. 3; Eph. 6. 23; Phil. 2. 11.

[33] Other passages using the Greek word for God, *theos,* without the definite article in a similar construction are always rendered 'God': e.g., Mark 12 . 27; Luke 20. 38; John 3. 2; 13. 3; Phil. 2. 13; Heb. 9. 14.

[34] Compare Rev. 4. 11, where the same construction is used in the plural ('our') instead of the singular ('my').

[35] The King James Version 'fails to bring out the deity of the Lord Jesus expressed very clearly in the Greek text. The latter conforms to the rule of Greek syntax known as Granville Sharp's rule, which states that when two nouns are in the same case and connected by *kai,* the first noun, articular, the second, anarthrous, the latter always relates to the same person or thing expressed or described by the first noun and is a farther description of it', Dana and Mantey, *A Manual Grammar of the Greek New Testament,* pg. 147. For the title 'great God' in the Old Testament, see Deut. 10. 17; Ezra 5. 8; Neh. 8. 6; Ps. 95. 3; Prov. 26. 10; Dan 2. 45.

our God and Saviour Jesus Christ', 2 Pet. 1. 1 RV and JND.[36] Thus John, Paul and Peter unite in giving the title 'God' to the Lord Jesus.

(2) ***Passages which indirectly assert the deity of Christ***.[37] For example:

(a) *His eternal existence*. 'I say to you, before Abraham was, I AM'.[38] For the Saviour to have said, 'before Abraham, I was' would have been no more than a claim to an existence prior to Abraham – a claim such as Michael the archangel could have made. Instead, Jesus asserted His self-existence and eternal being; that He was none less than the great 'I AM' of Exodus chapter 3 verse 14.[39]

(b) *His immutability*. 'Jesus Christ is the same yesterday, today, and forever', Heb. 13. 8.

(c) *His omniscience*. '**If** the mighty works which were done in you had been done in Tyre and Sidon, they *would* (not, we note, '**might**') have repented long ago in sackcloth and ashes'.[40] Only God can know for sure that 'if' such an event happened then certain consequences would follow.[41] Only God knows how every man, woman and child **would have** acted *if* their circumstances had been different to what they were. We mere mortals can only speculate.

(d) *His omnipotence*. His 'name shall be called Wonderful Counsellor,

---

[36] Again the King James Version 'fails to bring out the deity of the Lord Jesus expressed very clearly in the Greek text'; see note 21.

[37] The Lord Jesus knew that the acts of power which He had performed in the villages and towns of Galilee would have brought Tyre, Sidon and even Sodom to their knees in repentance. Note that our Lord does not say, '**If**. . . they **might** have', but '**If**. . . they/it **would** have'.

[38] John 8. 58. This is one of three instances where the Lord Jesus asserted His deity in discussion with the Jews, John 5. 18-19; 8. 58, 59; and 10. 30-39. In each instance, the Jews understood His claim to be that of equality with God and therefore attempted to kill Him, stone Him and arrest Him, respectively.

[39] 'He does not contrast Abraham's previous existence with His eternity of existence, but Abraham's coming into existence with His eternal being. There is a contrast between Abraham as a created being and our Lord as uncreated, the self-existent, eternal God'. KENNETH S. WUEST, *Bibliotheca Sacra*, July 1962, pg. 221.

[40] Matt. 11. 21; cp. v. 23.

[41] Compare Jer. 38. 17-18; and especially 1 Sam. 23. 12-13.

Mighty God', Isa. 9. 6 ESV.[42] The use of the title 'Mighty God' should be compared in its use in the following chapter: 'The remnant will return, the remnant of Jacob, to the **Mighty God** (which clearly refers to the Lord God)'.[43]

Note separately that those who, when speaking to Peter, Jesus described as 'my sheep' ('Shepherd {the Greek verb *poimainō*} my sheep', John 21. 16 JND), Peter later describes as 'the flock of God' ('Shepherd {*poimainō*} the flock of God', 1 Pet. 5. 2 JND).

(3) ***Passages which ascribe Old Testament divine titles to the Lord Jesus.***

(a) *Jehovah*. (i) 'In the name of Jesus every knee should bow, of things in heaven and things on earth and things under the earth, and that every tongue should confess that Jesus Christ is Lord', Phil. 2. 10-11 RV; compare, 'I the Lord . . . I am God, and there is none else. By myself have I sworn, the word is gone forth from my mouth in righteousness, and shall not return, that unto me every knee shall bow, every tongue shall swear', Isa. 45. 21-23 RV. (ii) 'All the churches shall know that I am He who searches the minds and hearts', Rev. 2. 23; compare, 'I the Lord search the mind and try the heart', Jer. 17. 10 RSV. (iii) Compare also: Matt. 3. 3 with Isa. 40. 3; Rom. 10. 13 with Joel 2. 32; Eph. 4. 8 with Ps. 68. 18; Heb. 1. 6 with Ps. 97. 7; 1 Pet. 2. 3-4 with Ps. 34. 8.[44] The confession 'Jesus is Lord' was the central confession of the early church, Rom. 10. 9; 1 Cor. 12. 3.

(b) *God* (*Elohim*). 'To the Son He says: Your throne, O God, is forever and ever; a sceptre of righteousness is the sceptre of your kingdom', Heb. 1. 8, 9; compare 'Your throne, O God, is forever and ever; a sceptre of righteousness is the sceptre of Your kingdom', Ps. 45. 6, 7.

(c) *The Lord of hosts*. (i) 'Sanctify in your hearts Christ as Lord', 1 Pet. 3.

---

[42] 'Father of eternity' may well mean simply eternal; compare other names formed with word 'father': *Abi-albon*, 'father of strength' = strong (2 Sam. 23. 31); *Abiasaph*, 'father of gathering' = gatherer (Exod. 6. 24); *Abigail*, a woman's name(!), 'father of joy/exultation' = exulting (1 Sam. 25 and 1 Chr. 2. 16).
[43] Isa. 10. 21. See also Jer. 32. 18.
[44] The repeated 'for' in this passage identifies the 'Lord' of Romans chapter 10 verses 12 and13 as the 'Lord Jesus' of verse 9.

15 RV; compare, 'The Lord of hosts, Him shall ye sanctify; and let Him be your fear', Isa. 8. 13 RV. (ii) 'The stone which the builders rejected (the Lord Jesus), the same was made the head of the corner; and a stone of stumbling, and a rock of offence', 1 Pet. 2. 7, 8 RV; compare, 'He (the Lord of hosts) will be a stone of stumbling and a rock of offence to both the houses of Israel', Isa. 8. 14. (iii) Compare also: John 12. 38-41 with Isa. 6. 3, 10; and note that John 12. 37 clearly identifies the 'Him' of verse 41 as the Lord Jesus.

(d) *The First and the Last*. 'He laid His right hand on me, saying to me, "Do not be afraid; I am the First and the Last. I am He who lives, and was dead, and behold, I am alive forevermore"', Rev. 1. 17; compare, 'Thus says the Lord, the King of Israel, and his Redeemer, the Lord of hosts: "I am the First and I am the Last; besides Me there is no God"', Isa. 44. 6. It is worth noting that the Lord God is called 'the First and the Last' three times in the Old Testament – always in Isaiah, Isa. 41. 4; 44. 6; 48. 12, and that the Lord Jesus is called 'the First and the Last' three times in the New Testament – always in the book of the Revelation, Rev. 1. 17; 2. 8; 22. 13.

(e) *The Ancient of Days*. 'The Ancient of Days was seated . . . the hair of His head was like pure wool', Dan. 7. 9; compare, 'One like the Son of Man . . . His head and hair were white like wool', Rev. 1. 13, 14.

(f) '*The Same*' ('The existing One who does not change'[45]). 'To the Son He (God) says . . . You, Lord, in the beginning laid the foundation of the earth . . . they will be changed. But you are **the same**', Heb. 1. 10-12; compare, 'Of old you laid the foundation of the earth, and the heavens are the work of your hands. They will perish, but you will endure; yes, they will all grow old like a garment; like a cloak you will change them, and they will be changed. But you are **the same**, and your years will have no end', Ps. 102. 25-27.

(g) '*The Rock*'. 'They drank of that spiritual Rock that followed them, and that Rock was Christ', 1 Cor. 10. 4;[46] compare, 'Ascribe greatness to our

---

[45] See the footnotes in J. N. Darby's *New Translation* to Deuteronomy chapter 32 verse 39 and Hebrews chapter 1 verse 12.

[46] In his statement that 'Christ' was the 'spiritual Rock that followed them', 1

God. He is the Rock', Deut. 32. 3, 4.[47]

Although not a direct reference to the Old Testament, it is useful also to note the title 'King of kings and Lord of lords', which is ascribed to God in 1 Timothy chapter 6 verses 15-16, and to the Lord Jesus in Revelation chapter 19 verse 16 (cp. v. 12).

(4) ***Passages which speak of the Lord Jesus being worshipped***. For example, Matt. 28. 9, 17 (where He did not reject worship, the worship of either the women or the eleven disciples). Note also that 'when He again brings the firstborn into the world, He says, Let all the angels of God worship Him', Heb. 1. 6, which is the more pointed when read in the light of the angel's replies to John in both Revelation chapter 19 verse 10 and Revelation chapter 22 verses 8 and 9: 'I fell at his feet to worship him. But he said to me, 'See that you do not do that! For I am your fellow servant . . . worship God!' It is interesting to note the limited use of the word 'worship' in Luke's Gospel, which occurs only in Luke chapter 4 verses 7 and 8 and Luke chapter 24 verse 52. It is, as our Lord said, the Father's purpose that 'all should honour the Son just as they honour the Father', John 5. 23.[48]

(5) ***Passages which record thanksgiving and prayer addressed to the Lord Jesus***. First, the example of Stephen, 'they stoned Stephen, praying, and saying, Lord Jesus, receive my spirit. And kneeling down, he cried with a loud voice, Lord, lay not this sin to their charge', Acts 7.

Cor. 10. 4, Paul was giving the word 'rock' a double meaning. The apostle has in mind the fact that the water which God gave Israel to drink had (on at least two occasions) come quite literally from a rock, Exod. 17. 1-7; Num. 20. 1-13. But, by playing on the word, he switches the meaning **from** a literal rock **to** a well-known title of God Himself – '**the** Rock'. It is worth noting that this particular title of God occurs five times in Deuteronomy chapter 32. It was Christ, Paul is saying, who accompanied Israel through the wilderness – and it was therefore 'Christ' whom they 'tempted' there, 1 Cor. 10. 9. It was, Paul is saying, Christ who constantly provided them with water to drink, and who therefore was their true source of refreshment for forty years.

[47] See also Deut. 32. 5, 18, 30, 31; cp. Ps. 62. 2, 6.

[48] See note 24 above.

59, 60.[49] Second, the example of Paul, (i) 'there was given to me a thorn in the flesh, a messenger of Satan to buffet me, that I should not be exalted overmuch. Concerning this thing I besought the Lord thrice, that it might depart from me. And he hath said unto me, My grace is sufficient for thee: for my power is made perfect in weakness. Most gladly therefore will I rather glory in my weaknesses, that the power of Christ may rest upon me', 2 Cor. 12. 7-9 RV,[50] and 'I thank Christ Jesus our Lord who has enabled me, because He counted me faithful, putting me into the ministry, although I was formerly a blasphemer, a persecutor, and an insolent man', 1 Tim. 1. 12, 13.

(6) ***Passages where doxologies are ascribed to Him***. Peter and Paul both close their last extant letters with very similar expressions concerning the Lord Jesus, 'to Him be glory forever and ever', 2 Tim. 4. 18, 'to Him be the glory both now and forever', 2 Pet. 3. 18. John, similarly, says concerning the Lord Jesus, 'to Him be glory and dominion forever and ever', Rev. 1. 5, 6.

(7) ***Passages which ascribe divine functions to the Lord***. I do not point to His miracles because any man can perform miracles with divinely communicated power.[51] I refer rather to those works and prerogatives which belong exclusively to God, such as (a) creation;[52] (b) providence and preservation;[53] (c) knowing the hearts of men, John 2. 25 (with 1 Kgs 8. 39[54]; 2 Chr. 6. 30), (d) the forgiving of sins, Mark 2. 5-12[55], and (e) the final raising of the dead and the settling of men's eternal destinies, John 5. 21-27.

---

[49] Note how Stephen's prayers echo our Lord's own prayers in Luke chapter 23 verses 34 and 46.

[50] Note that 'the Lord' to whom Paul prayed must have been the Lord Jesus because His 'my power' is spoken of by Paul as 'the power of Christ'.

[51] See also 2 Thess. 2. 9.

[52] See: John 1. 3; Col. 1. 16; Heb. 1. 10.

[53] See: Col. 1. 17; Heb. 1. 3.

[54] Solomon prayed, 'You alone know the hearts of all the sons of men'.

[55] Ultimately only God can forgive sins, for ultimately all sins are committed against God.

B. 3. The Spirit is God[56]

In Acts chapter 5, Peter implied clearly that to lie to the Holy Spirit was to lie to God, 'Peter said, "Ananias, why has Satan filled your heart to lie to the Holy Spirit . . . You have not lied to men but to God"'.[57] Equally clearly, Paul implied that to be a temple of the Holy Spirit was one and the same as to be the temple of God.[58] And John implied that to be born of the Spirit, John 3. 6, was to be born of God, 1 John 5. 4.[59]

Only God can know God in His fullness, yet 'the Spirit searches all things, yes, the deep things of God'.[60] There is nothing, not even in God, which baffles His scrutiny.[61] And the Holy Spirit is not only omniscient, but omnipresent, 'Where', David asked, 'can I go from your Spirit?'[62] The Holy Spirit is also eternal, 'Christ, who through the eternal Spirit offered Himself without spot to God'.[63]

C. The Father, Son and Holy Spirit are each personally distinct from one another

It is important to have clear in our minds the distinction between the persons of the Holy Trinity. There is little difficulty in proving the distinction between the Father and the Son. We read frequently of the Father having sent the Son.[64] We also read that the Father addressed the Son,[65] and that the Son addressed the Father in prayer.[66]

However, we need to ask a question about the Holy Spirit which it is unnecessary to ask about either the Father or the Son; namely, 'Is it correct to speak of the Spirit as a person?'

---

[56] See further, '*The Person of the Holy Spirit: Part 1*', JOHN F. WALVOORD, *Bibliotheca Sacra*, April 1940, pp. 166-189.
[57] Acts 5. 3, 4.
[58] 1 Cor. 6. 19; 2 Cor. 6. 16.
[59] See also 2 Cor. 3. 17, 18 ('the Lord the Spirit').
[60] 1 Cor. 2. 10.
[61] 1 Cor. 2. 10, 11.
[62] Ps. 139. 7.
[63] Heb. 9. 14.
[64] See, for example, 1 John 4. 14.
[65] See Mark 1. 11; John 12. 28; Heb. 1. 8.
[66] See Matt. 11. 25, 26; 26. 39, 42; John 17. 1.

We answer an emphatic 'Yes' for the following reasons.

(1) ***The way in which scripture speaks of the Holy Spirit***. Jesus claimed that the Father would give 'another Helper (or 'Counsellor')' to His disciples,[67] where the word translated 'another' (*allos*) suggests 'another of the same kind'.[68] That is, the Holy Spirit is as much a person as is the Lord Jesus. Again, the Holy Spirit is often referred to by the Greek masculine pronoun not the neuter pronoun.[69]

(2) ***The actions which are ascribed to Him***. He speaks (e.g. Acts 1. 16; 8. 29), referring to Himself as 'I', 10. 19, 20; He warns, 20. 23; He forbids, 16. 6; He appoints, 20. 28; He sends, 13. 4; He bears witness, John 15. 26; He prevents, Acts 16. 7; He predicts, 1 Pet. 1. 11; He groans, Rom. 8. 26; He leads, Luke 4. 1; Rom. 8. 14; He intercedes, 8. 27; He loves, 15. 30; He wills, 1 Cor. 12. 11; He helps, Acts 2. 4; Rom. 8. 26; He encourages, Acts 9. 31; He knows, 1 Cor. 2. 11; He shows, Heb. 9. 8; He searches, 1 Cor. 2. 10; He guides, John 16. 13; He invites, Rev. 22. 17; He reveals, Luke 2. 26; He teaches, John 14. 26; 1 Cor. 2. 13; He dwells, John 14. 17; 1 Cor. 3. 16; Eph. 2. 22, He gives, Acts 2. 4 etc. The Holy Spirit can be **grieved**, Isa. 63. 10; Eph. 4. 30; He can be **tempted**, Acts 5. 9; He can be **resisted**, 7. 51, and He can be **lied to**, 5. 3.

And I note that sometimes the Holy Spirit is closely associated in an action with believers, who are unquestionably persons! For example, we have the words of James, 'It seemed good to the Holy Spirit, and to us',[70] and of the Lord Jesus, 'The Spirit of truth, who proceeds from the Father, He will bear witness about me. And you also will bear witness'.[71]

---

[67] John 14. 16.

[68] '*Allos* expresses a numerical difference and denotes "another of the same sort"; *heteros* expresses a qualitative difference and denotes "another of a different sort". Christ promised to send "another Comforter" (*allos*, "another like Himself", not *heteros*), John 14. 16', W. E. VINE, *Expository Dictionary of New Testament Words*, article 'Another'.

[69] For example, 'when He, the Spirit of truth, has come, He will guide you into all truth', John 16. 13; cp. John 14. 26; 15. 13; 16. 7, 8. The word 'Spirit' in Greek is neuter and grammatical considerations sometimes require a neuter pronoun; e.g., John 14. 16-18.

[70] Acts 15. 28.

[71] John 15. 26, 27 ESV.

And we have the words of John, 'The Spirit and the Bride say, Come!'[72]

And it would surely be absurd to baptize in the name of a personal Father and a personal Son and an impersonal influence or energy![73]

4. New Testament references to the Holy Trinity

We find references and allusions to the Holy Trinity throughout the New Testament. We find, for example:

(a) ***A salutation***. 'From Him who is . . . from the seven Spirits . . . and from Jesus Christ';[74]
(b) ***A greeting***. 'The foreknowledge of God the Father . . . sanctification of the Spirit . . . the blood of Jesus Christ';[75]
(c) ***A thanksgiving***. 'God chose you . . . through sanctification by the Spirit . . . that you may obtain the glory of our Lord Jesus Christ';[76]
(d) ***A prayer***. 'The Father . . . His Spirit . . . that Christ may dwell';[77]
(e) ***A practical exhortation***. 'Praying in the Holy Spirit . . . the love of God . . . the mercy of our Lord Jesus Christ';[78]
(f) ***A doxology***. 'The grace of our Lord Jesus Christ . . . the love of God . . . the communion of the Holy Spirit'.[79]

Many doctrinal statements also bring together the three persons of the Trinity:

(g) ***Salvation announced***. 'The Lord . . . God also . . . gifts of the Holy Spirit';[80]
(h) ***Salvation experienced***. 'The love of God . . . the renewal of the Holy

---

[72] Rev. 22. 17.
[73] Matt. 28. 19. Again, references, such as Luke 4. 14; Rom. 15. 13, 19; Gal. 2. 29, provide evidence that 'the Spirit' is personal and is not to confused with an impersonal 'power'. Else in each case we would be reading of 'the power of the power'!
[74] Rev. 1. 4, 5.
[75] 1 Pet. 1. 2.
[76] 2 Thess. 2. 13, 14 ESV.
[77] Eph. 3. 14-17.
[78] Jude 20, 21.
[79] 2 Cor. 13. 14.
[80] Heb. 2. 3, 4.

Spirit . . . through Jesus Christ';[81]
(i) ***Salvation enjoyed***. 'Love of God . . . by the Holy Spirit . . . Christ died';[82]
(j) ***Access***. 'Through Him (Christ) . . . by one Spirit . . . to the Father';[83]
(k) ***Apostasy***. 'Partakers of the Holy Spirit . . . the good word of God . . . the Son of God';[84]
(l) ***Unity***. 'One Spirit . . . one Lord . . . one God and Father';[85]
(m) ***Spiritual Gifts***. 'The same Spirit . . . the same Lord . . . the same God'.[86]

Again, we find whole sections of scripture with a 'trinitarian' structure:

(n) ***Romans 1-8***. In very simple terms, the first eight chapters of Romans can be said to deal with (i) the wrath of God, 1. 3 - 3. 20; (ii) the work of Christ, 3. 21-7. 24, and (iii) the witness of the Spirit and life in the Spirit, 8. 1-39;
(o) ***Eph. 1. 3-14***. This passage is divided into three by the expression 'the praise of the glory of His grace', v. 6, and 'the praise of His glory', vv. 12, 14. Here we read of election and acceptance by ***the Father*** in verses 3-6, of redemption and forgiveness through ***Christ*** in verses 7-12, and of a seal and earnest in ***the Spirit*** in verses 13-14;[87]
(p) ***Hebrews 1-3***. In chapter 1, ***God*** speaks, vv. 2, 5-8, 10, 13; in chapter 2, ***the Son*** speaks, vv. 12-13; in chapter 3, ***the Spirit*** speaks, v. 7;
(q) ***Hebrews 10. 5-18***. Verses 5-10 speak of the ***will*** of the Father; verses 11-14 speak of the ***work*** of the Son, and verses 15-18 speak of the ***witness*** of the Holy Spirit.

From the above references and passages, we should note:

---

[81] Titus 3. 4-6.
[82] Rom. 5. 5, 6.
[83] Eph. 2. 18. See also the reference to the three persons of the Holy Trinity at the close of Ephesians chapter 2. Verses 20 to 22 speak of the Lord Jesus as 'the chief corner stone' of the church, which itself constitutes 'a dwelling place for God in the Spirit'.
[84] Heb. 6. 4-6.
[85] Eph. 4. 4-6.
[86] 1 Cor. 12. 4-6.
[87] We might say that this section teaches that salvation was planned by the Father, was executed by the Son, and is applied by the Holy Spirit.

(1) The wide variety of New Testament authors who contribute these;
(2) The unstudied and natural way in which the threefold pattern is introduced in each case;
(3) The varying order in which the three persons are mentioned. The apostolic writers clearly did not feel compelled to follow the order 'Father, Son, and Holy Spirit'. Indeed, the references and passages cited provide examples of every possible combination. To these writers the order clearly wasn't significant.

Consider the many things separately attributed to each of the persons of the Trinity:

	The Father	The Son	The Holy Spirit
Is eternal	Ps. 90. 2	Mic. 5. 2	Heb. 9. 14
Is holy	John 17. 11	Luke 4. 34; Acts 3. 14	Matt. 1. 18, 20; 3. 11 etc.
Is true/truth	John 7. 28	Rev. 3. 7	1 John 5. 6
Creates	Gen. 1. 1	John 1. 3; Col. 1. 16	Job 33. 4
Searches	Jer. 17. 10	Rev. 2. 23	1 Cor. 2. 10
Raises the dead	Acts 26. 8; 1 Cor. 6. 14	John 5. 28-29	Rom. 8. 11; 1 Pet. 3. 18
Is glorious	Eph. 1. 17	1 Cor. 2. 8	1 Pet. 4. 14
Loves	John 16. 27	Eph. 3. 19	Rom. 15. 30
Wills	1 Tim. 2. 4	John 17. 24	1 Cor. 12. 11
Invites	Isa. 1. 18 (Come and reason)	Matt. 11. 28 (Come and rest)	Rev. 22. 17 (Come and refresh)
Gives life	1 Tim. 6. 13	John 5. 21	2 Cor. 3. 6
Justifies	Rom. 8. 33	Gal. 2. 17	1 Cor. 6. 11
Sanctifies	Jude 1 ('by')	1 Cor. 1. 2 ('in')	1 Pet. 1. 2 ('of')
Indwells	2 Cor. 6. 16	Eph. 3. 17	John 14. 17
Pours out	Titus 3. 6	Matt. 26. 28	Rom. 5. 5
Known by Christians	1 John 2. 13	1 John 2. 3	1 John 4. 6
Our source of	Rom. 5. 11	Phil. 4. 4	1 Thess. 1. 6

joy			
Our fellowship with	1 John 1. 3	1 Cor. 1. 9	2 Cor. 13. 14

It is therefore no exaggeration to say that the New Testament is permeated by trinitarian teaching.

5. The Old Testament

It is obvious to even the most casual reader that the Old Testament offers no developed doctrine of the Holy Trinity.[88] We can, however, say two things at least.

(a) At no time is the teaching of the Old Testament inconsistent with the later revelation given in the New Testament. I note, for instance, that, when the Law says that 'Jehovah our God is one Jehovah' (or possibly, 'Jehovah our God, Jehovah is one'),[89] the Hebrew word translated 'one' can (and often does) include the idea of plurality in unity.[90] The idea conveyed by the word **can**, therefore, be that of 'one made up of more than one'.[91]

(b) There are several clear anticipations of the doctrine.[92] There are, for example, indications of the deity both of the Messiah[93] and of the Holy Spirit.[94] There are also the passages in Genesis and Isaiah where God

---

[88] Personally, I would not appeal to the plural *elohim* as evidence for plurality within the Godhead. I note, for example, that the plural *elohim* is used to describe Ba'al, Judg. 6. 31, Dagon, Judg. 16. 23-14, and even Samuel, 1 Sam. 28. 13.

[89] Deut. 6. 4.

[90] See, for example, Gen. 2. 24; Num. 13. 23; Judg. 21. 6; Ezek. 37. 17.

[91] See *New International Dictionary of Old Testament Theology and Exegesis*, Vol. 4, pp. 1217-1218. I am certainly not claiming that Deuteronomy chapter 6 verse 4 teaches the doctrine of the Trinity. But I think it fair to say that the verse is wholly consistent with it.

[92] See the reference to all three persons of the Trinity in Isaiah chapter 42 verse 1, and possibly in Isaiah chapter 48 verse 16.

[93] Isa. 9. 6; Zech. 13. 7; Mic. 5. 2.

[94] 2 Sam. 2. 2, 3; Job 26. 13; Pss. 104. 30; 139. 7.

speaks in terms of 'us': (i) 'Then God said, Let **us** make man in our image, after our likeness'[95]; (ii) 'The Lord God said, "Behold, the man has become like one of **us**, to know good and evil"'[96]; (iii) 'The Lord said . . . Come, let **us** go down and there confuse their language'[97]; and (iv) 'I heard the voice of the Lord saying, "Whom shall I send, and who will go for **us**?"'[98]

We may wonder why it was that the full revelation of the truth about the triune God was held back until New Testament times. We are not told but two observations may help us:

(1) I suspect that an early revelation of the triune God might have proved dangerous. As it was, Israel showed a constant tendency to idolatry and polytheism. It was wise therefore that the fact that there is only one God should be fixed firmly in their minds before the fuller revelation of one God in three persons was given.

(2) It was far easier for men to grasp and to accept the doctrine of the Trinity after the incarnation of the Son and after the coming of the Holy Spirit at Pentecost.[99]

6. Understanding and faith

Not that it is possible for any human mind to grasp how three persons can exist in one being. We believe the doctrine of the Trinity, not because we understand it, but because the Bible teaches it. We are altogether unable to fathom the depths of the divine being, and the doctrine of the Holy Trinity must therefore remain a sublime mystery which transcends human thought.[100] But God has spoken, and it is

---

[95] Gen. 1. 26. Clearly 'our image' is one and the same as 'the image of God', v. 27. That God was not talking to angels is clear therefore because, referring to the creation of man, the writer declares, 'in the image of God created He him'. God never created man in the image of angels, but in the divine image alone.

[96] Gen. 3. 22.

[97] Gen. 11. 6, 7.

[98] Isa. 6. 8.

[99] Indeed, the early Christians' very real trinitarian experience necessitated a doctrinal explanation. For that experience, see, for example, 'through Him (the Lord Jesus) we both have access by one Spirit to the Father', Eph. 2. 18.

[100] It has been said of the doctrine of the Trinity: 'Set out to understand it, and

enough!

7. The different roles and functions of the persons of the Holy Trinity

In the outworking of their eternal purpose and their counsels for time, the persons of the Godhead have adopted different roles and perform different functions.[101]

This must not be understood in terms of human arrangements, such as superiority-inferiority. But, although ever remaining equal with Him in nature and being, the Son and Spirit act in subjection to the Father. The Father sent the Son into the world,[102] and the Father and the Son sent the Spirit.[103] Throughout, the Father, the Son and the Holy Spirit co-operate in the administration of that eternal purpose which knows neither defeat nor frustration, and which will be consummated when 'God' is 'all in all'.[104]

It should surely fill us all with wonder and amazement that we should be the objects of the eternal purpose of the triune God.

'The grace of the Lord Jesus Christ, and the love of God, and the communion of the Holy Spirit be with you all'.

The Power of God* - A. Mellish

If we were to talk to one of our neighbours, or take a random survey in the local High Street, and ask for some descriptive words about God, I think it would be safe to say that the word 'power', or 'powerful', would be placed on the list very quickly. Further, whenever men have made

---

you'll lose your mind. But set out to deny it, and you'll lose your soul!'

[101] See the Additional Note to John 14. 28 in B. F. Westcott's *Commentary on the Gospel of John*. Consider the statement, 'Her Majesty Queen Elizabeth II is greater than I'. Clearly, I mean that she is greater than I am in terms of wealth, authority, status, influence, renown etc. No-one would take me to mean that she is more of a human being than I am. See further: https://www.cbmw.org/images/jbmw_pdf/15_2/10.pdf.

[102] Gal. 4. 4; 1 John 4 14.

[103] John 14. 26; 15. 26; 16. 7.

[104] 1 Cor. 15. 28.

up their own ideas of gods, in some capacity they will attribute some level of power to their god. There is something within all men that wants to attribute power to God, and, even in the case of the pagan, his gods.

When we come to the scriptures, we are faced not with a God who says He is powerful, but, by His actions, He demonstrates His power, and it is primarily this aspect that we will focus on in this paper. Before doing so, it will be worthwhile to consider the different uses of the word as we come upon them in the scriptures.
Rather remarkably, the exact expression 'power of God' is not found in the Old Testament, and the first person to use this expression was the Lord Himself, Matt. 22. 29, where He accused the Sadducees of not knowing the scriptures, nor the 'power of God'. If we lift this verse off the page of scripture in application for the current purpose, we can take from it that it is only by knowing, or, more accurately, discerning or perceiving the scriptures that we can come to a full appreciation of the power of God.

According to W. E. VINE, the use of the word in scripture describes for us God's ability, might, dominion, strength, and authority. There are two words that highlight God's power as one of His attributes. The first is the Greek word *dunamis*, and this, according to STRONG's Lexicon, is inherent power, power residing in a thing by virtue of its nature, or which a person or thing exerts and puts forth. The psalmist may well ask the question, 'For who in the heaven can be compared unto the Lord? who among the sons of the mighty can be likened unto the Lord?' Ps. 89. 6. For us, as we come to an understanding of scripture, this makes it significantly easier to comprehend that power is clearly a rightful attribute of God.

Another word used in scripture is the word *exousia*, and again we are indebted to VINE as he shows that it is 'the freedom of action, right to act', and, when used of God, it is absolute, and unrestricted, e.g., 'But I will forewarn you whom ye shall fear: Fear him, which after he hath killed hath power to cast into hell; yea, I say unto you, Fear him', Luke 12. 5. Yet, in every generation men in their ignorance rail against God with, they think, impunity!

The use of the word 'power' is also applied to Christ and His miracles; men, and authority that is delegated to them; and angels who, in Ephesians chapter 3 verse 10, are described as 'powers'.

Display of God's Power

Anyone looking for a description of God and opening a Bible at the first chapter and verse would be in awe as they see a demonstration of His power as the creation of this world is brought before them. In this demonstration of power we begin to learn about the character of God, as we see, for example, order and variety, and a remarkable expression of power as He creates the worlds out of nothing. As we see the order that God brings to the days of creation, we also begin to appreciate something of the mind of God. Job would have appreciated this when, in chapter 38, God speaks to him, and, in a series of questions, begins to show Job that His power had order to it, it was a power that did not introduce things randomly, 'Where wast thou when I laid the foundations of the earth? declare, if thou hast understanding. Who hath laid the measures thereof, if thou knowest? or who hath stretched the line upon it? Whereupon are the foundations thereof fastened? or who laid the corner stone thereof?' Job 38. 4-6. God, completely, and independently!

Outside of the creation of Adam, when we think of the physical creation of the world, there are two expressions that sum up God's power in the creation. First, 'And God said, Let there be light: and there was light', Gen. 1. 3. 'How simple! And yet how Godlike!' C. H. MACKINTOSH. 'He spake, and it was done. He commanded, and it stood fast', Ps. 33. 9. The unregenerate man might ask all the questions, and yet the newest believer can appreciate, by faith, it was by His power that all things came into being.

Second, 'he made the stars also', Gen. 1. 16. With the knowledge that men have acquired, *Encyclopaedia Britannica* brings the subject of stars under forty-one different sub-sections. While it should not surprise us that there was not one reference to the power of God, we can appreciate that to our God, it was nothing to put the stars in their place. In all their vastness and variety, they are immense distances away from our earth, and yet visible to the naked eye. We can look up and just wonder in amazement; 'he made the stars also'.

Again, we look to the appreciation of the psalmist to demonstrate to us not only God's power in creation but how He moves about His created universe, and in it we can come to value other facets of God. Momentarily, for example, 'He maketh the clouds his chariot: who walketh upon the wings of the wind', Ps. 104. 3. We know the power and force of wind, in hurricanes, and typhoons, and God reveals to us that He 'walks' on the wind. That which sinful man does not have the ability to harness, God simply walks on, and exhibits His absolute power over His creation.

With the establishment of the creation, God has not just stood idly back. His power is seen daily as He 'upholdeth all things by the word of his power', Heb. 1. 3, and, in every aspect of nature, including human life, we see the preserving power of God, for example, on the land from the oceans, or in the womb of a mother as she carries her unborn child. Similarly, God has placed ordered governments of men, and when men have failed to execute this justly, we see His power in judgement upon them.

Designation of God's Power

When God created this world, He gave it to Adam to look after. The psalmist tells us, 'Thou madest him to have dominion over the works of thy hands', Ps. 8. 6, and, as we know, Adam failed miserably. It was always God's intention that power would be invested in a man to be responsible for the creation, and yet, sadly, every dispensation has proved that sinful man does not have the ability to carry out this mandate. Today, what is the earth's condition? Our answer is found in Romans chapter 8 verse 22, 'For we know that the whole creation groaneth and travaileth in pain together until now'. Verse 19 of the same chapter tells us that, 'The earnest expectation of the creature waiteth for the manifestation of the sons of God'.

Beloved, we should be looking for the rapture, when we will see our blessed Lord, but can you take your mind further to the day when wondering worlds will see that Man of Calvary, and, in Christ, God's power (authority) will be designated to Him, the perfect Man, as He sets up His kingdom, and we, with Him, will rule and reign. For the first time, God's original intention will be displayed through His well-beloved Son, and perfect rule will be carried out.

He must have the pre-eminence, and, without taking anything away from Christ, I would exhort us not to lose sight of the truth, that this designation of God's power will be at our disposal too, as we participate in the rule and reign of Christ. Paul reminds the Corinthians, 'Know ye not that we shall judge angels?' 1 Cor. 6. 3, and that we will judge the world. 'To him that overcometh will I grant to sit with me in my throne, even as I also overcame, and am set down with my Father in his throne', Rev. 3. 21.

The earth was created for the habitation of men, and we, who we were created in His likeness and image and as those saved by grace, were saved to enable God to have a bride for His Son. John describes us as 'the bride, the Lamb's wife', 21. 9, we will share His throne and rule over God's universe with Him in power and authority. As God's power is demonstrated at the beginning of time, in all the majesty of the creation, when we come to the end of the Bible, we begin to get a glimpse of the purpose of it all. Just as God saw that it was 'not good that the man should be alone', Gen. 2. 18, God desired a bride for His Son, and, in a future day, presented to Christ without spot or blemish, we will be seated with Him upon the throne, ruling and reigning into all eternity.

The Sovereignty of God* - R. Collings

Scripture quotations are from the New King James Version unless otherwise stated.

Introduction

Being unique, incomparable, and ineffable, it is impossible for any created intelligence to have a comprehensive knowledge of God, for He is infinitely exalted above all His creatures. Thousands of years ago Zophar said, 'Can you search out the deep things of God? Can you find out the limits of the Almighty? They are higher than heaven – what can you do? Deeper than Sheol – what can you know? Their measure is longer than the earth and broader than the sea', Job 11. 7-9.

Yet, although He is unfathomable, God is not unknowable for He has chosen to reveal Himself to us. All that we shall ever know about Him, is the result of His choosing to make Himself known. But it doesn't stop there for God is not only knowable but is approachable. Like Abraham, we can say, 'Indeed now, I who am but dust and ashes have taken it upon myself to speak to the Lord', Gen. 18. 27.

As is true of every divine attribute, God's sovereignty is immeasurable. Even if it were possible to have the tongues of men and angels, we would have to agree with the hymn that 'all are to mean to speak His worth'. Therefore, it is important that we embark on this brief consideration of the sovereignty of God with a great sense of awe, and conscious inadequacy.

A definition

Before attempting to give a limited definition of the sovereignty of God there are two points we need to consider. First, the words 'sovereign' and 'sovereignty' do not occur in the Bible. However, that does not mean that God is not sovereign. From the beginning to the end of the scriptures we see the irrefutable evidences of this glorious truth. Second, it may be more accurate to suggest that sovereignty is not an attribute of God, rather it is the direct outcome of all His attributes. We say that God is love because love is an intrinsic element of His essential nature rather than because of something that He does or says. However, God is sovereign because He is almighty, spatially unlimited, ever-existing and measureless in knowledge.

Recognizing the limitations of any definition of divine sovereignty, we can state that, because of all that He is, God will achieve everything His perfect will determines. However, a mistake we need to avoid is to think that, because He is sovereign, God will act in any way contrary to His nature. For example, God cannot lie, Titus 1. 2. Sovereignty is exclusively His prerogative and He does not require the consent of anyone, or anything, to exercise it. Writing to the saints at Ephesus, Paul says of God that He 'works all things according to the counsel of His will', Eph. 1. 11.

An acknowledgment of the sovereignty of God

One of the clearest tributes to the sovereignty of God came not from the lips of a mighty prophet or a faithful priest, nor was it the overflowing worship of some devoted saint, but it was the confession of a heathen monarch. Nebuchadnezzar, the king of Babylon, declared, 'I, Nebuchadnezzar . . . blessed the most High and praised and honoured him who lives forever: for His dominion is an everlasting dominion and His kingdom is from generation to generation . . . he does according to His will in the army of heaven and among the inhabitants of the earth. No one can restrain His hand', Dan. 4. 34-35. Daniel describes Nebuchadnezzar as a king of kings and, in comparison with his kingdom, all subsequent world empires will be inferior, yet that Babylonian despot was brought to the point where he acknowledged that there is only one Ruler who is sovereign and he describes Him as being 'the most high'.

God's right to be sovereign

World history is littered with the names of people who have occupied a place of authority or power for which they had no merit, or suitability. By conniving, bribery or brute force, they have elevated themselves above their rightful station and exercised an influence they didn't deserve. However, in thinking about God's sovereignty we are contemplating one who not only has the ability, but has the unquestionable entitlement to be sovereign.

God has the ability to be sovereign because of what He is[105] and, in addition, He has the right because of who He is – He is God. His right to be the supreme governor derives from no other source than Himself. In Isaiah chapter 46, God gives a self-description, which is in direct contrast to the lifeless and powerless gods of the heathen, 'I am God, and there is no other; I am God, and there is none like Me', v. 9. In the previous chapter, God proclaims, 'I am the Lord, and there is no other; There is no God besides Me . . . that they may know from the rising of the sun to its setting that there is none besides Me. I am the Lord, and there is no other', vv. 5, 6.

In addition to His inherent right to be sovereign, there is something that God has done that also gives Him that entitlement – for sovereignty presupposes the fact of creation. Without any third party influence, for

[105] God is sovereign because He is eternal (not limited to, or by, time), omnipotent (all powerful), omnipresent (not limited by space), immutable (unchanging), and omniscient (all knowing).

there was no third party, God created the heavens and the earth. Before that there was nothing and nowhere save God and His eternal abode. The universe had not been formed, and creation existed only as a blueprint in the counsels of the Almighty, then God spoke 'and it was done; He commanded, and it stood fast', Ps. 33. 9. Furthermore, God created this vast universe for His own pleasure, hence the twenty-four elders in heaven cry out, 'Thou art worthy, O Lord, to receive glory and honour and power: for thou hast created all things, and for thy pleasure they are and were created', Rev. 4. 11 KJV.

A consequence of God's sovereignty

A direct consequence of God's sovereignty is that no one has the right to challenge what He does. Despite this, sin-corrupted and devil-blinded mortals who live on a planet that is miniscule against the backdrop of the universe, and whose lives are just a vapour, frequently question God in a disparaging manner. Such people would do well to heed those words of Nebuchadnezzar, 'All the inhabitants of the earth are reputed as nothing . . . no one can restrain His hand or say to Him, What have You done?' Dan. 4. 35.

However, even those who are Christians have to admit there are many times when we cannot understand what God is doing or what He allows. Why did God permit Herod to kill James with the sword and yet miraculously deliver Peter from his hand? There are many imponderables in life, so many of our questions will remain unanswered and the challenge for us is to acknowledge that because God is infinitely wise He cannot err, and because He is infinitely righteous He will not do wrong. Happy is that believer who doesn't see life as an unfolding drama of inevitable, predetermined consequences in which they are hapless pawns but who bows in faith and says, 'As for God, His way is perfect', Ps. 18. 30.

Another outcome that should derive from God's sovereignty is the peace we ought to enjoy knowing that He is in control. C. H. SPURGEON said, 'There is no attribute more comforting to His children than that of God's sovereignty'. We live in a chaotic world where the unpredictability of nations, climate conditions, financial institutions and of individual behaviour is reaching unprecedented levels. Despite the best efforts of governments and international organizations, these uncertainties continue on an inexorable downward spiral until the time will come when men's hearts will fail them for fear. How grateful we should be, and how reassuring it is to know, that despite the global disarray nothing takes place outside of the sovereign will of God. He dwells in an eternal tranquillity because nothing can overrun the boundaries that His sovereignty has decreed, and, as the Most High, He 'rules in the kingdom of men', Dan. 4. 17.

Demonstrations of God's sovereignty

One sphere in which God stamped His sovereignty is creation, for He was under no obligation to create; that He chose to do so was purely a sovereign act governed by His own good pleasure. At a point He chose, God spoke and from nothing the heavens and the earth were created! When Solomon built the temple in Jerusalem he used great stones, cedar trees, fir trees, iron and brass too heavy to weigh, 100,000 talents of gold and 1,000,000 talents of silver. He employed 183,300 men and it took him seven years to complete. God needed no materials and employed no one, He just spoke, and in six days the universe was complete.

There is another sphere in which God has displayed His sovereignty, a sphere even more amazing than His first creation; it is in the new creation. In Ephesians chapter 1 we discover that God has brought about our salvation by His own will and His own purpose and His own design and to the praise of His own glory. For these reasons Paul describes each Christian as being 'his workmanship', Eph. 2. 10. To create the universe God just spoke and it cost Him nothing; to bring about the new creation God sent His Son - and it cost Him everything. That this was a demonstration of His sovereignty is clearly emphasized by Peter on the day of Pentecost, 'Him, being delivered by the determinate counsel and foreknowledge of God', Acts 2. 23 KJV.

Conclusion

We have hardly scratched the surface of this vast subject; our consideration at best has been but a sketchy introduction. Despite this inadequacy may we make it our ambition to get to know God better for, 'Thus says the Lord: "Let not the wise man glory in his wisdom, let not the mighty man glory in his might, nor let the rich man glory in his riches; but let him who glories glory in this, that he understands and knows Me"', Jer. 9. 23, 24.

Angels and the Sovereignty of God* - K. Totton

Introduction

This paper briefly surveys the role of angels in supporting the sovereign purposes of God. The 'sovereignty' of God means that He is absolute in His decrees and actions and is accountable to no one. In the midst of a world of rebellion, this truth is deeply comforting to the believer. Scripture often designates God as 'Jehovah of hosts', alluding to the innumerable hosts of mighty angels at His direction.[106] In Old Testament times, as the armies of Judah dwindled in line with diminishing national fortunes this was great solace to the godly. What God has promised, He can, and will bring to pass.

The Constitution of Angels

First, we discern God's sovereignty in relation to the nature and constitution of angels. Angels are each **directly created** by God, hence their frequent designation 'sons of God'.[107] However, unlike mankind they are not a race, for they do not reproduce. Yet they can appear as men, interact with humans, and indeed eat food, Gen. 18. 8. The Hebrew word *malak* and the Greek *angelos* alike point to one of their basic functions – messenger.

In addition, a great variety of terms are used to refer to these mysterious spirit beings: holy ones (sometimes rendered 'saints' KJV); seraphim; cherubim; spirits; thrones; dominions; principalities; powers; rulers; and watchers.

A. W. Pink has a helpful comment highlighting the sovereignty of God in respect of their hierarchical orders, 'Consider the angelic hosts. Surely we shall find uniformity here. But no; there, as elsewhere, the same sovereign pleasure of the Creator is displayed. Some are higher in rank

---

[106] 1 Sam. 17. 45; Ps. 24. 10. As the 'host of heaven' designated the heavenly bodies, Gen. 2. 1, and heavenly beings, 1 Kgs. 22. 19, the title came to signify Jehovah as the ruler of all heavenly powers, the supreme sovereign of the universe.

[107] Job 1. 6; 2. 1; 38. 7.

than others; some are more powerful than others; some are nearer to God than others. Scripture reveals a definite and well-defined gradation in the angelic orders. From archangel, past seraphim and cherubim, we come to "principalities and powers" (Eph. 3. 10), and from principalities and powers to "rulers" (Eph. 6. 12), and then to the angels themselves . . . Again we ask, Why this inequality, this difference in rank and order? And all we can say is "Our God is in the heavens, He hath done whatsoever He hath pleased" (Ps. 115. 3)'.

In a primeval revolt, probably associated with the fall of Satan himself, multitudes of angels rebelled, and fell irretrievably. By contrast, holy angels are designated 'elect', reflecting their preservation, 1 Tim. 5. 21. As such, they constitute a heavenly council, 1 Kgs. 22. 19-23; they stand in close relationship to God.[108]

The following sections consider some of the more important activities of angels in the furtherance of God's purposes.

Serving

According to Hebrews chapter 1 verse 14 RV, angels are 'all ministering spirits, sent forth to do service for the sake of them that shall inherit salvation'. The psalmist celebrates their obedience in this capacity, 'Bless the Lord, ye his angels, that excel in strength, that do his commandments, hearkening unto the voice of his word. Bless ye the Lord, all ye his hosts; ye ministers of his, that do his pleasure', Ps. 103. 20, 21.

Angels do not select, opt into, or back out of assignments! On the contrary, they are versatile and fully at the disposal of God. For example, 'one of the seven angels which had the seven vials full of the seven last plagues . . . talked with me, saying, Come hither, I will shew thee the bride, the Lamb's wife', Rev. 21. 9. Moreover, if the conduct of the seraphim is indicative, their joyful service is mixed with deep reverence and worship, Isa. 6. 3, and they sing to the praise of the mighty creator.[109]

---

[108] Matt. 18. 10; 24. 36.

[109] Ps. 148. 2; Job 38. 7.

Communicating

There can be nothing more important than doing God's will, 'Thy will be done, as it is in heaven', Matt. 6. 10. It is, therefore, most fitting that amidst the awe-inspiring scenes of Sinai the transmission of God's law to Israel was 'ordained through angels by the hand of a mediator', Gal. 3. 19. In contrast to the gospel first announced by the Son of God, the law was 'the word spoken through angels'.[110] At Sinai Israel entered into a formal covenant with God, with associated blessings and penalties. Whilst Moses officiated on the side of Israel, angels functioned on the divine side.

Executing judgement

Throughout scripture, angels are seen as the executors of God's selective judgements. We might think of the destruction of Sodom, Gen. 19. 13; the Egyptian firstborn on Passover night, Exod. 12. 23; the Israelite rebels in the wilderness, 1 Cor. 10. 10; Israel under David, 2 Sam. 24. 16; Sennacherib's proud Assyrian army, 2 Kgs. 19. 35; Herod for his impiety, Acts 12. 23. In every instance the judgement is delivered with unerring accuracy and lethal effect. Especially in the book of Revelation, we see the central role played by angels in the forthcoming trumpet and vial judgements on unrepentant 'earth-dwellers', see especially Revelation chapters 8 and 16.

Safeguarding believers

Earlier, reference was made to the service angels perform on behalf of the people of God, Heb. 1. 14. Believers matter to God – He **guards** His people as the apple of His eye. Angelic ministry is often seen in relation to the patriarchs.[111] Later, we see an angel's tenderness in attending to the physically and spiritually exhausted Elijah, 1 Kgs. 19. 5. When Elisha was in Dothan, surrounded by Syrian hosts, and his servant cried, 'Alas! how shall we do?', the Lord opened his eyes to see the mountain full of chariots and horses of fire round about, 2 Kgs. 6. 15, 17. Amidst oppression in the alien environment of Babylon, Daniel was saved by God's angel in the lions' den, Dan. 6. 22.

Then, in the days of the early church, we see how the risen and

---

[110] Heb. 2. 2 RV, cp. Acts 7. 53.

[111] Gen. 19. 15; 28. 12; 32. 1.

sovereign Lord sent His angel at critical moments – undoing prison doors, directing evangelists, and reassuring Paul the apostle.[112]

Ministering to the Son of God

Angelic ministry in relation to the Lord Jesus may be regarded as a special case of the general protection and vindication just considered, and reveals how comprehensively God's determinate counsel was fulfilled. Thus, angels are seen in the annunciation both to Mary and Joseph, the directions to the shepherds, and the praises of the heavenly hosts, and the preservation of the infant Christ.[113] Following the temptations in the wilderness they 'ministered' unto their creator, Matt. 4. 11. What our Lord steadfastly refused under satanic temptation, the Father amply provided, Ps. 91. 11, 12. Again, amidst the gloom and anguish of Gethsemane, 'there appeared an angel unto him from heaven, strengthening him', Luke 22. 43. Yet for our eternal salvation, and in spite of the fact that more than twelve legions of angels were at His disposal, He chose to suffer alone, enduring the awful stroke of divine justice. Angels feature prominently in the accounts of the resurrection, attesting the vindication of the crucified One, 'Behold, there was a great earthquake: for the angel of the Lord descended from heaven, and came and rolled back the stone from the door, and sat upon it . . . He is not here: for he is risen, as he said. Come, see the place where the Lord lay', Matt. 28. 2, 6. The action of the angel shows the comprehensive power of God in the face of all human and infernal powers; the stone is rolled away not to let the Lord out, but rather to admit the witnesses of the empty tomb.

Agents of God's sovereignty in history

At several points in the book of Daniel we find intriguing disclosures of the role of angelic hosts in relation to world rulers. Michael the archangel is represented as Israel's champion against her accuser Satan, Dan. 12. 1. More generally, Daniel chapter 10 unfolds the mysterious truth that there are evil patron-angels in the spirit world, answering to the proud and defiant leaders of kingdoms in the political world, the 'prince of Persia' and the 'prince of Grecia' standing in antagonism to Michael. How good to rest assured that 'the Most High

---

[112] Acts 5. 19; 12. 7; Acts 8. 26; 27. 23.

[113] Luke 1; 2; Matt. 1. 20.

ruleth in the kingdom of men, and giveth it to whomsoever he will'! God decrees in relation to the dominion of His Son, 'I will overturn, overturn, overturn . . . until he come whose right it is; and I will give it him', Ezek. 21. 27.

Conclusion

The consideration of angels reminds us that God's merciful purposes cannot be thwarted, His power is unlimited, and His providential care of His people is incessant. For our part, as servants of God frequently marked by failure and unworthiness, we can learn much from the example of angels: their prompt and unquestioning obedience; their unceasing worship; and their staunch refusal of human adulation. Yet, by infinite grace, we are destined for greater glory, responsibility, and intimacy with God[114] – 'which things the angels desire to look into'.

Further reading

J. B. CURRIE, *Angels – a Biblical Survey*, Ritchie, 1999.
W. R. LEWIS, 'Angels', in *The Faith, a Symposium of Bible Doctrine*, F. A. TATFORD (Ed.), Pickering & Inglis, 1952, pp. 245-256.

The Holiness of God* - E. G. PARMENTER

No other book sets out the nature and character of God more realistically than the Bible. In it the transcendent glory, majesty, almighty power, righteousness and holiness that characterize Him are all revealed with great clarity.

The basic truth embedded in the word 'holy' is 'to be set apart, to be separate' – God is altogether separate and apart from all that is neither holy nor pure. God in essence is the 'Holy One'. The meaning of holiness in respect of God is stated by John, 'This then is the message which we have heard of him . . . God is light, and in him is no darkness at all', 1 John 1. 5.

In His purity, majesty and glory God is absolutely and intrinsically holy. At the outset, the Bible emphasizes God's holiness and, throughout, the subject holds sway – God is holy – this truth is stamped indelibly on the

[114] 1 Cor. 6. 3; Eph. 3. 10; 5. 29, 30; Heb. 2. 5-11; 1 Pet. 1. 12c.

pages of scripture. If the actions of God in the Garden of Eden express His righteousness when He drove out the man, setting the cherubim at its entrance with a flaming sword, Gen. 3. 24, then at Sinai, when the law of God was given, the mountain burning with fire expresses His holiness, at which Moses said, 'I exceedingly fear and quake'. God's holiness was further displayed in the wilderness when Moses, approaching the bush that burned with fire, unconsumed, heard God's voice, 'Put off thy shoes from off thy feet; for the place whereon thou standest is holy ground', Exod. 3. 5, indicating that the manifested presence of God in His holiness made the surrounding area where Moses was holy ground. When the tabernacle was set up, Aaron with his sons were given the privilege to draw near to God. Nadab and Abihu, sons of Aaron, approached God, but with strange fire, both being consumed by fire that came out from the Lord God. On that occasion God acted in His holiness as a consuming fire, Lev. 10. 1, 2, a solemn reminder that in our priestly service we ought 'to serve God acceptably with reverence and godly fear: for our God is a consuming fire', Heb. 12. 28, 29. The holiness of God is the reason behind the dietary laws given to Israel. On the basis of what God is, Moses commanded the people, 'Ye shall be holy, for I am holy', Lev. 11. 44, 45. The same truth is stated in Leviticus chapter 19 verse 2, 'Ye shall be holy, for I the Lord your God am holy'. Israel's relationship to God resulted in His holiness reaching into every department of life. In the New Testament, Peter lifts the truth of God's holiness from the references in Leviticus and applies the same principle to believers of this present day. 'But as he which hath called you is holy, so be ye holy in all manner of conversation [behaviour]; because it is written, Be ye holy; for I am holy', 1 Pet. 1. 15, 16.

Isaiah saw the Lord sitting upon a throne, high and lifted up, whose train filled the temple; the intrinsic holiness of the throne-sitter is seen in smoke, the incense of worship; and, before the throne, the seraphim, crying one to another, 'Holy, holy, holy is the Lord of hosts'. (The tense gives the sense that this was characteristic of their ministry continually). These burning ones are continuously occupied with the holiness of God, in whose presence they cover their faces. Isaiah responded, 'Woe is me, for I am undone'. Any contemplation we might have of God in the beauty and glory of His holiness will bring us to the same place.

Coming to the New Testament, when God was manifested in flesh, the angel's message to Mary was 'that holy thing which shall be born . . . shall be called the Son of God', Luke 1. 35. In the days of His flesh the Lord Jesus manifested the beauty of divine holiness in His sinless life. The quality of that holiness was now displayed in perfection in the person of Christ. The absolute holiness of God was recognized in the Lord throughout His sojourn here. Demons said, 'We know thee who thou art, the Holy One of God'. The writer to the Hebrews affirms, 'who is holy, harmless, undefiled, separate from sinners'. What He is now in heaven He was on earth in all the polluting atmosphere of sin in which He lived, moved and had His being. At Golgotha, in those hours of darkness when our Lord was 'made sin for us', there is evidenced the holiness of God. God who is of 'purer eyes than to behold evil and canst not look upon iniquity', Hab. 1. 13, forsook the Man of Calvary who had taken responsibility to be the sin bearer – 'My God, my God, why hast thou forsaken me?' The answer – 'But thou art holy', Ps. 22. 1, 3. The implication of this truth for believers today is be holy in all manner of conduct, holy in thought, word and ways, for 'it is written, "I am holy", saith the Lord'.

The Love of God* - B. OSBORNE

The apostle John tells us that 'God is love', 1 John 4. 8, 16. It is what He is essentially and eternally. He loves from everlasting. The statement is true quite independently of our being there to be loved. What then was the object of such love so that it could have been satisfied even without being poured out on mankind? We note the words of the Lord Jesus, 'Thou lovedst me before the foundation of the world', John 17. 24. Love in its essential nature exists in relationship and involves self-communication to another, and so if love and fatherhood belong eternally to God, there must be a distinction of persons within the Godhead. If we conceive of God as always and essentially living and loving, we must accept the doctrine of an eternal Son and Spirit of God. The relationship between the Father and Son is one of love. Most frequently the Father's love for the Son is brought before us.[115] We also learn of the Son's love for the Father.[116]

---

[115] Mark 1. 11; Matt. 12. 18; John 3. 35; 15. 9; 17. 23, 24, 26; Col. 1. 13 NIV.
[116] John 14. 31.

In the Old Testament the love of God is seen particularly in His relationship with Israel. The Lord chose Israel because He loved her.[117] It was not evoked by any intrinsic worth or qualities in Israel, but was rooted firmly in the personal character of God Himself. God's love has no cause prior to itself. It is not caused by any attractiveness or merit in its object. It is shown to be deeper than that of the love of a mother for her children, Isa. 49. 15. It is pictured in the paternal relationship and the marriage relationship. Israel is God's 'son'.[118] Hosea also poignantly paints the picture of a marriage relationship, and portrays a love that is willing to suffer.[119]

Writers have drawn attention to two types of love, one of complacence, and the other of benevolence. The love of complacence is drawn forth by the worth and excellency of the object. That of benevolence is a love that gives itself to lift the worthless, unlovely and undeserving into purity and beauty. That is the love, boundless and quenchless, which God has demonstrated to sinners. J. I. PACKER wrote, 'There was nothing whatever in the objects of His love to call it forth, nothing in man to attract or prompt it. Among men love is awakened by something in the beloved, but the love of God is free, spontaneous, unevoked, uncaused. God loves men because He has chosen to love them, and no reason for His love can be given save His own sovereign good pleasure'. To this we add the words of J. N. DARBY, 'In sovereign grace He rises above the sin, and loves without a motive save what is in His own nature and part of His glory. Men must have a motive for loving, God has none but in Himself, and "commended His love to us in that while we were yet sinners Christ died for us", the best thing in heaven that could be given for the vilest, most defiled and guilty sinners'.

God's love, then, is seen in the exercise of His goodness towards sinners. As such, it expresses itself in grace and mercy. Grace is the bestowal upon sinners of what they do not deserve; mercy is the withholding from sinners of what they deserve.

---

[117] Deut. 4. 37, 38; 7. 6-8; 10. 15; Isa. 43. 4.

[118] Exod. 4. 22, 23; Jer. 31. 20; Hos. 11. 1; Mal. 1. 6.

[119] This marriage metaphor is found elsewhere, Jer. 2. 1; 31. 32; Isa. 54. 5; 62. 4, 5.

God manifests His love in giving. This is the characteristic manifestation of love. The measure of love is how much it gives. God's love is measured by the gift of His only begotten Son, John 3. 16, whom He sent into the world to seek and to save the lost, to bring sinners back to Himself, and, in the course of this work, to suffer at their hands even to death. In the New Testament, the cross of Christ is the crowning proof of the reality and boundlessness of God's love.[120] In so far as God desires the salvation of all,[121] and has provided, in the sacrifice of His Son, for the salvation of all,[122] His love embraces the whole world, v. 16. God's love provides the propitiation which averts His wrath upon us, 1 John 4. 10. The Lord Jesus Christ is the propitiatory offering laid on the altar, exposed to the fire of God's wrath, meeting all the claims of divine justice as a perfect sacrifice for the guilty. On the basis of His sacrifice and death the sinner can say, 'God be merciful, be propitious, to me the sinner'.

The Faithfulness of God* - E. G. PARMENTER

A perusal of the New Testament Epistles reveals a number of direct references to God's faithfulness. 'God/He is faithful' is a recurring statement. 'Faithful' used of God means He is trustworthy, that He can be relied upon, that complete confidence may be placed in Him, and that we may have confidence in Him in the variety of circumstances of life.[123]

The Faithful God and Fellowship

Paul, writing to the church of God at Corinth, indicates the character of their corporate fellowship and then brings together a cluster of blessings, the last being, 'God is faithful, by whom ye were called unto the fellowship of his Son Jesus Christ our Lord', 1 Cor. 1. 9. This is a wonderful privilege; the faithful God willing to share His Son with us is

---

[120] 1 John 4. 9; John 3. 16; Rom. 5. 8.

[121] 1 Tim. 1. 15; 2. 4; 4. 10.

[122] 1 Tim. 2. 6; 1 John 2. 2; 4. 10.

[123] For example, the blessing of fellowship with God's Son is connected with God's faithfulness, 1 Cor. 1. 9. God is faithful in our trials, 10. 13. His word is true, i.e., faithful, 2 Cor. 1. 18. He is faithful to His promises, Heb. 10. 23; 11. 11. In circumstances of suffering according to His will, He is a faithful creator, 1 Pet. 4. 19. He is faithful in His forgiveness, 1 John 1. 9. These scriptures show God's unfailing faithfulness providing for the needs of His people in every experience of life with unremitting regularity.

a truth to thrill the heart. Of course, the enjoyment of this fellowship depends upon the spiritual state of the believer.

The Faithful God and Temptations

'No temptation', says Paul, '[hath] taken you, but such as is common to man', 10. 13. The Christian's trials are but common trials; others have like burdens and temptations. God is faithful. Satan is a deceiver. Men may be false, but God is faithful. Our strength and security are in Him. He will never disappoint His children.

God is wise as well as faithful, and proportions our burden to our strength. He will not allow us to be tempted above what we are able. He will take care that we are not overcome; He will make a way to escape, either from the trial itself or at least the mischief of it. There is no valley so dark but He can find a way through it, no affliction so grievous but He can prevent or remove it, or enable us to support it, and in the end overrule it to our advantage.

The Faithfulness of God and His Promise

The writer to the Hebrews, having set forth the value of the work of Christ and the witness of the Holy Spirit as to our forgiveness, reminds his readers of God's invitation to enter the holiest with boldness and to draw near in full assurance of faith, Heb. 10. 19, 22. Such privileges they were to hold fast. The motive or reason for this is 'he is faithful that promised', v. 23. God has made great and precious promises to believers, and He is true to His word; there is no fickleness with Him. His faithfulness should inspire and encourage us to enter boldly and draw near to God in the full assurance of being forgiven and accepted on the ground of the finished work of Christ.[124]

The Faithfulness of God and Suffering

The apostle Peter majors on the subject of sufferings in his First Epistle, first in relation to the Lord Jesus, and second in relation to those who

---

[124] Sarah bore a son when she was past age because she reckoned God was faithful who had promised, Heb. 11. 11. She had no other confidence or expectation than the faithfulness of God, whose promises are never broken even though a passage of time may elapse. Because God is faithful Sarah believed that what God promised He was able to perform.

are associated with Him, 'if any one suffers as a Christian', 4. 16. Suffering is the lot of every believer. The apostle links the truth of suffering with the 'will of God' and with God as a 'faithful Creator', v. 19. The will of God is introduced to assure us that such sufferings are permitted and controlled by Him having the best in view for us. In the experience of suffering in well-doing we are to commit our souls unto Him who is a faithful creator. The solitary reference here to God as creator in the New Testament tells us that He who created us will be faithful in His care of saints.[125]

The Faithfulness of God and Forgiveness

The Epistle to the Romans sets out the judicial side of forgiveness of sins. On the basis of the sacrifice of Christ, God has forgiven past, present, and future sins judicially, where faith has been placed in the Lord Jesus Christ. John, in his First Epistle, introduces the subject of God's family. All God's children can live in the enjoyment of fellowship with God and with His Son. That fellowship is disturbed when any of God's children commits a sin. As a result of the advocacy of Christ, the one who has sinned is made conscious of the sin committed. Upon confession of that sin, God is faithful and just to forgive and cleanse from all unrighteousness, 1 John 1. 9. God is liberal in forgiveness because of the provision made in the blood of Christ. Where true confession is made, a faithful God forgives what we did and cleanses from the unrighteousness which issues from the sin committed. Let us then reckon on God's faithfulness to us, 1 Thess. 5. 24.

God who is longsuffering* - K. TOTTON

Scripture quotations are from the New King James Version unless otherwise stated.

We live in an increasingly impatient age. People's 'fuses seem short' and new terms such as 'road-rage' have been coined to denote aggressive behaviour on the highways. Selfish intolerance fuels conflicts and injuries throughout society.

---

[125] This is seen in the first assembly prayer meeting, recorded in Acts chapter 4 verses 23 and 24.

What a refreshing contrast we find in the ways of the eternal God! Throughout the scriptures we delight to read statements such as, 'The Lord is merciful and gracious, **slow to anger**, and abounding in mercy'.[126]

The book of Proverbs extols this quality, 'He who is slow to anger is better than the mighty, and he who rules his spirit than he who takes a city', Prov. 16. 32. This restraint is seen to perfection in God. He is unhurried, for His timescales are radically different from ours, 'With the Lord one day is as a thousand years, and a thousand years as one day'.[127]

Definition

'Longsuffering is that quality of self-restraint in the face of provocation which does not hastily retaliate or promptly punish; it is the opposite of anger and is associated with mercy, and is used of God'.[128] If we wish to distinguish God's longsuffering from His mercy, perhaps it could be said that mercy pities sinners in their misery, whereas longsuffering is the exercise of forbearance in the face of their defiance. Longsuffering always relates to **persons** and their perversity, not to things.

Some scriptural examples

The Bible supplies numerous instances of God's longsuffering. 'The divine longsuffering waited in the days of Noah, while the ark was being prepared', 1 Pet. 3. 20. In respect of proud Pharaoh we read, 'God, wanting to show His wrath and to make His power known, endured with much longsuffering the vessels of wrath prepared for destruction', Rom. 9. 22.

Israel should have known much better, yet, in the wake of the flagrant apostasy of the golden calf, God disclosed Himself to Moses as, 'The Lord, the Lord God, merciful and gracious, longsuffering, and abounding in goodness and truth', Exod. 34. 6. The subsequent history of Israel and

---

[126] Ps. 103. 8, cp. 145. 8 [my emphasis].

[127] 2 Pet. 3. 8; Ps. 90. 4.

[128] Exod. 34. 6; Rom. 2. 4; 1 Pet. 3. 20, W. E. Vine, *Expository Dictionary*.

Judah is a sad record of provocation and backsliding.[129]

Saul of Tarsus is an outstanding example of Christ's longsuffering, 1 Cor. 15. 9. The apostle was ceaselessly amazed at the sheer wonder of it all.[130] If Christ could save a Saul, He can save anyone!

Implications

This glorious attribute of God is full of implications for our attitude and behaviour. Personally, we should maintain a profound personal appreciation of His goodness, forbearance, and longsuffering, that led us to repentance, Rom. 2. 4.

We may well ponder the enormity of the divine restraint as we contemplate the escalating wickedness of our world. Unbelief misinterprets this as indifference, but Peter warns, 'The Lord is not slack concerning His promise, as some count slackness, but is longsuffering toward us, not willing that any should perish but that all should come to repentance', 2 Pet. 3. 9. Again, he counsels, 'Consider that the longsuffering of our Lord is salvation', v. 15. The sheer dimensions of God's saving purposes, beyond all human comprehension, will magnify His name to all eternity! The Lord is certainly not slack. One day His judgement will fall, yet it remains His strange work, for He loves to save.[131] One thing is certain, the impenitent will never charge their Judge with impatience.

On the other hand, the tension between God's wrath and His restraint creates an age-long problem for the godly who suffer daily for righteousness' sake. The psalmist naturally yearns for vindication in the present, Ps. 13. However, the New Testament emboldens us to view the eternal perspective. In enduring adversity for the Lord's sake we experience fellowship with God in suffering as He bears patiently with

---

[129] 'Yet for many years You had patience with them, and testified against them by Your Spirit in Your prophets. Yet they would not listen; Therefore You gave them into the hand of the peoples of the lands', Neh. 9. 30.

[130] 'However, for this reason I obtained mercy, that in me first Jesus Christ might show all longsuffering, as a pattern to those who are going to believe on Him for everlasting life', 1 Tim. 1. 16.

[131] 'For the Lord will rise up . . . to do his deed – strange is his deed! and to work his work – alien is his work!', Isa. 28. 21 ESV.

the wicked.[132]

Our Lord's parable of the unforgiving servant, designed to teach forgiveness, serves to highlight the **expected link** between divine and human patience.[133] Forgiven much, how slow we in turn are to forgive, and how quickly we write people off, cp. Luke 13. 8! Let us learn well that 'love suffers long and is kind', 1 Cor. 13. 4, and part of the gracious composite fruit of the Holy Spirit is . . . longsuffering, Gal. 5. 22.

The Mercy of God* - S. Probert

The Merriam-Webster dictionary defines 'mercy' as, 'compassion or forbearance shown especially to an offender or to one subject to one's power'.

It is instructive that while angels are God's messengers to mankind and tell us many things about God, they never speak about the mercy of God. In scripture, we rely upon God's people to reveal something of God's mercy. They tell us that, as believers on the Lord Jesus Christ, we experience the mercy of God in two ways:

1. His mercy to us as sinners
2. His mercy to us as saints

We can learn much from the first occurrence of any word in the Bible, and Lot is the first person to use the word 'mercy', Gen. 19. 19. He used the word to describe the action of the two angels who were sent by God, and who physically pulled Lot out of the city of Sodom moments before it was utterly destroyed. When we, as sinners, called on the name of the Lord Jesus Christ and were saved, we also experienced the mercy of God. Our position was much more perilous than that of Lot, for being sinners we were 'offenders' towards God. We deserved eternal punishment but God showed mercy ('compassion' or 'forbearance') to us in providing a most wonderful and free salvation. Have we thanked God today for His great mercy towards us?

---

[132] 2 Cor. 4. 17, 18; cp. Acts 9. 4.
[133] Matt. 18. 21-35, particularly verses 26 and 29.

Speaking to Simon the Pharisee in Luke chapter 7, the Saviour used the example of two debtors: the one owed five hundred pence, and the other fifty. When the creditor frankly forgave them both, Simon rightly judged that the man with the greater debt would love the creditor most. His personal experience of the compassion and forbearance shown to him was greater, because he understood that he owed so much. The more that we recognize the sinfulness of our sin (and the overwhelming extent of our debt), the more we will love the One who showed such mercy towards us in taking that debt away from us, and nailing it to His cross.

But our experience of the mercy of God is not limited to the past, and/or the memory of our salvation from sin. Jude is the last writer in the Bible to refer to mercy. He wrote his brief letter to believers (or 'saints' – that is, those who are sanctified by God), and expressed his desire that they should keep themselves 'in the love of God, looking for the mercy of our Lord Jesus Christ unto eternal life', Jude 21. So God shows His mercy to saints as well as sinners. As before, the extent to which we appreciate this aspect of God's mercy will vary from one saint to another.

As saints living in this world we are in a dangerous environment, we are in enemy territory, for Satan is the ruler of this world, John 14. 30. We are also living in dangerous times, for Satan is the god of this age, 2 Cor. 4. 4. Without the mercy of God, the saint could not survive in such hostile conditions.

Most of us will admit that we fail our Lord from time to time; perhaps due to an attack from the adversary, but more likely because of the weakness of the flesh. As our sovereign Lord, He has the indisputable right to deal with us immediately for these failures because we are subject to His power and because, as the prophet Nathan explained to King David, our failures allow the enemies of our God to speak ill of Him, 2 Sam. 12. 14. That God does not immediately intervene in judgement and/or remove us from this scene is a sure indication of His mercy to us. Could it be that those of us who fail Him most (as believers), will come to have a deeper knowledge of God's mercy to His saints?

We may also benefit from the mercy of God in times of infirmity. Epaphroditus certainly experienced the mercy of God when he was sick unto death and God restored him to health, Phil. 2. 27. David tells us that God knows our bodies (our 'frame') and remembers that we are made from dust, Ps. 103. 14. In a similar vein, the writer to the Hebrews tells us that our Saviour understands our weaknesses, and is therefore able to demonstrate His compassion towards us in our infirmities. That is why he entreats us to 'come boldly unto the throne of grace, that we may obtain mercy, and find grace to help in time of need', Heb. 4. 16. If we follow his advice, we will soon discover that our God is 'full of compassion, and . . . plenteous in mercy', and, moreover, that He 'delighteth in mercy', Ps. 86. 15; Mic. 7. 18.

If this does not cause us to praise God for His great mercy to us, as sinners and as saints, we would do well to think briefly about the angels which 'kept not their first estate' and are even now 'reserved in everlasting chains under darkness unto the judgment of the great day', Jude 6. There is no mercy for them. Perhaps that is why angels never speak of the mercy of God.

The Wrath of God* - B. OSBORNE

The Bible is absolutely clear about the reality and terror of God's wrath, in contrast to the popular objection, 'Can a loving God eternally punish anyone?' To talk of divine judgement is not very popular in this day, yet the Bible refers to it constantly. A. W. PINK wrote that 'there are more references in scripture to the anger, fury and wrath of God than there are to His love and tenderness'. God's wrath was manifested in the lives of individuals and of nations when in self-will they pursued a course of sin, injustice and impiety. In the Old Testament the destruction of Sodom and Gomorrah[134] provides an illustration of this, as does the downfall of Nineveh,[135] and the fall of Belshazzar,[136] amongst others. The emphasis is found also in the New Testament. For example, we are told, among other scriptures, that 'the wrath of God is revealed from heaven against all ungodliness and unrighteousness of men, who hold the truth in unrighteousness', Rom. 1. 18, that a person can 'treasure up wrath in the day of wrath' by impenitence and hardness of heart, 2. 5,

---

[134] Gen. 19. 23, 24.
[135] Nahum 1. 2-8.
[136] Dan. 5. 25-28.

and that salvation from wrath is available.[137] Clearly, the inspired writers had no inhibitions about declaring God's wrath. When the Bible speaks so much about it, should we be silent?

What we have to be careful of is attributing to God unworthily the feelings and passions we experience as human beings. We must on no account think of anger in God as if it were the same in all aspects as anger in man. In man, anger may be aroused by malevolent feelings towards another, or by loss of self-control, by a feeling of powerlessness in a given situation, by wounded pride, or by bad temper. This would be to misunderstand the anthropomorphic language the Bible uses of God when it employs human feelings and actions to God in order that we might understand His person and purposes better. It is a divine condescension to our very limited ability to appreciate the greatness and person of God. What are our weaknesses and imperfections cannot be applied to God, and the Bible takes this for granted. God does not take delight in suffering. He does not act out of irritation. His wrath is not capricious, but is always a just response to moral evil.

God's wrath is seen not only in the future; it is a present reality, v. 18. Here we are told that it 'is revealed', and the present tense indicates that it is a present, continuous disclosure. It is against 'all ungodliness', that which blasphemes, denies, or ignores the Creator, and 'unrighteousness', that which wrests the claims whether of Creator, or of creature. The wrath is against those who 'suppress the truth in and by means of unrighteousness'. 'Holding down' conveys the idea of not being ignorant of the truth, but of deliberately suppressing it. That wrath is revealed in Bible history we have seen. In this chapter, Paul describes it in the phrase 'God gave them up', vv. 24, 26, 28, which is the present action of divine wrath. They had made their choice. God's wrath is something men have chosen for themselves. They chose to practise the lusts of their sinful hearts increasingly, and God gave them up to the consequences of their choice, and His decision was just.

God's wrath is always judicial, the wrath of a judge administering

[137] Rom. 5. 8, 9; 1 Thess. 1. 10.

justice.[138] The principles of His judging are stated.[139] Unsaved sinners are described as 'by nature children of wrath',[140] that is, those who belong to wrath, who are justly under God's wrath, the antagonism of eternal holiness to sin. The law cannot help them, for it 'worketh wrath', 4. 15. The law requires perfect obedience, but it stirs up sin within men as they rebel against its commands. It causes them to transgress its commands, and the transgression provokes God's wrath. How can the sinner be delivered from the wrath which is still future, treasured up until the day of wrath, the wrath to come?[141] God has made provision in the gospel whereby sinners can cease to be the objects of His wrath, and become the recipients of His grace. On the cross the Lord Jesus Christ bore the punishment which sinners deserve, the death in their stead, and our stead, being subject to God's wrath. In this way, He became 'the deliverer from the wrath to come' to all who put their faith in Him, who 'are justified by his blood' and 'saved from wrath through him', 5. 9.

The Goodness of God* - B. CARGILL

'There is none good but one, that is, God'. This is what the Lord Jesus said to a rich young ruler who came to Him one day with a question about inheriting eternal life. Addressing Him as 'Good Master', he received that rather unexpected reply, Matt. 19. 17. Did that young man learn that this 'Good Master' was God, the only One who is wholly and perfectly good? It is not a matter of good, better, and best. It is that God, who is infinitely great, is also totally and incomparably good.

Throughout the whole Bible we read of the goodness of God. Repeatedly, we see how His goodness is magnified in the way He reacts to the evil of man. We find also that whilst God cannot be tempted with evil, Jas. 1. 13, we can. The first reference in the Bible to 'good and evil' together is in Genesis chapter 2 verse 9 – 'the tree of knowledge of good and evil'. Our first parents had to make a choice, and what a consequential choice it was! The last reference is in 3 John verse 11, 'Follow not that which is evil, but that which is good'. We too have the

---

138 Rom. 2. 15.
139 Rom. 2. 2, 6, 11, 16.
140 Eph. 2. 3.
141 Rom. 2. 5; 1 Thess. 1. 10.

choice to make, habitually, and incidentally each day. To follow that which is good is to follow God. Furthermore, if and when we do good to those who hate us, we are demonstrating that we are truly the children of our Father which is in heaven, Matt. 5. 44, 45; for He is kind to the unthankful and to the evil, Luke 6. 35.

Goodness

Whilst a dictionary definition of 'good/goodness' is helpful (= morally excellent, wholesome, useful for a purpose, etc.) it is better to see how the scriptures define and describe it.

The word 'good' has two slightly different meanings:
(1) what is **intrinsically good** – good as opposed to evil. It is a ***root condition*** which may be described as morally excellent, and benevolent, as opposed to morally depraved and all that ***causes*** harm, grief, and ill;
(2) what is **beneficially good** – good as opposed to bad. It is ***an effect*** or ***an outcome*** which is wholesome, beautiful, and useful, as opposed to one that is hurtful, and damaging.

The two are together in Psalm 119 verse 68 to describe our God:

- 'Thou art good' – He is intrinsically good;
- 'and doest good' – He is beneficially good.

In what follows we will keep these two ideas before us. In all His intentions, purposes, and ways God is good, and in the outworking of all of these plans He does good. The opposite was seen in Joseph's brothers, Gen. 50. 20. They (1) meant it for evil in their hearts; and (2) treated him so cruelly with their hands. And yet, even here, the two aspects of the goodness of God are seen, for (1) 'God meant it unto good'; (2) 'to save much people alive'.

Hebrew and Greek words for 'goodness'

There are two Hebrew words used in the Old Testament for goodness. They also distinguish the two aspects of God's goodness:

> *chesed* which is also translated about seventy times as 'kindness', or 'lovingkindness'.

We have such verses as: 'The Lord God, merciful and gracious . . . abundant in goodness and truth', Exod. 34. 6; or, 'The goodness of God endureth continually', Ps. 52. 1. This is about God's unchanging character of intrinsic goodness.

> *tov* which means 'good things', as we read: 'I will make all my goodness pass before thee', Exod. 33. 19; and 'How great is thy goodness', Ps. 31. 19. This is about the good, and beneficial things God does for, and shows to, His people.

In a similar way the New Testament uses two different Greek words for 'good':

> *kalos* which carries the idea of what is 'honest, beautiful' or intrinsically good – as in 'good fruit', Matt. 3. 10; 'good ground', Mark 4. 8; 'good wine', John 2. 10; and the 'good word of God', Heb. 6. 5, etc.

> *agathos* which rather means beneficial – as in Matthew chapter 19 verse 17 (above); 'good and faithful servant', 25. 21; 'good works', Acts 9. 36; Heb. 13. 21; 'good conscience', 1 Tim. 1. 19, etc.

God is Good

Everything that God plans and does is totally good, i.e., perfect, in all His works and ways, 'The goodness of God endureth continually', Ps. 52. 1.

In Creation

In the great creation narrative of Genesis chapters 1 to 2, we read seven times that 'God saw that it was good' (once 'it was very good'). It was all good in His eyes, and it was for the good and benefit of all He created. In particular He saw how it was not good for the man Adam to be alone and so He graciously provided Eve, a help exactly suited to him and his physical and emotional needs for companionship. This is still true, in spite of the changes brought about by the fall and the entrance of sin into the world.

God's goodness continues to be expressed throughout His creation, in spite of man's continuing exploitation of land, sea, and atmosphere.

Read Psalm 104 verses 10 to 28 and be reminded again how He provides for all His creatures on the land, in the air, and in the sea, 'Thou openest thine hand, they are filled with good', v. 28. Paul told the people of Lystra that God 'left not himself without witness, in that he did good, and gave us rain from heaven, and fruitful seasons', Acts 14. 17. We can surely say today, 'The Lord is good to all: and his tender mercies are over all his works', Ps. 145. 9; 'His mercies fail not. They are new every morning', Lam. 3. 22-23. He satisfies our mouth with good things, Ps. 103. 5.

To Israel
God was continually good to His earthly people – Psalm 73 verse 1, 'Truly God is good to Israel'. He led them safely through a waste howling wilderness and brought them into a good and pleasant land, Deut. 8. 7. He gave them His good law to control and preserve them, Rom. 7. 12. Not one thing failed of all His good promise, Josh. 21. 45.

Their subsequent disobedience did not cancel God's goodness, though they reaped what they sowed. Although they asked for a king to suit their tastes, He gave them a better one, a man after His own heart. Even in their miserable captivity His prophets called them to remember how good God was, Zech. 9. 17. And He would (and He will) 'do them good at their latter end', Deut. 8. 16.

To Us
How good God is to us today, His heavenly people! Every good and perfect gift comes down to us from Him, Jas. 1. 17. The invitation is still, 'O taste and see that the Lord is good: blessed is the man that trusteth in him', Ps. 34. 8. He has given us 'everlasting consolation and good hope through grace', 2 Thess. 2. 16. He has begun a good work in us which He will complete at last in the day of Jesus Christ, Phil. 1. 6. He is good, 'a strong hold in the day of trouble; and he knoweth them that trust in him', Nah. 1. 7. Throughout the lives and changing circumstances of His people He works everything for good to them that love Him, Rom. 8. 28. Surely goodness and mercy follow us all the days of our lives, Ps. 23. 6.

To All
God is good to all, no matter what their attitude is to Him. He makes the sun to rise on the evil and on the good, and sends rain on the just and

on the unjust, Matt. 5. 45. He is longsuffering, not willing that any should perish. He is good and ready to forgive, Ps. 86. 5. The goodness of God leads men and women to repentance, as it did for Peter when the Lord Jesus filled his boat with fishes, Luke 5. 8. Yet, so many people refuse His offer of salvation and spurn His love. Think of the riches of His goodness, and forbearance, and longsuffering, Rom. 2. 4. Think too of the 'goodness and severity of God', Rom. 11. 22, for God's dealings with men depend on their attitude to Him.

In Christ our Lord

The Son of God, our Lord Jesus, called Himself the good shepherd, John 10. 11. Characteristically, He always 'went about doing good, and healing all that were oppressed of the devil', Acts 10. 38. Only a few, however, said, 'He is a good man', John 7. 12. Others did not notice or appreciate His goodness at all. Although He had done so many good works, they took up stones to kill Him on more than one occasion, 10. 32.

All of us who know God must surely respond to the great call, 'O give thanks unto the Lord, for he is good: for his mercy endureth for ever. Let the redeemed of the Lord say so', Ps. 107. 1, 2. Should we not 'say so' more often and more gratefully? (Psalm 136 finds reasons to say so twenty-six times!) And we must surely re-echo the longing expressed four times in Psalm 107, 'Oh that men would praise the Lord for his goodness, and for his wonderful works to the children of men'. 'How good is the God we adore'!

The Immutability of God* - R. CATCHPOLE

The word 'immutability' denotes 'unchanging' and 'unchangeable' and, in reference to the immutability of God, LEWIS SPERRY CHAFER succinctly says, 'He could not be less than He is and since He filleth all things He could not be more than He is'.[142] The actual word is used twice in the New Testament, in Hebrews chapter 6 verse 17, where the writer speaks of 'the immutability of his (God's) counsel', i.e., His purpose, while in the next verse the writer adds, 'That by two immutable things, in which *it was* impossible for God to lie, we might have a strong

---

[142] L. S. CHAFER, *Systematic Theology*, Vol. 1, pg. 217.

consolation'; those 'two immutable things' being God's promise and oath. But the immutability of God is not limited to His purpose and promise only, but is equally true of His person and perfections.

The immutability of God's person: As the 'Eternal God' He is not subject to change.

He was before all things, so that Moses, in praying, said, 'Before the mountains were brought forth, or ever thou hadst formed the earth and the world, even from everlasting to everlasting, thou art God', Ps. 90. 2. The psalm draws a contrast between the eternal existence of God and the mortality of man, the latter being likened to grass which flourishes and grows up, only to be cut down and to wither, and all within the expanse of a single day, a morning and evening, v. 6. In a similar vein, the writer of Psalm 102 says, 'My days are like a shadow that declineth; and I am withered like grass. But thou, O Lord, shalt endure for ever; and thy remembrance unto all generations', vv. 11, 12. The same psalm reminds us that God laid the foundation of the earth and the heavens are the work of His hands, but, while they are subject to change, the One who made them is not. 'They shall perish, but thou shalt endure . . . they shall be changed: but thou art the same, and thy years shall have no end', vv. 26, 27.[143]

He is eternally self-existent.

In Exodus chapter 3 verse 13, Moses, commissioned to go to the children of Israel, said, 'Behold, when I come unto the children of Israel, and shall say unto them, The God of your fathers hath sent me unto you; and they shall say to me, What is his name? what shall I say unto them?' In the scriptures, the various names of God are indicative of His nature and character, which find expression in His subsequent activity and operations. It is not that the children of Israel might question of whom Moses was speaking; did he not say, 'The God of your fathers'? But they might well have doubts about the nature and object of this visitation; hence, the anticipated question, 'What is his name?' In answer, 'God said

[143] Psalm 102 verses 25-27 is quoted in Hebrews chapter 11 in reference to Christ, vv. 11, 12, likewise Hebrews chapter 13 attributes immutability to Christ, 'Jesus Christ, the same yesterday, today and forever', v. 8.

unto Moses, I AM THAT I AM: and he said, Thus shalt thou say unto the children of Israel, I AM hath sent me unto you'. 'The repetition of I AM suggests the idea of uninterrupted continuance and boundless duration'.[144] In this character He had come to them, the eternal, self-existent, unchanging One, the faithful covenant-keeping God, who is dependent upon none, and thus able to carry through all He purposes and says.

The immutability of God's perfections: There can be no change in His character or nature.

He cannot increase in anything since He is perfect, nor can He decrease in anything for that, of necessity, would involve a loss of perfection. In His very nature God is light, and God is love, and all His ways are consistent with, and in perfect harmony with, what God is in Himself. In this connection a number of verses specify the immutability of particular divine attributes, such as God's truthfulness, 'God . . . cannot lie'; His mercy is 'From everlasting to everlasting upon them that fear him'; His goodness, 'Every good gift and every perfect gift is . . . from the Father of lights, with whom is no variableness, neither shadow of turning', Titus 1. 2; Ps. 103. 17; Jas. 1. 17.[145]

The immutability of His perfections that lies behind those verses suggests in one way or another that God does apparently change, such as in Exodus chapter 32 verses 9 and 10, 'The Lord said unto Moses, I have seen this people, and, behold, it is a stiffnecked people: now therefore let me alone, that my wrath may wax hot against them, and that I may consume them: and I will make of thee a great nation', or Psalm 18 verse 26, 'With the pure thou wilt shew thyself pure; and with the froward thou wilt shew thyself froward'.[146] Other passages speak of God 'repenting', 1 Samuel chapter 15 verse 11, 'It repenteth me that I have set up Saul to be king: for he is turned back from following me', or Jonah chapter 3 verse 10, 'God saw their works, that they turned from their evil way; and God repented of the evil, that he had said that he

---

[144] KEIL AND DELITZSCH, Vol. 1, pp. 442, 443. In this connection we should not forget the words of the Lord Jesus, 'Before Abraham was I am', John 8. 58.
[145] Cp. *No one Like Him* (The doctrine of God) by JOHN S. FEINBERG, pp. 265, 266.
[146] Cp. Pss. 18. 26, 27; 106. 44; Prov. 11. 20; 12. 22.

would do unto them; and he did it not'.[147] Regarding such passages L. S. CHAFER comments, 'God, though immutable, is not immobile'. Since God's ways are marked by absolute righteousness His attitude towards men responds to every moral change in men which in view of 'God's unchanging holiness requires Him to treat the wicked differently from the righteous'.[148] While in 1 Samuel 15 verse 11 God said, 'It repenteth me that I have set up Saul to be king', just eighteen verses later Samuel says 'the Strength of Israel will not lie nor repent: for he is not a man that he should repent', v. 29. There is no contradiction between the two verses, for verse 18 has in view God's response to Saul's failure to obey His command, while verse 29 concerns the revelation of God's purpose.

The immutability of God's purpose: What He determines He accomplishes.

In Psalm 33, calling upon men to fear and stand in awe of the Lord, the psalmist says, 'For he spake, and it was done; he commanded, and it stood fast. The Lord bringeth the counsel of the heathen to nought: he maketh the devices of the people of none effect. The counsel of the Lord standeth for ever, the thoughts of his heart to all generations', vv. 9-11. Men may purpose and plan but they cannot guarantee its fulfilment, for the Lord is able to bring their counsel to nought and make their intentions of no effect. But, with the Lord, He only has to speak and it exists, and what He commands, purposes, and intends abides throughout all generations. 'There are many devices in a man's heart; nevertheless the counsel of the Lord, that shall stand', Prov. 19. 21. 'The Lord of hosts hath sworn, saying, Surely as I have thought, so shall it come to pass; and as I have purposed, so shall it stand', Isa. 14. 24.

'I am the Lord, I change not; therefore ye sons of Jacob are not consumed', despite His judgement of them, Mal. 3. 6. Because of the immutability of His purpose God is able to declare what is to come, and in that He stands alone. In Isaiah chapter 46, as a comparison is drawn between the power and ability of God and lifeless idols, the Lord says,

---

[147] Cp. Judg. 2. 18; Ps. 106. 45; Jer. 26. 19; Amos 7. 3.

[148] L. S. CHAFER, *Systematic Theology*, Vol. 1, pg. 218. For a more detailed, and technical, consideration of this aspect of God's immutability, see *No one Like Him* by JOHN S. FEINBERG, pp. 266-273.

through the prophet, 'Remember the former things of old: for I am God, and there is none else; I am God, and there is none like me, declaring the end from the beginning, and from ancient times the things that are not yet done, saying, My counsel shall stand, and I will do all my pleasure . . . I have spoken it, I will also bring it to pass; I have purposed it, I will also do it', vv. 9-11. Thus, in respect of the dreams given to Pharaoh, Joseph says, 'God hath shewed Pharaoh what he is about to do'; 'because the thing is established by God . . . God will shortly bring it to pass', Gen. 41. 25, 32. Since God's counsel is immutable, several verses refer to eternal purpose, 'before the foundation of the world', Eph. 1. 4; 'the eternal purpose', 3. 11; 'his own purpose and grace which was given us in Christ Jesus before the world began', 2 Tim. 1. 9; 'promised before the world began', Titus 1. 2; 'foreordained before the foundation of the world', 1 Pet. 1. 20. Inherently linked to the immutability of God's purpose lies the ultimate destiny of all nations and men, i.e., the giving of the kingdoms of this world to Christ, the eternal security and salvation of those who believe, and the judgement of the ungodly.[149]

The immutability of God's promises: What He promises, He is faithful to fulfil.

God cannot lie, for Him to do so would involve a denial of His essential nature and holiness. Although Balak the king of the Moabites hired Balaam to curse Israel, and although Balaam was ready to comply, in Numbers chapter 23 verses 19 and 20 he has to acknowledge 'God is not a man, that he should lie; neither the son of man, that he should repent: hath he said, and shall he not do it? or hath he spoken, and shall he not make it good? Behold, I have received commandment to bless: and he hath blessed; and I cannot reverse it'. With men there can be change. Promises are not always fulfilled, either wilfully, or through changing circumstances, or sheer inability. Man's promises and plans can be affected by external events that necessitate alteration and change, but God is not a man, and therefore has no limitation in fulfilling His word, as men so frequently do.

Paul speaks of the 'hope of eternal life, which God, that cannot lie, promised before the world began', Titus 1. 2. Here is a promise made in

[149] See: Ps. 2. 8; John 6. 40; 2 Pet. 3. 7.

the eternal counsels to be fully realized in the coming eternal day. Referring to the promise given to Abraham the writer to the Hebrews says, 'When God made promise to Abraham, because he could swear by no greater, he sware by himself, saying, Surely blessing I will bless thee, and multiplying I will multiply thee . . . for men verily swear by the greater: and an oath for confirmation is to them an end of all strife. Wherein God, willing more abundantly to shew unto the heirs of promise the immutability of his counsel, confirmed it by an oath: that by two immutable things, in which it was impossible for God to lie, we might have a strong consolation, who have fled for refuge to lay hold upon the hope set before us', 6. 13-18. The very fact that it is God who gave the promise should have been sufficient for Abraham to believe it, but, in His grace, to His word God added an oath for confirmation, thereby placing the integrity of His name and character upon its fulfilment. That confirmation, having significance not only for Abraham but for all 'the heirs of promise . . . that we might have a strong consolation' concerning 'the hope set before us'. His promises can be counted upon.

Having considered something of the immutability of God we might well bow in reverence and say, 'Who is like unto thee?' Because He is immutable in His person, He is worthy of our trust. Because He is immutable in His perfections, His holy character is to be reflected in our character and conduct. Because He is immutable in His purpose we can be intelligent to His movements and will, and because He is immutable in His promise we can have full confidence as to our future.

The Eternality of God* - R. COLLINGS

Introduction

God is distinct from, and infinitely superior to, every facet of His creation, and that distinctiveness and superiority is emphasized by each inherent attribute of His being. In Isaiah chapter 40 the prophet details the incomparability of Jehovah and, in summary, asks, 'To whom then will ye liken me, or shall I be equal? saith the Holy One', v. 25. Thus, in meditating on His eternality, we are contemplating something that sets God apart from everyone and everything else.

The uniqueness of God's eternality

Whatever realm of the animal kingdom we consider there is a common link that runs through it all, for every creature has a beginning and an end. However, that principle cannot be applied to the human race. JACK HUNTER taught that there are three ways in which humanity began life on earth. Adam began by creation, Eve began by formation and, since then, everyone begins life by generation. Thus, all mankind has a beginning but, unlike animals, man has no ending. Those who are believers have 'eternal' life, and shall never perish; those who are unbelievers will also exist eternally, even though it will be in the Lake of Fire. Every created being – human, celestial, or infernal – will exist somewhere unendingly, therefore 'eternal', when applied to them, refers to the present and future, but not the past.

Even the cosmos has an origin. Whether people accept the viewpoint that the universe is billions of years old, or that it is relatively young, evolutionists and creationists concur that it had a beginning. Furthermore, 2 Peter chapter 3 and Revelation chapter 20 show that the universe, including the millennial earth, will also have an ending.

In total contrast to all these things, God is eternal in the absolute sense. The expression 'the eternal God' occurs just once in the scriptures when Moses, the man of God, blessed the children of Israel 'The eternal God is thy refuge, and underneath are the everlasting arms', Deut. 33. 27. When the Bible uses the word eternal in relation to God it not only indicates that He has no end, but also that He has no beginning.

The nature of God's eternality

Because we are creatures governed by time, we may contemplate God's eternality as just meaning that God pre-dates and succeeds time. We push our minds back into those pre-cosmic ages when there were no ages, and try to imagine what we inaccurately term 'eternity past'. Then we project our thoughts forward attempting to peer into 'eternity future', only to realize that these things are beyond the finite horizons of our understanding. All we discover is that God is at both points and beyond, unaffected by our inability to comprehend it all.

Our difficulty is compounded by the fact that the only way we can think of eternity is in terms of time. God created time, and subjected mankind to it, and therefore to us everything must have a beginning and an ending. 'To every thing there is a season, and a time to every purpose under the heaven: a time to be born, and a time to die', Eccles. 3. 1, 2.

To think rightly of the eternality of God we must think of a state of no-time, for eternity is not an extension of time. Eternity is not linear, consisting of a past, present, and future, but is timeless. As God is the Creator, He caused time to come into existence, He is its source and its sustainer, but He is never subject to it. He transcends time and exists outside of it. That's why, when Moses asked God what His name was, God said, 'I AM WHO I AM', Exod. 3. 14.

The consequence of God's eternality

If God is not eternal, then He is not almighty. A being that has a beginning cannot be omnipotent for whatever has a beginning was, prior to that beginning, non-existent and, thus, powerless. In addition, if God was not eternal then He must be the created product of someone else and, therefore, there must be someone greater than Himself. However, God is eternal, He is omnipotent, and beyond compare, 'Know therefore this day, and consider it in thine heart, that the Lord he is God in heaven above, and upon the earth beneath: there is none else', Deut. 4. 39.

The poet has rightly written, 'Change and decay in all around I see, Oh Thou who changest not abide with me'. Because God is eternal He does not change, He does not age, although He is referred to as the 'Ancient of Days' in Daniel's prophecy. Change is inevitable and irreversible, we may want to prevent it, and we may wish things didn't change but they do, and have done so since the dawn of time. The word that we use to describe the unchanging nature of God is 'immutable', and the Bible clearly presents to us God's immutability, 'Of old hast thou laid the foundation of the earth: and the heavens are the work of thy hands. They shall perish, but thou shalt endure . . . they shall be changed: but thou art the same, and thy years shall have no end', Ps. 102. 25-27.

God's eternality is one of the attributes which, combined with others, enables Him to be sovereign. A God that does not exist at some point could not be sovereign, for there would be events prior or subsequent to Him over which He had no control. As His children, we take comfort from the knowledge that everything that transpires in time falls within the compass of His sovereign will, for He works 'all things after the counsel of his own will', Eph. 1. 11. In addition, His eternality means that God knows all that has happened, is happening, and will happen and, because He is sovereign, He governs these events, 'I am God, and there is none like me, declaring the end from the beginning, and from ancient times the things that are not yet done, saying, My counsel shall stand, and I will do all my pleasure', Isa. 46. 9, 10.

God's eternality and us

An appreciation of God's eternality should be a real source of comfort and encouragement to every child of God in every age. We read through the Old Testament and see His faithfulness to Israel in general, and to certain individuals in particular. He is the God of Abraham, the God of Isaac, and the God of Jacob but, because He is eternal, He is our God today. Life in this fast-changing technological age bears no resemblance to the relatively primitive lifestyle that prevailed in the days of the patriarchs, and in the centuries that followed. In that sense, we might feel greatly detached from their situation.

J. I. PACKER writes, 'How can this sense of the remoteness from us of the biblical experience of God be overcome? It is true that in terms of space time and culture they and the historical epoch to which they belonged are a very long way away from us. The link between us is not found at this level, the link is God Himself for the God with whom they had to do is the same God with whom we have to do'.[150]

Because God is eternal our salvation is secure. In his letter to Titus, Paul wrote, 'In hope of eternal life, which God, that cannot lie, promised before the world began', 1. 2. This promise of eternal life, and our unending possession of it, is only relevant as long as God exists; were He to cease to be, what validity could be attached to His promises? God's pledges are dependent on His eternality and, because He is eternal, we can have total confidence in His word.

God's ultimate purpose is to make us like His Son and 'that we should be holy and without blame before him in love', Eph. 1. 4. We shall be in

---

[150] J. I. PACKER, *Knowing God*, Hodder and Stoughton, 1973.

His august company forever and, because He is eternal, our enjoyment of God will be constantly fulfilled. JOHN NEWTON, in the hymn 'Amazing Grace', refers to us being there 'ten thousand years', which, strictly speaking, is not true, for time will cease to exist. However, using that analogy, our delight in God will be no less then than when we were ushered into His presence at the first. The fullness of pleasure we find in Him will neither increase nor diminish, for He is changeless; we shall be perpetually and eternally satisfied by Him.

Conclusion

In this meditation we have focussed on the eternality of God the Father, but eternality is a quality possessed by each member of the Godhead. The eternality of the Spirit of God is specifically referred to in Hebrews chapter 9 verse 14, and the eternality of the Son of God is attested to in many scriptures, including John chapter 1 verse 1. He said of Himself, 'Verily, verily, I say unto you, Before Abraham was, I am', John 8. 58.

We live in a very insecure age; dictators rise and fall; governments come to power and then are toppled; nothing is permanent and temporality stamps its DNA on every human being. It is in contrast to this backdrop of frailty, and the brevity of life, that Moses opens Psalm 90 by referring to God being unchanging and the refuge of His people, 'Lord, thou hast been our dwelling place in all generations. Before the mountains were brought forth, or ever thou hadst formed the earth and the world, even from everlasting to everlasting, thou art God', Ps. 90. 1, 2.

> 'Before the hills in order stood, or earth received her frame,
> From everlasting thou art God, to endless years the same.
> O God our help in ages past, our hope for years to come,
> Be our defence while life shall last, and our eternal home'.
>
> ISAAC WATTS

The Glory of God* - J. GRIFFITHS

1. THE MATCHLESS GLORY OF GOD

'And he [*Moses*] said, I beseech thee [*God*], shew me thy glory', Exod. 33. 18.

The request of Moses is met by the response of God, 'I will make all my goodness pass before thee, and I will proclaim the name of the Lord before thee; and will be gracious to whom I will be gracious, and will shew mercy on whom I will shew mercy', v. 19. No man can look upon the unveiled glory of God, for He dwells 'in the light which no man can approach unto; whom no man hath seen, nor can see', 1 Tim. 6. 16. The only way that man can see God is in the person of the Son. 'No man hath seen God at any time; the only begotten Son, which is in the bosom of the Father, he hath declared him', John 1. 18. The Saviour could say, 'He that hath seen me hath seen the Father', 14. 9.

'Moses is to see the afterglow which is a reliable indication of what the full splendour is to be', HYWEL JONES.

The essential glory of God is matchless, peerless, and belongs to Him alone. We can only know anything of the glory of God by self-revelation on the part of God. The glory of God is the outshining of all that God is and has – His character, revealed through His attributes and actions. His glory is described as great and eternal.

In the Old Testament, out of a range of words translated 'glory', *kabod* is the most frequently used. It carries the sense of 'weighty' or 'important'. The New Testament equivalent is *doxa* which derives from a root meaning 'reputation', or 'opinion'. The manifest glory of God enables us to assert who God is and what He is like – His riches, His radiance, His reputation, and His revelation. It is essentially His presence, His aura.

When Moses stood on Mount Sinai and the Lord passed by before him, He revealed Himself by proclaiming His moral attributes. 'The Lord, The Lord God, merciful and gracious, longsuffering, and abundant in goodness and truth, keeping mercy for thousands, forgiving iniquity and transgression and sin, and that will by no means clear the guilty', Exod. 34. 6, 7.

The glory of God is revealed to us today in His attributes and activities. It has been manifested in time, from creation right up to, and including, the Lord's coming again.

2. **THE MANIFESTED GLORY OF GOD**

All three persons of the Godhead are linked with glory: 'the Father of glory', Eph. 1. 7; 'the Lord of glory', 1 Cor. 2. 8; and 'the Spirit of glory', 1 Pet. 4. 14.[151]

(a) ***The Glory of God and the*** CREATION

'The heavens declare the glory of God; and the firmament sheweth his handywork', Ps. 19. 1. 'For the invisible things of him from the creation of the world are clearly seen, being understood by the things that are made, even his eternal power and Godhead', Rom. 1. 20.

Sin has left its stain on creation but, even so, it still declares the glory of God its Creator. One day, Isaiah's words will be fulfilled, 'The whole earth is full of his glory', 6. 3; Hab. 2. 14.

(b) ***The Glory of God and the*** CREATURE – ***Man***

The writer of the Epistle to the Hebrews makes the point that Adam was crowned with glory and honour, prior to the fall, as God's vice-regent, or representative on earth.[152] Sadly, of Adam, he concluded, 'We see not yet all things put under him', Heb. 2. 5-9.[153] Indeed, the glory and honour has been transferred to another man, Christ Jesus, who, during the millennium, will have all things put under Him, 1 Cor. 15. 24-28! A worthy ruler over the earth during His mediatorial reign, He is the second man, the last Adam.

(c) ***The Glory of God and the*** CHOSEN NATION – ***Israel***

The scripture states, 'Israelites; to whom pertaineth the adoption, **and the glory**, and the covenants', Rom. 9. 4. 'The glory', refers to the shekinah, the abiding presence and dwelling of God amongst His people Israel, usually exhibited as a pillar of cloud by day or of fire by night, Exod. 14. 19, 20; 40. 34-38. It is linked in the first reference with the 'angel of God', which I believe is a pre-incarnate reference to the Lord

---

[151] We also read of 'the God of glory' appearing to Abraham, Acts 7. 2, and 'the King of glory' approaching Jerusalem, Ps. 24. 7-10.

[152] See, for example, Ps. 100. 3; Isa. 43. 7; 1 Cor. 11. 7.

[153] As a result of sin and the fall, the image has become distorted, and the glory dimmed, and it is only regained when we become new creatures, 2 Cor. 5. 17.

Jesus Christ, a Christophany. The glory of God is associated with the tabernacle and, in particular, with the ark of the covenant. God's presence dwelt between the cherubim carved in one piece of gold with the mercy seat, the 'lid' of the ark itself. When Israel lost the ark, they lost the sense of the presence of God with them. His glory had departed. Take note of the words of Phinehas' wife when she named her son Ichabod, 'The glory is departed from Israel: for the ark of God is taken', 1 Sam. 4. 22.[154]

The glory of God is linked with the temple in Solomon's day.[155] Haggai records the rebuilding of the temple after the deliverance from Babylon.[156]

Ezekiel also tells us of the departure of the glory of God to the threshold of the house, Ezek. 9. 3, to the city, and to the mountain to the east (Olivet), 11. 23.[157]

Thus, the glory of the Lord is seen to emphasize His presence when dwelling amidst His people. It is reflected in the shekinah, and the ark of the covenant, until Messiah comes personally to His temple in the millennium. 'Sing, O ye heavens; for the Lord hath done it: shout, ye lower parts of the earth: break forth into singing, ye mountains, O forest, and every tree therein: for the Lord hath redeemed Jacob, and glorified himself in Israel', Isa. 44. 23.

(d) ***The Glory of God and*** CHRIST

Uniquely, Christ is the outshining, the effulgence, the radiance of God's glory.[158] All the moral and spiritual glories of God beam out from Christ. He is also the precise representation of God's essential being. He

---

[154] See also Ps. 78. 60, 61.

[155] 2 Chr. 7. 1-3.

[156] 'Who is left among you that saw this house in her first glory'? 'The glory of this latter house shall be greater than of the former [Solomon's]', Hag. 2. 9.

[157] How perfectly this is fulfilled when our Lord left their house desolate, was taken outside Jerusalem's city walls to be crucified, and then departed to return to His Father from Olivet! This same prophet proceeds to tell us of a future millennial temple and exclaims, 'Behold, the glory of the Lord filled the house of the Lord', 44. 4, and he fell on his face awestruck.

[158] Heb. 1. 2, 3.

exactly, and accurately, represents God His Father. He reveals to man what God is really and truly like.

Paul, writing to the Romans, tells us that, 'All have sinned, and come short of the glory of God', 3. 23. The glory of God is the standard God has set and of which sinful man has fallen abysmally short. In the Old Testament, God's standard was the law. In the New Testament, God's standard is His Son. He is the glory of God.

The glory of God marked Christ's birth.[159] The disciples, during the days of His flesh, could say, 'And we beheld his glory, the glory as of the only begotten of the Father, full of grace and truth', John 1. 14. God's glory was manifested in Cana of Galilee when Christ performed His first miracle.[160] On the mount of transfiguration, Peter, James and John, 'saw his glory', Luke 9. 32.[161] Again, when Lazarus was restored to life, Jesus said to Martha, 'If thou wouldest believe, thou shouldest see the glory of God', John 11. 40.

The pinnacle of Christ's glory was achieved at Calvary. In Gethsemane, He prayed, 'Father glorify thy name'. The response from heaven, 'I have both glorified it, and will glorify it again', 12. 28; 17. 1. Calvary glorified both God and Christ.[162]

> 'O could I speak the matchless worth
> O could I sound the glories forth

---

[159] Luke 2. 9.

[160] John 2. 11.

[161] This led Peter to write, 'For he received from God the Father, honour and glory', 2 Pet. 1. 17.

[162] It should be noted that Jesus' resurrection was by 'the glory of the Father', Rom. 6. 4. Of His ascension, Paul says, 'received up into [in] glory', 1 Tim. 3. 16. John envisages believers in heaven enjoying the fruit of His desire, 'that they may behold my glory', John 17. 24. As great High Priest our Lord is now clothed with garments of glory and beauty. Simeon, having taken the babe into his arms could remark, 'Mine eyes have seen thy salvation . . . a light to lighten the Gentiles and **the glory of thy people**, Israel', Luke 2. 30, 32.
Although His external glory was veiled in flesh for the duration of His time on earth, we get a glimpse of it at the transfiguration, and it will be revealed during the millennium.

Which in my Saviour shine
In loftiest songs of sweetest praise
I would to everlasting days
Make all His glories known', SAMUEL MEDLEY

'To God only wise, be glory through Jesus Christ for ever, Amen', Rom. 16. 27.

(e) ***The Glory of God and the*** CHURCH

God is revealed in His glory in the church, and the church will be a source of glory to God, not only in time but for eternity![163] How amazing!

That great city, the abode of the church in eternity spoken of in Revelation chapter 21,[164] is illuminated by the glory of God, and lit by the presence of the Lamb. Such is the intensity of the light and the transparency of the materials used in the construction of the city that the Gentile nations are able to share the same source of light even though they are on earth.

(f) ***The Glory of God and the*** CHRISTIAN

In Exodus chapter 33, where Moses had requested of God, 'Shew me thy glory', God replied by stating that He would show mercy on whom He would show mercy. This is exactly what God has done to Jew and Gentile alike,[165] thus demonstrating the riches of His glory, 'Whom he justified, them he also glorified', Rom. 8. 30. Bless God, it is better on before! What a prospect lies before the believer! How certain it is when God speaks of the future in the past tense!

Not only have Christians experienced the riches of His glory, but they are to reflect His glory. 'God . . . hath shined into our hearts, for the shining forth of the knowledge of the glory of God in the face of Jesus

---

[163] 'That ye may know what is the hope of his calling and what **the riches of his glory . . . in the saints**', Eph. 1. 18. 'Unto him be **glory in the church . . .** [and in] Christ Jesus throughout all ages, world without end. Amen', 3. 21.
[164] 'And showed me that great city . . . having the glory of God', Rev. 21. 10, 11. 'And the city had no need of the sun, neither of the moon, to shine in it: for the glory of God did lighten it, and the Lamb is the light thereof', 21. 23.
[165] Rom. 9. 23-26.

Christ', JND. We are not just the terminals of this revelation but the means of channelling it to others, 2 Cor. 4. 6.

(g) ***The Glory of God and the*** COMING

Christ's second coming will be 'the appearing of His glory'.[166] Is this the rapture? 'Rejoice, inasmuch as ye are partakers of Christ's sufferings; that, when his glory shall be revealed, ye may be glad also with exceeding joy . . . for the spirit of glory and of God resteth upon you', 1 Pet. 4. 13, 14. Peter does not write about the rapture but about the return of the Lord relative to His kingdom, 'when his glory shall be revealed'. These two passages link the dual aspects of Christ's second coming with glory. Peter's references to the kingdom lead us to our final point.

(h) ***The Glory of God and the*** KINGDOM

Not only will the Lord's return be in power and glory but His kingdom will be glorious, for the King Himself is all glorious. Remarkably, we too have been called unto His own kingdom and glory, 1 Thess. 2. 12.[167]

3. **THE MAGNIFIED GLORY OF GOD**

The word 'glorify' has two meanings which are similar:
(a) To magnify, extol, praise . . . ascribing honour to;
(b) To do honour to; to make glorious.

We are expected to respond to the exhibition of God's glory and, in turn, glorify God. 'Worthy is the Lamb that was slain to receive power, and riches, and wisdom, and strength, and honour, and glory, and blessing', Rev. 5. 12. We can magnify the glory of God!

In Romans chapter 1 verses 21 to 23, we read of those that 'glorified him not as God . . . and changed the glory of the uncorruptible God into an image made like to corruptible man'. Believers, however, are exhorted, 'Whatsoever ye do, do all to the glory of God', 1 Cor. 10. 31.

We are to praise Him, for, 'whoso offereth praise glorifieth me', Ps. 50.

---

[166] Titus 2. 13.

[167] See, for example, Isa. 24. 23; 40. 3, 5; Ps. 102. 15, 16; Matt. 6. 10, 13.

23. We are to display good works before mankind so that men 'will glorify your Father which is in heaven', Matt. 5. 16. We are 'to be likeminded one toward another according to [after the example of] Christ Jesus: that ye may with one mind and one mouth glorify God', Rom. 15. 5, 6. We should be united in our worship of God and in testimony for Him.

Those of us who are Gentiles should glorify God for His mercy in extending salvation beyond the Jew to pagan, heathen sinners like ourselves, v. 9. As we have been purchased at infinite price, our bodies are no longer ours to do what we like with but they belong to God. We are to use our bodies to bring glory to God, 1 Cor. 6. 20. Male believers are the image and glory of God. To display this, and thus glorify God, a male should have short hair and an uncovered head in the gatherings of the Lord's people, 11. 4, 7.

This should be the touchstone of all our activities – not, is it right or wrong? – but rather, will it bring glory to God? If it glorifies God we can continue with a clear conscience. If it does not glorify God, then we should not do it. How truly amazing that we can magnify the glory of God and add to it. He is wholly worthy of it all! We can do no better than to conclude with Jude, 'To the only wise God our Saviour, be glory and majesty, dominion and power, both now and ever. Amen', v. 25.

The Jealousy of God* - J. BENNETT

'For thou shalt worship no other god: for the Lord, whose name is Jealous, is a jealous God', Exod. 34. 14. Because jealousy and envy have become synonymous in modern English usage many of us find the thought of a God who is jealous difficult to comprehend. How can a God who is holy, righteous, loving, gracious, and merciful also be jealous? Is there another side to the word 'jealous'?

Looking at its usage within the scriptures we can form an understanding of those things that cause God to exhibit His jealousy. He is moved to jealousy by:

- That which is not God, i.e., idolatry;[168]

[168] Deut. 29. 20; 32. 16, 21.

- Sin and vanities;[169]
- Immorality;[170]
- The arrogance of the enemies of Israel;[171]
- The maintenance of His holiness;[172]
- The state of His people Israel.[173]

In all these instances, and there is a degree of overlap, there is a sense in which God is seeking to maintain that which befits His person and character. He seeks to maintain:

- the uniqueness of His position as the object of human worship and praise. He stands no rival;
- His holiness. He moves in judgement against those who wilfully commit sin and immorality;
- the blessing and welfare of His own people, and zealously protects those who seek to maintain a relationship with Him.

In the biblical sense, then, jealousy is 'to burn with zeal; to be heated, to be zealous in the pursuit of good'.[174] For so many of us jealousy may degenerate into something bad, as when we feel frustrated and bitter because we cannot obtain what we want, or when we find fault with those who have what we want, or who keep us from getting it. For God, jealousy is only ever good. God wants what is His due: the exclusive devotion of His people, and it is only right that He should receive it.

The Meaning of God's Jealousy

From part of the definition above, the root idea in the Old Testament word 'jealous' is to become intensely red, to burn. It may be visible in the changing colour of the face or the rising heat of the emotions, also coupled with intense zeal or fervour. However, it is worth noting that both the Old Testament and New Testament words for jealousy are also translated 'zeal'.[175] There is a sense in which being jealous and being

[169] Josh. 24. 19; 1 Kgs. 14. 22.

[170] Num. 25. 11; 2 Cor. 11. 2.

[171] Ezek. 36. 5, 6; 38. 19.

[172] Ezek. 39. 25; 1 Cor. 10. 22.

[173] Zech. 1. 14; 8. 2.

[174] Thayer's Greek-English Lexicon, G2206, *zēlōō*.

[175] Num. 25. 11, 13; 2 Sam. 21. 2; Gal. 4. 17, 18; Rev. 3. 19.

zealous are essentially the same thing in the Bible. Hence, God is zealous, that is, eager to protect what is precious to Him.

The Manifestation of God's Jealousy

The prophet Isaiah records the words of the Lord, 'I am the Lord: that is my name: and my glory will I not give to another, neither my praise to graven images', Isa. 42. 8. Therefore, idolatry is an affront to God's name and glory, and God is jealous of His glory and expresses His desire for exclusive devotion and worship. To contemplate less, or to do less, would be to detract from His essential character.

Equally, idolatry is a challenge to God's sovereignty and supremacy over all things. For His creatures to ascribe His glory to other so-called gods, or to elevate them to a position equal with or above God, is to make Him less than the pre-eminent God He is. Hence, says God, 'Now will I . . . be jealous for my holy name', Ezek. 39. 25. It is in keeping with His character to maintain His high and holy position, and to want His creatures to attribute to Him an appropriate degree of honour. Unlike our jealousy, which is often associated with our insecurity, anxiety, pride, or spite, God's jealousy is the natural and necessary consequence of His absolute sovereignty.

It was Joshua who, anticipating his own death, warned the people, 'Ye cannot serve the Lord: for he is an holy God; he is a jealous God; he will not forgive your transgressions nor your sins', Josh. 24. 19. God is jealous of His holiness. He will not tolerate sin for it is an affront to His holiness, and He will not accept those who seek to approach Him without their sin having been dealt with. This is exemplified in the reign of Rehoboam when the idolatrous and immoral sins of the people brought Shishak, king of Egypt, as the instrument of divine judgement against Israel. It was a lesson too that God sought to teach the heathen when He said in relation to His judgement of Israel, 'According to their uncleanness and according to their transgressions have I done unto them, and hid my face from them', Ezek. 39. 24.

Although God may move one or other nation against His people as a means of bringing them into judgement for their idolatry and sin, God is also jealous for the preservation of His people. Israel, as a nation, were the people that carried the name of Jehovah, and their capital city was the place of God's sanctuary that bore His name.[176] God's honour is bound up in His people. God's jealousy is also an expression of His love as He takes positive steps to help His people. It is for this reason that He has afflicted the nation to bring it back unto Himself and it is also the reason why He will deliver it from its oppressors in a coming day. The Lord has said, 'I am jealous for Jerusalem and for Zion with great jealousy', Zech. 1. 14. Similarly, He wants only the best for us, that which will bring benefit and blessing to our lives.

The Message of God's jealousy

If God, by virtue of His essential being, is jealous for His glory and His supremacy above all, then those who know Him should be just as jealous for Him if they want to please Him. This can be demonstrated in a number of different ways. We should seek to exalt Him in our daily worship; we should be committed to living for His honour and glory; we should be zealous in doing His will. Our lives should demonstrate to the world that we believe in the one true and living God.

For many in our society, material possessions are the chief object of their life and worship. For others, Satan holds their adoration, as superstition grips the heart. There are many parallels with the time in which Elijah sought to serve God. He risked his physical safety to prove that Jehovah was God when he stood alone against the prophets of Baal, and called down fire from heaven on his water-soaked sacrifice. The fire of the Lord did fall, and it consumed the sacrifice, the wood, the stones, the dust, and licked up the water in the trench around the altar. It all happened because Elijah could say, 'I have been very jealous for the Lord God of hosts', 1 Kgs. 19. 14. The challenge is: will we stand against every expression of idolatry, and look solely to the Lord and His word for guidance and strength? Will we allow Him to control our lives so thoroughly that His sovereign power is evident to all who observe?

As God is jealous for His people, He wants us to have the same attitude toward fellow-believers. We should seek to be jealous for one another's best interests. The apostle Paul spoke of his jealousy for his converts at Corinth. He said, 'For I am jealous over you with godly jealousy; for I

---

[176] 2 Chr. 7. 14; Isa. 43. 7; Jer. 7. 10, 11, 14.

have espoused you to one husband, that I may present you as a chaste virgin to Christ', 2 Cor. 11. 2. As their spiritual father, he faithfully taught them the truth, at great personal sacrifice. Similarly, Paul said of Epaphras, 'For I bear him record, that he hath a great zeal for you, and them that are in Laodicea, and them that are in Hierapolis', Col. 4. 13. His jealousy for them led him to pray for them daily, faithfully bringing their needs to God's attention.

The challenge to us is whether we want the very best for the Lord's people. Are we seeking to live our lives according to God's word in order to try and bring the greatest possible good to fellow-believers?

Our God is a jealous God! Can it be said of us that we seek to demonstrate that same positive characteristic in our lives?

The Providence of God* - K. R. Keyser

God's activities encompass the totality of existence and there is no detail in the universe too small to merit His attention. The biblical doctrine of providence declares God's sovereignty in His creation, including its sustenance, government, and final destiny. Psalm 24 verse 1 speaks from this vantage point when it says, 'The earth is the Lord's, and the fullness thereof; the world, and they that dwell therein'. It dispels the myth cherished by lost men of their independence from their maker, while simultaneously giving assurance of the believer's security and eternal blessedness in Christ – no matter what occurs.

Omnipotence, Omniscience, and Omnipresence Applied

The Almighty's activity in the world flows from His attributes, including His omnipotence, omniscience, and omnipresence. No part of His universe is unaffected by His all-knowing, all-powerful will. He created the universe, and He maintains it.[177] As Hebrews chapter 1 verse 3 expresses it, 'Who being the brightness of his glory, and the express image of his person, and **upholding all things by the word of his power**, when he had by himself purged our sins, sat down on the right hand of the Majesty on high'. Planet earth is fine-tuned for life because of the Lord's provision for His creatures. The animals are fed by Him,

[177] John 1. 3; Col. 1. 16, 17.

sunshine and rain are provided by His merciful design, and the plant and animal kingdoms are outfitted by Him.[178] He appoints the boundaries of the sea, and regulates every aspect of the natural world.[179] He destroyed almost all of life previously by a global flood, and will destroy the future world by melting the elements with great heat.[180] The maintenance of the globe depends upon God, not on human, or mechanistic natural forces.

WALTER ELWELL points out the comprehensive scope of divine providence in these words:

'From beginning to end, from heaven to earth, from animate to inanimate, from individuals to nations, from hours to ages, from weeds to wheat, from birth to death, from catastrophe to calm – everything is within the loving presence and involvement of the heavenly Father. In his wisdom, power, righteousness, and love he is hastening slowly to work out his own eternal purposes for his own glory and for our eternal good'.[181]

The final phrase of this description highlights God's kindness towards mankind. His purposes are all encompassing, but they are in complete conformity with His desire to bless and love His creatures. As another teacher says, 'God's providence is never random. He always has a very definite and distinct purpose, and that purpose always flows from a heart of love'.[182] Unbelievers fear a deity who sees all and knows all, for they typically do not trust God, and, intuitively, expect His judgement. But experientially, Christians know that 'perfect love casteth out fear', 1 John 4. 18. Because of God's goodness shown to them in Christ, they rest in the knowledge of His providence.

---

178 Ps. 104. 11-15; Matt. 5. 45; Matt. 6. 26, 28-30.

179 Ps. 104. 9; Job 38-41.

180 Gen. 7. 23; 2 Pet. 3. 5-10.

181 WALTER A. ELWELL, 'Providence', in *Evangelical Dictionary of Biblical Theology*, ed. W. A. ELWELL, electronic ed., Baker reference library; Logos Library System (Grand Rapids: Baker Book House, 1996).

182 ROGER ELLSWORTH, 'When God's Arrows Fall Beyond Us: God's Strange Providence: 1 Samuel 20'. *Southern Baptist Journal of Theology Volume 2:3*. Fall 1998. Louisville, KY: Southern Baptist Theological Seminary, 1998, pg. 79.

What is Man that Thou art Mindful of Him?

The Lord's providential working extends beyond the natural world to embrace human affairs; in fact, this is His chief employment within His creation. He exalts nations and their leaders, and deposes regimes just as quickly, e.g., the visions regarding Babylon, Medo-Persia, Greece, and Rome in Daniel chapters 2 and 7. Romans chapter 13 verse 1 declares, 'Let every soul be subject unto the higher powers. For there is no power but of God: the powers that be are ordained of God'. The nations derive their authority from the Almighty.

God used Babylon to discipline Israel, but then brought this instrument of His chastisement into judgement because of their wickedness and idolatry.[183] More specifically, He enthroned Nebuchadnezzar, dethroned him by using temporary insanity, and then restored him to his throne once more, Dan. 4. As Daniel chapter 4 verse 17 explains, 'This matter is by the decree of the watchers, and the demand by the word of the holy ones: to the intent that the living may know that the most High ruleth in the kingdom of men, and giveth it to whomsoever he will, and setteth up over it the basest of men'. As further proof, when Peter exhorted the saints to 'honour the king', 1 Pet. 2. 17, Caesar Nero – a particularly depraved ruler – was sitting on the Roman throne. Obviously, believers are to render respect to political leaders based on the God who gives them their authority, rather than upon their own moral qualities. His judgement will bring to book the transgressions of the powerful in due time.

When rulers command something contrary to the Lord's commands, then His will supersedes their decrees.[184] Nevertheless, evil behaviour by human governments cannot thwart the divine purpose for the world. On the contrary, human wickedness is even used to further His will. This principle is clearly seen at the crucifixion, where men gave vent to their cruellest feelings against Christ. This notwithstanding, God used the occasion to lay human sin upon 'the Lamb of God who takes away the sin of the world', John 1. 29 NKJV, thereby making the suffering Servant a propitiation.[185] Peter's classic statement on the Day of

---

[183] Hab. 1. 5-17; 2. 8.

[184] Dan. 6; Acts 5. 27-29.

[185] Rom. 3. 25; 1 John 2. 1, 2.

Pentecost cogently expresses this truth as well, 'Him, being delivered by the determinate counsel and foreknowledge of God, ye have taken, and by wicked hands have crucified and slain', Acts 2. 23. Knowing that the Saviour who suffered is in control of the universe brings great comfort. As RYLE says, 'A crucified Saviour will never lay upon me anything that is not for my good. There is a needs be. It must be well'.[186]

Israel is My Firstborn

The history of the nation of Israel presents numerous examples of God's unparalleled providence. The fact that they still exist as an identifiable people is testament to the preservation of the Almighty's hand. They survived numerous foreign invasions – Egypt, Assyria, Babylon, Medo-Persia, Rome, various Muslim powers, Napoleon, etc. – as well as dispersion after the defeats of AD 66-70 and the 'Bar Cochba' rebellions.[187] Medieval Europe and North Africa did not absorb them into unrecognizability. What is more, persecutions by the Spanish Inquisition, Cossacks, Nazis, and others, did not destroy the Jewish people. The future assaults of world powers during the tribulation will similarly fail to wipe Israel off the map. Zechariah chapters 12 to 14, Romans chapters 9 to 11, and many other passages assure us that there is a future day of restoration for the believing remnant – it will come only when they nationally repent over the One who was pierced on the cross for them.[188] As Paul exults, 'And so all Israel shall be saved: as it is written, There shall come out of Sion the Deliverer, and shall turn away ungodliness from Jacob', Rom. 11. 26.

Unto Him be Glory in the Church

Currently Israel as a nation has been set aside until God resumes His direct work of restoration during the future tribulation period. During the current dispensation, the Lord is building His church,[189] a spiritual building, body, and family,[190] which is composed of Jews and Gentiles who receive Christ as their Lord and Saviour. In constructing this

---

[186] J.C. RYLE, 'The Cross of Christ', in *Old Paths: Being Plain Statements of Some of the Weightier Matters of Christianity*. London: Charles J. Thynne, 1898, pg. 261.

[187] AD 132-135.

[188] Zech. 12. 10 – 13. 1.

[189] Matt. 16. 18.

[190] Eph. 2. 14-22; 1 Cor. 12. 13.

church, the Lord Jesus promises to complete the work by thoroughly purifying it and presenting it to Himself as a spotless bride.[191] The Lord Jesus promises to build His church, and even does so amid the strongest opposition and trials.[192] His providential working uses all manner of circumstances to spread the saving gospel and sanctify His people.

To the individual believer the most wonderful aspect of God's providence is the working out of their personal destiny to be eternally in His presence, sharing in His glory. Romans chapter 8 verses 28 to 30 famously promise that God uses 'all things' for the ultimate 'good' – namely the saint's conformity to Christ's image and glorification with Him in heaven. This process is graphically depicted in God's dealings with Joseph, the Old Testament hero of the faith. Contrary to human thinking, his rough and unjust treatment at the hands of his older brothers was the first stage in his progression to the heights of glory and authority. As he later told them, 'But as for you, you meant evil against me; but God meant it for good, in order to bring it about as it is this day, to save many people alive', Gen. 50. 20 NKJV.

Abounding and Abasing in God's School

From an empty pit to slavery, to false accusation and imprisonment, the Lord sovereignly and skilfully used these trials to mould Joseph's character and prepare him for future service. His faithful labour in Potiphar's home, and subsequent service in the prison, sharpened his administrative skills for the relief work that he later performed during the famine.[193] Psalm 105 verses 17 to 23 make it clear that providentially the Almighty sent both the famine and the saviour Joseph, and that He used these events to reunite the Hebrew expatriate with his estranged brethren, and bring about the divine purposes for Israel. In addition to Joseph's prosperity, his family was also preserved, and Israel's national foundation was laid. The destiny of the world superpower and its surrounding nations was ordered in such a way that it performed God's desires for Israel and the patriarchs.

---

[191] Eph. 5. 25-27.
[192] Rev. 2. 9, 10.
[193] Gen. 41. 46-57.

The Blessedness of Providence

The Lord is described as the One who 'worketh all things after the counsel of his own will', Eph. 1. 11. The natural realm, political affairs of nations, the destiny of Israel and the church, the lives of individual believers, and the earthly ministry of Christ all demonstrate a supreme being who is directing His creation towards the end that He wills. He is not the author of evil and sin, but nor is He thwarted by them. In fact, He permits satanic and human wickedness, and sometimes uses it to further His own designs (much like modern doctors who use leeches to treat certain disorders). In the end, God will triumph over evil by judging all sin and unrepentant sinners, and consigning them to the lake of fire.[194] What is more, everything that happens to believers is within His perfect plan for glorifying us with the Lord Jesus. This doctrine makes sense of a chaotic world and gives great comfort to God's people. It shows that their prayers and hope are well placed in a sovereign Lord.

The Righteousness of God* - J. Scarsbrook

The righteousness of God pervades the whole of scripture from the initial unveiling of deity in creation's day, to the 'new heavens and a new earth, wherein dwelleth righteousness', 2 Pet. 3. 13. This fundamental attribute of God is displayed in a two-fold way. The first is condensed into the mode of address used by the Lord Jesus in the high-priestly prayer of John chapter 17 verse 25, 'O righteous Father'. The second aspect is acknowledged by the apostle Paul when he writes to Timothy of 'the Lord, the righteous judge', 2 Tim. 4. 8.

The title used by the Lord Jesus encapsulates what God is, He is righteous; fundamentally, eternally, intrinsically righteous. It is more than just a facet of His being; it expresses the very essence of deity.

The expression used by the apostle recognizes that everything God does emanates from what He is. He is righteous, therefore He will inevitably act, assess, and pass judgement in a righteous manner; He can do no other!

---

194 Rev. 20. 11-15.

Righteousness in its simplest definition is doing what is right. In our present society the concept of 'right' and 'wrong' has become a very subjective matter. Since 'God is not in all his thoughts', mankind, 'being ignorant of God's righteousness, and going about to establish their own righteousness, have not submitted themselves unto the righteousness of God', Rom. 10. 3. In his self-willed nature, man has come full circle from the days when the judges ruled, doing that which is right in his own eyes; and those perceptions fluctuate and are largely dependent on 'the desires of the flesh and of the mind' at any given time.

With God, the principles of right and wrong are established from eternity, and are immutable. To a vacillating people in Malachi's day He said, 'I am the Lord, I change not', Mal. 3. 6. Many years later, to those scattered abroad, in danger of wavering and instability, He is the One with whom is no variableness, neither shadow caused by turning. Such assurances instil confidence in the heart of the believer, enabling him to stand with faithful Abraham and say, 'Shall not the Judge of all the earth do right?' Gen. 18. 25.

It is precisely because God is righteous and man, on account of sin, is fundamentally unrighteous, that accusation is levelled against God for His actions toward men. We hear the familiar platitude, 'If God is a God of love, He would not allow this, or do that'. What people fail to appreciate is that love is not simply an aspect of His being, but rather, 'God **is** love', 1 John 4. 8, 16, while at the same time, and in full measure, He is holy, righteous and just. Only deity could hold and administer with absolute equity the multitude of perfections which are found in the Godhead; and in the person of the Lord Jesus, all are evident in a perfect Man, Col. 2. 9!

All the virtuous attributes of deity would, however, have remained unknown in a vast, eternal spirit realm unless infinite wisdom had chosen to prepare an arena in which they could be fully displayed. For this purpose the voice of God was heard, the universe came into being, with earth the centre of His purpose and man the object of His plan. We have no idea how long man lived in innocent harmony with his creator before sin entered and the bond was broken. But it was because God is righteous that Adam and Eve had to be expelled from the garden. Disobedience demanded it! However, without any compromise to His righteousness, in grace He provided a covering for them, in mercy He guarded access to the tree of life, and in love He made mention of the 'seed of the woman' who would ultimately defeat the adversary.

When again God looked down and 'saw that the wickedness of man was great in the earth', His righteousness called for judgement, and that was inevitable; but not before He made provision for those who would cast themselves upon His mercy, to be brought safely through the flood.

Righteousness could not stand by while the people of Sodom and Gomorrah indulged in their heinous practices; fire and brimstone were the only just remedy. Yet, even in such iniquitous circumstances, angelic beings were sent to carefully search through Sodom for just ten righteous, at the behest of 'the effectual fervent prayer of a righteous man', Gen. 18. 32; Jas. 5. 16.

Having called and formed a people for Himself, God gave to them a standard of righteousness written in stone, which became the benchmark for their life and behaviour. Repeatedly, they fell short, both individually and nationally, yet such was His heart of love towards them that for every transgression, provision was made for a substitutionary victim to bear the righteous judgement on behalf of the transgressor.

Throughout the wilderness journeys God 'suffered their manners' while they tempted and proved Him. But His longsuffering was never displayed at the expense of righteousness. Their murmuring brought hunger, thirst, and fiery serpents. A merciful God provided bread from heaven, water from a rock, and a brazen serpent as a life source. But righteous justice inevitably fell, and a generation of rebellious Israelites 'were overthrown in the wilderness', 1 Cor. 10. 5.

The years of Israel's occupation of the land graciously given to them repeatedly demonstrated the righteous character of their God. Obedience brought a just reward; disobedience, usually associated with idolatry, resulted in righteous retribution. Repeated warnings from faithful prophets fell largely upon deaf ears, to the extent that the righteous character of God was in danger of being compromised if action were not taken. Thus, the ten tribes of Israel were taken captive into Assyria, and the two tribes of Judah were led bound to Babylon for seventy years; the righteousness of God had been fully vindicated.

To a remnant of the nation returned from captivity, the revelation was given that, in a future day, the 'Sun of righteousness' would arise 'with healing in his wings', Mal. 4. 2; heaven then remained silent for four hundred years. The silence of God does not, however, indicate inactivity. Those years were running down the clock of Daniel's remarkable prophecy foretelling the nation's history, Dan. 9. 24-27. During those years the Medo-Persian empire fell to the relentless onslaught of Alexander the Great, the 'great horn' of Daniel chapter 8 verse 21, who lived, conquered and died, as foretold by the captive prophet, 8. 5-8, 21, 22. With the fragmentation and fall of the Grecian empire, the stage was prepared for Rome to exert its iron will, and, unwittingly, create conditions conducive to the furtherance of the divine programme. The fullness of the time had come!

The Lord Jesus did not need to submit Himself to John's baptism, which was a visible token of repentance. His life and character were exactly the same after His baptism as before. Yet, He would say to John, 'Suffer it to be so now: for thus it becometh us to fulfil all righteousness', Matt. 3. 15. In so doing He endorsed John's ministry, and publicly demonstrated His own righteousness; He was seen to be doing that which was accounted right. When later He spoke to cynical men of John's baptism, they could never accuse Him of unrighteousness by not practising what He preached!

In those few brief years during which the Lord Jesus walked His appointed pathway, He proved conclusively in word and action that righteousness belonged intrinsically to Him. Every statement, every act of mercy, every condemnation of hypocrisy was just and perfectly weighted. Commendation was given when merited, advice and encouragement were ready to hand. None could justly accuse Him of partiality or prejudice. In John chapter 7, the Jews sought Him out while He was in Jerusalem for the feast of tabernacles. Their approach, as so often, seemed innocuous. The Lord, however, read their hearts and knew that they were recalling the Sabbath-day healing of the man at Bethesda some time before, with a view to accusing Him. He exposed their hypocrisy, their selective compliance with the law, their inclination to judge matters by expediency, whereas in every situation

His own judgement was righteous, v. 24.

The events surrounding Calvary present to us the crowning demonstration of man's absolute unrighteousness; while at the same time, never was the perfect righteousness of God more clearly displayed. The essential details involved that day at Golgotha seem uncomplicated in the telling of them; their carrying through, and the implications for mankind both in time and eternity, are profound beyond measure.

Sin is abhorrent and alien to God. Man, since Eden, has a sinful nature. God's heart of love desired that man might be reconciled to Him. The only way this could be achieved was for a sinless substitute to bear the righteous judgement of God on behalf of man. No man, or angelic being, could undertake this consummate work. God became Man in the person of the Lord Jesus Christ, to live a perfect life and to willingly bear the wrath of God against sin. This He did fully and completely in the hours of darkness at Calvary, culminating in death, burial, and resurrection, signifying the absolute satisfaction of the heart of God in the work of His only-begotten Son.

Thus it was that provision was made for God to remain just, and yet become the justifier of all those who believe in the Lord Jesus Christ. In other words, His absolute righteousness is not compromised; sin, as a principle, has been fully dealt with in order that the sins of those who, by faith, accept the suffering and death of Christ on their behalf can be righteously forgiven. Amazing grace!

The righteousness of God with regard to those who believe does not end at Calvary. On the contrary, just as with Abraham of old, righteousness was reckoned, imputed, put to his account by God because he believed, so 'to him that . . . believeth . . . his faith is counted for righteousness', Rom. 4. 5.

Because of Calvary, the righteousness of God demands that the believer's greatest sin will never be remembered, Heb. 10. 17. By the same token 'God is not unrighteous to forget your work and labour of love, which ye have showed toward his name', 6. 10. Our smallest act of kindness will never be forgotten!

The Truthfulness of God* - A. de Ville

The purpose of this paper is to consider a selection of scriptures that refer directly to God's truthfulness. In addressing this subject, it is important to recognize the scope of the word 'truthfulness'. In everyday usage, the words 'truthful' or 'truthfulness' generally focus attention on the words of an individual. We say that a person is being truthful if what they say or write is true. While this is an integral part of a study of God's truthfulness, on its own it is too limiting. It is also necessary to consider the relationship between God and truth.

With this in mind, this article is structured as follows:

1. God and the truthfulness of His word;
2. God and the truth.

1. God and the truthfulness of His word

The scriptures make explicit claims in relation to the truthfulness of God's words, attesting the validity of the proposition: God's word is true.

First, scripture presents the testimony of men who came to the conclusion that God's words are true. For example, in 2 Samuel chapter 7 verses 28 to 29, David acknowledges to God that 'thy words be true'. For David, it was enough that, 'Thou, O Lord God, hast spoken it', v. 29. In the context, David is referring specifically to God's promise regarding the future blessing of the house of David. Why is David so sure? His knowledge and experience of God in his own life, coupled with the evidence of God's dealings with Israel, convinced him of the truthfulness of God's words. A more general claim is made in Psalm 119 verse 160 where the writer confesses, 'Thy word is true from the beginning'. Note that the writer is referring, not to any specific words of God, but to divine communication as a whole; hence, 'thy word'. The writer concludes that the totality of God's word is true. These two examples lead to the following claim: that each God-given communication is true and the sum of these is also true. God is truthful in His words!

Second, moving into the New Testament, two interesting passages are found in the Gospel of John relating to the claims of the Son of God. First, on three occasions in John chapter 8 the Son of God explicitly makes reference to telling the truth. In verse 40 the Lord says to the Jews, 'But now ye seek to kill me, a man that hath told you the truth, which I have heard of God: this did not Abraham'. They claimed Abraham was their father, but the Lord calls this into question on the basis of their reaction to the truth. Then, in verse 45, the Lord charges the Jews, 'Because I tell you the truth, ye believe me not'. Thus, their unbelief is the result of their reaction to the truth. Finally, in verse 46, 'And if I say the truth, why do ye not believe me?' Here, the Lord challenges them to respond appropriately to the truth presented to them. In John chapter 16 verse 7, now to the disciples, He says, 'Nevertheless, I tell you the truth, it is expedient for you that I go away'. Here, the Lord graciously takes account of the perplexity of the disciples at the news that He was leaving them. Though they may have found it hard to comprehend, it was to their advantage that He went away. Otherwise, they would not know the ministry of the Comforter, the Holy Spirit. In summary, in 2 Samuel chapter 7 verse 28, and Psalm 119 verse 160 the truthfulness of God's word is the conclusion of two men with plentiful experience of God. In John chapters 8 and 16, whether to unbelieving Jews or to His disciples, the truthfulness of God's word is the direct claim of the Son of God. God challenges us to accept that His word is true and to believe Him, just as 'Abraham believed God', Rom. 4. 3.

The closing three chapters of the Bible provide us with three further claims to the truthfulness of God's words.[195] For example, in Revelation chapter 21 verse 5, God Himself commands John from the throne thus, 'Write: for these words are true and faithful'. That they are **true** implies that they accurately describe the reality of events that are still future, including the description of a new earth that as yet does not exist. Since they are true implies they are **faithful**, they should be accepted and relied on.

The truthfulness of God's word is reinforced on two occasions by stating the impossibility of the negation of truthfulness. In Titus chapter 1 verse 2, Paul claims that God 'cannot lie'. In Hebrews chapter 6 verse 18, the writer assures his readers that it 'was impossible for God to lie'. The impossibility of the negative reinforces the positive; God's word is

[195] Rev. 19. 9; 21. 5; 22. 6.

true! When God speaks, it is necessarily true. In Titus chapter 1, Paul later makes reference to a Cretian prophet who had declared that 'the Cretians are alway liars', v. 12. In Crete, it seems that one could not rely on the word of any; however, God cannot lie and so His word is to be trusted.

2. God and the truth

There are three statements found in the scriptures that will aid our consideration of the relationship between truth and God Himself:

- The God of truth;[196]
- The true God;[197]
- God is true.[198]

The God of truth

The designation 'God of truth' involves more than the words of God. In Deuteronomy chapter 32 we find Moses' song. In verse 3 he calls on his hearers to ascribe greatness to God. In verse 4, Moses explains why, with the words, 'He is the Rock, his work is perfect: for all his ways are judgement: a God of truth and without iniquity, just and right is he'.

The title 'the Rock' views God as the source of unshakable stability; as to His work, it is perfect and, therefore, cannot be improved. The name of God here is *El*, signifying that God is the Mighty One, the first cause of all. In this context, God is the first cause of truth. For instance, as the Creator, He has established the reality that truth describes. The Hebrew word for 'truth' conveys the idea of what is established, stable, and firm. Truth, therefore, finds its source in God, the God who is the Rock. The terms which follow demonstrate that God is consistent with what He has established. He is without iniquity; the idea is that God does not distort; there is no perverseness in God and in His dealings. The God who is the first cause of truth is unfailingly consistent in His dealings with the truth He has established. Positively, 'just and right is He'. God is just, indicating that He is righteous; God is 'right' indicating that God

---

[196] Deut. 32. 4; Ps. 31. 5; Isa. 65. 16.
[197] John 17. 3; 1 Thess. 1. 9; 1 John 5. 20.
[198] John 3. 33; 7. 18; 8. 28.

is equitable in the nature of His dealings. Thus, as the God of truth, God is not only the source of truth, but His subsequent dealings are in harmony with truth.

The second reference to the God of truth is in Psalm 31 verse 5, where David states, 'Into thine hand I commit my spirit, thou hast redeemed me, O Lord God of truth'. In verses 1, 6, and 14, David expresses his trust in the Lord, leading to the committal of his spirit in verse 5. What is the basis of his trust? Surely, it is that he was convinced that the Lord is the God of truth. In verse 5, this is connected with the Lord redeeming David. The biblical account of redemption is, in itself, a demonstration that God is a God of truth. God has not ignored our condition, nor changed His own character (God is righteous), but has provided a way of salvation that is consistent with His own nature and yet meets our need.

The final two references are found in Isaiah chapter 65 verse 16, where God is again described as the God of truth. The word 'truth' here is the word 'amen'. God is 'the God of the amen'. The implication is this, what God has said will be; it is utterly reliable and sure.

The true God

The second triplet of references relate to God as the true God. In John chapter 17 verse 3, the Son addresses His Father as 'the only true God'. This does not exclude the deity of the Son and Holy Spirit, but does exclude the polytheism of pagan gods. Their many gods were but the invention of their own minds; the Father is true. The word 'true' conveys the thought of what is real, ideal and genuine. The contrast with idols is made plain in 1 Thessalonians chapter 1 verse 9, where Paul recalls that the believers had 'turned to God from idols to serve the living and true God'. They had left false gods and now served the One who is genuinely God. In 1 John chapter 5 verse 20, the Apostle John declares that 'this [He] is the true God'. Amongst the numerous claims to deity among the Gentiles, the God declared by His Son Jesus Christ is God in truth.

God is true

In John chapter 3 verse 33 we find the statement 'God is true'. Speaking of Himself, the Son of God declares in John chapter 7 verse 18 that 'the same is true'; and in John chapter 8 verse 26, concerning the Father, 'he that sent me is true'. The word 'true' carries the thought of what is manifest, unconcealed, actual, true to fact. God is all that He declares Himself to be. The Son, in John chapter 7 verse 18, was no deceiver, as some charged. The self-revelation of God is accurate and true to the reality of the nature of God. In the revelation given in scripture, no attribute has been misrepresented, no facet of character undisclosed. After all, 'God is light, and in him is no darkness at all', 1 John 1. 5.

Conclusion

In this brief consideration of God's truthfulness, there are three key messages:

1. The words of God are true, and the word of God as a whole is true;
2. God Himself is the source of truth, and His dealings are scrupulously consistent with that revealed truth;
3. God is, in actuality, all He has revealed Himself to be; there is no deception or distortion in the revelation that scripture gives of God.

The concept of truth is clearly fundamental. Accepting God's truthfulness places obligations on us. Our request should be that of the psalmist, 'Teach me thy way, O Lord: I will walk in thy truth', Ps. 86. 11, knowing that the God of truth desires 'truth in the inward parts', Ps. 51. 6.

The Wisdom of God* - K. TOTTON

Scripture quotations are from the New King James Version unless otherwise stated.

Introduction

The world is filled with the evidence of human progress. The accumulated knowledge and learning of the ages has been made accessible by the world-wide web in an unprecedented manner. Knowledge is one thing, but wisdom is quite another. As the poet TENNYSON put it, 'Knowledge comes, but wisdom lingers'. Wisdom is the ability to make right use of knowledge. Wisdom is concerned with the achievement of goals. Scripture reminds us that we could possess the most effective and profound worldly wisdom, and yet it could be 'earthly, unspiritual, demonic'[199] if applied to unworthy ends.

By contrast, wisdom, as an attribute of God, always has a *moral* component. The wisdom of God is not only supported by His boundless power to achieve its objectives, but, in addition, unerringly expresses His love, mercy, and goodness in its purposes. God knows the end from the beginning, and His wisdom is beyond our comprehension, 'For My thoughts are not your thoughts, nor are your ways My ways, says the Lord. For as the heavens are higher than the earth, so are My ways higher than your ways, and My thoughts than your thoughts'.[200] In contrast to our limited earth-bound perspective, the eternal God stands apart as the only **wise** God; His ways are past finding out.[201]

God in His wisdom invariably seeks His greatest glory, and the highest and most enduring blessing for the greatest possible number of His creatures. Scripture invites us to learn the wonders of God's wisdom as demonstrated by His actions. In this paper we consider the wisdom of God exhibited in creation, providence, and redemption.

Wisdom in Creation

What overwhelming evidence creation supplies as we admire the inexhaustible wisdom of the Creator! From the intergalactic to the sub-atomic we marvel at the order, coherence, and sheer beauty of God's handiwork. When we consider life on earth and the myriad diversity of its ecosystems, each creature perfectly suited to its environment, we can exclaim with the psalmist, 'The Lord is good to all, and his mercy is over all that he has made'; 'You open your hand; you satisfy the desire of every living thing'.[202]

'Thine almighty power and wisdom
All creation's works proclaim;

[199] Jas. 3. 15 ESV.
[200] Isa 55. 8, 9.
[201] Rom. 16. 27.
[202] Ps. 145. 9, 16 ESV.

Heaven and earth alike confess Thee
As the ever great I AM'.
J. G. DECK

Wisdom in Providence

Whilst we rightly marvel at the wisdom of God in the physical creation, not least the creation of man himself, as a responsible and rational creature in the image of his Creator, we also see the wisdom of God in His **providential** actions – the foresight, care, and protection He affords to those dependent on Him.

We see His wisdom, and sovereignty in that 'the Lord brings the counsel of the nations to nothing; He makes the plans of the peoples of no effect. The counsel of the Lord stands forever, the plans of His heart to all generations'.[203] God in His providential ways frequently overrules evil for good. This was classically demonstrated in the bitter experiences of Joseph, who at length graciously confessed to his brothers, 'As for you, you meant evil against me; but God meant it for good, in order to bring it about as it is this day, to save many people alive'.[204] Similarly, Balak king of Moab hired the false prophet Balaam to curse Israel, but God in His love for His people turned the curse into a blessing.[205]

Satan is a bitter opponent of God, and the cruel enemy of His people. Yet, we see in the life of Job that God can use Satan to achieve His gracious objectives. A divine boast plunges this godly man into an ordeal of suffering, yet he emerges to the glory of God, tried and restored.[206] James comments, 'You have heard of the perseverance of Job and seen the end intended by the Lord – that the Lord is very compassionate and merciful'.[207]

When Paul comes to sum up the merciful ways of God in justification and sanctification, with the goal of sharing God's glory, he affirms that 'we know that all things work together for good to those who love God,

---

[203] Ps. 33. 10, 11.
[204] Gen. 50. 20.
[205] Deut. 23. 5; Neh. 13. 2.
[206] Job. 1. 22; 2. 10; 42. 10-17.
[207] Jas. 5. 11.

to those who are called according to His purpose'.[208] Yes, **all** things! For His blood-bought people God blends our experiences, so that disappointments, circumstances which we might dread, even the tragedies of life in a broken world, are made to serve the inscrutable purposes of His eternal wisdom. What assurance and consolation this brings us! No wonder the Puritans could speak of the 'soft pillow of providence'!

Wisdom in Redemption

If nature stands as the universal testimony to the power and wisdom of God,[209] the great plan of redemption surely reveals the surpassing wealth of God's loving wisdom. To rescue guilty, helpless, and hopeless souls from the quagmire of sin, in a manner which magnifies His righteousness, is no trivial matter. In a world full of religious darkness and spiritual quackery, no wonder the apostle could exclaim, 'I am not ashamed of the gospel, for it is the power of God for salvation to everyone who believes'. The gospel works, and in it the transcendent wisdom of God shines forth. It solves the conundrum and delivers the result that has eluded all the theories and therapies, programmes and philosophies of the world, both ancient and modern: 'How then can man be in the right before God? How can he who is born of woman be pure?'[210]

In the drama of redemption we see that at every turn God delights to confound human thinking. How majestic the words of the first prophecy in respect of the seed of the woman's conquest of Satan, 'He shall bruise your head'. Not some mighty archangel, but One truly human would overcome the enemy. But consider the **manner** of His conquest: miraculously conceived by the Holy Spirit in the womb of the virgin; not born in a palace, but laid in a manger; raised in the obscurity and disadvantage of Nazareth, but delighting His Father; truly King, but with a kingdom not of this world; destined not for coronation, but crucifixion. The shameful crown of thorns must precede the crown of many diadems.

---

[208] Rom. 8. 28.

[209] Ps. 19. 1.

[210] Job. 25. 4.

'By weakness and defeat,
He won the meed and crown;
Trod all our foes beneath His feet
By being trodden down.

He Satan's power laid low;
Made sin, He sin o'erthrew;
Bowed to the grave, destroyed it so,
And death by dying slew'.
S. Whitlock Gandy

The Corinthians were influenced by displays of Greek wisdom and rhetoric. They were in danger of elevating the servants of God to the disadvantage of the Christ who had died for them – 'Christ the power of God and the wisdom of God'. But the apostle turns their attention to a new category of wisdom that simply beggars that of the world: the surpassing wisdom of God as demonstrated in the cross of Christ. Through His cross, Christ 'became for us wisdom from God – righteousness and sanctification and redemption'.[211] The Lion of the tribe of Judah, is none other than the little Lamb in the midst of heaven's throne with seven horns and seven eyes – plenitude of power, and plenitude of wisdom and knowledge.[212] The conqueror, destined to consummate the purposes of God and reign, is, at the same time, the lowly Lamb of God's providing, the perfect sin-atoning sacrifice.

Further, the church is the masterpiece of divine workmanship, the dazzling display to all wondering heavenly intelligences of the manifold (or, variegated) wisdom of God.[213] In it the ancient division between Jew and Gentile is done away; it is an eternal temple pervaded by God's presence, the body and complement of Christ the Head sharing His life, and also His bride – the supreme object of His love.

Practical considerations

The creature, however godly, can never attain to the perfect wisdom of God, yet Solomon is justly celebrated because he sought wisdom to

---

[211] 1 Cor. 1. 30.
[212] Rev. 5. 6; Isa. 11. 2.
[213] Eph. 3. 10; cp. 1 Pet. 1. 12; 1 Cor. 11. 10.

govern Israel.[214] We may feel that the complexity of the issues we face demands the wisdom of Solomon, but God promises wisdom to those who seek it from Him. On the other hand, we will be fools if we neglect the inspired storehouse of instruction of which the psalmist could declare, 'Your commandments make me wiser than my enemies; for they are ever with me. I have more understanding than all my teachers, for Your testimonies are my meditation'.[215]

To the Colossian church, endangered by speculative philosophies, Paul presents Christ as the sufficient repository of all the treasures of wisdom and knowledge.[216] Today, the world is delving afresh into the religions, mysticism, and philosophies of men; by contrast the Christian sees all God's wisdom and purposes of grace embodied in Christ, and needs nothing and no one else. In particular, we each need wisdom so to interpret our Father's disciplinary working in our lives as to be exercised thereby.[217] The Holy Spirit distributes divine wisdom,[218] reminding us that wisdom thoroughly characterizes the Trinity.

In conclusion, we may join Paul in prostration and worship in view of God's unfathomable strategies for the blessing of both Jew and Gentile, 'Oh, the depth of the riches and wisdom and knowledge of God! How unsearchable are his judgments and how inscrutable his ways . . . For from him and through him and to him are all things. To him be glory forever. Amen'.[219]

What is Thy Name? - C. E. Hocking

So many people today question the existence of God. Everywhere in the word of God His existence is taken for granted. After Jacob's encounter with that mysterious 'man' in Genesis chapter 32, he could not stand the suspense involved in not knowing 'him' any longer. 'Tell me I pray thee', said he, 'thy name', v. 29; cp. v. 27. Although given no direct answer to

---

[214] 2 Chr. 1. 10.
[215] Ps. 119. 98, 99.
[216] Col. 2. 3.
[217] Heb. 12. 11.
[218] Deut. 34. 9; Isa. 11. 2; Dan. 5. 14; Acts 6. 3; Eph. 1. 17.
[219] Rom. 11. 33-36 ESV.

that request, he was in no doubt, subsequently, that he had actually 'seen God face to face', v. 30. When God would send Moses to Pharaoh that he might bring Israel out of Egypt, God's servant was sure that the children of Israel would question his commission by God. He knew that he must be in a position to answer the question 'What is his name?' Exod. 3. 13.

Agur, deeply conscious of his ignorance of the Holy One asked, 'What is his name, and what is his son's name, if thou canst tell?' Prov. 30. 4. To know God's name meant nothing short of personally knowing Him, to know insofar as He had been pleased to reveal Himself. Hence, the final and complete revelation of God, even of the Father, was the purpose of the mission of the Son, our Lord Jesus, who said, 'I have manifested thy name unto the men which thou gavest me out of the world', John 17. 6, and 'I have declared unto them thy name', v. 26. On the very threshold of the study of divine self-revelation we are faced with 'the name', which, as B. W. ANDERSON has rightly assessed, is 'the key to the understanding of the biblical doctrine of God'. The phrase 'the name' is used to designate God frequently in the scriptures, especially in the Psalms, Isaiah, Jeremiah, and Ezekiel. It is with this use of the phrase that we are concerned here.

The Name Perfectly Expresses Character – Who God is

Following Moses' request to 'show me thy glory', God stood with him and 'proclaimed the name of the Lord', Exod. 33. 18, 19; 34. 5. What exactly was involved in this? The passage supplies the answer, for the Lord made Himself known as 'The Lord, the Lord, a God full of compassion and gracious, slow to anger, and plenteous in mercy and truth', 34. 6, 7 RV. Here, then, was a most detailed revelation of **the character** of the Lord, the God of the covenant, described as a proclamation of the divine name, v. 5. Little wonder that 'Moses made haste, and bowed his head toward the earth, and worshipped', v. 8.

The God of the Bible is not an 'It', but a 'Thou'. He is no faceless and nameless force, only to be feared and placated. Rather, He is the unchanging 'Thou', the initiator, controller, and consummator of all, who delights to reveal that which we are able to bear of His infinity in those terms which glorify Himself and do us good. Who can find a friend so faithful, a supporter so capable and strong, an offended One so forgiving, a tender One so compassionate, One who favours so munificently? God has chosen to reveal His nature and character, the God who is light, life and love, transcendent and yet so imminent. While the heaven of heavens cannot contain Him, He walks with men, He talks with them, He tells us that we are His own.

The various names and titles given to God in the course of the divine self-revelation each contribute something to our understanding of His person and attributes, for names describe the bearer, unveil something of His character, and therefore 'index personality'; see specially the next two chapters. The introduction of fresh names or titles, and, in the case of men or cities, a change of name or the giving of a new name alert both to the significance they bear, and to the progressive revelation being given of the bearer. Though stated in connection with Nabal particularly, it is true generally in the Bible that 'as his name is, so is he'. When God says that His people shall know His name, He is not referring to any one of His names or titles, but rather indicating in a 'shorthand' way that they shall come to comprehend, and apprehend, all that He has been pleased to reveal Himself to be for them, Ps. 9. 10; Isa. 52. 6. When He says of the temple 'My name shall be there',[220] He is assuring them that His presence will be known there, He will be among them; cp. Matt. 18. 20. So it is that 'the name' embraces 'the sum of the manifold revelations taken together as one supreme revelation'.

The Name Dramatically Influences the Bearer – What He does

In the course of revelation, we are left in no doubt that God is holy, e.g., Lev. 11. 44, or, to express it in another way, that He is the One 'whose name is Holy', Isa. 57. 15.

Consequently, His people glory in His holy name, 1 Chr. 16. 10; they even trust in His holy name, Ps. 33. 21. But if God's name is holy, then He is concerned for it; He must act so as to safeguard it, and will ensure that His great name is sanctified, Ezek. 36. 21, 23, and His holy name be made known among His people, 39. 7.

Again, His name is 'great in might', Jer. 10. 6, even 'glorious and fearful', Deut. 28. 58, 'dreadful among the heathen', Mal. 1. 14. But simply

[220] 1 Kgs. 8. 29; cp. 11. 36; 14. 21; Deut. 12. 5, 11, 21, etc..

because His name is great, and so closely bound up with the people that are called by His name, Jer. 15. 16, when they are exposed to extermination by their enemies, Joshua will cry out, 'What wilt thou do for thy great name?' 7. 9 RV. He must act, for He 'will not forsake his people for his great name's sake', 1 Sam. 12. 22. For His name's sake He defers His anger, Isa. 48. 9, and in judgement withholds His hand in measure for His name's sake. He says 'I wrought for my name's sake, that it should not be polluted before the heathen', Ezek. 20. 9, 14, 22, 44. God is thus seen to be self-consistent, acting in accord with His revealed character, 'Yea thou spakest with thy mouth, and hast fulfilled it with thine hand'.

Acting according to His nature as revealed brings further glory to Him; it enhances His name. On leaving Egypt, when He divided the water before them, did He not make Himself an everlasting name, Isa. 63. 12? In leading His people thus, He intended to make Himself a glorious name, v. 14; 'So didst thou get thee a name, as it is this day', Neh. 9. 10; Thou 'hast brought thy people forth out of the land of Egypt with a mighty hand, and hast gotten thee renown, as at this day', Dan. 9. 15. 'And what one nation in the earth is like thy people Israel, whom God went to redeem unto himself for a people, to make thee a name by great and terrible things', 1 Chr. 17. 21 RV.[221] Thus His fame is still further spread abroad, 'for they shall hear of thy great name'.

What an encouragement all this becomes to us! How often God's people move boldly into His presence rehearsing His earlier ways with them, reminding Him of past unveilings of His character which are still a support to them, and urging Him to take the initiative once again, and to deliver them 'for his name's sake'. 'Though our iniquities testify against us, work thou for thy name's sake, O Lord', Jer. 14. 7 RV. 'Where is he that brought them up out of the sea?' Isa. 63. 11; 'cause thy face to shine upon thy sanctuary that is desolate, for the Lord's sake'; 'behold our desolations, and the city which is called by thy name', Dan. 9. 17, 18. Hence, too, for 'thy name's sake . . . pardon mine iniquity', 'lead me, and guide me', 'quicken me', 'do not abhor us, for thy name's sake, do not disgrace the throne of thy glory: remember, break not thy covenant

[221] Cp. Jer. 32. 20.

with us'.[222]

If the name embraces all that He has revealed Himself to be, who He is, then what He does may be simply explained in the light of this. Further, because He is the unchanging One, He may be counted upon to act again consistently with who He is, as corroborated in His past interventions in history. His people look for Him, for, 'Behold, the name of the Lord cometh from far', Isa. 30. 27. During the days of His flesh, that revelation of God *par excellence*, the multitude said as the Lord Jesus entered Jerusalem, 'Hosanna to the son of David: Blessed is he that cometh in the name of the Lord', Matt. 21. 9. How this anticipation of the future glory at the second advent of our Lord causes His people to long for its fulfilment.[223]

'As is Thy Name, O God, so is Thy Praise'.

Happy that people to whom the Lord has made Himself known; 'My people shall know my name', Isa. 52. 6. For such, 'to thy name and to thy memorial is the desire of our soul', Isa. 26. 8 RV. They **'love thy name'**.[224] The reality of their personal encounter with Him prompts them to 'give thee thanks for ever, because thou hast done it: and I will **wait on thy name**, for it is good, in the presence of thy saints', Ps. 52. 9 RV. They **call** upon the name of the Lord.[225] From overflowing hearts they **sing praises unto His name**; 2 Sam. 22. 50, **sing forth the honour of His name**, Ps. 66. 2, 4; **praise His name**;[226] **give thanks to His name**;[227] **bless His name**;[228] they give unto the Lord **the glory due unto His name**, they **glory in His holy name**.[229]

Such a God who has made Himself known to them is worthy of their unwavering confidence, so they **'trust in the name** of the Lord'.[230] Their practical conduct will be regulated by their personal knowledge of Him,

---

[222] Pss. 25. 11; 31. 3; 143. 11; Jer. 14. 21.

[223] Matt. 23. 39; see Ps. 118. 25, 26.

[224] Pss. 5. 11; 119. 132; cp. Isa. 56. 6; Heb. 6. 10.

[225] 1 Kgs. 18. 24; 1 Chr. 16. 8; Gen. 4. 26; 12. 8; cp. Ps. 79. 6; 1 Cor. 1. 2.

[226] Pss. 74. 21; 145. 2; 1 Chr. 29. 13.

[227] Pss. 44. 8; 106. 47; cp. Eph. 5. 20; Heb. 13. 15.

[228] Pss. 100. 4; 103. 1; 145. 1, 21.

[229] 1 Chr. 16. 10, 29; Pss. 29. 2; 96. 8.

[230] Zeph. 3. 12; cp. John 1. 12; Acts 3. 16.

for they will **walk in the name** of the Lord their God for ever and ever, Mic. 4. 5; cp. Zech. 10. 12. Their **service will be done in His name**, Deut. 18. 5, 7, not only in the light of whose they are, and whom they serve, but also working by divine authority, on God's behalf, and in fact 'for his sake', cp. 3 John 7; Mark 9. 38. Many who know Him are commissioned to **speak and prophesy in His name.**[231] The building that counts with God is that which gives substance to His declared will, and is done out of a full heart in response to a God that is personally known. Hence Solomon said, 'I purpose to **build an house for the name** of the Lord my God, as the Lord spake unto David my father', 1 Kgs. 5. 5 RV, his intention being 'to dedicate it to him', 2 Chr. 2. 4. These, and so many other expressions, touch upon the response of hearts that have tasted for themselves that the Lord is good, and have found that the 'name of the Lord is a strong tower', Prov. 18. 10.

The theme 'the name' is carried over into the New Testament also.[232] However, the subject is greatly enlarged and enriched, the characteristic Old Testament phrases used of God's name being applied here to our Lord Jesus Christ. We have been reached and blessed by the Word who is God, and yet by that same Word who has become flesh. If, therefore, 'ye believe in God, believe also in me', John 14. 1, He says. If we trust in God's name, let us **believe in His name**;[233] Those who believe should be **baptized in the name**, Matt. 28. 19; Acts 2. 38. They have the privilege of **praying, asking in His name**, John 14. 14; 15. 16. They may be called upon to '**suffer for my name's sake**'.[234] We recall that 'God highly exalted him, and gave unto him the name which is above every name; that **in the name of Jesus every knee should bow**, of things in heaven and things on earth and things under the earth, and that every tongue should confess that Jesus Christ is Lord, to the glory of God the Father', Phil. 2. 9-11 RV. In response to Him, because of the enjoyed reality of who He is, and all that He has done, 'whatsoever ye do, in word or in deed, **do all in the name** of the Lord Jesus, giving thanks to God the Father through him', Col. 3. 17 RV.

---

[231] Jer. 26. 9, 16; cp. Luke 24. 47; Acts 4. 17; 5. 28.
[232] For example, Mark 11. 9, 10; Rom. 2. 24; 9. 17; 10. 13; 15. 9.
[233] John 1. 12; 2. 23; 3. 18; 1 John 3. 23.
[234] See Acts 9. 15, 16; cp. Phil. 1. 29.

Titles and Descriptive Titles of God in the Old Testament - F. F. BRUCE

Scripture quotations are taken from the Revised Version

YHWH, The LORD. The personal name of the God of Israel appears in the Hebrew Bible spelt with the four consonants YHWH or JHVH. After the return from the Babylonian exile this name, because of its pre-eminent sanctity, was almost never pronounced by Jews, so that its original pronunciation is doubtful. When, between AD 500 and 1000, points indicating the vowel sounds were added to the consonantal text of the Hebrew Bible to help with the pronunciation, the points attached to the consonants YHWH indicated the vowels of the word which was to be pronounced in its place, usually *Adonai*, 'Lord', but sometimes *Elohim*, 'God'. This is the origin of the form Jehovah, first attested in the Middle Ages, in which the consonants of the ineffable name are combined with the vowels of *Adonai.* In most editions of the English Bible YHWH is rendered 'the LORD', with four capitals, except when it is preceded by *Adonai*, then it is rendered 'GOD', with three capitals – 'the Lord GOD' representing *Adonai* YHWH. In Genesis chapter 2 verse 4 to chapter 3 verse 24 'the LORD God' represents YHWH *Elohim,* a compound form which marks the transition from 'God', *Elohim,* of Genesis chapter 1 verse 1 to chapter 2 verse 3 to 'the LORD' (YHWH) of chapter 4. In Isaiah chapter 26 verse 4 where 'the LORD JEHOVAH' has both words completely capitalized, 'the LORD' represents YH, Jah, a shorter form of YHWH, found also in Psalm 68 verse 4, 'His name is JAH', and Song of Songs chapter 8 verse 6, 'A very flame of the LORD [Jah]', and very frequently in the form -iah as an element in personal names, e.g. Zechariah, 'YHWH has remembered'.

The use of the name YHWH goes back to primeval times, according to Genesis chapter 4 verse 26, where it is said that in the time of Enosh, Adam's grandson, men began 'to call upon the name of the **LORD**'. But its special significance in the Old Testament marks God out as the covenant God of His people Israel. By this name He revealed Himself to Moses at the burning bush: He was at one and the same time the God of Abraham, Isaac and Jacob and the God who was bringing their descendants into a new relationship with Himself in which He would be their God and they would be His people. The meaning of the covenant name is unfolded as 'I AM THAT I AM', Exod. 3. 14, or perhaps, 'I will be what I will be' – the God of open-ended promise, 'This is my name for ever, and this is my memorial unto all generations'. Thenceforth YHWH is used as the personal name of the God of Israel; He has many titles, but this is peculiarly His name, 'I am the LORD; that is my name', Isa. 42. 8.

The LORD of Hosts. The LORD of hosts, YHWH *Seba'oth*, first occurs as the title by which God was worshipped at Shiloh, the sanctuary which in the period of the judges housed the ark, where the divine presence was enthroned upon the cherubim, 1 Sam. 1. 3; 4. 4. At that time the 'hosts' may have been envisaged as the hosts of Israel, as becomes explicit in David's challenge of Goliath 'in the name of the LORD of hosts, the God of the armies of Israel', 1 Sam. 17. 45. At a later time the hosts were thought of rather as the armies of heaven, the angelic powers that exist to carry out the Creator's commands, as in Psalm 103 verse 21; Daniel chapter 4 verse 35. In the Greek Septuagint the title was sometimes translated literally, sometimes as *pantokratōr*, 'Almighty', and sometimes left untranslated in the form Sabaoth, which appears in the New Testament in Romans chapter 9 verse 29 and James chapter 5 verse 4.

Other compounds with YHWH are used from time to time as expansions of the divine name, for example, 'the LORD that healeth thee', YHWH *ropheka*, Exod. 15. 26; 'The LORD . . . our righteousness', YHWH *sidqenu* in Jer. 23. 6; 33. 16; occasionally as place-names, like 'Jehovah-jireh', 'The LORD will provide', Gen. 22. 14; 'Jehovah-nissi', 'The LORD my banner', Exod. 17. 15; 'Jehovah-shalom', 'The LORD is peace', Judg. 6. 24; 'The LORD is there', YHWH *shammah*, Ezek. 48. 35.

Elohim, etc. The commonest Hebrew word for God in the Old Testament is *Elohim.* This belongs to a group of divine designations the root meaning of which appears to be 'power'. *Elohim* is a plural form, used either as a plural of majesty or in order to indicate that the living God comprises the totality of powers within Himself. When it is used of the living God, it is not a plural in sense; this is shown by the fact that, when it is the subject of a clause, the verb which accompanies it is regularly singular, like the verb *bara*, 'created', Gen. 1. 1. When *elohim* is used as a plural in sense, it denotes not the God of Israel but the gods of the other nations; the same is true of the Aramaic plural *elahin,* Dan. 2. 11, or *elahayya,* Jer. 10. 11. Sometimes the plural *elohim* denotes angelic powers or human judges, 'He judgeth among the gods', Ps. 82. 1, or 'Worship him, all ye gods', 97. 7. The 'sons of God', *bene Elohim,* are similarly angelic powers, Job 1. 6, etc., 38. 7; the sense of the same expression in Genesis chapter 6 verses 2 and 4 is debated.

The plural 'gods' in the title 'God of gods', Ps. 136. 2, may similarly denote angelic beings, as also, 'Who is like unto thee . . . among the gods?' Exod. 15. 11, and, 'a great King above all gods', Ps. 95. 3; on the other hand such a compound title may be a superlative formation, 'the supreme God'. On Nebuchadnezzar's lips the title 'God of gods', Dan. 2. 47, may mean that Daniel's God is greater than all the gods worshipped by the Babylonians or other peoples. The title 'God of heaven', used by Gentiles and Jews alike in exilic and post-exilic times, Ezra 1. 2; Neh. 1. 4, was an internationally recognized way of referring to the God of Israel. Jonah also speaks to the pagan mariners of his God as 'the LORD, the God of heaven', Jonah 1. 9.

The singular form of *Elohim* is *Eloah,* which is chiefly found in poetry. Its earliest occurrence is in the Song of Moses, Deut. 32. 15, 17; it is specially common in Job. The corresponding Aramaic form *Elah* appears in Ezra and Daniel; it is used, for example, in the title 'God of heaven', Ezra 5. 11, etc.; Dan. 2. 18, etc.

El. *El* has more of the nature of a personal name than *Elohim* or *Eloah*; it was used in the Canaanite religious vocabulary for the head of the pantheon. In the Old Testament it sometimes stands alone as a word meaning 'God': 'an altar unto God', Gen. 35. 1, 3; 'Heal her, O God', Num. 12. 13, and more especially in poetry, as in the oracles of Balaam, e.g. 'What hath God wrought!' Num. 23. 23; the Song of Moses, e.g., 'God that gave thee birth', Deut. 32. 18; Job and the Psalms. With the possessive suffix *-i* it has the meaning 'my God', Ps. 22. 1.[235]

The commonest use of *El,* however, is in compound titles and names. Examples are: 'a God that seeth', *El ro'i,* Gen. 16. 13; 'the Everlasting God', *El olam*, 21. 33; 'El-elohe-Israel', *El,* the God of Israel, 33. 20; 'El-

[235] Cp. Matt. 27. 46.

beth-el', the God of Bethel, 35. 7; 'a jealous God', *El qanna*, Exod. 34. 14; 'the living God', *El hai,* Josh. 3. 10. It occurs also in place names like Bethel, 'the house of God', Gen. 28. 19, and Peniel, 'the face of God', 32. 30; and as a prefix or suffix in personal names, like Elishua, God is salvation, Elishama, God has heard, Eliada, God knows, and Eliphelet, God is deliverance, sons of David, 2 Sam. 5. 15, 16, or Ishmael, God hears, Israel, God strives, Michael, who is like God?, Abdiel, servant of God.

The plural *elim* is occasionally used with the meaning 'gods'; 'sons of the mighty', *bene elim,* Ps. 29. 1, are angelic powers, like the *bene elohim* elsewhere.

Two important compounds containing *El* have not yet been mentioned: these are *El Elyon,* 'God Most High', and *El Shaddai,* 'God Almighty'; the other element in each of these is likewise a divine title in its own right.

Elyon, El Elyon. *Elyon* occurs as an ordinary adjective, with reference, for example, to the 'uppermost' basket carried by Pharaoh's baker, Gen. 40. 17. As a divine title its first occurrence is in Genesis chapter 14 verses 18 to 22. Melchizedek, king of Salem (probably Jerusalem), 'was priest of God Most High', in which capacity he bestowed a blessing on Abraham and received from him a tenth of the spoils of war. According to Genesis chapter 14 verse 22, Abraham acknowledged the LORD whom he worshipped to be identical with Melchizedek's God Most High. In the oracles of Balaam, Num. 24. 16, and the Song of Moses, Deut. 32. 8, *Elyon* ('the Most High') is used by itself as a title for God. It apparently came into more general use in Israel after David captured Jerusalem and made it his capital; in the Psalter *Elyon,* with its Jerusalem associations, and YHWH, alternate frequently in poetical parallelism. If YHWH speaks especially of God's relationship with His covenant people, *Elyon* speaks of His universal supremacy. This distinction appears as early as Deuteronomy chapter 32 verses 8 and 9, where *Elyon* 'gave to the nations their inheritance', while YHWH's 'portion is his people'.

Elyon was translated *hupsistos* in the Septuagint, and this became a link-word by which Jews and Gentiles in the Greek-speaking world could both refer to the one true God, as in the Philippian fortune-teller's cry, Acts 16. 17.

Shaddai, El Shaddai. *El Shaddai* was the name of self-revelation which God employed when he appeared to Abraham, Isaac and Jacob, according to His words to Moses, Exod. 6. 3. The etymology of *Shaddai* is uncertain; nowadays it is commonly related to a word meaning 'mountain', whereas in earlier days Jewish theologians explained it as meaning 'He who is [*sha*-] sufficient [*dai*]'. The Septuagint sometimes translates it by *hikanos,* 'sufficient', a rendering which may underlie Paul's words, 'our sufficiency is from God', 2 Cor. 3. 5, but more often by *pantokratōr,* 'almighty', 'ruler of all', a form reproduced in 2 Corinthians chapter 6 verse 18 and several times in Revelation. The traditional rendering 'Almighty' is adequate; almightiness implies all-sufficiency.

The first occurrence of *El Shaddai* is in Genesis chapter 17 verse 1, where God appeared to Abraham, introduced Himself as 'God Almighty', renamed him in accordance with His promise to make him 'the father of a multitude of nations' and gave him the covenant of circumcision. Isaac blessed Jacob in the name of God Almighty, 28. 3, and to Jacob himself God appeared as God Almighty on his return from Paddan-aram and confirmed His promises regarding descendants and land, 35. 11, 12.

Elsewhere *Shaddai* and YHWH are used as synonyms, as when Naomi says, 'the Almighty hath dealt very bitterly with me . . . the LORD hath brought me home again empty', Ruth 1. 20, 21. But Naomi soon had cause to confess that *Shaddai* was much more true to His name than she had supposed when she said that He had 'afflicted' her, 1. 21.

The God of the Fathers. Because God called Abraham, Isaac and Jacob, and established His covenant with them and their descendants, he 'is not ashamed of them, to be called their God', Heb. 11. 16. The Israelites knew Him as the God of their fathers, or more particularly, 'the God of Abraham, the God of Isaac, and the God of Jacob', Exod. 3. 6. Our Lord's inference from this self-designation is of great importance for the biblical doctrine of God and man, Mark 12. 26, 27, and parallels. Of the three patriarchs, Jacob is the one with whose name God most frequently links His own – a significant fact when Jacob's character and career are borne in mind. 'The God of Jacob is our refuge', Ps. 46. 7, 11. The title 'the God of Israel' refers more commonly to the nation than to the patriarch personally, but note Elijah's invocation, 1 Kgs. 18. 36. In some of these titles another word may be substituted for 'God': we read, for example, of the 'Fear of Isaac', that is, the one worshipped by Isaac, Gen. 31. 42, 53, and of the 'Mighty One of Jacob', 49. 24; the 'stone of Israel', 49. 24; the 'Strength of Israel', 1 Sam. 15. 29; the 'Holy One of Israel', Ps. 71. 22, and specially frequent in Isaiah.

Adonai. *Adonai*, 'the Lord', meaning literally 'my lords', is a plural of majesty from the singular *adon,* 'lord'. The plural of this word is sometimes used honorifically of high authorities, like Joseph in Egypt, 'the lord [plural] of the land', Gen. 42. 30. As used of God it expresses His limitless sovereignty. In such a statement as 'I am poor and needy; Yet the Lord [*Adonai*] thinketh upon me', Ps. 40. 17, there is an eloquent contrast between the speaker's inadequacy and the Lord's infinite resources. *Adonai* is sometimes used alone and also – often in the prophets, and very often in Ezekiel – in the combination *Adonai* YHWH, 'the Lord GOD'.

King. Another title designating God's sovereignty is King *(melek).* He is 'King of heaven', Dan. 4. 37; 'King of all the earth', Ps. 47. 7; King of His people Israel.[236] 'I am a great King, saith the LORD of hosts', Mal. 1. 14; His people acknowledge in response, 'the LORD is . . . a great King above all gods', Ps. 95. 3. Isaiah confesses his sinfulness when he sees 'the King, the LORD of hosts', Isa. 6. 5. Jerusalem is 'the city of the great King', Ps. 48. 2. The title forms part of personal names, e.g., Elimelech, 'my God is King', and Malchijah, 'YHWH is King'.

With the title 'King' are closely associated the verb 'reign', Exod. 15. 18, 'The LORD shall reign for ever and ever', and the nouns 'throne' and 'kingdom', 'The LORD hath established his throne in the heavens; And his kingdom ruleth over all', Ps. 103. 19. The Old Testament teaching about God's kingdom, including the kingdom which, according to Daniel chapter 2 verse 44, He is to set up in the latter days, forms the background to our Lord's proclamation of the kingdom of God in the Gospels.

Shepherd. In the ancient Near East the king was often called the shepherd of his people, as one who not only exercised authority and leadership over them but also had responsibility for their welfare. So it

---

236 See Judg. 8. 23; 1 Sam. 8. 7; Isa. 33. 22.

is with God, whether He is called 'Shepherd [*ro'eh*] of Israel' in general, Ps. 80. 1, or 'my shepherd' in particular, 23. 1. His people are 'the sheep of his pasture', 100. 3. The outstanding Old Testament passage which portrays God as the Shepherd of His people is Ezekiel chapter 34, against the background of which our Lord's parable of the shepherd and the sheep in John chapter 10 can be read with greater understanding.

Rock. Another designation which presents God as the refuge and strength of His people is 'The Rock', *sur.* It occurs repeatedly in the Song of Moses.[237] To the psalmist God is 'my rock, and my redeemer', Ps. 19. 14; He is 'the rock of our salvation', 95. 1. 'The LORD JEHOVAH is a rock of ages', Isa. 26. 4 mg. He Himself asks, 'Is there a God beside me?' and answers, 'yea, there is no Rock; I know not any', 44. 8.

Redeemer, Saviour. When God is addressed as 'my rock, and my redeemer [*go'el*]', the latter title suggests a personal bond between the Redeemer and the redeemed; He is their 'kinsman-redeemer'. 'Our redeemer, the LORD of hosts is his name, the Holy One of Israel', 47. 4. When He redeems His people from captivity, He need pay nothing to their captors, 'Ye were sold for nought; and ye shall be redeemed without money', 52. 3. But there are worse plights than captivity and exile, and when God is acclaimed as the One 'who redeemeth thy life from destruction', Ps. 103. 4, the stage is set for 'the redemption that is in Christ Jesus', Rom. 3. 24.

Nearly synonymous with 'redeemer' is 'saviour', *moshia*: when in Isaiah chapter 45 verse 21 God speaks of Himself as 'a just God and a saviour', it is the same God who is described in Romans chapter 3 verse 26 as 'just, and the justifier of him that hath faith in Jesus'.

Creator. The 'Creator [*bore*] of the ends of the earth', Isa. 40. 28, is more personally 'the Creator of Israel', 43. 15, and most personally 'thy Creator', Eccles. 12. 1.

Judge. The Creator of all at the beginning is the Judge of all at the end: so Abraham can appeal to God as 'the Judge [*shophet*] of all the earth', Gen. 18. 25 – the One who can be relied upon neither to commit nor to

---

[237] Deut. 32. 4, 15, 18, 30, 31.

tolerate anything that is unjust.

Titles and Descriptive Titles of God in the New Testament - F. F. BRUCE

Scripture quotations are taken from the Revised Version

God. The word most frequently used for 'God' in the New Testament is *theos.* This is a common noun in Greek, the ordinary term meaning 'god'. As Paul says, there were in the Graeco-Roman world 'gods many', *theoi polloi*, 1 Cor. 8. 5. Therefore, when *theos* is used of God it normally has the definite article before it, to mark Him out as *the* God. When *theos* in this sense is not prefaced by the article, there is usually some grammatical or stylistic reason for its absence. Occasionally *theos* is used with reference to the Son,[238] or to the Spirit, Acts 5. 4; but it predominantly denotes the Father: 'to us there is one God, the Father', 1 Cor. 8. 6. He is 'the only true God', John 17. 3; the 'living and true God', 1 Thess. 1. 9. As used of Him, *theos* fulfils the functions which *Elohim* fulfils in the Hebrew Bible.

Abba, Father. The distinctive title of God in the New Testament, His specifically Christian designation, is Father, Greek, *patēr*. Old Testament adumbrations of this usage may be seen, for example, 'thou art our father', Isa. 63. 16; and 'Like as a father pitieth his children, so the LORD pitieth them that fear him', Ps. 103. 13; as well as in God's claiming of Israel as 'my son, my firstborn', Exod. 4. 22. But the New Testament usage goes much farther than that. 'Father', as the Christian designation for God, reflects the Semitic Abba, which was not the 'my Father' of personal Jewish devotion or the 'our Father' of synagogue worship but the name by which children addressed their father or spoke about him one to another in the affectionate intimacy of the family circle. By this name, according to Mark chapter 14 verse 36, our Lord Himself addressed God; and it was after His example, no doubt, that (in common with a few other Semitic expressions like Amen and Hallelujah) Abba made its way at an early date into the vocabulary of Greek-speaking Christians. Paul assumes that the Roman Christians, whom he had not evangelized, were as familiar with it as his own Gentile converts in

[238] John 1. 1c; Rom. 9. 5; Heb. 1. 8, 9.

Galatia.[239] The relationship between the Father and His children is a spiritual one, established by grace on His part and by the response of faith on theirs. It is, more precisely, by faith in the Son of God that they come to know God as Father: it is thus that 'the God and Father of our Lord Jesus Christ' is confessed as their Father too. The spontaneous invocation of God as Father, for which non-Pauline testimony is provided in 1 Peter chapter 1 verse 17, is as much a token of the indwelling Spirit as is the acknowledgment of Jesus as Lord, 1 Cor. 12. 3. When we say 'Abba, Father', this is the Spirit of the Son of God, and the Spirit of our sonship too, bearing witness with our human spirit 'that we are children of God', Rom. 8. 16; cp. Gal. 4. 6. It is strange that so many children of God, especially in public prayer and praise, think it proper to pile up grandiloquent phrases in speaking to Him, when His delight is to hear them call Him 'Father'.

Lord. In the New Testament God is also designated 'Lord', Greek, *kyrios,* especially in quotations from the Old Testament, as in Romans chapter 14 verse 11, where Paul's statement in the preceding verse that 'we shall all stand before the judgement-seat of God' is reinforced by the quotation of Isaiah chapter 45 verse 23: 'As I live, saith the Lord, to me every knee shall bow'. For the most part, however, the designation 'Lord', even in quotations from the Old Testament where the Hebrew text has YHWH, belongs distinctively to the risen Christ. In Revelation, particularly, the title 'Lord' appears in a variety of compound designations, largely drawn from the Old Testament and emphasizing the eternity and supremacy of God, as in 'I am the Alpha and the Omega, saith the Lord God, which is and which was and which is to come, the Almighty', Rev. 1. 8. It is also noteworthy how many of these titles in this book are ascribed indiscriminately to the Son and to the Father.

The absolute sovereignty of God is occasionally denoted by *despotēs*: this title is used to address God by Simeon, Luke 2. 29, 'Now lettest thou thy servant depart, O Lord'; by the apostles and their associates, Acts 4. 24, 'O Lord, thou that didst make the heaven and the earth and the sea'; and by the souls of the martyrs, Rev. 6. 10, 'How long, O Master?' Another word with comparable meaning is *dynastēs,* translated 'Potentate', 1 Tim. 6. 15.

---

[239] Rom. 8. 15; Gal. 4. 6.

King. In accordance with Old Testament precedent, God is sometimes called 'King', Greek, *basileus*, in the New Testament. In the doxology of 1 Timothy chapter 1 verse 17, for example, Paul, reflecting on the wonder of that grace which saved the chief of sinners, ascribes everlasting honour and glory to 'the King eternal [margin 'King of the ages'], incorruptible, invisible, the only God'. Similarly in 1 Timothy chapter 6 verses 15 to 16 he speaks of God as 'the blessed and only Potentate, the King of kings, and Lord of lords; who only hath immortality'. We recall the ascription of very similar language to Jesus, Rev. 17. 14; 19. 16. The title 'King of the ages', with variant readings 'King of the nations', or 'King of saints' KJV, is used in Revelation chapter 15 verse 3.

Saviour. While 'Saviour', Greek, *sōtēr*, belongs more naturally to Christ in the New Testament, there are a few places where God the Father is so designated. Mary, using the language of Old Testament piety, speaks of her spirit as rejoicing 'in God my Saviour', Luke 1. 47. In the Pastoral Epistles reference is made repeatedly to 'God our Saviour'. Paul exercises his apostolic commission 'according to the commandment of God our Saviour', 1 Tim. 1. 1; Titus 1. 3. Prayer for rulers 'is good and acceptable in the sight of God our Saviour', 1 Tim. 2. 3. Slaves (but not slaves only) should be taught to 'adorn the doctrine of God our Saviour in all things', Titus 2. 10. When Paul, quoting a 'faithful saying', 1 Tim. 4. 10, speaks of 'the living God' as 'the Saviour of all men, specially of them that believe', he probably uses the word in the more general sense of 'preserver' as well as in the more specifically Christian sense.

Compound Titles. Various attributes of God are specified in such compound expressions as 'the God of hope', Rom. 15. 13; 'the God of peace';[240] 'the Lord of peace', 2 Thess. 3. 16; 'the God of love and peace', 2 Cor. 13. 11; 'the Father of mercies and God of all comfort', 1. 3; 'the God of all grace', 1 Pet. 5. 10. A number of Old Testament terms appear, sometimes with amplification, like 'the Most High', Luke 1. 32; Acts 7. 48, etc.; 'the Most High God', Mark 5. 7; Luke 8. 28; 'the righteous judge', 2 Tim. 4. 8; 'a faithful Creator', 1 Pet. 4. 19; the 'Holy One', 1 John 2. 20; Rev. 16. 5.

---

[240] Rom. 15. 33; 16. 20; Phil. 4. 9; 1 Thess. 5. 23; Heb. 13. 20.

God in Creation and Providence - E. W. Rogers

That matter is not eternal the Bible makes crystal clear, for 'all things were made by him; and without him was not any thing made that was made', John 1. 3. There was no exception to this. God was the great **eternal source** of all things, and His **Son was the agent** through whom He accomplished His purposes touching heaven and earth. 'By the word of the Lord were the heavens made; and all the host of them by the breath of his mouth', Ps. 33. 6. Scientists may investigate, but they cannot discover with certainty the origin of things; 'The secret things belong unto the Lord our God: but those things which are revealed belong unto us and to our children', Deut. 29. 29. In holy scripture we have the only reliable revealed disclosure of the true origin of things. The record given in Genesis chapter 1 should be read with the childlike simplicity of faith. It is not written for scientists, but for the plainest of the people. Just as we say that the watchmaker made the watch, but give no details touching all the complicated processes involved, so God states that 'in the beginning' He 'created the heaven and the earth', but gives no details as to all that was involved in so doing, Gen. 1. 'The works of the Lord are great, sought out of all them that have pleasure therein', Ps. 111. 2. Speculation must be avoided. Conjecture must be treated for what it is worth - merely as conjecture. Facts are to be distinguished from theories. God does not discourage research, but 'without faith it is impossible to please him', and that faith must be in His word, Heb. 11. 6, 3. Hence an unreserved acceptance of the statements of holy scripture touching the origin of things, as well as all else, is requisite if we are to be well-grounded in the truth touching the matters of creation and providence.

The Lord Jesus was both **the agent** in creation as well as **the object** of it. Such is the affirmation of John chapter 1 verse 3: 'by him' shows Him to be the agent, and 'without him' shows Him to be the object. This is restated in Revelation chapter 4 verse 11, 'Thou hast created all things, and for thy pleasure they are and were created'. Paul in his letter to the Colossians makes this crystal clear, Col. 1. 15, 16. He is 'the firstborn of all creation' RV, that is to say, He has priority to, and superiority over, all creation. The phrase does not mean that He is the first created being, for this is negatived by the following verse 16, which affirms that all things, that is the whole universe, were created by Him, be it in heaven or in earth. In fact, what the Spirit of God is saying is that the Lord Jesus is the designer, the maker, the maintainer, and the owner of the whole universe. The reader should carefully note the various prepositions which are used of the Lord Jesus in this context. He is the firstborn of all creation as having both priority to and superiority over it. For '**in** him' were all things created, He being the designer before anything came into actual existence, whether it be in heaven or earth, visible or invisible. They came into being '**through** him' as the agent producing their existence, v. 16 RV, and '**for** him' as the One for whose glory they exist. They 'consist', or 'hold together', **by** Him.

In all spheres the Lord Jesus is given the pre-eminence, no less in creation than in relation to God or to the church. For in the physical creation around us, He is its originator, maintainer, and owner. A consideration of this makes His incarnation, and all that was consequent upon it, all the more wonderful: that the Creator should come into His own creation, becoming man, and incurring for Himself those experiences which are the lot of sinless humanity, may well cause amazement, and should produce worship.

The Providence of God. We all well know that the globe, on which we dwell, revolves on its own axis and goes round in its own orbit. But the question will inevitably press itself upon us, who is maintaining it in working order so that it functions without error or mishap? The answer is categorically affirmed in scripture: it is the Lord Jesus who upholds 'all things by the word of his power', Heb. 1. 3, and 'in him all things hold together', Col. 1. 17 RVmg. God sits 'upon the circle of the earth', Isa. 40. 22, and its present orderly functioning, and its later disintegration, are dependent upon His fiat and will. A consideration of 2 Peter chapter 3 verses 5 to 7 will show that, as in the past God used water to destroy the world that then was, in the future He will use fire to destroy the present world. For He has stored the world with such fires, which at the moment He is holding in control, so that they are restrained from bursting forth in their destructive work. At His own appointed time the conflagration will ensue.

In the meanwhile, He provides unfailingly, and with unremitting regularity, for the maintenance of those creatures which He has made, whether it be man or beast. If He brings a drought with resultant famine, it is for judicial purposes, that man may return unto his maker and acknowledge his dependence upon Him. But such things are exceptional. The norm is the sequence of spring, summer, autumn and winter, each season having beneficial effects both upon man and beast, upon earth and trees. He daily loads us with benefits, so that the sun shines daily upon the just and the unjust, and the rain likewise falls on both without partiality.

The Lord Jesus, in His discourse recorded in Matthew chapter 6 verses 25 to 34, discourages anxiety by calling attention to the birds of the air and the lilies of the field. The birds neither sow nor reap, nor gather into barns, yet they are regularly fed by a heavenly Father. Likewise with the lilies of the field: they toil not nor do they spin, yet Solomon in all his glory was not arrayed like one of them. His glory was not part of himself, but the glory of the lily was part of itself, and inseparable from it. From both illustrations, the Lord Jesus argues that man is better than either birds or lilies, and he may, therefore, count upon the unfailing providing care of His heavenly Father in respect of food and clothing.

Is it not remarkable that every one of us comes into the world empty handed, and we leave it in the same way? We brought nothing into the world, and certainly we can take nothing with us when we leave it, 1 Tim. 6. 7. We, therefore, are entirely dependent upon a faithful Creator for our daily maintenance during our sojourn here. And what we have learned to sing, is what we have learned to prove by experience, that 'Great is Thy faithfulness'. His mercies are new every morning.

'Who', asks Job, 'provideth for the raven his food?' Job 38. 41. Yet we know that that carnivorous bird brought to Elijah regularly, morning and evening, day by day, meat which that servant of God accepted as God's provision for his sustenance. 'I have commanded the ravens to feed thee there', 1 Kgs. 17. 4, was God's word to His servant, and those unclean creatures did His bidding, thus sustaining His servant in times of famine. It is ever so; provided His people are in the right place, they can count on the faithfulness of God. Note the recurrence of the word 'there', vv. 4, 9: how it illuminates the word 'here' in chapter 19 verse 9: 'What doest thou here, Elijah?' God had sent him to the brook, and He had sent him to the widow, but He had not sent him to the wilderness of Beer-Sheba. He had strayed like a frightened sheep away from the

Shepherd, and virtually became useless to God as a witness for Him to the nation. He sat down, he lay down, he slept, and requested that he might die. He was not made of the stuff of which Nehemiah was made when he said, 'Should such a man as I flee? and who is there, that, being as I am, would go into the temple to save his life? I will not go in', Neh. 6. 11. We may be sure that, if we are in the place where God wants us to be, we can count on His protection and providing care, but should we go 'astray like a lost sheep', Ps. 119. 176, then we expose ourselves to many a danger. Or to change the metaphor, if we have lost our anchor, we are at the mercy of the storm and waves. It was in a time of famine that Abram went down to Egypt, instead of remaining where he was and trusting God. No wonder he denied his true relationship, and brought himself near to domestic disaster, Gen. 12. 10-20. Little wonder is it if his son behaved in a similar manner, 26. 7. Like father, like son!

The word 'providence' means 'seeing before', and God's providence is to be seen in many strange events of life. Take, for instance, the hatred of Joseph's brethren towards him which led to Joseph being sold to the Ishmaelites, and his ultimate descent into Egypt, where, under the remarkable overruling of God, he prospered, and became the second ruler in the land. Joseph states, 'It was not you that sent me hither, but God'. 'God sent me before you to preserve you a remnant in the earth, and to save you alive by a great deliverance', Gen. 45. 8, 7 RV. Time and space forbid our reciting all those instances recorded in scripture wherein is seen the overruling hand of God, such as, for example, in the case of the crying babe in the ark in the great river of Egypt, put there by a mother who could no longer hide her child at home. The very thing the mother hoped to accomplish, namely the successful hiding of the child, was not achieved, for it was discovered by one of the highest in the land, and her laudable intention of concealment was defeated. Yet behind it all was the providential hand of God, who had predetermined the early training and education of young Moses, thus qualifying him for later leadership when God's time had come, and the deliverance of God's captive people.

We have said that 'providence' means seeing beforehand. Our vision is far too restricted, and we are apt to judge things as they appear at the present, and not in the light of the future. But God ever has one goal in view, and that is the universal glory of His Son on the earth and in the heavens. To this end He works everything, Eph. 1. 10, and though it would seem that, from time to time, there are setbacks to the successful accomplishment of His purpose, we may be sure that the counsel of the wicked will come to nought, but the counsel of the Lord that shall stand. His will can never be finally frustrated. He is irresistible and almighty.

The Saviour God - J. ANDERSON

Bible doctrine has been said to fall under six main headings: (1) **Theology**, or the doctrine of God; (2) **Anthropology**, or the doctrine of man; (3) **Soteriology**, or the doctrine of salvation; (4) **Ecclesiology**, or the doctrine of the church; (5) **Eschatology**, or the doctrine of the last things; and (6) **Demonology**, or the doctrine of evil spirit beings. The present paper is devoted to an aspect of soteriology, especially as it was conceived in the mind and heart of God, and worked out by Himself as He intervened in human affairs. The sections of this book entitled 'The Doctrine of Christ' (**Christology**), and 'The Doctrine of the Believer's Blessedness' arising through Him, will develop in greater detail the wide range of God's salvation.

Much of this doctrine is linked up with the revelation of God in the divine titles previously treated in this section. The first reference to God in His saviour character must surely be that first mention of the Lord God, Gen. 2. 4. Liberal theologians have another method of explaining the changes in the use of divine titles in the Old Testament. Rather than see the end of a fragment of the so-called 'E' manuscript in Genesis chapter 2 verse 3, and the beginning of one from the so-called 'J' manuscript in verse 4, the spiritual will marvel at the way in which a new title of God indicates a new approach to man in his need.

DR. JAMES GRAY comments on Genesis chapter 2 verse 4 thus, 'Note the new name of God used here, "LORD God". The first of these words printed in capitals translates the Hebrew Jehovah while the second translates Elohim. Elohim is the far-off name, Creator. But Jehovah is the nearby name which distinguishes God relative to man, the covenant-making and covenant-keeping God. Hence its employment here where man is to be specially considered. Later on, when both Jehovah and Elohim are used in connection with human affairs, the former seems to be generally reserved for God's dealings with His own people'.

In furtherance of this kind of thought DR. GRAY goes on to say, 'Perhaps it is not too much to say that Jehovah is God entering into history in His redemptive relations with His people'. This idea is repeated by DR. A. T. PIERSON when he suggests that the name can mean 'the everlasting One, being connected with grace and salvation that have their origin in an eternal past, their outworking in a progressive present, and their perfect goal in an eternal future'. It is as well to point out that this is not to say that there is absolutely no reference to God being Saviour in His name Elohim.

The fact that God is a Saviour God stems from the fact that He is love. This explains His approach to man after Adam's fall. This truth is worked out in 1 John in several of the great 'herein' and 'hereby' passages. God is a Saviour God because of His love. This fact is introduced to explain His approach to Israel, Deut. 7. 7, 8, and His approach to us, Eph. 1. 4, 5, in which passage the Revised Version puts the words 'in love' at the beginning of verse 5, rather than at the end of verse 4. Nowhere is the truth better expressed than in John chapter 3 verse 16.

Salvation – Its Meaning and Scope. This calls for a definition of salvation. Perhaps evangelicals have been too narrow in their understanding of it. Salvation in Bible terms is not only personal and eternal. On the personal level it might be said that we are saved from the full consequence of Adam's fall, but on the broad scale it involves the rescue of God's ancient people, and indeed of the whole of creation from the effects of the fall.

On the personal level the Saviour God redeems, justifies, forgives, sanctifies and glorifies His people. Salvation is the inclusive word describing all that God does for His own. Both the Hebrew and the Greek words for salvation carry the idea of deliverance, safety, preservation, healing and soundness, all of which God does, or gives, when He saves.

The word is used to describe: (1) what happened to those rescued from the flood, 2 Pet. 2. 5; (2) what happened to Israel when they were delivered from Egypt, Exod. 15. 2; (3) what happened to Hannah when

God ended her barrenness and made her mother of a future ruler of His people, 1 Sam. 2. 1; (4) what happened to David when God intervened to make him king, and indeed in many another of his experiences;[241] (5) what happened to the Jews when they were brought back from their Babylonian captivity, Isa. 45. 15, etc.; (6) what is offered to the whole world in the gospel, Romans; 1 Tim. 2. 3-6; (7) what will be experienced by God's ancient people in a future day, Rom. 11. 26; (8) what will be brought to the whole world once all of God's enemies have been put out of the way.[242]

Salvation is of the Lord. Whatever the aspect of it, salvation always originates with God. Jonah was not alone in proclaiming this, 2. 9. He 'is become my salvation', chanted Israel after they had crossed the Red Sea, Exod. 15. 2. The psalmists tell us that salvation belongs to Him, Ps. 3. 8, that from Him is salvation, 62. 1, and that He is the God of salvation, 51. 14. Isaiah adds his quota with 'God is my salvation', and, 'The Lord Jehovah . . . is become my salvation', Isa. 12. 2.

This salvation was the subject of God's eternal counsel. The salvation mentioned in 1 Peter chapter 1 verse 9 was planned in eternity, v. 20. The passage previously quoted from Ephesians chapter 1 to prove that it was the love of God that caused it, also indicates that it dates from eternity. It constitutes divine intervention in human affairs, and it works in opposite directions, for so often salvation for the one party involved the destruction of another. Thus if Israel was saved, Egypt was destroyed; if David was brought to the throne it was because all his enemies were put under his feet; if salvation was brought to us, it was because the prince of this world was judged.

This salvation involved the virgin birth of the Lord Jesus. No wonder His mother Mary exclaimed, 'My spirit hath rejoiced in God my Saviour', Luke 1. 47. After all, if 'Christ Jesus came into the world to save sinners' every step of His way must form a part of salvation's story. The purchase price of salvation was His precious blood, and every part of the story led on to the obtaining of this eternal salvation for us.

---

[241] Pss. 18. 2, 3; 27. 1; 62. 1, etc.
[242] Rev. 7. 10; 12. 10; 19. 1.

But the provision of salvation must be made righteously. This teaching takes up a large part of Romans chapter 3. God is called 'a just God and a Saviour', Isa. 45. 21, while, describing the Lord's arrival in Jerusalem prophetically, Zechariah says, 'He is just, and having salvation', Zech. 9. 9.

Naturally, God's salvation must be like Himself – eternal. The grace of God brings it, Titus 2. 11. The longsuffering of God is the cause of it, and the power of God is demonstrated in it every bit as much as it is in creation or government.

God's Salvation Initiative - Old Testament Emphases. The subject of the Saviour God is more prominent in some Bible books than others. We have noted the beginning of the subject in Genesis chapter 2, but by its very nature it must be the prominent subject in Exodus.

Exodus. It was God who saw the affliction of His people in Egypt. It was He who moved first. There was no prospect of Israel taking the initiative; they were too helpless and oppressed for that. Chapter 3 particularly emphasizes this, telling of a God owing His existence to nobody, undertaking the cause of a nation of slaves, with the tremendous purpose in view of settling among that redeemed people in the land which He would give them. The book of Leviticus continues the theme telling of His dwelling place among them, and thus forming part of the same story.

Deuteronomy. This constitutes Moses' farewell address to his people, in which he makes much of what God had done for them. In chapter 4 he shows that the greatest thing that could happen to any people is to have God so nigh to them. Similar exclamations exult in the privilege of having God's law as their law, and His land as their land. The final paragraph of chapter 33 begins by saying that there was no God like the God of Jeshurun, and ends with the unparalleled superiority of a 'people saved by the Lord', v. 29. So ends the story which began in Exodus.

1 Samuel. All the ingredients of salvation's story are found in Hannah's song, 2. 1. The impossibility of the situation from the human point of view is found in Hannah's barrenness. The wonder of what God does is sung in figurative language; God takes the beggar from the dunghill and sets him among princes.[243]

Psalms. In psalm after psalm the subject appears, generally telling of David's experience, but also including that of others. Psalm 18 follows the pattern of 1 Samuel chapter 2, and is almost a repetition of 2 Samuel chapter 22. Both chapters begin by speaking of God as a horn of salvation and a saviour, and end on a similar note. Altogether the word salvation occurs thirty-four times in the Psalms.[244]

Isaiah. If Isaiah is the evangelical prophet, it is not surprising that the Saviour God is a prominent subject. Seventeen times salvation is mentioned in that great prophecy. Naturally, it is the salvation of God's ancient people, Israel, that is in view, first from the enemy of that time, Babylon, but undoubtedly from their future enemies as well. So similar is their deliverance to ours, that it escapes the notice of many that Isaiah chapter 53 is primarily theirs rather than ours. After all, salvation is obtained by repenting of wrongdoing, and then claiming the divine intervention which cost God so much.

But salvation's story in Isaiah begins in chapter 12, before the Babylonians were introduced in the book. What a collection of divine titles is mentioned within the context of salvation in that short chapter – Elohim, Jehovah Jah, and the Holy One of Israel!

The next great dividing line in the prophecy is chapter 40. The captivity was still future, but how aptly Isaiah entered into the ending of it with his exclamation, 'Behold your God'. When He comes He both rewards and punishes. There follow frequent references to the God of salvation in the subsequent chapters. Salvation's tidings are said to indicate that God reigns, 52. 7. This salvation reaches further out than to Israel, for 'all the ends of the earth shall see the salvation of our God', 52. 10.[245] It is interesting to note the link between God's salvation and His righteousness. He is called 'a just God and a Saviour', 45. 21, while His salvation and righteousness are both said to be near, 56. 1; cp. 63. 1.

---

[243] See 2. 1; 14. 45; 7. 8; 14. 6, 23, 39; 17. 47, etc.

[244] See especially for our theme: Pss. 18. 46; 24. 5; 25. 5; 27. 1, 9; 50. 23; 51. 12; 62. 7; 65. 5; 69. 13; 79. 9; 85. 4, 7, 9; 95. 1.

[245] See also 25. 9; 33. 22; 35. 4, etc.

Minor Prophets. Most of these mention the subject at some point, though none so clearly as Jonah when he sums up the subject in his exclamation, 'Salvation is of the Lord', 2. 9.[246]

God's Salvation Initiative – New Testament Emphases. This subject is most fully treated in the New Testament in connection with the Lord Jesus. However, we cannot ignore that the first mention of the gospel in Romans refers to it as 'the gospel of God' – He originated it before time began, cp. Phil. 1. 28; 2 Thess. 2. 13, and revealed it through His prophets in the Old Testament, cp. Luke 1. 69, 77. The subject is given prominence elsewhere.

Pastoral Epistles. Seven times in these three little letters God is called a Saviour God.[247] He is said to desire that all men should be saved, and the appearing of grace is linked with His being a Saviour, 2. 11.

Revelation. Only the book of Psalms exceeds Revelation for its number of songs and outbursts of praise. Three of them here specifically mention the word salvation. Each of these ascribes the provision, and the working out of salvation to God. Tribulation saints attribute their salvation to God, 7. 10. Salvation comes when the devil is cast out, 12. 10. Salvation is described as the outcome of the destruction of the false church, Babylon, 19. 1. This would indicate that salvation comes to the world at large when all of God's enemies are put out of the way. In other words, God's grand objective in intervening in human affairs is to bring salvation.

'Now unto him that is able to keep you from falling, and to present you faultless before the presence of his glory with exceeding joy, to the only wise God our Saviour, be glory and majesty, dominion and power, both now and ever. Amen', Jude 24, 25.

Manifestations of God - B. Osborne

In the Old Testament there are many occasions on which God

[246] See also Hos. 1. 7; 13. 4; Mic. 7. 7; Hab. 3. 13, 18; Zeph. 3. 17, 19; Zech. 8. 7, 13; 9. 16; 10. 6; 12. 7.

[247] 1 Tim. 1. 1; 2. 3; 4. 10; 2 Tim. 1. 9; Titus 1. 3; 2. 10; 3. 4.

condescends to the limitations of man's understanding, and expresses Himself in human terms. This is the case when God who is Spirit, John 4. 24, is said to possess human faculties, and His actions are described in human terms. Thus God walks in the garden of Eden, Gen. 3. 8. These are called **anthropomorphisms**.

Anthropomorphic Language. This was adopted to help man form a more definite conception of God. It is justified by the fact that man was made in the image of God, Gen. 1. 27, and became a living soul through the divine inbreathing, 2. 7. In the first chapter of Genesis God 'saw', v. 4, God 'said', v. 6, God 'called', v. 8, and these, in a sense, are quite as anthropomorphic as the statement in Genesis chapter 3 that He 'walked'.

The statements in Exodus chapter 24 verses 10 and 11 that Moses and the elders of Israel 'saw' the God of Israel, and those concerning His 'feet' and 'hand', **may seem** to indicate that He was regarded as having a material form. But other words of verse 10 indicate that all that they really saw was the heavenly glory which hid Him from mortal eyes. This was like a sapphire pavement under the feet of the heavenly king. That is, they saw no likeness of God, (cp. Deut. 4. 15), but only caught a glimpse of the glory that surrounded Him. Similarly, when Moses wanted to see God's glory, Exod. 33. 18-23, the language is anthropomorphic. He was permitted to see not God's 'face', but His 'back'. The latter word means what is 'after' or 'behind', and here may be described as 'the afterglow of the glory of the divine Presence'. Significantly the Hebrew word for the physical, bodily sense for 'back' is not used, but rather one, *achor*, which need not have such a sense at all.[248]

Occasions Where God is Seen in Vision. One of these is Isaiah chapter 6 verse 1. Here we are told that Isaiah 'saw' Jehovah in the temple. What he recalled was only that the train of His flowing robe filled the temple completely. The Lord's glory was seen. Then Ezekiel had a vision when

---

[248] One fruitful field for the study of the use of anthropomorphisms is the Psalms. The eyes, Pss. 11. 4; 17. 2; 31. 22; 33. 18, etc.; ears, Pss. 10. 17; 17. 6; 18. 6; 34. 15, etc.; hands, Pss. 8. 6; 10. 12; 31. 5; 32. 4, etc.; and feet, Ps. 18. 9, are referred to. These expressions are, of course, figurative.

in captivity. He saw the likeness of a man upon the throne, Ezek. 1. 26. This is a clear intimation that the man of God's counsels, the Lord Jesus Christ, is ever to occupy that place of power and majesty. It was the pre-incarnate Christ the prophet beheld. Now man's redemption is accomplished, the man Christ Jesus sits in His glorified human body on the throne of the Eternal. Daniel had a vision of 'the Son of man', Dan. 7. 13, 14. The title implies one descended from man, but as the person is spoken of being 'like' one of human descent, it follows that He was not merely a man. There can be no question as to the identity of this person – it could be no other than the Lord Himself. It was a title ascribed to Messiah, Ps. 80. 17, and one the Lord Jesus used some eighty times in the Gospels in reference to Himself, see the chapter 'The Son of Man'. Here the prophet sees Him receiving the kingdom and universal dominion – the rule of Jehovah entrusted to man in the person of Christ.

Old Testament Theophanies. Significant, too, are the occasions when the Lord appears as a 'man' to men prior to the incarnation. These theophanies are clearly intended to be preliminary to, and preparatory for, the incarnation. These appearances in human guise did not mean that manhood had been taken into union with deity. That took place at the incarnation, and only then.

The Lord appears as a 'man' to Abraham, Gen. 18. Three men stood by him, v. 2. Abraham does obeisance. The Lord speaks. The indication is that One of the three men is the speaker. The men go towards Sodom, the future of that city being told Abraham by the Lord, but 'Abraham stood yet before the Lord', v. 22. At evening two 'angels' came to Sodom, 19. 1.

A man wrestled with Jacob at the brook Jabbok, 32. 24. The 'man' blessed him, and the less is always blessed of the greater. For 'as a prince hast thou power with God . . . and hast prevailed', said the man to the supplanter who had ceased his wrestling, and now clung in dependence to his opponent. The place was named by Jacob, Peniel, because he had 'seen God face to face'. In referring to this incident, the prophet Hosea says of Jacob, 'He had power over the angel, and prevailed', Hos. 12. 4. This introduces another descriptive term used in connection with the theophanies. Angels of the Lord are many, but 'the Angel of the Lord' stands alone in His nature, and in His deeds. He wields divine authority, bears divine names, and receives divine worship. In His incarnation the Lord Jesus became the final revelation of God to man, but even before He became flesh He seems to be clearly indicated by the title 'the Angel of the Lord'.[249] Unlike the created angels, the Angel of the Lord accepts the worship offered to Him, whereas they, as mere creatures, refuse it; cp. Rev. 22. 8, 9. The appearances of the Angel of the Lord establish who He is.

His Care for Hagar, Gen. 16. 7-13. It is the Angel of the Lord who says, 'I will multiply thy seed exceedingly', v. 10. Who else but God could say such a thing? But further, the Angel is called 'Jehovah that spake unto her', v. 13, and she called Him, 'Thou God seest me'.

His Commendation of Abraham, Gen. 22. 11-12, 15-18. The voice of the Angel was the voice of the Lord. Again, the promised blessing is given by the Angel, this time upon Isaac, vv. 16-18. 'I know that thou fearest God', says the Angel, 'seeing thou hast not withheld thy son, thine only son from **me**'.

His Command to Jacob, Gen. 31. 11, 13. Here the Angel of the Lord speaks and reveals Himself as 'the God of Bethel'. That took Jacob back to his flight from Esau, 28. 12-22. The Lord who revealed Himself to Jacob in the vision, promising now to prosper Jacob's seed, whom Jacob recognized as Jehovah, v. 16, is the same person as the Angel of the Lord.

His Commission to Moses, Exod. 3. 2-18. The Angel of the Lord is spoken of as Lord and God, v. 4, whose presence made holy the very ground whereon His servant stood. He calls Himself 'the God of Abraham, the God of Isaac, and the God of Jacob', v. 6, and reveals His name as 'I AM THAT I AM', v. 14. In John's Gospel the Lord Jesus claims that divine name, John 8. 58; 18. 5, 8, etc.

His Counsel to Manoah's Wife, Judg. 13. 3-23. The visitor to Manoah is described as 'the Angel of the Lord', v. 3, and Manoah's wife described Him as the 'man of God'. The One who wrestled with Jacob was described as 'the man'. Asked His name, He says it is 'secret'. The same Hebrew word is found in Isaiah chapter 9 verse 6, of the child born, and

---

[249] Cp. Exod. 3. 2; Acts 7. 30-32.

of the son given. His name shall be called Wonderful. The 'man of God' whose name was 'Wonderful' was none other than the Son of God. Here we have a Christophany, as we have wherever the Angel of the Lord appears.

The Fatherhood of God - J. H. LARGE

Scripture quotations are taken from the Revised Version

A Special Revelation. Although there is a substantial and very important element of prediction in the Old Testament prophets, foretelling was not their main function. Their forth-telling was chiefly concerned with interpreting God to the people, and the student who reads the Old Testament with this leading idea in mind will reap a rich reward in enjoying the many and varied insights into the mind and heart of God. But despite the wealth of this revelation, the opening words of the Epistle to the Hebrews indicate that, after all, it was at various times and in various ways. It was not continuous but spasmodic, it was not complete but fragmentary. In contrast, God has now spoken finally and fully in One who is Son, inferring that the supreme revelation of God is that He is Father. Our Lord said that no one knows the Father save the Son, so obviously such a revelation could come only from Him. How thankful we are for the further statement 'and he to whomsoever the Son willeth to reveal him', Matt. 11. 27. Even a casual reader is conscious that when he turns from the Old Testament to the New Testament he is in a different atmosphere. Everywhere in the Gospels he finds the Son speaking of God, and the title constantly on His lips is 'Father'. In the prayer recorded in John chapter 17, He says, 'I made known unto them thy name'. We can hardly be in doubt as to what that name is, when, in the course of the prayer, we find the title 'Father' occurring six times. Moreover He went on to say 'and will make it known', referring no doubt to further insights to be granted by His continuing ministry from on high by the Spirit through the New Testament scriptures. See also John chapter 16 verse 25, I 'shall tell you plainly of the Father'. When toward the end of His earthly life He told them that if they had really known Him they would have known the Father also, Philip's response shows that he had sufficient penetration to see that if they could really be satisfied that God was indeed Father, with all that implied, then they could desire no more – 'show us the

Father, and it sufficeth us', 14. 8. Before we enlarge on what is implied for the child of God it may be well to glance briefly at various aspects of the Fatherhood of God if only to maintain a proper perspective.

Fatherhood in Eternity Past. Eternal Fatherhood obviously involves Eternal Sonship. 'O Father, glorify thou me with thine own self with the glory which I had with thee before the world was', 17. 5. But if there never was a point when the relationship began, how are we to understand the Son as being 'the only begotten from the Father', 1. 14? In our experience 'begetting' is an event taking place at some point in time, but temporal conditions are quite inadequate as a guide to the eternal state. Similarly, although human analogies are a necessary aid to our understanding they can never express the whole truth, but an illustration helps to clarify our thinking. Where we have a flame we also necessarily have light and heat. The light and heat are 'begotten' of the flame but there is no time sequence. Now if there were an eternal flame there would be eternal light and heat. So the Son is begotten of the Father, and the Spirit proceeds from the Father, but the generation and the proceeding are eternal. We shall have reason to elaborate later on the fact that the Sonship of Christ in this respect is, of course, absolutely unique.

Creatorial Fatherhood. Paul's quotation of the poet's words 'we are his offspring' must be understood in the light of his previous remark 'he himself giveth to all life, and breath, and all things', Acts 17. 25, 28. It is not justifying the false and misleading doctrine of the 'Universal Fatherhood of God', supported by a partial quotation from Galatians chapter 3 verse 26, 'ye are all sons of God', by unfairly omitting the following qualifying clause 'through faith, in Christ Jesus'. Similarly, we are referred to Ephesians chapter 4 verse 6, 'one God and Father of all', the context being ignored; 'the unity of the Spirit. . . one hope of your calling; one Lord, one faith', vv. 3-5, to say nothing of the fact that the Epistle is addressed to 'the saints. . . and the faithful in Christ Jesus', 1. 1. But this is not to deny that God has a fatherly concern for His creatures. He is the Saviour of all men in the sense of being their preserver, but 'specially of them that believe', 1 Tim. 4. 10. The Saviour indicates that there is a special providence over children, Matt. 18. 10. And who has not delighted in His declaration that our heavenly Father feeds the birds, and is present at the death of a sparrow, 6. 26; 10. 29.

So despite the agonizing problems which challenge and perplex faith, we are justified in believing in God's fatherly care over His creation.

National Fatherhood. God adopted the nation of Israel and spoke of them as His son, 'Israel is my son, my firstborn; and I have said unto thee, Let my son go, that he may serve me', Exod. 4. 22, 23; Rom. 9. 4. The appeal of the penitent in Isaiah chapter 63 verse 16 is based on this concept, which encouraged the godly to think of God as pitying like a father, Ps. 103. 13. But all this falls short of the relationship revealed by Christ.

Fatherhood in the Incarnation and the Resurrection. In the incarnation the Eternal Son, whilst remaining personally all that He ever was, nevertheless entered into a new aspect of sonship, 'He shall be great, and shall be called the Son of the Most High', Luke 1. 32. Some have taken, 'This day have I begotten thee', Heb. 1. 5, to refer to the incarnation, but the context in which it is repeated in 5. 5 is inconsistent with this idea. It is, of course, a quotation from Psalm 2 verse 7 which Paul at Antioch connects with the resurrection, Acts 13. 33, 34, when He became the firstborn of the dead, Col. 1. 18; Rev. 1. 5, and Head of the new creation.

Redemptive Fatherhood. The various aspects of Fatherhood have been touched upon very sketchily simply to clear the ground for the consideration of the relation of God as Father to the believer in Christ. Repentant and believing souls are 'born anew', and so become 'sons of God, through faith in Christ Jesus', Gal. 3. 26. 'Whosoever believeth that Jesus is the Christ is begotten of God', 1 John 5. 1. We must be clear that the Son's relation to the Father as 'the Only-begotten' is unique, and quite distinct from the sonship of the believer. 'And because ye are sons, God sent forth the Spirit of his Son into our hearts', Gal. 4. 6. He is **the** Son – we are sons. Christ taught His disciples to pray 'our Father' as indicating their common standing, but He never so prayed; cp. John 20. 17, 'I ascend unto **my** Father and **your** Father'. It is He who gives 'the right to become children of God, even to them that believe on his name: which were born . . . of God', John 1. 12-13. 'And because ye are **sons**, God sent forth the Spirit of **his Son** into our hearts, crying Abba, Father', Gal. 4. 6. So, where the believer in Christ is concerned, it is not simply a question of God's attitude to him being **like** that of a father to his child, but that he is virtually related to God as his Father. We shall now consider some of the implications of this tremendous fact.

Providential Fatherhood. Christ appealed to the natural care of imperfect human fatherhood as an argument for confidence in the greater care of our heavenly Father, Matt. 7. 11. Any father worthy of the name, out of **love** for his child, would wish to procure the best for him, and at the same time preserve him from evil. But even when his love is genuine it is never perfect. Moreover his **wisdom** is limited, and he cannot always be sure what would be good and what would be harmful. Yet even when he does know, he has not always the **power** to procure the good or to prevent the evil. But our heavenly Father's **love** can be measured only by His love for the Son, John 17. 23. Nothing can separate us from that love, Rom. 8. 39.

His **wisdom** knows perfectly what is good and what is evil, Matt. 6. 8, 32; Jas. 1. 17, and His **power** can secure the one and prevent the other. 'Abba, Father, all things are possible unto thee', Mark 14. 36, 'he is able even to subject all things unto himself', Phil. 3. 21; Jude 24, 25. This is not to guarantee that we shall be spared all difficulties, problems and trials. A father, foolish enough to shelter his child from every difficulty and disappointment would eventually earn, not the gratitude, but the reproach of his child when the latter found himself unfitted for adult life. Our heavenly Father's chief concern is the development of Christian character, and this helps to explain much that would otherwise be inexplicable in life. He wishes us to be fitted not only for our role in life here below, but also to be trained for privileges and responsibilities in His kingdom hereafter, see Heb. 12. 4-13. The Saviour, as in all else, gave us a perfect example of confidence in His Father when from a human standpoint things had seemed to go wrong, 'I thank thee, O Father . . . yea, Father, for so it was well-pleasing in thy sight', Matt. 11. 25, 26.

Fatherhood in the Future Eternity. Scriptures such as 'to us there is one God, the Father', 1 Cor. 8. 6, 'one God and Father of all', Eph. 4. 6, and many others which speak of 'God the Father', can be understood as indicating that in the Godhead the Father takes priority in function, without, of course, inferring any inequality between the persons of the Holy Trinity. Similarly an action attributed to God is likewise attributed to the Father, see e.g., 1 John 4. 9, 14. But is there also a suggestion that, quite apart from the personal distinctions of Father, Son, and Holy Spirit, there is a sense in which Fatherhood is the ultimate? In that grand passage, where Paul gives us a majestic account of the winding up of all things, he says, 'Then cometh the end, when he shall deliver up the kingdom to God, **even the Father**', 1 Cor. 15. 20-28. When He shall have abolished all rule and all authority and power, when the reconciled universe purged of all taint will be the congenial abode of righteousness, 2 Pet. 3. 13, when all is in beautiful accord with the perfect will of God, will God be known and worshipped in the new heavens and the new earth in His supreme character as Father? We bow our hearts 'unto **the Father**, from whom every family [mg Greek: fatherhood] in heaven and on earth is named . . . unto him be the glory . . . unto all generations for ever and ever', Eph. 3. 14-21.

THE DOCTRINE OF CHRIST

The Absolute Deity of Christ - E. L. LOVERING

'A Saviour not quite God is a bridge broken at the farther end', H. C. G. MOULE. Thus we proceed to consider the grand truth of the absolute deity of our Lord and Saviour.

Deity Defined. It would be well for us to be clear at the outset as to the meaning of the term 'deity', and to distinguish it from another familiar term, 'divinity', so widely used among those who, though not disputing the divinity, deny the deity of our blessed Lord. In the words of the 'New Theology', 'God is immanent (i.e., inherent) in human nature, and we are all His sons, whence Christ's title to divinity though undisputed is not regarded as exclusive or unique'.

There are two verses which will help us to appreciate the distinction between 'divinity' and 'deity', namely Romans chapter 1 verse 20 and Colossians chapter 2 verse 9. In the King James Version the word 'Godhead' appears in both cases, but different words are used in the original. In Romans chapter 1 verse 20 the word is 'divinity' – see RV: 'For the invisible things of him since the creation of the world are clearly seen, being perceived through the things that are made, even his everlasting power and divinity'. In Colossians chapter 2 verse 9 it is 'deity' - 'In him dwelleth all the fullness of the Godhead (i.e., deity) bodily'.

From these two passages it can clearly be seen that divine things, whilst they are an evidence of God, do not reveal God; they reveal the **fact** of God, but do not interpret the nature of God. By 'deity', therefore, we mean the very nature, essence, and being of God.

Further, John 1. 1 relates, 'And the Word was with God, and the Word was God' or better, 'God was the Word'.

Deity Disputed. It is sometimes argued that as the Lord Jesus was the Son of God, He must of necessity be subordinate to the Father. This is **not** so, for submission does not mean subordination. The fallacy arises from a misunderstanding of the term 'Son of God'. As 'Son of man' does not mean that He became son by a human father – (for He was the Son of man who 'descended out of heaven', John 3. 13 RV) – but rather that He was the perfection of humanity, 'very man', so the title 'Son of God' does not refer to a generation from God. He is Son of God because He is 'very God' and bears the character of God. The expression 'only begotten Son of God' does not refer to a 'time' when the Father begat the Son, but implies rather an expression of endearment, greatly beloved and 'only' Son, and hence with the meaning 'unique'. Here then we must beware of 'paraphrasing' what God has 'defined'.

Deity Described. Having thus begun at the beginning, we may now proceed to a consideration of the name and attributes by which deity is described.

Let us note:

(1) *the Proper Names of God* are applied to the Lord Jesus. He is Immanuel – God with us, Isa. 7. 14; God blessed for ever, Rom. 9. 5; God manifest in flesh, 1 Tim. 3. 16; the True God, I John 5. 20; The Mighty God, and Father of Eternity, Isa. 9. 6 RVmg; and the apostle Paul, writing to Titus, exhorts that we look for 'the blessed hope and appearing of the glory of our great God and Saviour Jesus Christ', Titus 2. 13 RV.

(2) *the Attributes of God* are also ascribed to Him. (1) His **eternity of being** is seen, Rev. 22. 13, where He says, 'I am Alpha and Omega, the first and the last'. This claim is all the more striking following upon the statement of God in 21. 6, 'I am Alpha and Omega, the beginning and the end'. There can be only one first and one last. He was 'set up from everlasting, from the beginning, or ever the earth was', Prov. 8. 23. (2) In His **omniscience** He has perfect knowledge of all men, John 2. 24, 25, and of the Father, for 'as the Father knoweth me, even so know I the Father', John 10. 15. (3) In His **omnipresenc***e* He promises to be where two or three are gathered together in His name, in the midst, Matt. 18. 20. (4) In **omnipotence** He claims, 'All power is given unto me in heaven and in earth', Matt. 28. 18. (5) He, too, is **immutable** and **unchanging**, for of the Son it is said, 'Thy throne, O God, is for ever and ever . . . the heavens . . . shall perish; but thou continuest . . . as a garment, they shall be changed: but thou art the same, and thy years shall not fail', Heb. 1. 8, 12 RV.

Deity Displayed. Let us refer briefly to the fact that the exercises and activities of God are ascribed to the Son.

(1) *He is the Creator* and *Sustainer* of all things, for we read in Colossians chapter 1 verses 16-18 RV that 'in him were all things created, in the heavens and upon the earth. . . all things have been created through him and unto him; and in him all things consist (or hold together)'. Compare this with Paul's assertion on Mars' Hill, Acts 17. 24, that it was 'God that made the world and all things therein'.

(2) *He it was who Inspired the Prophets* to write: 'the Spirit of Christ which was in them did point unto, when it testified beforehand the sufferings of Christ, and the glories that should follow', 1 Pet. 1. 11 RV.

(3) *The Scribes Reasoned* that, as it was the prerogative of God alone to **forgive sins**, our Lord Jesus must be a blasphemer, for He said to the sick of the palsy, 'Man, thy sins are forgiven', Luke 5. 20.

(4) *God is the Judge of all the Earth*, Gen. 18. 25; Heb. 12. 23, while Peter claims that He who is ordained of God is the Judge of quick and dead, Acts 10. 42, and Paul at Athens relates that God 'hath appointed a day, in the which he will judge the world in righteousness by the man whom he hath ordained', Acts 17. 31 RV.

(5) Further, let us note that **worship** is accepted by Him, and **prayer** addressed to Him. When the wise men from the east came into the house, and saw the young child, with Mary His mother, they fell down and worshipped Him (not her), Matt. 2. 11; a leper, 8. 2, a ruler, 9. 18, 'they that were in the ship', 14. 33, a woman of Canaan, 15. 25, His disciples, 28. 17, and a man of the tombs, Mark 5. 6, are among those who ascribed worship to Him. The martyr, Stephen, Acts 7. 59, prays, 'Lord Jesus, receive my spirit'.

For yet another display of deity we have space only to mention **the miracles**, for John tells us that these signs are written that ye may 'believe that Jesus is the Christ, the Son of God', John 20. 30, 31.

Finally, the glorious fact of **His resurrection** displays the power of deity. Who else but God could utter such words, 'I lay down my life, that I might take it again. No man taketh it from me, but I lay it down of myself. I have power to lay it down, and I have power to take it again', John 10. 17, 18.

Deity Declared. We now refer to His own claims to deity. It has been said that if Christ was not God, He was the greatest egotist the world has ever seen. He claims equal honour with the Father (as John chapter 5 verses 19 to 23 RV clearly indicates); in activity, 'for what things soever he (the Father) doeth, these the Son also doeth in like manner', v. 19; in quickening power, 'for as the Father raiseth and quickeneth (the dead), even so the Son . . . whom he will', v. 21; in judgement, for 'neither doth the Father judge any man, but he hath given all judgement unto the Son, that all may honour the Son, even as they honour the Father', vv. 22, 23.

He is the self-existing One, and claims that, 'Before Abraham was, I am', 8. 58, the name of God revealed to Moses in Exodus chapter 3 verse 14, 'I am that I am'.

Space would not permit a fuller exposition of this thought, except to refer to some of the claims of 'I am' in John's Gospel: I am the Light of the World, 8. 12; the Door, 10. 7; the Resurrection and the Life, 11. 25; the Way, the Truth, and the Life, 14. 6; the true Vine, 15. 1.

We conclude this outline by a quotation from the pen of a late expositor of the subject, 'If He is only man, then I am an idolater. If He is very God, then the man who denies it is a blasphemer. There can be no union among those who hold His deity and those who deny it'. We are not of those who doubt or deny, but bow in wondering and adoring worship.

'Thou art the Everlasting Word,
The Father's only Son,
God manifest, God seen and heard,
And heaven's beloved one;
The Lamb of God, exalted Lord!
Worthy art Thou to be adored!'

J. CONDER

The Names and Titles of Christ - C. E. Hocking

Scripture references are taken from the Revised Version

Our concern here is to provide a broad survey of the material supplied to us by the Spirit in the New Testament, both to instruct us, and to meet the yearnings of the human heart concerning God's Christ. Here and there, a little material will be given regarding those titles extensively used, and also concerning some not treated elsewhere in this book. The vast range of titles given to our Lord in the scriptures are invaluable pointers to His greatness, personally and officially, and, in an abbreviated form, they cover the field of Christology.

'Who do men say that I am?'. What appalling ignorance there was, generally, concerning who the Lord really was. To many He was 'Joseph's son', or 'the carpenter's son'.[1] With more truthfulness, but little more light, He was to others 'the son of Mary'.[2] Note in this connection the allusions to His 'parents', Luke 2. 27, 41, 43, and even Mary's reproving words, 'Thy father and I sought thee sorrowing', v. 48; cp. John 6. 42. The residents of Nazareth knew Him as the 'brother of James, and Joses, and Judas, and Simon', Mark 6. 3. To them He is but 'the carpenter', v. 3. These things, and much more, stand written in the Gospels, faithfully recorded by men who knew Him to be so much more than this, and in fact not Joseph's son at all, but 'being the son (as was supposed) of Joseph', Luke 3. 23.

How many of His contemporaries considered Him to be a mere man, whether 'gluttonous', or with 'no fault', Luke 7. 34; 23. 4. He was truly man, for apart from His coming into manhood, the purpose of God, and our eternal blessing, could never have been achieved. But His manhood is altogether unique, holy, for He is God manifested in the flesh, 'being made in the likeness of men', and 'being found in fashion as a man', Phil. 2. 7, 8, in order that He might become the 'one mediator also between God and men, himself man, Christ Jesus', 1 Tim. 2. 5. The Lord loved to illustrate His mission through parables in which He portrayed Himself

---

[1] Luke 4. 22; Matt. 13. 55; cp. John 1. 45.
[2] Mark 6. 3; cp. Luke 2. 34; Matt. 13. 55.

as 'man', e.g., Matt. 13. 44, 45. He is 'the second man', 'the last Adam', by whom comes, not death, but the resurrection, and 'the gift by the grace of the one man'.[3]

Many thought of Him as 'the Nazarene', Mark 14. 67, despising, persecuting, and rejecting Him. Others dismissed His ministry of exorcism as energized by Beelzebub, Matt. 12. 24. To the leaders of the nation He was 'that deceiver', 27. 63; how wilful blindness prevented these seeing Him as 'the truth'!

There were many who thought more highly of Him, using titles of great respect. To such He was 'Rabbi', or 'Rabboni', John 1. 38; 20. 16, a title which He accepted while discouraging His disciples from being so designated, Matt. 23. 7. Often, this Hebrew title is replaced by the Greek equivalent, 'Master' or 'Teacher' (mg) as is indicated in the verses cited above.[4] The Lord was happy to use this term of Himself, expressing, however inadequately, a truth as to His mission while here, 'for one is your teacher, and all ye are brethren', Matt. 23. 8. To another He was 'Good Master', Mark 10. 17. Here and there, it appears that the title connotes more than 'Teacher', bearing rather the significance 'Master' in a richer and more authoritative sense, cp. John 11. 28; Mark 14. 14.

Again, there were those who acclaimed Him as 'the prophet, Jesus, from Nazareth of Galilee', Matt. 21. 11, and while there was much confusion in the minds of the populace as to this, 'Jesus himself testified, that a prophet hath no honour in his own country', thereby endorsing that element of truth in applying the title to Him; see the chapter 'Christ as Prophet'.

'Thou shalt call his name Jesus'. He was to be so named 'for it is he that shall save his people from their sins', Matt. 1. 21. Jesus is an abbreviated form of the Hebrew name Jehoshua, a name made up of two

---

[3] 1 Cor. 15. 21, 45, 47; Rom. 5. 15.

[4] Note the three words used of the Lord and translated simply 'Master' in the Gospels, *didaskalos* and *epistatēs* (the latter in Luke only and exclusively of the Lord), e.g. Luke 8. 49 and 45 respectively; also *kathēgētēs* in Matthew 23. 10 only, signifying a leader, guide, 'for one is your master, even the Christ'. Another title found in parables, house-holder, lit., master of the house, *oikodespotēs*, is used both of God, Matt. 21. 33, and of Christ, 10. 25; 20. 1, 11.

parts, the divine title Jehovah, and the word for salvation. Jesus is, therefore, Jehovah the Saviour, the salvation of Jehovah, and while numbers of Jesus' contemporaries bore the same name, and such illustrious past deliverers as Joshua had been so named, He alone had the name divinely given, and embodied, in all its fullness, the truth contained in it; cp. v. 23, 'Immanuel'. It is a tribute to His uniqueness that once His name, expressing both who He is and what He has done, was heralded in the Near East and then further afield, Jesus was no longer used by parents, whether Jewish or Christian, for their children.

In the Gospels the name Jesus is used, without other additions, in the order of 550 times, some 250 of these being found, surprisingly, in John's record. This is incidental evidence for the historicity, and trustworthiness, of the four accounts, for here only in the New Testament is such extensive use made of the human name of our Lord. This would be appropriate only when describing the earthly, historic ministry of 'the man that is called Jesus', John 9. 11, though in the records men never directly addressed the Lord by His name. It is also to be observed that neither Luke nor John uses the name in isolation with such freedom in their other writings. In fact, throughout the remainder of the New Testament the name Jesus is found alone comparatively infrequently, some sixty-nine times, and mostly in Acts, thirty-two times, Hebrews, nine times, and Revelation, six times.

His contemporaries distinguished Him from others who bore the name with some descriptive words: Jesus of Nazareth; Jesus the, or thou, Nazarene; the Nazarene Jesus; Jesus the Galilean; the prophet Jesus who is from Nazareth of Galilee; Jesus the son of Joseph; Jesus of Nazareth the son of Joseph; Jesus, Master; Jesus the son of David; Jesus the King of the Jews; another king, one Jesus; Jesus surnamed Christ; Jesus the Christ; the Christ who hath been appointed for you, even Jesus; Jesus, the Son of God; Jesus, thou Son of the Most High God; Jesus His Son; Jesus the mediator of a new covenant; the Apostle and High Priest of our Confession, even Jesus; Jesus, the author and finisher of faith; a Saviour Jesus; Jesus our Deliverer.

Jesus, how much that name unfolds!

'The mention of Thy name shall bow

Our hearts to worship Thee;
The chiefest of ten thousand Thou,
The chief of sinners we'.

MARY B. PETERS

'Sir, we would see Jesus', John 12. 21.

'What think ye of the Christ?' The ready answer given to this question asked by our Lord was, 'The son of David', Matt. 22. 42. Herod, when asked by the wise men concerning the One born as the King of the Jews, rephrased their question, enquiring of the religious authorities 'where the Christ should be born', 2. 2, 4. From these, and other passages in the Gospels, we are made aware of the popular Messianic expectations of that time. For instance, many said, 'What, doth the Christ come out of Galilee? Hath not the scripture said that the Christ cometh of the seed of David, and from Bethlehem', John 7. 41. Although so sure of the lineage of Christ, and the location of His birth, it was generally felt that his appearance would be somewhat mysterious for 'when the Christ cometh, no one knoweth whence he is', 7. 27. He would certainly be preceded by a messenger sent from God, even Elijah himself.[5] The Christ would be a great national hero, a deliverer, a King of Israel, to whom total victory was guaranteed. Suffering, shame, and death were out of the question for him, for, 'We have heard out of the law that the Christ abideth forever', John 12. 34; hence, too, the challenge in Matthew chapter 27 verse 42.

Much of this popular, and more eschatological, interpretation of the Messianic office is in harmony with the teaching of the Old Testament. The word transliterated 'Christ', *christos,* meaning 'anointed', is the Greek equivalent of the Hebrew *Mashiah*, the Aramaic form of which is twice found in the New Testament, transliterated 'Messiah', John 1. 42; 4. 25. The word is used in the Old Testament for the anointing of the prophet, 1 Kgs. 19. 16; the high priest, Lev. 8. 12; and frequently of the king, in particular of Saul, David, Solomon, Zedekiah, and of the future Davidic King.[6] We read of mine anointed, thine anointed, his anointed, and the anointed of the God of Jacob. The three offices in the old economy were literally 'christed', and in this pointed the way,

---

5 Matt. 17. 10-13; Mal. 3. 1; 4. 5.

6 See 1 Sam. 24. 6; 2 Sam. 19. 21; 2 Chr. 6. 42; Lam. 4. 20; Ps. 2. 2.

somewhat subconsciously, to the Christ. The word is used of the Messianic Prince that was to come, and who would 'be cut off', having nothing, Dan. 9. 25. That this is a clear forecast of the death of our Lord is beyond dispute, the application of Psalm 2 in Acts chapter 4 verses 25 to 28 adding further detail concerning those who pitted themselves 'against the Lord, and against his anointed'. It was this aspect of truth related to the Christ of which Jesus' contemporaries were appallingly ignorant. The extra-biblical Hellenistic Jewish literature crystallized the Messianic hope which was so popular in the Lord's day.

Consequently, during His public ministry, the Lord refrained from using the title, and urged others 'that they should tell no man that he was the Christ', Matt. 16. 20; hence John chapter 10 verse 24. Nonetheless, He claimed to be the Christ to the woman of Samaria; the Father unveiled Him as 'the Christ, the Son of the living God', and He answered the high priest's question as to His claim to be the Christ in the affirmative.[7] He, and He alone, is the One who combines in Himself the three great anointed offices of the Old Testament, His ministries as Prophet, Priest and King enveloping within their folds the past, present and future. He is the Prophet like unto, yea greater than, Moses; He is the great High Priest who excels Aaron, and whose order was foreshadowed by Melchizedek; He is the King of kings far greater in victories than David, and One whose reign of peace will surpass the dazzling glories of Solomon, and to which the king-priest character of His rule will add its measureless benediction.

The use of the title in the Gospels has special reference to the Messianic office.[8] Acts, too, has a similar emphasis and pattern of use.[9] Hebrews, and especially 1 Peter among the catholic Epistles, carry on the theme, though in the case of 1 Peter with less official and formal emphasis.[10] Elsewhere in the catholic Epistles and Revelation the title is found six times only.[11] There is a marked increase of usage in Paul's Epistles

---

[7] John 4. 25; Matt. 16. 16; Mark 14. 61.

[8] 'The Christ' occurs some thirty-three times, the simple 'Christ' only six times. Mark has only one example of each.

[9] Christ with the definite article occurs nine times, once without it.

[10] With the article: Hebrews (six); 1 Peter (two). Without the article: Hebrews (three); 1 Peter (eleven).

[11] Only with the article: 1 John (one); 2 John (one); Revelation (four).

however, where the title is found about 200 times.[12] The official and more formal use of the title is less emphasized, giving place rather to its use as a personal name. However, there are still numerous instances of its use with a heavy official and formal overtone, and even in those many instances where Christ is clearly a personal name, an undertone of a Messianic character remains.

The title is found in a number of different combinations. He was the Lord's Christ, Luke 2. 26; His Christ or his Anointed;[13] the Christ of God, Luke 9. 20; the Christ of God, His chosen, Luke 23. 35; the Christ, the Son of God, Matt. 26. 63; John 20. 31; the Christ, the Son of the Blessed, Mark 14. 61; the Christ, the Son of the living God, Matt. 16. 16; the Christ, Jesus, Acts 5. 42 lit.; cp. 18. 5, 28; the Christ appointed for you, even Jesus*,[14] Acts 3. 20; Christ a King, Luke 23. 2; the Christ the King of Israel, Mark 15. 32; Christ the Lord, Luke 2. 11; the Lord Christ, Col. 3. 24; cp. 1 Pet. 3. 15; our Lord Christ, Rom. 16. 18; Jesus called Christ*, Matt. 1. 16; 27. 17, 22; Messiah, John 1. 41; 4. 25. It will be noticed that the majority of these variants are found in the Gospels and Acts. Throughout the remainder of the New Testament, 'Christ' is frequently linked with the name Jesus, though this is seldom found in the Gospels.[15] There is a massive increase both in the number, richness, and fuller forms of the titles that are given to Christ following His ascension to heaven.

Jesus Christ. There are approximately sixty references to this title, all but 5 of them from Acts onwards.[16] Jesus, the one called the Christ, of

---

[12] With the article: eighty-one times. Without the article: 129 times.

[13] Acts 3. 18; 4. 26; Rev. 11. 15; 12. 10.

[14] The grouping of titles combining more than one name/office is a subjective matter in part. Normally the initial name/title has a certain emphasis, though in the case of the title 'Apostle and High Priest of our confession, even Jesus', the reverse is the case, 'Jesus' occupying an emphatic place by being held in reserve until the end! In this chapter we have arranged the titles topically so as to assist a preliminary investigation, and consequently, here and there, it was felt desirable to repeat a combination title. So that readers are aware that a given title has appeared in the article before, **an asterisk*** will mark each such repetition.

[15] Matt. 1. 1, 18; Mark 1. 1; John 1. 17; 17. 3.

[16] It is not found in Luke, Colossians, 1 and 2 Thessalonians, Philemon, and 3 John.

the Gospels, Matt. 27. 17, 22, is now named universally Jesus Christ, His vindication by God in resurrection leading the way to this, Acts 2. 36. The dignity and authority belonging to the office is from henceforth vitally linked with the person Jesus, the Messianic note providing an undertone in the name Jesus Christ. Here again there are many combinations found, adding something to our apprehension of His fullness. Initially He is still Jesus Christ the Nazarene, Acts 3. 6; 4. 10 lit., but as the unfolding of His glories proceeds He becomes Jesus Christ our Saviour, Titus 3. 6; Jesus Christ the Righteous, 1 John 2. 1; Jesus Christ, the faithful witness, the firstborn of the dead, the ruler of the kings of the Earth, Rev. 1. 5. He is also Jesus Christ the same, a divine title in the Old Testament now given to Him, Heb. 13. 8; cp. 1. 12; our God and Saviour Jesus Christ, 2 Pet. 1. 1; our great God and Saviour Jesus Christ, Titus 2. 13. Jesus is the Son of God, 1 John 4. 15, hence we read of Him as Jesus Christ, the Son of the Father, 2 John 3; the Son of God, Jesus Christ, 2 Cor. 1. 19; His Son Jesus Christ, 1 John 1. 3; 3. 23; 5. 20; and His Son Jesus Christ our Lord, Rom. 1. 3 KJV; 1 Cor. 1. 9.[17]

Christ Jesus. Remarkably, this title is found only once outside Paul's Epistles, and even then it is used of his ministry concerning the faith in Christ Jesus, Acts 24. 24. It occurs about seventy-five times in all, being therefore not only unique to Paul, as was the character of his conversion and selection as an apostle on the Damascus road, but it is greatly emphasized by him too.[18] It seems to underscore the dignity of the bearer, and consequently that amazing grace consciously enjoyed by the apostle who, though 'chief of sinners', was put into the ministry. He was truly 'apprehended by Christ Jesus', Phil. 3. 12. A number of combinations involving this title are found also, Christ Jesus our Saviour, Titus 1. 4; our Saviour Christ Jesus, 2 Tim. 1. 10; Christ Jesus our hope, 1 Tim. 1. 19.

While Jesus Christ and Christ Jesus are often associated with similar facts concerning the Lord, e.g., 'him whom thou didst send, even Jesus

---

[17] For instances of Jesus Christ and Christ Jesus combined with the title Lord see earlier article. Note that there is a much wider range, and more frequent use, of titles created by combinations with Jesus Christ.

[18] Note it is found more frequently in Paul's Epistles, than the simple title Jesus Christ is found in the whole of the New Testament.

Christ' and 'Christ Jesus came into the world to save sinners'; 'the resurrection of Jesus Christ from the dead' and God 'raised up Christ Jesus from the dead'; 'the revelation of Jesus Christ' and 'the appearing of our Saviour Christ Jesus', yet there are certain important distinctions to be observed and pondered. Passages where the two titles occur in close proximity provide a starting-point for closer study.[19] The two titles are each used with a characteristic preposition, providing another distinguishing feature. The phrase 'through [*dia*] Jesus Christ' is often found, the same preposition appearing when Lordship supplements the title. However, the title Christ Jesus is never joined with 'through', though the phrase 'in [*en*] Christ Jesus' is frequently found, the same preposition being adopted when the title is supplemented with 'Lord'. The phrase 'in [*en*] Jesus Christ' is never found. Jesus Christ is the one 'through' whom the blessings of God's salvation are channelled to us, and 'through' whom our responses to God in thanksgiving, worship, and the offering of our spiritual sacrifices are made. It is 'in Christ Jesus', cp. 'in Christ', that God's eternal purpose is created and executed. He is the One in whom we are made alive to God, sanctified, and set at liberty. He is that divine sphere in whom the blessing of Abraham has come upon even the Gentiles; He is that altogether new element into which we all have been brought so that neither circumcision nor uncircumcision avails further, for in Christ Jesus we are all sons of God. **Through** a risen and glorified Christ as an infinite source of blessing to all those who are **in** Him, we taste the riches, yea the extravagance of divine grace.

'Jesus Christ is Lord'. Such was the simplest, pithiest 'creed' of the early church. To confess this was essential to salvation and baptism, Rom. 10. 9, and it will yet be owned universally, as all bow the knee before the One that God has highly exalted, Phil. 2. 9-11. Now both of these passages include references to the resurrection or ascension, that memorable, epoch-changing event which gave the title 'Lord' prominence, and an enriched significance. The word translated 'Lord' is *kurios,* meaning at root one who has power and authority, and its use in the Gospels prior to the resurrection is more restricted, and the meaning less revelatory. 'Lord' when used in direct address to Jesus[20]

---

[19] For example: Gal. 2. 16; Phil 2. 5-11; 1 Tim. 1. 12-16.

[20] 'Lord' is used frequently in the vocative in the Gospels, *kurie,* the references illuminating the range of meaning in the minds of the users.

demonstrates the great respect shown Him by many.[21] Sometimes it is the equivalent of Teacher, or Rabbi. In some cases the addressee expressed much more than respect as, for example, when Peter said, 'Depart from me; for I am a sinful man, O Lord', or 'Lord, save me', Luke 5. 8; Matt. 14. 30. On the part of His disciples and followers there was an increasing tendency thereby to express their submission to, and reverence for, One altogether unique.

The Lord's use of the title in parables portraying both God and Himself led to a further enriching of its significance in their estimation, 18. 25; 25. 18; consider, too, 'the Lord of the harvest', and 'Lord of the Sabbath', 9. 38; 12. 8.

Two specially important uses are found on the Lord's lips during that last fateful week in Jerusalem. In the case of the two that were sent to bring the colt to Him, they were instructed to say to any that might query their action 'The Lord hath need of him', Mark 11. 3. A still further unfolding of who He is, though baffling to His opponents, resulted from His quotation from Psalm 110, 'The Lord said unto my Lord. Sit thou on my right hand', Mark 12. 36, for 'my Lord' here represents the Hebrew divine title *Adoni.*

The writers of the Gospels indicate also that, in the varying incidents of His earthly career, Old Testament scriptures were fulfilled which equated Jesus with *Jehovah* of the former covenant; e.g., Matt. 3. 3 = Isa. 40. 3.

Among the four evangelists Luke alone substitutes often in his narrative 'the Lord' for 'Jesus',[22] the name more usually adopted in narrative by the other writers, crowning all with the thrilling words, 'the Lord is risen indeed', Luke 24. 34. From the time of that glad announcement, the title comes into its own, cp. Acts 2. 36, as is indicated by its frequent use from then on in the resurrection account in John's Gospel.[23] The

---

[21] cp. Matthew 27. 63 where the Jewish authorities address Pilate as 'Sir', the word being *kurios*.

[22] For references to 'the Lord' in the narrative of Luke see 7. 13, 19; 10. 1, 39, 41; 11. 39; 12. 42; 13. 15; 17. 5, 6; 18. 6; 19. 8, 31, 34; 22. 61 (2). Of these only 19. 31, 33 have parallels in the other Gospels.

[23] John 20. 18, 20, 25, 28; 21. 7 (2), 12.

climax of the Gospel records is the confession 'my Lord and my God', John 20. 28. It is understandable, therefore, that only twice in these records do we find the title 'the Lord Jesus', Mark 16. 19; Luke 24. 3, and both are in the setting of the resurrection event.

From Acts onwards, the literature of the New Testament is dominated by titles, simple, descriptive, and compound in form, emphasizing the **Lordship** of Christ[24]. Gentiles as well as Jews had received the Christ, Him whom they had found to be Jesus the Lord; see Col. 2. 6. The early preachers presented Him as the divine Lord, the One whose person and work had been delineated throughout the Old Testament from which, as their only Bible, they found it so easy to preach Jesus, Acts 8. 35, as the Christ, 17. 2, in fact Christ Jesus as Lord, 2 Cor. 4. 5. The Greek translation of the Old Testament by its adoption of *kurios* as the replacement especially for the divine titles *Jehovah,* and *Adonai,* caused the Spirit-anointed eyes of the disciples to see, biblically, fresh glories in their ascended Lord.[25]

To this existing revelation the Spirit added, by taking of the things of the One who is 'My Lord and my God', and revealing them. Were we to ask, 'Who art thou, Lord?' Acts 9. 5, the New Testament would answer 'the Lord', v. 11; my, thy, his, their Lord, and the Lord, *kurios*, of the house, cp. the Master of the house, *oikodespotēs;*[26] Jesus our Lord, 1 Cor. 9. 1; Lord Jesus, the Lord Jesus, Acts 7. 59; 1 Cor. 11. 23; our Lord Jesus, 1 Cor. 5. 4, the Lord Christ*, Col. 3. 24; our Lord Christ*, Rom. 16. 18; Lord Jesus Christ, the Lord Jesus Christ, 1 Cor. 1. 3 lit.; 2 Cor. 13. 14; our Lord Jesus Christ, Rom. 5. 1; Jesus Christ our Lord, 5. 21; Christ Jesus the Lord, Col. 2. 6; Christ Jesus our Lord, Rom. 6. 23; Christ Jesus my Lord, Phil. 3. 8; One Lord; One Lord, Jesus Christ, Eph. 4. 5; 1 Cor. 8. 6; the Lord and Saviour, 2 Pet. 3. 2; the Lord and Saviour Jesus Christ, 2. 20, a Saviour, (the) Lord Jesus Christ, Phil. 3. 20; our Lord and Saviour Jesus Christ, 2 Pet. 1. 11; our only Master, *despotēs*, and Lord, Jesus Christ, Jude 4; the Master, *despotēs*, that bought them, 2 Pet. 2. 1; the Lord of peace, 2

[24] Apart from Titus and the Epistles of John, every NT book from Acts onward contributes to the theme.
[25] Note because of this, the difficulty of knowing, in some cases, whether God or Christ is meant when the title 'Lord' is used. This is a further incidental witness to the deity and equality of the Lord Jesus.
[26] Luke 12. 36, 43, 45; Matt. 25. 21; Mark 13. 35; Matt. 10. 25.

Thess. 3. 16; the Lord of glory, 1 Cor. 2. 8; our Lord Jesus Christ, the glory, Jas. 2. 1 lit; the Lord, the righteous judge, 2 Tim. 4. 8; the Lord of lords, and King of kings, Rev. 17. 14; the King of kings, and Lord of lords, 19. 16; in fact He is Lord of all, Acts 10. 36. See further the chapter 'The Lord'.

Christians, those who were ever beloved of or by, *hupo*, the Lord, 2 Thess. 2. 13, begin their course by believing on, *epi*, the Lord Jesus, Acts 16. 31, for turning to, *pros*, the Lord causes the veil to be removed, 2 Cor. 3. 16. Believers draw fresh supplies of grace, mercy and peace from, *apo*, the Lord daily, 1 Tim. 1. 2; they have eternal life in, *en*, the Lord, Rom. 6. 23, and can never be separated from the love of God in the Lord, 8. 39. They have tasted and seen that the Lord is gracious, 1 Pet. 2. 3, immeasurable benefits of peace and salvation coming to them through, *dia*, the Lord, Rom. 5. 1; cp. v. 19. They count all things loss for the excellency of the knowledge of their Lord, Phil. 3. 8, their overflowing thanksgivings ascending to God through, *dia*, Him, Rom. 7. 25; cp. 1 Cor. 15. 57. They set apart Christ as Lord in their hearts, 1 Pet. 3. 15, and although often not understanding His ways say, 'Behold, I am here, Lord', Acts. 9. 10; 'What shall I do, Lord?' 22. 10. With what confidence they look for that day when they shall be forever with, *sun*, the Lord, 1 Thess. 4. 17. Maranatha – our Lord comes!

'Whose Son is He?' Upon the correct answering of this question the eternal destiny of men depends. We shall briefly consider the distinctive aspects of our Lord's Sonship as demonstrated in the New Testament.

He is the **Son of Abraham**, Matt. 1. 1, the promised seed, Gal. 3. 16. Consequently, 'the promise by faith in Jesus Christ might be given to them that believe', 3. 22. Old distinctions are set aside for those who were baptized into Christ, and 'ye all are one man in Christ Jesus', v. 28. Abraham is 'the father of us all (as it is written, A father of many nations have I made thee)', Rom. 4. 16, Isaac, the son of Abraham according to promise, may suggest to us the route via which the true 'Seed' would travel, in order to lay the divine foundation essential for such unrestricted blessing from God. He was the submissive son, destined for the altar, and yet, from whose obedience unto death, Abraham 'in a parable' did 'receive him back', Heb. 11. 17; cp. Paul's hint directing us back to Genesis chapter 22 by his use of the title 'his own Son' of our Lord, Rom. 8. 3, 32.

He is the **Son of David**, Matt. 1. 1. This title is most prominent in Matthew.[27] The fact of our Lord's Davidic descent according to the flesh is clearly and fully substantiated. Gabriel's forecast to Mary was that 'the Lord God shall give unto him the throne of his father David', while later Zacharias could sing 'the Lord, the God of Israel. . . hath raised up a horn of salvation for us in the house of his servant David', Luke 1. 32, 68. The two genealogies of Matthew chapter 1 and Luke chapter 3 establish this fact, and more, and of Him it can be truly said 'Jesus, thou son of David'*, Mark 10. 47.

The Lord was born King of the Jews, Matt. 2. 2, in the city of David, Bethlehem, Luke 2. 4, 11; cp. John 7. 42. Considerably later, He entered Jerusalem, the city of the Great King, Matt. 5. 35, in a manner designed to alert the people to the fulfilment of His mission to her as 'thy King' that 'cometh unto thee', 21. 5; Zech. 9. 9. Pilate's interrogation, the soldiers' mockery, the title-board on His cross, and the mocking of the religious leaders, were all prompted because of His link with the royal house of David and the kingly rights associated with this. He is the King of the Jews, Jesus the King of the Jews*, the King of Israel, even Christ a king*.[28]

Paul states that He was 'born of the seed of David according to the flesh', and in the course of a challenge to Timothy to be prepared to suffer hardship he wrote, 'Remember Jesus Christ, risen from the dead, of the seed of David, according to my gospel', Rom. 1. 3; 2 Tim. 2. 8. Paul and his companions were even accused of preaching contrary to the decrees of Caesar 'another king, one Jesus'*, Acts 17. 7. Though rejected by men Christ is 'the root of Jesse, and he that ariseth to rule over the Gentiles', 'the root of David', 'the root and the offspring of David', having 'the key of David', and to Him are guaranteed 'the holy and sure blessings of

[27] 'Son of David' occurs nine times in Matthew, 1. 1; 9. 27; 12. 23; 15. 22; 20. 30, 31; 21. 9, 15; 22. 42. Mark and Luke both use it four times, these all having parallels in Matthew, Mark 10. 47, 48 = Luke 18. 38, 39 = Matt. 20. 30, 31; and Mark 12. 35, 37 = Luke 20. 41, 44 = Matt. 22. 42.

[28] Matt. 27. 11, 29, 37, 42; Luke 23. 2.

David'.[29] God is the 'King of the ages', 1 Tim. 1. 17 mg; Rev. 15. 3, and has decreed that the Lord is yet to return and overcome the future political confederacy as 'Lord of lords, and King of kings'*, or 'King of kings, and Lord of lords'*, and to set up His own throne, 'the throne of his glory', as the King, Matt. 25. 34, 40, when He will be manifestly 'the ruler of the kings of the earth', the Lion that is of the tribe of Judah, and a governor of Israel.[30] Taunt though it was on Pilate's lips, we see the truth in the words 'Behold, your King!' John 19. 14.

He is the **Son of Man**, Mark 14. 61. The Lord generally preferred to use this title when speaking of Himself. Over eighty occurrences of His use of it are recorded by the four evangelists. Apart from one occasion when the people's complete inability to comprehend who was meant by it caused them to ask 'Who is this Son of man?' John 12. 34, it is found on the Lord's lips alone in the Gospels. As the Son of man He came from heaven to serve, and to suffer, following which He would sit at the right hand of God in exaltation until His return in power and great glory, when all things would be seen as made subject to Him. For a detailed consideration of the many references to this title see the chapter 'The Son of Man'.

He is the **Son of God**, John 20. 31. This title related to Sonship is often used by the Son Himself in speaking of His relationship to the Father, but it is frequently found on the lips of men too. It is in the Gospels that this family of titles predominates, John giving special emphasis to it. Stress is placed upon the doctrinal implications of His Sonship, by means of which we are able, so far as revelation permits us, to enter into the 'distinctions within the unity of the Godhead'. Throughout the remainder of the New Testament, Sonship features most in Hebrews, twelve occurrences, 1 and 2 John, twenty-four, and the Epistles of Paul, seventeen.[31]

The subject is enriched by the use of a vast range of titles: consider Jesus His Son*, 1 John 1. 7; His Son Jesus Christ*, 1. 3; 3. 23; 5. 20; His Son Jesus

---

[29] Rom. 15. 12; Rev. 22. 16; 3. 7; Acts 13. 34.

[30] Rev. 17. 14; 19. 16; Matt. 25. 31-46; Rev. 1. 5; 5. 5; Matt. 2. 6.

[31] Sonship is referred to twice in Acts, 9. 20; 13. 33, once in 2 Peter, 1. 17, and once in Revelation, 2. 18. It is not treated in 2 Thessalonians, 1 and 2 Timothy, Titus, Philemon, James, 1 Peter, 3 John and Jude.

Christ our Lord*, Rom. 1. 3 KJV; 1 Cor. 1. 9; Jesus Christ, the Son of the Father*, 2 John 3, the Christ, the Son of God*, Matt. 26. 63; the Christ, the Son of the living God*, Matt. 16. 16; the Christ, the Son of the Blessed*, Mark 14. 61, Son of the Most High, Son of the Most High God, Luke 1. 32; 8. 28; Son, Heb. 1. 2 lit, the Son, 1. 8; my Son, 1. 5; 5. 5; my Son, my (the) chosen, Luke 9. 35; my beloved Son, Matt. 3. 17, (cp. the Beloved, Eph. 1. 6, my Beloved, Matt. 12. 18); the Son of His love, Col. 1. 13; Thy Son, John 17. 1; His SON, Rom. 5. 10; His own Son, Rom. 8. 3, 32; the only begotten, John 1. 14; the only begotten Son, 1. 18; the only begotten Son of God, 3. 18; His only begotten Son, 3. 16; the Son of God, 5. 25.

The eternal, unique, intimate and unbroken relationship enjoyed by the One who is in the bosom of the Father is further unveiled as the Son speaks of 'the Father', and 'my Father'. The men of His day sensed that this was nothing short of making Himself 'equal with God', while He specifically taught that all should 'honour the Son, even as they honour the Father', John 5. 18, 23. In addition to the absoluteness of the personal and eternal being of the Son as the Only-begotten, the essential and loving relationship experienced between the Son and the Father, and the immensity of the gift of God's love suggested by its expression in One who is 'his only begotten Son', 'his own Son', it follows that we reach here the inexpressible, for 'no one knoweth the Son, save the Father', Matt. 11. 27. Yet 'our fellowship is with the Father', and nothing so delights Him as sharing with His children that concerning His beloved Son which He alone can communicate.

It will be convenient for us to enumerate here other titles which relate to the **Godhood** of our Lord, which further focus attention upon the majesty and deity of Christ. He is the Alpha and the Omega, the first and the last, the beginning and the end, Rev. 22. 13. He is the firstborn of all creation (cp. the beginning, the firstborn from the dead, Col. 1. 18, and the beginning of the creation of God, Rev. 3. 14), Col. 1. 15; He is Immanuel, Matt. 1. 23; the image of the invisible God, Col. 1. 15; the effulgence of his (God's) glory, the very image of his (God's) substance, Heb. 1. 3. He is the Word, the Word of God, the Word of Life;[32] the life, the eternal life, 1. 2; the living One, Rev. 1. 18; the Prince (or Author) of life, Acts 3. 15; the resurrection, and the life, John 11. 25; the way, and

[32] John 1. 1; Rev. 19. 13; 1 John 1. 1.

the truth, and the life, 14. 6; the great 'I am'.[33] He is the Lord of glory*, 1 Cor. 2. 8; cp. Jas. 2. 1; the light of the world, John 8. 12; 9. 5; the power of God, and the wisdom of God, 1 Cor. 1. 24. He is God, Heb. 1. 8; God blessed forever, Rom. 9. 5; our God and Saviour Jesus Christ*, 2 Pet. 1. 1; our great God and Saviour Jesus Christ*, Titus 2. 13; the true God, and eternal life, 1 John 5. 20; and, by matchless grace, He is 'My Lord and my God'*, John 20. 28. He is the Yea to the promises of God, 2 Cor. 1. 20, and the Amen, Rev. 3. 14; cp. Isa. 65. 16 mg.

'Behold, my servant whom I have chosen'. It is Matthew who clearly forges the link between our Lord and the Servant of Isaiah by his quotation of Isaiah chapter 42 verses 1 to 4 in chapter 12 verses 18 to 21, and Isaiah chapter 53 verse 4 in chapter 8 verse 17. The voice heard from heaven at the baptism, 'This is my beloved Son, in whom I am well pleased', drew attention to both the fact of His Sonship and that He was the Servant of Isaiah.[34] The Servant Songs also provide the background for the Lord's predictions of His coming sufferings, death and resurrection.[35] Note the connection is made also between the Servant and the Son of man. The One referred to as my servant, Matt. 12. 18, is called his servant Jesus, his servant, and thy holy Servant Jesus, *pais*, by the early church, Acts 3. 13, 26; 4. 27. There are allusions to all the Servant Songs in the New Testament, but the one most frequently used is Isaiah chapter 52 verse 13 to chapter 53 verse 12.[36] With that Spirit-given insight the early church read these Songs, finding their consummation in the crucified and crowned Christ.

Another word for servant, *diakonos*, is applied to the Lord as a minister of the circumcision, Rom. 15. 8, and this to maintain God's trustworthiness in connection with His promises to the Jew. How ready He was to serve the interests of Israel and become the 'Yes' to God's

---

[33] John 8. 24, 28, 58; 13. 19; 18. 5, 8.

[34] Matt. 3. 17; Ps. 2. 7; Isa. 42. 1.

[35] Matt. 16. 21; 17. 12, 22; 20. 18; Luke 22. 37

[36] New Testament uses of Isaiah 52. 13 to 53. 12 are: **52. 13** in Acts 3. 13; Phil. 2. 9; **52. 15** in Rom. 15. 21; **53. 1** in John 12. 38; Rom. 10. 16; **53. 3** in Mark 9. 12; **53. 4**. in Matt. 8. 17; Rom. 4. 25; 1 Pet. 2. 24; **53. 6** in 1 Pet. 2. 25; **53. 7.** in Acts 8. 32.; 1 Cor. 5. 7; Rev. 5. 6, 12; 13. 8; **53. 9** in 1 Pet. 2. 22; Rev. 14. 5; **53. 11** in Acts 3. 13; 13. 39; 1 Pet. 2. 24; **53. 12** in Luke 22. 37; 23. 34; 1 Pet. 2. 24; Heb. 9. 28; Phil. 2. 9.

promises. Thus He said, 'I am in the midst of you as he that serveth', Luke 22. 27. But God's objective included glory to be brought to Himself through His mercy to the Gentiles also, for, as the Son of man, Christ 'came not to be ministered unto, but to minister, and to give his life a ransom for many', Mark 10. 45.

Wonder of wonders that He, 'being in the form of God', should take upon Himself 'the form of a servant', the word here, *doulos*, bondslave, indicating His utter submission to the will of God. Consequently, now highly exalted, He has obtained a more excellent ministry, being a minister, *leitourgos*, of the sanctuary, and of the true tabernacle, Heb. 8. 2.

'For mine eyes have seen thy salvation'. 'Salvation is of the Lord', sang Jonah, thereby expressing a basic tenet of the Old Testament faith. Confined within the great fish, Jonah waited on the Lord to save him. When finally removed from danger, brought to safety on the dry land to breathe the fresh air of liberation, delivered from all that which had menaced his well-being, into a new set of circumstances designed to give him room for spiritual expansion, he was a monument to God's saving activity. The meaning of the Old Testament word-family for save/salvation is thus illustrated in Jonah's experience, perhaps needing further expansion with the ideas of victory and triumph, Ps. 20. 5-9.

Israel at the Red Sea, and in a variety of other impossible situations, were encouraged to 'stand still, and see the salvation of the Lord', Exod. 14. 13. Beside Him there is no Saviour, Isa. 43. 11. Yet God not only directly intervenes as a Saviour God, but frequently raised up saviours for His people. These Old Testament anticipations find their climax and final consummation in the New Testament, where the words for save, salvation and Saviour occur about 175 times. In the Lord Jesus, God 'hath raised up a horn of salvation for us', so that Israel might know 'Salvation from all our enemies, and from the hand of all that hate us', Luke 1. 69, 71. Fundamental to this is their acceptance of Jesus, Jehovah the Saviour, for He alone can 'save his people from their sins', Matt. 1. 21.

Saviour, one of the Old Testament titles for God, though also used of

Him in the New Testament,[37] is here used twice as often for Christ, another indication of His equality with God, His deity. We rejoice in Him as a Saviour, which is Christ the Lord, Luke 2. 11; thy salvation, 2. 30; the Saviour of the world, John 4. 42; 1 John 4. 14; a Prince and a Saviour, Acts 5. 31; a Saviour, Jesus*, 13. 23; the saviour of the body, Eph. 5. 23; a Saviour, the Lord Jesus Christ*, Phil. 3. 20; our Saviour Christ Jesus*, 2 Tim. 1. 10; Christ Jesus our Saviour*, Titus 1. 4; Jesus Christ our Saviour*, 3. 6; Our Great God and Saviour Jesus Christ*, 2. 13; Our God and Saviour Jesus Christ*, 2 Pet. 1. 1; our Lord and Saviour Jesus Christ*, 1. 11; 3. 18; the Lord and Saviour Jesus Christ*, 2. 20; the Lord and Saviour*, 3. 2. He is the author of their salvation, Heb. 2. 10, and being the eternal One is the author of eternal salvation to all them that obey Him, 5. 9.

Praise God, we are not appointed to wrath 'but unto the obtaining of salvation through our Lord Jesus Christ', 1 Thess. 5. 9. It is well to include here the statement that the Lord is, literally, our deliverer from the wrath to come, 1. 10, and also the guarantor of Israel's national salvation for 'there shall come out of Zion the Deliverer', Rom. 11. 26. He will be then the embodiment of (the) consolation, *paraklēsis*, of Israel, Luke 2. 25; cp. His past and present ministries as the Comforter, and advocate, *paraklētos,* John 14. 16; 1 John 2. 1.

Other Official Titles. Among the more important and most used of these, we may notice briefly: priest, Heb. 5. 6; another priest, 7. 11; A great priest, 10. 21; a high priest, 5. 10; a high priest of the good things to come, 9. 11; a merciful and faithful high priest, 2. 17; the Apostle and High Priest of our confession, even Jesus*, 3. 1; a great high priest, 4. 14; see further the chapters 'The Priesthood of the Lord Jesus Christ' and 'The High Priestly Work of Christ'.

Associated with this mediatorial ministry from the throne of God, cp. Rom. 8. 34, is the work of the Lord as an advocate with the Father, Jesus Christ the righteous, 1 John 2. 1, and as the one mediator between God and men, 1 Tim. 2. 5; the mediator of a better covenant, the mediator of a new covenant, even Jesus the mediator of a new covenant*, Heb. 8. 6;

[37] See Luke 1. 47; 1 Tim. 1. 1; 2. 3; 4. 10; Tit. 1. 3; 2. 10; 3. 4; Jude 25.

9. 15; 12. 24; see further the chapter on 'Mediator and Advocate'. As mediator He is the One through whom the terms of the covenant are to be effected, but He is also personally the **guarantor**, or the **surety** of a better covenant, Heb. 7. 22. We may also conveniently include here that aspect of Christ's work suggested by the blood-sprinkled mercy-seat in the Old Testament to which the New Testament draws attention by the words 'whom God set forth to be a **propitiation** [or propitiatory, mercy-seat], through faith, by his blood', Rom. 3. 25. He is the propitiation for our sins, 1 John 2. 2; 4. 10.

From yet another standpoint, our Lord is the **head**, Col. 2. 19; the head of every man, 1 Cor. 11. 3; the head of all principality and power, Col. 2. 10, head over all things, Eph. 1. 22; the head of the body, the church, Col. 1. 18; the head of the church, Eph. 5. 23; the head, even Christ, 4. 15. Christ as the head is one with the church, His body, directing its functions by His wisdom, commanding its operations, co-ordinating and uniting its many parts, the source and dynamic of its life. While He is over it and above it, at the same time He is its inseparable, vital head, the body providing the vehicle of expression for all that He is, 'the fullness of him', Eph. 1. 23. It is also the subject of His care and concern as He provides for its well-being and protection as the Saviour of the body*, 5. 23.

Then He is the **bridegroom**, suggesting a more personal and intimate relationship with His people. Those joyous days leading to the blessing of restored Israel are the subject of many prophecies, e.g., Hos. 2. 14, 20; Isa. 54. 5; cp. Song of Songs. No doubt John the Baptist had this in mind when he referred to Jesus as the bridegroom, John 3. 29. The Lord thus referred to Himself, Matt. 9. 15, even more colourfully in parables, 22. 1; 25. 1. He, too, is the one husband who loved the church, giving Himself up for her, meantime preparing His bride for the glad day of presentation, Eph. 5. 26; cp. 2 Cor. 11. 2. If nuptial joys commence with the marriage supper, Rev. 19. 7, they will never cease to be enjoyed nor will they wane throughout the eternal day. In glad anticipation of love fully realized 'the Spirit and the bride say, Come', 22. 17.

The Lord is also the **Firstborn**, *prōtotokos,* a term indicating both His dignity and priority where relationship with things or men is concerned. By contrast, 'only-begotten', *monogenēs,* denotes a relationship with the Father, at once eternal, essential, and in which He stands alone. In connection with the universe He is 'the firstborn of all creation', Col. 1. 15, while in resurrection He is 'the beginning, the firstborn from the dead', 1. 18; cp. Rev. 1. 5. God's predestining purpose for each one called in the gospel is that, when glorified, they shall be eternally conformed to the image of His Son, 'that he might be the firstborn among many brethren', Rom. 8. 29. But He is also appointed heir of all things, Heb. 1. 2, the right of the firstborn, and as the messianic King He is yet to come into His inheritance, Ps. 89. 27. This He will do when God 'again bringeth in the firstborn into the world', Heb. 1. 6. Perhaps we may conveniently include here the title A forerunner Jesus, *prodromos*, 6. 20, with its encouraging reminder that our Lord has gone in advance of us, going to prepare a place for us, John 14. 2, guaranteeing that all of His own will be one day where He is.

Both the Old and New Testaments teach us that God is the **Judge** of all; e.g., Ps. 50. 6; Heb. 12. 23. Yet God has decreed that 'he will judge the world in righteousness by the man whom he hath ordained', Acts 17. 31. As the Lord, the righteous judge*, He will review and reward His people in a future day.[38] As the Judge of quick and dead, He is the One before whom all are to stand, Acts 10. 42; cp. 2 Tim. 4. 1. Let us live in the light of the fact that 'the judge standeth before the doors', Jas. 5. 9.

Our Lord's appointment by God to fill so many offices is telling evidence for His unique fullness, as also for His moral fitness. Numbers of titles ascribed to Him insist on this. Only the One owned of God as 'my **righteous** servant', Isa. 53. 11, could suffer as 'the righteous for the unrighteous', 1 Pet. 3. 18. He alone is the righteous One, the holy and righteous One, who was denied and killed.[39] Some owned Him as such, 'this (or that) righteous man', 'a righteous man', in the very context of that glaringly unjust trial and murder. God vindicated Him, raising Him and taking Him to heaven, appointing Him also as an advocate with the Father, Jesus Christ the righteous*, to meet the case of His children who sin, 1 John 2. 1.

---

[38] 2 Tim. 4. 8; cp. 1 Cor. 4. 4; 2 Cor. 5. 10.

[39] Acts 7. 52; 22. 14; 3. 14; cp. Jas. 5. 6.

He was also selected by, and set apart for God here, 'my Son, my chosen', Luke 9. 35; cp. 1 Pet. 2. 4, being referred to as thy Holy One, *hosios*, Acts 2. 27; 13. 35. Unquestionably, He was morally that for which He had been equipped, the Holy One of God, the holy and righteous One*, thy holy Servant Jesus*, the Holy One.[40]

To righteousness and holiness is added His faithfulness. He is the faithful witness, the Amen*, the faithful and true witness, and the One called Faithful and True.[41]

A Cluster of Metaphorical Titles. In the scriptures the Spirit has adopted metaphorical means to express further glories of the One who described Himself not only as being a greater than Jonah, and a greater than Solomon, but also as one greater than the temple, Matt. 12. 41, 6. In this field of titles perhaps the most used of metaphors is that related to the **Stone**. It is upon 'this rock', the bedrock foundation fact of His deity as Son of the living God, that He will build His church, Matt. 16. 16. The foundation that is fundamental for each local church is Jesus Christ, and Him crucified, 1 Cor. 3. 10. As far as the architects and builders of Israel, the politico-religious leaders of Christ's day, were concerned, He could not be fitted into their schemes. Consequently, He was the stone which the builders rejected;[42] the One 'set at nought of you the builders' in Peter's challenging words, Acts 4. 11. To all that refused the faith-righteousness offered in the One who is the end of the law for righteousness, He became A stone of stumbling and a rock of offence, Rom. 9. 32; 1 Pet. 2. 8. He is the test of all man's schemes, many of His contemporaries being broken to pieces through their attitude to Him, falling on this stone, and many upon whom He shall fall in the future will be scattered as dust, Matt. 21. 44. What a contrast to those who believe on, *epi*, Him as the foundation of their faith, for they will never be put to shame, their faith in Him will not prove ill-founded. The One once laid as God's foundation in Zion, is now seen as A living stone, with God elect and precious, 1 Pet. 2. 4, and also as the chief corner stone binding together the walls upon the firm foundation, 1 Pet. 2. 6; Eph. 2.

---

[40] Mark 1. 24; Luke 4. 34; John 6. 69; Acts 3. 14; 4. 27, 30; 1 John 2. 20; cp. Rev. 3. 7, *hagios*.

[41] Rev. 1. 5; 2. 14; 19. 11.

[42] Matt. 21. 42, 44; Mark 12. 10; Luke 20. 17; 1 Pet. 2. 7.

20. He is also the head of the corner exalted by God, guaranteeing the completion of the whole, and giving to the whole building its strength and beauty, e.g., 1 Pet. 2. 7. Regarding Israel, in the past Christ was to them the **rock**, a spiritual rock that followed them, 1 Cor. 10. 4. In the future He is to be brought forth as the head stone with shoutings of 'Grace, grace, unto it', Zech. 4. 7.[43] By means of catastrophic judgement upon Gentile world power, Christ, described as a stone cut out of the mountain without hands, is yet to smite and break it in pieces, and become Himself as a great mountain filling the whole earth, Dan. 2. 31-45.

Pressing into service sacrificial imagery, we are taught that He is the Lamb of God, John 1. 29, 36, of whom a bone was not to be broken, 19. 36; cp. Exod. 12. 46. Before His accusers He was like a lamb dumb before His shearers, and was led as a sheep to the slaughter, Acts 8. 32; Isa. 53. 7, while His precious blood, as that of a lamb, *amnos*, without blemish and without spot, is the means of our redemption. He is to the believer Christ our **passover** that has been sacrificed for us, 1 Cor. 5. 7 KJV. Throughout Revelation He is pre-eminently the lamb, *arnion*, a diminutive form of the word being used of Him some twenty-eight times. Then, too, He is the **door**, the door of the sheep, John 10. 9, 7; the **Shepherd** smitten by God;[44] a shepherd, the shepherd of the sheep, the good shepherd, one shepherd, the great shepherd of the sheep, the Shepherd and Bishop of your souls, and the chief Shepherd.[45] Whereas Israel and the nations have been as sheep without shepherds, and remain so until now, when Christ returns in glory He will be shepherd of my people Israel, Matt. 2. 6, and all the nations shall know Him as their shepherd ruler also.[46]

God is **light** and He has sent the dayspring from on high to visit us, Luke 1. 78. He came as A light for revelation to the Gentiles, and the glory of God's people Israel, 2. 32; A light of the Gentiles, Acts 13. 47. He was the light, John 1. 7, the true light, v. 9, the light of the world, 8. 12; 9. 5. he is

---

[43] See also for the Old Testament background: Ps. 118. 22; Isa. 8. 14; 28. 16.
[44] Matt. 26. 31; Mark 14. 27; cp. Zech. 13. 7.
[45] John 10. 12, 2, 11 (2), 14, 16; Heb. 13. 20; 1 Pet. 2. 25; 5. 4.
[46] Rev. 12. 5; 19. 15; 7. 17; cp. 2. 27; see the chapter 'The Lamb and the Shepherd'.

the daystar, 2 Pet. 1. 19; the bright, the morning star, Rev. 22. 16; cp. the sun of righteousness, Mal. 4. 2, and of that city which is yet to come down out of heaven from God it is said, that it has no need of sun nor moon for 'the glory of God did lighten it, and the lamp [*luchnos*] thereof is the Lamb', Rev. 21. 23. Today, those into whose hearts God has shined have the light of the knowledge of the glory of God in the face of Jesus Christ, 2 Cor. 4. 6.

To sustain His people, Christ is the true **bread**, John 6. 32; the bread of god, v. 33; the bread of life, vv. 35, 48; the living bread, v. 51; the bread which came down out of heaven, vv. 41, 50, 58; and this bread, v. 58. How completely He satisfies the deepest needs of men, God's provision for a starving world, the counterpart now, though surely much richer, of that manna given by God to Israel in the wilderness, v. 31; Exod. 16. 1. The overcomer of Pergamum was promised still further the hidden manna laid up in God's presence, Rev. 2. 17.

We have had occasion to refer to numbers of the '**I am**' titles of our Lord elsewhere.[47] The eternal One who said 'Before Abraham was, I am', John 8. 58, referred to Himself metaphorically with the words 'I am the true vine', and 'I am the vine', 15. 1, 5.

'In the Apocalypse the veil is lifted, and we see the extent of the change wrought by the Resurrection and the Ascension . . . the Lord's face shines as the noonday sun, the eyes flash, the hair is white as snow, the feet glow like metal in a furnace, the voice is like the thunder of the waterfall', H. B. SWETE. The opening vision of chapter 1 influences the selection of those descriptive titles found prefacing the letters to the seven churches in chapters 2 and 3, another proof that names and titles are intended to describe the person that bears them. In the brief compass of these two chapters a range of descriptive revelation concerning our Lord is given to which we have made no reference so far. He is he that holdeth the seven stars in his right hand, he that

---

[47] The significant uses of 'I am' are: John 6. 35, 41, 48, 51; 8. 12; 10. 7, 9, 11, 14; 11. 25; 14. 6; 15. 1, 5 – all these are followed by descriptive titles: in John 8. 24, 28, 58; 13. 19; 18. 5, 8 'I am' stands alone. Compare also John 6. 20 and Matt. 14. 27; Mark 6. 50, and the Lord's answer to the Samaritan woman following her remarks regarding the Messiah, John 4. 26.

walketh in the midst of the seven golden candlesticks, 2. 1, he that hath the sharp two-edged sword, v. 12, the Son of God, who hath his eyes like a flame of fire, and his feet are like unto burnished brass, v. 13, he that hath the seven spirits of God, and the seven stars, 3. 1, he that is holy, he that is true, he that hath the key of David, he that openeth, and none shall shut, and that shutteth, and none openeth, v. 7, the Amen*, the faithful and true witness*, the beginning of the creation of God, v. 14. 'To the members of His church the ascended Christ is all in all. He loves them, He redeemed them, and He has made them what they are . . . He is in their midst, regulating all the affairs of the churches; removing, punishing, guarding, giving victory, as He sees fit. From Him are to be obtained all spiritual gifts and helps; from Him are to be expected the final rewards', SWETE *ibid,* for of Him it is revealed, 'I am He which searcheth the reins and hearts: and I will give unto each one of you according to your works', 2. 23.

It will be appropriate to bring this rehearsal of the titles of our Lord Jesus to a close with one that stimulates our hope. How thankful we are for the wealthy revelation of His person and work, together with those ensuing official glories, which are concentrated in the vast range of titles that are borne by Him. Truly, were we to

> 'Join all the glorious names
> Of wisdom, love, and power . . .
> All are too mean to speak His worth,
> Too mean to set my Saviour forth'.
>
> ISAAC WATTS

But soon we are to see Him, faith is to give place to sight, for He is the **Coming One**. We wait expectantly, 'For yet a very little while, he that cometh shall come, and shall not tarry', Heb. 10. 37. Though the mocker says otherwise, suggesting that 'all things continue as they were from the beginning of the creation', 2 Pet. 3. 4, we know that among those who survive the great tribulation there will be some that say, 'Blessed is he that cometh in the name of the Lord', Matt. 23. 39, when He comes in His kingdom, Luke 23. 42. The Glorified One says, 'Yea: I come quickly'. To which our glad response is, 'Amen: come, Lord Jesus', Rev. 22. 20.

The Title 'Only Begotten' - T. HOLLIDAY

In the original scriptures there is a sweetness in this title which is not apparent in the English translation 'only begotten', and if the emphasis is placed only on the word 'begotten' then the meaning is altogether obscured. For example, Isaac is called Abraham's 'only begotten' son, Heb. 11. 17, so that if a question of generation were involved then this would not be true, since Abraham had other sons. Rather, Isaac had no rival in Abraham's affections; he was Abraham's **only one – his darling**.

The word is used in: (1) 'the **only** son of his mother', Luke 7. 12; (2) 'he had **one only** daughter', Luke 8. 42; (3) 'he is mine **only** child', Luke 9. 38. These verses indicate that 'only begotten' means one standing alone, the sole object of the thoughts and love of the heart. Add to this both intimacy of relationship and community of nature, then we have clearly the meaning of this title as it belongs to the Lord. Christ ever did and ever will occupy this peculiar and unique place in the Father's thoughts and affections; He is the Father's 'only begotten'.

The Holy Spirit uses this title '**only begotten**' at least five times in reference to Christ; on each occasion it is very beautiful and impressive.

To exalt to the uttermost the glory of the Word become flesh, the Spirit declares through John, 'the glory as of the **only begotten** of the Father', John 1. 14.

When the Spirit would convey to our hearts the perfect eternal intimacy and union between the glorious persons of the Godhead, the unspeakable endearment of the Son to His Father, the loftiest possible idea of the majesty of the revelation of the truth, the perfection of the manifestation of God in Christ, the Spirit again declares through John, 'No man hath seen God at any time; the **only begotten** Son, which is in the bosom of the Father, he hath declared him', 1. 18.

To show the benevolence of God in highest splendour towards the world, the Spirit says, 'For God so loved the world, that he gave his **only begotten** Son, that whosoever believeth in him should not perish, but have everlasting life', 3. 16.

To show unbelief as the extreme of human guilt, putting man under condemnation at the present time, the Spirit warns, 'He that believeth not is condemned already, because he hath not believed in the name of the **only begotten** Son of God', 3. 18.

To show both the magnificence of the benevolence of God toward His people, and God's great desire for a living response, the Spirit affirms, 'In this was manifested the love of God toward us, because that God sent his **only begotten** Son into the world, that we might live through him', 1 John 4. 9. Observe that it is not a matter of possessing life, but of living. This involves responding in a practical way, exhibiting in our lives the beneficent features of the divine nature in the power of the Holy Spirit, so that God Himself may be seen and known in His family (all born again persons) while in this scene of contrariety and evil – a magnificent triumph for God.

How the glory and beauty of God's only begotten Son, Jesus Christ our Lord, shine in the sacred page so as to impress our hearts and thoughts with a yearning to know Him in a deeper and fuller way, so that there may be in our hearts no rivals or idols.

It is most impressive to note that Christ anticipatively uses the word 'only one – darling' of His bride the church, when He was in the midst of the most intense sufferings, 'Deliver my soul from the sword; my **darling** from the power of the dog', Ps. 22. 20 (the word 'darling' is in the feminine form). The bridegroom, speaking of the bride, says, 'She is the **only one** of her mother', S. of S. 6. 9. How profoundly touching to contemplate that the church holds this unique place in the affections of Christ!

May the divine love of the Father, Son and Holy Spirit have a larger place in our hearts, so that our service of praise may increase in volume until that glad day when every chord in the vast universe will reverberate with His praises.

The Word - J. Boyd

John, in the prologue to his Gospel, 1. 1-18, introduces us to the central figure of his evangel by the name of 'the Word'. Why he does so we cannot easily prove, but we note that in current Jewish and Greek thought there was a conception of the Creator of the world under this title. The term was used by John without explanation, as though such an expression had a meaning well-known to his readers.

The Jew knew it. He appreciated the fact that creation was the outcome of the speaking of God, Ps. 50. 1, the work of the word of Jehovah, 33. 6. In the Old Testament the word of God is also personified as a physician, 107. 20, and as a messenger, 147. 15.

Greek philosophers had been searching in vain for some means of making God intelligible to man. In their speculations they also had employed this term. Philo, an Alexandrian Jew, steeped in Greek philosophy, had propounded an erroneous view of the Word. It may well be that John's Gospel was written partly to counteract this false conception.

John was conscious that he possessed the true answer to this hitherto insoluble enigma, and used the expression that human reason had chanced upon in its search after truth. But with him it was removed from the precarious foundation of philosophy and mythology, and set upon the imperishable rock of inspiration. For him the Word was identical with the historical Christ.

The introductions of the first three Gospels present to us one view of the Lord Jesus Christ, namely. His humanity. Matthew is taken up with the nature of His advent; Mark straight away launches us into His work; Luke explains the conditions on earth into which He came. John's introduction is different. He raises us above the earth. He is coupled not so much with His humanity as with His deity; not so much with His appearance in time as with His eternal pre-existence; not so much with His earthly as with His heavenly relationship. While the Synoptists show that Jesus who was a real man was the Christ, John demonstrates that the Christ was God Himself.

In the New Testament the Lord Jesus Christ is called the Word only in John's writings. In his Gospel, John 1. 1, 2, he tells of the person thus designated, and in verses 3 to 5, of His work prior to His incarnation. Verse 1 sets before us three propositions concerning the Word: (1) His eternal pre-existence; (2) His personal distinction and intimate association in the Godhead; (3) His essential identity as God.

In the Beginning was The Word. Three times in scripture the words 'the beginning' are used without directly specifying what was begun.[48] In 1 John chapter 1 verse 1 we get the beginning of the manifestation of Him who was the eternal life, a time fixed by the qualifying terms that follow. In Genesis we get the beginning of creation, but in John chapter 1 verse 1 'the beginning' is anterior to the other two. It is the earliest beginning towards which our thoughts could search. The verb 'was' (imperfect tense) reminds us that, however far our thoughts go back to what we conceive as the beginning, then He had prior existence for then 'the Word was'. This verb affirms the existence of One called the Word even before the creation of the world, for He who was in the beginning created these things. In Him was hidden from all eternity all that God has to say to man. By the term 'the Word' is meant the One who was the expression of deity, Heb. 1. 2. He expressed God in creation, John 1. 3; Rom. 1. 20; in speech, John 12. 49; in works, John 5. 36. 'The Word', we are told, was eternally the expression of God.

The Word was with God. The Word had a close relationship to God, yet a distinct personality. The Greek preposition used here is *pros,* towards, with the implication that the Word was face to face with God. Mere man could not thus dwell with God, Exod. 33. 20. While it postulates a personal distinction in the Godhead, it infers an intimate knowledge and understanding the One of the Other. Compare John 1. 18.

The Word was God. To say that the Word was only divine might suggest a plurality of gods. This would be error. Yet He was God. He possesses all the attributes of the essence of God; He was in the form of God, Phil. 2. 6; His essential being was God, Heb. 1. 3. So essentially was He one with God that all things we attribute to God are true of the Word.

What a marvellous crescendo of wonder and worship is produced in our hearts by this description of the Word! He existed eternally, and in that existence He ever possessed an intimate relationship with God. Yes, He

---

[48] Gen. 1. 1; John 1. 1; 1 John 1. 1.

is God in very essence. In verse 2 we get these three thoughts linked together, not a mere repetition of facts, but a further lesson. The Word, who was God, who had such an intimate relationship with God, possessed the same relationship to God in the beginning. Verse 2 informs us that His connection with God was eternal, just as verse 1 states that His existence was eternal. Throughout all the ages He was with God. Eternally He was God.

All Things were Made by Him. This is a definite act of the Word, an act of expression of God. Creation sets forth the everlasting power and divinity of God, Rom. 1. 20. Creation is the work of Him whom John calls the Word. Thus the thought of the Word being the expression of God is grander than merely being His mouthpiece, for to the Word here is ascribed power, wisdom, might. In the former part of the verse the emphasis is laid on the 'all things', stressing the magnitude of the work. In the latter part we are told that no detail of all the created things, no matter how small or insignificant to our eyes, had its origin **apart from** the creative act of the Word. The consideration of the vast universe impresses us with the mighty work of creation, but the realization that each petal of the wayside flower is a result of the handiwork of the same Creator causes us to marvel at the particularizing greatness of the One who has become our Saviour. We need not fear, for the very hairs of our head are all numbered. Each one of us is precious in His sight.

In Him was Life. This expresses a further stage in the work of creation. Only One who was God could produce life, Exod. 8. 16-19. The Word, who made all things, gave them life. He was the well-spring of life for all living things – vegetable, animal, and human.

While life was given to all animate things, to man alone was light given. Light is more than truth. It is the revelation and understanding of the reason for things; it is the knowledge that He who is over all is God. As man saw life in evidence in creation, he should have appreciated this light. This was Paul's argument in his address on Mars' Hill. God made all things; God gave life, and man ought through these to seek and find God. Thus the Word, through creation and through life, revealed God to man. Men failed to apprehend this light, even though it was shining in their hearts. Their hearts had become darkened because, while knowing God in creation, they glorified Him not as God, Rom. 1. 21. Note the gradual descent, John 1. 1-5, from the sublimity of the eternal relationship in the Godhead to the depths of man's misapprehension of the purposes of God. In verses 1 and 2 we get the Godhead supreme, eternal; in verse 3 the creation of all things; in verse 4 life is given to some of these created things, and light is made possible to man; in verse 5 light is not apprehended by man.

The Word Became Flesh. In these words we have set before us another activity of the Word, another expression of God. This is God's last word to man. In this the apprehension of God's light was realized in His fullness of grace and truth. Through the Word becoming flesh it was possible for us to become children of God.

The manifestation on the stage of history of the divine Word is set before us in verses 6 to 18 as follows:

1. **The Revelation of the Incarnate Word**, by John the Baptist, vv. 6-9.
2. **The Rejection of the Incarnate Word** by the world in general, and by Israel in particular, vv. 10-11.
3. **The Reception of the Incarnate Word**, by those who thus become the children of God, vv. 12-13.
4. **The Recognition of the Incarnate Word**, by those who have received Him, vv. 14-18.

The Word partook of our human nature in all its frailty and necessities, but without its sinfulness. The Word tabernacled among us. Just as the tabernacle was Jehovah's dwelling-place in the wilderness in the midst of His people, so the flesh was the tent in which the Word dwelt, in the wilderness of this world amongst His own. As the glory of Jehovah filled the tabernacle in the wilderness, Exod. 40. 34, so there was a glory filling the body in which the Word tabernacled, for He was 'full of grace and truth'. 'We beheld his glory', says John. As they listened to His teaching; as they saw His mighty works; as they witnessed His sufferings, they saw manifested in Him grace and truth. They saw His glory, a glory such as became Him who was the only begotten of the Father, a glory like unto the Shekinah glory of the tabernacle in the wilderness.

With John, the word 'glory' is used here of the sum total of the attributes of God. It is the revelation of the grandeur of Him who is the Object of our faith. Through the incarnation of the eternal Word has been displayed to us the grace of God: grace that brought salvation; grace to help in time of need; grace that is about to be revealed as the Lord comes for His own. Well might John say, 'and grace for grace', a phrase that implies one supply of grace superseding the former. The believer is taught to expect a more remarkable display of the grace of God in the future than that which has astonished him in the past. The Word becoming flesh brought also the truth, the revelation of God to men. The only begotten Son dwelling in the place of intimate communion, the bosom of the Father, and penetrating into the thoughts and intents of the Father's heart, reveals to us His father-character, His heart of love towards those who have become His children. In the Word was life; through Jesus Christ by grace came life eternal, given to those who have become children of God. The life which was in the Word was the light of men; through Jesus Christ came the truth, the revelation of the loving heart of God to His children. Thus is the identity of the Word with the historic Jesus Christ firmly established.

Let the believer rejoice as he appreciates the far-reaching effects to him personally of the incarnation of the Son of God. He worships the eternal Word, the Creator, the giver and sustainer of life, the One who brought light to man. If that were all, he might still be in the darkness of verse 5. But, glory be to His name, the Word became flesh, tabernacled among us, and fully revealed the Father's heart by dying for us. By reason of this the believer has been received into the family of God, has been made a partaker of the divine nature, and joys in the love of God his Father. Well might he bow the knee and worship Him to whom one day every knee shall bow.

> 'Thou art the Everlasting Word, the Father's only Son,
> God manifestly seen and heard, and heaven's Beloved One.
> In Thee most perfectly expressed, the Father's glories shine,
> Of the full deity possessed, eternally divine!
> Worthy, O Lamb of God, art Thou,
> That every knee to Thee should bow!'
>
> JOSIAH CONDER

The Son of God - J. M. Davies

It is with unshod feet, subdued spirits, and bowed hearts that we should approach this most important and absorbing subject, for if we are in error in our answer to the question, 'What think ye of Christ? whose son is he?' Matt. 22. 42, or 'Dost thou believe on the Son of God?' John 9. 35, we will end in the blackness of eternal darkness.

The Title 'Son' – Its Significance and Scope. The word occurs upwards of 300 times in the New Testament. Primarily the word denotes a male offspring, but in many passages it is used in a metaphorical sense, suggestive of certain moral characteristics; e.g., sons of light, Luke 16. 8; sons of the evil one, Matt. 13. 38 RV (cp. Acts 13. 10 RV), sons of thunder - Boanerges, Mark 3. 17. It is also used to describe certain characteristics other than moral; e.g., sons of the kingdom, Matt. 8. 12; 13. 38 RV; son of exhortation, Acts 4. 36. In these metaphorical usages there is no thought of derivation, generation, birth, or sex. This is important when we consider the title 'son' in relation to the Lord Jesus as 'Son of God', or 'Son of man'. In this connection four couplets in which the title 'son' is used may be noted.

1. 'Being (as was supposed) the son of Joseph', and 'the son of Mary', Luke 3. 23; Mark 6. 3.
2. He was the son of David and the son of Abraham, Matt. 1. 1.
3. He was 'the Son of the Highest' – the Most High – *Elyon*, Luke 1. 32, and 'the Son of the Blessed', a title used only of God in the New Testament, Mark 14. 61.
4. He claimed the two titles, Son of God, and Son of man.[49] It is with the first of these that we are especially concerned in this study.

Some of the ways in which the Sonship is referred to are 'Son' in contrast to servants;[50] 'the Son', Matt. 11. 27; 'his Son', Rom. 1. 9; 1 Thess. 1. 10; 'his own Son', Rom. 8. 32; 'my beloved Son', Matt. 3. 17; 'the, his only begotten Son', John 1. 18; 3. 16; and 'the Son of his love', Col. 1. 13 RV.

---

[49] John 5. 25-27; 9. 35-37; 10. 36; Matt. 16. 13.
[50] Matt. 21. 37; Heb. 1. 1-3; 3. 1-6.

The Title Son – Its Importance. This may be gauged by the prominence given to it in the New Testament. It was because he claimed to be the Son of God that the Jews condemned Him to be crucified, John 19. 7; Matt. 26. 63. Each of the four historians make reference to it. Mark commences his chronicle with the words, 'The beginning of the gospel of Jesus Christ, the Son of God', 1. 1. And John wrote his evangel for the specific purpose that his readers 'might believe that Jesus is the Christ, the Son of God', 20. 31. Along with the signs which he records to establish the truth of this divine Sonship, there is interwoven the Lord's own claims to the title Son of God, which must be considered.

Following the healing of the cripple at the pool of Bethesda, the Lord made some startling statements. There was no doubt in the mind of the Jews as to the nature of His claims. They 'sought the more to kill him, because he not only had broken the sabbath, but said also that God was his Father, making himself equal with God', 5. 18; cp. 1. 14. Some eight times in John chapter 5 He refers to Himself as 'the Son', once as 'the Son of God', and once as the 'Son of man'. The references to the Son are always to Himself as the Son of God, and not as the Son of man. Twelve times he refers to 'the Father'. He does not act independently of the Father, but claims equality of authority, power, and honour with the Father. He who fails to honour the Son fails to honour the Father. This is again emphasized by John in his First Epistle as we shall see. The Lord cites the witness of John Baptist, His own works, and the direct witness of the Father from heaven on the banks of the Jordan, 'This is my beloved Son', Matt. 3. 17.

The Only Begotten. This title is used five times in the New Testament, all in the writings of the Apostle John.[51] He is 'the only begotten from the Father', John 1. 14 RV. 'This indicates that as the Son of God He was the sole representative of the being and character of the One who sent Him. In the original, the definite article is omitted before "only begotten" and before "Father", and its absence in each case serves to lay stress on the characteristics referred to in the terms used. The apostle's object is to demonstrate what sort of glory he and his fellow-apostles

[51] John 1. 14, 18; 3. 16, 18; 1 John 4. 9.

had seen'.[52] The word[53] 'only begotten' is used in Hebrews chapter 11 verse 17 of Isaac; 'Abraham . . . offered up his only begotten son'. This indicates that Isaac was Abraham's son in a unique way, different from the other sons. The relationship of the Lord Jesus with the Father is unique. It is not shared with, or by, any other. Of Him it is stated 'which is [or being] in the bosom of the Father', John 1. 18. 'The word *being* is not merely a statement of fact, but what is essential and characteristic of it'. The mutual love between the Father and the Son is an eternal reality, as was the glory He had with the Father, 17. 5, 24. This relationship was not a thing of time, or of birth, or of becoming, but an eternal and essential relationship. So He stated, 'I and the Father are one', 10. 30 RV. AUGUSTINE'S comment on this verse is noteworthy, 'The two nominatives and the plural verb exclude the identification of the Father with the Son, which would involve a denial of a plurality in the Godhead (Sabellianism). The predicate 'one' is singular and neuter, thus affirming the unity of the Father and the Son in essential being, and excluding their separation as unto creator and created (Arianism)'.

The Sonship in Romans. When Peter made his historic confession 'Thou art the Christ, the Son of the living God', the Lord stated that it was upon this rock, the truth embodied in the confession, that He would build His church. Hence it is but natural that in the exposition of the gospel, the Epistle to the Romans, the truth of this Sonship should be prominent. It is referred to seven times. To Paul there had been given a similar revelation to that which had been given to Peter. Flesh and blood had not revealed it to them, Matt. 16. 17; Gal. 1. 16. The gospel is God's good news 'concerning his Son' and it is 'the gospel of his Son'. The fact of the divine Sonship was powerfully determined, or established, by the resurrection from among the dead, Rom. 1. 1-4, 9. Immediately after his conversion Paul 'preached Christ. . . that he is the Son of God', Acts 9. 20, and this was his first message when he went to Corinth, 'the Son of God. . . who was preached among you by us'. Hence the assembly at Corinth is referred to as 'the fellowship of his Son', 1 Cor. 1. 9. It is His Sonship that gives value to His death. It is 'by the death of his Son' that we are reconciled to God, Rom. 5. 10. God 'spared not his own Son, but delivered him up for us all', 8. 32. It is 'the Son of God, who

---

[52] W. E. VINE, *Expository Dictionary of New Testament Words.*
[53] It is one word in the Greek.

loved me, and gave himself for me', Gal. 2. 20. Little wonder we read of the 'precious blood', 1 Pet. 1. 19. We are 'purchased with the blood of his own', Acts 20. 28 JND.

The Sonship in Hebrews. Just as chapters 1 to 8 of Romans is the exposition of the gospel in legal terminology to the Gentile, so the letter to the Hebrews explains it in ceremonial terms to Jewish believers. In order to show the superiority of the new covenant over the old, and thereby wean the Christians away from the temple with its ceremonial system and priesthood, the superiority of Christ as the mediator over those who mediated the old covenant is established. Angels and Moses were but servants, and the priests were but men, mortals. He is the Son.[54] The Epistle opens with what may be termed a very definitive statement regarding His Sonship. In chapter 1 verses 1 to 3 there are three finite verbs, 'appointed', 'made' (created), and 'sat down'. These are in a historical sequence. The appointment of the Son as heir ante--dated creation. It was in eternity. As heirship is contingent upon Sonship it follows that His Sonship also ante-dated creation. It is eternal. This is confirmed, 7. 3; Melchizedek was 'made like unto the Son of God' in that, in the historical record, he has no beginning of days or end of life. This cancels out the suggestion, and interpretation, that the title 'Son' was one which was given to the Lord at His birth, or at His incarnation. 'It was His ages before the incarnation; this is the plain implication of the statement that God spake to us in His Son, Heb. 1. 1-2. He inherits the title Son as He inherits all things by the Father's eternal appointment'.[55] As the Son He is the effulgence of God's glory, and the express image of His character.

The Sonship in John's First Epistle. In this letter there are twenty-one references to the Son, and seven to the Son of God. It is evident that just as the sonship of Jesus of Nazareth was the rock of offence to the Jews initially, so it became the stumbling stone to those who were denying the faith at the close of the apostolic era. There were those who preached 'another Jesus', 2 Cor. 11. 4. They denied both His essential deity, and the reality of His humanity; Arianism, Docetism, Mormonism and the Kenosis Theory. Hence John very effectively combats both by

---

[54] Heb. 1. 1-3; 3. 1-6; 7. 28; 8. 6.
[55] F. F. BRUCE, *Hebrews*, pg. 8.

his affirmation that it is the 'blood of Jesus his Son' that cleanses, and that faith in Jesus as the Son of God is the smooth stone which brings down this Gnostic Goliath, giving the believer complete victory over the world in its opposition to the truth, 1 John 1. 7 RV; 5. 5. Anyone who denied the Son automatically denied the Father. Such a person is branded a liar and an antichrist, 2. 22, 23. It was this Sonship that was the target of Satan's temptation in the wilderness, as well as the taunt of the rulers when Jesus was on the cross. This citadel of the Christian faith – Jesus is the Son of God – is still the rock against which the enemy continues to marshal his assaults through the many cults that are propagated with such vigour in the West, and is militantly opposed by all oriental religions. This Satanic enmity and hatred of this truth should not surprise us, for the Son of God was manifested to destroy the works of the devil, 3. 8.[56]

The implications of the title are clear in the light of John 1. 1, 14. The Word who became flesh – the only begotten of the Father – is the One of whom three things are predicated in verse 1: eternal existence, distinct personality, and absolute Godhood; cp. Col. 1. 19; 2. 9. In Him all the attributes of deity in all their totality reside eternally.

'Dost thou believe on the Son of God?'; if so read John chapter 9 verse 38. But if not, read John chapter 3 verse 36; 1 John 2. 23.

The Son of Man - A. Naismith

Old Testament Occurrences and their Significance.

In the King James Version of the Old Testament, in addition to the ninety-three times, according to *Strong's Concordance*, by which the prophet Ezekiel is addressed, the title 'son of man' invariably alludes to the weakness and incompetence of man as a creature on earth. Human instability is emphasized in Balaam's address to Balak, Num. 23. 19. Man's inefficiency and sinfulness are the themes of the two verses in Job in which the title appears, 25. 6; 35. 8; his insignificance and unreliability in the occurrences in the Psalter, Pss. 144. 3; 146. 3; and his weakness and failure to fulfil his moral responsibility in Isaiah's

[56] Compare the other references to the Son of God: 1 John 4. 15; 5. 5, 10, 12, 13, 20.

prophecy, Isa. 51. 12; 56. 2. The angel Gabriel in his message to Daniel refers to man's lack of understanding and need for instruction, Dan. 8. 17.

In the Septuagint, with the one exception of Psalm 146 verse 3, both the words 'son' and 'man' are in the singular number in each occurrence. In Psalm 146 verse 3 both nouns are in the plural and could literally be rendered 'sons of men'. The definite article is absent from every Old Testament use of the title, including all in Ezekiel's prophecy.

Thus the 'son of man' is man on earth in whom, apart from the bestowal of grace and power by Jehovah, man's generic infirmity and frailty are apparent. In Jehovah's address to Ezekiel as 'son of man', God's design is to teach the prophet that, apart from the importance of his work as observer and recorder, he too was subject to all the weakness inherent in human nature.

Origin of the Title and its Implications. The Old Testament scriptures that are relevant to our Lord's application of the title to Himself during His life on earth are those in Psalm 8 verse 4, cited Hebrews chapter 2 verse 6, in Psalm 80 verse 17, and in Daniel 7 verse 13. The question, 'What is man?' indicates the insignificance of humanity before God; the words that follow, 'that thou art mindful of him', show mankind to be the object of divine consideration. 'Ben-adam', translated 'son of man', links man with earth and with our original forefather. Applied to the Lord Jesus, the phrases, 'made a little lower than the angels' and 'crowned with glory and honour' fittingly describe His self-humiliation and His exaltation. By faith the believer can now see the man, Jesus, who came to this earth in poverty, crowned with glory and honour because then He tasted death for everything. Man's lost glory has thus been restored by the Son of man to whom all things will be put in subjection according to the divine purpose. The sinless sharer of human weakness is to share divine glory in His coming kingdom as 'King of kings' and 'Lord of lords'.

The Targum attributes Asaph's words in Psalm 80 verse 17 to the Messiah, the person whom Jehovah has made strong for Himself. Psalm 110 can refer to no one other than our Lord Jesus: it opens with the statement, 'The LORD said unto my Lord, Sit thou at my right hand'. The prophet Daniel saw in a vision the Son of man come to the Ancient of days to receive everlasting dominion and an indestructible kingdom, Dan. 7. 13, 14. This prophetic scripture will have its fulfilment in Jesus Christ.

In the New Testament, 'the Son of man' is the designation that Christ most frequently applied to Himself while here on earth. In His use of it, with the exception of John chapter 5 verse 27, the definite article precedes both words 'son' and 'man'. It always relates Him to the earth and establishes His absolute identification with mankind. JOHN R. ROLLO wrote, 'The humanity of Jesus was real, genuine and true, naturally or physically like that of all men. His humanity was perfect morally, possessing the quality of sinlessness, unlike that of any other man'. In addition, it involves and implies the widest range of relationship, including all the peoples of the earth. Thus, though truly man, 'the Son of man' was devoid of the moral weakness that characterizes the human race.

The Jewish people understood the title to apply to the Messiah and linked it with Daniel's vision. Jesus, the Messiah rejected by man on earth, was, as 'the Son of man', directing His people's thoughts from the expected 'son of David' to His universal mission and ministry. He thus identified Himself with humanity in a way that manifested His deity. He daily rubbed shoulders with men of all classes, yet was morally and spiritually different from all. His heavenly pre-existence, earthly life of humility, and future glory are all wrapped up in the title 'Son of man'. In Him there was nothing local as to place, nothing transient as to time, and nothing merely national as to race.

Occurrences of the Title in the New Testament. The Gospel records show that Jesus used this designation eighty-four times – eighty-five if we include Mark chapter 13 verse 34 where the words, 'For the Son of man is' are in italics and therefore do not occur in the original manuscripts.[57] In the King James Version – in Matthew's Gospel it appears thirty-two times, in Mark fifteen times, in Luke twenty-six

---

[57] The title is not used in the Revised Version, Matt. 18. 11; 25. 13; Mark 13. 34; Luke 9. 56, and therefore there are only eighty-one occurrences in that version of the four Gospel records.

times and in John twelve times. Those interested in the several occurrences in detail may find them in a good concordance, in Appendix 98 of *The Companion Bible*, or on page 521 of *A Guide to the Gospels* by W. GRAHAM SCROGGIE.

There is an impressive contrast between the first and last uses of this designation by our Lord in the Gospels. The first is, 'The Son of man hath not where to lay his head', Matt. 8. 20; the last is, 'Now is the Son of man glorified, and God is glorified in him', John 13. 31. In these, poverty and glory are contrasted, the poverty of the Son of man and the glory of the Father and the Son.

The first and last occurrences in the New Testament also stand in striking contrast. We read, 'Upon the cloud one sat like unto the Son of man, having on his head a golden crown', Rev. 14. 14. When on earth He had not where to lay His head: in heaven His head is crowned with gold. The first and last mentions in each Gospel may also be profitably considered.[58]

Our Lord's last recorded use of the title to His disciples after Judas Iscariot had left the company occurs in John chapter 13 verse 31. The last time Jesus employed it before men of the world was in reply to Caiaphas the high priest; and in it He affirms accurately, yet briefly, His coming glory.

It is significant that, after Stephen's martyrdom, the designation 'Son of man' never passed into the language of the early church, and is not found in any of the canonical Epistles. Why is this? Is it not because the title was specially associated with the life of the Lord Jesus on earth? The writers of the Epistles, and the literature of the early church, view Him as glorified in heaven. Within four years of Christ's cross and resurrection, Stephen testified before his death that he saw 'the Son of man standing on the right hand of God', Acts 7. 56. This is the only other time that the designation so frequently used by Jesus is employed with the definite article before 'Son' and before 'man'.

---

[58] Compare and contrast, Matt. 8. 20 with 26. 64; Mark 2. 10 with 14. 62; Luke 5. 24 with 24. 7; John 1. 51 with 13. 31.

The relationship between Psalm 8 verse 4 and Hebrews chapter 2 verse 6 has already been established in the consideration of the Old Testament usage of the term. There remain only two other mentions of our Lord Jesus as 'Son of man' in the New Testament, both in the book of Revelation and both in visions, Rev. 1. 13; 14. 14. In each He appeared to John the beloved apostle; in both, Jesus glorified is seen to be like unto the Son of man, *homoion huiō anthrōpou.* In the glory of heaven He still bears the title He employed so often on earth, and it will still be His in His future advent as Judge of all the earth.

Occasions of its Use in Natural/Chronological Order

In the New Testament there seem to be just exactly a score of such, and their enumeration may be helpful. On some such occasions there will be reference made to more than one aspect of our Lord, but that which is most pronounced has been selected.

1. He is in heaven, John 3. 13, His real and permanent home, though He came to live on earth as a man.
2. He is the theme of prophetic scripture, Dan. 7. 13; Luke 18. 31.
3. The prophetic scriptures were fulfilled in all that He said and did, 18. 31.
4. He had a normal humanity, eating and drinking like most other men, Matt. 11. 19; Luke 7. 34.
5. Paul tells us, 2 Corinthians chapter 8 verse 9, that 'though he was rich, yet. . . he became poor', and poverty marked His life on earth, Matt. 8. 20; Luke 9. 58.
6. He was unknown and misunderstood by the men of His day, and He told them, 'When ye have lifted up the Son of man, then shall ye know that I am he'. The crowds were puzzled by His title.[59]
7. In all His words and deeds He claimed full authority on earth.[60]
8. He continually met with opposition to His teaching and to His claims, Matt. 12. 32; Luke 12. 10. Yet the officers whom the Pharisees sent to arrest Him said of Him, 'Never man spake like this man', John 7. 46.
9. He claimed to be a God-sent sign to His people, the Jews, Matt. 12. 39, 40; Luke 11. 30.
10. He spoke of Himself as a sower scattering the word of God

[59] Matt. 16. 13; John 8. 28; 12. 34.
[60] Mark 2. 10, 28; Luke 5. 24; 6. 5.

among men, Matt. 13. 37.

11. He came as the Saviour of men, seeking the lost and laying down His life for their salvation.[61]
12. He was nefariously betrayed by one of His followers, Judas Iscariot.[62]
13. He foretold His sufferings, persecution, rejection and death.[63]
14. He predicted His resurrection from the dead, Matt. 17. 9; Mark 9. 9, 31; the Son of man's dominion was unbroken by death.
15. He portrayed His ascension into heaven whence He had come to the earth, John 6. 62.
16. He was seen, glorified in heaven, by Stephen and by the apostle John, Acts 7. 56; Rev. 1. 13.
17. The most frequent use by our Lord of this designation is in connection with His second advent, its certainty, signs and suddenness.[64]
18. He uses the title to hail His coming glory.[65]
19. Because of His humanity, the prerogative of judgement is His at His advent.[66] When the Son of man judges the nations there will be a clear and complete division, the sheep on His right hand and the goats on His left.
20. The reward of reproach borne for His sake and for confessing Him before men will be bestowed by the Son of man, Luke 6. 22; 12. 8.

The above, with the scriptural references to them, are all connected with the designation, 'Son of man'. By its use, He presents Himself as a supra-mundane being, who has entered a sphere of earthly life in fulfilment of the purpose of His Father.

---

[61] Matt. 18. 11; 20. 28; Mark 10. 45; Luke 9. 56; Luke 19. 10; John 6. 27, 53.

[62] Matt. 17. 22; 20. 18; 26. 2, 24, 45; Mark 14. 21, 41; Luke 22. 22, 48.

[63] Matt. 17. 12; Mark 8. 31; 9. 12, 31; 10. 33; Luke 9. 22, 44; 24. 7; John 3. 14; 8. 28; 12. 23, 34.

[64] Matt. 10. 23; 16. 27, 28; 24. 27, 30, 37, 39, 44; 25. 13; 26. 64; Mark 13. 26; Mark 14. 62; Luke 9. 26; 12. 40; 17. 24, 26, 30; 18. 8; 21. 27.

[65] Matt. 19. 28; Luke 22. 69; John 1. 51; Rev. 14. 14.

[66] Matt. 13. 41; 25. 31; Luke 21. 36; John 5. 27.

The Lord - A. NAISMITH

A missionary colleague in India for many years used in the postage of all his letters an envelope with the words in bold lettering – 'Preaching peace by Jesus Christ: He is Lord of all'. Its purpose was to convey the tremendous fact that Jesus Christ is the universal Lord to a Hindu community which esteemed their god Krishna, one of the incarnations of Vishnu, to be lord of all India. In Imperial Rome the emperor claimed to be divine, and it was a crime to refuse to call him 'Lord'. For their refusal to do so, multitudes of Christians who firmly believed that the title 'Lord' belonged to One alone, suffered martyrdom.

Occurrences and Renderings of 'Lord'. On one occasion in two parallel passages in the New Testament, Matt. 22. 41-45; Luke 20. 41-44, the word 'Lord' in an Old Testament scripture was cited by the Lord Jesus Himself as a reference to His deity and His relationship to David. The citation was from Psalm 110 verse 1, where the Hebrew names are, 'The Lord [*Jehovah*] said unto my Lord [*Adon*], Sit thou at my right hand, until I make thine enemies thy footstool'. *Adonai* means 'Sovereign Lord', and is a 'plural of majesty'.

In the New Testament the Greek word *kurios* is rendered 'lord' 719 times, sometimes with a capital 'L' and sometimes without the capital. It is rendered 'sir' 13 times, and of these Jesus was addressed as 'sir' six times without the knowledge that the person to whom it was addressed was the Lord Jesus.[67] Once it is translated 'owner'. Twelve times, chiefly in our Lord's parables when He refers to others, *kurios* is rendered 'master', while twice 'Master' obviously refers to Jesus, Matt. 23. 8, 10.

In the book of Acts, the combinations, 'name of the Lord', 'word of the Lord', and 'way of the Lord' frequently recur, and these expressions are found to a lesser extent in the Epistles. In his letters Paul frequently employs the terms 'the Lord', 'the Lord Jesus Christ', 'Jesus Christ our Lord' and 'Christ Jesus our Lord'. Six times, chiefly in doxologies, God is spoken of as 'the God of peace', this being most frequently applied to Him. In only one such doxology Jesus is described as 'the Lord of peace', 2 Thess. 3. 16.

---

[67] John 4. 11, 15, 19, 49; 5. 7; 20. 15.

The expression 'the day of the Lord' occurs again and again in the Old Testament scriptures.[68] Twice in the New Testament the title 'Lord' with the Hebrew phrase 'of Sabaoth' occurs, whereas in the Old Testament the appellation is found many times, and always as 'the Lord of hosts'. There is a very interesting and significant similarity between the first two occurrences of the term, 1 Sam. 1. 3, 11, and the two uses of the title in the New Testament, Rom. 9. 29; Jas. 5. 4, as applied to a godly remnant and an afflicted people.

Jesus Christ is Lord. Isaiah wrote, addressing Judah in chapter 26 of his prophecy, 'O Lord our God, other lords beside thee have had dominion over us: but by thee only will we make mention of thy name', Isa. 26. 13.

For Judah, those other lords would be the rulers of the nations during the period of their captivity, the Babylonian, Medo-Persian, Grecian and Roman kings and emperors. In a moral sense the nation had been subject to many forces controlling the lives of its people such as lust, covetousness, pride, envy, malice, guile and slander. Before regeneration the believer too was brought into captivity to indwelling sin until he believed the proclamation, 'sin shall not have dominion over you'. Now our emancipator has become our master, and we address Him as Lord, as did the apostles and Mary and Martha in His life on earth, as did the dying thief at the cross, as did doubting Thomas at His resurrection, and as did Saul of Tarsus when the Saviour appeared to him in heavenly glory.

Several epithets applied to our Lord Jesus Christ enable us to trace chronologically His story from His first advent to His return in glory.

He is 'the second man . . . the Lord from heaven', 1 Cor. 15. 47. Heaven is the realm from which He came and to which He has returned. This is a claim no other member of the human race can make. We note that the Revised Version rendering is 'the second man is of heaven'. However, the number of manuscripts retaining the words 'the Lord' and the

---

[68] But in the New Testament only in: Acts 2. 20; 1 Thess. 5. 2; 2 Thess. 2. 2 RV; 2 Pet. 3. 10.

number omitting it are about equal.

He is 'Lord even of the sabbath day', Matt. 12. 8. Here the ministry of our Lord while here on earth is in view, for many of His acts of compassion and healing as He 'went about doing good' were performed on the Sabbath.

On the cross, despised and rejected, He is 'the Lord of glory', 1 Cor. 2. 8, whom the princes of this world crucified.

He is 'Lord both of the dead and living', for 'to this end Christ both died, and rose, and revived', Rom. 14. 9. Here His resurrection is in view. Jesus was declared to be the Son of God with power by the resurrection from the dead.

Now seated at the right hand of God, our exalted Saviour is 'the Lord of the harvest', Luke 10. 2, who, issuing His commands to the labourers and renewing the promise of His constant presence and help, is responsible for the service of each sower and reaper in the world's harvest field.

He is, and will remain all the time His people need Him, 'the Lord of Sabaoth', encouraging the revived remnant and strengthening His afflicted saints, Rom. 9. 29; Jas. 5. 4.

He will come again to the world that rejected Him, having 'on his vesture and on his thigh a name written, King of kings, and Lord of lords', Rev. 19. 16. Then every tongue shall confess that 'Jesus Christ is Lord, to the glory of God the Father', Phil. 2. 11. Philippians chapter 2 verses 5 to 11 is one of the great doctrinal statements of scripture. We believe that 'Jesus Christ the Lord' is the name that is above every name, for many men other than our Lord have borne the simple name of Jesus.

Christ Jesus my Lord, Phil. 3. 8. Consider now what the experience of the Lordship of Christ should mean for each and every believer.

1. The primary evidence of the recognition of Jesus as Lord is our belief in His deity, Matt. 22. 43-45; Luke 20. 42-44. Ten centuries before the Word became flesh, David prophetically called Him 'my

Lord': we who live in the Christian era recognize Him who, in accordance with Micah's prediction, was born in Bethlehem-Judah, to be 'God manifest in the flesh'.

2. Elisabeth, the cousin of the mother of Jesus, who was visited by the virgin before the birth of her own son John and of Mary's Son Jesus, called Mary 'the mother of my Lord', Luke 1. 43. Every true Christian today acknowledges the virgin birth of our Lord Jesus.
3. Confession with the mouth of 'Jesus as Lord', Rom. 10. 9 RV, and belief in His resurrection from the dead form the basis of our salvation individually. Apart from such confession and faith, none can claim Jesus as his or her Lord.
4. The step that follows confession with the mouth is the sanctification of Christ as Lord in the heart, 1 Pet. 3. 15 RV. This inward expression 'in your hearts' has practical and visible results in various spheres of life. In his exhortation Peter quotes Isaiah chapter 8 verse 13, 'Sanctify the Lord of hosts himself'. Instead of the Lord of hosts being sanctified, Christ is to be sanctified in our hearts as Lord.

In the New Testament there are three passages in which the title 'Lord' is applied to Jesus Christ more frequently than in any other New Testament scriptures within the same number of verses. In Romans chapter 14 verses 6 to 9 it occurs eight times in four verses; it is repeated seven times in ten verses, Col. 3. 16-25; and the Lord is spoken of seven times in ten verses, 1 Cor. 11. 23-32. When we sanctify Christ as Lord in our hearts, His authority is seen in our eating and drinking, in our life and in our death. It is stamped, too, on every relationship of life, and it comes into prominence in our observance of the Lord's Supper.

1. The Lord Himself will be the object of the believer's worship. It was so with the man blind from birth to whom the Lord restored the faculty of sight, John 9. 36-38, and with the apostle Thomas so often called the doubter, John 20. 28.
2. The assurance that we have none in heaven but Jesus our redeemer whom God has made 'both Lord and Christ', Acts 2. 36, and that He is our advocate with the Father and our great High Priest, is imparted to all who believe. Thus we depend upon 'the Lord Christ' in heaven for all our service for Him on earth, Col. 3. 24.

3. In witnessing to the Lord, as Jesus ordained, Acts 1. 8, Christ is the centre and circumference of our message, 'We preach not ourselves, but Christ Jesus the Lord', 2 Cor. 4. 5.

Thus every realm of Christian life and experience is regulated and controlled by Christ Jesus the Lord.

'He's the Lord of life and glory, now exalted far on high,
And we love to tell the story of His coming down to die;
And He's coming, quickly coming, all His glories to display:
We shall see Him and be like Him through heaven's eternal day'.

The Lamb and the Shepherd - K. T. C. Morris

It is natural to associate a shepherd with a lamb, but very strange to think of a person as being both shepherd and lamb at the same time. This is part of the wonder of the person of our Lord Jesus Christ. He who was eternally God, the shepherd of Israel, became really man so that He might be offered as a lamb in sacrifice for sin.

The disciples first knew Him as a man, the prophet of God, the Messiah. They exclaimed, 'What manner of man is this?'. But in time each true disciple came, like Thomas, to own Him as 'my Lord and my God'.

The Lamb of God. When John the Baptist cried, 'Behold the lamb of God, which taketh away the sin of the world', John 1. 29, his hearers would have thought of Abraham's words, 'God will provide himself a lamb for a burnt offering', Gen. 22. 8, or of the passover lamb that sheltered their sinful ancestors from judgement in Egypt, or of the lambs offered every morning and evening in the temple. The lamb was especially the animal for sacrifice. Peter says that we have been redeemed with the 'precious blood of Christ, as of a lamb without blemish and without spot', 1 Pet. 1. 19. This turns our thought to the Old Testament sacrifices. Each animal had to be without blemish within or spot without. Each had to be perfectly healthy, without deformity or superfluity, Lev. 22. 19-25. Christ's life on earth demonstrated that He was perfect. Men acknowledged, 'Never man spake like this man', John 7. 46. Thus He was marked out as the lamb, 'foreordained before the foundation of the world'. He was God's appointed provision for our need long before sin reared its ugly head.

But other animals were sacrificed also: bullocks, suggesting strength and unwearied labour; rams with their reserves of strength and virility; goats, noted for their sure-footedness; and doves, gentle and mournful. All spoke of Christ. But the lamb speaks particularly of the meekness and gentleness of Christ, of His ready submission to the will of God, and of His yieldingness to the cruelties of men. He was 'brought as a lamb to the slaughter, and as a sheep before her shearers is dumb, so he openeth not his mouth', Isa. 53. 7. He who taught us to 'resist not evil' was ever an example, returning good for evil. Later John, looking upon Jesus as He walked cried again, 'Behold the Lamb of God'. One may often learn much of a man's spirit from the manner of his walk. It was the demeanour, the carriage and conduct of our Lord that impressed men as He passed step by step through this world. His humble yet majestic progress proved His suitability to be the lamb for sacrifice. He was never moved to vengeful thought or retaliatory action. Moving among unclean men He remained undefiled Himself. Though really man He was different from all others.

The Good Shepherd. The Lord Jesus repeatedly warned His disciples of His impending crucifixion, but He never once referred to Himself as the Iamb. More than any other He doubtless had a vivid sense of what it meant to Isaac to be bound to the altar on Mount Moriah, and to see his father's hand raised to slay him. There was something unspeakably sacred about that transaction. The faithful trained servants of Abraham had to be left at the foot of the mount. Yet the Saviour knew that there would be something far more sacred when He would become the lamb slain at the cross. No creature could enter into what took place in the dark hours when God's sword awoke and smote the shepherd, Zech. 13. 7.

Yet the Saviour twice assures us, 'I am the good shepherd', John 10. 11-15. First, He says, 'The good shepherd giveth his life for the sheep'. It was costly to be a good shepherd. It meant facing the lion and the bear; it meant going over the mountains to find lost sheep. Christ assured His own that unlike the selfish and cowardly hireling, He Himself would never fail them. A lamb cannot lay down its life, but Christ speaks of the length to which He will voluntarily go for the sake of His sheep. He will not only risk His life, but will lay it down for them.

Second, He says, 'I know my sheep, and am known of mine'. He knows the true from the mere professor. He knows those who love Him in sincerity. The phrase 'my sheep' is an echo of the repeated word of the Lord in Ezekiel chapter 34, 'I will seek out my sheep. . . I will save my flock', vv. 11-31. He distinguishes them from the 'fat cattle' who push with their horns, but more. It is not just that He calls us each by name; He understands the idiosyncrasies, the peculiar problems and needs of each. He knows the sheep intimately even as the Father knows Him; see the words 'even as', John 10. 15 RV.

His claim to be the good Shepherd was a claim to deity, for the eternal One, Jehovah, was the shepherd of Israel, Ps. 80. 1. His words recall Psalm 23 verse 1, 'The Lord is my shepherd'. He is saying that all the provision, protection, and comfort of the psalm they would find in Him. 'I will feed my flock, and I will cause them to lie down, saith the Lord God. I will seek that which was lost, and bring again that which was driven away, and will bind up that which was broken, and will strengthen that which was sick', Ezek. 34. 15, 16.

The Great Shepherd and the Chief Shepherd. All is secured to the believer today because the God of peace 'brought again from the dead our Lord Jesus, that great shepherd of the sheep', Heb. 13. 20. In Revelation we see Him as the little lamb slain and as the living shepherd. Concerning saints coming out of the great tribulation we read, 'for the lamb which is in the midst of the throne shall be their shepherd, and shall guide them unto fountains of waters of life', Rev. 7. 17 RV. He still goes before and the sheep follow.

You have returned, says Peter, to 'the Shepherd and Bishop of your souls', 1 Pet. 2. 25. The work of a shepherd and of an overseer are much akin; the Chief Shepherd has given some men as shepherds ('pastors', is really the same word; Jer. 3. 15; Eph. 4. 11), and elders must so care for the flock that when He appears they may receive a crown of glory, 1 Pet. 5. 1-4. They must give account to Him.

In that day He, who pledged that His sheep will never perish, will say again in resurrection triumph, 'Of them which thou gavest me I have lost none', John 10. 28; 17. 12; 18. 9.

Our Lord's Incarnation and Virgin Birth - F. F. BRUCE

'"What think ye of Christ?" is the test
To try both your state and your scheme:
You cannot be right in the rest,
Unless you think rightly of Him'.

JOHN NEWTON was thinking primarily of a man or woman's personal relationship to Christ when he wrote the verses which begin with these lines. But a right personal relationship to Christ and right thinking about Him, doctrinally speaking, cannot be dissociated from each other – as indeed Newton went on to point out.

The mystery of our Lord's person filled His disciples with wonder. 'What manner of man is this?' they asked. And not until the Holy Spirit came to guide them into all the truth did they receive an adequate answer to their question. Even then the mystery was not removed; it remains as true today as it was when our Lord spoke the words 'no man knoweth the Son, but the Father', Matt. 11. 27. But the answer which they received to their question, under the Holy Spirit's guidance, finds its ultimate expression in the opening words of John's Gospel, 'In the beginning was the Word, and the Word was with God, and the Word was God... and the Word became flesh, and dwelt among us ... No man hath seen God at any time; the only begotten Son, which is in the bosom of the Father, he hath declared him', John 1. 1, 14, 18 RV. In the light of this revelation, John and his fellow-disciples could look back with understanding on words and actions of their Lord which at the time they had utterly failed to comprehend.

That our Lord Jesus Christ is the eternal Son of God, who became man for our salvation, is the historic Christian faith going back to the apostolic witness itself. He is altogether God and altogether man, His human nature is as perfect as His divine nature, and He unites Godhead and manhood in one person. We cannot think of Him as a dual personality, and we should not yield to the temptation of saying that He did or said such-and-such as God, and did or said something else as man. Such distinctions may seem to be effective in preaching, but they represent the thin end of a very dangerous wedge. Since His coming into the world, in all that He is as well as in all His actions and words, it is the God-man, the Word become flesh, that we see, and seeing Him we see the Father.

Yet some Christians may feel that it is difficult to avoid seeing our Lord as in some sense a 'dual personality' or as acting in some capacities as God and in others as man. The perfection of His Godhead and manhood, on the one hand, and the unity of His person, on the other, can best be safeguarded by the classical Christian recognition of the two natures in one person. That in some cases His deity is more prominent, and in others His humanity, is true. Yet the humanity is never entirely excluded from the former, nor the deity from the latter. To take one crucial example: God is immortal, but Jesus died. We have scriptural warrant for believing that He became man in order that He might die, Heb. 2. 14. The statement that 'God died' belongs to the poetic licence of hymns and not to sober theological prose. Yet, while it was the man Christ Jesus who died, it remains true that He never revealed God more fully than in the hour of death, 'God was in Christ reconciling the world unto himself', 2 Cor. 5. 19. We must in the end recognize with humility that the poverty of our thought and language will never do justice to the person of Him whom 'no man knoweth . . . but the Father', Matt. 11. 27.

When we speak of our Lord's incarnation, we refer to the fact that He became Man – became Man without ceasing to be God. His Incarnation is a miracle, a unique miracle; nothing of the sort has ever happened before or since. It would not be surprising if something of its miraculous character were manifested in the means by which it took place. And the witness of the New Testament is that it did take place by miraculous means, for our Lord, as the ancient creed puts it, 'was conceived by the Holy Ghost, born of the Virgin Mary'.

We should indeed keep our Lord's incarnation and His virgin birth distinct in our minds. His incarnation is the **fact** that He became man; His virgin birth is the **means** by which He became man. There are people who accept the incarnation but deny the virgin birth, just as there are others (Muslims, for example) who accept His virgin birth but deny the incarnation. God could, had He so willed, have adopted some other means for sending His Son into the world as man. But the testimony of holy scripture is that the virgin birth was the means which He adopted, and to accept the one while denying the other is to put asunder two things which God has joined together. And it may well be asked whether those who accept the incarnation while denying the virgin birth really believe in the same kind of incarnation as do those who accept both.

There is certainly a fitness in the virgin birth as the means of the incarnation. Our Lord came forth from God in a **sense** in which no one else ever did; does it not follow that He came forth from God in a **way** in which no one else ever did? (This way of putting it is not original; it comes from JAMES DENNEY.) Besides, as we trace the Christian faith back to its foundations, we find the two doctrines – the fact of the incarnation, and the virgin birth as the means of the incarnation – held side by side. The fact and the means alike are miraculous through and through. It is irrelevant, and indeed impossible, to give any explanation of the virgin birth in terms of biological parthenogenesis; it cannot be brought within the framework of any natural process. Here God is supremely at work, and the only human agency was that of the submissive maiden of Nazareth who said, 'Behold, the handmaid of the Lord; be it unto me according to thy word', Luke 1. 38.

But for those to whom the holy scriptures are the ultimate authority, the virgin birth is amply attested as the means by which the eternal Word became flesh. Matthew and Luke both bear witness to it, and there is no alternative account in all the scriptures. Matthew and Luke's accounts of our Lord's nativity are completely independent; there is no question of one having drawn upon the other. Indeed, so independent are they that well-known problems arise for those who try to dovetail the details of the two narratives together. All the more impressive, then, are those points on which the two agree. Of these points three demand special mention: (a) our Lord was born in Bethlehem; (b) He was born to Mary, who was betrothed to a member of the family of David named Joseph; (c) He was conceived within her while she was yet a virgin, by the supernatural working of the Holy Spirit. Of these three points of agreement it is the third that constitutes the miracle.

The scriptures testify to Christ. Apart from their testimony, our knowledge of Him would be infinitesimal, and our knowledge of the way of salvation through faith in Him would be non-existent. Moreover, their testimony concerning Him is one, and self-consistent. The Christ to whom they bear witness as our Saviour and Lord is a supernatural Christ and yet an intensely human Christ, Son of God and Son of man. None ever lived or died as He did; none ever rose from the dead as He did. The course of His life on earth was unique, the consummation of His life on earth was unique; it is but fitting that the beginning of His life on earth should have been unique. And unique it was, for the Christ to whom the scriptures bear witness is the virgin-born Christ.

'Christ, the Son of God, became man, by taking to Himself a true body, and a reasonable soul, being conceived by the power of the Holy Ghost, in the womb of the Virgin Mary, and born of her, yet without sin.' – *Westminster Shorter Catechism, Answer* 22.

The Perfect Humanity of Christ - E. L. LOVERING

Preliminary. The stability of a building depends upon the reliability of its foundation, and we may well ask upon what foundation does the whole structure and fabric of the Christian faith depend.

Mark writes in the first verse of his Gospel, 'The beginning of the gospel of Jesus Christ, the Son of God', and it is surely here that the whole Christian doctrine finds its source. The message of the angel to Mary was, 'Thou shalt call his name Jesus, for he shall save his people from their sins', and if there is to be a Saviour for mankind, there must be a 'man to die', for God had decreed that without the shedding of blood is no remission of sins. But the psalmist wrote that 'none can by any means redeem his brother, nor give to God a ransom for him', 49. 7, for the sacrifice must be as perfect as God Himself. Here then must be the basis of salvation, a person who is perfect man and very God.

Job complained, 'Neither is there any daysman betwixt us, that might lay his hand upon us both', Job. 9. 33. But when the fullness of the time came, 'God sent forth his Son, born of a woman, born under the law, that he might redeem them which were under the law, that we might receive the adoption of sons', Gal. 4. 4, 5 RV.

Like the pillars of stability and strength, Jachin and Boaz, which in the days of Solomon stood before the temple, so the perfect humanity and absolute deity of the Lord Jesus stand upon the threshold of the glorious structure revealed to faith's vision. May we, therefore, consider the perfect humanity of the Saviour.

The Mystery. Let it be said at the outset that 'without controversy, great is the mystery of godliness: God was manifest in the flesh', 1 Tim. 3. 16, and on this declaration faith must rest where reason fails. When the angel announced to Mary the glad tidings of the Saviour's birth, she herself asked, 'How shall this be?' and, though reason could find no logical answer to the question, her faith found perfect repose as 'the bondmaid of the Lord, and . . . according to thy word', Luke 1. 38 RVmg.

I quote C. H. MACKINTOSH: 'The truth respecting Christ's humanity must be received with Scriptural accuracy, held with spiritual energy, guarded with holy jealousy, and confessed with heavenly power. If we are wrong as to this, we cannot be right as to anything. It is a grand, vital, fundamental truth, and if it be not received, held, guarded, and confessed, as God revealed it in His Holy Word, the entire superstructure must be unsound'.

Let us then beware of mystic theory in this subject and seek to abide by spiritual accuracy.

Some Heresies. There have been very ancient and numerous heresies in connection with the humanity of our Lord. The Docetist denied the reality of His body; some held that it was a body only in appearance; others that it was of a peculiar heavenly texture. The Apollinarians denied that He had a human soul. The Monophysites held that there is only 'one nature' in Christ. The Monothelites held that although our Lord had two natures, He had but 'one will'; thus they denied His perfect humanity, for His human nature must have had a human will.

Scriptural Accuracy. When God sent forth His Son, He did not create an alliance of two persons. He who was born in Bethlehem, grew and waxed strong in spirit, suffered and died at Calvary, was the One who said, 'Before Abraham was, I am', John 8. 58. He it was who had glory by the Father's side before the world was, 17. 5, and, though He was 'in the form (i.e., possessed the manifested essence) of God', 'took the form of a bondservant', and obeyed 'even unto death', Phil. 2. 6, 8; He is God, He became man. 'And the Word became flesh, and dwelt [tabernacled, pitched His tent] among us (and we beheld His glory, glory as of the only begotten from the Father) full of grace and truth', John 1. 14 RV.

Reality of His Manhood. Christ's manhood is not a strange manhood alien to our own. He 'was in all points tempted like as we are, yet without sin', Heb. 4. 15. 'For verily not of angels doth he take hold, but he taketh hold of the seed of Abraham. Wherefore it behoved him in all things to be made like unto his brethren', Heb. 2. 16, 17 RV. He becomes complete and perfect man, possessing body, soul, and spirit, for in the garden of Gethsemane He said, 'My soul is exceeding sorrowful, even unto death', Matt. 26. 38; and on the cross, 'Father, into thy hands I commend my spirit', Luke 23. 46.

Luke further portrays for us the fact that our Lord Jesus as a child, Greek, little child, 'grew and waxed strong, [becoming full of, RVmg] filled with wisdom; and the grace of God was upon him', Luke 2. 40 RV. He is asking questions, and receiving instruction; then from boyhood to maturity, 'Jesus advanced in wisdom and stature, and in favour with (by the side of) God and men', Luke 2. 52 RV.

At the words of the centurion 'he marvelled', Matt. 8. 10, at finding such great faith outside Israel; at the death of Lazarus the Jews seeing Him weep said, 'Behold how he loved him', John 11. 35, 36. He knew real temptation and hunger in the wilderness; real weariness as He sat and talked with the woman at Sychar's well; and real thirst, pain, and anguish upon the cross.

He was both angry and grieved at the hardness of men's hearts, Mark 3. 5, and rejoiced 'in the Holy Spirit' because the profound things of the kingdom of God were clear to 'babes' though hidden from 'the wise and prudent', Luke 10. 21 RV.

Perfection of His Manhood. Testimonies to the perfection of His manhood come from all quarters of society. Pilate beholds the man in whom is found no fault at all; the hardened centurion witnessing before the cross sees one who was indeed a righteous man, whilst from the lips of the dying criminal comes the rebuke to his fellow, 'We indeed justly .

. . but this man hath done nothing amiss', 23. 41.
To us, He is the chiefest among ten thousand and the altogether lovely One, S. of S. 5. 9, 16.

> 'Fullness divine in Thee I see,
> Wonderful Man of Calvary!'

The Sinless Christ . . . the Impeccable Christ* - G. S. Beck

The subject of our article, which simply means, 'Christ was not able to sin', is a truth that needs to be stated firmly, for we are living in days when, in certain quarters, Christ's sinless impeccability is under severe attack. Some will know teachers both past and present, though teaching that Christ did not sin, teach that as He was human as well as divine, He could have sinned! In other words, He was not impeccable! The problem is that these teachers divide the person of Christ suggesting that as God He could not sin, but as man he could have sinned. The Lord Jesus Christ is one divine person, with two perfect natures, and what He could not do in His Godhood, He could not do in His manhood. At all times and in every circumstance of life, He was 'God manifest in flesh', 1 Tim. 3. 16.

To support the scriptural position that Christ was impeccable we will look at Christ's incarnation, a truth that has two sides. The Lord Jesus Christ is fully God and fully man.

Firstly, let us look at Him in His deity: the One who is described as the 'great God and our Saviour Jesus Christ', Titus 2. 13; the One who is the object of human and angelic worship.[69] He does what only God can do, such as the creation of the universe.[70] Again, He does what only God can do in regard to the matter of forgiveness of sin, and also the judging of men at the final judgement. [71] He is addressed in prayer.[72] He also possesses divine attributes, such as omnipresence,[73] omniscience,[74]

---

[69] Phil. 2. 9-11; Heb. 1. 6.
[70] John 1. 3; Col. 1. 16; Heb. 1. 2.
[71] Mark 2. 1-12; Col. 3. 13; John 5. 22; Acts 10. 42; 2 Thess. 1. 7-9.
[72] 1 Cor. 1. 2; 16. 22; 2 Cor. 12. 8.
[73] Heb. 1. 3; Eph. 4. 6.
[74] Rev. 2. 23.

omnipotence,[75] and immutability.[76] Further, the fullness of the Godhead dwells in Him[77] and He bears, and is given, titles that are given alone to God in the Old Testament, Isa. 44. 6; cp. Rev. 1. 17. He is the co-author of divine blessing.[78] Further, He describes angelic beings as His own.[79] In all these, we have the Lord Jesus Christ as fully God in His deity.

The scriptures also speak of His humanity, 'the man Christ Jesus', 1 Tim. 2. 5, and His humanity is beautifully brought before us throughout the New Testament. In Matthew chapter 4 verse 2, we have the Lord Jesus experiencing hunger in the wilderness, and we see He knew weariness and thirst at Sychar's well.[80] He wept tears of sympathy at the death of Lazarus.[81] When we come to the Garden of Gethsemane, we see Him in agony.[82] Coming to the apex of His sufferings at the cross, He bled and died, for it is here we see the fullness of His humanity for though God cannot die, He who died on the cross was God manifest in flesh, 1 Tim. 3. 16. It is important to distinguish things which differ. Truly the hymn-writer was right in this matter when he wrote, 'Verily God yet became truly human – lower than angels – to die in our stead', H. d'A. CHAMPNEY. And truly we can say, fully man as to His humanity in all aspects yet with one essential difference, 'sin apart', Heb. 4. 15. Peter testified to the fact that the Lord 'did no sin', 1 Pet. 2. 22, supported by the Apostle Paul who states that He 'knew no sin', 2 Cor. 5. 21, confirmed by John who wrote that 'in Him is no sin', 1 John 3. 5. When the Lord Himself speaks on the subject He attests His impeccability when He challenges, 'Which of you convinceth me of sin?' John 8. 46. He had a conscience that was clear of sin, 'The prince of this world cometh, and hath nothing in me', John 14. 30. Satan had no claim upon Christ, for He was impeccable; never sinned nor could sin.

Again, in Christ there was no inherent sin, 1 Pet. 1. 19. He was 'without blemish and without spot', the One who is described as 'holy, harmless,

[75] Matt. 28. 18-20.
[76] Heb. 13. 8.
[77] Col. 1. 19; 2. 9.
[78] Rev. 1. 4, 5; Titus 1. 4.
[79] Matt. 13. 41.
[80] John 4. 6, 7; cp. John 19. 28.
[81] John 11. 35.
[82] Luke 22. 43-46.

undefiled, separate from sinners', Heb. 7. 26. In all this, though truly human He was so unlike us. There was nothing within that Holy One to respond to sin, for Luke refers to Him as 'that Holy One who is to be born', Luke 1. 35 NKJV. He had no desire to engage in sin for, as the Bible shows, Christ said, 'I do always those things that please him', John 8. 29.

In conclusion, we have sought to show that the scriptures deny that Christ could have sinned, for sinful thinking and actions are absent in the person of the Lord Jesus Christ.

Christ as Prophet - A. T. SHEARMAN

All Quotations are taken from the Revised Version

The role of the prophet in the nation of Israel was an important one. The office involved standing as the mouthpiece of God to the people. Prophetic exercise was usually a sign of times of spiritual decline in the nation. The prophets were sent from God to make the people aware of their sin and departure. They were sent to call the nation to repentance. It is well to understand that prophecy is not always associated with prediction, that is, foretelling future events. The prophet **forth**-told, told forth the mind of God, and he was a spiritual link among the people for the understanding of divine revelation. In the book of Samuel he is referred to as a 'seer', 1 Sam. 9. 9, which means one who sees with the natural eye. Yet in its application to Samuel, it had deeper implications. Whatever shades of meaning are included in the word, it was true of the days before Christ that God spoke unto the fathers by the prophets, Heb. 1. 1, 2. It is also noteworthy that there were companies and schools of prophets, indicating circles of those who were trained in prophetic thought and wisdom.

Deuteronomy chapter 18 verses 15 to 22 has an important bearing on the office of the prophet, especially in relation to the Lord Jesus Christ. Here Moses outlines the kind of ministry attached to the ideal prophet. He would be **raised up from among the people**, v. 15; thus he would be in touch with contemporary needs and conditions. He would **stand between the people and God** in His transcendence, v. 16. The **words of God would be in his mouth** – he would speak by divine command, v. 18. **Responsibility would be upon the people to listen**, v. 19.

Fulfilment of the word would be the sign of authority, vv. 21-22. The words 'like unto me', v. 15, show us the character of Moses as the prophet among his people, cp. Hos. 12. 13. It would seem that here we have the pattern for the true prophetic office.

Many modern writers do not see in this passage any direct reference to the Lord Jesus in His office as prophet. But those who appreciate rightly His excellent character, cannot but see in Him the fulfilment to perfection of each office of prophet, priest and king. Acts chapter 3 verses 22-26 makes abundantly clear that the words of Moses were fulfilled in Christ. The days of the inauguration of the church were unique days indeed. Peter shows how 'these days' were the burden of much prophetic ministry beginning with Samuel, and continuing with those who followed afterwards, v. 24. Notice how the Jews of that day are referred to as the sons of the prophets, v. 25. And at the heart of Peter's thinking is Christ, for, 'Unto you first God, having raised up his Servant, sent him to bless you', v. 26.

Christ Came as the Great Fulfiller of Prophecy

Matthew's Gospel presents Him as such. Often in this Gospel the writer uses such words as 'that it might be fulfilled which was spoken by the Lord through the prophet'. This is so in relation to **His birth**, 1. 22; cp. 2. 6. Regarding **the location of His public ministry**, He fulfilled the word of Isaiah, Isa. 9. 1-2; Matt. 4. 14-16. Again, regarding **the character of His ministry**, prophecy is quoted, 12. 17-21. So it is with **His rejection and death**. On His journey with the two disciples to Emmaus, 'beginning from Moses and from all the prophets, he interpreted to them in all the scriptures the things concerning himself', Luke 24. 27. It is well to enquire the true significance of this. We say, quite rightly, that fulfilled prophecy gives divine authority to the mission of Christ. His pathway was prepared by prophecy. But deeper still, these fulfilments gave confirmation to the authenticity of the prophetic office in times before He came. For many prophets there was no credence given to their words during their lifetime. Their voices went unheard and were often rejected. It is good for us to realize that, coming into the world as the fulfilment of the ideal of the prophetic office, Christ gave approval and credence to every God-given prophetic mission in the fulfilment of their word in Himself. This is a great truth.

Christ Came as the Great Revealer of the Mind of God

All those tests of authenticity given as the ideal of the prophetic office were found in Him. It is clear in several places in the Gospels that 'the prophet' was expected by the people. John's Gospel records how the Pharisees asked John the Baptist if he was 'the prophet', 1. 21. When the multitude heard the words of Jesus they said, 'This is of a truth the prophet', 7. 40. The prophecy of Moses spoken so long ago, could have laid the foundation for such an expectation. John presents Christ as the Word – the Word eternal, with God, and yet made flesh, dwelling among men, 1. 1-18. In the world He came to reveal all that men in their sins needed to know about the purpose of God in salvation. And His voice was the voice of the true prophet. Notice John 3. 31-34. The Son reveals that He came 'from above', and therefore His status is 'above all'. Hence the things seen and heard in this realm form the burden of His message, v. 32. Thus He could say, 'For he whom God hath sent speaketh the words of God: for he giveth not the Spirit by measure', v. 34. Here is the qualification of the true prophetic office. So in 7. 14-16, as the source of His teaching was questioned, Jesus could say, 'My teaching is not mine, but his that sent me'. Again in 12. 49, 'For I spake not from myself; but the Father which sent me, he hath given me a commandment, what I should say, and what I should speak'. It is good to ponder these claims in the light of Deuteronomy chapter 18.

In the exercise of His office, Christ was the true forth-teller of the mind of God, and also the foreteller of His purpose. The test of the value of the predictive words of Christ can be applied without reserve. Concerning His own mission, He could state what would be its end. He foretold His own death and resurrection. His prophecies of the end times did not contradict the prophecies that had gone before, but confirmed and amplified them. Matthew chapter 24 contains the Olivet discourse, the answer of the Lord Jesus to His disciples concerning their question of the end times. Some of them would live to see the 'fulfilment' of His words concerning the initial judgement on Jerusalem, and its destruction by Titus and the Romans. As he told of the Son of man 'coming on the clouds of heaven with power and great glory', v. 30, He not only foretold His coming at the climax of the ages, but He gave confirmation to the expectation of Jewish prophets expressed many years before, cp. Dan. 7. 13, 14.

It is good to review the ministry of the Lord Jesus in the light of the prophetic office. Many of His contemporaries considered Him, rather nebulously, as 'a prophet', or 'one of the prophets', Mark 6. 15; 8. 28. The Lord Himself remarked poignantly that, as had been the case with many before Him, 'A prophet is not without honour, save in his own country, and among his own kin, and in his own house', 6. 14. On entering Jerusalem in a manner fulfilling Zechariah chapter 9 verse 9, many expressed the conviction that 'this is the prophet, Jesus, from Nazareth of Galilee', Matt. 21. 11. Even the two on the road to Emmaus spoke of Him as 'Jesus of Nazareth, which was a prophet mighty in deed and word before God and all the people', Luke 24. 19. One deed in particular linked Him with Moses in the popular mind, the feeding of the five thousand. Although Moses did not give Israel the bread out of heaven, after this miracle the people seeing the sign said, 'This is of a truth the prophet that cometh into the world', John 6. 14.

As in everything else associated with Him, our Lord fulfilled the prophetic office to perfection. None of His words fell to the ground, nor will they ever lack fulfilment. We can say with those of old, 'Never man so spake', 7. 46. And to those that hear them there is blessing. To those who refuse them, those very words will form the basis of their judgement, 12. 47, 48.

Christ was 'Made' - H. PALMIERI

It may be profitable to meditate upon seven passages where (in the King James Version) the word 'made' is applied to the Lord Jesus Christ, after making it clear that He was not actually 'made' anything. But since the phraseology is so familiar, we retain the word for our present purpose, after remarking that the idea is rather that He 'became' these things and not that He was 'made' them. Moreover, He 'became' without for a moment ceasing to be, what He ever was, very God of very God.

1. **'Of a woman',** Gal. 4. 4 – *INCARNATION.* This is the most startling doctrine ever announced to the world. It sets forth the Creator becoming man by the door of being 'made of a woman'. In this, He seems only to be a mere man, but not so. He was the God-man. His conception was unique. There never was, nor will there ever be, another like it. The angelic announcement to the virgin states this unique mode of

conception – 'The Holy Ghost shall come upon thee, and the power of the Highest shall overshadow thee: therefore also that holy thing which shall be born of thee shall be called the Son of God', Luke 1. 35. It has been said, and rightly so, that there is a special signification attached to this expression, 'made of a woman'. Paul here distinguishes the Lord's birth from all others. If not, why state a known fact of common experience? Would not that be wasting words? Surely this is not the case. Have you ever read a biography which stated 'he was born of a woman'? No, and there is no reason to. Here Paul is testifying to His divine pre-existence as the Eternal Son and by supernatural birth becoming man. This doctrine then can be told briefly. God has become man in the person of the Lord Jesus Christ.

'Amazing, that the Christ of God,
The Lord's Anointed King,
To take the guilty rebel's place,
To put away his sin,
And sinners ransomed by His blood
Back unto God to bring,
Should come to earth as Jesus –
The lowly Nazarene'.

2. **'Of the seed of David'**, Rom. 1. 3 – *DELINEATION.* Matthew tells us that the Lord Jesus Christ is the Son of David, and as such He is the king who is to reign on the throne of David, Isa. 9. 6, 7. He descended from David through His mother, the Virgin Mary, who was Heli's daughter. This being the case, He had full legal title to the throne. 'Consonant with his purpose to set forth the Christ in His kingly majesty as the One "born King of the Jews", Matthew traces the royal lineage from Abraham through 'David the king'. Luke, whose object was to delineate the glory of Christ's humanity as the Son of man, traces His ancestry back to "Adam, the son of God", Luke 3. 23-38. In both cases, the genealogy was essential, the one to prove His kingly claims, cp. John 18. 37, and the other to show that His humanity belonged to the race', A. E. LONG.

'All nations soon shall praise Him,
And speak His wondrous fame,
When Christ the Lord's Anointed
Shall take His power and reign;

All that hath breath shall praise Him,
His Name alone shall be
Through heaven and earth exalted,
And praised eternally'.

3. '**Like unto His brethren',** Heb. 2. 17 – *IDENTIFICATION.* Here we have one of the main purposes of the incarnation. The object of His being 'made like unto his brethren' was for the work of propitiation and that He might be a merciful and faithful High Priest. In order for Him to take hold of the seed of Abraham (believers on Him), it was imperative that He should be 'made like unto his brethren'. This verse then teaches the position that our Lord Jesus Christ assumed as the One who alone could come to the help of poor helpless, hopeless and hell-bound sinners. And in order to provide salvation for mankind, He had to become man. 'For verily the Lord did not undertake the cause of angels, but that of the seed of Abraham, and in order to proclaim the work that was necessary for them and to represent them efficaciously and really before God, He must needs put Himself into the position and the circumstances into which that seed were found, though not the state they were personally in' JND.

'Though in the very form of God,
With heavenly glory crowned,
Thou didst partake of human flesh,
Beset with sorrows round.
Thou wouldst like sinful man be made
In everything but sin,
That we as like Thee might become,
As we unlike have been'.

J. Stennett

4. **'Himself of no reputation',** Phil. 2. 7 – *HUMILIATION.* The blessed Christ of God emptied Himself that we believers might be filled. What humiliation! He could go no lower. Indeed, He 'was stripped of all His glory and His rights, at Calvary, that we might be clothed and stand before our God in all the infinite worth and beauty of His own dear Son'. He was rich, and for our sakes became poor; He had not where to lay His head; He had no money to pay the tax; no colt to ride upon; no place in which to keep the Passover; and no grave in which to be buried.

'Oh, what wondrous love and mercy –
Thou didst lay Thy glory by;
And for us didst come from heaven
As the Lamb of God to die!

Thou wast poor that we might be
Rich in glory, Lord, with Thee'.

5. **'A curse',** Gal. 3. 13 – *DEGRADATION.* What a wonderful message is this, redeemed from the curse of the law. How? By 'Christ being made a curse for us'. The curse was the sentence pronounced upon those who did not obey the law's demands. And who could? So the offender fell under the wrath of a righteous God. But the Lord Jesus Christ bore its curse, thus redeeming and liberating those who were subject to this curse, who now believe on Him. He never violated God's law. He was perfect. God's Son, God's only begotten Son, God's Son in whom was all His delight. Yet, He became man to redeem those who were under the sentence of the law. But redemption is ours, for being under the curse, as Paul states, Christ was Himself made a curse. What a glorious message indeed, that the Lord Jesus Christ exhausted for the believer – who before was subject to the law and guilty of breaking it – all the curse that it pronounced on the guilty.

'Beneath the curse, in grace He dies –
He dies for sinful men;
Redeemed we upward turn our eyes –
Lo, Jesus lives again'.

6. **'Under the law',** Gal. 4. 4 – *OBLIGATION.* As to the Lord Jesus Christ's responsibility, He was 'made under the law', taking His place as others, subject to its demands. As through the law man is under the sentence of the law, the Lord Jesus puts Himself under the law also. He places Himself in the position where man is found, in grace, though not the state they were personally in, 'but with the responsibility that belonged to it – a responsibility which He alone has met'. Of necessity He kept the law for He was sinless. He never came under its curse for He never failed, and, because He never failed, He was able to go to Calvary's cruel cross and give Himself a ransom for many, to bear the curse of the

broken law, to redeem them that were under it, 'that we', states Paul, 'might receive the adoption of sons'.

> 'Behold I come, O God, to do Thy will,
> Become Incarnate God with men to dwell;
> Thy law to keep, its righteousness fulfil,
> To conquer sin and Satan, death and hell'.

7. **'Sin for us',** 2 Cor. 5. 21 – *RECONCILIATION.* This is the solid basis of the marvellous ministry of reconciliation. Christ was 'made sin for us'. Are they not wonderful words? Can we enter into them? Can we fathom their depths? I think not. Under the Levitical economy when sin was charged to any Israelite, he was to bring an offering before Jehovah, put his hand on the head of the victim, thus typifying the transferring of his guilt to the victim, who is made 'sin' or a 'sin-offering' (for the word is identical in both Hebrew and Greek), and it was slain in his stead. 'The sin-offering was presented to God of old as the "sin" of the one who presented it', F. W. GRANT. Seeing that the Lord Jesus Christ had no sin of His own, for the Offerer must be spotless to be accepted, He stood before God as identified with our sins which He took and which were placed upon Him, and bore their awful judgement. He not only bore our sins in His own body on the tree, but He was made sin, being charged with the entire sin-question.

If to get the full meaning of this text, we take special notice of the contrast made between 'sin' and 'righteousness', we will adoringly exclaim 'him . . . sin for us' and then 'we . . . righteousness of God'. Glory be to God.

> 'All thy sins were laid upon Him,
> Jesus bore them on the tree;
> God who knew them, laid them on Him,
> And believing, thou art free'.
>
> J. DENHAM SMITH

The Death of Christ - E. L. LOVERING

The Event Declared. The Apostle Paul, in his summary of the Christian message, wrote to the church at Corinth in these words, 'I delivered unto you **first of all** . . . how that Christ died for our sins according to the scriptures; and that he was buried, and that he rose again the third day according to the scriptures', 1 Cor. 15. 3, 4. To the death, burial and resurrection of the Lord Jesus Christ, Paul attached supreme importance.

In the Old Testament we see the event

foreshadowed in the coats of skin provided for the pair in Eden's garden; in Abel's sacrificial lamb; in the Levitical ritual and offerings, and in the Day of Atonement and the Passover.

foretold by the prophets, the main theme of prophecy. Peter reminds us that 'the things which God foreshewed by the mouth of all the prophets, that his Christ should suffer, he thus fulfilled', Acts 3. 18 RV. To the two on the way to Emmaus, Luke 24. 26-46, the Saviour said, 'O fools, and slow of heart to believe all that the prophets have spoken: ought not Christ to have suffered these things, and to enter into his glory?' vv. 25, 26. What details are listed in Psalm 22 – the shooting out of the lip and the shaking of the head in mockery; the pierced hands and feet; the extreme thirst as His tongue cleaves to His jaws; the gambling for His only possession, a garment without seam!

In the New Testament we find this event

fulfilled. The Saviour said, in John chapter 6 verse 51, 'I am the living bread . . . which I will give for the life of the world'; and in Matthew chapter 20 verse 28, 'the Son of man came not to be ministered unto, but to minister and to give his life a ransom for many'.

In the Acts we find this event **the theme of preaching**. Peter declared, Acts 2. 23 RV, that 'him, being delivered up by the determinate counsel and foreknowledge of God, ye by the hand of lawless men did crucify and slay'. It was 'in the name of Jesus Christ of Nazareth whom ye crucified, whom God raised from the dead', Acts 4. 10 RV, that Peter explained the healing of the man at the Beautiful gate. To the eunuch in the desert of Gaza, Acts 8. 35, Philip preached Jesus, as he read, 'He was led as a lamb to the slaughter'; whilst Paul reminds the elders of Ephesus, Acts 20. 28, to feed the church of God, 'which he hath purchased with his own blood'.

Some Aspects Described. The death of our Lord Jesus Christ was

1. ***voluntary***. The Saviour said, 'Therefore doth my Father love me, because I lay down my life, that I might take it again', John 10. 17. He said to Peter who would resist those who came, armed with swords and staves, to take Him, 'Thinkest thou that I cannot beseech my Father, and he shall even now send me more than twelve legions of angels?', Matt. 26. 53 RV. He 'offered himself without spot to God', Heb. 9. 14 – the perfect burnt offering.

2. ***vicarious***. He died 'for' us, 'for' sinners, and 'for' our sins. It was on our behalf that He died. 'He that spared not his own Son, but delivered him up for us all', Rom. 8. 32; 'the Son of God, who loved me, and gave himself up for me', Gal. 2. 20 RV; 'our Saviour, Jesus Christ; who gave himself for us, that he might redeem us from all iniquity', Titus 2. 13, 14.

3. ***substitutionary***. He died 'instead of us'; 'the Son of man came . . . to give his life a ransom for many', Matt. 20. 28; 'Christ Jesus; who gave himself a ransom for all', 1 Tim. 2. 5, 6. This little word 'for' may not only mean 'on behalf of' and 'instead of' but also 'on account of' and here we discover that the death of Christ was

4. ***penal***. He 'was delivered up for our trespasses, and was raised for our justification', Rom. 4. 25 RV, that is, the Lord Jesus died on account of our sin and need, certainly not for Himself, but on the sinner's behalf and established the law by enduring its penalty, death, Gal. 3. 13; 2 Cor. 5. 21. 'He was wounded for our transgressions, he was bruised for our iniquities: the chastisement of our peace was upon him . . . for the transgression of my people to whom the stroke was due', Isa. 53. 5, 8 RVmg.

5. ***propitiatory***. 'Christ Jesus: whom God hath set forth to be a propitiation [sacrifice] through faith in his blood', Rom. 3. 24, 25. The 'mercy-seat' was sprinkled with atoning blood on the Day of Atonement, Lev. 16. 14, in token that the righteous sentence of the law had been (typically) carried out. A judgement-seat becomes

righteously a mercy-seat, a place of communion, Exod. 25. 21, 22. We must note, however, that there is no thought in propitiation of placating a vengeful God, but of doing right by His holy law and so making it possible for Him righteously to show mercy.

6. ***redemptive.*** 'In whom we have redemption through his blood, the forgiveness of sins', Eph. 1. 7; 'Ye are not your own: for ye were bought with a price: glorify God therefore in your body', 1 Cor. 6. 19, 20 RV. The slaves of sin can be delivered from its power and its guilt.

7. ***reconciling.*** Man is not only a slave in the power of sin and Satan and in need of liberty, but he is by nature an enemy to God and needs to be reconciled. And so we read in 2 Corinthians chapter 5 verse 19 that 'God was in Christ reconciling the world unto himself'. Further, 'And you . . . hath he reconciled in the body of his flesh through death, to present you holy and without blemish and unreprovable before him', Col. 1. 21, 22 RV.

8. ***revealing.*** Here is the supreme evidence of divine love for fallen man, for 'God *so* loved . . . that he gave his only begotten Son', John 3. 16; 'Herein was the love of God manifested in us, that God hath sent his only begotten Son into the world, that we might live through him', 1 John 4. 9 RV.

9. ***efficacious and victorious.*** The Lord Jesus, speaking of the manner of His death, said, 'And I, if I be lifted up from the earth, will draw all men unto myself', John 12. 32, 33 RV. What blessings and effects flow to us from the cross of Christ! 'Justified by his blood', Rom. 5. 9; 'made the righteousness of God in him', 2 Cor. 5. 21; 'made nigh by the blood of Christ', Eph. 2. 13; 'loosed [washed] from our sins in his own blood', Rev. 1. 5 RV.

Some Effects Desired in the Christian experience.

1. ***Separation from the World.*** It was the apostle Paul's desire to glory alone in the cross of our Lord Jesus Christ, 'through which the world hath been crucified unto me, and I unto the world', Gal. 6. 14 RV. The death of Christ divides us from the world.

2. ***Identification with Christ.*** In the symbol of baptism we acknowledge our identification with Christ. Going down into the water, the believer witnesses to his acceptance of God's judgement in death. In his immersion in the water he signifies his burial, the severance of the last links with sin and its service, the world and its ways, Col. 2. 20. Emergence from the water is symbolical of the fact of resurrection here and now by the operation of God, Col. 2. 12, 13, to walk and live as one 'risen with Christ', 3. 1, to seek the things above.

3. ***Proclamation of His Death.*** What a privilege and joy it is for believers in Christ to gather together on the first day of the week to remember their Lord and to proclaim His death! 'For as often as ye eat this bread, and drink this cup, ye proclaim the Lord's death, till he come', 1 Cor. 11. 26 RV.

4. What does 'the word of the cross' mean to you? Is it foolishness, or is it the power and wisdom of God? Shall we join with BUNYAN in his *Pilgrim's Progress*? –

> 'Blest cross! blest sepulchre! blest rather be
> The Man that there was put to shame for me!'

The Messiah's Sufferings in the Epistle to the Hebrews

- F. CUNDICK

The great spiritual force of the presentation of a suffering Messiah will be felt when a reader bears in mind three simple matters concerning this great Epistle.

1. The Chief Characteristic. It contrasts the past order with the present. Old Testament personalities and ceremonies are considered and attention is repeatedly drawn to the 'better' aspects of the present new order.[83]

2. The Chief Consideration. It emphasizes the superiority and excellency of the priesthood of Christ over the old Aaronic order.

---

[83] Heb. 1. 4; 7. 19, 22; 8. 6; 9. 23; 10. 34; 11. 16, 35, 40; 12. 24.

3. The Chief Cause. In some locality unknown to us, there were some Jews who had accepted the despised Jesus of Nazareth as the true Messiah. Through the preaching of the apostles, 2. 3, they had been converted to the Christian faith, and consequently turned away from the obsolete forms of Judaism. Persecution for their response to the Christian faith had been endured, and it seems that there was a likelihood for this persecution to increase. Because of this some were in danger of being drawn back to their former religion, thus to forsake the Christian faith with its now invisible Christ. It is not difficult to imagine how the first readers of the Epistle had been taunted and reproached for their acceptance of a faith without external ritual. To reinforce their faith the inspired penman wrote.

As he did so, he was not unmindful of their sufferings. He writes, 'But call to remembrance the former days, in which, after ye were illuminated, ye endured a great fight of afflictions . . . for ye . . . took joyfully the spoiling of your goods, knowing in yourselves that ye have in heaven a better and an enduring substance', 10. 32-34. This deep experience of heavenly realities is what the writer wished to be retained. Spiritual joy comes not by possessing material wealth, but by 'seeing the invisible'. Furthermore, it was essential to reveal from scripture that the Messiah must needs suffer to enter into His glory. The Jewish theologians seemed to have overlooked this feature of the Messianic prophecies. In the Epistle these sufferings appear and their distinctive purposes are made known to inspire the people of God in their pathway of obedience to the will of God.

1. The Divine Kinsman-Redeemer. As the glories of the divine-human Redeemer are expounded, and the great purposes of God declared in the Messianic advents of grace and glory in the opening of the Epistle, the writer draws attention to the Messiah's sufferings in life and death. First, let us think of His sufferings in life. 'He himself hath suffered being tempted', 2. 18, amplifies the Gospel records revealing that He was exposed to temptation. This for Him was suffering. His holy nature recoiled from the awful character of sin. Here is a fact that men of depraved nature and hardened by sin are unable to comprehend. Suffering is a relative term; the measure of its acuteness is determined by the degree of one's refinement. The same burden weighs unequally on different men. Christ alone knew the full strength of temptation, for His life had in no wise been scorched by the fire of sin. The more we realize the uniqueness and beautiful refinement of His being, the more likely we shall be able to interpret in some small degree the intensity of His sufferings in life.

Then 'the suffering of death' is mentioned, 2. 9, that is, not merely death, but the suffering of death. Its bitterness He tasted in His vicarious sufferings. To remove the disastrous effects of sin, and to bring the many sons to glory, God in grace sent His Son to die. In the Son's patient path of obedience and in His endurance of the cross, He has wrought the eternal salvation of His people, and all in perfect harmony with divine requirements. Both aspects of suffering, in life and death, focus attention on the reality and intensity of the work undertaken by the kinsman-redeemer. There could not be any pretence in dealing with the consequences of sin in the universe. The Son, who alone could measure the responsibility involved, has adorned the throne of God with the glory of redemption.

2. The Qualified Priest. 'Though he were a Son, yet learned he obedience by the things which he suffered; and being made perfect, he became the author of eternal salvation unto all them that obey him', 5. 8, 9. The Son did not need to be made perfect in His relationship with the Father, or in His moral character in manhood. In these matters He is inherently perfect. But to become the author of eternal salvation, the way of the cross must be trodden. The corn of wheat must die to bring the harvest. The words 'learned he obedience' point to the practical cost of doing the will of God in His manhood. Our salvation is dependent on this priest who with His fullness of experience discharges His ministry perfectly. The experience of suffering has given Him the qualification to interpret our feelings aright, so He cannot intercede in vain.

The incident is related of a boy who lost his right hand. The reaction of the boy to this severe injury was one of deep despondency. He did not want to see anyone. In hope of restoring the boy, his father said, 'I am going to bring a special visitor to see you'. 'I don't want to see him', replied the boy. But the father brought the visitor and when the boy looked up he saw that the kind man had no right arm; there was an empty sleeve. He came over to the boy and said, 'I haven't any hand either. I lost mine when I was a boy, and I know how it feels'. Their mutuality of suffering made them friends immediately.

3. The Perfect Sacrifice. 'Nor yet that he should offer himself often, as the high priest entereth into the holy place every year with blood of others; for then must he often have suffered since the foundation of the world: but now once for all in the completion of the ages hath he appeared to put away sin by the sacrifice of himself', 9. 25, 26 NEWBERRY. The great hinge of the argument relative to the ceremony of the Day of Atonement in chapters 9 and 10 is the remark, 'But Christ', 9. 11. His sacrifice is eternally efficacious and absolutely independent of time. The writer reasons if Christ's sacrifice had availed only for a time like the annual sacrifices of the Levitical order, then there would have been need for a repetition of His offering whenever the time expired. But Christ's sufferings are valid as a single, non-repeated act, and their vicarious character permanent. Consequently the salvation that ensues is eternal in quality.

4. The Great Sanctifier. 'Wherefore Jesus also, that he might sanctify the people with his own blood, suffered without the gate', 13. 12. Here the sacrifice of Christ is the antitype of the Day of Atonement. The ritual of that complex ceremony is doubtless in view, for the character of the offering considered is national. The blood was brought into the sanctuary, v. 11, this expression including the most holy place; further, the high priest is the official who functions as representative of the people. Christ has fulfilled this great type in His own sufferings in sacrificial death. Not merely His dying but His vicarious sufferings are we asked to consider. By the divine overruling of circumstances in Christ's death, the ritual pertaining to the sin offering was fulfilled. Outside the camp He knew the shame of a malefactor's death. The great issue is the sanctification of His people. From the practical point of view 'the people' are expected to accept the divine verdict of man in the flesh. According to verse 13 we should learn to take sides with God, and judge all that is a product of man's endeavour, be it religious, intellectual, political or all that is depraved and unacceptable before God.

The motive behind the Epistle becomes clearer as these themes of perfect substitution, sympathy, salvation and sanctification are reviewed. Did not the identification of faith with the suffering Messiah

first give the readers **a link with the past**? Their experience of suffering was by no means exceptional. The illustrious men of chapter eleven had known suffering for their faith. For example, 'By faith Moses, when he was come to years, refused to be called the son of Pharaoh's daughter; choosing rather to suffer affliction with the people of God, than to enjoy the pleasures of sin for a season; esteeming the reproach of Christ greater riches than the treasures in Egypt', 11. 24-26. Could they not estimate comparative values as did Moses the man of faith? **Second**, identification with the despised Christ brought them **grace for the present**. The pathway of suffering by which the captain of their salvation was made 'perfect' is the pathway along which He brings His people. Not all royal sons are capable for rule. But training and discipline fit the 'many sons' for the coming regency of glory, and there is grace for every emergency. **Third**, there is **glory for the future**. In the eternal commonwealth of the heavens, 12. 22-24, there will be no grief at the loss of pleasures and prospects of this doomed world. The measure of the clarity and vision of the beauty and stability of this heavenly order, will determine the measure of the believer's endurance in the pathway upwards and homewards.

Christ our Saviour* - I. AFFLECK

The lovely title of the Lord that we are considering in this study is that of Christ our Saviour and it is a powerful reminder to all our hearts of what the Lord Jesus did for us. He saved us from the penalty of sin and saves us from the power of sin day by day. Then, one day, He will save us from the presence of sin altogether and what a glorious day that will be! 'When He takes us by the hand and leads us through the promised land', J. HILL, it will be a land of stainless beauty and unsullied glory, even heaven itself.

We shall consider the subject under five headings:

The promise of the Saviour – Acts 13. 22, 23

Paul is in Antioch in Pisidia, Asia, preaching in a synagogue using King David as an illustration and He reminds his Jewish audience of the lovely testimony of God concerning David. God said of him:

> He is a man after mine own heart

He shall fulfill all my will.

What delight and confidence God had in David, for he had a tender yet faithful heart. But, in verse 23, Paul turns the attention of his audience to the seed of David, the long promised Messiah, He who would be Israel's **Saviour,** even Jesus the despised Nazarene. How much more confidence would God have in great David's greater son, for He would bring even more delight to His heart. Indeed, God publicly declared, 'This is my beloved Son, in whom I am well pleased', Matt. 17. 5. Now, David did the will of God, of that there is no doubt, and he saved Israel from a life of servitude under the Philistines, when he slew their champion Goliath of Gath, but the Lord Jesus saves from greater foes, even Satan himself and from sin. The salvation which the Lord Jesus provides is not for the sons of Israel only but also for the sinful sons of Adam's ruined race, therefore, for the whole world. John corroborates this, for, in his First Epistle and in chapter 4 verse 14, we read the words, 'The Father sent the Son to be the Saviour of the world'.

The provision of the Saviour – Luke 2. 11
'Unto you is born this day in the city of David a **Saviour,** which is Christ the Lord'.

What a wonderful message the angel brought to the shepherds that day. It was a message of joy and hope for all the people. The angel told of the birth of a Saviour, who would save His people from their sins, and that Saviour was for all the people. But, before He could be the Saviour, He must become a man. Therefore, in Hebrews chapter 2 verse 14 we read, 'Forasmuch then as the children are partakers of flesh and blood, he also himself likewise took part of the same'. The angel also told them of the sign by which they would know Him, 'Ye shall find the babe wrapped in swaddling clothes, lying in a manger', v. 12. What a sight to behold, Messiah, the very Son of God, not born in one of the great palaces of men nor in a home, however humble, but in the outside place, even a lowly cattle shed. The poet has penned the words so beautifully:

'Down from His glory ever living story,
My God and Saviour came and Jesus was His name,
Born in a manger to His own a stranger,
A man of sorrows, tears and agonies.

> Oh, how I love Him, how I adore Him
> My breath, my sunshine, my all in all.
> The great creator became my Saviour
> And now God's fullness dwelleth in Him'.
>
> WILLIAM E. BOOTH-CLIBBORN

The purpose concerning the Saviour – Acts 5. 30-32
Peter and John have been released from prison on condition that they would not teach in the name of Jesus and now stand accused of breaking the conditions of bail. They respond by saying, 'We ought to obey God rather than men', thus setting an example to saints of every generation. They go on to state two important facts concerning the Lord Jesus:

- The nation put Him to death, but God reversed their judgement when He raised him from the dead.
- Then God exalted Him by His power and made Him a Prince and a **Saviour** for the very people who crucified Him, so that their sins might be forgiven.

Surely, this was God's purpose in relation to the Saviour, that He would be exalted and extolled and made very high. From that high position He would be able to save to the uttermost all that come unto God by Him.

The apostles state that both they and the Spirit of God are witnesses to these things and, therefore, they will not fear what man shall do to them. Surely, they would have sung the words of the old hymn, if it had been written:

> 'I'm not ashamed to own my Lord or to defend His cause,
> Maintain the honour of His word, the glory of His cross'.
>
> ISAAC WATTS

The prospect of the Saviour – Phil. 3. 20
'For our conversation is in heaven; from whence also we look for the **Saviour**, the Lord Jesus Christ'.

What a blessed assurance to know that the man whom this world crucified is alive in heaven today. But it is also a comfort to know that this self-same Saviour will come from heaven to fulfill the work He has begun in every believer. To Paul, this must have been a precious truth, for he had suffered much for his faithfulness to his Saviour and I have no doubt his body was showing signs of premature ageing because of this. What joy then for Paul to look up and wait patiently for his Lord as he anticipated the wonderful change, when he would be clothed upon with a glorious body. May the prospect of the Saviour's return encourage all who know the burden of passing years and the feeble frame of mind, for He shall do what no doctor can do, that is, deliver us from the ageing process! Paul, when writing to Titus, adds another dimension to this thought when he says, 'Looking for that blessed hope, and the glorious appearing of the great God and our **Saviour** Jesus Christ', Titus 2. 13. Here, the thought is not only that the Saviour is coming for His own to take them out of this world, but the fact that He is coming back to this world where He was rejected and ridiculed to set up His kingdom. He shall reign throughout the whole world, for every knee shall bow and 'every tongue . . . confess that Jesus Christ is Lord to the glory of God the Father', Phil. 2. 11.

The picture of the Saviour as seen in Joseph – John 4. 42
'We believe . . . and know that this is indeed the Christ, the **Saviour** of the world'.

This was the name that Pharaoh gave to Joseph after he, by his God-given wisdom, made known the meaning of Pharaoh's dream. By such wisdom, Joseph ensured that provision would be made against a forthcoming famine and certain death. Joseph is a lovely type of Christ the Saviour, for his way to the throne was by suffering.

Joseph was rejected by his brethren who hated him and could not speak peaceably to him. They sold him to merchantmen after having cast him into a pit and then faked his death so that their old father mourned for his son and would not be comforted. Joseph became a servant in Egypt but was falsely accused by Potiphar's wife and so was put in prison, there to await his fate. But, in the providence of God, he was brought to the palace and was made ruler throughout the land of Egypt with all being caused to bow the knee before him. This came about because Joseph was a man who brought the word of God to the people of this world and also because the Spirit of God was in him. What a fitting type of the Lord Jesus, the man of sorrows who daily suffered grief, and was rejected by His own people. Men crucified Him, but God raised Him to a throne, for He not only brought the word of God to the people but He is the Word of God, the Spirit abode in Him, and He brought a greater salvation to this world than Joseph did in his day.

Is it any wonder that Mary, His mother, lifts up her heart in song and says, 'My soul doth magnify the Lord and my spirit hath rejoiced in God my **Saviour'**, Luke 1. 47. Surely, it becomes us who are saved to blend our voices with hers and, in the words of the hymn, say from the depths of redeemed hearts:

'Praise the Saviour ye who know Him
Who can tell how much we owe Him,
Gladly let us render to Him,
All we are and have'.
THOMAS KELLY

Substitution - M. J. PARKER

The effects of the death of Christ are revealed to us in expressions with which we are familiar. Such terms as ransom, redemption and reconciliation are, of course, only word-pictures, windows that allow the light of truth to enter our minds and hearts. But even when we feel that we have understood the ideas behind them, we have not advanced far into the mysteries surrounding the cross. God's indescribable gift, 2 Cor. 9. 15, cannot be brought within the scope of human language. In our consideration of the death of Christ, we are therefore on safe ground when we keep close to the phraseology of scripture; difficulties arise when we go beyond this.

This is particularly the case in the usage of the word 'substitution'. Although the word has found a permanent place in the teaching of the atonement, it is not a scriptural expression, but has been deduced from phraseology found there. It is therefore quite reasonable to inquire into its accuracy. Substitution means 'the putting of one in the place of another'. With reference to the death of Christ, have we sufficient authority for using such a term? Moreover, to whom is it applicable?

The Old Testament offers many illustrations. We at once recall the scene recorded in Genesis chapter 22, where Abraham's faith is tested even to the offering of his only son as a burnt offering, and the climax when a ram is provided in his stead. This, without doubt, foreshadows Calvary, cp. Gen. 22. 14 RVmg, John 8. 56. In Exodus chapter 13 verse 13, the firstborn of an ass was redeemed with a lamb; it went free because another had died in its place. In the sin offering, we may say that the death of the offering was in the place of the one who had sinned, because he had identified himself with the victim.

This brings us to an important point in our usage of the term 'substitution'. It is possible that we shall be misunderstood if we present Christ to the unsaved as their substitute, because this would at once cancel all individual decision and the response of faith. To claim Christ as our substitute is to have identified ourselves with the sacrifice, to have appropriated by faith the saving value of His death. Care must therefore be taken in our application of the word 'substitution'.

The New Testament makes it clear that Christ died on **behalf** of all, making salvation available for all mankind. This, however, is different from saying that He died **instead** of all, which is substitution. The place substitution occupies in the New Testament in relation to other aspects of the death of Christ may be seen from the following references:

1. It was for sins;[84]
2. It was for all;[85]
3. It was for believers, Luke 22. 19-20; Gal. 2. 20.

In these passages, 'for' translates the preposition *huper,* and the general opinion is that *huper* has as its leading thought the sense of 'on behalf of' rather than 'instead of'. We may, of course, draw the sense of substitution from the context, in which case we are confined to the quotations where the believer is particularly in view.

There are a few more explicit statements:

In 1 Timothy chapter 2 verse 6 we read, 'Who gave himself a ransom [*antilutron,* "of a substitutionary character", W. E. VINE] for [*huper,* "on behalf of"] all'. Here the substitutionary aspect of His death is

[84] Heb. 10. 12; 1 Cor. 15. 3; Gal. 1. 4.
[85] 1 Tim. 2. 6; Heb. 2. 9; 2 Cor. 5. 15; John 6. 51.

introduced together with its scope for all mankind.

The words of the Lord Jesus 'to give his life a ransom for many' occur twice in the Gospel records, Matt. 20. 28; Mark 10. 45. In both of these cases, 'for' translates the preposition *anti.* DR. BASIL ATKINSON has written, 'The meaning of the preposition, which is a very important word in the sentence, is "in exchange for", "as the equivalent of", "instead of". The sentence teaches the substitutionary doctrine of atonement, and I think it safe to say that no other view of its meaning can be safely entertained'.[86] In these verses, the word 'many' stands in contrast to 'all', 1 Tim. 2. 6. Those only who accept Him as Saviour may claim Him as their Substitute.

In Isaiah chapter 53 we see the suffering substitute: 'with his stripes we are healed'; 'the chastisement of our peace was upon him'; 'He bare the sin of many'. This chapter is apparently in Peter's thoughts in the closing verses of the second chapter of his first Epistle. The thoughts 'as a lamb that is led to the slaughter, and as a sheep that before her shearers is dumb; yea, he opened not his mouth', Isa. 53. 7 RV, prefigure Him as the One who 'committed his cause to him that judgeth righteously', 1 Pet. 2. 23 RVmg, and as the One who 'his own self bare our sins in his body upon the tree'. It is here that the obligations of those who claim Him as substitute are felt – 'That we, having died unto sins, might live unto righteousness'. This is beautifully expressed for us in the words of JAMES DENNEY:

'How this effect is mediated the apostle does not say. Once we understand what Christ's death means – once we receive the apostolic testimony that in that death He was taking all our responsibilities upon Him – no explanation may be needed... Whoever says 'He bore our sins' says Substitution; and to say Substitution is to say something which involves an immeasurable obligation to Christ, and has therefore in it an incalculable motive power. This is the answer to some of the objections which are commonly made to the idea of Substitution on moral grounds. They fail to take account of the sinner's sense of debt to Christ for what He has done, a sense of debt which is not too much to designate as the most intimate, intense and uniform characteristic of

---

[86] B. F. C. ATKINSON, *Theology of Prepositions,* Tyndale Press, pg. 6.

the New Testament life. It is this which bars out all ideas of being saved from the consequences of sin, while living on in sin itself. It is so profound that the whole being of the Christian is changed by it'.

Propitiation - J. M. Davies

It will be necessary to note the references to the word in its different forms in the New Testament, and its Old Testament equivalent. Thereby, as we compare scripture with scripture, its meaning will be established, its importance evaluated, and our experience should be enriched as we enter into the enjoyment of its procured blessings.

The New Testament References. The word in its verbal and noun forms is used in the following passages:

1. The prayer of the publican, lit. 'God, be propitious to me, the sinner', Luke 18. 13;
2. In connection with the Lord's priesthood, 'Wherefore it behoved him in all things to be made like unto his brethren, that he might become a merciful and faithful high priest in things pertaining to God, to make propitiation for the sins of the people', Heb. 2. 17 RV. In cases 1 and 2 the word is *hilaskomai*;
3. In the context of justification, 'Whom God hath set forth to be a propitiation through faith, in [or in virtue of] his blood', Rom. 3. 25. The word here is *hilastērion*, the word used for the 'mercy seat', Heb. 9. 5. Sprinkling the blood of the sacrifice on and before the mercy seat was an essential and integral part of the ritual on the great Day of Atonement, Lev. 16;
4. In connection with sins and the believer, 'he is the propitiation for our sins; and not for ours only, but also for the whole world', 1 John 2. 2 RV;
5. Connected with the love of God, 'he loved us, and sent his Son to be the propitiation for our sins', 1 John 4. 10. In cases 4 and 5 the word is *hilasmos.*

The Meaning of the Words. Green's *Lexicon* gives the following. The verb *hilaskomai* – to appease, render propitious. Make an expiation. And in Luke chapter 18 verse 13 it suggests, 'be gracious, show mercy, pardon'. The noun *hilastērion* – propitiatory, invested with propitiatory power. The noun *hilasmos* – propitiation or expiation. The difference between propitiation and expiation will be clarified later.

Its Old Testament Equivalent. The Old Testament word is *kaphar,* and it is rendered atonement. It is used in connection with each of the five offerings mentioned in Leviticus, and of the offering of the ram for consecration for the high priest and his family, Exod. 29. 33. A most important text in this study is, 'I have given it [the blood] to you upon the altar to make an atonement for your souls: for it is the blood that maketh an atonement for the soul', Lev. 17. 11.

From a consideration of these verses in the New Testament, and some fifty occurrences of the word in connection with the tabernacle ministry in Exodus, Leviticus and Numbers, certain facts emerge. These establish very clearly its meaning and its message. Sin and its consequences were the root cause for the need of propitiation.

Propitiation Meets the Demands of God. In Leviticus chapter 16 emphasis is laid upon the 'uncleanness of the children of Israel', and on their 'transgressions in all their sins'. This makes it clear that it was because of the demands of holiness and righteousness that atonement was necessary. Holiness and righteousness are the two pillars of the throne of God, therefore it is imperative that their demands should be met. Sin, whether it be sacrilege in the holy things of the Lord, or selfishness in relation to one's responsibility to a neighbour, had to be atoned for by a sacrifice. These two aspects of sin cover both tables of the law. Failure to love the Lord, or failure in the matter of love to one's neighbour, is guilt. This had to be atoned for by sacrifice. Atonement, or propitiation, then, has in view the satisfying or exonerating of the demands of divine righteousness and divine holiness. Guilt incurs judgement which involves the wrath of God. That wrath must be appeased. It must be propitiated, before God can show His kindness, or bestow His favour and blessing. This aspect of the death of Christ is basic in connection with God's great plan of salvation. If guilt was to be expiated, the inexorable demands of law and justice, or holiness and righteousness, had to be honoured.

Propitiation was Initiated by God. Man cannot accomplish this, he is without strength, a sinner and ungodly, and at enmity with God. The plight of man is such that he has a built-in consciousness of guilt, and of unfitness to enter God's presence. In his *Expository Dictionary*, W. E. VINE draws attention to the fact that 'in non-biblical Greek the word propitiation (*hilaskomai*) meant to conciliate, to appease, to propitiate, cause the gods to be reconciled; their goodwill was not regarded as their natural condition, but as something to be earned. They believed their gods to be alienated in feeling from man. But in the New Testament it never means to conciliate God'. On the contrary the New Testament indicates that propitiation was initiated by God. 'God so loved . . . that he gave his only begotten Son', John 3. 16. It was because of His love towards man that He sent His Son to be the propitiation for our sins, 1 John 4. 10. God, being infinite, and His love being infinite, He provided a propitiation which is infinite.

Propitiation and the Son of God. The Lord Jesus Christ is the propitiation, 2. 2, and what He is gives character to the propitiation. It cannot in any sense be limited in its potential value. It is for the whole world. That cancels any idea of a limited atonement. Not only is He the propitiation, but He accomplished it when He offered up Himself as a sacrificial victim, Heb. 2. 17; 9. 14, 26, 28.

'In Hebrews 2. 17 Christ is called a "high priest", and not merely a "priest" as in Psalm 110. 4. The verse views His redemptive work as the anti-typical fulfilment of the sacrificial ritual of the Day of Atonement, where the high priest in person was required to officiate'.[87] In connection with the Passover, no priest was called upon to officiate. The lamb was slaughtered by the head of the house for his family, a man who had no official priestly status. So from the Passover aspect, the death of Christ was not a priestly act, but from the aspect of the Day of Atonement it was the action of the high priest.

As already noted, in Romans chapter 3 verse 25 it is the word for the mercy seat that is rendered 'propitiation', better 'the propitiatory'. The mercy seat was the lid or cover of the ark. The word cover is connected with the covering or the removal of sin, Ps. 32. 1. The ark contained the law, the golden pot of manna and the rod that budded, the reminders of the three great sins of Israel in the wilderness, those of idolatry, of

---

[87] F. F. BRUCE, *Hebrews*, pg. 52.

despising the manna, and of the rebellion of Korah. These correspond to the sins of the three great sections of humanity arraigned by the apostle, Rom. 1. 20 – 3. 20; the derelict idolater, ch. 1, the despiser of the goodness of God, ch. 2, and the rejecters of Christ, 2. 16 – ch. 3. The pagan idolater, the proud philosopher, and the Pharisee were represented in the three languages written on the title board on the cross, a wonderful demonstration of the fact that Christ is the propitiation for the whole world. It is important to note the change introduced by the Revised Version in Romans chapter 3 verse 25. The Lord is not the propitiation because we believe, but because of His blood.

The Fundamental Character of Propitiation. Luke chapter 18 verse 13 shows that justification depends on propitiation. The publican went down to his house justified. He had evidently stood in the outer court, and as he saw the blood-sprinkled altar he cried for mercy because of the blood. 'God, be propitious to me'. Not only justification, but cleansing depends on propitiation. This is made clear in the instructions for the Day of Atonement. Propitiation is also the basis for expiation and reconciliation. Because of sin man merited the wrath of God, but as Christ endured the wrath of God upon sin, expiation was made, and the barrier to peace with God was removed. The word *kaphar* (atonement) is the word used of the pitch with which the ark was covered, Gen. 6. 14. It preserved the ark and those within it from destruction in the deluge. The propitiatory sacrifice of Christ is our security from judgement also.

'Sin atoning sacrifice,
Thou art precious in mine eyes,
Thou alone my rest shall be,
Now and through eternity'.

H. GRATTAN GUINNESS

The Cross of Christ and the Blood of Christ - K. T. C. MORRIS

The preaching of the gospel of Christ was to Paul the preaching of the cross. The cross was the heart and centre of the message. In the resurrection of our Lord Jesus we see the exceeding greatness of God's power; in the cross the exceeding greatness of His love. Only divine love could give such a Son to such a death for such rebels; and Christ was obedient to God right up to that appalling death on a cross.

Paul reminds the Corinthians of the true character of the Gospel, 1 Cor. 1. 17-23. The crucifixion was not a mighty wonder, a sign for which the Jews looked; neither did it appeal to the philosophies of the worldly-wise Greeks. It was a thing of shame; it was reserved for the worst of criminals; the common crowd derided the helpless victim. Therefore Christ crucified was 'unto the Jews a stumblingblock, and unto the Greeks foolishness'. The Jews had expected deliverance from national and physical ills by an overwhelming display of Messiah's power. The Greeks scoffed at the notion that blessing could come through faith in one who was put to such a death. But to those who believe, Christ is seen as the power and the wisdom of God. They perceive their dire need as sinners, guilty and unclean, fully met at His cross.

The truth of the cross corrects the common and subtle thought that religious observances can contribute something towards our salvation. This was the error of the Galatians. But Paul says, in effect, 'I have been crucified with Christ. Really it was I who was put to shame; I, so proud of my zeal for my God-given religion; I, stopping my ears to the testimony of Stephen, and closing my eyes to the light on his face as he suffered martyrdom. The cross was the end of the old me in the sight of God, and now it is in my sight also'. Ours was the place of ignominy and shame that Christ took on the cross. It was the flesh with its 'affections and lusts' which really needed to be impaled, Gal. 5. 24. We recognize with Paul that in our old evil nature we have been finally condemned and disgraced. But with Paul each can say, 'Nevertheless I live; yet not I, but Christ liveth in me', 2. 20.

Glorying in the Cross. The Galatians were warned that insistence on the rite of circumcision was due to pride in religion, and to fear of suffering persecution for the cross of Christ. Men find the cross offensive. It certainly does not flatter them. 'But', Paul says, 'God forbid that I should glory, save in the cross of our Lord Jesus Christ, by whom the world is crucified to me, and I unto the world', Gal. 6. 13, 14. At the cross we see the world in its true colours. It was the princes of this world, the leaders, who crucified the Lord of glory, 1 Cor. 2. 8. So Paul says that to him the world of men in alienation from God was put to shame. Just before the crucifixion the Lord said, 'Now is the judgment of this world: now shall the prince of this world be cast out', John 12. 31. At the cross Paul sees not only the world-system in its true character, but also himself in relation to it: I am crucified unto the world. Not only had he finished with the wisdom, wealth and way of the world, but now the world despised and derided him as it had previously despised and derided his master. In this he boasts. All is seen clearly and judged at the cross. We glory now neither in circumcision nor uncircumcision, neither in religious observances nor in the lack of them. We boast in the work of the cross which prepared the way for the new creation where Christ is all, Gal. 6. 15.

The cross was not only the display of man's enmity with God, of his miserable myopia and malignity, nor was it only the display of the moral majesty of the king praying for, and ministering to those around Him. Rather for Christ the cross presented the most intense agony. But the scriptures do not regard the cross of Christ with mere sentimental pity for the sufferer, though the images and art of Christendom tend to make us think of the physical suffering. But there was something far more terrible in the darkness, when Christ's soul was made an offering for sin. Then God's Son, in whom was all His delight, was made sin, that abominable thing which He hates with all the intensity of His being. Suffering unsparing judgement against sin, and the horrors of abandonment by His God, He cried, 'My God, my God, why hast thou forsaken me?' Matt. 27. 46. The cross was the place where, in a way beyond our ken, mercy and truth met together, righteousness and peace kissed each other, Ps. 85. 10.

Blood: Life Taken and Life Given. The cross of Christ speaks of the humiliating and agonizing aspect of His death as seen by men. His blood speaks of the expiatory value and preciousness of His death to God.

Blood is first mentioned in scripture in reference to the death of Abel, a death by violence. God said to Cain, 'The voice of thy brother's blood crieth unto me from the ground', Gen. 4. 10. Again blood is the evidence of a violent death as when Jacob was shown the blood-stained garment of Joseph, 37. 31-33. When God gave man permission to eat the flesh of animals He said, 'But flesh with the life thereof, which is the blood thereof, shall ye not eat', 9. 4. This reminds us that all life belongs to God. God has so constituted man that when his blood is poured out his 'life in the flesh' is 'taken from the earth', and is terminated, Acts 8. 33.

Turning to the law of sacrifice we find no atonement for sin and no acceptance with God apart from the death of another, death evidenced by shed blood. 'For', God says, 'the life of the flesh is in the blood: and I have given it to you upon the altar to make an atonement for your souls: for it is the blood that maketh an atonement for the soul', Lev. 17. 11-13. So blood speaks not only of life taken, whether wrongfully as in the case of Abel, or rightly as in the case of a murderer; it speaks also of life given, given upon the altar in expiation of sin. The blood of the offering poured out at the base of the altar suggests divine judgement executed and justice satisfied. Blood shed is not the liberation of life to be enjoyed by others, as has been taught. Christ's own life was laid down that He might take it again. When the priest made atonement for Israel's sins, he entered the holy presence of God 'alone, once in the year, not without blood, which he offereth for himself, and for the errors of the people', Heb. 9. 7 RV. He sprinkled the blood on the mercy seat for the satisfaction of God, and seven times before it, providing in figure adequate and ample ground on which man could stand before a holy God. So believers today have boldness to enter the holiest by virtue of the atoning and cleansing value of the blood of Jesus, Lev. 16. 14, 30; Heb. 10. 19.

Covenant Sealed, and Cleansing by Blood. When the first covenant was made the blood of sacrifice was sprinkled on book and people, and ceremonial cleansing was by blood. Apart from shedding of blood there is no remission. 'How much more shall the blood of Christ . . . cleanse your conscience . . . to serve the living God', Heb. 9. 13-22 RV. The cup at the Lord's Supper is a token of the new covenant sealed, ratified, by His blood; it assures us that the benefits of the covenant relevant to ourselves are secured to us by His death.

First, 'the blood of Jesus Christ his Son cleanseth us from all sin', 1 John 1. 7. This is its permanent effect. Its cleansing, that is, clearing from defilement in the sight of God, is unlimited, unlike the blood of bulls and goats. In the old economy washing was always in water, cleansing by blood. So also in the new, Rev. 1. 5 RV.

We were redeemed 'with the precious blood of Christ'; we were redeemed to God by His blood; 'we have redemption through his blood, the forgiveness of sins'; the ransom price has been paid and the church has been purchased (acquired RV.) by His own blood.[88] Also, writing of Christ's death Paul says that we are 'justified by his blood'; God has set forth His Son as a propitiatory sacrifice that enables Him righteously to justify the ungodly, Rom. 3. 25; 5. 6-9. So Christ's death deals with both man's defilement and man's guilt. Gentiles, once far off from God, on conversion are now brought into a place of privilege, 'made nigh by the blood of Christ', to enjoy peace made by the blood of His cross, Eph. 2. 13; Col. 1. 20.

So then the cross speaks of our Lord's rejection, shame and suffering. His blood speaks of the value of His death by which God cleanses and redeems men to Himself.

The Cross Today - T. Stephen

1. Standing by the Cross, John 12. 26; 19. 25, 26. These scriptures would indicate to us that to follow Christ and to identify ourselves with His cross and all that it means, we need to be moved in our spiritual affections for Him. The little company of women and the disciple whom Jesus loved formed an illustrious group that day as they stood by the cross: when others had fled, the devoted affections of these disciples held them fast by His cross. The supreme hour had come and with it rejection, reproach, and shame. How precious that company must have been in the sight of God as they stood by the cross of their Lord, with their love for Him rising above all the hatred and scorn of men!

Beloved reader, do you subscribe to His cross only in its historical sense, or has it entered into your life as a spiritual power? Is your heart so filled with love for Him who hung there, that you are presently prepared to 'stand by His cross' and all that that means to you in its moral implications, and to apply to your life the doctrines of the Epistles built upon the cross? May our hearts be kept tender so that the Holy Spirit can impress them by the wondrous love of Him who filled that cross for us.

---

[88] 1 Pet. 1. 19; Rev. 5. 9; Eph. 1. 7; Acts 20. 28.

2. On the Cross with Christ, Rom. 6. 1-10. Here, we have the ordinance of baptism associated with the cross. Whilst it is the will of God for every believer to be baptized, acknowledging the authority of His Holy Word, it is more blessed if its real meaning has entered into our experience. Romans undoubtedly gives us that experimental aspect of this truth. What does it mean? The cross, or crucifixion, was the form of capital punishment adopted by the judiciary of Imperial Rome: to be crucified was to be doomed to die, there being no hope for such a person, for their life was going to be ended. And God has incorporated this system of judgement into the understanding of spiritual truth. He has sentenced our 'old man' (i.e., our sinful nature or the evil principle that operates in our ruined nature – 'the flesh') to death in its capital sense. Therefore, in the cross we must learn that God has no intention of reforming or repairing our old nature, but that He has condemned it absolutely as something that is unfit to live. In the cross we learn that God has brought our sinful nature to a moral terminus. Its practical issues are resolved in this that, if I allow sin to operate in my life, I allow something to act that the Lord died to put away. What a serious reflection on our baptism if this is the case! May we ever live in the light of our baptism and, in doing so, we'll never go wrong. Burial is what follows death, its first mention in scripture being when Abraham bought the sepulchre from the sons of Ephron to bury his dead 'out of his sight'. This is where God would have the 'old man', dead and buried out of sight. In rising out of the waters of baptism we are brought into the light of resurrection and under moral obligation to live unto God and to walk in newness of life. God delights in living things and in this way we can minister pleasure to Him in our lives: we live unto God.

3. The Death of the Cross, Phil. 2. 1-8. This aspect of the cross has nothing to do with sin – something which is never mentioned in this Epistle. This should not startle the believer, but should make him endeavour to know and learn the will of God in this particular presentation of His cross. The cross in the Philippian Epistle is to teach the believer how to behave in the local assembly, especially in regard to its service and how that should be carried on. Thus, the injunction that nothing should be done through strife or vainglory would indicate, that in this otherwise good and happy assembly there was an element which caused some disturbance in the service of God. In fact, at the time of writing it amounted to something of the nature of a crisis. Because of the appeal to these two sisters, Euodias and Syntyche, 4. 2, it can be safely assumed that they had made a definite contribution to the disturbance of the assembly and were exposing its very existence to vital danger. It was this that caused the apostle to write these words contained in the second chapter, and never have words like them come from an inspired writer's pen. They stand unequalled, unique, profound as they describe the humiliation of Christ from His Godhead glory right to the death of the cross. Paul prefaced these words by this request, 'Let this mind be in you, which was also in Christ Jesus'. The mind of Christ was to come down, as can be seen from our passage.

Beloved, if pride of place in the assembly has been allowed to grip our hearts, we need to learn the meaning of His cross afresh. And how can this be done? Most of us have, in our assembly experience, been faced with situations whose solutions have meant the renunciation of our personal rights (not of divine principle), our complete humiliation being involved and not a shred of dignity left in us. How can we descend to such a level? Remember, however far we come down in this way, beloved child of God, we shall always find One who has come down farther. He in His obedience and service came down to the death of the cross. Can pride really exist in our hearts; can strife and vainglory influence; can murmurings and disputings mark us in our assembly life as we learn the meaning of His cross? How far is it true of us when we sing those well-known, yet profound words,

> 'When I survey the wondrous cross,
> On which the Prince of Glory died,
> My richest gain I count but loss,
> And pour contempt on all my pride?'
>
> ISAAC WATTS

What a test the cross is to us as to our spiritual development! The cross then in the Philippian aspect is to teach us the mind of Christ. And having learned this lesson, we arrive at the apostle's exhortation to work out our own salvation (i.e., the salvation of the assembly in its local testimony) with fear and trembling. For it is God that worketh in us both to will and to do of His good pleasure.

4. Enmity Slain by the Cross, Eph. 2. 15, 16. The context of the passage helps us to understand yet another aspect of the cross. The mystery, having been hid from all ages, has now been revealed to us by the apostle, that is, the Jew and Gentile have now been brought together in one body. That which formerly separated them was the enmity caused by the law, and this has now been abolished. The law gave the Jew his standing above the other nations, and he was such an elevated person with respect to the old covenant that other nations and people are called Gentile dogs! This law made him a proud aristocrat amongst other peoples but, in the light of the new revelation, national distinctions were levelled at the cross: the privileged Jew, as well as the alienated Gentile, required to be reconciled to God. The dividing wall – pride of place, race, and privilege – was broken down completely at the cross.

The truth thus given us, would teach us that in the church, the new creation, there is no place for national distinction but one body, making of the twain one new man. Whilst the politicians of this world sometimes find the problem of racial discrimination difficult, let us who, in this present dispensation have been called by His grace, rejoice in that we form part of that glorious body, that heavenly corporation where nothing exists which distinguishes men from men. And should this fundamental principle, which has its universal bearing in Ephesians, be lost to us locally? No! For everything that would separate believers from each other – the distinctions which men love to make and which obtain in this world, racial, social, etc. – have been removed by the cross. Oh, may our hearts respond in a practical way so that we may endeavour to give the necessary expression of our love to those of other nations in the body of Christ and in our local churches. Let us refuse to recognize the distance that men create between men, embracing all in our love and affection as being in the body of Christ, ' the cross, having slain the enmity thereby'.

5. The Offence of the Cross, Gal. 5. 11; 6. 12. The Epistle to the Galatians is not in its primary sense direct revelation, but is rather one of recovery, written to recapture the ground lost by the Galatian error. For they had gone back on the basic doctrines of the faith. They were guilty of submitting to the Judaizers who taught them that it was necessary to keep the law for their justification. The exacting nature of the law had destroyed their Christian character. Works of the law will never justify the believer, 2. 16; legality will take every mark of Christ out of our characters, 4. 19; it will destroy our relationships with our brethren, 5. 15, until nothing is left. Let us beware of all these dangers! We are directly referred to the rite of circumcision and the cross, 5. 11; 6. 12, as that which is radically opposed to such a practice. This is probably referred to by the apostle as that which represented or betokened the whole system of rites and ceremonies. It left its mark in men's flesh, and provided something in which they could glory. The Lord gave Himself to deliver us from this present evil world, 1. 4, and the apostle speaks of himself as being crucified unto the world, 6. 14. Now to give these passages their contextual value, 'the world' must of necessity incorporate into its meaning that part which the obsolete Judaistic system gave to it, and, although other features are certainly there, this is its primary connection in chapter 6.

Has it not its counterpart in the often worldly-religious systems existing in Christendom today? Many believers are there and we love them for Christ's sake, but we often have to repudiate the unholy systems with which they are associated. May the offence of the cross never cease in this sense with us! And, if we feel that our present association with the people of God, gathered to His name, be characterized by outward insignificance, may we find our compensation in this, saying with the apostle, 'God forbid that I should glory, save in the cross of our Lord Jesus Christ, by whom the world is crucified unto me, and I unto the world'.

6. The Preaching of the Cross, 1 Cor. 1. 18. The cross to the unbelieving Jew, was a stumbling block; to the educated Greek, foolishness. Seeing it is the preaching of the cross, would it not have a strong bearing on our evangelical service, in our gospel meetings, both inside and out? To preach the cross is to make nothing at all of man, whether he be religious or educated, its preaching coming as a fresh challenge to all. To preach the cross with such effect needs much of God's presence and power. The cross will be forever isolated in all its solitary grandeur from the cheap accompaniments that are found in modern methods of preaching. No one in the will of God can glamorize the cross or make it appeal to natural man, for it reduces him to the very dust. Although the preaching may be regarded as foolishness, and the preacher very often a fool, to the saved it is the power of God. Thus, God in His infallible word has linked the cross and salvation together. May the message of the cross lie at the heart of all our spiritual exercises in evangelical labours. Whilst it exposes man and all that he is in the sight of God, it also accomplishes salvation to those who believe.

'So while the cross my sin displays,
In all its blackest hue,
Oh wondrous mystery of grace,
It seals my pardon too'.

JOHN NEWTON

The Suffering and Exalted Servant - H. BEATTIE

Often, when we want to underline the sorrows and the humiliation of our Lord, we quote the well-known verses from Isaiah chapter 53. There He is so minutely described as 'a man of sorrows, and acquainted with grief' that the prophet's message has come to be associated almost exclusively with this aspect of His redeeming work.

Yet running through the section Isaiah chapter 52 verse 9 to chapter 53 verse 12 is another line of thought that wonderfully balances the presentation of the suffering Messiah, and casts its rays of heavenly light across the dark background of sorrow. In a study Bible, I once wrote beside these verses: Heaven's Response!

The four contrasts are connected with:

1. The changed site of burial, 53. 9;
2. The Messianic line, 53. 8, 10;
3. The world rulers' silence, 53. 7; 52. 15;
4. The divine might revealed, 53. 1; 52. 10.

The Changed Site of Burial. The heavenly reaction is clearly seen beginning in Isaiah chapter 53 verse 9. The plans of the authorities were to consign the body of the Lord Jesus to the degradation of the communal pit. There was no ceremonial burial for common criminals. '**They** made his grave with the wicked', RV. The precious body, formed in the womb of the virgin by the power of the Holy Spirit, was thus planned by men to be defiled. The wonderful body of Christ, culminating point of creation and to become the perfect basis of the new creation, was to have joined the corpses that had been removed from so many other crucifixions.

But heaven intervened. How fragrant is the scene in the garden, John 19. 38-42. A good man and just, Joseph of Arimathea, pleads with Pilate for the body of the Saviour. Loving hands carefully remove the nails from His wounded hands and feet, and gently lower Him from the cross. Surrounded by the sweet-smelling myrrh and aloes, the precious body is placed in the pure white linen and laid in the clean new rock tomb in the midst of the garden. What a contrast willed by God! They had planned His grave with the wicked ones, but He was with the rich one in His death. Heaven's response!

The Messianic Line. Then comes the prophet's query concerning the lineage and the posterity of the suffering Servant. Who shall declare His generation?, Isa. 53. 8. This question is all the more poignant when one remembers how the Messianic line had been divinely protected across so many centuries. Through Egyptian bondage and the Babylonian deportations, through the domestic crises of Judah and David, through links with unexpected incomers like Rahab and Ruth, the line of the Promised Seed was maintained. The wicked queen Athaliah thought she had destroyed all the seed royal, but the Lord preserved the tiny Joash. What a slender thread! Now the Messiah has come in fulfilment of all the promises, and His life has abruptly ended. There are no successors! Have all God's purposes fallen to the ground? Who shall declare His generation, Acts 8. 33?

How infinite is the vision inspired by the words of Isaiah chapter 53 verse 10 – 'He shall see his seed'. One hundred and twenty gathered in the Upper Room had become three thousand one hundred and twenty on the day of Pentecost. Many more thousands were soon added. Syria, Cyprus, Greece, Italy, Spain and the uttermost parts of the earth were to join the risen, glorified Lord in the power of the new creation on resurrection ground, as new believers from every region became true Christians. 'Behold I and the children which God hath given me', Heb. 2. 13. The once lonely, despised man of sorrows, in whom the Messianic line seemed to have irremediably terminated, is now surrounded by the countless myriads of the redeemed. He shall see of the travail of His soul. He shall be satisfied!

The World Rulers' Silence. Our Lord's silence in the presence of His accusers and judges surprised them. 'As a sheep before her shearers is dumb, so he openeth not his mouth', Isa. 53. 7. One appeal from His lips and twelve legions of angels or more would have sped to His rescue. The silent sufferer, wrists bound, does not protest. His only desire is meekly to accomplish His Father's will.

What a contrast in chapter 52 verse 15 NKJVmg, 'So shall He startle many nations. Kings shall shut their mouths at Him!' Here is a scene of regal glory, when our Lord will be revealed as the King of kings and the Lord of lords. In the full-orbed vision of His multiple glories all earthly authority will bow in the dust and not a voice will be heard in the vast assembly but that of Him who was so silent before those who thought they were His judges. Now, as in Psalm 29. 4, the voice of the Lord is powerful, the voice of the Lord is full of majesty. He who wore the crown of thorns in mockery will then have on His head many diadems.

The Divine Might Revealed. The expression 'the arm of the Lord' occurs several times in the book of Isaiah, speaking of the revealing of His strength in domination and in salvation. The question, to whom is the arm of the Lord revealed, Isa. 53. 1, seems to use it as a title of our Lord Jesus. How difficult though to discern the infinity of divine strength in the One presented in the following verses. A tender plant, a root out of a dry ground, no form nor comeliness, no beauty, despised, rejected, stricken, smitten of God, afflicted . . . these terms epitomize the totality of weakness and defeat. The final scenes at Calvary only seemed, to the natural man and to the outward eye, to confirm the hopelessness of the position of Jesus of Nazareth. Then comes the heavenly reaction, 'The Lord hath made bare his holy arm in the eyes of all the nations; and all the ends of the earth shall see the salvation of our God', Isa. 52. 10. 2 Thessalonians chapter 1 verse 7 comes to mind, 'The Lord Jesus shall be revealed from heaven with his mighty angels, in flaming fire taking vengeance on them that know not God. . . when he shall come to be glorified in his saints'. Heaven's response to all iniquity, rebellion and sin will once again grant to our beloved Lord the central and supreme position, revelation of the eternal infinity of the light and life and love of God.

The Resurrection of Jesus Christ - E. L. Lovering

It has been said that, 'the glory of our Christianity is that it never views life as being complete in this world. It always has its eyes lifted to the morning, and gazes out upon the eternities, recognizing that we belong to eternity as well as to time'.

The resurrection of Jesus Christ was, therefore, the essential sequel to His atoning death, that 'as in Adam all die, even so in Christ shall all be made alive'. B. F. Westcott wrote that 'taking all the evidence together, there is no single historic incident better or more variously supported than the resurrection of Christ'.

We shall content ourselves in this paper with a study of the great resurrection chapter, 1 Corinthians chapter 15.

1. Let us first consider, **three important testimonies** to the fact of the resurrection of Christ, vv. 1-11, as given in this chapter.

The Testimony of Experience. It is interesting to notice that the first evidence of the resurrection is not documentary or evidential but the living experience of a Christian soul. The apostle writes, 'Now I make known unto you, brethren, the gospel . . . which also ye received, wherein also ye stand, by which also ye are saved', vv. 1, 2 RV.

> 'He lives, He lives, Christ Jesus lives today,
> He walks with me and talks with me,
> Along life's narrow way;
> He lives, He lives, salvation to impart;
> You ask me how I know He lives,
> He lives within my heart'.
>
> A. H. Ackley

The Testimony of the scriptures. The scriptures here referred to are no doubt the Old Testament Hebrew scriptures. Throughout these scriptures there ran the principle of resurrection, of life out of death, of triumph through travail. This was the pathway of the Saviour, 'when thou shalt make his soul an offering for sin, he shall see his seed, he shall prolong his days . . . He shall see of the travail of his soul and shall be satisfied', Isa. 53. 10, 11. Concerning Israel we read, 'He hath torn, and he will heal us; he hath smitten, and he will bind us up. After two days will he revive us; in the third day he will raise us up, and we shall live in his sight', Hos. 6. 1, 2.

The Testimony of Eye-witnesses. 'He appeared to Cephas [Peter]; then to the twelve; then he appeared to above 500 brethren at once . . . then he appeared to James; then to all the apostles, and last of all, as unto one born out of due time, he appeared to me also', 1 Cor. 15. 5-8 RV. Surely here are sufficient witnesses for any court of law!

Modern rationalists maintain that they can account for the appearances of our Lord Jesus Christ by the ordinary laws of psychology, without introducing supernatural agency. Hallucinations, they say, are known to occur to persons afflicted with certain physical diseases; to insane persons; to persons, not insane, but suffering from certain disorders of the nervous system; to healthy persons intensely preoccupied with an idea which they have allowed to obtain exclusive possession of their minds. We note here, however, that none of those who saw the risen Lord were sick, nor insane. It is hardly credible that Mary Magdalene who came to a graveyard in the dim light of early morning, was suffering from disorders of the nervous system, and in any case it cannot be said of the twelve, or of James, or of the 500 brethren. As to the idea of preoccupation, the disciples showed no intense preoccupation with this thought. Rather, the Gospels indicate that our Lord's prophecies of His resurrection fell upon deaf ears, Matt. 16. 22; Mark 9. 10, and depict the despondency of the disciples, Matt. 26. 56; Mark 16. 10, and their unwillingness to believe the good news.[89]

2. The apostle continues his theme, 1 Cor. 15. 12-34, by showing the resurrection message to be a **central fact** in: (a) his preaching, vv. 12-19; (b) God's plan and purposes, vv. 20-28; and (c) his own personal experiences, vv. 29-34.

His preaching is empty, unreal and frustrated, if Christ hath not been raised, vv. 14, 15, and those who have placed their hopes in Christ are of all people most to be pitied, v. 19.

---

[89] Matt. 28. 17; Mark 16. 11-14; Luke 24. 11.

Moreover, in **God's plan** Christ has been raised from the dead, the firstfruits, the pledge of harvest, of them that are asleep. Paul scans the whole plan of the ages from Adam to the time when God shall be all in all.

His own conduct would have been entirely illogical and unwarranted if the dead are not raised at all. Surely his motto for living would have been 'let us eat and drink, for tomorrow we die', v. 32. Instead he 'died daily', holding his life 'in jeopardy every hour', fighting even 'with beasts at Ephesus'. This thought demands no compromise with evil, but a bestirring of the soul to righteous living, v. 34.

3. Two **questions** now present themselves in the next section of the chapter, vv. 35-49. There were those who asked, How are the dead raised up? and with what manner of body do they come? It was not surprising to find these difficulties arising in an atmosphere permeated with the philosophies of the Corinthian schools. The Epicurean philosopher denied any existence beyond death. The Stoic said that at death the soul would be burnt or return to be absorbed in God, and so the personality would be lost. Platonism, though believing in the immortality of the soul, denied the idea of bodily resurrection.

In answering these questions Paul begins by referring to the miracle of harvest. The bare unclothed grain is placed in the ground, it dies and is quickened. God gives it a 'body', clothed with stalk, ear and full corn in the ear. It is different from that which was sown, yet essentially the same. In nature, death is the necessary prelude to life.

Bodies are adapted to environment; there is one flesh of men, another of beasts, another of fish, and another of birds. So also is the resurrection of the dead, v. 42. The sun, moon, and stars have varying glories; there is variety in God's creation, but each has its own peculiar glory. Thus, there is something much more than Epicurean materialism; and, contrary to the Stoical and Platonic teachings, the soul does not lose its personality, or its bodily form in resurrection.

The natural body is sown in corruption, it is raised in incorruption; it is sown in dishonour, it is raised in glory; it is sown in weakness, it is raised in power; it is sown a natural body, it is raised a spiritual body. As we have borne the image of the earthy, we shall also bear the image of the heavenly, v. 49.

4. The apostle finally calls for special attention while he discloses **a revelation hitherto kept secret**, vv. 50-57. 'Behold', he declares, 'we shall not all sleep [die] but we shall all be changed, in a moment, in the twinkling of an eye, at the last trump'. Here is an event which will take place in time, when Christians who are living their ordinary lives will be suddenly and wonderfully changed, just as really as those who are fallen asleep in Jesus. Then the final triumph of resurrection will be realized, for death is swallowed up victoriously. And so the challenge rings out to the last great enemy, 'O death, where is thy sting? O grave, where is thy victory? Thanks be to God, which giveth us the victory, through our Lord Jesus Christ'.

Thus, having challenged death as to its sting and the grave as to its victory, Paul concludes with a **note of encouragement**, 'Wherefore, my beloved brethren, be ye stedfast, unmoveable, always abounding in the work of the Lord, forasmuch as ye know that your labour is not in vain in the Lord', v. 58.

The harvest is sure and your reward for labour and toil will surely find its recompense.

> 'Toil on, and in thy toil rejoice –
> For toil comes rest, for exile home;
> Soon shalt thou hear the Bridegroom's voice,
> The midnight peal, "Behold, I come!"'.
>
> H. BONAR

Resurrection - T. W. CARRON

It has been said: 'Christianity begins where religions end . . . with the Resurrection'. How true this is! The two great world religions, Buddhism and Islam, to which hundreds of millions of the human race are enslaved, know nothing of a living Saviour, or indeed of a Saviour at all. The same is true of all the other religions, which are either ancient superstitions, demon worship, Satanic delusion, or human speculation.

Christianity alone can boast of a living Saviour. It stands unassailably on the impregnable rock of Christ's resurrection. Men have striven to disprove it, and some are still trying, but they only expose themselves to ridicule in the attempt. One who critically examined the account of the resurrection in the Gospels with the object of disproving it, finished up with the conviction that the resurrection was an indisputable fact.

In that inspired treatise on the resurrection in 1 Corinthians chapter 15 the apostle Paul deals with a number of different facets of the subject.

The Doctrine of the Resurrection. He writes, 'For I delivered unto you first of all that which I also received, how that Christ died for our sins according to the scriptures; and that he was buried, and that he rose again the third day according to the scriptures', 1 Cor. 15. 3. When Christ rose again, He did not return to the old condition of flesh and blood. He had given that life up. He was raised in a new condition of life, a new kind of life. He said to His disciples on the resurrection day, 'handle me, and see; for a spirit hath not flesh and bones, as ye see me have', Luke 24. 39. It was not a spirit they saw, but a man with flesh and bones, not flesh and blood. Yet He left the grave clothes undisturbed, and the stone needed not to be moved to allow Him to leave the grave. The closed doors of the upper room needed not to be opened to Him. He stood in the midst of His disciples, and ate before them. Such was His resurrection body.

The Proof of the Resurrection. Paul cites the appearances of Christ as proof of His resurrection: to Cephas, to the twelve, to 500 at once, most of whom were alive when Paul wrote, to James, and to all the apostles. Finally he tells of his own experience when Jesus appeared to him from heaven, 1 Cor. 15. 5-9.

From the Gospels we can add other witnesses, Mary Magdalene and the other women, the two whom He overtook on the Emmaus road, and that hard-to-convince disciple Thomas. These were not the hallucinations of excited men and women. When the Spirit came on them at Pentecost, they realized that Christ's resurrection had been foretold in scripture, and remembered His own assurance that He would rise again. The Jews themselves had not forgotten this, and to make assurance doubly sure, they had the tomb sealed and a guard posted at the entrance. How futile it was!

The Importance of the Resurrection. It seems incredible that there should have been men in the assembly at Corinth who doubted the resurrection. Yet there were. And there are professors of Christianity today who doubt or deny it. To such Paul answers, 'and if Christ be not raised, your faith is vain; ye are yet in your sins. Then they also which are fallen asleep in Christ are perished. If in this life only we have hope in Christ, we are of all men most miserable', vv. 17-19. There can be no true gospel without the resurrection.

The Consequence of the Resurrection. The consequence of Christ's resurrection is that others will be raised too. He is the firstfruits of a great harvest, v. 20.

This is beautifully typified in the sheaf of firstfruits offered year by year according to the law, and doubtless offered on the very day Christ rose from the dead. Nearly 1,500 years earlier God had given this command, 'Speak unto the children of Israel, and say unto them, When ye be come into the land which I give unto you, and shall reap the harvest thereof, then ye shall bring a sheaf of the firstfruits of your harvest unto the priest', Lev. 23. 10. The month Abib, also called Nisan and the first month of the sacred year, was the month the barley ripened. This commandment follows that of the passover and the sheaf was to be offered on the day after the Sabbath, that is, the first day of the week. This is the type. Here in 1 Corinthians 15 we have the antitype, 'Christ the firstfruits; afterwards they that are Christ's at his coming', v. 23.

The Manner of the Resurrection. 'But some man will say', writes Paul, 'How are the dead raised up? and with what body do they come?' v. 35.

Using the illustration of the seed and the different kinds of flesh he demonstrates that the resurrection body differs from the body that goes into the grave. We have already noticed the wonderful change in the Lord's own body. And we are told that in the resurrection we shall have bodies like His; 'when he shall appear, we shall be like him; for we shall see him as he is', 1 John 3. 2.

The Glory of the Resurrection. Our resurrection bodies will be bodies of glory, 'it is sown in dishonour; it is raised in glory: it is sown in weakness; it is raised in power . . . And as we have borne the image of the earthy, we shall also bear the image of the heavenly', 1 Cor. 15. 43, 49. Moreover, we are told in Philippians chapter 3 verses 20 and 21 RV, 'Our citizenship is in heaven; from whence also we wait for a Saviour, the Lord Jesus Christ: who shall fashion anew the body of our humiliation, that it may be conformed to the body of his glory [or, his body of glory]'.

The Victory of the Resurrection. 'Behold, I show you a mystery; We shall not all sleep, but we shall all be changed, in a moment, in the twinkling of an eye, at the last trump: for the trumpet shall sound, and the dead shall be raised incorruptible, and we shall be changed . . . So when this corruptible shall have put on incorruption, and this mortal shall have put on immortality, then shall be brought to pass the saying that is written, Death is swallowed up in victory', 1 Cor. 15. 51, 52, 54.

The emphasis here is on the **resurrection**. In 1 Thessalonians chapter 4, it is the **rapture**, our being caught up to meet the Lord in the air, which is emphasized. Here, it is the actual resurrection. Ascension is not mentioned. On the first Easter Day our blessed Lord stood upon this earth, a Man, raised from the dead. He had vanquished death. On that coming day when the trumpet sounds, the raised dead and the changed living, a vast host, will stand – if only for a moment – upon this earth, glorious demonstration of Christ's victory over death.

'Death is swallowed up in victory. O death, where is thy sting? O grave, where is thy victory?' 1 Cor. 15. 54, 55.

The Lord's Ascension and Exaltation - M. Jones

The departure from earth and arrival in heaven of the Lord of glory is an enthralling study for the believer. The event introduced a whole range of heavenly glory for the Lord, of which we, by grace, are partakers. For our present position as strangers and pilgrims is not the end of the story. It has yet to be exchanged for an eternal and exceeding weight of glory, into which the Lord Himself has already entered.

In order to clarify our thinking we will look at the Lord's ascension and exaltation from four viewpoints.

1. The Reality of it. To those who accept the divine authority of the scriptures, there can be no doubt as to the historical and bodily ascension of the Lord of glory. That the event actually occurred is seen from the detailed record of it in more than one place.

As to His Ascension, two evangelists, Mark and Luke, include the event in their writings, and the other two evangelists clearly write in full knowledge of it, Matt. 28. 20; John 20. 17. Four interesting expressions are used of Christ's ascension, as follows:

a) He was 'received up', Mark 16. 19.[90] The perfect Servant was welcomed to the place of highest honour – the right hand of God;
b) He was 'carried up', Luke 24. 51. The perfect Man, while blessing others, was Himself escorted in triumph, perhaps by angels – 16. 22, into heaven whence He continues to bless His people;
c) He was 'taken up', Acts 1. 9. Here the power of God is seen as the means whereby the Lord was lifted from earth to heaven;
d) He 'ascended up', Eph. 4. 8. Both the resurrection and the ascension were not only effected by the glory of the Father, but also by the personal power of Him who is one with the Father, John 20. 17.

It is important to observe that the ascension was not missed by sleeping men, nor imagined by dreaming men, but was beheld by credible and dependable witnesses, Acts 1. 9.

As to His Exaltation, the scripture is equally detailed and emphatic. For when the cloud, possibly the Shekinah, received Him from their sight, He did not just vanish. He returned to the place whence He came, John 16. 28. The following expressions are given to help our understanding.

a) He 'passed through the heavens', Heb. 4. 14 RV. The triumphant Saviour journeyed through the territory of His defeated enemy, Eph. 2. 2, with none to withstand Him, Dan. 10. 13. 'Up through the skies the Conqueror rode'.

---

[90] See also Acts 1. 2, 11, 22 RV; 1 Tim. 3. 16.

b) He 'ascended far above all the heavens', Eph. 4. 10 RV, by His own authority as the mighty Victor.
c) He is 'made higher than the heavens', Heb. 7. 26, by the divine decree of the God who is well satisfied with the sent One.
d) He entered 'into heaven itself', Heb. 9. 24. 'No place too high for Him is found'. He entered the immediate and eternal dwelling place of God.
e) He 'is on the right hand of God', 1 Pet. 3. 22. The writer of the Epistle to the Hebrews describes this position of supreme authority in similar terms. The Lord is seen there in view of His successful sin-purging, 1. 3, His high priesthood, 8. 1, His one final sacrifice, 10. 12, His enduring the cross, 12. 2.

The Reasons for it. It was necessary that all things written concerning Him in the sacred writings should be fulfilled, Luke 24. 44.

In the Law of Moses, Lev. 16, we observe a high priest entering into the holy of holies to make atonement annually on the great Day of Atonement. In glorious fulfilment of this ritual, Christ has 'entered in once for all into the holy place, having obtained eternal redemption', Heb. 9. 11, 12 RV. The superiority of His sanctuary is also to be noted, 8. 2.

In the Prophets we find it foretold that Jehovah's Servant would be 'exalted and extolled, and be very high', Isa. 52. 13. The fulfilment of this verse is clearly recorded by Paul, Phil. 2. 9.

In the Psalms David records Jehovah as saying to Messiah, 'Sit thou at my right hand, until I make thine enemies thy footstool', 110. 1. These words are quoted or referred to seven times in the New Testament, and Peter specifically relates them to the ascension in Acts 2. 33-36.

It was also necessary that the Lord's own words concerning His ascension should find their fulfilment.[91]

But not only was the Lord's ascension necessary to fulfil divine words. It was essential for the welfare of His people. For we now have in

[91] See, for example, John 6. 62; 7. 33; 14. 2, 3; 16. 28; 20. 17.

heaven an 'advocate with the Father', and a 'merciful and faithful high priest' concerned with our present needs. Not only so, but we understand from John chapter 14 verses 2, 3 that the Lord is occupied with our future needs. 'I go to prepare a place for you' were His words of assurance.

The Results of it. For the Lord His ascension brought:

a) *Vindication.* The estimation of men was then reversed. He who was despised and abhorred on earth, Isa. 49. 7; 53. 4, has been welcomed in heaven, Acts 2. 36; 4. 11.
b) *Glorification.* From John chapter 17 verse 5 we would gather there was a glory which the Lord 'veiled' on coming into the world, cp. John 1. 14. No doubt it was the enjoyment and glory of a heavenly supremacy with the Father, contrasted temporarily for the indignities of earth. Having glorified the Father on earth, He himself was immediately glorified upon ascending to heaven, John 13. 31, 32.
c) *Pre-eminence.* This the Lord enjoys among His people by reason of being Head of the body, the church, Col. 1. 18. But His supremacy in heaven extends far above all forms of rule, authority and power, whether present or future, whether submissive or hostile.[92]

For us His ascension has brought about:

a) *The Descent of the Spirit.* This could not take place until the Lord's return to heaven, John 7. 39; 16. 7, and its occurrence is evidence of the Lord's exaltation, Acts 2. 33;
b) *The Giving of Gifts to men,* for the well-being of the church, over which He is the exalted Head, Eph. 4. 8-13;
c) *His Constant Presence,* Matt. 18. 20; 28. 20. The disciples, while losing the bodily presence of their Lord when He ascended, exchanged it for something better. Prior to the ascension the Lord spent certain time in their company; subsequently He never left them. His words, moreover, are not just a promise of what shall be, but a statement of what is. He said, 'lo, I am with you all the days, even unto the end', 28. 20 RVmg. There is never a single day, nor a

---

[92] Eph. 1. 20, 21; Phil. 2. 10; 1 Pet. 3. 22.

moment of a day, when we are denied His presence;

d) *His Constant Help,* Mark 16. 19, 20. Luke describes his Gospel as consisting of things that 'Jesus began both to do and teach', Acts 1. 1. The Acts is a continuation of these things, for though He has ascended on high He still works with His disciples below, 'the Lord working with them';
e) *Assurance of our Ascension.* The Lord's ascension to glory is the pledge of our arrival there, for He has entered heaven as our forerunner, Heb. 6. 20. Before He left the disciples the Lord left on record the promise of His return to receive us to Himself forever, John 14. 3. And when we ascend with Him to the Father's house, it will be in a state totally conformed to our Lord, Phil. 3. 21; 1 John 3. 2.

4. **The Response to it.** The study of scripture is not an academic exercise having its end in itself. The record of the Lord's ascension and exaltation should produce within us:

a) *Concentration* on heavenly things. The Lord has linked us with Himself where He is, and our earnest desire should be for 'those things which are above', Col. 3. 1. Our attention and affection should be directed to them, and not to the passing things of earth.
b) *Confidence.* Fear of future condemnation need never terrorize the true child of God. We are so certainly the objects of divine love eternally, that we are encouraged to have great boldness 'because as he is, so are we in this world', 1 John 4. 17.

The Priesthood of the Lord Jesus Christ - J. Boyd

In the New Testament, explicit teaching concerning the Priesthood and the priestly work of the Lord Jesus Christ is confined to the Epistle to the Hebrews, and to an example of His functioning as such in John chapter 17.

His Qualifications for the Priesthood.
(How He qualified for His priestly office).

His Incarnation. He was made like unto His brethren, Heb. 2. 17.
His Call. He was called of God, 5. 6, 10. He was made a priest by the oath

of God, 7. 21.

His Experience:

He was tempted in all points like us, 2. 18; 4. 15.
He offered up prayers in the days of His flesh, 5. 7.
He experienced obedience through sufferings, 5. 8.
He was perfected through sufferings, 5. 9; 7. 28.

His Work. He offered Himself a sacrifice, 8. 3; 9. 12, 14. He passed through the heavens, 4. 14.

The Type of His Priesthood.

The nature of His Priesthood is seen in type in Aaron's, in that He, like Aaron:

1. Was taken from among men, 2. 17; 5. 1;
2. Was called of God, 5. 4, 5;
3. Could enter within the veil, 6. 19, 20; 9. 7, 12;
4. Was a minister of the sanctuary, 8. 1, 2; cp. Lev. 16. 16;
5. Was appointed to offer gifts and sacrifices, Heb. 8. 3;
6. Cleansed the tabernacle and the vessels of the ministry, 9. 21-24;
7. Offered a sacrifice for sin, 10. 11, 12.

The Order of His Priesthood.

(The rank, or class in which He was included).

a) It was of the order of Melchizedek's priesthood, 7. 1-3, ***in that***
   He was a King-Priest.
   He had no genealogy.
   He had no beginning, nor ending.
   He abideth a Priest for ever.
b) It was a different rank from that of Aaron, ***because***
   He was of a different tribe, 7. 12-14.
   He had a different tenure of office, 7. 15-19.
   He received His appointment in a different manner, 7. 20, 21
c) It was superior to that of Aaron, ***because***
   Aaron was blessed by Melchizedek, 7. 6.
   Aaron paid tithes to Melchizedek, 7. 6, 9.
   Christ was the surety of a better covenant, 7. 22-28, because:
      They of Aaron's order died. He ever liveth;
      They were sinful. He was sinless;

They had infirmities. He was perfected;
They were earthly. He was made higher than the heavens;
They never led the people into the holiest. He is our Forerunner, 6. 20.

The Ministry of His Priesthood.

(a) His Past Ministry.

He made propitiation for the sins of the people, 2. 17; 7. 27.
He appeared to put away sin, 9. 26.
He became the surety of the new covenant, 7. 22.
He sanctified believers, 10. 10.
He offered one sacrifice for sins, 10. 12.
He perfected the sanctified, 10. 14.
He entered into heaven – As Forerunner, 6. 20.
– As Redeemer, 9. 12.
– As Purifier, 9. 23, 24; cp. Lev. 16. 16.

(b) His Present Ministry (In the true tabernacle, Heb. 8. 2).

He succours the tempted, 2. 18; cp. Luke 22. 31, 32.
He encourages us to draw near to the throne of grace, Heb. 4. 16; 10. 22.
He brightens our hope of being in heaven, 6. 20; 10. 23.
He saves to the uttermost those who come unto God through Him, 7. 25.
His salvation is initial, continual, eternal.
He makes intercession, 7. 25; cp. Lev. 16. 12; Ps. 141. 2.
He is the Mediator of the new and better covenant, ensuring that believers receive the promises of it, Heb. 8. 6; 9. 15; cp. 1 Tim. 2. 5.
He appears before God for us, Heb. 9. 24; cp. Exod. 28. 29. He presents our sacrifice of praise to God, Heb. 13. 15.

c) His Future Ministry.

He will appear a second time for the consummation of our salvation, 9. 28.

The Excellence of His Priesthood.

Because of the excellence of:

a) *The Priest Himself;*

Without sin, 4. 15; 7. 27.
Perfect, 5. 9; 7. 28.
Undying, 7. 16, 24.

b) *His Ministry;*

A perfect sacrifice, 7. 27; 9. 14, 23, 26.
A perfect salvation, 7. 25.
A perfect covenant, 7. 22; 8. 6.
A perfect approach through Him, 10. 20.

c) *The Sphere of His Ministry;*

Within the veil, 6. 19.
The true tabernacle, pitched by God, not by man's hand, 8. 2; 9. 11.
Heaven, 9. 24.
Before the face of God, 9. 24.

The Character of the Priest.

Merciful, faithful, 2. 17.
Sympathetic, 4. 15.
Experienced, 4. 15.
Unchanging, 7. 16, 24.
Holy, guileless, undefiled, separated from sinners, made higher than the heavens, 7. 26.
Perfect, 7. 28.
Majestic, 8. 1.

An Example of His Priestly Work, John 17.
He prays for the believers that:

1. They might be kept in the knowledge of God's will, v. 11;
2. They might have His joy, v. 13;
3. They might be kept from the evil in the world, v. 15;
4. They might be sanctified, separated to the ministry of the word, vv. 17, 19;
5. They might be one with all believers, v. 21;
6. They might be with Him in eternity, and see His glory, v. 24.

Christ Our High Priest* - B. CLATWORTHY

When we consider the work of the high priest in Israel, we immediately think of sacrifice and ritual. But, in fact, the work of the high priest began after the sacrifice had been ritually killed at the brazen altar. This prefigures the high priesthood of Christ whose intercessory work for us began after His ascension, once he had secured eternal redemption, Heb. 9. 12. As SIR ROBERT ANDERSON writes, 'And on earth it was that His **sacrificial** work in redemption was accomplished. That work, therefore, must have been complete before He entered on His High-priestly office'.[93] This is an important point since on earth Christ could not have officiated as a high priest as He belonged to the tribe of Judah, not Levi, 7. 14.[94] Yet, He made purification for our sins, a feat that no other high priest could accomplish, 10. 11, and then sat down on the right hand of God.[95] This is a remarkable statement because no high priest had ever sat down in the presence of God, v. 11. What is even more significant is that Christ's present ministry for us is not associated with a material world and an earthly sanctuary, things indicative of a former covenant, 9. 1. Christ now intercedes for us in the very presence of God Himself, i.e., in the heavenly sanctuary and the true tabernacle, which God pitched not man, 8. 2; 9. 11, 12. This reflects the mediatory order of a new covenant, which crucially has been ratified by the blood of Christ, 9. 14, 15. This calls for further explanation as to why a system of worship introduced by God appears to be flawed. Essentially, the question is why it was necessary then for Christ to become our High Priest? A question that is interestingly anticipated for us in Hebrews chapter 7 verse 11.

This latter question can be answered only as we compare and contrast the high priesthood of Christ with that of Aaron. This is without doubt the intention of the writer to the Hebrews as he carefully constructs an argument to show how Christ not only fulfils all the requirements of the Aaronic priesthood, but surpasses it. So to prove fitness for high priesthood according to the law, i.e., the old covenant, Christ must be shown to comply with the pattern of Aaron's ministry. The writer to the Hebrews consequently provides incontrovertible proof of this in two

---

[93] *Types in Hebrews,* pg. 27.

[94] But this does not mean that the form of Christ's ministry for us was not anticipated, e.g., His high priestly prayer in John 17.

[95] The expression 'majesty on high' in Hebrews chapter 1 verse 3 is simply a periphrasis for God. See also: Ps. 110. 1; Heb. 1. 3; 8. 1; 10. 12.

ways. First, because Aaron was human he was able to understand human frailty as he ministered before God in his capacity as a high priest, 5. 1-4. He was taken in all his human weakness, 7. 28, to represent those who were physically alive, but spiritually dead in trespasses and sins. This did not, however, mean that Aaron was sinless, as he also had to offer sacrifices for his own sins, 5. 2, 3. Hence the inherent weakness of the Aaronic priesthood! Christ, through incarnation, 2. 14-17, is likewise fitted to exercise priesthood amongst men, 5. 5, but is shown to be impervious to sin, Rom. 8. 3; Heb. 4. 15. The fact that Christ was impeccable does not mean that His temptations were unreal, 2. 18;[96] but He remained unstained by them, 4. 15, and is therefore able to provide us with sympathetic assurance when we are tempted, 2. 18; 4. 16. In contrast then to Aaron, Christ was taken from among dead men in resurrection glory to intercede for those who were once dead in trespasses and sins, but He is declared to be holy, innocent, unstained, separated from sinners, and exalted above the heavens, 7. 26 ESV.

Second, even though Aaron featured prominently in Israel's history, Exod. 16. 33, he did not just assume the position of high priest; he needed a definite call by God to the office, 28. 1; Heb. 5. 4. Similarly, Christ was called of God to be a high priest, but notably His ministry is after the order of Melchizedek. Contrast the different words used for 'call' in Hebrews chapter 5. The word used in verse 4 of Aaron's call, *kaleō*, merely confirms that he had been called by God. But the word used in verse 10 of Christ's call, *prosagoreuō* – a word used only once in the New Testament – can be translated as 'saluted', suggesting a public proclamation. WILLIAM LANE goes further when he states that the word conveys the idea of a formal and solemn ascription of an honorific title.[97]

In the Old Testament, leadership and high priesthood were regarded as separate functions within Israel, 2 Chr. 26. 18. Herein, then, lies the

---

[96] 'Sympathy with the sinner in his trial does not depend on the experience of sin but on the experience of the strength of the temptation to sin which only the sinless can know in its full intensity', B. F. WESTCOTT, *The Epistle to the Hebrews*, pg. 59.
[97] *Hebrews*, pg. 110.

greatness of Christ's high priesthood, which is after the order of Melchizedek. He combines in His ministry both priesthood and kingship – this is foreshadowed in 2 Samuel chapter 6 when David, as king, danced before the ark wearing a linen ephod, a symbol of sacerdotal vesture.[98]

The mysterious figure of Melchizedek is referred to in only two passages in the Old Testament, Gen. 14. 18-20; Ps. 110. 4, yet he also plays a significant part in our understanding of the High Priesthood of Christ as reflected in the New Testament letter to the Hebrews. Melchizedek is introduced to us when he suddenly appears to Abram, at the same time as the king of Sodom, Gen. 14. 18-20. He provides refreshment to Abram and his hired servants on their return from battle. The name Melchizedek literally means 'my king is righteous', cp. Heb. 7. 2. Melchizedek is described in Genesis chapter 14 verse 18 as the king of Salem, and as being a priest of God Most High. Salem is usually understood as referring to Jerusalem, cp. Ps. 76. 2. Melchizedek is referred to on eight occasions in the letter to the Hebrews,[99] but nowhere else in the New Testament. Melchizedek's sudden appearance and then disappearance, plus the omission of any family genealogy in Genesis chapter 14, is used by the writer of Hebrews to typify the timelessness of the priesthood that resembles that of the Son of God. Melchizedek's priesthood did not depend upon succession, since there was no record of his death. Similarly, Christ's high priesthood is seen to be eternal, never to be passed to another, unlike that of Aaron who would eventually die and thereby be subject to the rules of succession, Ezra 2. 62-63; Neh. 7. 63-65. This means that Christ's ministry for us is always consistent, never subject to change or weakness, Heb. 13. 8. It has been well said that when Aaron assumed the role of a high priest, the office dignified the man. But when we think about Christ as our High Priest, it is the Man that dignifies the office!

We posed the question earlier as to why it was necessary for Christ to

---

[98] ANDREW LINCOLN, *Hebrews – A Guide*, pg. 69, suggests that Psalm 110 verses 1 and 4 contain the major theme of Hebrews – the exaltation of Christ at God's right hand, v. 1, and specifically His exaltation as Priest after the order of Melchizedek according to God's oath, v. 4.

[99] Heb. 5. 6, 10; 6. 20; 7. 1, 10, 11, 15, 17.

become our high priest. The simple answer might be the failure of those who served under the old covenant to fully meet the standards and requirements of God. But, that is only part of the equation. Priestly activity under the Aaronic order was directly linked with ineffective sacrifices, 10. 1-4, so, irrespective of the value of their service, and the volume of sacrifices, they could not produce the desired effect, v. 11. A precedent is therefore established with the priesthood of Christ in that by His one single oblation, i.e., His death on the cross, the question of sin has been dealt with once and for all, v. 14. This now means that access into God's presence is assured for us at all times as the veil separating us from God has been removed, vv. 19, 20.

We might finally ask ourselves the question, 'Why then do we need a High Priest under a new covenant with God?' As we have indicated previously, priesthood has to do with intercession, principally, but not exclusively, the maintenance of communion and fellowship with God. The substance of Christ's activity for us now is summarized in the table below:

Present Activity	**Reference**
He orchestrates the worship of God's people – the great song leader in God's presence	Heb. 2. 11-13
He continues to reconcile believers to God, because He has removed the barrier of sin thus effecting unbroken communion with God. Believers can go boldly where others were previously excluded	Heb. 2. 17; 10. 19, 21, 22; 1 John. 2. 1
He provides a source of strength and encouragement to believers in times of temptation/testing, because He too has experienced severe testing/temptation	Heb. 2. 18; 4. 14-16
He ensures that our spiritual worship is acceptable to God since it is made through and by Him	1 Pet. 2. 5
Every charge/allegation brought against us on account of sin is rejected as Christ makes intercession for believers	Isa. 53. 12 Rom. 8. 33-35

We have touched only the hem of the high priest's garment, and there is so much more that could be said about Christ our High Priest. Perhaps, however, the verse of an old hymn now made popular by a modern tune, will cover our inadequacy.

> 'Before the throne of God above
> I have a strong, a perfect plea –
> A great High Priest, whose name is Love,
> Who ever lives and pleads for me'.
>
> C. L. BANCROFT

The High Priestly Work of Christ - E. H. TRENCHARD

High Priestly Functions. The key verse for the understanding of the functions of a high priest, whether in type or fulfilment, is Hebrews chapter 5 verse 1, 'For every high priest taken from among men is ordained **for men in things pertaining to God**, that he may offer both gifts and sacrifices for sins'. A high priest, then, stands between God and man, and it is an essential condition of his service that he should have perfect contact with one and the other. The work is a special form of the mediatorial office. Paul speaks of the One Mediator between God and man, Himself Man, Christ Jesus, 1 Tim. 2. 5, and refers to the intercessory ministry of Christ at the right hand, Rom. 8. 34. John delights to remind us that we have an advocate, a *Paraclete,* with the Father, 1 John 2. 1; but the detailed working out of the implications of the High Priestly type is unique to the writer of the Hebrews. He sees deep spiritual import in the oft-repeated command, 'See . . . thou make all things according to the pattern showed to thee in the mount', and sees each material detail of the tabernacle and its service as being a visible and imperfect expression of the invisible and perfect heavenly reality, with Christ as High Priest mediating between God and man in the heavenly sanctuary.

The Contact Godward. This contact was exceedingly faulty in the Aaronic type, and could only be maintained in symbol. Natural man is unsuited to the divine presence, and the Old Testament saints rightly felt that the logical outcome of seeing God face to face was death. Even Moses confessed in the presence of God, 'I exceedingly fear and quake',

Heb. 12. 41. Aaron was not 'at home' in the Holiest of All, and, even in the earthly shadow, could only approach tremblingly and lift the veil once every year. Moreover, he was not only a natural man, but personally a sinner and exposed to the wrath of God. For that reason, on the great Day of Atonement on which so much of the teaching of Hebrews is based, he had first to offer sacrifice for his own sins, and afterward, typically covered by the blood, he could begin to exercise his office on behalf of this people. The sinful, natural man was also mortal, and thus his ministry was necessarily cut short by death. 'They truly were many priests, because they were not suffered to continue by reason of death', Heb. 7. 23, and for this reason the Aaronic priesthood was hereditary so that there should be no break in continuity in the earthly shadow.

The weakness of the Aaronic type was felt even in the old dispensation, and in Psalm 110 there was the looking forward to a permanent priesthood associated with the Messiah. By this prophetic reference, the brief appearance of Melchizedek, the mystical priest-king, of whom no ancestry or descent is recorded, and who received tithes at the hand of Abraham, acquired new significance. The Hebrew Christians to whom the letter is addressed, and whose thoughts were turning longingly back to the old ritual, are reminded that there was no finality about the Aaronic priesthood, even in the inspired thoughts of David, and are thus helped to see in Christ the perfect fulfilment of both types.

The Godward contact, so faulty in Aaron, was perfect in 'Jesus the Son of God', Heb. 4. 14, whose very title thus given emphasizes perfect humanity and perfect deity. For this reason the writer opens his treatise with a sublime demonstration of the full deity of the Lord Jesus, so that the faltering Hebrews might understand how much greater was the heavenly High Priest than the earthly one to whom their thoughts were returning. **He** is perfectly 'at home' in the sanctuary for He belongs there and, as of right, when He had purged our sins, He sat down on the right hand of the majesty on high. Our hearts can therefore perfectly rest in His all sufficiency in 'things pertaining to God'. In all things here He stands in contrast to Aaron, for He knows no limitation in regard to moral requirements, for His only contact with sins was when He purged them. Neither is there any failure of continuity for, having once offered Himself for sins, He 'continueth ever' in an unchangeable priesthood, and saves to the uttermost since He ever liveth to make intercession. 'For such an high priest became us [answered to our need] . . . holy, harmless, undefiled, separate from sinners, and made higher than the heavens', Heb. 7. 26, 27.

The Contact Manward. Aaron's qualifications, which were so deficient on the Godward side, were such on the manward side that he could indeed 'have compassion on the ignorant, and on them that are out of the way; for that he himself also is compassed with infirmity', Heb. 5. 2, so that, in the essential matter of understanding the people's needs and appearing on their behalf, his very sinnership was a qualification.

What was easy and natural for the type was infinitely difficult for the antitype whose very deity and absolute moral perfection as a man rendered Him so different from poor, weak, struggling, sinful humanity. How was He to be 'touched with the feeling of our infirmity'? How could He enter into the experience of those who were immeasurably removed from His calm, sinless sphere? Only the full riches of divine wisdom and grace could supply the answer in the mystery of the incarnation, temptation, and suffering of the Son of God. We get glimpses of that tremendous and heart-moving process by which the Son of God, the Lord of all, could appear as a 'merciful and faithful high priest' on behalf of a halting and failing people.[100] What wealth of grace and love that He should wish to 'perfect' Himself for such an office! We are staggered at the thought that such a process, unthinkable in human systems of religion, should have been 'becoming' or 'seemly' to the Godhead, doubtless as expressing divine nature in relation to man in a way otherwise impossible, 2. 10.

By incarnation the Son of man really and in very fact partook of flesh and blood, that is, of human nature, 2. 14, for those with whom He was to be united in one family, and for whom He was to minister, shared in this nature, and in God's purpose the infinite gap between God and man was to be bridged in the one who was God and man. This is the first great step by which He could stand at the side of men and appear for them in the presence of God.

---

[100] See: Heb. 2. 9-18; 4. 14-16; 5. 7-10; 7. 26-28.

The temptation of the Son of man is a deep mystery, but holy scripture assures us that it was a reality and that He was in all points tempted as we are, sin apart. The reality and the potency of the solicitation to evil was made clear to Him in the attacks of the devil, of which the temptation in the desert is but a sample, though in His case the devil could never breach the protecting walls for, as Son of man, His will was in perfect submission to that of His Father. In this way He acquired the power of being touched with the feeling of our infirmities from the standpoint of tested man, 4. 15.

'Though he were a Son, yet learned he obedience by the things which he suffered', 5. 8. Suffering deity learning in the school of obedience would be folly to natural religion, but the mystery has been revealed to us, and bows our hearts in worship more than any outward manifestation of divine glory could do. There was before Him in divine-human personality what was impossible to deity alone, the path of supreme anguish which was in God's will for the salvation of man. Thus, in Gethsemane, we hear not 'my will' but 'thy will', an antithesis which was resolved by the perfect obedience of the divine Servant who thus 'learned' obedience as a practical reality of anguished anticipation.

The participation in flesh and blood; the experience of the impact of temptation; the dread discipline of suffering; the penetrating insight of love; all these have given our High Priest the same perfect contact on the manward side as was His by essential nature on the Godward side. This is what the inspired writer means by 'being made perfect', Heb. 5. 9; obviously nothing could be added to the moral perfection of the Son of God and perfect Man, but a tremendous process was involved in His representing sinners and interceding for them. This 'perfection' is now also His 'that in all things he might have the pre-eminence', and we rest with a worshipping joy, which serves to make the conscience the more tender, in His blessed ministry on our behalf of guarantee, 6. 18-20, of intercession, 7. 25, and of succour, 2. 18 – a far greater Aaron and a heavenly Melchizedek.

Mediator and Advocate - S. EMERY

Mediator. The word so translated, *mesitēs*,[101] has to do with

a) Moses at the giving of the law;
b) Christ as the Mediator in the work of salvation;
c) Christ as the Mediator of the new covenant.

The word means 'a go-between', and as so used means:

a) One who can put his hand on both parties, bridge the gulf between, and bring them together, 1 Tim. 2. 5;
b) One who acts as a guarantee to secure what otherwise would not be obtained, as in the passages in Hebrews.

The Mediator, therefore, is one who has essential oneness with both parties he is seeking to reconcile. This was the case with our great Mediator. Paul says there is one God, and, by inference, one kind of man, sinful man who is at variance with God, and one Mediator, Christ Jesus. He has oneness with God, possessing deity, and oneness with man, sin apart, for says Paul, He is 'the man Christ Jesus', or, perhaps more correctly, 'himself man', for He mediates not for certain men, but for man universally. How Job longed for such a Mediator, Job. 9. 32, 33 – a 'daysman'! The mediation of this Man, however, was not effected by His simply being man. More than His living as man was required; His dying was essential, for sin was involved, so Paul adds 'who gave himself a ransom for all', 1 Tim. 2. 6.

As Mediator, in the work of reconciliation, or the new covenant, the death of the Mediator was required. Hence, we read 'how much more shall the blood of Christ, who through the eternal Spirit offered himself without spot to God, purge your conscience from dead works to serve the living God? And for this cause he is the mediator of the new testament', Heb. 9. 14, 15. Therefore, as Mediator He brings us to God, 1 Tim. 2. 5, whereas in Hebrews He brings blessing to us.

Advocate. The word *paraklētos* is only used by John.[102] In the Gospel

---

[101] It occurs in the following scriptures: Gal. 3. 19, 20; 1 Tim. 2. 5; Heb. 8. 6; 9. 15; and 12. 24.
[102] It occurs as follows: John 14. 16, 26; 15. 26; 16. 7; 1 John 2. 1.

occurrences, the Spirit is presented as the *Paraclete.* By inference, however, the Lord Jesus is also a *Paraclete*, for we note that the word 'another' in John chapter 14 verse 16 is *allos,* meaning another of the same sort. In 1 John chapter 2 verse 1, the Lord Jesus is so designated directly. The word means 'one called to one's side', 'to one's aid'. It is used in the legal sense as 'counsel for the defence', one who pleads another's cause. Therefore, John says here that he is writing so that the word might prevent us from sinning as believers, 'that ye sin not'. Nonetheless there is an Advocate with the Father to plead if we should sin. This advocate is a provision, not when we confess our sin, or at the moment of our sinning, but 'we **have** an advocate', a glorious present fact, to meet our case when and if we should sin. This advocate is 'with [*pros*] the Father', before His face, as it were, the erring child's constant and unfailing plea. The value of the Lord's advocacy, like the value of His mediation, is based upon His crosswork, for 'he is the propitiation for our sins', 1 John 2. 2. Moreover, having a faithful and merciful High Priest, we also have a righteous advocate, 'Jesus Christ the righteous'; hence our case is righteously presented by the One who has given full satisfaction for us by His death. His valid ministry, therefore, on our behalf, is not on the basis of an effective, verbal and persuasive pleading before the Father, but on the basis of a perfect satisfaction for all our sins ever before the Father's face. He is our propitiation of abiding value. It could be said of the child of God who sins, in the words of that gospel hymn which many sang when they first believed, 'He looks on Him and pardons me'. His very presence before the Father is the plea. Continuance in the family of God is never in question, but forgiveness of our sins, and cleansing from all unrighteousness, is experienced only when we make confession, 1 John 1. 9.

Summary. These two ministries of Christ may thus be compared. His work of mediation was effected on earth, through His finished work on the cross; His work of advocacy is effected in heaven, the work on the throne, but on the ground of His propitiatory sacrifice. The former is past and final, but the latter present and continuous. As a past work, His mediation is because of what He did, while His present work of advocacy is because of what He now is in the Father's presence. As Mediator, His work was finished as before God and to His satisfaction, but as advocate He is with the Father. Hence, His ministry as Mediator was on the behalf of sinners, but as advocate it is on the behalf of the children of the Father. As a Mediator He 'brings us to God'; as advocate He maintains us before the Father. The need for His mediation is because 'all have sinned', whereas His advocacy is to meet the need 'if any man [i.e., a believer] [should] sin'. As Mediator, His work is one of divine grace, but His advocacy is linked with parental government.

Faithfulness of Christ* - J. Bennett

There are times when we can be fulsome in our praise and generous with our plaudits, building the reputation of men higher than we should. Scripture is much more measured in what it has to say and there are very few to whom the word 'faithful' is applied. Old Testament saints such as Abraham, Moses, David and Daniel are all called such. These were men who accomplished much for God in adverse circumstances. In the New Testament, we have Paul, and he writes of Timothy, Tychicus, Epaphras, and Onesimus. However, whatever the character and achievements of these men, all were marked by failure at some stage in their lives.

Only one can carry this title of faithful to its full height. Only the Lord was perfect in every aspect of His service, unfailing in His fulfilment of all that the Father required. It is the purpose of this paper to explore some of the features of faithfulness as displayed in the life and testimony of the Saviour and that we might also rejoice in all that means for us.

Faithful in His work for the Father

Twice in the early chapters of the book of Revelation, John acknowledges the title of the Lord Jesus as the faithful witness.[103] Of whom was the Lord a witness? In John's Gospel we read the words of the Lord to Philip, 'He that hath seen me hath seen the Father', John 14. 9. In the Lord Jesus there was one who told out the character and person

[103] 'And from Jesus Christ, who is the faithful witness, and the first begotten of the dead, and the prince of the kings of the earth. Unto him that loved us, and washed us from our sins in his own blood', Rev. 1. 5; 'And unto the angel of the church of the Laodiceans write; These things saith the Amen, the faithful and true witness, the beginning of the creation of God', Rev. 3. 14.

of the Father in all His fullness. If we need to know what God is like, in any particular facet of His person, we can look to Christ who is the fullest revelation of deity.[104]

It is the writer of Hebrews who draws our attention to Christ as if to say, 'Contemplate Jesus, who is faithful'.[105] The Jewish readers of that epistle might look to Moses as the supreme example of fidelity, but he cannot be compared with Christ. Only of the Lord could it be said that faithfulness was a designation of inherent character; He was faithful, He is faithful, and He will always be faithful! ARTHUR PINK in his commentary states, 'Faithfulness signifies two things: a trust committed, and a proper discharge of that trust'. In His prayer to the Father, the Lord could say, 'I have glorified thee on the earth: I have finished the work which thou gavest me to do', John 17. 4. This is what faithfulness really means!

There is, in the word 'witness', Rev. 1. 5, a reminder of the extent of the Lord's faithfulness. The word *martus* is also translated 'martyr', signifying one who has been prepared to give up his life in order to remain faithful. Of the extent of the Lord's faithfulness, Paul writes, 'He humbled himself, and became obedient unto death, even the death of the cross', Phil. 2. 8. The Lord knew the cost but did not shrink from paying it in order that the work of the Father might be accomplished.

> 'Faithful amidst unfaithfulness, midst darkness only light,
> Thou didst Thy Father's Name confess, and in His will delight'.
> JAMES G. DECK

In the work of the Father that was accomplished on the cross by the Saviour, there was that which was necessary to 'make reconciliation for the sins of the people', Heb. 2. 17. Here is a demonstration of the Lord's faithfulness in completing the work of the Father and, also, faithfulness in offering the sacrifice that God required to deal with sin. He is 'a merciful and faithful high priest in things pertaining to God'.

But scripture indicates that there is a work that the Lord has yet to fulfil,

---

[104] Cp. John 1. 18.
[105] 'Who was faithful to him that appointed him', Heb. 3. 2.

'And I saw heaven opened, and behold a white horse; and he that sat upon him was called Faithful and True, and in righteousness he doth judge and make war', Rev. 19. 11. As the Lord has been faithful in all that He has accomplished to date, we can be assured that judgement will fall upon the unrighteous and all rebellion will be put down. He will not fail!

Faithful in His work for us

It is also worth thinking about what the faithfulness of Christ means to us.

His Keeping Power

It is Paul who writes to the relatively young assembly at Thessalonica to say, 'Faithful is he that calleth you, who also will do it', 1 Thess. 5. 24. We need have no doubt or fear in respect to the security of our salvation. We should not focus upon the trials and difficulties of the Christian life, as real as these may be. We look to the Lord who is faithful and, as He has called us out of darkness into His marvellous light, so we can be assured He will deliver us home to glory.[106]

But what of the trials? The scriptures furnish us with many examples of those who suffered for their faith, many to death. It is not easy to remain faithful in the midst of the furnace of persecution. The example of the Lord may remain before us to encourage us, but to what can we cling as we face the violence? Paul reminds the believers at Thessalonica, 'But the Lord is faithful, who shall stablish you, and keep you from evil', 2 Thess. 3. 3. We may face the wrath of 'unreasonable and wicked men', v. 2, but 'the Lord is faithful'. He is set to make us firm and to guard us. The Lord does not save us to leave us to the mercy of the evil one. In the midst of the conflict, He provides the guard that will keep us. In His hands, the testimony will not fail.[107]

It is Peter who offers more practical advice, 'Wherefore let them that suffer according to the will of God commit the keeping of their souls to him in well doing, as unto a faithful Creator', 1 Pet. 4. 19. In the midst of trials we also have the resource of prayer. We can commit ourselves and

---

[106] 'Let us hold fast the profession of our faith without wavering; (for he is faithful that promised;)', Heb. 10. 23.

[107] See also 1 Cor. 10. 13.

the welfare of our souls to the Lord. This commitment should not be a single action but a constant attitude and is exemplified for us elsewhere in Peter's Epistle.[108] However, the apostle appeals to his readers to appreciate 'a faithful Creator'. He reminds them of One who has and continues to demonstrate His faithfulness in 'upholding all things by the word of His power'.[109] Equally, as the Creator, He knows our frame and understands all the intricacies of our beings. Perhaps Peter remembered the time when the early church faced persecution from the Jewish authorities. On that occasion, when released from prison, they gathered with fellow believers for prayer and lifted up their voices to God, 'which hast made heaven, and earth, and the sea, and all that in them is'.[110]

His Cleansing Power

One of the most vital things for any Christian is fellowship. John reminds us that 'our fellowship is with the Father, and with his Son Jesus Christ', 1 John 1. 3. However, that fellowship can be broken. It may be that the manner of our life is incompatible with our confession of faith. Do we seek the fellowship of One who is light or are we pursuing those things that pertain to the shadows? John exhorts his readers that if we want the fellowship of divine persons and the fellowship of fellow saints then we should 'walk in the light as he is in the light', v. 7. If we think of the high priest in the most holy place of the tabernacle we can get an appreciation of what it should really mean to walk in the light – the Shekinah glory of God's presence. What a responsibility is upon us! How careful we should be!

But the major barrier to fellowship is sin. John is clear in stating that although sin might not be the controlling force in our lives, it can and does intrude to damage our communion with God and fellow saints. How, then, can fellowship be restored? This is where we can rely upon the faithfulness of God in Christ, 'If we confess our sins, he is faithful and just to forgive us our sins, and to cleanse us from all unrighteousness', 1 John 1. 9. As E. W. ROGERS puts it, 'Confession is literally "speaking the

---

[108] 1 Peter chapter 2 verse 23 furnishes the perfect example of what the apostle is teaching here.

[109] Heb. 1. 3.

[110] Acts 4. 23-31.

same thing"; we side with God in regard to the gravity of the thing done: we do not argue or plead or excuse: we own up and make acknowledgement of guilt'.[111] In faithfulness to the work of Christ and the word of God, and on a just basis, God can and will forgive and fellowship can be restored. How precious that we can rely upon the work of Christ in salvation, and in cleansing from that defilement that we contract through our movements in this scene.

As we think, then, of the faithfulness of Christ, let us remember that it is a testimony to His deity, an assurance of His finished work at Calvary, and the pledge of His ability to keep us throughout life's journey into His presence. What a truth!

Christ as Judge* - J. SCARSBROOK

The thought of a judge or of judgement immediately brings to the minds of many the picture of a courtroom, a charge against the accused and the distinct possibility of a penal sentence. The early chapters of Paul's Epistle to the Romans present such an image, as the whole of mankind stands before the Judge of all the earth and a guilty verdict is pronounced, 'For all have sinned, and come short of the glory of God', Rom. 3. 23. While this is undoubtedly true, and an essential foundation for the doctrine developed in the epistle, the underlying presentation of divine judgement, demonstrated clearly in the Roman Epistle and throughout scripture, is not one of retributive vengeance meted out by a remote and impassive arbiter. It is rather the application of righteous justice, administered in a manner which is entirely consistent with the essential nature of a loving, merciful and longsuffering God.

God was entirely justified in His actions toward Adam and Eve when sin entered the world. His righteous character had been challenged, His veracity offended. He could have ended man's existence there and then, but instead His heart of love reached out to fallen man and the promise of a deliverer was given; One through whom salvation would be accomplished in such a way that God 'might be just', there could be no compromise of His holy character, and yet He would become 'the justifier of him which believeth in Jesus', v. 26.

---

[111] *Thoughts on the First Epistle of John*, pg. 26.

As mankind multiplied, so also did their sinful ways, until the righteous judgement of the flood became inevitable. Here, also, the gracious attributes of God were seen, not only in the preservation of Noah and his family, but also in His longsuffering toward mankind as He waited while the ark was being prepared, 1 Pet. 3. 20. Later, in the days of Abraham, Sodom and Gomorrah reaped a harvest for the sin they had sown and suffered 'the vengeance of eternal fire', Jude 7, in which context Abraham declared, 'Shall not the Judge of all the earth do right', Gen. 18. 25.

With the giving of the law a standard was set in stone for man's acceptance before God. With a detailed written code covering all aspects of life and behaviour, whether social, moral or ceremonial, provision was in place for leaders, rulers and priests to administer justice and, as necessary, sit in judgement upon their fellow men, subject, of course, to the ultimate authority of heaven. The difficulty was, however, that although the law was 'holy, and the commandment holy, and just, and good', Rom. 7. 12, obedience to its commands and absolute righteousness in its administration were impossible, because of the sinful nature of man and the weakness of the flesh, 8. 3. It required One with the authority and perfection of deity, yet, at the same time, the experiential sympathy of true humanity, Job's daysman who could put a hand upon both God and man. So, to a place and to a people prepared, 'when the fullness of the time was come, God sent forth his Son', Gal. 4. 4. He came 'in the likeness of sinful flesh', Rom. 8. 3, yet was never a partaker of Adam's fall; perfect, sinless humanity, holy, harmless, undefiled and separate from sinners, One fully qualified to judge not by appearance but according to righteous judgement, John 7. 24.

The intrinsically righteous character of the Lord Jesus was, in itself, a condemnation of those who opposed Him. Their critical spirit served only to enhance the perfection of His nature. Their cruel accusations were countered by gracious words; false allegations were met with meekness. What all but a few failed to grasp was that this first advent was essentially a mission of grace. 'I came', He would say, 'not to judge the world, but to save the world', 12. 47. Nevertheless, righteous justice must be brought to bear upon all men and, because the Lord Jesus is perfectly and uniquely fitted, He made it known that in the purposes of the Father, 'all judgement', in its administration, its severity, its sentence and reward, has been committed to the Son, 'because He is the Son of man', 5. 22, 27.

Just consider, for a moment, what mortal judge or jury could possibly make allowance for every factor, every facet and every nuance of individual human behaviour for everyone who has ever lived? Who could take into account the variations of ability and disability, intellect and ignorance, opportunity and misfortune, from the tribal people of the rain forests, the Inuit of Alaska, and the desert dwellers of the world, to the global leaders in education, industry, commerce and religion? Only the One who 'needed not that any should testify of man: for He knew what was in man', 2. 25; the One 'in whom are hid all the treasures of wisdom and knowledge', Col. 2. 3. Only He can safely take responsibility for such an onerous task!

Scripture makes it abundantly clear that there are a series of events, yet future, in which the Lord Jesus will exercise His authority in the administration of righteous justice. The first of these is imminent; others will follow as the purposes of God in relation to the earth are realized. Some will be swift and brief, others over, or after, a period of time. The rapture of the church, as clearly described in 1 Thessalonians chapter 4 verses 13 to 18, will be followed by the unfolding plan of God, at present enshrined in prophetic scripture. Immediately, on being called from earth, believers who comprise the church will be assembled before the judgement seat of Christ.[112] This is not a penal judgement on account of sin; for the believer, that was dealt with at Calvary. Rather, this is an assessment of service with a view to reward. As the name indicates, the judge will be the Lord Jesus and He will justly and perceptively evaluate not necessarily the volume of activity we have achieved but the value of it, not only the magnitude but more importantly the motive. With this appraisal completed, the believer can truly and fully enter into the joy of the Lord's presence and begin to appreciate the wonder of being forever with Him.

Meanwhile, back on earth, the rapture of the church has provided the

[112] Rom. 14. 10-12; 1 Cor. 3. 12-15; 4. 5; 2 Cor. 5. 9, 10.

catalyst for the prophetic programme to develop as outlined from Revelation chapter 6. The breaking of the seals, the blowing of trumpets and the bowls of wrath outpoured describe in graphic detail the awful devastation which will fall upon a world ripe for judgement. The specified time of tribulation will end with the return of the Lord Jesus from heaven in 'power and great glory', Matt. 24. 30; Rev. 19. 11-16. He comes not only in character as the warrior King, but also in His capacity as Judge. It would seem that Armageddon, which follows His return to earth, will be a brief encounter resulting in total defeat for the earth's armies and summary judgement visited upon the beast and false prophet, v. 20. Preparatory judgements follow to determine who will enjoy the kingdom reign which occupies so much of prophetic scripture in both Old and New Testaments. First, those of the nation of Israel, gathered from all countries wherein they had been scattered, will be brought to the wilderness border of the land and be made 'to pass under the rod', to purge out 'the rebels and them that transgress', Ezek. 20. 33-44. As a result of this judgement a regathered, restored, redeemed nation will be brought into the land promised to their forefathers.

There follows a judgement usually described as 'the judgement of the living nations', the 'sheep and goats' of Matthew chapter 25. Again, this assize, also presided over by the Lord Jesus, will apply certain criteria, particularly of behaviour toward Israel in tribulation days, to determine the occupants of the millennial earth. With Satan then bound for a thousand years, a reign of perfect righteousness is established with the Lord Jesus Himself taking the place of authority. These years will be characterized by flawless government and equitable justice. The earth, ravaged by the preceding years, will be restored and blessed, becoming abundantly fruitful.

At the end of this time, Satan will be released and, amazing as it may seem, will find an army ready to gather to his banner in opposition to the perfect administration of the Lord Jesus; proof indeed that the heart of man, even in such favourable circumstances, does not change! No battle ensues, 'fire . . . from God out of heaven' destroys the rebels and Satan is finally cast into the lake of fire, Rev. 20. 7-10.

One more judgement follows before the new heaven and new earth are ushered in. A great white throne is seen, apparently independent of any terrestrial foundation. Before this awesome justice bar stand 'the dead, small and great'! The books are opened, evidence of wasted lives and sinful works recorded; the book of life is there for inspection, bearing witness to all that their names are not recorded. This is not a trial but a sentence, all are lost. The Judge who utters the awful words once reached out and cried, 'Come unto me . . . and I will give you rest'; they refused, to their eternal loss.

The greatest blessing one can enjoy is to know the Lord Jesus as Saviour; to never live in fear of judgement on account of sin. Yet, may we ever remember to live our lives in light of that day of assessment and reward that we may 'not be ashamed before Him at His coming', 1 John 2. 28.

THE DOCTRINE OF THE HOLY SPIRIT

The Titles of the Spirit of God - C. E. Hocking

Our objective is to review those parts of the biblical revelation which provide us with the contexts, and the foundation facts, for a doctrine of the Holy Spirit. As men are obsessed with themselves, the seen, the tangible, the physical, they prefer, generally, to ignore the unseen, the intangible, and the spiritual. But the God with whom we have to do is Spirit, John 4. 24. Further to this, He is the Creator of a whole spirit world which we cannot see. He is the director of the affairs of the universe through spirit agencies. He even controls, and restricts the activities of hosts of fallen spirit beings, demons, Satan and his infernal hosts. But this God is also the Creator of the physical, the tangible things, things visible as well as things invisible. He made man in His own image, and set eternity in his heart. He not only gave to man a body and soul, but also a spirit, 1 Thess. 5. 23. Man, to be satisfied therefore, must fulfil that for which the Creator-God built him, namely to 'glorify God, and to enjoy Him forever'. There is intended to be an enriching communion between man and his God, who is 'the God of the spirits of all flesh', Num. 16. 22, 'the Lord, the God of the spirits of all flesh', 27. 16, even 'the Father of spirits', Heb. 12. 9. The Spirit of God makes such communion a reality, and so many other blessings that involve the realization of the power and presence of the unseen God in the 'real' world in which we live.

The biblical doctrine of the Holy Spirit is given considerable space. The Old Testament introduces the subject, and provides some essential elements concerning God's **activities** by His Spirit. The New Testament completes and crowns this revelation, bringing into clearer focus, along with the many ministries of the Spirit, **His personality**. At the very threshold of our study we are shut up to the Spirit Himself, for apart from Him we have no Bible – He is its divine author, 2 Pet. 1. 21. But further to this, apart from His aid, we are not able even to understand the scriptures. The human instruments taken up by the Spirit in the writing of the word of God turned back to the One prompting them, in order to gain light on God's purpose and its timescale, 1 Pet. 1. 11, 12. While we are encouraged to apply ourselves diligently to the word, it is the Spirit who must flood the page with divine light. The Spirit must be given His rightful place, and as if to alert us to this He features on the first and last pages of the divine revelation, Gen. 1. 2; Rev. 22. 17.

The Use and Meaning of the Words for Spirit. In our English translations the word 'spirit' occurs frequently in both Old and New Testaments.

In the Old Testament the Hebrew word translated 'spirit' is *ruach.* It covers a wide range of ideas, as the variety of English words used to translate it would indicate. It is replaced in English by air (once), blast (four times), cool (once), tempest or wind (ninety times), windy (once), breath (twenty-eight times), anger (once), courage (once), mind (five times), side (six times), quarters (plural once), and spirit some 232 times. Where it is translated 'spirit' it is used of the spirit of men, of good and evil spirits, in addition to those cases when reference to the Spirit of God is intended. The range of use of the Hebrew word results in differences of views as to the most likely meaning in certain passages, and consequently this results in slightly different assessments of the number of occasions when it specifies the Spirit of God. There are approximately 100 instances where it is so used.

It should be noted that 'the Holy Spirit' is never used absolutely in the Old Testament, but 'thy Holy Spirit', and 'his Holy Spirit' are found on three occasions. The Spirit is the power of God in operation generally, Ps. 104. 30, and that which creates and develops a thirst for, and a joy in, God, together with devotedness to Him, 51. 10-12; 143. 10. By the Spirit are made known the glories of the coming age, the inauguration of which is largely associated with the Spirit of God.[1]

In the New Testament, the Greek word translated 'spirit' is *pneuma.* English words used to replace this in translation are, wind (once), life (once), breath (once), spirit (151 times), Spirit (137 times), Spirit with Holy (four times), Ghost with Holy (eighty-nine times), ghost (twice), spiritual gift (once), spiritually (once). The meaning of this word for the New Testament has been more heavily influenced by the Hebrew understanding of *ruach,* rather than the content of *pneuma* for Greek

---

[1] Isa. 61; Ezek. 43. 5; Zech. 12. 10; Joel 2. 28-32.

writers. The way had been prepared for this by the translation of the Old Testament into Greek, in which the word *ruach* had become replaced by the Greek word *pneuma.* But the New Testament revelation concerning the Holy Spirit is considerably richer. The individualizing tendency, evident in the Old Testament, is crystallized in the unfolding of the personality of the Spirit in the New Testament.[2]

The word's incidence relating to the Spirit of God in both Testaments is revealing. There are approximately 100 references to the Spirit in the Old Testament, yet, in the New Testament, which only extends over about one-third of the space of the Old, there are some 230 references. Hence the Spirit has a much more prominent place in the New Testament revelation, and we may say that the present phase of God's dealings with men is pre-eminently that of the Spirit.

Titles of the Spirit in the Old Testament. The variety of titles used for the Spirit here is one of the means used to convey to us something of the fullness of the Spirit. Those most frequently found are:

- The Spirit of the Lord.[3]
- The Spirit of God.[4]
- The Spirit.[5]
- My Spirit.[6]

The lesser used designations are: His Spirit;[7] The Spirit of the Lord God, Isa. 61. 1; The Breath (inspiration) of the Almighty, Job 32. 8; 33. 4, cp. the breath of his mouth, Ps. 33. 6; His Holy Spirit, Isa. 63. 10, 11; Thy

---

[2] See especially John chapters 14 to 16.

[3] Judg. 3. 10; 6. 34; 11. 29; 13. 25; 14. 6, 19; 15. 14; 1 Sam. 10. 6; 16. 13, 14; 2 Sam. 23. 2; 1 Kgs. 18. 12; 22. 24; 2 Chr. 18. 23 (used in mockery); 2 Kgs. 2. 16; 2 Chr. 20. 14; Isa. 11. 2; 40. 7 (? breath), 13; 59. 19(?); 63. 14; Mic. 2. 7; 3. 8; Ezek. 11. 5; 37. 1.

[4] Gen. 1. 2; 41. 38; Exod. 31. 3; 35. 31; Num. 24. 2; 1 Sam. 10. 10; 11. 6; 19. 20, 23; 2 Chr. 15. 1; 24. 20; Job 27. 3(?); 33. 4; Ezek. 11. 24.

[5] Num. 11. 17, 25(2), 26; 27. 18; 1 Chr. 12. 18; 28. 12; Isa. 32. 15; Ezek. 2. 2; 3. 12, 14, 24; 8. 3; 11. 1, 24; 43. 5; Mal. 2. 15(?).

[6] Gen. 6. 3; Prov. 1. 23(? Wisdom's); Isa. 30. 1; 42. 1; 44. 3; 59. 21; Joel 2. 28, 29; Ezek. 36. 27; 37. 14; 39. 29; Hag. 2. 5; Zech. 4. 6; 6. 8(?).

[7] Num. 11. 29; Job 26. 13; 34. 14; Ps. 106. 33; Isa. 34. 16; 48. 16; Zech. 7. 12.

Holy Spirit, Ps. 51. 11; Thy Spirit;[8] Thy Good Spirit, Neh. 9. 20; (Thy) Free (or willing) Spirit: Ps. 51. 12(?); The Spirit of wisdom, Exod. 28. 3; Deut. 34. 9; The Spirit of wisdom and understanding, Isa. 11. 2; The Spirit of counsel and might;[9] The Spirit of knowledge and of the fear of the Lord, Isa. 11. 2; The Spirit of grace and of supplications, Zech. 12. 10; The Spirit of judgement and the Spirit of burning, Isa. 4. 4; The Spirit of judgement, Isa. 28. 6; Another Spirit, Num. 14. 24; A New Spirit, Ezek. 11. 19 (cp. 18. 31); 36. 26; An Excellent Spirit, Dan. 5. 12; 6. 3.[10]

Some Emphases in the Old Testament Revelation of the Spirit. God is the great Creator, and has under His control all that He has brought into being. He is not only over all things, but also governs in the course of history, intervening both in judgement and salvation. It is by means of the transcendent, Isa. 40. 13, unrestricted, Mic. 2. 7, and almighty Spirit, Job 33. 4, that He effects His sovereign purposes.

On this account, we read of the Spirit in connection with creation.[11] To control and influence the course of history, both in judgement and salvation, the Spirit is sent forth by God, Ps. 104. 29, 30; Isa. 40. 7. He comes upon men, Judg. 3. 10, sometimes mightily, 14. 6, but equally we read of His departure from men, 1 Sam. 16. 14, and hear one plead that the Spirit be not taken from him, Ps. 51. 11.[12] The Spirit falls upon a prophet, Ezek. 11. 5, even carries him, 37. 1. He imparts to men skills, enabling them to make and to build according to the divine pattern, Exod. 28. 3; 35. 31. To the Spirit can be traced special capacity for leadership, Deut. 34. 9; 1 Sam, 16. 13, and that wisdom that sees beyond the merely outward, 1 Chr. 12. 18.

Revelation of the mind and will of God, and the unfolding of the divine purposes and plans through God's servants and prophets, are evident pointers to the Spirit's work; in fact this is the most characteristic sphere of the Spirit's operation. A Balaam, and a Saul, can know the

---

[8] Neh. 9. 30; Ps. 104. 30; 139. 7; 143. 10.

[9] Isa. 11. 2; cp. Isa. 28. 29; Jer. 32. 18, 19.

[10] Note, too, similar expressions on the lips of idolaters: the spirit of the holy gods, Dan. 4. 8, 9, 18; 5. 11, and the spirit of the gods, Dan. 5. 14.

[11] Gen. 1. 2; Ps. 104. 30; Job 33. 4.

[12] To be contrasted with John chapter 14 verse 16.

Spirit's compelling, overpowering influence,[13] can even be 'turned into another man', 10. 6. How the Spirit is able to impose the divine will! In a special way David could say that the Spirit spoke by him, 2 Sam. 23. 2; cp. Neh. 9. 30. The words of the Lord of hosts, sent by His Spirit, came to the people by the hands of the prophets, Zech. 7. 12. Sadly, despite the Lord's multiplied mercies, we read that Israel 'rebelled, and vexed [grieved] his holy Spirit', Isa. 63. 10.

Yet, through God's steadfast, determined love toward Israel, His gifts and calling prove to be without repentance. In contexts treating the restoration of Israel, and her glorious future, the prophets unfold the blessedness in terms of the outpouring of the Spirit. God would 'pour upon the house of David, and upon the inhabitants of Jerusalem, the spirit of grace and of supplication', Zech. 12. 10 RV. He would put a new Spirit within them, Ezek. 36. 26; 37. 14. The prophet yearns for the day when 'the spirit be poured upon us from on high', Isa. 32. 15, when, God says, 'I will pour out my spirit upon all flesh', Joel 2. 28. That glad day, to be ushered in by the arising of the Sun of righteousness, is still awaited. Yet throughout the Old Testament, the Spirit's activities present God at work, the divine power furthering His plans in human history toward the goal of that final age, fundamental to the establishing of which was the advent of our Lord Jesus Christ.

Titles of the Spirit in the New Testament. If space considerations are taken into account, along with the actual number of references to the Spirit of God in the two Testaments, the proportionate frequency of instruction concerning Him in the New Testament is in the order of seven to one. There are only three books where no reference is made to Him, Philemon, 2 and 3 John, though only one reference to Him is found in each of seven others, Colossians, 2 Thessalonians, and 2 Timothy, Titus, James, and 2 Peter. All the historical books of the New Testament present the person and the work of the Spirit, Luke and John among the Gospels most heavily working the theme. The Acts, far from restricting itself to the theme of the deeds of the apostles, is more characteristically 'the Acts of the Holy Spirit'. The book opens with the record of the Lord's ascension to heaven, quickly following this with the account of the descent of the Spirit. The characters featuring in that dynamic history

[13] Num. 24. 2; 1 Sam. 10. 6, 10; 19. 23.

could be aptly described as, 'his witnesses of these things; and so is also the Holy Ghost, whom God hath given to them that obey him', 5. 32. Upon these historical foundations, the teaching of the Epistles and Revelation regarding the Holy Spirit is erected.

The titles of the Spirit most frequently found in the New Testament are listed below, literal translation being adopted in some cases to highlight differences in the original text.

- Spirit;[14]
- The Spirit;[15]
- Spirit Holy;[16]
- Holy Spirit, 1 Cor. 6. 19;
- The Holy Spirit (the Spirit, the Holy One);[17]
- The Holy Spirit;[18]
- Spirit of God;[19]
- The Spirit of (the) God;[20]

---

[14] Matt. 1. 20; 22. 43; John 1. 33; 3. 5; 7. 39; Acts 6. 3; Rom. 8. 4, 5, 9, 13; 15. 19 (NESTLE); 1 Cor. 2. 4, 13; 14. 2; 2 Cor. 3. 6(?); Gal. 3. 3; 4. 29; 5. 5, 16, 18, 25(2); Eph. 2. 22; 3. 5; 5. 18(? see RVmg); 6. 18; Phil. 2. 1; Col. 1. 8; 2 Thess. 2. 13; 1 Pet. 1. 2; Jude 19; Rev. 1. 10; 4. 2; 17. 3; 21. 10.

[15] Matt. 4. 1; 12. 31; Mark 1. 10, 12; Luke 2. 27; 4. 1, 14; John 1. 32, 33; 3. 6, 8, 34; 7. 39; Acts 2. 4; 6. 10; 8. 18, 29; 10. 19; 11. 12, 28; 20. 22(?); 21. 4; Rom. 8. 2, 5, 6, 10, 16, 23, 26(2), 27; 15. 30; 1 Cor. 2. 10(2), 12; 12. 7, 8; 2 Cor. 1. 22; 3. 6, 8(?), 17(?); 5. 5; Gal. 3. 2, 5, 14; 5. 17(2), 22; 6. 8(2); Eph. 4. 3; 6. 17; 1 Thess. 5. 19; 1 Tim. 4. 1; 1 John3. 24; 5. 6(2), 8; Rev. 2. 7, 11, 17, 29; 3. 6, 13, 22; 14. 13; 22. 17.

[16] Matt. 1. 18; 3. 11; Mark 1. 8; Luke 1. 15, 35, 41, 67; 2. 25; 3. 16; 4. 1; 11. 13; John 20. 22; Acts. 1. 2, 5; 2. 4; 4. 8, 25; 6. 5; 7. 55; 8. 15, 17, 19; 9. 17; 10. 38; 11. 16, 24; 13. 9, 52; 19. 2(2); Rom. 5. 5; 9. 1; 14. 17; 15. 13, 16; 1 Cor. 12. 3; 2 Cor. 6. 6; 1 Thess. 1. 5, 6; Titus 3. 5; Heb. 2. 4; 6. 4; 2 Pet. 1. 21; Jude 20.

[17] Matt. 12. 32; Mark 3. 29:12. 36; 13. 11; Luke 2. 26; 3. 22; 10. 21; John 14. 26; Acts 1. 16; 2. 33; 5. 3, 32; 7. 51; 10. 44, 47; 11. 15; 13. 2; 15. 8, 28; 19. 6; 20. 23, 28; 21. 11; 28. 25; Heb. 3. 7; 9. 8; 10. 15.

[18] Matt. 28. 19; Luke 12. 10, 12; Acts 1. 8; 2. 38; 4. 31; 9. 31; 10. 45; 13. 4; 16. 6; 2 Cor. 13. 14.

[19] Matt. 3. 16; 12. 28; Rom. 8. 9, 14; 1 Cor. 7. 40; 12. 3; Phil. 3. 3.

[20] 1 Cor. 2. 11, 14; 3. 16; 1 John 4. 2.

The lesser used designations are: One Spirit, the One Spirit, the Same Spirit, the One and the Same Spirit;[21] The Spirit, the Dweller in you, Jas. 4. 5; Spirit Holy, the Dweller in us, 2 Tim. 1. 14; The Spirit of our God, 1 Cor. 6. 11; The Spirit of your Father, Matt. 10. 20; The Spirit (the) Holy of God, Eph. 4. 30; Spirit of God, a living One, 2 Cor. 3. 3; Spirit of Him, Rom. 8. 11; The Spirit of Him, Eph. 3. 16; 1 John 4. 13; The Spirit of Him that raised up Jesus from the dead, Rom. 8. 11; The Spirit of Him, the Holy One, 1 Thess. 4. 8; My Spirit, Matt. 12. 18; Acts 2. 17, 18; Spirit of (the) Lord, Luke 4. 18; Acts 8. 39; The Spirit of (the) Lord, 5. 9; 2 Cor. 3. 17(?); The Spirit of Jesus, Acts 16. 7; Spirit of Christ, Rom. 8. 9; 1 Pet. 1. 11; The Spirit of Jesus Christ, Phil. 1. 19; The Spirit of His Son, Gal. 4. 6; Spirit Eternal, Heb. 9. 14; The Spirit of grace, 10. 29; The Spirit of (the) truth;[22] Spirit of adoption, Rom. 8. 15; The Spirit of glory and of God, 1 Pet. 4. 14; The Spirit of prophecy;[23] An Anointing, 1 John 2. 20; The Anointing, v. 27; His Anointing, v. 27; cp. Acts 10. 38; The Spirit of promise, the Holy, Eph. 1. 13; The seven Spirits, Rev. 1. 4; The seven Spirits of God, Rev. 3. 1; 4. 5; 5. 6; The promise of the (my) Father, Acts 1. 4; Luke 24. 49; Power of the Most High, Luke 1. 35 (cp. 24. 49); Another Comforter, John 14. 16; The Comforter, v. 26; 15. 26; 16. 7; cp. Acts 9. 31; The like Gift;[24] Lord Spirit, 2 Cor. 3. 18; God, Acts 5. 4.

To this list some would add: the Spirit of holiness, Rom. 1. 4; The Spirit of power, love, and self-control, 2 Tim. 1. 7; The Spirit of life (rather than link to read 'life in Christ Jesus'), Rom. 8. 2; The Spirit of faith, 2 Cor. 4. 13; The Spirit of wisdom and revelation, Eph. 1. 17.

In most cases where the definite article precedes 'Spirit', the person Himself is in view. The omission of the article before 'Spirit' often points to a ministry, an operation, a power, a gift, or an influence of the Holy Spirit. The context has to be carefully considered in each instance as there is no inflexible rule in these things however. Ponder, also, the force and significance of the different prepositions, and the personal pronouns,[25] that are used in the contexts unfolding the person and work

[21] 1 Cor. 12. 13(2); Eph. 2. 18; 4. 4; 1 Cor. 12. 9; 12. 4, 8, 9, 11.
[22] John 14. 17; 15. 26; 16. 13; 1 John 4. 6(?).
[23] Rev. 19. 10(?); cp. Acts 1. 16; 11. 27, 28.
[24] Acts 11. 17; cp. 8. 20; 10. 45; 1 John 3. 24.
[25] John 14. 16; 15. 26; 16. 7, 13; Rom. 8. 16, 26 RV.

of the Holy Spirit.

Some Emphases in the New Testament Revelation of the Spirit. The pronounced use of 'Holy' in the titles by which the Spirit is made known, the emphasis upon His personality, His large role in connection with the first advent of our Lord, the enriching influence of His continuous in-dwelling of every child of God, and His ceaseless work in the church are prominent features of the New Testament revelation. It is the Spirit of God who sets men apart for new creation, cp. Gen. 1. 1, 2, in order that they may be brought into the blessing of the eternal counsels of God, 1 Pet. 1. 2; 2 Thess. 2. 13, and experience the renewing of the Spirit, Titus 3. 5. We receive the Spirit when we believe, Acts 19. 2 RV; Gal. 3. 2, 14, and consequently begin our career as believers in the Spirit, 3. 3.

The Holy Spirit and our Lord's First Advent. The forerunner of our Lord is peculiarly endowed, filled with the Spirit 'from the womb', Luke 1. 15. The Spirit was the begetter of our Lord's holy humanity.[26] Elizabeth, Zacharias, and Simeon were filled by the Spirit to speak reverently and intelligently of the Coming One, Luke 1. 41, 67; 2. 25. Many years after His birth, that same Spirit descended, and abode upon the Son of God on the occasion of His baptism,[27] evidence indeed that the Lord was the One who would baptize in the Holy Spirit.[28] Thereafter, the Son of God, full of the Holy Spirit, was led, even driven, into the temptation,[29] from which He returned in the power of the Spirit, Luke 4. 14. Throughout His unique vocation as the Servant, the Spirit of God upon Him was His equipment for service.[30] The kingdom of God had, indeed, drawn near in that One upon whom the Spirit rested, Isa. 11. 2; 42. 1; 61. 1. In collision with the authority of Satan, the Lord demonstrated His superior strength by casting out demons by the Spirit, such miracles being wrought by the power of God, Matt. 12. 28; Luke 11. 20.[31] What blissful triunity is unveiled to the privileged 'babes' as the Son rejoiced in the Spirit while communing with the Father, Luke 10. 21 RV.

---

[26] Luke 1. 35; Matt. 1. 18, 20.

[27] Matt. 3. 16; Mark 1. 10; Luke 3. 22; John 1. 32; Acts 10. 38.

[28] Matt. 3. 11; Mark 1. 8; John 1. 33.

[29] Matt. 4. 1; Mark 1. 12; Luke 4. 1.

[30] Matt. 12. 18; Luke 4. 18; Acts 4. 27; 10. 38.

[31] Note the equating of the Spirit of God with the finger of God here, cp. Exod. 8. 19; 31. 18.

The Spirit and the Church-Corporate. The many members have been incorporated into the one body through the once-for-all baptism in the Spirit, 1 Cor. 12. 12, 13. Jew and Gentile alike may now have access by the Spirit, Eph. 2. 18. Local churches come into being through the ministry of the Spirit, 1 Thess. 1. 5, 6. These companies of God's people know the indwelling of the Spirit, 1 Cor. 3. 16, 17, which sets them apart as God's sanctuary, 2 Cor. 6. 16. There is one Spirit, the Creator of the unity which believers are exhorted to keep, Eph. 4. 3, 4. Happy that assembly not only endowed of the Spirit, but with the beauty of the Spirit's graces, where by lowliness, meekness, patience, and forbearance in love, the unity of the Spirit is maintained! True fellowship among the saints is established and promoted by the Spirit, 2 Cor. 13. 14; Phil. 2. 1. The Spirit speaks to the churches through the word of God, and we are wise in the present, and will be rewarded in the future, in the measure in which we heed His messages.[32] It is the Spirit who makes overseers, Acts 20. 28, who apportions gifts to each one individually as He wills, and it is He that operates them too, 1 Cor. 12. 4, 7, 11. Men preach, 1 Pet. 1. 12, and speak by the Spirit, 1 Cor. 7. 40; 12. 3. Service is to be discharged in the demonstration of the Spirit and power, 1 Cor. 2. 4; 1 Thess. 1. 5.

Some Other Emphases. Toward the close of His ministry, the Lord gave detailed instruction to the apostles concerning both the person and work of the Spirit, His personality and deity and His many-sided ministries as the Comforter whom the Father and the Son would give and send.[33] The Lord also spoke of the Spirit's activities toward a world that neither saw Him nor knew Him, but in which He would create conviction of sin, and lead some to conversion.[34] The chapters immediately following this one will develop these and other aspects of the person and work of the Holy Spirit of God more particularly.

For further information relating to the Spirit, readers may consult the *Precious Seed* publications *The Person and Work of the Holy Spirit,* and *Church Doctrine and Practice.* May their consideration encourage us the more to live by the Spirit, Gal. 5. 25, to walk in the Spirit, both as

---

[32] Rev. 2. 7, 11, 17, 29; 3. 6, 13, 22.
[33] John 14. 16, 26; 15. 26; cp. 1 Thess. 4. 8; Gal. 3. 5; 4. 6; 1 John 3. 24; 4. 13.
[34] John 14. 17; 15. 26, 27; 16. 7-11; cp. 3. 5, 8.

individuals and as companies, Gal. 5. 16, 25, to sow to the Spirit, Gal. 6. 8, to mortify the deeds of the body by the Spirit, Rom. 8. 13, to abound in hope, in the power of the Spirit, Rom. 15. 13, to guard the deposit through the Spirit, 2 Tim. 1. 14, and to pray in the Spirit, Jude 20, 21. For this Guide and Comforter bequeathed we give thanks to God, knowing that

> 'Every virtue we possess,
> And every victory won,
> And every thought of holiness,
> Are His alone'.
>
> HARRIET AUBER

The Personality and Deity of the Holy Spirit - F. CUNDICK

The holy scriptures speak of the Spirit of God from cover to cover. On its first page there is painted the impressive picture of chaos, when darkness was upon the face of the deep; but the Spirit of God was brooding like a mother-bird upon the face of the waters. From the last page there rings out the evangelical challenge of the church to the world, 'the Spirit and the bride say, Come'. The central point of instruction on the Spirit between the above mentioned boundaries is the farewell Paschal discourse of our Lord to His disciples, John 13-16. From this central peak we look back over the Old Testament landscape and afterwards turn to scan the fields of New Testament truth. The outlook creates within the heart an impression of the immensity and comprehensiveness of the subject of the person and work of the Spirit of God, and, at the same time, deep feelings of thankfulness to God for the vantage-ground on which we are able to stand. The priceless ministry of our Lord to His own banishes many of the difficulties that existed in the minds of men long ago. Living as we are in the brighter light of Christ's revelations, we can strengthen our apprehension of the personality and deity of the Holy Spirit. This is essential for the believer because of 'natural' inclinations towards opposite views. It is natural to think of God the 'Father' as personal, manifested by the 'Son' who became incarnate, and walked in lowly grace among men. But of the Spirit who is invisible, and whose operations are secret and silent, we are disposed to think otherwise.

Added to this inclination there is the influence of translation difficulties which translators were unable to avoid. Examples are:

1. *The word 'Spirit'*. In the language of both the Old Testament and the New Testament, the words for Spirit denote 'wind', 'breath'. This means that it is not always easy to decide the meaning of obscure passages. An Old Testament example would be, 'When the enemy shall come in like a flood, the Spirit of the Lord shall lift up a standard against him', Isa. 59. 19. Is the Spirit mentioned here the Holy Spirit, or 'a blast of wind' as some translators think? A New Testament difficulty of a distinct kind is provided by the words of the apostle Paul, 'Are ye so foolish? having begun in the Spirit, are ye now made perfect by the flesh?' Gal. 3. 3. Does the apostle refer to the Spirit of God, or the quickened spirit of the believer? See also Romans chapter 8 verse 10.

2. *The Use of the word 'It' in reference to the Spirit.* Such passages are found in Paul's Epistle to the Romans. 'The Spirit itself beareth witness with our spirit, that we are the children of God', 8. 16; 'The Spirit itself maketh intercession for us with groanings which cannot be uttered', 8. 26. Students of the Greek language point out that the word for 'Spirit' is neuter, and, accordingly, the strict rules of grammar demand reference to Spirit as 'it'; we return to this matter later.

3. *Scripture Passages which Give Emphasis to the Work of the Spirit.* Because of this feature, it is reasoned by some that the Spirit is but a symbol for God spiritually working. It is true that often it is difficult to distinguish between an operation of the Spirit and the Spirit Himself the Operator. The important thing is to endeavour to understand properly the viewpoint and purpose of such passages.

These are some of the influences that unfortunately produce hazy, nebulous ideas of the Spirit of God. Another has asked, 'Is the Spirit a divine faculty or a mode of action, in brief, a divine thing or a divine person?'. The answer comes not from the imagination of man's mind, nor traditions of men, but from the inspired scriptures. In the present age it is obvious to one regardful of the light of Christ's ministry that the Spirit's work proves His personality. No mere non-moral energy is contemplated but a living person.

What Constitutes Personality? Some of the elements of personality – personality in a theological sense – are individuality, intelligence and will. Holy scripture bears evidence that these are possessed by the Spirit of God. The Spirit's **individuality** is declared in the words of our Lord, 'I will pray the Father, and he shall give you another Comforter', John 14. 16. What is meant is 'another of the same kind'. The Lord spoke of a personality distinguishable from His own. As He had been a personal Comforter to His disciples, so the Holy Spirit became to them and still is to the disciples of the present day. We may now revert to the exceptional use of the masculine pronoun 'He' with the neuter word 'Spirit' mentioned in paragraph two above.[35] This 'phenomenon of grammar', as another has called it, denotes that John thought of the Spirit as a person, scripture using the common masculine form to denote both 'Comforter' and 'Spirit'.

The **intelligence** of the Spirit is unmistakably taught by Paul in the First Epistle to the Corinthians: 'The Spirit searcheth all things, yea, the deep things of God', 1 Cor. 2. 10. The actions of intelligence, such as speaking, hearing, guiding, are ascribed to Him in the holy scriptures.[36]

Whilst writing of the ministries of the Spirit, Paul attributes to the Spirit **will**. After enumerating the spiritual gifts in the assembly, Paul writes, 'All these worketh the one and the same Spirit, dividing to each one severally even as he will', 1 Cor. 12. 11 RV. **Will** is the characteristic activity of personal life; therefore, the Spirit must be a person. He is not some*thing* but some*one*, a being in His own right.

Deity. The Spirit is not only a person but the third person of the triune Godhead. He is co-equal, co-eternal, and co-substantial with the Father and the Son. Three well-known passages of the New Testament associate the Spirit with the Father and the Son. (1) In the work of redemption, 'How much more shall the blood of Christ, who through the eternal Spirit offered himself without spot to God', Heb. 9. 14. (2) In the great commission, 'Go ye therefore, and make disciples of all nations, baptizing them into the name of the Father, and of the Son, and of the

---

[35] See John 14. 16, 17; 15. 26; 16. 7, 8, 13.

[36] See, for example, Acts 28. 25; John 16. 13.

Holy Ghost', Matt. 28. 19 NEWBERRY. It is helpful to note in this reference the unity of the three persons as implied in the singular word 'name'. (3) In the words of benediction, 'The grace of the Lord Jesus Christ, and the love of God, and the communion of the Holy Ghost, be with you all', 2 Cor. 13. 14.

The essential qualities of Godhead, or 'attributes' as they are known theologically, are absolute and moral. When these come into view in the references of scripture to the Spirit, one has to recognize unhesitatingly that the Spirit is equal in His personality and deity with the Father and the Son. We may mention the following absolute attributes. **Omnipresence** is attributed to the Spirit, 'Whither shall I go from thy spirit? Or whither shall I flee from thy presence?' Ps. 139. 7. Again, 'For in one Spirit were we all baptized into one body, whether Jews or Greeks, whether bond or free', 1 Cor. 12. 13 RV. The Spirit must be in every locality to perform this ministry. **Omniscience**: 'The Spirit searcheth all things, yea, the deep things of God', 1 Cor. 2. 10. The nature of the knowledge possessed by a believer is spiritual, surpassing human knowledge in value because his tutor is the Spirit who knows those things that belong to the very nature of God. **Omnipotence**. The work of salvation is ascribed to the Spirit, 'not by works of righteousness which we have done, but according to his mercy he saved us, by the washing of regeneration, and renewing of the Holy Ghost', Titus 3. 5. The mighty act of resurrection is likewise: 'If the Spirit of him that raised up Jesus from the dead dwell in you, he that raised up Christ from the dead shall also quicken your mortal bodies by his Spirit that dwelleth in you', Rom. 8. 11.

Practical Considerations. These remarks remind us that the doctrine concerning the Spirit of God is of great importance. The practical import of the facts of the Spirit's personality and deity reaches out to every branch of Christian experience. The believer's increase of spiritual knowledge depends upon the gracious Spirit's operations. The devotion of a saint is vitally affected by what he knows of the Spirit's ministry. One's thoughts in this connection are regulated by the deep, unfathomable and inscrutable relationship of the Spirit's eternal 'procession' in the deity, John 15. 26. As the 'Spirit of life', He is the creative energy. Whether in creation or salvation, this is so, as consideration of scripture will show. Compare Genesis chapter 1 verse

14 with Job chapter 26 verse 13 for the work of creation, and Romans chapter 6 verse 8 with chapter 8 verse 2 for the work of salvation. This 'well is deep', but, through the ministry of our Lord, we are taught that the Father was in the Son, 'the Father that dwelleth in me', John 14. 10, and that the Son is in the Father, 'Believe me that I am in the Father', John 14. 11, and again, that both the Father and the Son are in the believer by the Spirit, 'In that day ye shall know that I am in my Father, and ye in me, and I in you', John 14. 20 NEWBERRY. All believers should understand that, in their devotions, the Spirit directs them to the Father and the Son, and hence the Spirit has no objective place in any prayer of the Lord Jesus or of the apostles; nor in any doxology, prologue to an Epistle nor in any solemn charge, which are always before the Father and the Lord Jesus Christ and, in one case, the elect angels. If the Lord, the apostles and the scriptures are silent as to prayer to the Holy Spirit, can we be voluble? This is not creating an artificial distinction, but giving full respect, as should always be the case, to the silence and omissions of scripture. Then as regards service, is it not necessary, in the somewhat 'jaded' conditions that obtain in general, to consider afresh that what has been brought to us through the grace of Christ can be enjoyed and used effectively through the power of the Spirit alone? However clever or fertile the mind of man may be in inventing ideas, methods, technique, etc., one thing is evident that all is useless without the power and operations of the indwelling 'Heavenly Guest'.

The Work of the Holy Spirit - E. L. LOVERING

The wide scope of this important subject will not permit more than a brief consideration of the activities of the Spirit of God in a fourfold aspect of truth. We shall deal with His work in creation, conviction, and conversion, concluding with His work in the Christian.

The Work of the Spirit in Creation. Verse one of the Bible declares the fact of creation, 'In the beginning God created the heaven and the earth', Gen. 1. 1. Here it seems was God's original creation of the heaven and the earth, and, as such, we can only believe, it was good and perfect. It is striking, therefore, to find in verse 2 the earth described as being 'waste' and 'void,' and that 'darkness was upon the face of the deep'. In Isaiah chapter 34 verse 11 the same Hebrew words are translated 'confusion' and 'emptiness'. We can only gather from this that a condition of chaos and disorder replaced the original order of creation. It is not our purpose here to attempt an explanation of this, as it could, at best, be only suggestive. It is, however, in connection with this condition of things that the Spirit of God first appears. Here He is represented as brooding over the face of the deep. A beautiful foreshadowing is this of the work of the Holy Spirit in the spiritual awakening of souls in darkness. He broods over the chaos and darkness of our fallen nature, bringing order out of chaos, light out of darkness.

It has been noted that the activities of the Spirit in the material creation bear a close analogy with the work of the Spirit in the moral creation. **Restoration** follows ruin, 2 Cor. 5. 17 RV – 'if any man is in Christ, there is a new creation: the old things are passed away; behold, they are become new'. **Illumination** follows darkness, 'Seeing it is God that said, Light shall shine out of darkness, who shined in our hearts, to give the illumination [RVmg] of the knowledge of the glory of God in the face of Jesus Christ', 4. 6 RV. A further step in the divine activity is seen in the **separation** of light from darkness, good from evil. The Corinthian believers were reminded that there can be no compromise with evil, for, 'What fellowship have righteousness and iniquity? or what communion hath light with darkness?' We are a sanctuary of the living God, and there can, therefore, be no agreement of a sanctuary of God with idols. 'Wherefore, come ye out from among them [idolaters] and be ye separate, saith the Lord, and touch no unclean thing', 6. 17 RV. Then follows **liberation**, Gen. 1. 9, for the waters were 'gathered together unto one place' and 'dry land appeared'. Every mountain, valley and plain were freed from the desolating embrace of the mighty waters. Thus, we read, Gal. 5. 1 RV, 'For freedom did Christ set us free'. **Fruit bearing** comes next, 'And God said, Let the earth bring forth grass, the herb yielding seed, and the fruit-tree bearing fruit after its kind', Gen. 1. 11. So, too, with the believer, we are set free for purposes of divine fruitfulness. In the words of our Lord, 'Herein is my Father glorified that ye bear much fruit', John 15. 8. And so to **witnessing**; God said, 'Let there be lights in the firmament of the heaven . . . and let them be for signs, and for seasons, and for days, and years . . . and let them be for lights to give light upon the earth', Gen. 1. 14, 15. It is the privilege of the child of God not only to bear fruit, but also to witness in the world which has rejected the Saviour. 'Ye are the light of the world. A city that is set on a hill cannot be hid', Matt. 5. 14. As the only representatives of the Lord here on earth, we are to be holy, living, beautiful witnesses to Him and for Him. May the evidences of the work of the Holy Spirit be seen in all our lives.

The Work of The Spirit in Conviction. It will be remembered that on the day of Pentecost, Peter stood up with the eleven and declared that the event then being witnessed was a fulfilment of the Old Testament prophecy, 'And it shall come to pass in the last days, saith God, I will pour out my Spirit upon all flesh', Acts 2. 17; Joel 2. 28. This takes in the whole human family. This is the work of the Spirit in the world today striving with the unbeliever as the **Spirit of conviction**, seeking to bring men into the ways of God.

Our Lord in His Paschal discourse spoke of the Spirit as the One who 'when he is come, will convict the world in respect of sin, and of righteousness, and of judgement. Of sin, because they believe not on me; of righteousness, because I go to my Father, and ye see me no more; of judgement, because the prince of this world hath been judged', John 16. 8-11 RV. Here, the root sin is that of unbelief, 'because they believe not on me'. Three spheres are clearly distinguished, that of sin, of righteousness and of judgement, dealing with the past, the present and the future. The sin is that of the sinner, the righteousness is that of the Saviour, whilst the judgement (already accomplished in the purposes of God) is that of Satan, the prince of this age. How much we need to thank God for the work of the Spirit in convicting us of sin, and pointing us to that righteousness now available to us because the Lord Jesus has ascended to the Father.

The Work of the Spirit in Conversion. *Its absolute necessity.* That no person can be a child of God but by the renewing work of the Holy Spirit is clearly and finally expressed in the Saviour's words to Nicodemus, 'Ye must be born anew', John 3. 7 RV. We have no doubt as to the utter sincerity of this man, but sincerity in itself could never make him a child of God. 'That which is born of the flesh is flesh, and that which is born of the Spirit is spirit'. Here are two kingdoms, that of the natural realm and that of the spiritual.

Its astonishing nature. How then can a child of Adam's guilty race, become an inheritor of the kingdom of God? This was the problem confronting Nicodemus, and it still confronts us today. We cannot afford to be wrong about this, for it will decide our eternal destiny. In only one way can any member of the human race step into an inheritance, namely, by birth. So it is here. 'Except a man be **born of water and of the Spirit**, he cannot enter into the kingdom of God', John 3. 5. Interpretations of this phrase differ, but it is certainly clear that there must be a new birth of water and of the Spirit. May it be that Nicodemus would remember the symbolic cleansing of the water of the laver? 'Wherewithal shall a young man cleanse his way? by taking heed thereto according to thy **word**', Ps. 119. 9. The New Testament seems to link this thought consistently. 'Having been begotten again, not of corruptible seed, but of incorruptible, through the **word** of God', 1 Pet. 1. 23 RV; 'Of his own will he brought us forth, by the **word** of truth', Jas. 1. 18 RV; 'Already ye are clean because of the **word** which I have spoken unto you', John 15. 3 RV. That water is symbolic of the word of God is clearly the teaching of these scriptures. Thus, the Spirit of God takes up the word of God, applies it to the heart and mind, and the soul is born of God.

As we have already stated, new life will inevitably express itself, revealing unmistakably its nature and character. The mind alienated from the life of God is enmity against Him, Rom. 8. 7, for **love** is absent. The understanding of the 'natural man' in spiritual matters is darkened, Eph. 4. 18, for **light** is absent. The life without Christ is **no life at all**, for we are all 'dead in trespasses and sins', Eph. 2. 1. The being is enslaved by the power of darkness, Col. 1. 13, for **liberty** is lost. All these, however – love, light, life and liberty – are the cherished and assured portion of the one who is 'born anew' by the Spirit of God.

We shall now refer to His work in relation to the Christian.

The Promise of the Spirit. In John chapter 14 verses 16 and 17, our Lord gave to His disciples the promise of the Spirit. 'And I will pray the Father [that is, make request of, as one on equality with the Father], and he shall give you another Comforter, that he may abide with you for ever; even the Spirit of truth; whom the world cannot receive, because it seeth him not, neither knoweth him: but ye know him; for he abideth with you and shall be in you'. 'He abideth **with you**'! What consolation, courage and comfort do these words convey to the trusting soul in a world in which he often finds himself misunderstood and rejected. How much the disciples would need the promised Holy Spirit as they went forth to face a hostile world, was known only to our Lord Himself.

The Presence of the Spirit. Further, the Holy Spirit was not only to be 'with them', as their Guide, Comforter and Helper, He was to be **'in them'**. The apostle Paul writing to the Corinthians, amongst whom existed divisions, disputes and desecrations, reminds them of the fact that they were not only God's tilled land or husbandry, but also a temple, shrine or sanctuary of God. 'Know ye not that ye are a sanctuary of God, and that the Spirit of God dwelleth in you? If any man destroyeth the temple of God, him shall God destroy; for the temple of God is holy and such are ye', 1 Cor. 3. 16, 17 RVmg. What shall be the practical outcome of this astounding fact? 'Ye are bought with a price; therefore glorify God in your body', 6. 20.

The Purpose of the Spirit. The grand purpose of the Spirit when He came, was not to declare Himself, it was not to fasten attention upon Himself; the grand purpose of the Spirit would be to fix our gaze on the Saviour. For these disciples Christ was to be the object of their faith, and although there were many things which the Lord Jesus could not say unto them because they were not able to bear them, the time would come when the Spirit of God would say these things for Him. 'Howbeit when he, the Spirit of truth is come, he shall guide you into all truth: for he shall not speak from himself . . . he shall glorify me: for he shall receive of mine . . . declare it unto you', John 16. 13, 14 RV.

The Power of the Spirit. The work of the Spirit is a demonstration of power. Power came with the coming of the Holy Spirit. The letter to the Galatians provides a most revealing and comprehensive study of the activities of the Spirit of God in the life of the believer, and in view of its importance we shall confine ourselves here to this Epistle. The subject is manifold in its scope. Briefly we note the following:

The Spirit of God and Christian Privilege, Gal. 4. 6-8. When we were the children of this world we were held in bondage under the rudiments of the world, the A.B.C. of letters; but when the fullness of the time came, that is, the time appointed of the Father – a legal term – 'God sent forth his Son, born of a woman, born under the law, that he might redeem them which were under the law, that we might receive the adoption of sons'. In the natural realm how often it occurs that, though the adoption of the child is legally transacted and the child enters into all the privileges of the adopted son, the nature or spirit of the parent is not found in the child. Is it not wonderful, therefore, to find that in the spiritual realm, 'because we are sons, God sent forth the Spirit of his Son into our hearts, crying, Abba Father'?

The Spirit of God and Christian Conflict, Gal. 4. 28-31. An historical parable is here. Two sons were born to Abraham, one by the handmaid, Hagar, and one by the freewoman, Sarah. The first was born according to natural laws, after the flesh; the second according to the promise of God. The coming of Isaac into the home created conflict and resulted in the expulsion of the son of the bondmaid. So it is now; that which is born after the flesh persecutes that which is born after the Spirit. But we are not children of a handmaid, but of the freewoman, 'For freedom did Christ set us free: stand fast therefore, and be not entangled again in a yoke of bondage', Gal. 5. 1 RV.

The Holy Spirit and Christian Activity, Gal. 5. 16. 'But I say, walk by [the rule of] the Spirit and ye shall not fulfil the lust of the flesh'. Whatever may be our walk or calling in life, by those rules of our calling we are expected to conduct ourselves. By this standard alone can we maintain the honour and dignity of our profession. So, too, in our Christian activities; let us walk by the rule of the Spirit, and we shall not fulfil the lust of the flesh. No promise is given that there will be no lust, but that we shall not fulfil that lust. It has been aptly said that 'the best way to keep tares out of a bushel is to fill it with wheat'.

The Holy Spirit and Christian Guidance, Gal. 5. 18. 'If ye are led by the Spirit ye are not under law'. Alas, how often we are led and directed by much that is not of the Spirit's mind and purpose, with devastating results in our lives. Self-will can only produce bondage and barrenness, but giving ourselves up to be led by the Spirit results in a 'service which is perfect freedom'.

The Holy Spirit and Christian Fruitfulness, Gal. 5. 22. The fruit of the Spirit is love, joy, peace, (inward realization); long-suffering, gentleness, goodness, (outward manifestation); faithfulness, meekness, temperance, (upward culmination). What a contrast presents itself in these verses! The works of the flesh, and the fruit of the Spirit, the former plural word denoting conflict and disunity, the latter singular word indicating one harmonious whole. Where shall we look for the perfect demonstration of the godly, Spirit-filled life? Were not all these beautiful virtues exemplified in the life and character of our Lord Himself? Love characterized His life, and triumphed in His death; joy, deep and unchanging, even in the darkness of the cross filled His holy soul; He constantly moved in an atmosphere of peace, unruffled by storms, the anxieties of His disciples, or the threats of His foes. Long-suffering, He bore with unbelief, unfaithfulness, and misunderstanding; gentle and tender, He was ever courteous and kind; going about doing good. Never for one single moment was He guilty of self-indulgence, or self-will, or self-interest. He alone could say, 'I do always those things which please the Father'.

The Holy Spirit and Christian Service, Gal. 6. 8. 'He that soweth unto the Spirit shall of the Spirit reap eternal life', RV. What opportunities are presented to the Christian for sowing to the Spirit and reaping the reward. For the fallen one, overtaken in a fault, there is an opportunity to 'restore in meekness, looking to thyself, lest thou also be tempted'. The restoration here perhaps implies the tenderness of one who seeks to restore the dislocation of a limb, the tenderness and resourcefulness of a nurse with a patient. For the overburdened one, an opportunity to 'bear one another's burdens [weights] and so fulfil the law of Christ', v. 2; by a right idea of one's own burden and infirmity, 'for each man shall bear his own burden [load]', v. 5. By a practical responsibility to those to whom it is due, 'let the taught communicate unto him that teacheth', v. 6. By resolute well-doing, as opportunity arises, for 'let us work that which is good toward all men, and especially toward them that are of the household of faith', and 'let us not be weary in well-doing: for in due season we shall reap, if we faint not', vv. 9, 10.

The Ministries of the Spirit for the Believer - F. Cundick

There are good reasons for diligent enquiry into this subject. One leading reason is the greatness of the blessing of the unique work of the Spirit in the church and in the individual believer. 'It is expedient for you that I go away', said our Lord, 'for if I go not away, the Comforter will not come unto you; but if I go, I will send him unto you', John 16. 7 RV. Think of this, the gift of the Spirit came by virtue of Christ's atonement and glorification! How precious then is the gift! One has said, 'Rediscovery of the unique and essential work of the Holy Spirit in the church and in the individual was one of the greatest bequests of the Reformation divines'. Another reason is the development of spiritual intelligence that respects the precise and perfect language of scripture. Phraseology of ignorant sentiment such as, 'A fresh baptism of the Spirit', 'Send Thy Holy Spirit', or 'Waiting for the Spirit', is inexcusable in those who have had time enough to consult the word of truth. In respect of these reasons alone we may consider some of the range of ministries the Spirit of God performs for us. Selections are made bearing in mind that some of the ministries are perfect and permanent in character being the result of a divine work in the believer. Others are progressive and are known in experience according to the measure of the believer's personal appropriation.

The Gift and Gifts of the Spirit, As Paul traces the characteristics of the believer's hope in the Epistle to the Romans, the statement he makes regarding its power is soul-stimulating, 'and hope maketh not ashamed; because the love of God is shed abroad in our hearts by the Holy Ghost which is **given** unto us', Rom. 5. 5. This gift is universal to everyone who knows redemption through the blood of Christ. Justification is accompanied by this gift of the Holy Spirit. Without the gift one does not belong to Christ, 8. 9. The relationship of fellowship, the personal presence and individual indwelling of the Spirit as a gift were distinctly announced by our Lord to His disciples. 'I will pray the Father, and he shall **give** you another Comforter, that he may be with you for ever, even the Spirit of truth: whom the world cannot receive; for it beholdeth him not, neither knoweth him: ye know him; for he abideth with you, and shall be in you', John 14. 16, 17 RV.

Later Paul writes of Christian responsibility saint-ward: 'And having **gifts** differing according to the grace that was given to us, whether prophecy, let us prophesy according to the proportion of our faith', Rom. 12. 6 RV. There are three great passages in Paul's writings dealing with the subject of gifts in the church. In Romans chapter 12 verse 4 the gifts are imparted by **God**; in Ephesians chapter 4 verse 7 they are bestowed by the **Christ**, the ascended Head of the body; in 1 Corinthians chapter 12 verse 11 the gifts are given by the **Spirit**. It does not follow that everyone who has received the gift of the Spirit is possessor of all these gifts enumerated by Paul. Much that is unprofitable would be avoided if believers would give studied attention to the proper use of these gifts given for the edification of the body of Christ. The gifts do not all function the same way, at the same time, or even to the same end. Let all seek grace to minister according to the gift received.

The Baptism and Fullness of the Spirit. In the New Testament there are six references to baptism 'in the Spirit'.[37] This was announced prophetically in the Gospels, historically fulfilled in the Acts of the Apostles, and its doctrinal meaning expounded in First Corinthians. The following facts are found in the scriptures:

1. The baptism in the Spirit was introduced on the day of Pentecost. It is, therefore, a distinctive truth and blessing of the present age, Acts 1. 5;
2. It is received at conversion to God, and not as an attainment of advanced spirituality. Paul spoke of this baptism as a completed act in the past history of the believers at Corinth. Despite their carnality and sectarian strife this was true of them, 1 Cor. 12. 13; cp. Acts 11. 15, 16;
3. It incorporates a believer in the body of Christ. It is not a passing phase of experience but a great foundation fact. Whilst personal joy and power in service may flow out of its initial work, its primary purpose is to unite the believer in the one body of Christ, 1 Cor. 12. 13.

Closely related to the baptism in the Spirit is the filling of the Spirit. Let the reader consider in the Acts of the Apostles the four references to companies,[38] and the four individuals that were filled: Peter, 4. 8; Stephen, 6. 5; 7. 55; Saul, 9. 17; 13. 9; Barnabas, 11. 24, and it will become apparent that the filling of the Spirit meets the recurring need of spiritual power for the life of devotion to and service for God.

---

[37] See Matt. 3. 11 RVmg; Mark 1. 8; Luke 3. 16; John 1. 33; Acts 11. 16; 1 Cor. 12. 13 RV.

[38] See Acts 2. 4; 4. 31; 6. 3; 13. 52.

The Earnest and Enduement of the Spirit. We read of the Spirit as the **earnest** for the believer in the following three passages: 2 Cor. 1. 22; 5. 5; Eph. 1. 14. In the first, the earnest is connected with the promises of God, in the second, with the future 'clothing upon' of the believer, and in the third, with the coming inheritance of the saints. The word 'earnest' applied originally to the part-payment money deposited by a purchaser, but later was used to denote a pledge of any sort. The Spirit of God is in the believer as a pledge of all that God has promised relative to the future in glory. The olive leaf in the mouth of the dove that returned to the ark was a pledge to Noah of the coming new inheritance, Gen. 8. 10, 11. The two bracelets given by Abraham's servant to Rebekah were a pledge of her coming marriage to Isaac, 24. 22. And so the blessed presence of the Spirit in the heart of a saint of God is a pledge of glorious things to come. God's pledge will be honoured!

The **enduement** of the Spirit directs our attention not to our prospect of glory, but to the need of power in witness. 'But ye shall receive power, when the Holy Ghost is come upon you', Acts 1. 8 RV. The Christian witness at the beginning was sustained by this power alone, and today God knows of no other kind of power. 'Music was not to be the power, nor eloquence, nor subtle argument, nor personal magnetism, nor mass psychology. The Holy Spirit was to be the power; and the heralds of the gospel were to go forth with the assurance that He would be with them, enabling and empowering them, and backing up their message with the working of His might', H. P. BARKER.

The Regeneration and Renewing of the Spirit. Both these ministries are mentioned in Titus chapter 3 verse 5. The first, '**regeneration**', birth again, is used of a spiritual event introducing a new state of things. The same truth is found in the record of our Lord's conversation with Nicodemus, John 3. Physical birth brings one into a world with a fallen, corrupt nature. Nothing of that is used by God in the new birth. A new life is communicated which is altogether heavenly and holy. It is a transaction that is complete and essential for all who would enter the kingdom of God. The terms '**regeneration**' and '**born again**' refer to the same event, but are not synonymous. One has rightly said, 'The new birth stresses the communication of spiritual life in contrast to antecedent spiritual death; regeneration stresses the inception of a new state of things in contrast with the old'. It was most suitable that Paul should use the word 'regeneration' relative to the work of God's grace in the island of Crete where lawlessness abounded in so many forms. This is the reason why the thought of government pervades the whole of the Epistle. How appropriate, then, was Paul's choice of the word to teach the saints that they were brought into a new spiritual state, to own the government of God over their lives.

The **renewing** of the Holy Spirit refers to the Spirit's power in the development of the new life.[39] The subject of renewal is 'the new man', 'the inward man', 'the mind', which is not the mind in its natural powers, but 'the mind of the spirit', Rom. 8. 6 RV. The pattern of renewal is 'the image of him that created him', and the process of renewal is 'day by day'.

The Anointing and Teaching of the Spirit. These ministries are found together in the same context, 1 John 2. 20, 27 RV. The anointing draws attention to the Old Testament symbol of the sacred oil which was used in the anointing of prophets, priests and kings to set them apart for their respective offices. John uses the term, by metonymy, of the Holy Spirit. Believers have 'an anointing from the Holy One', and are thus set apart to God. In the context, John teaches how saints can be kept from imbibing the spirit of antichrist. **First**, there must be obedience to the revealed will of God in His word, 'the word of God abideth in you', v. 14; 'he that doeth the will of God abideth for ever', v. 17. **Second**, they were to recognize the separate character of the Christian fellowship, v. 19. Only those who possess eternal life can know the true place of the present family of faith. **Third**, by a practical use of the anointing of the Holy Spirit; John seems to say, 'You have the true chrism (anointing) while others have the counterfeits, the antichrisms'. That this anointing is permanent cannot be gainsaid. It is divine, indwelling and abiding. The oil poured upon David's head, 1 Sam. 16. 13, was a pledge that he would one day wear the kingly crown. Despite the jibes of his brethren, Eliab's reproof and Saul's doubt, David knew he would not fall under the sword of the Philistine because the oil of his God was upon him. The believer, likewise, can look forward with confidence to the day of royal manifestation, 1 John 2. 28.

---

[39] Confirmation of this meaning is found by noting the use of the same root word: Rom. 12. 2; 2 Cor. 4. 16; Col. 3. 10.

The next fact must be observed, 'his anointing teacheth you concerning all things', v. 27 RV. By the anointing the believer has the spiritual potentiality to discern error. 'Knowing all things' is definitely not perfection of knowledge. Neither is it intended to encourage independence of God-given teachers, a conceit which unfortunately has led many to leanness of soul. But just as there is a natural instinct and impulse in beasts, birds and insects, so is there in the Christian a spiritual awareness of what is of God.

The Baptism of the Holy Spirit - T. Holliday

Paul, by the Holy Spirit, wrote, 'Now I beseech you, brethren, by the name of our Lord Jesus Christ, that ye all speak the same thing, and that there be no divisions among you; but that ye be perfectly joined together in the same mind and in the same judgement', 1 Cor. 1. 10. Why, then, is there such a diversity of opinion on the subject of the baptism of the Holy Spirit? Certainly this state of affairs is not of the Holy Spirit who indited the word, for He has only one interpretation. Otherwise, we have the principle, 'To the law and to the testimony: if they speak not according to this word, it is because there is no light in them', Isa. 8. 20. Let us see, then, what the scripture says concerning the baptism of the Holy Spirit.

In the Historical Books. In the four Gospels, the baptism of the Holy Spirit is mentioned in contrast to baptism by water.[40] In Acts chapter 1 verse 5 the Lord said, 'but ye shall be baptized with the Holy Ghost not many days hence'. Acts chapter 2 verses 1 to 4 gives the account of the descent of the Holy Spirit. In chapters 1 and 2, we have the four basic facts of Christianity: (1) The death of Christ; (2) The resurrection of Christ; (3) The ascension of Christ; (4) The descent of the Holy Spirit, the greatest antitype of the feast of weeks, Lev. 23. 15-21; thus, when the day of Pentecost was fully come, the Holy Spirit came down from heaven. Therefore, there are two facts that characterize this Christian era, namely, there is a real man on the throne of God, and the Holy Spirit is present on earth.

---

[40] Matt. 3. 11; Mark 1. 8; Luke 3. 16; John 1. 33.

How this Baptism Took Place. When 'they were all with one accord in one place . . . suddenly there came a sound from heaven as of a rushing mighty wind, and it filled all the house where they were sitting . . . And they were all filled with the Holy Ghost', Acts 2. 1-4. They were merged in the Spirit – He took complete possession of them, while there appeared on each one cloven tongues like as of fire. Moreover, they all spake with tongues as the Spirit gave them utterance.

When did this Take Place? On the day of Pentecost for the Jews, and in the house of Cornelius for the Gentiles, Acts 10. 44. In giving an account of this to those at Jerusalem, Peter linked what took place in the house of Cornelius with Pentecost, 'as I began to speak, the Holy Ghost fell on them, as on us at the beginning. Then remembered I the word of the Lord, how that he said, John indeed baptized with water; but ye shall be baptized with the Holy Ghost', 11. 15, 16. Thus, the baptism of the Holy Spirit was completed, never to be repeated. It was complete as was the work of Christ.

What is the Object of the Baptism of the Holy Spirit?
The final teaching on this subject has been given by Paul who wrote, 'For by [in the power of] one Spirit are we all baptized into one body', 1 Cor. 12. 13. This last mention of the baptism of the Holy Spirit gives us the result of this baptism; by, or, in the power of, the Holy Spirit, Christians are formed into one body. They are linked together by the Holy Spirit, and have a living link with Christ in glory by the same Spirit. This oneness is such that we are members one of another, and are to have the same care the one for the other.

Christ is still Here. When Christ was crucified, the world thought that they had eliminated Him, but no! Christ is still here by the Holy Spirit in His people. As we express ourselves through or in our bodies, so Christ now expresses Himself through His body, so that what was seen in Christ when on earth is now to be seen in His body, the church. Subsequent to the descent of the Holy Spirit, 'the Lord added to the church', Acts 2. 47, and God is still adding to this unique company. Attention should be drawn to the fact that Paul writes of this baptism in the past tense, and the words 'we' and 'ye' are emphatic; we do not read of any particular individual being baptized with the Holy Spirit.

In 1 Corinthians chapter 12, we find the structural unity or the oneness of the various members of this one body – the human body is used as an illustration. It is a most important chapter for the present day when the presence and power of the Holy Spirit are being discarded or ignored. This unity formed by the Holy Spirit is called 'Christ', properly, 'the Christ', v. 12, and also Christ's body, v. 27.

From the above scriptures, we learn at least four things concerning the baptism of the Holy Spirit and its results:

1. It was completed once and for all; there is no baptism of the Holy Spirit today;
2. The baptism of the Holy Spirit has formed a living link between the saints on earth and Christ in glory;
3. By the baptism of the Holy Spirit, the saints were formed into one body, the church;
4. This one body is to express Christ on earth during the period of His absence.

For God's pleasure and glory, may He help us to realize the greatness of what we have in the personal and corporate indwelling of the Holy Spirit, and give us grace to hear what He is saying to the churches.

The Leading of the Spirit - J. Boyd

This is a phrase which many associate only with the Holy Spirit guiding believers as to what part they may take at the Lord's Supper, in a prayer meeting, or at an 'open conference', as though these were its only expression. We do well, therefore, to examine its occurrences in the New Testament in order to find out its meaning, and to learn its true application to the gatherings of the saints.

The term 'led of the Spirit' is used four times altogether, twice of the Lord, Matt. 4. 1; Luke 4. 1, and twice of believers, Rom. 8. 14; Gal. 5. 18. In no instance is it applied specifically or exclusively to the functioning of the believer at the Breaking of Bread meeting, or at any other gathering.

The Holy Spirit and the Lord. Notice first the leading of the Lord Jesus

Christ by the Holy Spirit. We are here on holy ground, and must tread softly – one person of the triune God leading another! But we can learn much from the temptation of the Lord in the wilderness of what is implied in being led by the Spirit. Note the three expressions used of the Lord's going into the temptation: He was 'led up of the Spirit into the wilderness to be tempted of the devil', Matt. 4. 1; 'the Spirit driveth him into the wilderness', Mark 1. 12; 'Jesus being full of the Holy Ghost was led by [RVmg in] the Spirit into [RV in] the wilderness', Luke 4. 1.

Matthew's account stresses the Lord's submission to the Holy Spirit, and co-operation with Him. Jesus was led for a special task – 'to be tempted of the devil'. The word Mark uses – 'driveth' – suggests the force and strength with which the Holy Spirit was able to direct the movements of the perfect Servant. From Luke's account we notice that the leading goes side by side with being full of the Spirit. Note, too, that Luke says Jesus was led **in** (RV) the wilderness. Not only was the initial move indicated by the Spirit, but every succeeding step was directed by Him. The verb in Luke is in the imperfect tense. He was constantly being led; even after the temptation, the Lord returned in the power of the Spirit to Galilee, Luke 4. 14.

The Holy Spirit and the Believer. Let us apply the Lord's example to the believer today. As the Holy Spirit directed the Lord to the wilderness so does He teach the believer His will. To be assured of His leading one should be filled with the Spirit, continually seeking to walk under His control. The Spirit's direction will be easily appreciated if one is constantly listening for it. A readiness to co-operate with the Holy Spirit is essential, even though the task be difficult or to the flesh unpleasant. Not only will the Spirit indicate when one should commence an undertaking, but He will continue to support and direct in that task.

Consider now the other two references to the leading of the Spirit. First, that in Romans chapter 8 verse 14 is in the middle of a section which teaches that though those in Christ Jesus are not under condemnation, yet in them are two conflicting powers – the flesh and the Spirit. The believer is either 'after the flesh' or 'after the Spirit'. The former is opposed to God, and submission to it cannot please God; the believer ought not to walk after the flesh but after the Spirit. Paul gives a threefold reason for this:

1. Those who are after the flesh are dead as far as communion with God is concerned, v. 13;
2. Those who are led by the Spirit manifest the dignity of sons of God, v. 14. The Son of God was led by the Spirit, and so may the sons of God be;
3. Those who are born again have received the position of adopted sons, v. 15. The believer should rejoice in his dignity as a son, manifesting it by submission to the leading of the Spirit rather than to the dictates of the flesh.

The last reference is in Galatians chapter 5 verse 18. In chapter 5 verse 13 Paul envisages the believer as one freed from bondage – of the law in the case of the Jew, 4. 3, and of idolatrous practices in the case of the Gentile, 4. 9. Both of these were fleshly activities. Paul was concerned lest the Galatians should be again entangled by the flesh in submitting to legal ordinances. If they walked by the Spirit they would overcome the tendency to fleshly desires, for the flesh and the Spirit are irreconcilable opposites in their lives. Walking by the Spirit means that the whole round of the Christian's activity is directed by the Holy Spirit. One who willingly submits to being led by the Spirit is controlled by a different power from that of obedience to the law. A picture of this is seen in the life of Rebekah. When she placed herself under the control of Abraham's servant for the wilderness journey she was no longer under the compulsion of the law either of her family, or her city, Gen. 24. 61.

Thus the leading of the Spirit takes us out of the realm either of fleshly desires or legal impositions. We must dispense with these. Instead of engaging in fleshly activities we should produce the fruit of the Spirit. Paul sums up in a practical way, Gal. 5. 25, 26. Seeing that we have life through the Spirit we ought also to keep step with the other, each controlled by the Spirit. This will prevent self-seeking or envying others.

When His guidance is sought the Holy Spirit leads in every department of our lives. The Lord who told Peter where to find fish still enables His children to make business decisions. The Spirit guides in family matters, Gen. 24. 40; He advances those who put God's kingdom first, Dan. 6. 28;

He gives directions in church matters, Acts 13. 2.

How is Guidance Given? The question will now be asked, How is the leading of the Spirit known? Paul deals with this in 1 Corinthians chapter 2 verses 9 to 16. It is spiritually discerned by faith. He who unreservedly casts himself on the Holy Spirit for His leading will ultimately recognize that he has been so led. Note the testimony of Abraham's servant, 'I being in the way, the Lord led me', Gen. 24. 27. It can be asserted after the event has taken place, not when it is taking place.

This guidance is never at variance with the word of God for the Holy Spirit will not contradict Himself. He speaks through the word, Heb. 3. 7, and leads in accordance with what is written therein. For example, the Holy Spirit will not lead a believer into an unequal yoke with an unbeliever, 2 Cor. 6. 14. A mind stored with the word of God will know how the Spirit is likely to lead, and will be quick to discern His guidance.

In Acts chapter 16 verses 6 to 10 divine guidance is illustrated. Note the expressions, 'the Holy Ghost forbade', v. 6, 'the Spirit of Jesus [RV] suffered them not', v. 7, 'they came down to Troas', v. 8, 'a vision appeared to Paul', v. 9. How they came to know God's call is indicated in the words 'assuredly gathering' (*lit.*, joining things together). **Thus the confluence of circumstances can point to the Spirit's leading.**

What must one do to expect the leading of the Spirit? It is given in response to prayer, as David requested, 'Let thy good spirit lead me', Ps. 143. 10 RVmg. In Luke 11. 13 the Lord said that the Father would 'give the Holy Spirit to them that ask him'. This is explained by comparing it with the parallel passage, Matt. 7. 11, where Matthew uses 'good things' instead of 'the Holy Spirit'. The gift, Luke 11. 13, is the 'good things' that pertain to the Holy Spirit – His guidance and His instruction.

Again, those will be guided who are filled with the Spirit, and live in the conscious enjoyment of His presence. As the Spirit is opposed to the flesh, the believer cannot expect to be led by the Holy Spirit if he seeks the lusts of the flesh. These must be eschewed. The flesh – the old sinful, selfish nature in us – has been crucified, and must be constantly reckoned so. The desires to which the natural appetites impel us must be subdued.

The Breaking of Bread Meeting. Let us now consider a particular leading of the Spirit – that pertaining to the breaking of bread meeting. Here we do well to inquire whether or not it is scriptural for several to take audible part at this gathering, necessitating the direction of the Spirit. Our knowledge of the functioning of a remembrance feast is confined in scripture to two portions, Acts 20. 7-12; 1 Cor. 11-14.

In Acts chapter 20 Paul appears to have been the sole speaker. This was, however, a special occasion, when the company desired to obtain the maximum benefit from the apostle's visit. The Holy Spirit was using one with an outstanding gift – who could edify the church, and who did so for its profit. The circumstances guided them as to the Spirit's leading.

Chapters 11 to 14 of 1 Corinthians are concerned with the normal functioning of the Lord's Supper, and are left for our present-day instruction. The frequent use of the expression 'when ye come together' in chapters 11 and 14 show that both chapters refer to the same meeting. Thus, at the Lord's Supper in Paul's day there was an opportunity for the exercise of various gifts by several brethren, 14. 16-29. All gifts were not resident in one person, 12. 24.

Now the question arises, How did a brother know when to take part? How did they avoid confusion? Whilst there is no mention of the Holy Spirit in chapter 14, it is reasonable to suppose that He who had led the believers during the week would not desert them at the Lord's Supper. **The Spirit leads in the gatherings of the saints precisely as He does in everyday living**. His guidance is not a supernatural prompting; not an emotional crisis; not a sudden impulse. It comes not through feelings, but out of an intelligent assessment of what is suitable for the occasion; it is an exercise of the understanding, 1 Cor. 14. 20; it is the consequence of coming to the meeting with a full basket – a mind stored with God's word, a heart filled with God's worship. God prepares the heart and mind before the meeting. He may or may not provide the opportunity at the meeting to use what He has given. The leading of the Spirit will take hold of the opportunity when it presents itself.

Praying, singing, thanksgiving and speaking are all functions of the believer's spirit. This is under the control of the man himself, 1 Cor. 14. 32, but is also the sphere of the Holy Spirit's operations, Rom. 8. 16.

How the Holy Spirit controls the spirits of the saints in these exercises is seen in 1 Corinthians chapter 14, where several principles are given as to when one should take part.

1. His exercise should be for the profit of all – to their edification, v. 26.
2. He should seek God's glory, v. 25.
3. Several should take part, v. 29.
4. There should be waiting one for another – 'one by one', v. 31; no undue haste; no unseemly rushing, 11. 33.
5. There should be nothing done that would lead to strife or confusion, but rather that which harmoniously fits in with what has already gone, v. 33, if that bears the marks of being Spirit-led.
6. A brother who, after commencing, realizes that he is not being helped by the Spirit should quietly take his seat again, that another whom the Spirit is guiding may find room, v. 30.
7. Each one must be activated by love – love that desires to profit others, 13. 1; love that does not envy another, 13. 4; love that seeks not her own, 13. 5.

The Spirit's guidance at the breaking of bread meeting will be more readily appreciated if the believer has been consciously led by Him throughout the week, if he has not been walking after the flesh. How is the Saturday evening spent? If one is not then walking by the Spirit he cannot expect His leading on the Lord's Day. Hatred, wrath, strife and envying amongst brethren are works of the flesh, and prevent the discernment of the Spirit's leading. Such a brother would do well to obey the Lord's words in Matthew chapter 5 verse 24. A conscious dependence on the Holy Spirit is essential, recognizing one's own unworthiness and inability. A brother wanting to take part must learn to distinguish between the leading of the Spirit and the promptings of the flesh. His own glory must not be considered – not what credit he can get out of what part he takes. Nor must he be bound by traditions – 'We have always done this', 'This is the best way to do it'. Circumstances will often guide the believer as to what part, if any, the Holy Spirit would have him take.

Thus does the Spirit lead in the assemblies of God's people. Ever seek to walk by the Spirit, to be so led by Him in the secular life that church life will be but a continuance of that control. Thus, in all things God will be glorified.

THE DOCTRINE OF EVIL

The Devil and his Angels - E. W. Rogers

That there is in existence such a person as the 'devil', and that he has his angels, the scriptures make plain. To satisfy the mind, one has but to refer to Matthew chapter 13 verse 39, where the Lord Jesus categorically states that the enemy that sowed the tares is the devil, or to John chapter 13 verses 2 and 27, where we are told that the devil himself entered into Judas, having put it into his heart to betray the Lord Jesus. Further, Acts chapter 5 verse 3 attributes to Satan the terrible work of deception that was enacted by Ananias and Sapphira. Again, the devil goes about as a roaring lion nowadays, seeking whom he may devour, 1 Pet. 5. 8.

Modern man may dismiss the idea in unbelief, but scripture from beginning to end, by its various writers, is unanimous in its testimony that such a person has for long existed, doing his nefarious work against God and His Christ, and, of course, against the saints and their best interests.

The Devil – a Fallen and Defeated Foe. He is a fallen, created being. He is not self-existent, nor is he eternal in being. He was the 'anointed cherub that covereth', Ezek. 28. 14, and from the earliest human history played a hostile part in diverting the loyalty and obedience of man from God to himself. The Lord Jesus describes Satan as a liar and murderer from the beginning, John 8. 44, and the record of Genesis chapter 3 confirms this. He is called a 'serpent' because of his wiliness and subtlety. Paul speaks of his beguiling Eve, 2 Cor. 11. 3, and fears lest he may be at his same evil work among the Corinthian Christians.

It was he who incited David to number the people, with such disastrous consequences, 1 Chr. 21. 1. His very name, Satan, means adversary, which describes what he is, both in relation to God and man. He showed himself to be this at the threefold temptation of the Lord Jesus in the wilderness, when he sought to deflect Him from the path of the will of God, and simple dependence upon Him. He also showed himself in like manner when he endeavoured to divert the Lord from going to the cross, which elicited the reply, 'Get thee behind me, Satan: thou art a stumblingblock unto me: for thou mindest not the things of God, but the things of men', Matt. 16. 23 RV. It was at the cross that the Lord Jesus put out of action 'him that had the power of death, that is, the devil', Heb. 2. 14. This was made evident by His resurrection and ascension to the right hand of God in heaven, for then He 'put off from himself the principalities and the powers', and 'made a show of them openly, triumphing over them in it [the cross]', Col. 2. 15 RV. Consequently, at the present time, the devil and his hosts are potentially conquered foes, and although they have an extension of the time of their freedom, the certainty of their ultimate doom is not in doubt. Satan will be bound for a thousand years, and cast into the abyss which will be sealed, so that he will not be able to deceive the nations for that period, Rev. 20. 2, 3.

The Devices of the Devil. Meanwhile he opposes the servants of God, and gives to such a man as Paul a thorn in the flesh, whatever that may have been, that it might buffet him. Whilst under the providence of God it was permitted, it was, none the less, a messenger of Satan, 2 Cor. 12. 7; permitted, no doubt, to prevent Paul from being over-elated by reason of the excellence of the revelations granted to him, yet designed by Satan to buffet him, and to hinder his further evangelistic work.

It is not only by such violent means that Satan seeks to hinder God's work. Jason and others, Acts 17. 9, had given the local authorities security against Paul's revisiting their city, and they, having received such, let him go. This would appear to be the hindrance to which Paul alludes in 1 Thessalonians chapter 2 verse 18. Paul had made one or two attempts to revisit the Thessalonian believers but had not been successful, and he discerned the work of Satan in the matter. When writing to the Romans, he attributed his hindrance to the claims of the unevangelized regions where the name of Christ had not been heard, and he was ambitious that he might have the honour of proclaiming Him to such people. But that was not the case with the Thessalonians. Behind this hindrance was the sinister hand of Satan, who sought by all means to hinder the progress of the word of God. He took advantage of the kindly thought of those early Christians, and used the security, given out of gracious consideration for the well-being of Paul, for the effective closing of the door to further evangelistic work by him in that place.

No wonder Paul says, 'we are not ignorant of his devices', 2 Cor. 2. 11. He either adopts the garb of an 'angel of light', or that of a 'roaring lion', whichever suits him at a particular time and toward a particular company. As one reads the scriptures, whether the Old Testament or New Testament, one cannot fail to see that the 'seed of the woman' and the 'old serpent, the devil' are opposed to each other, and the latter ceaselessly opposes and seeks to frustrate the work of the former. He sows tares among the wheat. He used a man and wife to spoil God's first creation, and he seeks to do the same in regard to the new creation, Acts 5. 3. In fact, earlier the Lord had forewarned Peter thus, 'Simon, Simon, [the duplicate of emphasis] behold, **Satan** asked to have you, that he might sift you as wheat: but I made supplication for thee, that thy faith fail not', Luke 22. 31, 32 RV. Peter's courage failed: his denial ensued, but his faith remained intact. His denial showed that his courage failed: his tears proved that his faith was intact. Peter had fallen victim to 'the wiles of the devil', and had denied the Lord, as He had forewarned. Later he was to become the victim of 'the fiery darts' of the devil, Eph. 6. 11, 16. The one produced tears, the other produced prayers.

The Devil's Forces - Desperate and Dangerous Foes. Our contest is not against flesh and blood, but it is against spiritual foes. It is true that betimes earthly enemies assault, and try to hinder the servants of God, but their real foes are spiritual – 'principalities', 'powers', 'the world rulers of this darkness', 'the spiritual hosts of wickedness in the heavenly places', Eph. 6. 12 RV. These concentrate their opposition, not merely on those who are doing specific work for the Lord, but on the people of God in general. It is a common foe which all God's people have to confront, and for which they are provided with adequate armour, vv. 10-18. If verse 11 speaks of the devil, verse 12 speaks of those who operate under him, and at his bidding. So that at the present time there are in the world two unseen mighty forces at work: the Spirit of God, and all the powers who do His bidding for the service of the saints; and the devil and his hosts, who are antagonistic to these, and seek to frustrate God's designs as to them. This is not surprising. It was foretold in Genesis chapter 3 verse 15, which verse also foreshadows whose will be the ultimate final victory.

In 1 Timothy chapter 3 verses 6 and 7, mention is made of the condemnation and the snare of the devil. That 'condemnation' is the self-importance of pride, a trait that must not be found in one who seeks the laudable work of caring for the people of God. He must, on the contrary, be like His Lord, whose self-humiliation is described in Philippians chapter 2 verse 5. The devil's 'snare' is the trap which he lays in the path of God's people, to which Paul alludes, 2 Tim. 2. 26. Typically, it was laid for Samson, and when his hair was cut off, sign of his separation to the service of God, he became as other men, devoid of his erstwhile power. It was the snare into the meshes of which Lot got entangled in Sodom, and from which Abram was used to deliver him. In fact, if we read 2 Timothy chapter 2 verse 26 aright, we may liken such an one to an animal in a zoo, which is encaged, having lost its freedom.

Should anyone have the praiseworthy desire of liberating such a captive, he himself must take heed to the doctrine and continue in it, for in so doing he will both save himself, and those that hear him from the many pitfalls that beset the believer's pathway, 1 Tim. 4. 16. Otherwise, he may be entrapped.

Paul observes that 'even Satan fashioneth himself into an angel of light', 2 Cor. 11. 14 RV, thereby successfully deceiving the unwary. It is no wonder, therefore, if his servants adopt a similar deceptive role with like results. In fact, the words 'the deceiver' are used in reference to the devil himself, Rev. 12. 9 RV, for he will deceive the whole world of men – no small achievement. God's people are, therefore, enjoined not to be deceived; not merely evil communications but evil company corrupts good manners, 1 Cor. 15. 33, and each are to be eschewed.

The Devil – the Great Accuser. The 'great dragon', 'the old serpent', that is called 'the Devil, and Satan', 'the deceiver of the whole world' is also called 'the accuser of our brethren', Rev. 12. 9, 10 RV. The word 'devil' actually means an accuser, or a slanderer. This is what the devil, Satan, does, both in regard to God, and in regard to His people. He slanders man to God and God to man.[1] Doubtless there is much truth in his accusations against the brethren, but they overcome him because of the blood of the Lamb, and because of the word of their testimony, Rev. 12. 11, having accepted by faith and are, therefore, bold to confess that 'the blood of Jesus Christ his Son cleanseth us from all sin', 1 John 1. 7.

---

[1] See: Job. 1. 6-11; 2. 1-5; Rev. 12. 9, 10; Gen. 3. 5.

Their words are:

> 'I hear the accuser roar
> Of ills that I have done.
> I know them well, and thousands more;
> Jehovah findeth none'.
>
> S. W. GANDY

Let the reader ponder Zechariah chapter 3 verses 1 and 2. Satan may stand at the right hand of God with the view to being the adversary of Joshua, the high priest, but God's work, and God's word, are each sufficient to meet the situation, and Satan is effectively rebuked. Did not the Lord Jesus say of His own that they were 'clean every whit', John 13. 10? Did not the Spirit throw out the challenge, 'Who shall lay anything to the charge of God's elect'? God is the justifier: who is the condemner, Rom. 8. 33, 34? Has He not said 'as he is, so are we in this world'? That is, He is the other side of judgement, and it can no more touch Him, and we are in the same immune position, 1 John 4. 17.

The Doom of the Devil and His Hosts. But for the devil there awaits, first, his incarceration in the abyss for a thousand years, Rev. 20. 1-3. Thereafter, he will be released and instigate an abortive rebellion against Christ, which will result in his being cast into the lake of fire where he will be the most wretched of all God's created beings for eternity, 20. 7-10.

The angels of the devil will share a similar fate, for the lake of fire was prepared for them as well as for him, Matt. 25. 41.

Moreover, in Jude 6 RV, we read of 'angels which kept not their own principality', which explains why there are both good and bad angels. Then, in Revelation chapter 12 verse 7, we read of a conflict between Michael and his angels, and the devil and his, the latter suffering defeat, they being cast down to earth from the heavenly position hitherto occupied by them.

The ultimate and complete triumph of the Lord Jesus over every foe is everywhere asserted in scripture as the following scriptures, selected at random, testify: Genesis chapter 3 verse 15 – He bruises the serpent's head, thus dealing a fatal and final blow, while the devil bruises His heel, a temporary injury; Luke chapter 10 verse 18 RV – 'I beheld Satan fallen as lightning from heaven'; John chapter 12 verse 31 – 'now shall the prince of this world be cast out'; John chapter 16 verse 11 RV – 'the prince of this world hath been judged'. The whole tenor of scripture has to do with the conflict of Christ and Satan, darkness and light, evil and good, and it leaves us in no doubt as to the final issue, the ultimate triumph of God, and all that is good, and the defeat of Satan, and all that is evil. Ponder Isaiah chapter 14 verse 12; though this may be true of what will yet be exhibited in the man of sin, the great head of the revived Roman Empire, who will claim universal worship as though he himself were God, yet he is the incarnation of the devil himself, and what is written is true of Satan.

He is called 'the prince of this world', John 16. 11, and is regarded as already judged, the victory of the cross being then in view, and now, of course, an accomplished fact. The empty tomb, and the ascended Christ, are each a demonstration that the one who 'had the power of death', and is 'the prince of the power of the air', has been conquered, since he was not able to keep Christ in the grave, nor to retain Him on the earth. Peter speaks of 'the resurrection of Jesus Christ; who is on the right hand of God, having gone into heaven; angels and authorities and powers being made subject unto him', 1 Pet. 3. 21, 22. He is the Eternal Victor.

The Personality and Power of Satan* - A. T. Shearman

It is perhaps quite surprising to us, that in a day of increasing evil, when wickedness is practised more openly than ever before, the thought of a personal agent behind it all is consistently denied. To much of the world, Satan is a legend or a funny story. In many religious quarters, infected by the teachings of liberal theology, he is a medieval myth, long since forgotten in the more mature developments of religious thought. This is very much to Satan's satisfaction and makes his work much easier. Delusion is certainly a vital weapon in his programme of disaster. More to the devil's taste is the increasing fascination of many people with the powers of evil. During the last decade or so we have witnessed a growth in the outward manifestations of the works of the 'kingdom of darkness' that is quite striking, and, to thinking Christians, very significant. The practice of occult sciences, black magic, and communications with evil spirit forces through spiritism, has grown at an alarming rate in this country. In many of our schools, the Ouija board has become the basis of gaming – many young people being trapped unawares in the acts of evil.

These facts are no exaggeration of the true state of affairs, as many evangelists and teachers will affirm. 'Spectacularism' has been one of the devil's most successful gambits during recent times. In the pursuit of Christian warfare it is essential to know the enemy we face. His personality and power are real. It is not wasting words to state this, although we are certainly aware of it. There is no place for relaxation in our dealings with him. His energies are unflagging and his experience vast in dealing with the weaknesses of human lives. The object of these two studies is to outline something of the nature of scriptural teaching as to his personality and power.

The Personality of Satan. From beginning to end, the Bible leaves us in no doubt as to the fact that Satan is a person. If we look at the record of the events of Eden in Genesis chapter 3 this is evident. 'The serpent was more subtil than any beast of the field that the Lord God had made', v. 1. This identifies the character of the serpent straight away. But then we notice, '**he** said unto the woman, "Yea, hath God said?"' Personality is implied. We feel that we are confronted by a person who by intent, as a result of careful and cunning planning, was determined to destroy the humans he was tempting. More than that, we realize that through their fall he was furthering a deadly plan, aimed at overthrowing all the purposes of God. God's severe curse upon Satan in verses 14 and 15 also makes clear the personal nature of the conflict between God and the serpent himself. Amidst much discrediting of the early teaching of Genesis in our day, belief in the fall of man and the origin of human sin revolves around the work of a **person** determined to destroy both God and man in his activities. So much for the beginnings of divine revelation.

When we come to the end of our Bible we find, significantly, the marking out of the personality of the evil one. In Revelation chapter 20 we read of the ultimate climax of Satan's activity on earth. Here personality is ascribed to him. We notice that his names are spelled out, so that there shall be no mistaking his person, v. 2. Referring to the angel out of heaven with the chain, we read that he 'laid hold on the dragon, that old serpent, which is the Devil, and Satan, and bound him a thousand years'. While he is in the abyss, the earth knows millennial peace and prosperity. Eventually, after a release for a brief while, we read that 'the devil which deceived them was cast into the lake of fire and brimstone' with the beast and the false prophet. The torment will be everlasting, 20. 10. We can thus learn that teaching concerning the personality of Satan encompasses the whole of scripture. He enters as a person, with all attributes of personality; he is seen at the end to be judged as a person. It is a sad reflection here that hell was created for the devil and his angels and that so many unbelievers will share its terrors.

For the **origin** of Satan we go back before time began. He is a created being and it is obvious that he was not created as the evil one. This would make God the author of evil, a false proposition. There are two outstanding Old Testament passages which give us an indication as to where Satan began. In Isaiah chapter 14 verses 4 to 23 we have words against the king of Babylon. It incorporates a parable taken up against him and speaking of his overthrow. All the pomp and pride of the nation is to be brought down, v. 11. Then, in verse 12, Lucifer, son or star of the morning, is addressed. Here a creature of beauty and power is seen, aspiring to the throne of heaven. 'I will ascend above the heights of the clouds; I will be like the Most High', v. 14 RV. This describes vividly Satan's origin – the powerful Lucifer cast down to Sheol because of his pride and rebellion. We notice here the will of a person raised in rebellion against the will of God. This picture is confirmed in Ezekiel chapter 28 verses 11 to 16 – a remarkable prophecy concerning the king of Tyre. We read of the 'anointed cherub that covereth' – one in whom was sealed or measured the sum, full of wisdom and perfect in beauty. Yet of this person we read that there came a time when unrighteousness was found in him and he was cast out of the mountain of God.

What can we learn from these passages concerning the person of Satan? He is a person of great intelligence and power. Long ages ago he held high office in the realms of the highest created beings before God. In his pride he sought to rise, and led a rebellion with many other beings against God and His will. He was cast down, bringing with him a train of fallen angelic beings, 2 Pet. 2. 4. The exact nature of Satan's position and power before he fell we cannot fully know, But we are bound to feel that his could have been the highest place that a created intelligence could hold under God Himself. How great his fall!

In closing our thoughts concerning the personality of Satan, we can look at the manifestation of his **character** in Bible history. There are three interesting Old Testament passages which describe Satan's intentions to damage the lives of men. In each of these cases we see him as the **adversary** bent on evil work against God's people.

'Satan stood up against Israel, and moved David to number Israel', 1 Chr. 21. 1 RV. 'There was a day when the sons of God came to present themselves before the Lord, and Satan came also among them', Job 1. 6. 'He showed me Joshua the high priest standing before the angel of the Lord, and Satan standing at his right hand to be his adversary', Zech. 3. 1 RV. Here is a threefold witness to the personal nature of the aggression of Satan. He moves David to do wrong before God. He assails with questions before the Lord the integrity of Job, gaining by his pleas the permission to tempt Job with adversity. It is obvious from Zechariah chapter 3 that he was set to do the same work with Joshua, but the Lord rebuked him. How essential for us as Christians today to gain insight into the personal character of our great adversary. How good to know that we meet him with the power of a **personal Saviour**.

The New Testament also indicates the reality of Satan as a personal adversary. Notice the following scriptures:

1. Regarding the final temptation of the Lord in the wilderness, the Lord Jesus says to the devil, 'Get thee hence, Satan . . . for it is written, Thou shalt worship the Lord thy God', Matt. 4. 10 RV;
2. In rebuking Peter, the Lord Jesus says, 'Get thee behind me, Satan: thou art a stumblingblock to me', Matt. 16. 23 RV;
3. Words of the Lord Jesus again, 'Simon, Simon . . . Satan asked [obtained you by asking] to have you, that he might sift you as wheat', Luke 22. 31 RV.

Here, again, is a threefold witness to the character of the enemy we deal with. The Lord Jesus confronted him with His majesty and superior power. There is no doubt as to the personal character of the conflict which was constantly emerging until it found its deadly climax in the triumph of the cross.

Let us not underestimate the powers of darkness with which we deal. We need to take to ourselves constantly the whole panoply of God, divinely provided for those who have to do battle with the enemy of souls.

We now look at some of the features of his **power**, outlined for us in the scriptures. Of one thing we can be completely sure. Satan does not share the attributes of deity. He is not omnipotent – his powers, though great, are limited. He is not omniscient – there is a veil drawn over his ability to know all circumstances, though he knows much more than we do. He is not omnipresent – his movements are much restricted although, through his agents, he moves behind the world scenes and behind the lives of men. This is obvious from Job chapter 1 verses 6 to 12. The conversation between the Lord and Satan concerning Job demands careful thought. From going to and fro in the earth, the enemy of souls presents himself, with the sons of God, before the Lord. As the Lord calls attention to the character of His servant, Satan takes issue with the Lord about His reasons for integrity. Satan implies that Job only serves the Lord because of blessing and prosperity. Notice the words of the Lord to Satan, v. 12, 'Behold, all that he hath is in thy power; only upon himself put not forth thine hand'. Then out of this confrontation we can learn something of the mystery, yet reality, of the power that Satan can wield. And he is allowed to exercise it by divine permission. We may be sure that he exercises it to the full, but we can be glad that his is not a sovereign power. He works only as long as he is permitted to do so. God in His sovereignty has the final word.

As we look at the scriptures we can learn much about Satan's activities from the titles that are given to him. What he is called very often gives an indication of those things which he does, especially if we read them in the context in which they are written.

He is called Satan. We have already noted some of these passages and also noticed that the meaning of the name is the Adversary. In this role he is set for the discrediting and spoiling of every believer. Even in the presence of the Lord he is seen as the adversary to accuse and debase. Thank God that for every activity of the Adversary we have an advocate with the Father, Jesus Christ the righteous, 1 John 2. 1, 2. When Paul would have visited the Thessalonians, it was Satan that hindered him, 1 Thess. 2. 18. When Paul spoke of his 'thorn in the flesh', he viewed it as a messenger of Satan to buffet him, 2 Cor. 12. 7. With the evils at Corinth and their possible permanent damage to the church, Paul was concerned lest Satan should gain an advantage over them. 'We are not ignorant of his devices [or methods]', 2. 11. So we could go on. As Satan, he works for the damage, discredit and debasement of every believer. How good that we can count on the constant ministry of the Lord Jesus in the presence of God our Father to meet the strategies of Satan.

He is called the devil. Let us look more closely at this. Scripture seems to use this title for the enemy as an epitome of all that is vile and evil about him. So 'the devil sinneth from the beginning', 1 John 3. 8. Speaking to the Pharisees, Jesus said they were of their father, the devil. Note how he is described, 'He was a murderer from the beginning', John 8. 44; 'he is a liar, and the father of it'. Peter tells us 'your adversary the devil, as a roaring lion, walketh about seeking whom he may devour', 1 Pet. 5. 8. Thus, he is called the 'evil one' and the 'wicked one'. We can thank God that 'for this purpose was the Son of God manifested, that he might destroy the works of the devil', 1 John 3. 8. And through death, He has destroyed 'him that had the power of death, that is, the devil', Heb. 2. 14, 15. It is good to ponder again on the complete answer of Christ in His person, to the evil, sinister, power of the devil.

We notice now that he is described as the serpent or, that old serpent. This is significant in that it takes us back to the events of Eden, Gen. 3. 1. It presents the enemy in his subtlety and cunning. It is essential to notice his approach to Eve. The seed of doubt is sown with 'hath God said?' Bewildered, Eve states the command of God to them in the garden. Soon the doubt cast in her mind is followed by a flat denial of God's command, 'Ye shall not surely die'. It was not long before the dreadful deed was done and the beginning of enslavement of the whole human race was effected. The subtlety of Satan has caused the downfall of many. He will quote scripture to suit his ends. He will approach any saint in the guise of an 'angel of light', 2 Cor. 11. 14, if through this means he can achieve his ends. Today, we need to beware of the insidious suggestions of evil which have their source in the serpent's mind. We are told about the perils of 'seducing spirits, and doctrines of demons', 1 Tim. 4. 1, 2 RVmg. These are all too prevalent in our generation.

He is called 'the prince of the power of the air', Eph. 2. 2. This description of Satan suggests that the high court of evil administration is higher than, and outside of, the realm of time and space. Ephesians chapter 6 verse 12 confirms this when it speaks of the spiritual wickedness in heavenly places. We face the devil here as the ruler of unseen forces of wickedness which infiltrate into human lives and affairs and do their damaging work. We can praise God that, however high the realm of evil is, Christ is higher. His location, through resurrection and ascension, is far above every principality and power and every name that is named, 1. 21.

Again he is called the 'prince of this world', John 12. 31; 14. 30. This designation of Satan is used by the Lord Himself. The Lord Jesus was in the cosmos and, as He moved, He faced the antagonism of the one He describes as the prince of the cosmos – the ordered, material substance of the world, whose people God loved and into which He was sent. The crisis of the cross marked the judgement of this person. The wonder of the experience of Christ in the world is that He could say about the prince of this world that he 'hath nothing in me'. The perfect man had the only effective answer to the power of Satan, and eventually destroyed him.

We notice also that he is called the 'god of this world', 2 Cor. 4. 4. Here it is not the cosmos but the 'age' of which Satan is called the god. It is called this 'present evil age', Gal. 1. 4 RVmg – that from which the Lord Jesus gave Himself to deliver us. This speaks to us, not of a place, but of a period of time throughout which Satan has power. And for this time, which includes our generation, he has dominion over those who inhabit the cosmos, to blind and seduce and destroy. We can be sure that during this 'age' the devil is seeking to move against God with all the forces he possesses, and to enslave as many souls as will obey him.

We close our study with the description of the devil in Revelation chapter 12. Here he is called the dragon. All the marks of power that are evil are gathered to him. His object is to destroy the 'man child' born to the woman. There is a climax of warfare between the forces of heaven and the forces of the evil one. He is eventually cast down to earth, there to pursue wickedness. It is noteworthy that just as Satan was the originator of all that is evil, so he will be the one who brings evil to its climax. Revelation chapter 13 describes how, through the beast and the antichrist, the 'man of sin', Satan will make this world the scene of his final desperate bid for dominion and power.

Satan is a reality. Perhaps the impact of his power is becoming more evident today. How essential it is to face facts concerning the growing evils of the last times. There is no room today for compromise or slackness in spiritual things. The words of the Lord Jesus in Gethsemane come to us in vital force, 'Watch ye and pray, lest ye enter into temptation', Mark 14. 38. Thank God, we serve a triumphant Saviour, who, through the conflict of Calvary, conquered in resurrection the great enemy of souls. We follow in His train.

Man - His Constitution, Uniqueness, and Supremacy in the Creation - E. H. Betts

'What is man, that thou art mindful of him? and the son of man, that thou visitest him?' Ps. 8. 4.

An examination of scripture shows without the least room for doubt that man is unique in his constitution. In God's thought and purpose he is supreme amongst the creatures, being the image or representative of God Himself, having been made in His likeness. It is the determinate purpose of God to make all this good in man. In Christ, the Son of man, it is His plan to give him forever the headship and authority over all things, to the glory of God.

Such teaching we find woven into the texture of scripture. But the passages which draw our attention to it more directly are three or four.

The Constitution of Man. In Genesis chapter 1 verse 26 we have the inspired account of the creation of man. It differs in every respect from that of the animals and other parts of the creation. The creation formula used is different. Instead of 'light be', and other such simple creative imperatives, we have the deliberative formula 'let us make man in our image, after our likeness'. We hear the deliberations of the Godhead in counsel, 'let us make man'. And how is that making described as having been effected? Only by a fresh creation, 'God created man in his own image, in the image of God created he him; male and female created he them'. Just as the work of the fifth day was a step upwards from the creation of inanimate beings, plants, etc., to that of 'living souls', and accordingly the word 'created' was there used instead of merely 'made', v. 21, so the creation of man was a step yet higher upwards; and here, as we have noted, we have: (a) the deliberative act of divine persons; (b) the use, once more, of the word 'create'; and (c) of the result, God saw that it was, this time, not merely 'good', but 'very good', for now creation had been crowned by the bringing in of its head. But: (d) further still, we see how much higher was this culminating act of the creation of man than of all that went before. This we see pointedly in chapter 2 verse 7, 'And the Lord God formed man of the dust of the ground, and breathed into his nostrils the breath of life; and man became a living soul'.

What was not said when God created animal life, 1. 20, 24, is expressly stated with respect to man: God 'breathed into his nostrils the breath of life; and man became a living soul', 2. 7. Here it is completely in accord with the genius of the original Hebrew to understand the word 'so' or 'thus': 'and **so** man became a living soul'. Indeed, in at least one translation it has been rendered accordingly: 'This was how man became a living soul', for that was the mode of his creation, for there was included in man's very constitution that which was derived from God Himself. Man is unique.

The Dominance of Man. Man was also dominant. We hear the divine voice continuing, 'and let them have dominion over the fish of the sea, and over the fowl of the air . . . and over every creeping thing . . . upon the earth', Gen. 1. 26. The purpose of the Creator is made clear from the commencement. As man was uniquely created, so is his place in the creation to be unique. Under God, and as His representative, he is to wield dominion over creation.

According to scripture then, man is unique, and dominant. And what says science? Let us cite a most distinguished biologist. SIR JULIAN HUXLEY says, 'Man is unique in virtue of his power of conceptual thought' and he proceeds to specify a score or more of human characteristics which raise man far above the animals and place him in an order of being distinct and incomparable. Included explicitly is man's dominance over the rest of creation. Man is truly unique and dominant, even as viewed from the observational level of science.

The eminent scientist we have above cited has been a foremost champion of evolutionary doctrines. He has advocated also 'religion without revelation', being a bitter opponent of holy scripture. Nevertheless he is compelled to furnish unintended confirmatory evidence of the truth of the very book opposed, since according to his scientific observations, as according to the Bible, man is unique, and man is dominant. He does not, however, give the credit to God the Creator for the truly striking assemblage of qualities which raise man above the beasts. We surely owe no apology for differing from him. God the Creator Himself finds pleasure in the creation of the infinitely varied and variable beauties of form, line, tone, material, colour, light, shade and harmonies of nature, for He repeatedly pronounces them all 'good', Gen. 1; Rev. 4. 11. Is it not a verification of the Bible story of our origin if we His creatures find similar delights, for 'we are also his offspring' says Paul, Acts 17. 28? Our very aesthetic sense – our feeling for the beautiful – is a legacy from God Himself. We love beautiful things because our divine Originator loves them, and we are His offspring. To the poverty-stricken mind of the **mere** scientist, a beautiful fragrant rose is the end-product of the chance-play of natural forces. To us, if taught by scripture, it is the handiwork of a God who delights in beauty.

The Paradox of Man. Man, then, derives from God. He was made in His likeness. What light on this great thesis have we outside the creation story of Genesis chapters 1 and 2? In Psalm 8 the Spirit of God takes up the theme, and, at once, we face a paradox. Man, viewed against the background of the majestic heavenly bodies, the work of God's fingers, is truly little and puny. 'What is man, that thou art mindful of him? and the son of man, that thou visitest him?' The writer uses the words *enosh* and *adam* which speak of man's weakness and lowly origin. But, on the other hand, in strongly marked contrast we read, 'Thou hast . . . crowned him with glory and honour. Thou madest him to have dominion over the works of thine hands; thou hast put all things under his feet', vv. 5, 6. How is this paradox to be resolved? Well, the psalm itself gives us, not the solution, but a pointer to it. 'Out of the mouth of babes and sucklings hast thou ordained strength because of thine enemies, that thou mightest still the enemy and the avenger', v. 2. For the express purpose of securing His own glory, God takes up the weak and despised things of the earth. And the result? This is indicated in the first verse of our psalm, giving the theme, as so often in the psalms, and reverted to in the last verse, 'How excellent is thy name in all the earth'.

A Clue. Yet the psalm furnishes only a moral clue. The full solution awaited a New Testament revelation. It is the 'babes and sucklings' of Matthew chapter 21 verses 15 to 16 who direct us to the real solution – the person of Christ, the true Son of man. For we cannot agree that in his use of the common forms of poetic parallelism the psalm writer is merely saying the same thing in different words. That would be to attribute wantonness to the Spirit of God. On the contrary, even when the parallelism may be styled identical it is hardly synonymous. No! To say, 'What is man . . . and the Son of man?', far from merely saying the same thing twice, carries a real enlargement of thought in the second limb of the parallelism, suggestive of the divine interpretation of the whole paradox.

The Solution. For when our blessed Lord revealed a significant preference for the designation 'Son of man' as a title for Himself, for He used it thus eighty times, He was speaking, yearningly perhaps, of a heavenly glory that was once His. He tells us distinctly that as Son of man He came down from heaven. 'No man hath ascended into heaven, but he that descended out of heaven, even the Son of man which is in heaven', John 3. 13 RV; and, again, 'What and if ye shall see the Son of man ascend up where he was before?' John 6. 62. Thus, we learn that 'Son of man' is the designation of One of heavenly standing and glory. And in answer to the psalmist's question, 'What is man . . . and the Son of man?' we discover Him who is the divine and heavenly archetype of the race – the Son of man, who came down out of heaven.

Confirmatory Summary. A third passage, Heb. 2. 5-10, having a direct bearing on our theme can here receive only cursory reference. This passage asserts:

1. It is a moral requisite of the nature of God that the leader, *archēgos,*

of man's salvation **must** suffer and die, v. 10;

2. That this Jesus, the Son of man, must as racial head – like Adam – be crowned with glory and honour, in order that it might be on behalf of every man that He should fully taste death; and
3. That thus, and thus only, could the many sons be brought to glory, and the full purpose of God for man be accomplished.

'Son of man, His incarnation
Opened first the tale of grace;
Son of man, in new creation,
Leader of a chosen race;
Well may glory
Crown Him in the ordered place!'
H. K. BURLINGHAM

What is Man?* - R. V. COURT

Normally, when we ask this question our thoughts instinctively go to Psalm 8 verse 4, but in fact the question is asked four times in the Old Testament. If we were to try to answer the question without reference to the word of God, but by human reasoning alone, our answers would be very varied, and would depend on our outlook on life. The physiologist would speak of him, if he is honest, as the most wonderful thing he knows – the human body so complex that even now, after hundreds of years of close examination, men have to say that they are still only slowly discovering its marvels. They would, of course, only be talking of the body. The evolutionist would speak of him as something which has developed over a period of millions of years from the very lowest form of life to its present exalted position, without stopping to think of where and how the original something originated. Both of these positions leave God out of the picture – there is no place for Him.

When we turn to the word of God we are in the realm of fact and not fancy, and there we discover that man came directly from the hand of God, Gen. 1. 26, 27. He is declared to have been made in the 'image of God'; he was made with the ability to have communion with God, and was destined to know the glory of God. Positionally, he was made only a little lower than the angels, Ps. 8. 5. Alas, the divine record, following his history, shows him to be now one who, because of sin, has fallen from his privileged position.

It is interesting to note that four different Hebrew words are translated 'man' in the Old Testament. They are: (1) *Adam*, meaning a human being, a created being, therefore a dependent being; (2) *Ish*, an individual, one not lost in the crowd; (3) *Enosh*, mortal, subject to death; (4) *Gibbor*, a mighty man, indicating great possibilities.

The Bible, which asks the question 'What is man?' and shows us what he is now as a fallen creature, also looks to the future, and tells us what man can become – a new creation, the possessor of divine life, to become Christlike, to again have communion with God, and ultimately dwell in glory.

In considering these four questions it may be well to begin with the one so well-known to us, Ps. 8. 4, bearing in mind that the Holy Spirit draws our special attention to it and its context in Hebrews chapter 2 verses 6 to 8. In the Psalm the Hebrew word used is *enosh* – one that is mortal and subject to death, and the psalmist is expressing his amazement that the One who was so great that the universe came from His hand, the One who with His fingers had put the moon and the stars in their places, and kept them there, should be interested in such a creature as man in all his frailty and failure. The degree of interest shown by the Creator in His frail creature is indicated by the terms 'thou art mindful of him [or rememberest him]' and that 'thou visitest him [inspects him that He might know all about him]'. The words indicate a special attention to this created being. Verses 5 to 8 of the Psalm show us what God intended for him when He placed him in the Garden of Eden – 'to have dominion'. But, as David writes these words, he sees man as one fallen from that position, and he marvels that God the Creator should still be so interested in the rebel.

When we consider the divine comment in Hebrews chapter 2 verses 9 and 10 we begin to see what the psalmist could never have imagined, what was involved in God's remembrance and visitation. The writer of Hebrews is led to show us the One who never failed, but who, for a time, became lower than the angels in becoming a man. He tells us that this man was the One who made all things, and yet was mindful of and came and visited man, that here in the place which had been marred by sin,

He might know the suffering of death, and taste death for every man.

Do we experience a surge of wonder as again we think of this well-known and well-loved truth? David, led by God, could ask in awe and amazement why man in his sin should be the object of God's love and care; and we too may well ask, 'And what am I that I should be the object of God's love and grace?' It is, of course, beyond understanding. In Psalm 144 verses 3 and 4 the psalmist is again amazed that God should be interested in man. This time the word translated 'man' is a*dam* – a created, dependent being. The preceding verses, 1 and 2, reveal to us the thoughts of the psalmist in relation to God Himself. He sees Him as the mighty One, the all-sufficient One, the One who is completely dependable in every experience of life. The succeeding verses, 5 to 10, show his understanding of Him as the mighty Deliverer, before whom no enemy can stand – He is God.

It may be that as David was meditating quietly in the presence of God, these thoughts came to him and he contemplated his God in the wonder of His person, and the grandeur and might of His works, and he saw himself against the background of this glory, and wondered why this exalted being should be so interested in him. He speaks of God 'taking knowledge of him', or 'considers his ways', and 'makest account of him', suggesting that man has a place in His plans. This is all the more wonderful when we note that he also speaks of 'the son of man'. This is even lower. In Luke's genealogy of the Lord Jesus from the human angle, Luke 3. 38, Adam is spoken of as 'the son of God', but David sees himself as the 'son of man' (Adam – a created one?) – i.e., the son of his mother. He did not see himself as coming straight from the hand of God.

Both these lines of thought in verses 3 and 4 are worthy of our consideration. God 'takes knowledge' of us in spite of our nothingness. These words should have a sobering effect upon us, as behind them is the realization that our God has knowledge of us in detail, what we are doing, what we are thinking – nothing is hidden from this omniscient One, not even our innermost thought. Equally wonderful is the fact that He takes us into account – we have a specific place in His eternal plans. This is all the more wonderful when we consider the words of verse 4 – 'man is like to vanity: his days are as a shadow that passeth away'.

As we turn to Job chapter 7 verses 17 and 18 let us remember that we are now reading what may be the oldest book known to man, probably written well before the giving of the law. So far as we can judge whoever wrote the book did not have before him other spiritual literature from which to draw his thoughts, but there was certainly an exalted conception of God. DR. C. I. SCOFIELD comments, 'the book sheds a remarkable light on the philosophic breadth and intellectual culture of the patriarchal age'.

The words on either side of our verses are full of Job's despondency and of complaint at God's dealings with him – why does He do it? Verses 17 and 18 seem to be an expression of incredulity. It appears that, although he had spoken of God almost as a persecutor, and takes up this theme again later, there comes to him a recognition, based on past experience, that God is not really at all like that. He speaks now of God magnifying man, i.e., making him large and great; he speaks of Him as setting His heart upon him, not laying His hand upon him. Surely, here he is thinking of God's love for him – man, *enosh* – mortal man, subject to death. He then thinks of God visiting him every morning, and testing him every moment. Is this so that the continuing trial should not be more than he could bear, 1 Cor. 10. 13? It seems almost like a sudden gleam of light into his darkness. He reverts to his complaint, but his thought of God taking such an interest in him stirs him further, and we hear him saying, 'I have sinned', v. 20, and he asks the question, 'why dost thou not pardon my transgression and take away mine iniquity?' v. 21.

We look at our verse 17 in the light of the fuller revelation of God in the person of Christ, and the triumph of the cross, and we marvel at the intention of God to 'magnify' those who trust Him, Rom. 8. 28-30, and the glorious fact that He sets His heart upon them. We must remember that Job had no knowledge of the purpose of all that he experienced. He did not know of Satan's charge against him, and of God's permission that he should be tested in this way. And it says much for his spiritual state that although everything points to God's apparent harshness in His dealings with him, he can still marvel that He should have any thought for him at all, and that he can also consider God's enlargement of him, and His constant watchfulness. FRANCIS ANDERSEN, in his *Tyndale Commentary* on Job says, 'All Job has known about God he still believes.

But God's inexplicable ways have his mind perplexed to breaking point. Job is in the right: but he does not know that God is watching with silent compassion and admiration until the test is fully done and it is time to state His approval publicly, Job 42. 8'.

The question 'What is man?' is asked again, Job 15. 14, not by Job this time but by one of his friends, Eliphaz. He uses the same word that Job used, *enosh,* mortal man, subject to death. With regard to Job, who first asked the question, and David, who repeated it many years later, we can say that they are the words of godly men. It is difficult to know how to describe Eliphaz. He is certainly not of the spiritual calibre of either Job or David. It has been suggested that Eliphaz is seeking to put Job in his place by denigrating 'man' completely. What he says about man he is really saying about Job, and, without meaning to, about himself. But whatever purpose he had in uttering verses 14 and 16 they are, alas, true, and with the fuller revelation of God's ways in grace we see again that man, in spite of his wretched failure and sin, is loved by God. Eliphaz may well ask the question, 'what is man that he should be clean . . . that he should be righteous?' His words in verse 16 are probably intended to refer to Job primarily – 'abominable and filthy and drinking iniquity like water', a jaundiced view indeed, but they apply to mankind in general. And, if this is so, how is he going to be made clean and righteous? In spite of all his fine swelling words, Eliphaz cannot answer his own question – indeed no human reasoning could produce an answer.

It is said concerning the Lord Jesus in John chapter 6 verse 6, 'He knew himself what he would do', and without any doubt this is true concerning God as He listened to the words of His two servants and Eliphaz concerning:

1. The faithfulness of God and His visiting man, Ps. 8. 4;
2. The taking knowledge of man and including him in His plans, Ps. 144. 3;
3. God magnifying man and setting His heart upon him, Job. 7. 7;
4. God making man clean and making him righteous, Job. 15. 14.

As we turn to Hebrews chapter 2 we see God dealing with these problems, and we discover it is through 'The Man' in whom there was no sin, no failure, the One who came from the throne and was made for a little while lower than the angels for the suffering of death. The writer of Hebrews, while acknowledging the failure of man, says triumphantly, 'But we see Jesus'. And he is then able to speak of this One as 'tasting death for every man', v. 9. He goes on to speak of sanctification and the bringing of many sons to glory, v. 10. He also speaks of them as His 'brethren' and of deliverance from the power of Satan and death, Yes, God knew that He would do! Those who now know God's saving and keeping power, as they are asked the question 'What is man?' must surely reply, 'I'm only a sinner saved by grace'.

'Now what is man, when grace reveals
The virtues of a Saviour's blood?
Again a life divine he feels
Despises earth and walks with God.
And what in yonder realms above
Is ransomed man ordained to be
With honour, holiness and love
No seraph more adorned than He!
Nearest the throne and first in song
Man shall his hallelujahs raise,
While wondering angels round Him throng
And swell the chorus of His praise'.
JOHN NEWTON

The Fall - P. F. W. PARSONS

[Read: Gen. 3; Rom. 5. 12-21; 8. 18-25; 1 Cor. 15. 21-22]

Adam had been installed in the garden on the condition, or 'law', of Genesis chapter 2 verses 16 and 17; he had, in Eve, been given a suitable helpmeet; he had, in conjunction with her, the capacity for multiplying; his food was fruit; his occupation to dress, and 'guard' the garden, 2. 15, using it as a 'base' whence he was to 'subdue' the earth, 1. 28. The terms 'guard', 'subdue', and 'evil' ('the tree of the knowledge of good and evil') suggest that the enemy was lurking near even before man was created.

Genesis chapter 3 shows that after a relatively short time, the enemy came out into the open, attacking the weaker partner. She soon succumbed, the downward steps being (1) doubt, v. 1; (2) distortion, v. 3; (3) denial, v. 4, and (4) disobedience, v. 6. The appeal was, v. 6, to the lust of the flesh – 'good for food', the lust of the eye – 'pleasant to the eyes', and the pride of life – 'to be desired to make one wise'; cp. 1 John 2. 16.

Adam, in eating, disobeyed the 'law' which he, before Eve was formed, had received from God; he became a sinner, fell a victim to a far less formidable opponent than Eve faced, showed that Eve, taken from him, had done only what he would have done in her circumstances, and condoned her action.

Adam then tried to (1) hide himself, v. 8; see: Rev. 6. 15, 16; 20. 11; (2) excuse himself, v. 12; see: Rom. 1. 20; 2. 1; (3) clothe himself, v. 7; see: v. 21 - guiltless victims, their death providing a covering satisfactory to God.

Effects of the entry of sin into the lives of Adam and Eve and their world were immediate, far-reaching, and indescribably devastating. Sin struck:

Upwards, challenging God's authority.

Inwards, alienating man from God, and bringing straight away **spiritual** death. He found himself the possessor of a conscience, i.e., the knowledge which a man has, **within himself** of what is right and wrong in the **moral** sphere, and a defiled conscience at that. It caused a change in **the physical** constitution of both man and woman, with an accompanying downgrading in their diet, which was to include herb, and grass (corn is a grass). Ultimately the body was to die, and decay. The woman was to yield obedience to the man, in place of spontaneous co-operation. Both were to experience sorrow, the woman in conception, necessarily multiplied to repair the ravages of death. Children would bear the stamp of their fallen parents.

Downwards. The animal and vegetable creations were cursed and their natures changed. Animals became aggressive; the vegetable creations deteriorated, and noxious and abortive growths were produced. The earth was cursed, and yielded reluctantly. Throughout the realm of nature a lack of balance, and consequent instability ensued, to display itself eventually in storms, floods, volcanoes, and such things.

Forwards. Sin struck through all the future ages of time, laying the whole of man's posterity under the doom of death.

Satan heard his doom pronounced, so that the Bible became largely the account of a conflict between him and 'the seed', and in Revelation he is seen as the dragon, ready to devour the 'man child', Christ, ch. 12, through whom restoration, and more, will be effected.

During the past century or so, the history of the fall has been challenged by the theory of evolution, which owes its popularity to its supposition that man, so far from having fallen from a high estate, with progressive deterioration, has by some inward urge, and his own efforts, evolved from something very primitive, and will continue to advance to great heights. This theory not only does away with the fall, but with sin, conscience, human responsibility and man's unique relationship to God. Scientists base their speculations upon buried remains, and geological discoveries; they assert that millions of years were required for the formation of the earth, and its inhabitants; they ignore divine interventions in the two catastrophes of the fall and the flood.

1. The fall may well have involved the immediate wiping out of a large section of the animal creation straight away, particularly of the largest forms of life. It would be neither unscriptural nor unreasonable for us to **assume** that through the fall they quickly acquired offensive means and a ferocity which rendered them a menace to man, particularly as his control over them had been lost. Such a quick physical change, but in reverse, is mentioned in Isaiah chapter 11 verses 6 to 8, while Nebuchadnezzar affords yet another example, Dan. 4. 33. The wiping out of animals on a vast scale finds its parallel later in that of the human race in the flood (with eight exceptions).

2. In describing the flood, Genesis chapter 7 verse 11 refers to 'the great deep' being broken up; nowhere else is the phrase used; it suggests volcanic action and the turning of the earth into a vast swamp to a great depth. It may well have been that the

concentration of such vast forces, compressed in their operations into forty days, had effects which would normally be produced in those vast ages which science requires in explanation of its theories; it would explain many geological puzzles and discoveries of mammoth remains scattered over wide areas.

Romans chapter 5 enlarges upon the fall by bringing Adam forward as 'the figure of him that was to come', i.e., Christ. Adam was the 'figure' in that: (1) he was the head of a family; (2) he did one outstanding act; and (3) the effects of that one act spread to all who were, by heredity, linked with him, even to those who lived before Moses, when no law had been given which they could transgress. So Christ did one outstanding act of obedience, in contrast with Adam's; He is also the head of a family; and the blessed effects of that one act pass to all those who, by faith and the Spirit, are linked with Him.

In 1 Corinthians chapter 15 verses 45 to 47 Christ is referred to as the 'last Adam', i.e., finality, and 'the second man', as displacing the first, and carnal head, Adam. In Christ, man is given a hope of heaven which he never would have possessed, even if Adam had not fallen, for at best he was earthy. Christ has brought life and immortality to light in the gospel; in Adam there was no hope of a resurrection. Verses 20 and 23 of the chapter are selective, referring to the godly, but verses 21 and 22 are universal in their application, for as universal as the death of the body became, so universal will be its resurrection, either to glory or for judgement, cp. Rev. 1. 18.

Man as a Sinner - Sin and its Synonyms - E. W. ROGERS

That God did not create man as a sinner is categorically affirmed in scripture which states that 'God made man upright', Eccles. 7. 29. Sin is not part of humanity; it is, rather, an invader which had proved its ruination. Sin in its original Hebrew meaning signifies missing the mark, and denotes a failure on the part of man to fulfil the purpose that God had in his creation.

By a peculiarity in the Hebrew language, sin, an offering for sin, and the punishment of sin, are all represented by the one Hebrew word which throws light on 2 Corinthians chapter 5 verse 21. God made the One who knew no sin to be sin for us, a phrase whose depth of meaning we shall perhaps never be able to fathom. It alludes to God's judicial dealings with His Son when He hung on the cross. There He bore the punishment that we deserved for our sins, He having none of His own. There He was made 'an offering for sin', Isa. 53. 10. There He was made sin for us. It was this that accounted for the three hours of darkness, and the forsaking by God of the Lord Jesus which elicited the cry, 'My God, my God, why hast thou forsaken me?'

Sin is universal: 'all have sinned, and come short of the glory of God', Rom. 3. 23. It was 'by one man sin entered into the world, and death by sin; and so death passed upon all men, for that all have sinned', 5. 12. In the one federal head, Adam, the whole human race was involved, and his sinful action affected them all. Its consequences were passed on to all his posterity. There was only One, who voluntarily came into the human race, that was free from the taint of sin, and whose advent was designed 'to put away sin by the sacrifice of himself', Heb. 9. 26. This was effectually accomplished when He died on the cross at Calvary, and it was proved by His resurrection, Rom. 4. 25.

Sin, we repeat, is an invader into God's creation. It was brought in by the serpent by his subtle approach to the woman, Eve, in the garden of Eden, the record of which is given in Genesis chapter 3. The plan of campaign was first to cast a **doubt** upon God's word: then to **distort** it: then to **deny** it, and, as a final achievement, to get the man and his wife to **disobey** it. The point at issue was quite simple – merely the taking of forbidden fruit, but that prohibition was as a kind of peppercorn rent, reminding Adam and Eve that they were but tenants in the garden and not the owners thereof; they were responsible to a superior proprietor. In their downfall was the downfall of all their posterity which was, as yet, unborn in their loins.

The meaning of the Hebrew word translated sin is 'missing the mark', (see Judges chapter 20 verse 16, where it is translated in its literal sense in regard to accurate slinging of stones), and man has certainly done this in that he has failed to come up to the purpose of God in His creation of him. Or, to change the figure, he has gone astray like a stupid sheep, turning to its own way.[2] That is why man is so frequently described as 'lost'. The bewilderment of such a state, the inability to recover one's bearings, and the despair that is apt to come over one's soul, is almost indescribable.

Satan has a way of causing his dupes to be satisfied with their condition, but as soon as there is a realization of the true position the cry is wrung forth, 'O wretched man that I am! who shall deliver me?'. We may be grateful that the situation is not altogether hopeless. The response is, 'I thank God through Jesus Christ our Lord', Rom. 7. 24, 25.

Other words are used in scripture to describe 'sin'. Turn, for example, to Psalm 32 verses 1 and 2, where occur the words 'transgression', 'iniquity', and 'guile'. These are all aspects of the one heinous thing generalized as 'sin'. 'Transgression' is the infringing a limit which has been laid down by an existing authority who is entitled so to act. It virtually says, 'thus far and no farther', and should anyone exceed that restriction he would be guilty of 'transgression'. 'Iniquity' denotes lawlessness, injustice, springing from a total disregard for what is legal and just. It springs from a spirit of rebellion within. 'Guile' marks a strong degree of moral turpitude in the individual.

It is David who used these words in the cited Psalm, and who doubtless was conscious of personal guilt in the matter of his sin in relation to his adultery with Bathsheba, and his murder by proxy of her husband, Uriah – one of his mighty men. Doubtless he saw his sins in their true light, and in his confessional Psalm 51, and his blissful Psalm 32, he alludes to his conduct in appropriate terms.[3]

Sin is lawlessness, 1 John 3. 4 RV. It is not merely a breach of the law, but it is a mental repudiation of its legitimate claims over one – a casting off of its proper restraint. Indeed 'all unrighteousness is sin', 5. 17.

The question may be asked, what is 'sin unto death'? Various answers have been given. It would appear that it is not such a sin as occurred in

---

[2] Ps. 119. 176; Isa. 53. 6; 1 Pet. 2. 25.

[3] For further concentrations of synonyms for sin, see: Ezra 9. 6, 7; Prov. 6. 12-14; Isa. 1. 4-6; Dan. 9. 5, 6.

Acts chapter 5 when Ananias and Sapphira were visited by death; it is an identifiable sin as being a 'sin unto death', and the present writer believes it to be such a sin as cannot be put right in one's life time. For example, the sin of theft can be adjusted by repayment of the principal and interest, but there are other sins that admit of no such adjustment in a lifetime. The sin is identified as 'sin unto death', which does not, in the writer's view, mean that it will be visited by judicial death, but that it cannot be adjusted during one's life on earth. 1 John chapter 5 verse 16 appears to discourage enquiry as to what sin unto death actually is; it will become known as such at the time.

In 1 John chapter 1 verses 7 to 9 the occurrences of the word 'sin' and 'sins' denote the root and the fruit; the one has to do with our sinful nature, the other has to do with our sinful deeds. It is the deeds which are 'forgiven', as we read, 'whosoever believeth in him shall receive remission of sins', Acts 10. 43. This is reasonable. The spring of all the trouble in the human race was man's distrust of God, and his unbelief of His word in the garden of Eden, recorded in Genesis chapter 3. Man believed the lie of the devil that God was not interested in the well-being of man, but was fearful of a rival, for He knew that in the day that man took of the forbidden fruit he would be as God knowing good and evil. The devil did not tell man that in the day he took of the forbidden fruit he would know good but have no power to do it, and he would know evil yet have no power to resist it. Man fell for the suggestion with all the age-long sad issues that have flowed therefrom. How can the damage be undone? If the damage was done through man distrusting and disbelieving God, the remedy lay in man going back on that very action, and to believe God and trust Him. This is the very heart of the gospel: believe Me; trust Me. All who believe will be saved from the consequence of the fall.

The way of recovery for man lies in the way of his returning to God in humble confession of his guilt. A touching picture of this is given in that of the prodigal as recorded in Luke chapter 15, 'Father, I have sinned against heaven, and in thy sight, and am no more worthy to be called thy son', v. 21. The father would not allow him to proceed further with the request that he be made as one of his hired servants. The father did not intend that his son should be relegated to the kitchen; he must be given the son's place in the father's home.

God said, 'your iniquities have separated between you and your God', Isa. 59. 2, and this certainly was the case with the son of Luke chapter 15 who left a good home and a good father and went into a far country to live a life of independence and lawlessness. But it was not long before famine brought him to want and degradation. He compared his lot (and he was his father's son) with that of the lot of the servants in the old homestead, and bemoaned his folly. Nor was it long before he resolved to arise and return to his father making confession of his sin, and request to be installed as one of the servants. But his father's heart was too kind for that!

'Sin' is regarded as a merciless taskmaster who recompenses his servants with death; 'the wages of sin is death', Rom. 6. 23, such death not merely being physical and spiritual in this present time, but also eternal in time to come. It is also regarded as the product of lust's conception – lust when it hath conceived bringeth forth sin, and sin when it is finished bringeth forth death, Jas. 1. 15. Sin, therefore, is not an original integral part of human nature. It is the product of human 'lust'. No wonder, therefore, it manifests itself in many ways, such as the lust of the flesh, the lust of the eyes, and the pride of life, 1 John 2. 16. To this our first parents fell: the woman saw that the tree was good for food (the lust of the flesh), and that it was pleasant to the eyes (the lust of the eyes), and a tree to be desired to make one wise (the pride of life). She disobeyed God, and took of it, and gave to her husband. Along those three lines Satan attempted to overthrow the Son of God, but in each case he was unsuccessful. God's word was a sure resource for each assault.

Because of this the Lord Jesus was able to challenge His enemies thus, 'which of you convicteth me of sin?' John 8. 46 RV. They might charge Him with it, but they could not bring home to His heart a sense of guilt. Paul, the man of knowledge, said that He knew no sin, 2 Cor. 5. 21. Peter, the man of action, said He did no sin, 1 Pet. 2. 22. John, the man of contemplation, said, in Him is no sin, 1 John 3. 5. He was the Holy One of God. He was 'holy, harmless, undefiled', and in resurrection was 'separated from sinners' RV, though at the cross He had been 'numbered with the transgressors', Isa. 53. 12; Heb. 7. 26.

In Isaiah chapter 53 verse 5 sin is regarded as transgression, iniquity, enmity, and a disease. It exposes in its true and full light the dreadful plight in which the sinner is: as a transgressor of the law of God he is under its curse; his iniquity reveals him to be a rebel; his enmity is the open display of his inward hatred, which inward hatred reveals the diseased state of his moral nature. That such terms should lie embedded in this verse must cause wonder as we ponder the substitutionary work of the true subject of Isaiah chapter 53, a perplexity which the Ethiopian eunuch had, and which was solved for him by Philip the evangelist, Acts 8. 34.

The eternal, absolute, and unchangeable holiness of the Son of God must ever be borne in mind when considering Him as the One who bare in His own body our sins on the tree, 1 Pet. 2. 24. Never was He more pleasing to His Father than then, when He was made 'sin for us'. He remained for ever personally untainted by that which at the cross He was for ever putting away. That is why His body saw no corruption.

Sin 'is lawlessness' – 'All unrighteousness is sin', 1 John 2. 4; 5. 17. Lawlessness is an utter disregard of those claims which God has embodied in His word; unrighteousness is a failure to comply with His commandments. The chief sin of which man is guilty is stated, John 16. 9. The Holy Spirit will convict the world of sin 'because they believe not on me'. This is man's chief sin. It is not the only one for which men will be judged, for their judgement will be according to their works, Rev. 20. 12, but it is that sin which decides their eternal destiny of judgement. Had they believed on Him they would not have come into judgement, John 5. 24.

The World - A. T. Shearman

The enemies of the Christian are usually described in a threefold way as the world, the flesh, and the devil. While, in one sense, these represent one united trinity of opposition to that which is godly in life and practice, each has its own distinct feature of danger to the believer. It is good to know what the scriptures teach about these alien forces, so that they can be recognized and repelled in every way. Thank God, 'in all these things we are more than conquerors through him that loved us', Rom. 8. 37. We shall consider here some features of the New Testament teaching regarding the world, to assess its character and influence.

The World – Definition. There are two words mainly used in the New Testament to express the ideas of the world, *kosmos* and *aiōn.*

Kosmos. The primary meaning of this word is order, arrangement, or adornment. Its opposite is chaos, disorder. The ordered universe, the sum of creation as made by God's hand, is described as the world. This includes the heaven and the earth, for God is the One 'that made the world and all things therein . . . being Lord of heaven and earth', Acts 17. 24 RV. But this word is also used of the dwelling place of the human race, 'that order of things in which humanity moves, or of which man is the centre'. Then, it is used of mankind itself. Hence the Lord Jesus came into the world, and left it again, John 16. 28, and 'God so loved the world', meaning the whole human race, 3. 16. Finally, sadly, it depicts that order of things which is alienated from God by the fall, and which is dominated by the evil one himself, 1. 10; 1 John 5. 19.

Aiōn. This word is used to denote an age or period of time, the course of life or the time of life. The Son is said to be the Creator of the 'ages', Heb. 1. 2 RVmg. Then Ephesians chapter 3 verse 11 speaks of 'the purpose of the ages', or dispensation, RVmg. The Lord Jesus gave Himself for our sins that He might deliver us 'out of this present evil age', Gal. 1. 4 RVmg. It is clear from this passage that the word is used to represent the moral and spiritual characteristics of the time. So we read of: its disputers, 1 Cor. 1. 20; its rulers, 2. 6, 8; its cares, Matt. 13. 22; and, Satan as its god, 2 Cor. 4. 4. The word is used to denote 'the unbounded time, past or future, in which the history of the world is accomplished'.

In Hebrews chapter 1 verse 6 another word is used which denotes the inhabitable earth.

God and the World. We live today in a world that is increasingly godless. Many say that God has either abandoned the world or was never interested in it at all. The whole burden of scripture, however, presents a God who is intimately involved in its affairs. One has said 'This is God's world, not man's, and whilst men are, up to a point, able to choose their actions, they are not able to choose the results of those actions'.

The **creation** of the world was God's work. Both the Old Testament and

New Testament state this, cp. Isa. 40. 28; Acts 17. 24. The 'cosmos' and the 'ages' are the result of His mighty power. John chapter 3 verse 16 states that 'God so loved the world, that he gave his only begotten Son'. Though the world in its sin rebels against its Creator, yet God loves mankind. While the hand of God creates, the heart of God loves – this is the core of the gospel message. Yet, the attitude of the world is one of rebellion and opposition to God's will in every sense. Therefore, scripture speaks consistently of the judgement of God upon the inhabitants of the world. Paul winds up his address on Mars Hill saying, 'Inasmuch as he hath appointed a day, in the which he will judge the world in righteousness by the man whom he hath ordained', Acts 17. 31 RV. Thus the gospel urges all to repent.

Christ and the World. 'He was in the world, and the world was made by him, and the world knew him not', John 1. 10. John so describes the reaction of the cosmos to the presence of the Saviour in it. He was sent into it, 3. 17, that He might be the Saviour of the world, 1 John 4. 14. Nothing was made without Him, John 1. 3; through Him the ages came into being, Heb. 1. 2 RVmg. Yet history has on its pages the tragic record that the world was the place where Jesus was crucified. This is mystery indeed, that a world should put to death its maker. If the 'rulers [or princes] of this age', and 'the rulers [or princes] of this world', had known Him, they would not have crucified the 'Lord of glory', 1 Cor. 2. 6, 8 RV and mg.

The Lord said 'I am not of the world', and of His own He could say 'they are not of the world', John 17. 14. We are not always as clear about this as the Lord Himself was. Of the boundaries of His first advent He said, 'I came out from the Father, and am come into the world: again, I leave the world, and go unto the Father', 16. 28 RV. The climax of the ages will come when, 'The kingdom of the world is become the kingdom of our Lord, and of his Christ', Rev. 11. 15 RV. He will be the world's rightful King.

Satan and the World. Satan is described as the 'god of this age', 2 Cor. 4. 4 RVmg. He is also called by Christ Himself the 'prince of this world [cosmos]', John 12. 31. As the 'god of this age', he is the director of its principles, and sets its tone. Behind the outward trends of world society, through the generations of mankind, there have been the workings of a mastermind of evil. Consider those unseen forces of Satanic evil, those 'world-rulers of this darkness' with which the Christian has to do battle, Eph. 6. 11, 12 RV. In our day we are becoming more conscious of the breaking through into the open of these unseen powers. As the 'god of this age', Satan blinds the minds of those that believe not. As the 'prince of this world [cosmos]' we see the great usurper of authority in God's world – the one who offered the kingdoms of the world to Christ when he tempted Him in the wilderness.

Satan's authority is evident in the world today. Yet, the Lord Jesus could say 'the prince of this world cometh, and hath nothing in me', John 14. 30. As to the extent of Satan's influence, 'the whole world lieth in the evil one', 1 John 5. 19 RV.

The Believer and the World. What is God's purpose in saving men and women from a world that is under His condemnation? Acts chapter 15 verse 14 RV says, 'God did visit the Gentiles, to take out of them a people for his name'. So, too, the Lord Jesus could define His own in a threefold way as those who were given to Him by God **'out of the world'**, John 17. 6, as those who, like Himself, were **'not of the world'**, v. 16, and yet they were those whom He sent **'into the world'**, v. 18. These verses clearly indicate that a believer's pathway is one of separation from the world system of things. Notice 1 John chapter 2 verses 15 to 17 in this connection, 'Love not the world, neither the things that are in the world'. It is possible to live on the fringe of the devil's domain. Positive action is needed, 'be not fashioned according to this age: but be ye transformed', Rom. 12. 2 RVmg. We need to take the stand that Paul felt necessary, so that 'the world is crucified unto me, and I unto the world', Gal. 6. 14.

The World – Destiny. What is to be the end of this present world – both cosmos and age? The destiny of the universe does not rest in man's hand, but God's. In God is cause and finality in all that He has made. He is the Alpha and Omega, the First and the Last, the Beginning and the End. In these words the idea of destiny is implicit. 2 Peter chapter 3 is interesting in connection with the climax of the ages. Looking back to **the past** we read of 'the world that then was', vv. 5, 6. This primeval creation perished in the flood. Then we read of the heaven and the earth which **now are**; they are 'stored up for fire, being reserved against the day of judgement and destruction of ungodly men', v. 7 RV. Finally, **the hope** of all who are Christ's is 'for new heavens and a new earth, wherein dwelleth righteousness', v. 13.

The Flesh - A. T. Shearman

Scripture quotations are taken from the Revised Version

The use of the word 'flesh' in scripture is associated with human weakness. It is often meant to designate those qualities that have to do with the body. Yet it also means more than this. It has spiritual connections, expressing the outworking in experience of the passions of man's fallen nature. It is therefore reckoned as a relentless enemy of spiritual growth and progress. We can describe it as **the enemy within**, as the world represents **the enemy without**.

In the Old Testament 'flesh' usually means the whole of man's earthly nature. In the days of Noah it is recorded that 'all flesh had corrupted his way upon the earth', Gen. 6. 12. God saw the evil in humanity, and the corruption of man in his practices. This led to the judgement of the flood. Man's frailty is associated with the flesh. Even before the flood God took account of man's moral weakness in the flesh. 'My spirit shall not strive with man forever, for that he also is flesh' ('in their going astray they are flesh', mg), v. 3. Within himself sin had weakened man's moral resistance to evil. The Old Testament also consistently teaches that flesh is perishable, having no enduring qualities. It is subject to corruption and death. 'All flesh is as grass, and all the goodliness thereof is as the flower of the field: the grass withereth, the flower fadeth', Isa. 40. 6, 7. Man was made from the dust. In the day that Adam fell in his sin, the words were spoken 'dust thou art, and unto dust shalt thou return', Gen. 3. 19. Death and corruption lay in those dreadful words. Yet, in two places at least there seems to be some glimmer of hope in connection with the idea of the flesh. David could say as he considered the grave, having set the Lord always before him, 'Therefore my heart is glad, and my glory rejoiceth: my flesh also shall dwell in safety [KJV hope]', Ps. 16. 9. And Job, as he averred that his redeemer lived, could say that in his flesh he would see God, Job 19. 25, 26. From these two scriptures, as they look beyond the grave, the whole of man's being is seen to be contained in the word 'flesh'. A much wider use is made of the idea of the flesh in the New Testament.

It is used of human generation or kinship. There is that which has to do with 'flesh and blood'. Flesh and blood cannot inherit the kingdom of God, 1 Cor. 15. 50, as they have to do with the natural order of being. In Hebrews chapter 2 verse 14 the children are 'sharers in flesh and blood [blood and flesh, mg.]'. This is their constitution as natural beings. Significantly, Christ, that He might die, 'partook of the same' constitution, taking hold of the seed of Abraham in incarnation. He 'was born of the seed of David according to the flesh', Rom. 1. 3. His natural lineage could be traced, although He was 'declared to be the Son of God with power, according to the spirit of holiness, by the resurrection'. Thus, Hebrews chapter 5 verse 7 refers to 'the days of his flesh'. His earthly life could be measured in terms of time and sense. In the same way, Paul could speak of those who were his 'kinsmen according to the flesh', Rom. 9. 3. He had great compassion for those who were of his nation.

Flesh is used, also, of that which is imperfect, that which speaks of human limitation. Paul was conscious of the weakness and infirmities of his own flesh, Gal. 4. 12-16. Despite this, he had preached to the Galatians. Whatever the disability was, they did not despise him because of it. Thus, in the same connection he could speak of the 'thorn in the flesh, a messenger of Satan to buffet me', 2 Cor. 12. 7. Imperfection in one way or another is linked with the flesh. It is noteworthy that God chooses that which men despise that 'no flesh should glory before God', 1 Cor. 1. 26-29. In this, divine wisdom is displayed.

Weakness is attributed to the flesh in the sphere of man's will. In Gethsemane, perhaps with understandable sadness, the Lord Jesus said of His sleeping disciples, 'the spirit indeed is willing, but the flesh is weak', Mark 14. 38. Paul speaks of the fickleness in the purpose that is according to the flesh, 2 Cor. 1. 17. Neither his speaking nor his actions were after this fashion, v. 18.

By far the most important teaching concerning the flesh in the New Testament has to do with its relationship to the life of the believer. In this connection, it is well to distinguish between the use of 'body' and 'flesh'. Paul says 'in me, that is, in my flesh, dwelleth no good thing', Rom.

7. 18. But he says concerning believers in Corinth, 'know ye not that your body is a temple of the Holy Ghost which is in you', 1 Cor. 6. 19. Again, he refers to believers as those who have 'crucified the flesh with the passions and the lusts thereof', Gal. 5. 24. But he beseeches believers to 'present your bodies a living sacrifice, holy, acceptable to God', Rom. 12. 1, and to 'glorify God therefore in your body', 1 Cor. 6. 20. The flesh is looked at, therefore, as that which is incurably evil, the agent through which Satan can damage and destroy the spiritual growth of the believer. 'That which is born of the flesh is flesh; and that which is born of the Spirit is spirit', John 3. 6. So the Lord Jesus described the kind of life that enters into, and lives in the sphere of, the kingdom of God. Hence, in the life of the believer there is constant tension. 'For the flesh lusteth against the Spirit, and the Spirit against the flesh; for these are contrary the one to the other', Gal. 5. 17. 'Now the works of the flesh are manifest, which are these', v. 19, following which Paul enumerates many evils which emanate from man's lower nature, the passions of his sinful heart. Not that the list is exhaustive as is indicated by Paul's 'and such like', v. 21. What place can any of these have in a life of true spiritual worth? It is only those 'after the flesh' who 'mind the things of the flesh', Rom. 8. 5. The 'mind of the flesh is death', v. 6; it is 'enmity against God', v. 7; it is not subject to the law of God, neither indeed can be; they that are in the flesh cannot please God, vv. 8, 9.

Though we are a new creation in Christ Jesus we have to reckon, day by day, with the desires of the flesh. Yet Paul reasons, 'we are debtors, not to the flesh, to live after the flesh', Rom. 8. 12. In other words, we owe the flesh no allegiance – we owe our life and living to the Spirit of God. The answer to the damaging effects of the lusts of the flesh is surrender to the power of the Spirit. In Galatians chapter 5 verses 22 to 23 the apostle speaks of 'the fruit of the Spirit'. The beauty of these graces as they develop in Christian experience replaces the works of the flesh. Against them there is no law. The positive rule of life for dealing with the flesh is made clear. 'Walk by the Spirit, and ye shall not fulfil the lust of the flesh', v. 16.

THE DOCTRINE OF THE BELIEVER'S BLESSEDNESS

Foreknowledge, Election and Predestination - M. Horlock

Few things afford greater stability to the believer's faith than the discovery that God is working all things according to His own plan and purpose, Eph. 1. 11. The present article attempts to relate God's sovereignty to His dealings with sinful men. The New Testament stresses that the initiative in salvation lay with God. The doctrine of God's sovereignty in salvation influences and pervades the teaching of the New Testament to a greater extent than is suggested by the occurrences of the three words under consideration. See, for example, John 6. 37, 44, 45 and Acts 13. 48. God has not been influenced in His saving purpose by any merit, seen or foreseen, in the recipients of His salvation. The roots of foreknowledge, election, and predestination are all firmly planted in His own unfathomable love. God is His own motive, Deut. 7. 7, 8. His love is not drawn out by any loveliness or good in us, but springs up spontaneously from the depths of His nature, 1 John 4. 8-10.

Distinction in the Terms. Foreknowledge, election, and predestination refer to facets of God's purpose concerning some of our sinful race who should be made the voluntary partakers of His salvation in Christ. The terms are not, however, synonymous. Election is distinguished from predestination, Eph. 1. 4, 5; predestination from foreknowledge, Rom. 8. 29; foreknowledge from election, 1 Pet. 1. 2. **Foreknowledge** has to do with **persons**, and brings into focus **the objects** of God's purpose in salvation. **Election** refers to the actual **selection and choice** for salvation of the persons foreknown. **Predestination** concerns **the goal and glorious destination** toward which the objects of God's foreknowledge and election are moving.

Foreknowledge. In the New Testament the noun *prognōsis* occurs only twice, and signifies a knowledge in advance or beforehand. The corresponding verb occurs five times. The verb is used in a non-theological way in Acts chapter 26 verse 5 and 2 Peter chapter 3 verse 17. In relation to God's foreknowledge, Peter uses the verb of Christ in His office as Redeemer, 1 Pet. 1. 20, and he uses the noun of Christ's sufferings, Acts 2. 23, closely linking it with God's determinate counsel.

Paul once uses the verb of Israel, Rom. 11. 2. The other two references concern the believer.

The verb occurs in Romans chapter 8 verse 29. In the face of distressing earthly circumstances, Paul assures the Roman saints of God's providence and sovereignty. He reminds them that they were the subjects of foreknowledge and predestination, the recipients of calling and justification, and the heirs of glorification. In the light of these truths, they could be confident that all things in the present would work for their good. Foreknowledge is therefore the first of five successive steps in the spiritual history of the believer. The steps are clearly co-extensive: all men are not foreknown any more than all men are predestinated, etc. Before the world began, of course, God **knew about** all men, but He did not 'know' all men. Foreknowledge indicates something other than mere prevision.

Before God formed any plans or intentions for the objects of His special interest, predestination, He first brought them into view and focus, foreknowledge. It may be that, as often in scripture, the knowledge in mind involves more than mere intellectual apprehension. 'Knowledge' sometimes includes the idea of an intimate awareness and love, and suggests special favour and affectionate regard.[1] God's foreknowledge might therefore imply that He lovingly 'unites Himself beforehand' with the believer. It certainly reveals the unplumbed depths and infinite range of the divine wisdom, together with the detailed character of God's knowledge, both of which are stressed in another context given to the discussion of God's sovereignty, Rom. 11. 33-36.

It should be noted that foreknowledge concerns persons, and not anything in, or about them. Romans chapter 8 verses 29 to 30 expands Paul's statement in verse 28 that those that love God are the called according to His purpose. The apostle does not base everything upon God's contemplative foresight of man's efforts or response.

God's foreknowledge appears finally as the basis also of election, 1 Pet. 1. 2.

---

[1] For example: Amos 3. 2; Matt. 7. 23; 1 Cor. 8. 3; 2 Tim. 2. 19.

Election. With a single exception, 2 Thess. 2. 13, the New Testament references to the believer's election derive from one family of Greek words. The verb *eklegō* signifies to choose or to pick out, and its basic meaning is apparent from its non-technical use.[2]

The phrase 'the elect' is often used to denote the remnant of Israel who are yet destined for future blessing.[3] The Lord Himself is described several times as 'the chosen', Luke 9. 35 RV; 23. 35; 1 Pet. 2. 6, stressing His eminence, worth, and excellence. Compare also the use in Romans chapter 16 verse 13 and 2 John verses 1 and 13. It is frequently used of Jesus' choice of the twelve apostles.[4] The title 'the elect' was commonly used by the apostles to describe believers in general.[5]

One of the principal texts is Ephesians chapter 1 verse 4. God has chosen us 'in Christ'. Israel's relationship to Abraham was the ground of, and reason for, its blessings. Similarly, our election to blessing is bound up with a person – Christ. Note that we are chosen **that** we might be holy, and not **because** we would be. There was nothing attractive about the objects of God's election. He was not moved by those considerations that influence men's choice. Generally He chooses the poor, Jas. 2. 5, the foolish, the weak, etc., that no flesh should glory before Him, 1 Cor. 1. 27-29. All human merit is excluded from God's gracious choice in 2 Timothy chapter 1 verse 9, which also, as Ephesians chapter 1 verse 4, anchors God's purpose of salvation in eternity. Again, this is stressed in 2 Thessalonians chapter 2 verse 13, where the association of election (*lit.* a taking for oneself) with the love of God should be noted, cp. 1 Thess. 1. 4 RV.

Paul considered it possible to know, not only one's own election, 1 Cor. 1. 26, 27, but also that of others, 1 Thess. 1. 4. The power that accompanied his preaching, the zeal with which the gospel was embraced, and the fruit it bore, vv. 5-10, provided clear evidence to the apostle that the Thessalonians were the objects of God's loving choice.

---

[2] See: Luke 10. 42; 14. 7; Acts 6. 5; 15. 22, 25.
[3] Matt. 24. 22, 24, 31; Rom. 11. 28; cp. Isa. 65. 9, 15, 22.
[4] Luke 6. 13; John 6. 70; Acts 1. 2 (see verse 24).
[5] Rom. 8. 33; Titus 1. 2; 1 Pet. 1. 2; 2. 9.

Peter says that the believer's calling and election can be confirmed and attested by the exercise of the qualities and graces which serve to make the Christian fruitful in the knowledge of God, 2 Pet. 1. 10. Here 'calling' precedes election because the viewpoint is the recipient's rather than God's.

Election is depicted as a basis of the believer's security, Rom. 8. 33, as an incentive and encouragement to personal holiness, Col. 3. 12, and as a spur to evangelism, 2 Tim. 2. 9, 10. Paul endured amidst all his afflictions both because he realized that God's word was not bound as he was, and because he had regard for God's elect that they might 'obtain the salvation'. Paul knew that God had appointed both the end – salvation, and the means – evangelism; cp. also Acts 18. 9, 10. It was One greater than Paul who linked together God's sovereignty in salvation and the universal invitation of His gospel, Matt. 11. 25-30.

In Romans chapters 9 to 11 Paul maintains that God's attitude to Israel is to be gauged by His promises to the patriarchs, and His steadfast love to His people – not by their present rejection on account of unbelief. In the passage, the word 'election' refers both to individual Jewish believers of the present church age, 11. 5, 7, and to the restored nation of the future, 11. 28. In both spheres 'the purpose of God according to election' stands, 9. 11.

Predestination. The verb 'to predestinate', *proorizō,* means to determine beforehand, to mark out in advance, to foreordain. It occurs only six times in the New Testament. In Acts chapter 4 verse 28 it is used to stress that even men's sinful actions are drawn into the outworking of God's counsel, not that this absolves men in any way from guilt, Luke 22. 22; Acts 2. 23. The word is also found in 1 Corinthians chapter 2 verse 7 of God's wisdom 'foreordained before the worlds unto our glory' RV. God's all-wise plan antedates all of man's boasted wisdom, and purposes glory for the believer, vv. 9, 10.

The other references apply predestination to persons only, and describe **that to which** they have been foreordained, Rom. 7. 29, 30; Eph. 1. 5, 11. In each case it is traced back to God's purpose, and the counsel which had its origin in His will.

In Romans chapter 8 verses 29 and 30 predestination represents the second link in a chain of salvation which binds together two eternities. This chain cannot be broken; it is forged in heaven, vv. 35, 38, 39. In the spiritual realm, as well as in the natural, God's ultimate aim is the supremacy and pre-eminence of Christ, Col. 1. 18. God has foreordained that all those whom He has foreknown shall be altogether like His Son, that He might occupy the place of firstborn among them.

Predestination also involves the dignity of our relationship to God as sons, Eph. 1. 5 RV, and the enjoyment of our prospective possessions in that new order of things to be introduced by Christ's return, Eph. 1. 11; also see v. 14.

A Balanced View. Three points must be made.

God's ways are just. It is a matter of pure grace that any guilty and condemned sinners should be saved at all. The lost suffer no more than the due reward of their deeds.

Scripture carefully avoids any suggestion that God chooses any men to be damned (the theory of reprobation). Election is always to salvation, and never to destruction. The kingdom is divinely prepared for the 'sheep', but eternal fire is not said to be prepared for the 'goats', though they can sin themselves into everlasting punishment, Matt. 25. 34, 41, 46! Paul attributes to divine preparation the glorification of 'vessels of mercy', but not the destruction of 'vessels of wrath', Rom. 9. 22, 23.

'God chooses certain to be saved'. 'Man is free, and has the power to choose for himself'. Which of these statements is true? The truth **does not lie in either** of the statements nor somewhere between them, but **in both**. Man is both free **and** under the control of God. True, we cannot reconcile these things in our minds, but that does not prevent their being reconciled in God's mind. Remove man's freedom and there are no persons to save; remove God's sovereignty and no persons will be saved.

Grace - B. Osborne

The word 'grace' is found over 160 times in the Bible, and 128 of these are in the New Testament. God is spoken of as 'the God of all grace', 1 Pet. 5. 10. We are told that 'grace and truth came by Jesus Christ', John 1. 17, who is said to be 'full of grace', v. 14. The grace of the Lord Jesus Christ we 'know', 2 Cor. 8. 9. The Holy Spirit is referred to as 'the Spirit of grace', Heb. 10. 29. Thus, the three persons of the Godhead are closely linked with grace. The fact that grace is received from Christ, Rom. 5. 15, and from God the Father, 2 Cor. 1. 12, is a testimony to the deity of Christ. Grace is seen as an attribute of Godhead. What then is grace?

The English word 'grace' is sometimes used in our Bible with the meaning of 'graceful' in the sense of comeliness, cp. Jas. 1. 11, where the Greek word is *euprepeia.* More usually the word 'grace' is used in the New Testament to translate the Greek word *charis,* which means favour without recompense or equivalent. It is rendered in our English version variously.[6]

Grace Defined. Whilst it is impossible for man to define fully the richness of God's grace, yet some statements are helpful towards an appreciation of what is involved:

- 'Grace is God's free, unmerited favour, graciously bestowed upon the unworthy and sinful'.
- 'Grace is something in God which is at the heart of all His redeeming activities, the downward stoop and reach of God, God bending from the heights of His majesty, to touch and grasp our insignificance and poverty'.
- 'Grace is love which passes beyond all claims to love. It is love which after fulfilling the obligations imposed by law, has an unexhausted wealth of kindness', R. W. DALE.
- Grace 'means, first, love in exercise to those who are below the lover, or who deserve something else; stooping love that condescends and patient love that forgives', MACLAREN.
- 'God is love; but when He bestows that love on guilty, unclean,

---

[6] Grace, John 1. 14; Rom. 1. 5; Eph. 2. 5, etc; favour, Luke 1. 30; 2. 52; Acts 2. 47; pleasure, Acts 24. 27; 25. 9; liberality, 1 Cor. 16. 3; benefit, 2 Cor. 1. 15; joy, Philem. 7; acceptable, 1 Pet. 2. 20; gift, 2 Cor. 8. 4; and thanks, 1 Cor. 15. 57; 2 Cor. 2. 14; 8. 16; 9. 15. Some conception of the richness of the content of the word is thus seen.

rebellious sinners, then it is grace'.

- 'Grace is God showing nothing but love and mercy when we deserve nothing but wrath and judgement. It is God bending toward us in infinite love'.
- 'Love that looks up is adoration; love that is on its own level is affection; love that descends is grace'.
- 'Grace is energy. Grace is love-energy. Grace is redeeming love-energy ministering to the unlovely and endowing the unlovely with its own loveliness', DR. JOWETT.
- 'Grace is love indeed, but it is love to creatures, and to creatures who do not deserve His love. And therefore all He does for us in Christ and all that is disclosed to us of His goodwill in the gospel is called grace', ALEXANDER WHYTE.
- 'The grace of God is His free love and unmerited favour, imparted to men through Christ', F. F. BRUCE.
- 'The idea is that of a gift which a man never deserved and could never earn, and which is given to him in the generous goodness and love of the heart of God', W. BARCLAY.

These statements are helpful and instructive, but the word of God has its own descriptions of grace.[7]

In grace God acts out from Himself towards those who have deserved not His favour but His wrath. Grace refers to that act of God in Christ whereby man's sin is put away and salvation made available as a free gift. Grace is freely bestowed by God apart from man's deserving. If there were any compensatory act or payment, however slight or inadequate, it would be no more grace. When speaking of God's grace towards man, the matter of human merit or deserving is utterly excluded. It is freely bestowed by God apart from man's deserving. Grace is the free, spontaneous, unmerited love of God to sinful man.

Grace Contrasted. In the New Testament grace comes into contrast and conflict with the following concepts:

Antinomianism. This is the denial of all rule over the lives of believers, the affirmation that because saved by God's free grace, wholly without

---

[7] Cp. Titus 2. 11; Eph. 2. 7; Rom. 5. 8.

merit, men are not required to live holy lives. But this is not so. The very first thing that grace does for the lost sinner is to bring him salvation, and when he receives this salvation it teaches him to deny 'ungodliness and worldly lusts', and to live 'soberly, righteously, and godly, in this present world', Titus 2. 12. Grace teaches the Christian how he is to live. He is to live 'soberly', with inward self-government. The grace that saves teaches the control of temper, thought, tongue. He is to live 'righteously', in his relationships with men. He is to live 'godly', in his relations with the world above.

Ceremonialism. This reared its head early in the church. In its first form the demand was that believers should observe the Levitical ordinances, cp. Acts. 15. 1. In its modern form it is seen in the idea that Christian ordinances are essential to salvation.

Works. Grace is not to be confused with works. Works are a ladder that we ourselves set up and painfully attempt to ascend; grace is an elevator which God provides, into which we pass by faith, and where all the lifting power is God's alone. Salvation by works is the choice of the Pharisee; salvation by grace is the hope of the publican, Luke 18. 10-14. The two cannot be blended, for 'if it is by grace, it is no more of works; otherwise grace is no more grace', Rom. 11. 6 RV.

Law. 'For the law was given by Moses, but grace and truth came by Jesus Christ', John 1. 17. Grace then characterizes the present age, as law characterized the age from Sinai to Calvary. That is not to say that law did not exist before Sinai, or that there was no grace revealed before the coming of Christ. The forbidding of the fruit of the tree of knowledge of good and evil was a law, Gen. 2. 17, as God's seeking the sinful couple and clothing them manifested grace, 3. 21. Law and grace as some revelation of God's ways and dealings have always existed, but law as a rule of life was given by Moses, and dominates the period from Sinai to Calvary, just as grace has prevailed since Calvary, and will do so until the end of this age.

There were teachers who came to Galatia who wanted to 'put the clock back'. They proclaimed a mingling of grace and law – justification partly by grace and partly by law; cp. Gal. 3. 2, 3; 1. 6-8. The two cannot be co-mingled in this way. Law brings a work to do; grace tells of a work that is done. Law reveals sin, Rom. 3. 20; grace reveals salvation, Titus 2. 11-13. Law is a ministry of condemnation, Rom. 3. 19; grace of forgiveness, Eph. 1. 7. Law is God prohibiting and requiring, Exod. 20. 1-17; grace is God beseeching and bestowing, 2 Cor. 5. 20. Law curses, Gal. 3. 10; grace redeems from that curse, 3. 13. Law kills, Rom. 7. 9, 11; grace makes alive, John 10. 10. Law shuts every mouth before God; grace opens every mouth to praise Him. Law puts a great and guilty distance between man and God, Exod. 20. 18, 19; grace makes guilty man nigh to God, Eph. 2. 13. Law says, do and thou shalt live, Luke 10. 26, 28; grace says, believe and live, John 5. 24. The law lays down what man must do; the gospel lays down what God has done. Law utterly condemns the best man, Phil. 3. 4-9; grace freely justifies the worst.[8]

Grace Evaluated. What grace provides causes the believer to exclaim,

> 'Oh, to grace how great a debtor,
> Daily I'm constrained to be'.

Grace brings salvation, Titus 2. 11-13, and justification, 3. 7. It gives us a standing, Rom. 5. 2, and an inheritance, Acts 20. 32. It secures acceptance, Eph. 1. 6, 7, and help when we need it, Heb. 4. 16, and strength, 2 Cor. 12. 9. It is the secret of successful service, 1 Cor. 15. 10, the power of a blameless walk, 2 Cor. 1. 12, the deliverer from the dominion of sin, Rom. 6. 14, and the means of consolation, 2 Thess. 2. 16. To grace is ascribed instruction, Titus 2. 11, 12.

> *In the past,* grace provided salvation, Titus 2. 11; Eph. 2. 5, 8.
> *In the present,* grace pledges sufficiency, 2 Cor. 12. 9.
> *In the future,* grace promises satisfaction, Eph. 2. 7.

The church is to exhibit to men and angels throughout endless ages the exceeding riches of His grace. Paul sees in the future a long vista of ages coming on, in every one of which God desires that His grace should be known as passing all bounds in its riches; and His kindness to us in Christ is so wonderful, that it is fitted to be an exhibition through all ages, and to all ranks of God's intelligent creatures, of the vastness of the grace that is in Him.

---

[8] Luke 23. 43; Rom. 5. 8; 1 Cor. 6. 9, 11.

The General Call. God's wisdom of old had been expressed vocally, in the places of concourse, in the cities and everywhere by those who testified in the fear of the Lord. The appeal went forth, calling men to the wisdom of the just. God stretched out His hand in loving invitation, desiring the hearer's proper response.[9]

This word of invitation became personalized in the Word incarnate among men.[10] He came to call sinners, not the righteous, Matt. 9. 13. He usually sat to teach, but He stood, and called loudly, to those athirst, John 7. 37. He invited men to the royal feast of bountiful grace, and confirmed the call by yet another call. Many were called, but few were chosen, Matt. 22. 1-14. He commanded the blind man to be called, to whom the disciples rightly said, 'Be of good comfort, rise; he calleth thee', Mark 10. 49. The risen Lord still commands His called-servants to go into the highways and hedges with the invitation to His fully-finished grace.[11]

This call is the invitation to 'whosoever', and is as extensive as the love God has shown to the world.[12] With His whole heart and soul God desires the good of all.[13] The propitiation and the ransom are in the interest of all, 1 Tim. 2. 6; 1 John 2. 2. Alas, so many refuse, with dire results in judgement.

There is a general 'drawing'; there is an effectual 'drawing', John 12. 32; 6. 44. Similarly, there is a general calling, and an effectual calling. In the Gospels, the 'call' is general and is sometimes unheeded; in the Epistles it is always effectual.

The Effectual Call. Human responsibility to respond to the call of God is explicitly stated, and implicitly inferred. The believer is instructed, and soon realizes that it was God who effected the call. The One 'that

---

[9] Prov. 1. 20-24; Luke 1. 17; 11. 49.

[10] Prov. 8. 4, 31; Heb. 1. 2; John 1. 14, 18.

[11] Luke 14. 16-24; Acts 16. 10; 2. 39.

[12] John 3. 15, 16; 4. 14; 7. 17; Acts 2. 21; 10. 43; Rom. 10. 13; Rev. 22. 17.

[13] Jer. 32. 41; 1 Tim. 2. 4; 2 Pet. 3. 9.

calleth', and 'he who calls', both emphasize this fact, Rom. 9. 11; Gal. 5. 8. To this agrees the statement of our Lord, 'No man can come to me, except the Father . . . draw him', John 6. 44. The calling is always referred to the Father.

The saved are described as 'the called', that is, the called-ones, who belong to Jesus Christ, Rom. 1. 6, 7; 1 Cor. 1. 2, 24. They gladly acknowledge that their responding to His call, and God's answer to their response, are divine in inception, progression, and consummation,[14] for all this is consistent with His very being, Rev. 21. 6.

According to God's Purpose. The believer's calling is according to God's own purpose, which was 'before times eternal', 2 Tim. 1. 9 RV. It was 'his own purpose', being of His own good will, uninfluenced by anything outside of Himself. Romans chapter 8 verse 28 sees the counsels of a past and a future eternity converging on the call. The purpose was not an arbitrary decree, but His love set upon its object, the believer. Thus 'elect', 'beloved', and (effectually) 'called' are inseparable expressions.[15]

From the eternal viewpoint of the past, the sequence is: foreknown, predestinated, called. From personal experience in time, the called look back to their call, and further back to their being foreknown and chosen, Rom. 8. 29; 2 Pet. 1. 10.

According to God's Mercy. The calling is according to God's mercy, 'who saved us, and called us with a holy calling, not according to our works, but according to his own purpose and grace, which was given us in Christ Jesus before times eternal', 2 Tim. 1. 9 RV. It was calling in grace, Gal. 1. 6, for God made known 'the riches of his glory upon vessels of mercy, which he afore prepared unto glory', Rom. 9. 23 RV. It was not of man's effort, but of God that has mercy on those whom He called, not from the Jews only, but also from benighted Gentiles, 9. 16, 24. To this agree Peter's statements that it is the God of all grace that called us, and that He called out of darkness into His marvellous light those who were 'no people' and who had 'not obtained mercy', 1 Pet. 2. 9, 10 RV; Hos. 2.

---

[14] Rom. 11. 36; 2 Cor. 5. 18; Phil. 1. 6.
[15] Jude 1 RV; Rom. 1. 6, 7; Col. 3. 12; Eph. 1. 4-6 RVmg; 1 Thess. 1. 4.

23. The call comes whilst still in the circumstances of everyday life, whether bond or free, 1 Cor. 7. 20, 22, 24. Not many 'wise' are effectually called, and they do not sense their real need before the God of all wisdom, 1 Cor. 1. 26. But 'unto them which are called . . . Christ the power of God, and the wisdom of God', 1. 24.

Called by the Gospel. God effectually calls by the gospel through sanctification of the Spirit, and belief of the truth, 2 Thess. 2. 13, 14. God took the initiative both in His eternal counsel, and in the time-experience of the called. 'He made His electing grace effectual through the gospel', C. F. HOGG AND W. E. VINE, through obedience to the gospel, which obedience is of faith, 1 Pet. 1. 2; Heb. 11. 8.

'In 2 Thessalonians 2. 13 and 1 Peter 1. 2 sanctification of the Spirit is associated with the choice, or election, of God: it is a divine act preceding the acceptance of the gospel by the individual. . . set apart by the Holy Spirit that they might obey the truth and so come under the shelter of the sprinkled blood of Jesus Christ'.[16]

The called are the justified, and the glorified, Rom. 8. 30. Of the five divine acts stated in Romans chapter 8 verse 29, four are totally of God's sovereign grace. 'Called' is central to the five, being the only one which has within it some element of human responsibility. Even so, it is linked in the unbreakable chain of unfailing purposes, so that the predominant force is God's effectual working in the call. The gospel of the glory and virtue of God called us to the knowledge of Him in His own excellencies, 2 Pet. 1. 3 RV.

Security of the Called. The called belong to Jesus Christ,[17] and as such their security is assured. His sheep are His in His prescience and purpose, before His calling them by name, 10. 3, 27, for the Father gave them to Him long before their effectual calling in time, 10. 29.

The calling is joined to unfailing foreknowledge, predestination, justification and glory, Rom. 8. 29, 30. The words 'them' and 'also' of these verses are to be observed, for they describe all so designated. 'The

---

16 C. F. HOGG AND W. E. VINE, *Notes on Thessalonians.*

17 Rom. 1. 6 RV; Jude 1 RV; John 17. 11, 12, 24.

called' in verse 28 and verse 30 are those who are assured that God is working all things for their good, because of His eternal purpose and coming glory. 'Faithful is he that calleth', for 'the gifts and calling of God are without repentance' on His part, 1 Thess. 5. 24; Rom. 11. 29.

The Goals of the Calling. These may be enumerated as follows:

1. *Called unto Sainthood.* We are 'the called of Jesus Christ . . . beloved of God, called [to be] saints', i.e., saints by calling. It is status conferred, for we are sanctified in Christ Jesus, who is Himself our sanctification, Rom. 1. 6, 7; 1 Cor. 1. 2, 30.

The status is absolute, for it is 'in Christ'. Yet those so graced are to comport themselves as saints in experiential holiness of character, for He that called them is holy, 1 Pet. 1. 15. They are to walk worthy of the calling wherewith they are called, for they were called unto holiness, Eph. 4. 1 RV; 1 Thess. 4. 7. By so doing they would make (for themselves) their calling and election sure; that is, they would confirm in their lives what God has done for them in His calling, 2 Pet. 1. 10. Again, this would be laying 'hold on eternal life, whereunto thou art also called', 1 Tim. 6. 12.

2. *Called unto Sonship.* Called out of darkness into God's marvellous light, 1 Pet. 2. 9, they are called children of God (not denominated such, but 'called'), 1 John 3. 1 RV. So much is this calling beyond man's doing, that the world no more knows them than it knew the Lord. What manner of love is this!

3. *Called unto the Fellowship of God's Son.* In both what they share with Him, and what He shares with them, there is fellowship because of the effectual call, 1 Cor. 1. 9. They are joint-heirs with Christ, Rom. 8. 17, so they shall see and share His glory, John 17. 22. They have fellowship with Him in His rejection, Rom. 8. 17, and in distresses for Christ's sake.[18]

4. *Called unto Fellowship in One Body.* Their calling was the effectual working of God in their individual souls, yet they were called

[18] 2 Cor. 1. 5; 12. 10; Phil. 1. 29; 1 Pet. 4. 13.

in one body so that the peace of God should rule in their hearts in practical Christian unity, Eph. 4. 4; Col. 3. 15.

5. *Called unto Eternal Glory.* Whom God called He glorified (as viewed from past eternity).[19] He called them to His kingdom and glory, 1 Thess. 2. 12, and to an eternal inheritance, Heb, 9. 15.

Faith - D. C. Hinton

Faith has been described as the personal confidence of the awakened soul on the ground of divine truth and promise (Handley Moule). Therefore, there is no room in faith for human wisdom, education or reasoning, for faith must rest utterly and completely upon the infallibility of God and therefore of His word.

The patriarchs had faith in the words spoken to them personally by Jehovah; the children of Israel should have had faith first in the words spoken by Moses and subsequent prophets, and then, in later years, in the written scriptures of the Old Testament. Those of this dispensation are to have faith in the whole canon of scripture, which contains the complete and final revelation of the mind of God.

It is only by a childlike reliance on the truth of God's word that it is possible to accept without question the record of events in the past that are beyond human comprehension, and at the same time rest with confidence upon God's statements concerning the future. Thus, we accept that the worlds were framed by the spoken word of God. Science must fit in to this statement; if not, we accept the testimony of scripture, not the wisdom of men.

Faith, not reason, is the basis of all relationship with God. 'Without faith it is impossible to please him', Heb. 11. 6. This is a very sweeping statement, covering both the sinner and the saint. All one can ever do to please God must be in response to His word. Every soul that has ever been brought into relationship with a thrice-holy God has been blessed on the ground of faith, never of deeds. Every believer that has brought joy to God has done so through faith, a faith that was the basis of his

---

[19] Rom. 8. 30; 1 Pet. 5. 10; 2 Thess. 2. 14.

deeds.

Faith in the Old Testament. The word 'faith' is found only in two places in the Old Testament: Hab. 2. 4 (quoted three times in the New Testament); and Deut. 32. 20. However, Hebrews chapter 11 makes it plain that the worthies of those days knew much of faith. It was not only the basis of their relationship with God, it also regulated their daily living.

The often-used word 'believe' has the same thought as 'faith'. The first mention of this word is in Genesis chapter 15 verse 6, and the manner in which this record is taken up in Romans chapter 4 and James chapter 2 proves its importance.

Abraham, a childless man well-advanced in years, had been told by Jehovah to look up to the heavens, studded with innumerable stars, and had heard the momentous words, 'So shall thy seed be'. Although this was impossible by human reasoning, he and his wife being as good as dead physically, Abraham believed what was said, simply because of who had uttered the words. He had complete confidence that his God would bring to pass that which was humanly impossible. By this act of faith he earned the title of the 'father of the faithful'.

Faith in the New Testament. How fitting, therefore, that this scripture is taken up in Romans chapter 4 verse 3 to illustrate the truth that only on the ground of faith is it possible for a holy God to justify a sinner. In other words, a sinner must acknowledge his own inability to deal with the problem of his sin, just as Abraham owned his inability to produce children. The sinner must then believe what God has said concerning the Saviour, the Lord Jesus Christ, just as Abraham believed God. Concerning the Saviour, God has said that when He, the only sinless one to have ever lived, died on Calvary's cross, He sustained judgement from a holy God on account of the sin of the world. The sinner must believe that His death was sufficient to deal with his sins. Then forgiveness is obtained, by repentance toward God and faith in our Lord Jesus Christ.

By such an act of faith, God reckons the sinner as righteous. This is saving faith, which is illustrated in the Gospel records by the miracles of healing when the words were so often spoken, 'thy faith hath saved thee', or made thee whole, Luke 8. 48.

Faith a Matter for Life. But the faith that saved was intended to become a permanent characteristic of the believer's life, and not to be put to one side after salvation. Once we are justified by faith we are to live by faith; it is to be the guiding principle of our life, extending into every aspect of the daily round of duty.

Faith enabled Enoch, who had never seen Jehovah, to accept His reality, and to live in His presence as though He was visible. So it is recorded that he walked with God, Gen. 5. 22; Heb. 11. 5. It was faith that enabled the patriarchs to live as strangers and pilgrims, because they appreciated the reality of the city which God had prepared for them.

So other Old Testament worthies, who suffered much at the hands of ungodly men, had faith in the person of God. This alone enabled them to endure. There was nothing in them, personally, mentally or physically, that empowered them to undergo privation – simply their childlike faith.

The great roll-call of men and women in Hebrews chapter 11 is a record of faith. They came from every walk of life, and every period of history. Their faith gave them a confidence in God that grasped, even before the scriptures were written, the truths of substitution, translation without dying, the pilgrim character, resurrection from the dead, and a right valuation of earthly glory as compared with the unseen riches of heaven.

So believers of this age are exhorted to direct their gaze away from earth to a risen Lord, who is the 'author and finisher' of faith, Heb. 12. 2. As a man, He has left us the perfect example. He had complete faith in His God from Bethlehem to Calvary: 'thou didst make me hope when I was upon my mother's breasts'; 'thou wilt not leave my soul in hell; neither wilt thou suffer thine Holy One to see corruption', Pss. 22. 9; 16. 10. Having experienced a life of faith, a faith that was tested to extremes far beyond anything which we shall ever be called upon to pass through, He is able to succour us as we endeavour to follow His example.

Faith a Matter of Practice. Moreover faith is intensely practical. If there is a true faith in the living God, then the effects will be seen in that believer's behaviour. Thus, James emphasizes that faith must prove itself by its works, otherwise there is no living faith there. Here again Abraham's faith as recorded in Genesis chapter 22 is the illustration, Jas. 2. 17-26.

Faith is predominantly for this life, in the sense that it requires belief in an unseen God. When we shall know as we are known, faith will give place to sight. Therefore our opportunities for exercising faith are limited to our present life. No wonder that Timothy, the man of God, was exhorted to follow after (namely to pursue) righteousness, godliness and faith, 1 Tim. 6. 11.

Faith grows only as it is put to the test. By trusting God for small things, the child of God will find his faith strengthened and will be encouraged to trust Him more. This is what glorifies God, for the testing of our faith produces that which will add to the display of His glory in that future day when our Lord will be manifested in glory and power, 1 Pet. 1. 7.

The exercise of faith is clearly seen in Peter walking on the water, Matt. 14. 29. He obeys the word of his Lord, putting all human support to one side (the boat), and trusts his Lord to meet his needs in circumstances which, to human logic and science, were impossible, though in the following verses there is 'little faith' and 'doubt'.

Faith must not be confused with the expression 'the faith', such as in Titus chapter 1 verse 13. The latter refers to the whole body of revealed truth contained in the scriptures which is to be the subject of our faith.

To sum up, we will use the words of a young Sunday School scholar, 'faith is taking God at His word and asking no questions'.

Quickening, New Birth, Regeneration, New Creation - E. W. Rogers

Nicodemus acknowledged the Lord Jesus to be a teacher come from God, John 3. 2. He, therefore, must be prepared to be taught by Him, and the first lesson that he must learn is 'Ye must be born again'. The word 'again' implies not merely another birth, but another **kind** of birth. The word 'again' signifies not merely repetition, but a different source – 'Ye must be born **from above**' 3. 7 RVmg. Natural birth, earthly parentage, is of no avail and of no account in divine and spiritual matters. 'That which is born of the flesh is flesh; and that which is born of the Spirit is spirit', v. 6. And it is this latter that counts with God.

New birth is essential if the kingdom of God is either to be seen or to be entered into, vv. 3, 5. That kingdom is the sphere where God's rule not only obtains, but is acknowledged. At present that kingdom has nothing to do whatever with the earthly and natural; therefore entrance into it is not by a repetition of the natural process. The word 'again' means 'from above' or 'anew', denoting a different source and, in consequence, a different nature. To enter that kingdom, a man must be born 'of water and of the Spirit', a truth already set forth in Ezekiel chapter 36. The 'water' here alluded to could not have any reference to Christian baptism, for that was not known till after the resurrection of the Lord Jesus. Yet whatever this was, it was a thing Nicodemus was expected to have known. The prophecy of Ezekiel chapter 36 was available to him, whence he could have gleaned the facts, see John 3. 10.

New birth is a necessity. 'Ye must be born again'. 'Except a man be born again, he cannot see the kingdom of God'. 'Except a man be born of water and of the Spirit, he cannot enter into the kingdom of God', vv. 3, 5, 7. Nicodemus, as a ruler of the Jews, should have been well acquainted with Ezekiel chapter 36 verses 25 to 26, which reads thus: 'Then will I sprinkle clean water upon you, and ye shall be clean . . . and a new spirit will I put within you'. Thus the negative and positive sides of the matter are presented: the water removes all that is unfitted for the kingdom of God, and the Spirit brings in the power that is requisite for being a subject in such a kingdom.

New birth is not a repetition of the first and natural birth. It is 'not of bloods, nor of the will of the flesh, nor of the will of man, but of God', John 1. 13 RVmg. It is not of bloods, therefore it is not by natural birth; it is not by the will of the flesh, therefore no one can give to himself this new life; it is not by the will of man, nor indeed can any other man impart it to him, but it is of God, that is, it is of divine origin, and is a free gift from God. For the gift of God is eternal life, not independently of but in Christ Jesus our Lord. This life is in His Son, Rom. 6. 23; 1 John 5. 11.

We must ever be careful in drawing analogies between human nature and divine operations. There may, in some cases, seem to be parallels, but in other cases there are contrasts and differences, and spiritual discernment is necessary to discriminate where necessary.

When God 'quickens' a person, He imparts to that person divine life; He does it in response to the exercise of faith. He makes them alive after their being 'dead in trespasses and sins'. Whereas in their unregenerate state there was no response to God's various calls, yet immediately the person obeys God's call, accepts God's invitation, and draws nigh to Him, he finds that God will also draw nigh to him, and the distance is not bridged but is destroyed.

Human logic has been brought into this matter, and arguments which seem to be unanswerable have been introduced, such as: if, as you say, man is spiritually dead, what is the use of making any appeal to him? But let the reader consult Ezekiel chapter 37 and the problem therein set forth: 'can these bones live?', and the instructions given: 'say to them, O ye dry bones, hear the word of the Lord'. How apparently illogical to address many, and very dry, dead bones, and call on them to hear and to expect them to live. But so it came to pass. Admittedly, man is 'dead in trespasses and sins', Eph. 2. 1, but to such the gospel is to be preached; they are called upon to 'Believe on the Lord Jesus Christ', and if they do so the promise is sure they will 'be saved'. Human logic in divine things will oftentimes lead one into a morass of confusion and error. From one point of view the sinner is dead spiritually, but from another point of view he has a conscience, is a responsible creature Godward, and is morally capable of responding to the message of the gospel, and according to the manner of his response so will be determined his eternal destiny.

The chief trouble with man lies in his perverted will, 'ye will not [do not wish to] come to me, that ye might have life', John 5. 40. Yet it was available to them on God's terms.

Paul, in his great letter to the Ephesians, traces the matter back to its very source; he says it was 'for [on account of] his great love wherewith he loved us', Eph. 2. 4. This was the spring of all, whence the river of His mercy flowed out to both Jew and Gentile in all its rich fullness, breaking down the middle wall of partition between them, and forming those who believed into one harmonious body of which Christ was the Head and the Spirit was the power, the apostles and prophets being the foundation of the household of God.

We should carefully note the phrase 'quickened us together with Christ', v. 5. The implications are these: we were dead through trespasses and sins, the positive and negative sides of our own natural state before God. But the Lord Jesus became dead through these trespasses and sins, but He did this vicariously and substitutionarily for He had no sins of His own. He came to where we were, and when God quickened Him He quickened us; when He raised Him He raised us, and so on, till we are found seated with Him in the heavenlies. So that He went to the lowest in order to take us to the highest. How wonderful!

This truth, it should be noted, was written to the Ephesians, who were erstwhile worshippers of the goddess that they alleged had fallen down from heaven, Acts 19. 35, but now their interests were altogether transferred and centred on One who had 'ascended up far above all heavens', Eph. 4. 10. Everything had thus become new for them; instead of their eyes being earthbound they were heaven-bound. Instead of being concerned with dead idols they were occupied with a living Lord. For them, old things had passed away, and all things had become new, 2 Cor. 5. 17.

It should furthermore be observed that the operations of God to which we have referred took place in what we call a past eternity, and their consummation is in a time which we call a future eternity, though all time is present with God. But to accommodate Himself to our finite minds, He uses the three tenses of past, present and future to enable us the better to understand these mighty movements of the Godhead toward us.

The Epistle to the Ephesians is the Mount Everest of divine revelation in scripture. There is no higher truth anywhere else within the sacred volume. Horizontally it stretches from the two extremes of what we are in the habit of calling the past and the future. Vertically the eternal purpose of God determined to take us from the lowest pit of corruption and elevate us to the highest height of glory.

The caption of this paper speaks of four things:

1. *Quickening.* To this Paul alludes in Ephesians chapter 2 verse 1, with which we should read the parallel passage Colossians chapter 2 verse 13. In marvellous grace the Lord Jesus came down to where the sinner was in order that He might bring the believing sinner out of his sinful state into the purposed state of eternal glory. He became dead through trespasses and sins, not His own, but vicariously, so that when God quickened Him, He, pursuant to His eternal purpose, quickened the believer with Him. Who but God can quicken the dead?[20]

2. *New Birth.* This is but another way of speaking of the same experience as 'quickening', which latter word simply means 'making alive'. The individual was born in a state of alienation from God, dead in trespasses and sins, inheriting man's guilt since he belonged to the Adamic fallen stock. But pursuant to the eternal purpose of God, and realized on believing in Christ, the individual passed from death to life, was born again.[21]

3. *Regeneration.* This is referred to in Titus chapter 3 verse 5. This 'washing' here mentioned is the initial washing that needs no repetition seeing it is the washing of regeneration. Now regeneration cannot be repeated any more than new birth can be repeated. By means of it, a new state of things is introduced, a new 'genesis'. The word is found elsewhere only in Matthew chapter 19 verse 28, where it refers to the new condition of things brought in with the future age, the millennium. The 'renewing' alluded to in the verse in Titus is a continuous process which will go on to the end of life's journey.

4. *New Creation.* This is spoken of in 2 Corinthians chapter 5 verse 17, and is contrasted with the 'old things' which have passed away. These 'old things' are our former standing 'after the flesh', and are enumerated in the early part of Philippians chapter 3. The new

---

[20] John 5. 12; 6. 63; Rom. 4. 17; 8. 11; 1 Cor. 15. 45; 1 Tim. 6. 15.

[21] John 1. 13; 3. 3, 5-8; 1 John 2. 29; 3. 9; 4. 7; 5. 1, 4, 18.

creation is what the believer is in Christ. He discovers experimentally that his interests, his outlook, his hopes, and everything are new, 'all things are become new'. 'For neither is circumcision anything, nor uncircumcision, but a new creation', Gal. 6. 15 RVmg; let us walk by this rule.

He cannot attribute any of these changes to himself or his own endeavours. The whole thing is 'of God', 2 Cor. 5. 18, and we have to say 'Not unto us, O Lord, not unto us, but unto thy name give glory, for thy mercy, and for thy truth's sake', Ps. 115. 1. 'God, who is rich in mercy' has created 'one new man', Eph. 2. 4, 15, 'according to the good pleasure of his will, to the praise of the glory of his grace, which he freely bestowed on us in the Beloved', Eph. 1. 5, 6 RV.

This new man replaces the old man, and whereas in the first creation fallen man dishonoured his Creator, in the new creation redeemed man glorifies His redeemer.

Repentance - D. Wilson

'And that repentance and remission of sins should be preached in his name among all nations', Luke 24. 47.

'For godly sorrow worketh repentance to salvation not to be repented of: but the sorrow of the world worketh death', 2 Cor. 7. 10.

A 'Threshold' Word. God has placed repentance at the threshold of the door to salvation, and there it must remain if sinners are to be truly saved. God has also placed repentance at the threshold of the door to fellowship with Himself, and there it must remain if saints would enter into the sanctuary. Repentance has to do with sin: in the first place with the sin of the creature against a holy God; in the second place with the sin of a child against a holy Father.

That repentance is a threshold word is evident from the following:

1. The forerunner of our Lord appears on the scene and announces His coming with the following words, 'Repent ye: for the kingdom of heaven is at hand', Matt. 3. 2;

2. The Lord then comes forth, and His first command is, 'repent ye, and believe the gospel', Mark 1. 15;
3. The twelve were sent forth, and we read that they 'went out, and preached that men should repent', 6. 12;
4. The command of our risen Lord is that 'repentance and remission of sins should be preached in his name', Luke 24. 47;
5. On the day of Pentecost we hear Peter saying to the convicted Jews that they should repent, Acts 2. 38;
6. At Athens, Paul sounds forth the universal command for 'God . . . now commandeth all men everywhere to repent', 17. 30;
7. Paul declared to the elders at Ephesus that his universal testimony, to Jews and Greeks, had been 'repentance toward God, and faith toward our Lord Jesus Christ', 20. 21. Later in life he said to Agrippa that from the beginning of his ministry he had preached that men 'should repent and turn to God, and do works meet for repentance', 26. 20;
8. As the last plagues of God's judgements are being poured out upon the earth-dwellers, they refuse to do one thing that would bring deliverance – 'they repented not', Rev. 16. 9, 11.

Is it not evident from these scriptures that repentance has to do with our attitude toward God? Is it not an attitude of a very practical nature and of the utmost importance? 'Have I repented?' is a question of **vital importance** to every soul, for out of it are the issues of life and of death. If sinners do not repent they will be lost eternally. 'I tell you, Nay: but, except ye repent, ye shall all likewise perish', Luke 13. 3, 5. God desires that all men come to repentance, and is said to be longsuffering for this reason, 2 Pet. 3. 9.

Meaning of the Word. From the foregoing scriptures we can see that all who are saved must have repented. Therefore, by examining the conversions recorded in the word we should be able to discover the true meaning of repentance. The definition of the word is – 'a change of mind', but as one can change his mind about many things, the definition does not tell us much. Many say that it is a change of mind about God's character, while others say that it is a change of mind about the way of salvation. Such differences simply emphasize the importance of searching the scriptures for God's meaning.

In 1 Thessalonians chapter 1 verses 9-10 we read how the Thessalonians '**turned** to **God** from idols **to serve** the living and true God; and to wait for his Son from heaven'. The Colossians were told how that God had delivered them from the **power** of darkness and had translated them into the **kingdom** of His dear Son, Col. 1. 13. Paul was told to **turn** the Gentiles from the **power** (authority) of Satan unto God, Acts 26. 18. 'Serve', 'kingdom', 'power', all speak of authority, so they were changed from one sphere of rule to another. The heads of these two kingdoms are Satan and the Lord Jesus Christ. Satan rules through the flesh and minds of unbelievers; the Lord Jesus rules through the Holy Spirit and the word in the hearts of believers. That which characterizes many of the 'children of wrath' is not moral or spiritual wickedness, but this – 'they do the desires of the flesh and of the mind'; that includes the most refined of sinners. That which characterizes the children of God is this – they 'serve the living and true God'; they **hear** the voice of their Lord and **follow** Him. That which brings one out of the kingdom of Satan and into the kingdom of the Son is 'Repentance toward **God**, and faith toward our **Lord** Jesus Christ'.

Now we believe that it can be shown clearly that repentance is a **change of mind as to who shall rule over us**. It is a decision of the will that God shall reign over us, and self and Satan be deposed. Repentance toward God is the heart-acknowledgment of God as my God. Faith toward our **Lord** Jesus Christ is the heart-confession of the risen and glorified Jesus as my **Lord** – the One to whom God has given all authority and power.

The message to Israel was 'Repent'. Israel's reply was 'We **will not** have this man to **reign** over us'. On the day of Pentecost, Peter said, 'Let all the house of Israel know assuredly that God hath made that same **Jesus**, whom ye have crucified, both **Lord** and **Christ . . . Repent**'. They had rejected God and His Anointed. They must reverse their decision and accept the enthroned Jesus as their Lord. There cannot be a divided house in God's kingdom, some being subject to God, and some to self and Satan. There may be stumbling and wandering on the part of God's own, but not the rejection of His authority.

God is not willing that any should perish, but all who would be saved **must** come to repentance, 2 Pet. 3. 9. To reject Jesus as **Lord** now, is to meet Him later as the One who meets out vengeance to those who know not God and obey not the gospel, 2 Thess. 1. 8. A common tragic error of many is to speak of God's Son as 'Saviour and Lord', thus giving Him the pre-eminence as 'Saviour'. The Holy Spirit always reverses this order by speaking of Him as 'Lord and Saviour'. 'Hold fast the form of sound words' is an exhortation that is greatly needed, because little heeded in these days of much spiritual laxity. This reversal of the divine order is the natural result of forgetting that God requires repentance.

The apostle Paul says, 'We preach. . . Christ Jesus the **Lord**', 2 Cor. 4. 5. Acts abounds with proofs of this, and the Epistles as well.

Scriptural Illustrations. *The Two Sons of Luke chapter 15.* Further proof of the truth of our definition of repentance is given to us in the record of the two sons in Luke chapter 15. The father was the divinely-ordained ruler of these two sons. Like many modern sons, the younger one decided that the father's rule was not good. He asked for his portion in order that he might get away from his father's control and fulfil the desires of his flesh and of his mind unhindered. He turned his back on God and his father, and went out to become his own 'boss'. Note that verses 7 and 10 speak of the repentant sinner. Verse 11 starts the record of the two sons. Is it not plainly evident from this that our Lord is giving us His own definition of repentance, and lack of repentance, in the record of these two sons? The elder son was far away (in heart) from his father, and remained unrepentant.

The younger son is in the far country. He had a glorious time (so he thought) as long as his money lasted, but, in the end, he became a starving swineherd. Finally 'he came to himself'. He wakes up to see his sin and folly. While still in the far country he says, 'I will **arise** and **go** to my father, and **will say** unto him, Father, I **have sinned against heaven [God], and before thee**, and am no more worthy to be called thy son: **make me as one of thy hired servants**'. He acknowledges his **rebellion** and confesses his willingness to take the place of **subjection**. He returns to his father with this attitude of heart; he confesses his sin; he is restored to his place as a son. The stubborn elder brother refused to repent, and shut himself out from the joy in the father's house; his body was nearby but his heart was in the far country, so he refused to go in. Is it not plain from this record that repentance is a turning of the will to God with a heart-desire to be subject to Him?

The People of Nineveh. We have another example in the book of Jonah. We read in Matthew chapter 12 verse 41 that 'The men of Nineveh shall rise in judgement with this generation, and shall condemn it: **because they repented** at the preaching of Jonas; and, behold, a greater than Jonas is here'. Now what did they do? We read that 'the people of Nineveh believed God, and proclaimed a fast, and put on sackcloth, from the greatest of them even to the least of them', Jonah 3. 5. Moreover, the king and the nobles said, 'let man and beast be covered with sackcloth, and cry mightily to God: yea, **let them turn** every one from his evil way, and from the violence that is in their hands', v. 8. What was the result? 'God saw their works, **that they turned** from their evil way', v. 10. So here again we see that repentance is a change of mind as to who shall govern us.

The Two Sons of Matthew 21. Another example is given by our Lord in the record of the two sons, Matt. 21. 28, 29. Here it is – 'But what think ye? A certain man had two sons; and he came to the first, and said, Son, **go work** today in my vineyard. He answered and said, **I will not**: but afterward he **repented, and went**. And he came to the second, and said likewise. And he answered and said, I go, sir; and went not. Whether of them twain did the will of his father? They say unto him, The first'. Finally, He says to the priests and elders that the publicans and harlots believed John, 'and ye, when ye had seen it, **repented not** afterward, that ye might believe him'.

Repentance the Forerunner of Salvation. Salvation may not follow immediately after true repentance because of ignorance of the Lord Jesus Christ; yet every truly repentant soul will undoubtedly be saved in due time, for repentance is a work of God, and He never begins a good work but what He finishes it. Cornelius had repented long before Peter was sent to tell him words whereby he might be saved. The Holy Spirit tells us that he was a **devout** man who **feared God** and gave much alms. He is not told to repent but is told of the One who had been crucified and whom God had raised from the dead – the Lord of all and the God-ordained Judge of quick and dead. It is to this **person** that all the prophets give witness, that **through His name** whosoever believeth **in Him** shall receive remission of sins.

Distinction between Repentance of Saint and Sinner. We read in 2 Corinthians chapter 7 verse 10 that godly sorrow worketh repentance to salvation not to be repented of. This is the sorrow of a child of God when the Holy Spirit causes him to realize his sin, when he has been walking contrary to the will of God. It leads him to turn from his sin and bow to the will of God. Such was the repentance of the Corinthians, and such will be the repentance of all saints who are caused to sorrow after a godly sort. Therein you have the restoration of 'backsliders'. **Saints** need to be saved from their sins. Thou shalt call His name Jesus for He shall save **His people from their sins**.

If the sinner refuses to repent, then judgement and punishment await him after death, Acts 17. 30, 31. If the saint fails to repent, then judgement and punishment, as the Father's child, will be his portion in this life; and he must render an account at the Judgement Seat of Christ.[22] Just as the invalid must submit to the authority of the doctor if he would be cured, even so must the sinner submit to Jesus as **Lord** if he would be saved with God's salvation. Also the saint who would enjoy God's present salvation, must own the Lordship of Christ over his daily life; the 'backslider' is one who has failed in this.

Just as a drowning person can do nothing for his rescuer until he submits to him and is saved, even so the sinner can do nothing for God until he repents, is delivered from the power of Satan, and translated into the kingdom of God's dear Son. The 'backslider', also, can do nothing to please his Lord until he repents and is restored to fellowship.

Repentance of the sinner is connected with relationship – that of being brought into the family of God – so it never needs to be repeated. Its effect is eternal. Linked with faith in the Lord Jesus Christ it takes one out of Satan's kingdom and gives one an eternal inheritance in the kingdom of God. Repentance of the saint is connected with fellowship, so it needs to be repeated as often as the fellowship with his Lord is broken.

The Lordship of Christ. The title of 'Saviour' is given to our Lord only sixteen times in the New Testament. He is called 'our Lord' about

---

[22] 1 Cor. 11. 31, 32; Rom. 14. 10; 2 Cor. 5. 10.

seventy-five times, and is given the title of 'Lord' about 700 times. Is not this because God insists that His Son be given His rightful place as 'Lord of all'? In view of these facts, and the facts presented in this paper, can we afford to set aside repentance and make our Lord simply a purveyor of pardons to anyone who will accept one, a Saviour from hell for all who will accept Him as Saviour, though they will not have Him as Lord? A thousand times NO! God is receiving no rebels into His kingdom. Where there is no willing **submission** there is no **remission**. There **must** be repentance toward **God**, and faith toward our **Lord Jesus Christ**.

The Lord Jesus is 'the author of eternal salvation unto all them that **obey him**', Heb. 5. 9. This word 'obey' means to **hearken submissively** (YOUNG). The Revised Version of John chapter 3 verse 36 is 'He that obeyeth not the Son shall not see life, but the wrath of God abideth on him'.

Conclusion. From the foregoing we can see why Satan is so strongly opposed to the preaching of repentance. He has duped many with his lies about its meaning; duped even 'Bible Teachers' into setting it aside or nullifying its meaning. If there is to be a 'revival' there must be a return to the preaching of repentance, a return to the preaching of God's Son as a living, once-wounded, flesh-and-bones **Man** in glory, and a return to the preaching of Him as **Lord**. The book of Acts is **not out of date**, as some would have us believe, but the Holy Spirit's own revelation of His methods with and His messages to **sinners**. Paul's message to sinners was identical with Peter's, and the messages of both are identical with that of our Lord, 'Through this man is preached unto you the forgiveness of sins'.[23]

Conversion - R. L. DAWES

In these days of easy profession, it is possible that some associated with the activities of a local church and passing as believers have not had a personal experience of Christ in conversion. One is caused to suspect at times, with genuine concern, the reality of some professing Christians,

---

[23] The following scriptures should grip our minds and hearts: Acts 17. 30; 20. 21 and 26. 18-20.

whose lives show little evidence of subjection to Christ and His word. The challenge of Paul to 'Examine yourselves, whether ye be in the faith', needs to ring out again today, and practical evidence of conversion to be provoked, 2 Cor. 13. 5.

It is a healthy exercise, however, for us all to reflect upon our conversion. Some may not be able to remember the day and hour, but can recollect what led to their conversion. The remembrance of it causes us to magnify the overflowing grace of God and recognize afresh our own wretched unworthiness. Hence there is praise to God and preservation from pride, 1 Tim. 1. 12-16. Many things perplex us but of this we should be sure. With one of old we should confidently testify that 'one thing I know, that, whereas I was blind, now I see', John 9. 25.

The scriptures recall the experience of conversion again and again. The psalmist prays, 'Restore unto me the joy of thy salvation', 51. 12; Paul when warning the Corinthians of fornicators, thieves, adulterers, drunkards, adds pertinently 'And such were some of you', 1 Cor. 6. 11; and again, to the Ephesians, pointing back to their unconverted days he says, 'at that time ye were without Christ, being aliens . . . and strangers . . . having no hope, and without God in the world', Eph. 2.13. The Corinthians had been washed and sanctified, the Ephesians had been made nigh. When? At their conversion! We must all thank God for such an experience and sing:

> 'O happy day, that fixed my choice
> On Thee, my Saviour and my God!
> Well may this glowing heart rejoice,
> And tell its raptures all abroad',
>
> PHILIP DODDRIDGE

The Meaning. The word conversion means 'a turning around' in order to face the opposite direction. It is the word used in 1 Thessalonians '**ye turned to** God from idols', 1. 9, and in Acts chapter 26 'to **turn** them from darkness to light, and from the power of Satan unto God', v. 18. Its spiritual significance becomes immediately apparent from these verses. Thus, at our conversion, we who were occupied with idols turned around to the true and living God; we, who were in darkness, turned to the light, and we, who were in Satan's power, turned to Christ. In the words of the Psalmist, 'I thought on my ways, and **turned** my feet unto thy testimonies', Ps. 119. 59.

The Need. The need to be converted is fundamental. Man's condition demands it. Notice again the three things from which we must turn: from idols; from darkness; and from the power of Satan. What an awful state this depicts!

Idolatry. Many are not idolaters in the literal sense of that word, but in principle they are. An idol is anything that fills the place that God should have in man's heart and affections. Even the desire to have things without bringing God into our thoughts is spoken of as 'covetousness which is idolatry', Col. 3. 5. O the multitude of things that occupy the hearts of men to the exclusion of God – money and possessions, which the Lord Jesus personified as 'mammon', saying 'Ye cannot serve God and mammon', Matt. 6. 24. To serve mammon is to be guilty of idolatry. How many indeed worship silver and gold! Many too in this generation worship at the altar of pleasure. Sport, entertainments, music, gambling, even the fine arts and culture fill the hearts of thousands who are 'lovers of pleasures more than lovers of God', 2 Tim. 3. 4. These are some of the idols of life which claim men's utter devotion. Such is their fascination that John warns believers to 'keep yourselves from idols'.

Darkness. Without God, man's moral condition is necessarily affected. Paul concludes that, as a result of idolatry, 'their foolish heart was darkened', Rom. 1. 21. If God, who is Light, is displaced from the heart by idols, darkness follows. Man's moral state is still one of darkness, in spite of the fact that light is come into the world in the person of Christ. Men prefer darkness to light, John 3. 19. Their moral blindness is shown in the fact that Christian principles of morality, which have raised the standards of life wherever they have been heeded, are being relentlessly attacked and immorality is being justified. Isaiah's words are strangely pertinent today, 'Woe unto them that call evil good, and good evil; that put darkness for light, and light for darkness', 5. 20. Learning and material prosperity are at an unprecedented peak, but men still grope in moral darkness, unable to discern moral truth. Reasonings are perverted, consciences are dull; the shaft of divine light by means of conversion is still needed to chase away the night of sin from the soul.

Satan. Behind it all there lurks the sinister power of Satan, in whose hand the world lies, 1 John 5. 19 RV. He and his spirit forces are 'the world rulers of this darkness', Eph. 6. 12 RV, and unconverted men and women walk 'according to the course of this world, according to the prince of the power of the air, the spirit that now worketh in the children of disobedience', Eph. 2. 2. The Lord Jesus said to some of old, 'ye are of your father the devil', John 8. 44. No man can match his might. Apart from Christ, men are helpless in his power, cp. Heb. 2. 15.

What a terrifying condition this is – engrossed with idols, swallowed up in darkness and in the grip of Satan. No religious rite, no moral reformation, no lofty resolve, no cultural pursuit can meet such a desperate plight. We must be converted to God and turn to Him from idols, from darkness to light, from Satan to Christ. Conversion is absolutely essential, it provides the only solution to the situation.

The Experience. How is conversion effected some may ask? Psychologists have tried to rationalize it but it defeats them. First, conversion is through the word of God, that living word which is the inspired revelation of God, for 'The law of the Lord is perfect, converting the soul', Ps. 19. 7. The world is marked by imperfection and impotence, but this word is perfect and powerful, which, if believed, will effectually turn the soul to God, 'And this is the word which by the gospel is preached unto you', 1 Pet. 1. 25; cp. v. 23. Second, humility is needed. All pretension must be abandoned, worldly wisdom shunned and we must become as little children to be converted, Matt. 18. 3. Third, as regards our sins, we must repent and be converted as Peter declared in Acts chapter 3 verse 19. The word, when heard and believed with humility and repentance within the realm of the soul, brings conversion. It is a decisive act of the will to repent and believe, thus turning to God. Conversion brings the soul into a personal experience of God that becomes a sheet anchor for the soul. For when doubts arise and Satan assails, this experience remains undeniable and unshakable.

In turning from idols we find a God who is true and lives eternally. It was a true report that we heard. O the glorious discovery of God when once the soul turns to Him! He is the same God of glory who appeared to Abraham, Acts 7. 2, the creator of the universes, the Almighty, yet He becomes for the first time a great reality to the soul at conversion. We turn from darkness, and God, who commanded the light to shine out of darkness, shines into our hearts, 2 Cor. 4. 6. The blind eyes of the soul open and become filled with light, so that one newly converted can say, 'Truly the light is sweet, and a pleasant thing it is for the eyes to behold the sun', Eccles. 11. 7. Also, we turn from Satan, escaping from his grip, into the hand of the Son, thus, to be eternally free and safe, John 8. 36. For the moment we turn, the mighty hand of Christ snatches us from our evil captor, never to be returned into his grasp. In brief then, at conversion we turn to find the living God, who imparts **life** to dead souls, **light** to dark souls and **liberty** to dominated souls.

Has this been our experience? Or, is there an idol set up in the heart and Christ is still outside? Do we grope uncertainly in the moral darkness of this world, in need of divine revelation? Has Satan still the real power over our soul, or have we been made free by the Son of God? Ponder the questions deeply, nothing is of greater importance; eternal issues are involved, 'for except ye be converted . . . ye shall not enter into the kingdom of heaven', Matt. 18. 3.

For those who have definitely turned to God, conversion places us on the threshold of spiritual life marking the beginning of experience with God. Although immediately fitted for heaven, we are thus also fitted for earth, to walk with God, worship Him and witness for Him. Divine life, light and liberty are ours, and God wants them developed and manifested in us now. What tremendous possibilities and opportunities are latent in the new convert, and what unspeakable loss therefore, if these things are neglected. Let us remember, as we reflect on our conversion, 'only one life 'twill soon be past; only what's done for Christ will last'.

Remission - E. L. LOVERING

The apostle Paul, writing to the saints at Ephesus and to the faithful in Christ Jesus, reminds them that they have been blessed with every spiritual blessing in the heavenlies in Christ. Such a position of privilege brings corresponding responsibilities and obligations. Thus the writer to the Hebrews warns us against neglecting 'so great salvation', and it is one aspect of the wealth and scope of these blessings and the greatness of this salvation that we desire to consider in this article. We shall deal with the blessing of **remission**, noting:

The Price of Remission. The Lord Jesus, gathered with His disciples, revealed to them the true significance of His death, for as 'they were eating, Jesus took a loaf and blessed and brake it; and he took a cup and gave thanks and gave to them, saying, Drink ye all of it; for this is my blood of the new testament, which is shed for many unto remission of sins', Matt. 26. 28 RV. It had always been true that apart from 'shedding of blood there is no remission', Heb. 9. 22, and now the blood of Christ (not the bleeding, but the fact that Christ died) could bring the sinner into the blessing of perfect forgiveness and remission. 'In whom we have redemption through his blood, the forgiveness [remission] of our trespasses, according to the riches of his grace', Eph. 1. 7 RV. To this we add the testimony of Mark, 'John came, who baptized in the wilderness and preached the baptism of repentance unto the remission of sins', Mark 1. 4.

The Proclamation of Remission. Immediately after His resurrection our Lord appeared unto His disciples and said, 'Thus it is written, and thus it behoved Christ to suffer, and to rise again from the dead the third day: and that repentance and remission of sins should be preached in his name among all nations, beginning at Jerusalem', Luke 24. 46, 47. 'The story must be told'; remission is of God and from God, and it must be proclaimed – and in Christ's name. The blessing derives its value from His death, and partakes of His character and perfection. In its scope it is universal, it is to 'be preached in his name among **all** nations'. Thus, in Peter's discourse with Cornelius he will not discriminate between Jew and Gentile, but perceives, of a truth, that 'God is no respecter of persons: but in every nation he that feareth him and worketh righteousness, is accepted with him', Acts 10. 34, 35. This brings us to:

The Promise of Remission. This great blessing is not to him that worketh for salvation, but that 'through his name whosoever believeth in him shall receive remission of sins', Acts 10. 43. Remission of sins is given not to the deserving but to the believing.

Let us now consider some aspects of truth contained in this word 'remission'. The original Greek word *aphesis* is richly suggestive. In our English Versions it is variously translated remission, forgiveness, deliverance and liberty. So that this comprehensive word expresses **the plenitude of remission**. Remission not only means **forgiveness** absolutely and completely on the ground of sovereign grace alone; it also includes **liberty** and **deliverance** from bondage. Our Lord Himself made this very clear and plain when He stood up in the synagogue on the Sabbath day to read. 'And there was delivered unto him the book of the prophet Esaias. And when he had opened the book, he found the place where it was written, The Spirit of the Lord is upon me, because he hath anointed me to preach the gospel to the poor; he hath sent me to. . . preach deliverance [*aphesis*] to the captives and recovering of sight to the blind, to set at liberty [*aphesis*] them that are bruised', Luke 4. 17, 18. For the believer in Christ there is freedom as well as forgiveness.

'He breaks the power of cancelled sin,
And sets the prisoner free',
C. WESLEY

More than this, the believer is not only forgiven, delivered and set at liberty, he is **reinstated** and **restored**. We are not only delivered out of the power of darkness, we are translated into the kingdom of the Son of His love. The blood of Christ is 'of sin the double cure, saving from its guilt and power'.

Further, we may note that in remission there is not only the idea of payment, deliverance and forgiveness, but it is commonly used in a court of law by a judge **discharging one from a penalty or fine** and, on occasions, by a sovereign in the **pardoning of guilt or annulling the penalty.** Herein lies the difference between pardon, forgiveness and justification. In pardoning us, God acts as sovereign, it is His royal prerogative; in forgiving us, God is acting as Father, and so it is our privilege to ask His forgiveness by confession to Him alone; whilst in justification, God is acting as Judge, justifying us from all our guilt – the guilty one thus leaving the presence of the Judge as if he had never sinned. 'Being justified freely by his grace through the redemption that is in Christ Jesus', Rom. 3. 24.

It might also be noted that the word 'remission' is used in a medical sense by a physician, meaning to abate or relax a fever or disease. Here, therefore, we have the thought of **healing and enrichment**. The One who pardons, justifies, forgives and delivers us, is not only our sovereign to rule over us, our Father to bless us, and our Judge who pronounces us guiltless; He is also our great Physician to restore us. In the words of our Lord, 'They that are whole need not a physician; but they that are sick. I came not to call the righteous, but sinners to repentance', Luke 5. 31, 32. He has not only accomplished a great work **for** us, He begins and continues a great work **in** us.

We conclude with a story from the autobiography of DR. GUTHRIE, who described an old Scottish parishioner who died as he had lived, a curious mixture of benevolence and folly. The lawyer who drew up his will, after writing down several legacies, of £500 to one person, £1,000 to another, and so on to many more, at last said: 'But Mr.______, I do not believe that you have all that money to leave'. 'Oh!' was his reply, 'I ken that as well as you, but I just want to show them **my good will**'.

God's goodwill toward men is no mere pretence of bestowing gifts. May it be ours to discover the benefits and blessings He has left us in His will, and seek by His grace and help to enjoy them to the full.

Justification - J. M. DAVIES

Justification is one of the great cardinal truths of the gospel. Its importance cannot be over-estimated. References to it are scattered with a liberal hand throughout the Old and New Testaments. The verb *dikaioō* occurs in Romans thirteen times, Galatians eight times, James three times, Timothy and Titus once. Of these references three may be taken to establish its meaning.

1. In Romans chapter 3 verse 4 we read that God is 'justified', indicating that He is righteous in all His ways and judgements in accordance with his character as 'a just God'.
2. Christ was 'justified in the Spirit', 1 Tim. 3. 16. His resurrection proved that He had been unjustly condemned, cp. Ps. 37. 6. His claims were vindicated. He was declared righteous.
3. Not 'the hearers' but 'the doers of the law shall be justified', Rom. 2.

13. No charge could or would be brought against anyone who would perfectly fulfil all its commandments. He would be declared righteous.

A justified person then is one who is free from any charge of guilt, and therefore has a righteous standing before God.

The noun form *dikaiōsis* is only used twice in the Epistle to the Romans. It denotes a judicial sentence, or an act of pronouncing righteous, or acquittal; see VINE'S *Expository Dictionary.* The other word *dikaiōma* occurs some twelve times in the New Testament, and is rendered in various ways. In Romans chapter 1 verse 32 and chapter 2 verse 26 it represents a just or righteous decree, while in Romans chapter 5 verse 16 it represents acquittal from guilt. But in chapter 5 verse 18 it denotes a righteous act. This is evident from the way it is contrasted with the one trespass of Adam. There are other words which are important in the consideration of the subject, e.g., the word *logizomai* which, figuratively speaking, refers to something being credited to a person's account. In the King James Version, it is translated 'impute'.[24] In the Revised Version it is rendered 'reckon'. Then there is the word *ellogaō*, only used twice in the New Testament, Rom. 5. 13; Philem. 18. Until the law came sin could not be imputed, or put to their account as transgression.

Along with these words there is the word righteousness: *dikaiosunē.* Altogether it occurs some eighty times in the New Testament, in both the historical and the doctrinal sections. It is used in John chapter 16 verse 10 for instance. It occurs some thirty-five times in Romans, and the expression the 'word of righteousness', Heb. 5. 13, could well serve as a title of the Epistle to the Romans. In some cases it denotes the righteous nature or character of God, e.g., Rom. 3. 24, 25. The way sin was judged in the death of Christ reveals God's righteousness; see also Acts 17. 31. In the five references to it in Romans chapter 6, it refers to a mode of living, a righteous conduct.[25] But in Romans chapter 5 verse 17 we read of the 'gift of righteousness', later referred to as the 'free gift', and as 'the gift of God', 6. 23. This is its connotation in many, if not

---

[24] See Rom. 4. 6, 8, 11, 23, 24; 2 Cor. 5. 19; Jas. 2. 23.

[25] See also Eph. 4. 24; 5. 9; 6. 14.

most, of its occurrences. This is specially so in the case of the two witnesses cited by the apostle, Abraham and David.

Having thus briefly considered the meaning of the various words used, we must now seek the answer to the age-long problem raised by Job, 'how should man be just with God?' Job 9. 2. Justification, being a legal term, demands that there should be a definitive statutory law, a confirmatory law with some clear illustrations of its operations, and also consideration of any seemingly counteracting principle.

1. The Statutory Law, the definitive and confirmatory statements. In the Epistle to the Romans, the only full exposition of the gospel that we have, the apostle lays down the definitive principle by which a man may be justified. There is a note of finality in the way Paul quotes the words from Habakkuk chapter 2 verse 4, 'The just shall live by faith', Rom. 1. 17. This is a very definitive statement; hence, it is quoted three times in the New Testament, each reference having a different emphasis.[26] Very few Old Testament quotations introduced into the New are quoted three times, but this is one of them. Faith, then, according to this unconditional principle, in contrast to, and independent of, the deeds of the law, is the way, the only way, a man may be justified before God. This is established by a confirmatory statement, Gen. 15. 6, which is quoted four times in the New Testament: 'Abraham believed God, and it was counted unto him for righteousness'.[27]

2. Case Law. To establish his statement that now the righteousness of God independent of the law 'is manifested, being witnessed by the law and the prophets', Paul cites two witnesses, Abraham from the books of the law, and David from the prophets. These two are representative of the two sections of the human race, the Gentile and the Jew. Abraham was justified some 430 years before the law was given, and some twenty-five years or so before he was circumcised, as he was ninety-nine years old when he was circumcised. In Romans chapter 4 verses 1 to 8 Abraham represents the uncircumcised Gentile, while David represents the circumcised Israelite. But in chapter 4 verse 18 as a circumcised man waiting for the fulfilment of the promise, he

---

[26] Rom. 1. 17; Gal. 3. 11; Heb. 10. 38.

[27] Rom. 4. 3; cp. v. 9; Gal. 3. 6; Jas. 2. 24.

represents the faithful in Israel who were waiting for the Messiah. In James chapter 2 verse 21 the reference is to Mount Moriah, when his hope was that Isaac would be raised from the dead whence he received him in a figure. There he represents the tested disciples, Luke 24. 21-35.

David acknowledged his iniquities, transgressions and sin, words that were used by the high priest on the great Day of Atonement. And he appropriated its propitiatory value in faith. Propitiation then is the basis for justification as seen in Luke chapter 18 verses 13 to 14. It is stated that Christ was delivered for our trespasses, Rom. 4. 25. So the justification of chapter 5 verse 1 is similar to that of David; that is, it is from sins committed and guilt incurred. But we read of being freed, or justified from sin, 6. 7. By the one sin committed by the one man, Adam, we were all constituted sinners, and under condemnation. Similarly by the one act of righteousness, the one act of obedience by the Lord, Phil. 2. 8-11, the free gift is extended to all unto justification of life, and the believer is viewed as in Christ crucified, buried and risen. He not only sees that his sins were laid upon his substitute, thereby being justified from guilt. He also sees himself as the criminal crucified, and thereby the extreme penalty of the law has been meted out to him in the person of the One with whom he is identified, and he is to reckon this as a judicial fact, Rom. 6. 11.

3. A Seemingly Counteracting Principle to that already enunciated. James insists that 'by works a man is justified and not by faith only'. As Paul and James both wrote by the inspiration of the Spirit there can be no conflict. They must be confirmatory. The words faith and works appear often in James' letter; faith ten times and works thirteen. He speaks of the trial of faith, of being rich in faith, and of the prayer of faith. So there is no devaluation of a true and living faith. He condemns a lifeless, barren, and corrupt faith, which is only a corpse. He draws an illustration from life, and from nature, to elucidate this.[28] He condemns the barren faith of the merely orthodox Jew. He commends the faith of the true believer, as illustrated in Abraham and Rahab. Their works were the fruit of a true and genuine faith. What they did was never seen by men, nor would what they did have been applauded by men, so their

[28] Jas. 2. 14-20, 26; cp. Luke 16. 19-21; 18. 11, 12.

justification was not before men. Their works were the works of faith, so highly appraised by the apostle Paul in his first letter to the Thessalonians. So the silver trumpets which Paul and James blow are in tune with each other.

By way of summary, the truth of justification is manifested:

1. Authoritatively by God, Rom. 3. 26; 8. 33;
2. Representatively and substitutionally by Christ, Gal. 2. 17, 20;
3. Sacrificially by His propitiatory work – His blood, Rom. 3. 25; 5. 9;
4. Judicially or legally by His resurrection, Rom. 4. 25; 8. 34;
5. Gratuitously or freely by grace, Rom. 3. 24;
6. Instrumentally by faith, Rom. 5. 1;
7. Evidentially by works – the works of faith, Jas. 2. 14-26.

The scriptures considered establish that the believer is justified immediately he believes, Gen. 15. 6; Luke 18. 13, 14. He is justified freely, Rom. 3. 24; fully, Acts 13. 38-39; finally and eternally, Rom. 8. 33-34. Moreover it is not a process, or progressive. All believers are justified in exactly the same way, and to the same degree, for Christ is our righteousness, and the believer has been made the righteousness of God in Him.

Reconciliation - E. L. LOVERING

God deviseth means (literally, thinketh thoughts) that he that is banished be not an outcast from Him. These were the words of the wise woman of Tekoah, as, at the instigation of Joab, she sought to persuade David to recall the outcast Absalom, 2 Sam. 14. 14.

Man, by his own sin and on righteous grounds, is banished from God, for God cannot tolerate sin in His presence. However, the outcast is not abandoned by God, for His love is unchanged toward the sinner, even though His wrath is kindled against his sin. God would devise means whereby He could be just and the justifier of the ungodly. His thoughts are thoughts of holiness and thoughts of love, and by the means of the cross and the death of His Son, He has been able to effect a righteous reconciliation for the sinner. If while we were enemies, alienated and hostile to God, 'we were reconciled to God [not God to us but we to Him] by the death of his Son, much more, being reconciled, we shall be saved by his life', Rom. 5. 10. It is interesting to notice in our study of the word 'reconciliation' that two distinct thoughts emerge from its usage. First, that in which the change is on the part of one party induced by an action on the part of another – the reconciliation of men to God by the death of His Son. Secondly, that in which there has been mutual hostility, yielding to mutual concession, e.g. Matt. 5. 24, between man and man. Let us note then:

Reconciliation Between Man and Man, Matt. 5. 24. This is the only occurrence of the Greek word in the New Testament, and, as we have already observed, implies that where there has been mutual hostility there must be mutual concession. There is no such idea as 'making it up' where God and man are concerned. It is well to remember that unless there is mutual agreement between man and man, it is vain to offer our gifts to God.

Reconciliation Between Believing Jew and Gentile. 'That he might reconcile both unto God in one body by the cross, having slain the enmity thereby', Eph. 2. 16. DR. HANDLEY MOULE beautifully expresses this union, when he writes, 'the apostle cannot let the Ephesians forget the past, lest they mistake the blissful present. He is indeed in the act of reminding them that they have been brought not only into a place of mercy, but into all the wealth of a covenanted privilege. They are incorporated . . . no more resident aliens, lodged in the suburbs of the Holy Zion, but full citizens of the place, aye, members of the royal family of its king . . . they cannot be nearer to God, for they are in His Christ. They were outsiders once. They had not the slightest claim upon salvation. Not only as they were, men, fallen and sinful, but also as they were 'Gentiles' they stood upon ground where redemption found them outcast and outlawed . . . it was mercy from first to last'.

Reconciliation Between Man and God. 'And you, that were sometime alienated and enemies in your mind by wicked works, yet now hath he reconciled in the body of his flesh through death, to present you holy and unblameable and unreprovable in his sight', Col. 1. 21. Here, it is not the union of Jew and Gentile which is in view, but the change wrought in the individual believer from alienation and enmity. Reconciliation is what God accomplishes in grace towards man on the ground of Christ's death. He bore the judgement due to sin, and God reconciled us (believers) to Himself through Christ, giving us the ministry or word of reconciliation, 'that God was in Christ, reconciling the world unto himself', 2 Cor. 5. 18, 19. The thought here is not that of the unity of the Godhead (God in Christ), but that what God has done in the matter of our reconciliation He has done in Christ. It is based upon the fact that the One who knew no sin He made to be sin on our behalf, that we might become the righteousness of God in Him. Hence, as ambassadors for Christ we beseech men to be reconciled to God, that is to change their attitude and accept the provision God has made for them. Until this change of attitude takes place, men are under condemnation and exposed to God's wrath. The death of the Lord Jesus is the ground upon which this can be removed and by which we can 'receive the reconciliation', Rom. 5. 11 RV. The rendering 'atonement' in the King James Version is incorrect; atonement is the offering itself of Christ under divine judgement upon sin. We do not receive 'atonement', but its result, namely 'reconciliation'. It may be asked, 'Does not the removal of God's wrath contravene His immutability?' The answer is that God is light and God is love, and we must distinguish between these and between indignation and anger against evil, and between wrath and hostility. When our Lord was criticized for healing on the Sabbath day we are told that 'he looked round about on them with anger, being grieved for the hardness of their hearts', Mark 3. 5. Here was anger without enmity, righteous indignation combined with fervent love. The change in God's relative attitude towards those who receive the reconciliation only proves His real unchangeableness. Not once is God said to be reconciled; the enmity is alone on our part.

Reconciliation of all Things. It is the divine purpose 'to reconcile all things unto himself . . . whether they be things upon the earth or things in the heavens', Col. 1. 20 RV. God will 'in the dispensation of the fullness of times . . . gather together in one all things in Christ, both which are in heaven, and which are on earth; even in him', Eph. 1. 10. Things 'under the earth', though not reconciled, will be subdued, for 'at the name of Jesus every knee should bow, of things in heaven, and things in earth, and things under the earth; and that every tongue should confess that Jesus Christ is Lord, to the glory of God the Father', Phil. 2. 10, 11.

Cleansing - J. M. Davies

In the concordance there are several columns of the various words used in relation to this subject. The words unclean, defiled, pollute and their antitheses clean, purify, purge and washing, unlike propitiation and justification, are words that are in daily use. They are common currency. The verb *katharizō* denotes to make clean, to cleanse from physical stains or dirt, Matt. 23. 25, and, in a moral sense, from the defilement of sin, Acts 15. 9, and from the guilt of sin, 1 John 1. 7. It is also used in a Levitical sense of pronouncing someone clean, or to consecrate by cleansings.[29] The compound form *diakatharizō,* to cleanse thoroughly, is used in Matthew chapter 3 verse 12 RV, 'he will thoroughly cleanse his threshing-floor', see *Expository Dictionary of New Testament Words,* W. E. Vine. In its connotation it implies purity and holiness, for that should be its effect or result.

It is the aspect of the redemptive work of Christ emphasized in the Epistle to the Hebrews. In its opening verses we read 'when he had made purification of sins', and of a conscience purged 'from dead works', 9. 14. As the Epistle draws so much from the Old Testament Levitical sacrificial system, it is necessary to consider the citations and references to it in the book.

The basic chapter dealing with the question of cleansing is Leviticus chapter 16 with its record of the instructions for the Day of Atonement, or propitiation. Cleansing followed, and was dependent on the propitiation. Apart from it there could be no cleansing. The claims of the throne of God must first be met, as grace reigns through righteousness. It is by virtue of the demands of righteousness having been exonerated that grace has been enthroned.

Along with Leviticus chapter 16 we have in Numbers chapter 19 the record of the provision made for cleansing from defilement while in the wilderness during the 38 years. These two ceremonies, and their significance, are linked together in Hebrews chapter 9 verse 13. The reference to 'the blood of bulls and of goats' is to the Day of Atonement, while 'the ashes of an heifer' refers to the important ordinance

[29] Mark 7. 19; Acts 10. 15; Heb. 9. 22, 23; 10. 2.

instituted after Kadesh-Barnea. They are also linked together in Hebrews chapter 10 verses 19 to 22, at the beginning of the practical section of the Epistle. The reference to the blood connects it with Leviticus chapter 16 when the blood was sprinkled on the mercy seat, while 'having our hearts sprinkled from an evil conscience, and our bodies washed', refers to Numbers chapter 19.

These two ordinances are complementary to each other. The second may be said to be supplementary to the first. The one prefigures the permanent, the never-to-be-repeated cleansing by the blood of the propitiation, 1 John 2. 2. The other prefigures the provision for cleansing from defilement through contact with that which is corrupt, the corruption that is in the world through lust, or the corrupting 'old man' for instance, 2 Pet. 1. 4; Eph. 4. 22. A similar dual aspect is to be seen in the instructions regarding the Day of Atonement. Along with the sacrifice for their cleansing, there was the celebration of the Sabbath of rest and the affliction of soul, a true and genuine contrition; see Psalms 32 and 51.

While the verses in Hebrews that have been referred to relate the two ordinances to the believer's present experience, it is well to remember that they will both have a future fulfilment in relation to the nation; see Isa. 53; Ezek. 36, 37.

Then in Leviticus chapters 13 to 14 we have two long chapters regarding leprosy, or the leper and his segregation, and the sacrifice for his cleansing, with which the cleansing of the defiled Nazarite may be compared. Israel, the once Nazarite nation, now defiled, leprous, and rejected, is yet to be restored. The prophet Isaiah saw himself as a leper like king Uzziah, and saw that the nation was leprous. In his agony he cried, 'Woe is me . . . I am a man of unclean lips, and I dwell in the midst of a people of unclean lips', Isa. 6. 5. He was cleansed by a touch of the live coal from the altar; propitiation had been made, so he was cleansed.

The passages we have considered, with their emphasis on sin as uncleanness and defilement, indicate the absolute necessity for cleansing in view of the holiness of God. They also indicate that 'God, being rich in mercy', has made provision for such cleansing. This provision we shall now analyze in summary.

Cleansing by Blood. The 'blood of Jesus his Son cleanseth us from all sin', 1 John 1. 7 RV. The present tense does not suggest a continual cleansing. It is rather a definitive statement as to the cleansing value, or power, of the blood of Jesus in contrast to that of the Old Testament sacrifices. He takes away sin; cp. Heb. 10. 4, 11. It purges the conscience, 9. 14; 10. 2. The tabernacle, the pattern of things in the heavens, was cleansed, but by the blood of Jesus 'the heavenly things themselves ' are to be cleansed, 9. 23.

Cleansing by Water. At their consecration the priestly family underwent a ceremonial bath which was never repeated. But in, and by virtue of their ministry, it was necessary for them to wash their hands and feet at the laver continually, Exod. 30. 17-21. The verse 'He that is bathed needeth not save to wash his feet, but is clean every whit', John 13. 10, is its New Testament application. 'Clean every whit, thou saidst it Lord, shall one suspicion lurk?'

Cleansing from Defilement, the water of separation, Num. 19. 13. The camp was the camp of the dying, so contact with a dead body was at times unavoidable. One sacrifice provided for every such emergency for the whole period. The blood was sprinkled seven times before the tabernacle. The sacrificial victim was burnt, and into the fire, cedar, hyssop and scarlet, representing nature at its extremes, were thrown. The ashes were kept, and, when needed, running water was poured on a little of it, and sprinkled on the defiled person, or tent. If the individual or tent was not cleansed, the sanctuary would become defiled. The water containing the ashes symbolizes the word or message of the cross. A clean person, not necessarily a priest, did the sprinkling. After that he was to wash his clothes and bathe. The ceremony is an illustration of 1 John chapter 1 verse 9, 'If we confess our sins, he is faithful and just to forgive . . . and to cleanse us'.

Cleansing with a Razor. This was done with the leper when he was cleansed, to remove all traces of defilement, Lev. 14. 5-9. It was also done with the Nazarite when he had lost his Nazariteship by defilement, cp. Samson. It was also done, strangely enough, when the Levites were consecrated, Num. 8. 7, suggestive of a complete cleansing on entering upon a path of service. The sharp, heart-searching question of the Lord to Peter, 'Lovest thou me more than these?', may be considered a New

Testament counterpart.

Cleansing by the Knife, the fruit-bearing branch, John 15. 2. The washing of the feet was a ministry committed to the disciples, but the pruning knife is in the Father's hand. The pruning is not because of sin, but to produce more fruit.

Cleansing by Fire, Mal. 3. 2. The fiery trial, 1 Pet. 1. 7; 4. 12, was a reference to the persecution that had already begun. In Hebrews chapter 12 verses 3 to 11 it is referred to as chastisement, the evidence of the Father's love. Gold is tried in the fire to get rid of any and all dross. Job's sufferings brought to the surface his self-righteousness. Israel, the threshing floor, is to be thoroughly purged in the time of the tribulation looming on the horizon.

The Ordering or the Preparing of the Lamps, Exod. 27. 21. The lamps had to be cleansed daily if they were to give light and shine over against the lampstand to reveal its beauty. The flame produced the ash, and reduced the oil supply. So there had to be a daily removal, and a daily renewal, two important lessons.

Sevenfold Salvation - E. W. HUMPHREYS

The orthodox evangelist will say that there is one way and only one way of salvation, and he emphatically quotes Acts chapter 4 verse 12, 'Neither is there salvation in any other: for there is none other name under heaven given among men, whereby we must be saved'. Yet scripture speaks of salvation from seven points of view.

Saved by Grace, Eph. 2. 8. This is God's side of salvation. The ruin and guilt of the sinner are alike complete, and he is quite incapable of doing anything to remedy his sad condition. Like Mephibosheth he is lame on both his feet, and as helpless as the poor man who had spent thirty-eight years by Bethesda's pool. It is a case where God must intervene and act if blessing is to come to the poor sinner. God was under no obligation to save but He abounds in grace, that is, free unmerited favour to those who had no claim upon Him. 'The grace of God that bringeth salvation hath appeared', Titus 2. 11, and this grace is seen in its fullest display at Calvary's cross where God's infinite justice had its demands fully met, with the sequel that His love can now flow out without hindrance to the vilest of sinners. We can each say with the apostle, 'by the grace of God I am what I am', 1 Cor. 15. 10. When we get home to heaven, from full hearts we shall exclaim, 'Not unto us, O Lord, not unto us, but unto thy name give glory, for thy mercy, and for thy truth's sake', Ps. 115. 1.

Saved by Faith, Luke 7. 50. This is our side of salvation. If God has acted in such marvellous grace and if the merits of the sacrifice of Calvary are sufficient for the whole human race, why, then, are not all saved? The answer is that we must believe it and appropriate it for ourselves; 'And let him that is athirst come. And whosoever will, let him **take**', Rev. 22. 17. There must be the taking, and this is the act of faith; it is because men do not take that they are not saved. The Israelite child of old was preserved because his father believed the word of God and sprinkled the blood. The power of God to protect was there all the time, but faith had to be exercised for that power to be made effective. In his valuable book, *The Gospel and its Ministry,* SIR ROBERT ANDERSON has illustrated faith by referring to the chains that hang from the Thames Embankment to the water's edge. They are provided to save life but the drowning person must grasp one of them if his life is to be saved. This is faith.

Saved by Works, Jas. 2. 24. There is no contradiction between Paul and James; they both wrote by inspiration of the Holy Spirit. Paul is writing of our salvation as viewed by God; James is writing of it as seen by man, and one of his key phrases is 'if a man say' or some similar expression. If I say I am saved, I must have something to show for it before the men around me. I see a tree that appears barren and leafless in the winter; I am told that it is an apple tree. Then I expect to see evidences of this in the bursting forth of leaves and blossom in spring, and, later, I shall look for a crop of apples. In the absence of these evidences, I am entitled to doubt the truth of the statement.

The reference in Philippians chapter 2 verse 12 to working out your own salvation probably refers to the salvation of the local assembly rather than that of an individual. At Philippi there were the beginnings of a serious trouble, namely the lack of unity among the Lord's people. Paul refers to it in each of the four chapters. A divided assembly would have no standing nor influence before the eyes of onlookers.

Saved by Baptism, 1 Pet. 3. 21. The salvation in question here is not the salvation of the soul from sin, but the salvation of the believer from an accusing conscience. How quickly the Spirit of God adds the words 'not the putting away of the filth of the flesh'. This verse cannot be taken by those who teach baptismal regeneration to support their terrible error. There can be no hesitation in saying that this error is another of Satan's delusions in blinding people's minds to the grand truth of the gospel. No, the salvation by baptism is the answer of a good conscience. Suppose that I, as a Christian of several years' standing, had never been baptized. My conscience should always be reminding me, 'You ought to be baptized; it is one of the Lord's commands'. When I have taken this step my conscience is satisfied and I am saved from its accusations. Our text tells us that baptism is a figure – it is a figure of identity with the Saviour in His death, burial and resurrection.

Saved by His Life, Rom. 5. 10. The 'we' in this verse is addressed to those described as 'beloved of God, called . . . saints', 1. 7. It cannot refer to our salvation from death and hell. Nowhere are the sufferings that the Lord endured during His life down here said to be for us. The reference is to His resurrection life and His intercession for us at God's right hand, where, Hebrews chapter 7 verse 25 tells us, He ever lives to make intercession for us. When we get home to heaven, we shall discover how much we have owed to His high priestly ministry there on our behalf. Salvation here refers to our being preserved from falling. We are living in perilous times; we have a bitter enemy who is always on the alert. Believers are often his special target, but we are kept because the Saviour lives and intercedes. He said to Simon Peter, 'I have prayed for thee, that thy faith fail not', Luke 22. 32. He still prays similarly for us, so 'Let us therefore come boldly unto the throne of grace, that we may obtain mercy, and find grace to help in time of need', Heb. 4. 16. On one occasion when sorely pressed, Paul wrote, 'the Lord stood with me, and strengthened me', 2 Tim. 4. 17. He was being saved or preserved by His life.

Saved by Fire, 1 Cor. 3. 15. Day by day God is taking note of our doings. We can either be filling up the days and moments with loving and loyal service for our Saviour, or we can be living for self, courting the favour and approval of our brethren and even of the world. All this will be brought under review at the Judgement Seat of Christ. No saint will be lost – there are abundant scriptures to prove that, but some will be rewarded with their Saviour's commendation and a crown, while others, alas, will suffer the loss of these blessings. The fire of His searching review will decide with perfect fairness and righteousness. Those whose works are but wood, hay and stubble will be saved by fire; they will see their endeavours consumed under His kind but searching eye, but they will themselves be brought through safely.

Saved by Hope, Rom. 8. 24. Here the believer's present life is in view, not his eternal salvation. He is kept going by the glorious hope of the wonderful future that is just ahead for him. Around him is a world that is rapidly drifting from bad to worse, but just before him is a precious promise, 'Surely I come quickly', Rev. 22. 20. On every hand, men and women of the world are giving way to despair, but the child of God looks ahead and knows that the body of his humiliation is soon to be exchanged for a body of glory like unto that of his Lord. Many today can see no hope for the world, but the Christian lifts up his head and sings with TREVOR FRANCIS:

> 'I can almost hear His footfall
> On the threshold of the door,
> And my heart is longing, longing
> To be with Him evermore'.
>
> S. T. FRANCIS

He is thereby being saved by hope.

Redemption - C. E. HOCKING

The prodigal son of Luke chapter 15, when he came to himself, made his way home to the father's house. The prodigal spouse of Hosea chapter 3 was neither free nor able to do this. She was a slave in the market-place, awaiting the visit of her purchaser. Slavery was a repugnant feature of the past. Degraded and often maltreated humanity was for sale. The slave, once purchased, was little more than a live chattel. He knew no freedom, the will of his master being the law in every department of his 'existence'. What a state of helplessness and hopelessness is suggested by this.

Much is said in both Old and New Testaments in connection with slavery. Reference is made to ransom, redeem, deliverance and freedom, etc. In not a few cases the subject is treated literally. The more important doctrinal use of these words, however, is where a figurative sense is found. God takes up the sad outward condition of the slave to depict the awful inward condition of mankind through the fall. The Old Testament has so often revealed the vital connection between sins and oppressions in the history of Israel (cp. Judges). In the New Testament we read 'of whom a man is overcome, of the same is he brought into bondage', 2 Pet. 2. 19.

Sin is slavery. Sinners are slaves, John 8. 34. By nature, men are the slaves of sin, and Satan;[30] they are subject to his power, Acts 26. 18, and not free to do the things they would, though they idly boast of 'free will', etc., Rom. 7. 14, 15. Even the Jew with his lofty privileges is a slave under law and needs deliverance from its curse, Gal. 4. 1-7. Hence, men are debtors and in the shackles of a bondage they are powerless to break. This is so universally true that the Psalmist says 'none of them can by any means redeem his brother, nor give to God a ransom for him', 49. 7. If a ransom is to be found, it must come from above, Job 33. 24. God must send redemption to His people, Ps. 111. 9; God must be their redeemer, Isa. 63. 16, if men are to be liberated. The Beloved must come 'in whom we have redemption through his blood, the forgiveness of our trespasses, according to the riches of his grace', Eph. 1. 7 RV. The infinite cost involved in procuring this redemption was the precious blood of Christ, 1 Pet. 1. 19; cp. Acts 20. 28. Christians are thus 'bought with a price', 1 Cor. 6. 20; 7. 23, and are free, Gal. 5. 1. 'If the Son shall make you free, ye shall be free indeed', John 8. 36.

In the Old Testament the word 'redeem', in all but two cases, is the translation of two words and their derivatives. Both of these are sometimes used in a literal sense. The first is used for the payment required of the firstborn, Num. 3. 46-49; 18. 15, or release of persons from slavery, Exod. 21. 8. The second is used of the recovery of property which has passed into other hands, Lev. 25. 26; Ruth 4. 4.

However, both of these words are frequently used when referring to the

---

[30] Rom. 6. 17, 20; Titus 3. 3; Heb. 2. 14, 15.

God-wrought deliverances in the history of the nation of Israel, Isa. 29. 22; 48. 20, and in the experience of individuals, Ps. 34. 22. When this figurative use of the words is considered, it becomes apparent that the idea of money payment recedes and the emphasis is placed rather on the salvation or deliverance effected. Nonetheless, the contexts always suggest the mighty effort and personal cost that brought about the deliverance as, with an outstretched arm, God wrought their redemption. God was no disinterested observer but took up the cause of His own people and demonstrated the greatness of His love. He delivered Israel in the past from Egypt, Deut. 7. 8, and Babylon, Isa. 48. 20, and will yet redeem them in the future, Zech. 10. 8, etc.

One of the derivatives is of particular interest. It is *go'el,* a participle meaning one who asserts a claim, or has a right of redemption, one who vindicates the right of a murdered man, avenging his bloodshed, Num. 5. 8; Ruth 2. 20. The right, in each case, belonged to the nearest kinsman or a near relative, Ruth 4. 1-4. Hence the word came to be used to denote a near kinsman. This particular word is often used in Isaiah of God Himself. He is emphatically 'the Redeemer'. Breathtaking grace is revealed in this title. The nation's political and spiritual deliverance is His prerogative and He who has them graven on the palms of His hands would intervene and save them. Through this title the heart of God is revealed as also His might,[31] and the very helplessness of the people, Isa. 41. 14; 59. 20, was the occasion for a rich unveiling of His character.

In the New Testament two words and their derivatives are used in connection with the subject of redemption. The first is akin to the contemporary literature in deeds of sale. It means 'to buy', emphasizing the fact that the payment has been made, Matt. 13. 44. The word is used in connection with the death of Christ, highlighting the cost of liberation. Freed from all liabilities, those purchased are now His.[32] Whilst believers are purchased unto God, we are not told that the price was paid to anyone. Old Testament usage prepared us more particularly to appreciate the grace, self-sacrifice and might displayed that He might make us His own.

---

[31] Isa. 43. 14; 44. 24; 54. 5; 60. 16.

[32] 1 Cor. 6. 20; 7. 23; Rev. 5. 9; 14. 3, 4.

A passage where this word occurs has caused difficulty to some. In 2 Peter chapter 2 verse 1 RV we read of those who are guilty of 'denying even the Master that bought them, bringing upon themselves swift destruction'. Of course such purchase does not mean that the false teachers were among the redeemed. Purchase is not redemption. The infinite price of the cross work of Christ has made all His, though many deny His absolute right over them. He is the only Master, the absolute Despot, and ultimately every knee will bow and every tongue confess His Lordship. As the parable teaches, He has purchased the whole field on account of the treasure in it.

A strengthened form of this word brings in the thought of redemption alongside that of purchase, Gal. 3. 13; 4. 5. The Jew, under the law and its curse, through faith in Christ, is liberated from it. It is also used in the exhortation to the Christian to redeem the time, Eph. 5. 16; Col. 4. 5. We are thus encouraged to buy up every opportunity and use it for the furtherance of Christ's interests.

The other word and its derivatives used frequently in the New Testament come from a verb meaning 'to loose' and stresses the setting at liberty which results on payment of a ransom. There are occasions when a physical or political deliverance is in mind.[33] However, when used in connection with the death of Christ, spiritual liberation is connoted. The Christian has been redeemed from a vain manner of life, 1 Pet. 1. 18, and from all iniquity, Titus 2. 14. The shedding of Christ's precious blood, Heb. 9. 12; Eph. 1. 7, has loosed us out of bondage to the traditions of the life of self-will. The Son of man has come 'to minister and to give his life a ransom for many', Matt. 20. 28. We note here the restricted circle of those who would come into the good of His redemptive work and know forgiveness, Col. 1. 14, and justification, Rom. 3. 24. The laying down of His life was the ransom paid in the stead of the many who would appropriate it. This needs to be discriminated from the teaching of 1 Timothy chapter 2 verse 6 where a kindred word is found. There the context teaches that God desires the salvation of all, and the finished work of Christ is shown to be available for all and for the advantage of all. We do not read, however, that He died in the stead of all. 'He gave himself a ransom [an adequate ransom] for [i.e., on behalf

[33] See Luke 1. 68; 2. 38; 24. 21.

of] all.' Such is the perversity of the human heart that whilst God has made adequate provision for the blessing of all, multitudes reject His offer of mercy.

Redemption by blood is the portion of every believer now. Redemption by power is to be the experience and blessed portion of such in the future. Every true child of God is longing for that bright day when we shall see the Lord and be like Him. Sin abounds around us and we feel the downward tug as it appeals to the old nature within us. We await that moment when we shall be delivered from the presence and power of sin for ever with our redemption completed.[34] These bodies of our present low estate are subject to corruption and are yet to come into the good of redemption. Hence, the redemptive work of Christ not only deals with our past, e.g., Col. 1. 14; Gal. 3. 13, and affects our present lives, Titus 2. 14, but also will be brought to full fruition in the future. We must unite in praise to God for Him who is a High Priest of the good things to come, who, 'through his own blood, entered in once for all into the holy place, having obtained eternal redemption', Heb. 9. 12 RV.

Adoption - J. M. Davies

Adoption means taking into a family one who is either an orphaned or unwanted child. Generally there is a legal procedure to follow in such cases. However, the biblical significance of adoption is very different. God never adopts anyone as His child, or any group as His children. All believers are **born** into the family of God by the new birth, thereby imparting to them a new and divine nature. Even though adopting parents may sincerely love, and genuinely care for, their adopted child or children, they cannot impart to them their own peculiar nature.

The word rendered adoption in the New Testament is *huiothesia.* It is made up of two words, the word for a son *huios*, and the word for placing *thesis.* In his *Expository Dictionary of New Testament Words,* W. E. Vine states that it signifies the place and condition of a son given to one to whom it does not naturally belong. Paul is the only New Testament writer who uses the word adoption, but he also uses the word children in Romans chapter 8. It is as children that we are heirs of

---

[34] 1 Cor. 1. 30; Eph. 1. 14; 4. 30.

God, and joint-heirs with Christ, and not by virtue of any attainment. As sons, referred to in Hebrews as the 'church of the firstborn . . . written in heaven', Heb. 12. 23, we shall be manifested with Christ in glory. Being children highlights our relationship, as emphasized in 1 John, where the word 'little children' occurs seven times. On the other hand, sonship relates to, and signifies, the place and position given to one who is regarded as a son. We shall consider the passages where the word 'adoption' is used in the New Testament.

1. National: Adoption and Election, Rom. 9. 4. In the catalogue of nine blessings, or privileges, or priorities, over other nations bestowed on the nation of Israel, the apostle lists 'adoption' as the second, in what seems to be a historical order. The term 'Israelites' establishes their connection with Jacob, to whom the name Israel was given by the Lord at Peniel, Gen. 32. 28. This was later confirmed when he arrived at Bethel, and had established an altar there, 35. 6-15. Then, when Moses was commissioned to return to Egypt, he was given an ultimatum to deliver to Pharaoh, demanding the release and liberation of the nation of Israel from its slavery and bondage. The first words he was to utter were, 'Thus saith the Lord, Israel is my son, even my firstborn', Exod. 4. 22.

It is to this statement that the phrase 'to whom pertaineth the adoption' refers. It indicated that Israel, the nation collectively, was recognized or claimed by the Lord as being in a position of peculiar relationship with Himself, not enjoyed by any other nation. That was a position they had before God by virtue of His electing grace. And, centuries later, when the curtain was about to fall on Israel's history as an independent nation in the land, the prophet Jeremiah re-emphasized that relationship as he prophesied of Israel's future regathering from a worse, and longer, period of exile than the one spent in Egypt. He says, 'I am a father to Israel, and Ephraim is my firstborn', 31. 9. In that prophecy the term Ephraim stands for the whole nation. The Exodus passage, coupled with Romans chapter 9 verse 5, establishes the meaning to be given to adoption in the other passages. It has to do with their position, its privileges and prospects. Israel's adoption was due entirely to God's sovereign electing grace. Thus, electing grace is the cornerstone of adoption. This adoption, being to a position of national priority, did not ensure eternal blessing to any individual Israelite, but the privileges which flowed from it made such spiritual blessings possible, or available.

2. Individual: Adoption and Predestination. Having 'foreordained us unto adoption as sons through Jesus Christ unto himself, according to the good pleasure of his will, to the praise of the glory of his grace', Eph. 1. 5, 6 RV. In contrast to Israel's national adoption, this is personal. It has both a present, and an eternal dimension, for it relates to eternity as well as to time. A comparison of the passage in Ephesians with Romans chapter 8 verses 29 to 30 and its four-fold repetition of the word 'whom' shows that, although predestination may have a collective aspect, it is the individual or personal aspect that is indicated when referring to adoption. The importance of the change from 'as children' in the King James Version, to 'as sons' in the Revised Version, should be noted in view of the difference between children and sons. The believer is a member of the family of God, one of His children, through the spiritual experience of the new birth by the operation of the Holy Spirit, whereas our adoption as sons is through Jesus Christ according to the sovereign will of God.

3. Dispensational and Experiential: Adoption and Redemption. This leads us to a consideration of adoption, and its significance in relation to Christian experience. But 'when the fulness of the time came, God sent forth his Son, born of a woman, born under the law, that he might redeem them which were under the law, that we might receive the adoption of sons', Gal. 4. 4, 5 RV. The illustration that the apostle uses makes very clear the difference between the Jew under law, and the believer under grace. The heir as long as he is a child is under tutors and governors until the time appointed by the Father. This was Israel's position under law. The word translated 'tutors', v. 2, does not refer to a teacher, but a guardian or a steward, one who had a responsibility with regard to the care of the house, and of the children. The law, then, was not given to lead them to Christ. It was given to meet an emergency, as a stop-gap until Christ came. With the death of Christ by which the curse that it had pronounced, and the penalty it had demanded, were righteously satisfied, the curse was removed, and its dominion was cancelled or annulled. The believer, then, is not under the law. He is delivered from its condemnation. He is not under rules and regulations to control his life. Sonship means freedom from the law as a mode of living, and as a means of sanctification. In its place, those constituted sons by redemption have been made the recipients of the 'Spirit of his Son', the 'Spirit of adoption, whereby we cry, Abba, Father'. The two words conjoined in Romans chapter 8 verse 15 and Galatians chapter 4 verse 6 combine the language of the lisping child – Abba, and of the mature son – Father. Being a son by adoption does not cancel his relationship as a child. Believers are both children of God and sons of God. The law not only meant bondage, it generated, and still generates, fear in all who put themselves under its yoke. This was the net which the Judaizers spread for the Galatians, and they were in danger of substituting for their past bondage to idolatry, a bondage to the law and its beggarly elements, instead of entering into their blood-bought liberty as sons.

4. Eschatological: Adoption and its Future Manifestation. 'For the earnest expectation of the creation waiteth for the revealing of the sons of God', Rom. 8. 19 RV. The whole creation groans. All its songs are in the minor key. The roar of the waves, the howling of the wind, the lowing of the cattle, and the bleating of the sheep are all mournful in their tone. Even the spiritually minded Apostle Paul groaned, saying, 'O wretched man that I am! who shall deliver me from this body of death?' 7. 24. He longed for the final phase of the adoption, the redemption of the body, 'the liberty of the glory of the children of God', Rom. 8. 18-25. If the angelic sons of God shouted for joy at creation's dawn, what will the acclamation be like when the assembly of the first-born, the sons of God by election, predestination and redemption, will all be gathered home: 'O that with yonder sacred throng, we at His feet may fall; join in the everlasting song and crown Him Lord of all'.

Eternal Life - D. CLAPHAM

In the King James Version of the New Testament, the word 'eternal' translates three Greek words, viz: *aidios*, Rom. 1. 20, where it would be better rendered 'everlasting'; *aion,* Eph. 3. 11, 1 Tim. 1. 17, where it should be 'of the ages'; and *aionios*, which occurs seventy-one times in all and is translated 'eternal' forty-two times, 'everlasting' twenty-five times, 'world' three times, and 'forever' once. In the sixty-seven occurrences where *aiōnios* is translated 'eternal' or 'everlasting', these two words are practically synonymous, and are used interchangeably in relation to:

	times		times		times
God	1	Consolation	1	Damnation	1
Glory	2	Covenant	1	Destruction	1
Glory, weight	1	Gospel	1	Fire	3
Habitations	1	Inheritance	1	Judgment	1
House, heavenly	1	Life	44	Punishment	1
Kingdom	1	Redemption	1		
Power	1	Salvation	1		
Spirit	1				
Unseen things	1				

The four Greek words which are translated 'life' are: *bios, pneuma, psuchē* and *zōē. Zōē* (English: zoo, zoology), which is the word invariably connected with *aiōnios,* is rendered 'life' 133 times, and 'lifetime' once; and it refers to life as a principle, life in the absolute sense.

The Apostle John's Gospel and Epistles are full of instruction regarding eternal life, and it is principally from these that we learn about it, John 20. 31; 1 John 5. 13. He uses three terms to describe life under different aspects:

1. 'The life' *(hē zōē),* life which is truly life;
2. 'Eternal life' *(zōē aiōnios)*;
3. 'The eternal life' *(hē aiōnios zōē).*

Connected with these terms are four verbal phrases to be noted:

4. 'To live' *(zaō),* John 5. 25; 6. 57; 11. 25; 14. 19; 1 John 4. 9;
5. 'To live forever' *(zaō eis ton aiōna),* John 6. 51, 58;
6. 'To have life' *(exein zōēn),* 10. 10; 20. 31; 1 John 5. 12;
7. 'To have eternal life' *(exein zōēn aiōnion),* John 3. 15, 36; 5. 24; 6. 40, 47, 54; 1 John 5. 13.

A valuable additional note (1), on 1 John 5. 20, entitled 'The Ideal Life', in B. F. WESTCOTT'S *Commentary on the Epistles of John,* should be consulted in this connection, if possible.

Eternal Life, being divine life, is distinct from the life of angels, men, beasts, birds and fishes. It is, therefore, in essence uncreated, underived, without beginning or end, unchanging. One has written, 'This life is not merely a principle of power and mobility, however, for it has moral associations which are inseparable from it, as holiness and righteousness'. From this life man has become alienated in consequence of the fall, Eph. 4. 18, so that to him it is said, 'ye have no life in you', John 6. 53. He is 'dead in trespasses and sins', Eph. 2. 1, and, remaining in unbelief, he 'shall not see life', John 3. 36.

Given below is a selection of scriptures gathered under a number of headings for the purpose of drawing attention to various important facts relating to eternal life:

1. *It existed before the world began.*
   'The living God', 1 Tim. 4. 10.
   'The living Father', John 6. 57.
   'As the Father hath life in himself', 5. 26.
   'Given to the Son to have life in himself', 5. 26.
   'That eternal life, which was with the Father', 1 John 1. 2.
   'In him was life', John 1. 4.
   'I am the living bread which came down from heaven', 6. 51.
   'Eternal life, which God, that cannot lie, promised before the world began', Titus 1. 2.

2. *It was alluded to in Old Testament times.*
   'The eternal God', Deut. 33. 27.
   'There the Lord commanded the blessing, even life for evermore', Ps. 133. 3.
   'Many of them that sleep in the dust shall awake, some to everlasting life', Dan. 12. 2.

What relation Old Testament saints had to God does not seem to be clearly revealed. No doubt they were individually given life by the Spirit, as they came to believe in God for their personal salvation. But, whatever may have been the result of their spiritual change, they knew nothing of the new life and sonship as it is opened up to us in the New

Testament.

3. *The coming of the Son into the world fully manifested it.*
'For the life was manifested, and we have seen it, and bear witness, and show unto you that eternal life, which was with the Father, and was manifested unto us', 1 John 1. 2.
'This life is in his Son', 5. 11.
'The life was the light of men', John 1. 4.
'Thou hast the words of eternal life', 6. 68.

4. *The Son is the sole communicator of it.*
'The bread of God is he which cometh down from heaven, and giveth life to the world', John 6. 33.
'I am the bread of life', 6. 35, 48, 51.
'I am come that they might have life', 10. 10.
'I give unto them eternal life', 10. 28.
'That he should give eternal life to as many as thou hast given him', 17. 2.
'The Son quickeneth whom he will', 5. 21.
'The last Adam . . . a quickening spirit', 1 Cor. 15. 45.
'Ye will not come unto me, that ye might have life', John 5. 40.

5. *How it becomes a present possession.*
'Ye must be born again', John 3. 3, 7.
'Even so must the Son of man be lifted up: that whosoever believeth in him should . . . have eternal life', 3. 14, 15.
'For God so loved the world, that he gave his only begotten Son, that whosoever believeth in him should . . . have everlasting life', 3. 16.
'He that believeth on the Son hath everlasting life', 3. 36.
'He that heareth my word, and believeth on him that sent me, hath everlasting life', 5. 24.
'He that eateth my flesh, and drinketh my blood, hath eternal life', 6. 54.
'But these [signs] are written, that ye might believe that Jesus is the Christ, the Son of God; and that believing ye might have life through his name', 20. 31.
'The free gift of God is eternal life in Christ Jesus our Lord', Rom. 6. 23 NEWBERRY.

'He that hath the Son hath life', 1 John 5. 12.

6. *The future aspect of it.*
   'They that have done good . . . the resurrection of life', John 5. 29.
   'He that hateth his life in this world shall keep it unto life eternal', 12. 25.
   'In hope of eternal life', Titus 1. 2.
   'That being justified by his grace, we should be made heirs according to the hope of eternal life', 3. 7.
   'Looking for the mercy of our Lord Jesus Christ unto eternal life', Jude 21.

7. *Misconceptions concerning it.*
   'For in them [the scriptures] ye think ye have eternal life', John 5. 39.
   'What shall I do that I may inherit eternal life?' Mark 10. 17.
   'If there had been a law given which could have given life, verily righteousness should have been by the law', Gal. 3. 21.

8. *The awful alternative to the possession of it.*
   'Depart from me, ye cursed, into everlasting fire, prepared for the devil and his angels', Matt. 25. 41.
   'Everlasting punishment', 25. 46.
   'Shall perish', John 3. 16.
   'Shall not see life; but the wrath of God abideth on him', 3. 36.
   'Abideth in death', 1 John 3. 14.
   'He that believeth not is condemned already', John 3. 18.

9. *How it is illustrated by the Prodigal Son,* Luke 15. 11-32.

Into a far country, v. 13.	In the Father's house, v. 25.
Wasting substance, v. 13.	Making merry with friends, v. 29.
Spent all, v. 14.	Best robe, ring, shoes, v. 22.
In want, v. 14.	Bread enough and to spare, v. 17.
Hungry for pig swill, v. 16.	Fatted calf, v. 23.
Perishing, v. 17.	Gladness, v. 32.
Dead, v. 24.	Alive again, vv. 24, 32.

From this it will be perceived that eternal life for the repentant and forgiven one involves relationship with the Father, and nearness to

Him; being in the position of a son, and in possession of the inalienable rights of one; experiencing fellowship and full satisfaction, peace and unbounded joy; and all this begun here and now, and continuing evermore.

Perhaps the nearest approach to a definition of eternal life is found in John chapter 17 verse 3, 'And this is life eternal, that they might know thee the only true God, and Jesus Christ, whom thou has sent'. It is not a definition in the usual sense of the word, but it is Christ's own description of eternal life, and reveals His conception of it. It is to **know** God and His Christ. 'This knowledge is vastly more than mere intellectual perception or understanding. It is moral knowledge, it is personal acquaintance, it is fellowship, a contact, if we may so speak, of personality with personality, an inner affinity and sympathy, an experience of similar thoughts, emotions, purposes, motives, desires, an interchange of the heart's deepest feelings and experiences. It is a bringing of the whole personality of man into right relationship with the personality of God. This relation is ethical, personal, binding the two together with ties which nothing can separate. It is into this experience that Jesus Christ came to bring men' (J. J. REEVE).

Such a knowledge is not arrived at all at once. As B. F. WESTCOTT pointed out in his comment on John chapter 17 verse 3, the 'that', *hina,* expresses an aim, an end, and not only a fact. So, too, the tense of the verb **know** marks continuance, progress, and not a perfect and past apprehension gained once for all. It is always advancing from glory to glory, 2 Cor. 3. 18; cp. 4. 6.

Sanctification - E. L. LOVERING

The Old Testament words rendered sanctify, or sanctification imply a setting apart to sacred purposes or to consecrate, and have various applications in the Old Testament. We read, for instance, of holy **places**: Jerusalem – the holy city; Mount Sinai – the holy mount. Or again, the word is used of **persons**. It is written of the Lord Jesus that He sanctified Himself, 'for their sakes I sanctify myself, that they also might be sanctified through the truth', John 17. 19. Aaron and his sons and their garments were sanctified, Exod. 28. 41; Lev. 8. 30. **Things** also are said to be sanctified – the anointing oil, Exod. 30. 25; the seventh day, Gen.

2. 3; feasts and the year of Jubilee.

From these and other passages of scripture it seems clear that the fundamental idea underlying the word 'sanctification' is that of separation or setting apart for God. As a skilfully-cut diamond has one beauty but many facets, so this priceless blessing has several aspects, some of which we shall now consider.

Pre-conversion Sanctification. 1 Peter chapter 1 verse 2 records, 'Elect according to the foreknowledge of God the Father, through sanctification of the Spirit, unto obedience and sprinkling of the blood of Jesus Christ'. Included in this are the activities of the triune God – the foreknowledge of God the Father, the sanctification of the Holy Spirit, and the sprinkling of the blood of Jesus Christ. The same order is evident in 2 Thessalonians chapter 2 verse 13, 'God hath from the beginning chosen you to salvation through sanctification of the Spirit and belief of the truth'. God chose us in His sovereignty, and the Holy Spirit sanctified and separated us to believe the truth. Thus, 'the sanctification of the Spirit is associated with the choice or election of God; it is a divine act preceding the acceptance of the gospel by the individual'.[35]

Positional Sanctification. The New Testament describes believers in the Lord Jesus Christ as saints or sanctified ones, and even to the church at Corinth, where there was so much to bring discredit upon the name of the Lord, the apostle wrote 'unto the church of God which is at Corinth, to them that are sanctified in Christ Jesus, called saints', 1 Cor. 1. 2. All believers in the Lord Jesus are, therefore, saints, and, because of this, it behoves them to be saintly in their walk and character. The Epistle to the Hebrews tells us that 'by one offering he hath perfected for ever them that are sanctified', Heb. 10. 14. This is positional sanctification, our standing before God, which is not determined by our state. Further, Hebrews chapter 3 verse 1 speaks of 'holy brethren, partakers of the heavenly calling', and Christians are said to be 'of him in Christ Jesus, who was made unto us wisdom from God, and righteousness and sanctification and redemption', that he that glorieth should glory in the Lord, 1 Cor. 1. 30, 31 RV. One has written, 'Sanctification is that relationship with God into which men enter by

---

[35] C. F. Hogg and W. E. Vine, *Notes on Thessalonians*, pp. 115, 271.

faith in Christ, Acts 26. 18; 1 Cor. 6. 11, and to which their sole title is the death of Christ'.[36]

Practical Sanctification. There is, in the New Testament, the aspect of sanctification which involves a separation of the believer from evil things and ways. As in Old Testament times the individual Israelite might be 'positionally' sanctified and yet be ceremonially and practically unclean, so may be the believer of New Testament times. Sanctification is God's will for all His people: 'this is the will of God, even your sanctification', 1 Thess. 4. 3. And this was His purpose in calling us by the gospel, 'for God called us not for uncleanness but in sanctification', v. 7 RV. How is this worked out in the life of the believer? It involves a path of separation in the normal walk and activities of life, whether domestic, social, business, friendships or any other relationships into which we might be brought. The Old Testament principle was, 'Thou shalt not plough with an ox and an ass together', Deut. 22. 10, and the New Testament makes it plain that there must be no 'unequal yoke' for Christians, 2 Cor. 6. 14. Practical sanctification involves separation from evil, in desire, motive and act from the 'world', which is enmity against God and His Christ; all that is of the world, the lust of the flesh, the lust of the eye and the pride of life. Further, it involves separation from false teachers, vessels unto dishonour, 2 Tim. 2. 20. Separation is not from contact with evil in the world or church, but from complicity and conformity to it. 'I pray not that thou shouldest take them out of the world, but that thou shouldest keep them from the evil', John 17. 15. Failure to observe this fact has produced a monastic system, alien to the teaching and spirit of Christ. What, then, if we should happen to sin? 'We have an advocate with the Father, Jesus Christ the righteous', 1 John 2. 1. 'Wherewithal shall a young man cleanse his way? by taking heed thereto according to thy word', Ps. 119. 9. The priest in the tabernacle needed the altar and the laver for his cleansing. Christ also 'loved the church, and gave himself for it; that he might sanctify and cleanse it with the washing of water by the word', Eph. 5. 25, 26.

Progressive Sanctification. It is God's will that the believer should pursue, earnestly and undeviatingly, that 'sanctification without which

---

[36] See: Eph. 5. 25, 26; Col. 1. 22; Heb. 10. 10.

no man shall see the Lord', Heb. 12. 14 RV. Practical sanctification and holiness of life are essential if we would see God. Many believers see little of God in their circumstances, in their afflictions, in world affairs, in the daily round and common task – because they know little of practical sanctification. Sanctification is not an instantaneous act, but a steady growth in grace as a result of obedience to the word of God and of following the example of Christ in the power of the Spirit. The believer is sometimes chastened that he may be partaker of His holiness, Heb. 12. 10; he is to present his body a living sacrifice, holy, acceptable unto God, Rom. 12. 1; he is to be transformed into the likeness of Jesus Christ day by day, 2 Cor. 3. 17, 18, and reckon himself dead unto sin and alive unto God, Rom. 6. 11. May God grant that in all things we may grow up into Him!

Perfect and Prospective Sanctification. 'Christ loved the church, and gave himself for it; that he might sanctify and cleanse it with the washing of water by the word, that he might present it to himself a glorious church, not having spot, or wrinkle, or any such thing; but that it should be holy and without blemish', Eph. 5. 25-27. 'Beloved, now are we the children of God, and it is not yet made manifest what we shall be. We know that if he shall be manifested, we shall be like him, for we shall see him even as he is', 1 John 3. 2 RV.

The Unity of the Spirit* - W. E. Vine

At the beginning of the fourth chapter of Ephesians believers are exhorted to walk 'worthily of the calling' wherewith they were called, a walk to be characterized by 'all lowliness and meekness with longsuffering, forbearing one another in love'. For this it is necessary to give diligence (not merely to endeavour, but to make it their business) 'to keep the unity of the Spirit in the bond of peace'.

Unity can exist only where we have a right estimate of ourselves, a realization of our own littleness and demerit, and that unassuming self-abasement which is a reflection of the lowliness of Christ; when, too, we exercise that spirit of glad submissiveness to God's dealings which produces considerateness towards others even when under provocation, the 'invincible might of meekness', which reflects the meekness of Christ and overcomes evil with good. To these is to be added the longsuffering which patiently bears with unreasonableness and meets disappointments with quiet fortitude. Only so can we forbear one another in love. That kind of forbearance is not studied courtesy or frigid endurance, but is characterized by the holy attachment which binds believers together in the bonds of Christian love.

The unity is there; it is not for us to make it. The church is one, a Divine entity. The Spirit of God makes it so. As the presence of the Holy Spirit imparts to the church its fitness to be God's temple, Eph. 2. 22, so His power imparts its unity to it. That unity is not formed by man, nor by any ecclesiastical organization on earth. Human arrangements and institutions may devise, and have devised, something which possesses a show of uniformity from the natural point of view, but the unity of the true body of Christ of which scripture speaks, is spiritual in its course of development and heavenly in its position and character, its design and destiny.

There is no hint here, or anywhere else in the New Testament, of anything like unity consisting of the combination of a number of communities, or assemblies, delimited by geographical conditions, or formed into earthly associations or circles of fellowship, nor is there any hint of a number of churches bound together by the bonds either of formulated religious creeds or of human tradition. No matter whether such communities are organized by mutual consent or under a church council or any form of ecclesiastical authority centralized in a given locality, all such combinations are a distinct departure from the plain teaching of Christ and His apostles. They do not constitute the unity spoken of in this passage or any other in the word of God. They satisfy the aspirations of men but are contrary to the mind of the Lord.

All bitterness, and wrath, and anger, and clamour and railing, and all malice are to be put away from us; we are to be kind one to another, tender-hearted, forgiving each other, even as God also in Christ forgave us, Eph. 4. 31, 32. In maintaining unity thus in the local church, our harmonious conduct would be in conformity with the unity of the Spirit which pervades the whole spiritual body.

The risen and glorified Head has made provision for the spiritual direction and care of each local assembly. The traditions of men and the bondage, or confusion, which has been brought about by them have naught to do with the unity formed by the Holy Spirit. Where a local church acts in conformity with the teaching of the word of God, it is thereby an expression of the unity of the Spirit.

There are elements of unity which characterize the whole. These are enumerated, Eph. 4. 4-6: 'There is one body, and one Spirit, even as ye were also called in one hope of your calling; one Lord, one faith, one baptism, one God and Father of all, who is over all and through all and in all'. The mention of the Trinity, 'one Spirit', 'one Lord', 'one God and Father of all', is significant. The Spirit is put first, for the immediate subject dealt with is the unity of the Spirit. Associated with Him are the spiritual and heavenly unities of the body and the hope of our calling.

The next three unities are associated with Christ. They have to do with public witness; first, the acknowledgment of Christ as Lord; second, the one faith, the complete Divine revelation, which testifies of Christ; he who holds it confesses Him; third, the one baptism, an ordinance involving the public recognition of, and identification with, Christ as Lord. Then, to crown all, 'there is one God and Father of all, who is over all' (His transcendence and supremacy), 'and through all' (His pervading and controlling power), 'and in all' (His indwelling and sustaining presence).

All these constitute 'the unity of the Spirit', v. 3, and they are enumerated as inducements for us to give diligence to keep this unity in the bond of peace. They have to do with the one church, the body of Christ, in which all believers are thus united to Him. Its unity is not yet visible, for the Head is not visible, but it will become so when He is manifested and His saints with Him.

Evidences of the New Birth - A. BROWSE

The First Epistle of John is the complement of the Gospel by the same writer. The latter was written 'that ye [believers] might **have** life'; the former, 'that ye may **know** that ye have life'. In the Gospel we are taught the way of life through God's Son, and in the Epistle we learn the nature of that life as possessed by His children. The three great words prominent in the Gospel recur here and show that life to be a **life** dwelling in **love** and walking in the **light**.

John, the apostle of love, writes to the little children who have been born into the family of God and seeks to make them at home there. He tells them what kind of a life is expected of them, towards both their Father and their brethren, and before the world.

The words 'born of God' occur nine times in the Epistle, and, as it was written to teach how the new life manifests itself, we shall naturally expect to find stated in it some of the marks that distinguish and characterize those who have really been brought into this wonderful filial relationship with God.

Selecting five passages containing the phrase 'born of God', which indicate what some of the evidences of the new life are, let us, as we consider them one by one, apply them to our own hearts and lives and see if they prove whether we are the children of God.

'Whosoever believeth that Jesus is the Christ is born of God', 1 John 5. 1. If one has been born again, his life will be a **life of faith**; for faith in Christ and in God is an evidence of spiritual life. Note the continuous tense – 'believeth'. There is not only the **initial act** of believing by which a person becomes a child of God, but the **continued habit** of believing by which the spiritual life, received at the new birth, is maintained and developed. As it was by faith in the Son of God that we were saved from the guilt and penalty of sin at the commencement of the Christian life, so it is by faith in Him all along the Christian course that we are being saved from the power of sin and enabled to live lives that are pleasing to Him. 'Kept by the power of God **through faith**'. Real faith is far more than the intellectual acceptance of a creed; it is a force which expresses itself in life, growth and fruitfulness. How do we stand this test? Are we all alive, and 'living by faith in the Son of God'?

'Whosoever is born of God doth not commit sin', 1 John 3. 9. If one has been born of God, this means a **life of freedom from sin**. Here note carefully the following scriptures. 'All unrighteousness is sin', 5. 17; 'sin is lawlessness', 3. 4 RV. 'Everyone that committeth [practises] sin is the bondslave of sin', John 8. 34 RV. 'He that committeth sin is of the devil . . . For this purpose the Son of God was manifested that he might destroy

[undo] the works of the devil', 1 John 3. 8. 'He was manifested to take away our sins; and in him is no sin. Whosoever abideth in him sinneth not; whosoever sinneth hath not seen him, neither known him', 3. 5, 6. Verse 9 does not teach that it is impossible for a born-again person to fall into sin. John is writing of the general marks which characterize the people of God and distinguish them from the unconverted. It is the characteristic of the latter that they live in sin; it is their habit to work iniquity. It is the characteristic of the former that they flee from sin; holiness is their habit and their element. The born-again one 'doth not **practise** sin, for his seed remaineth in him'. Sin is repugnant to his spiritual nature and sanctified affections. The following rendering of chapter 5 verse 18 is worth considering: 'We know that whosoever is begotten by God does not commit sin; but He (Jesus Christ) who was begotten by God keeps him, and the wicked one does not lay hold of him'; see MERCER WILSON and WEYMOUTH's translations.

Here is what an old theologian says on this subject: 'There is that *light in his mind* that shows him the evil and malignity of sin. There is that *bias upon his heart* that disposes him to loathe and hate sin. There is that *spiritual seminal principle* (or disposition) which breaks the force and power of sin. There is that *love to God* which makes him delight to do His will, so that it is contrary to the nature of his new-born soul to commit sin; and when temptation is presented, instead of yielding to the suggestions of the enemy as the ungodly habitually do, he repels the tempter, exclaiming, "How can I do this great wickedness, and sin against God?"'

But whilst the new nature implanted at the new birth is impeccable, and power to overcome temptation can be realized by the one who abides in Christ, 3. 6, we need to recall the teaching contained in the first twelve verses of the Epistle, namely: (a) that believers are not sinless; and (b) that the Father has provided a way of forgiveness and cleansing, and restoration to communion for His erring children, who do not 'practise' sin. The difference between the unbeliever and the believer regarding sins may be illustrated by the reactions of a pig and a sheep to falling into a muddy pond. The former would enjoy it as being agreeable to its nature, but the latter would not be happy until it was out of it and clean again.

'Every one that doeth righteousness is born of him [God]', 1 John 2. 29. A **righteous life** is another result and evidence of the new birth. The true and healthy Christian life is not merely passive and negative; it does not consist of **not sinning** only – not doing this and that, which the world does; it is active and positive. The born-again one 'doeth righteousness'. 'He that doeth good is of God', 3 John 11, and 'every one that doeth righteousness is born of God'. He no longer **practises** sin, but righteousness.

Consider 1 John chapter 3 verses 7, 8 RV, 'My little children, let no man lead you astray; he that doeth righteousness is righteous, even as he is righteous: he that doeth sin is of the devil'. Then, verse 10, 'In this the children of God are manifest, and the children of the devil: whosoever doeth not righteousness is not of God'. 'All unrighteousness is sin', 5. 17. 'Lord, who shall abide in thy tabernacle? He that . . . worketh righteousness', Ps. 15. 1, 2. The grace of God teaches us that, denying ungodly lusts, we should live righteously, Titus 2. 11, 12.

'Every one that loveth is born of God', 1 John 4. 7. The new life is a **life of love**.

(a) *There will be love for God the Father.* There was a time when what the Lord Jesus said to the Jews, John 5. 42, could be said of us, 'ye have not the love of God in you'. But now, having been born into the family of God, we have the love of God shed abroad in our hearts.

The most natural thing in the world is for a child to love its parents, and our heavenly Father expects His children to love Him supremely. 'Love for God' means 'obedience to His commands', 1 John 5. 3. 'O love the Lord, ye His saints.'

(b) *There will be love for the Son of God.* How can we help loving Him when He first loved us and laid down His life for us? Our love for Him will be proved by obedience to His word, by keeping His commandments and doing those things that are pleasing in His sight. 'If ye love me, ye will' – what? – 'keep my commandments', John 14. 15 RV – 'Be baptized' – 'Do this in remembrance of me'. 'If God were your Father, ye would love me', 8. 42. 'If any man love not the Lord Jesus Christ, let him be Anathema. Maranatha', 1 Cor. 16. 22.

(c) *There will be love for the brethren* – our Father's other children. 'Every one that loveth him that begat loveth him also that is begotten of him', 1 John 5. 1. 'This is the message . . . that we should love one another', 3. 11. 'Beloved, if God so loved us, we ought also to love one another . . . If we love one another, God dwelleth in us, and his love is perfected in us', 4. 11, 12. True love is practical; it does not consist of words, but deeds, 3. 17, 18. Did not our Lord say that our love for one another would be a proof of our love for Him, and a proof to the world that we are His disciples, 3. 13-15; John 13. 35?

(d) *There will be love for the lost,* and for our enemies. Having been 'found of him', we are to be actuated by the same purpose and motive that brought Him into the world, i.e., 'to seek and to save the lost'. May our prayer be:

'Lord crucified, give me a heart like Thine!
Teach me to love the dying souls of men,
And keep my heart in closest touch with Thee;
And give me love, pure Calvary love, to bring the lost to Thee'.

(e) *There should be no love for the world.* 'Love not the world, neither the things that are in the world. If any man love the world, the love of the Father is not in him', 1 John 2. 15-17. 'Know ye not that friendship with the world is enmity with God? Whoever therefore is minded to be the friend of the world is constituted enemy of God', Jas. 4. 4 JND. 'Demas has forsaken me, having loved this present world', 2 Tim. 4. 10.

'O cold ungrateful heart that can from Jesus turn,
When living fires of love should on His altar burn.

'Whatsoever is born of God overcometh the world', 1 John 5. 4. If one has been born from above, his will be a **life of victory**.

(a) *Victory over the power of indwelling sin.* 'Whosoever abideth in him sinneth not', 3. 6. 'Sin shall not have dominion over you'; see Rom. 6. 14.

(b) *Victory over the world.* 'All that has been begotten of God gets the victory over the world; and this is the victory which has gotten the victory over the world, our faith. Who is he that gets the victory over the world, but he that believes that Jesus is the Son of God?' 1 John 5. 4, 5 JND. Resolve on 'no compromise with the world'.

(c) *Victory over the flesh.* 'Walk in the Spirit, and ye shall not fulfil the lust of the flesh', Gal. 5. 16, the cravings of your lower nature. The Spirit and the flesh are antagonistic to each other, 'that ye may not do the things that ye would', v. 17 RV.

The works of the flesh are only evil continually, and until the flesh is crucified there can be no fruit of the Spirit. 'And they that are of Christ Jesus have crucified the flesh with the passions and the lusts thereof', v. 24 RV.

(d) *Victory over the devil,* 1 John 2. 13, 14. As the Lord Jesus overcame the devil's temptations by the word of God, so can every one of us. We are strong to overcome only as we 'abide in him' (our impregnable Fortress), and His word ('the sword of the Spirit') abides richly in us. We need to put on the panoply of God that we may be able to stand firm against all the artifices of the devil. By his death on the cross the Lord Jesus rendered powerless him that had the power of death. 'The God of peace shall bruise Satan under your feet shortly', Eph. 6. 10-18.[37]

(e) *Victory over false teachers,* 1 John 4. 4. These tools of Satan deny that Jesus Christ is God incarnate. But the children of God, indwelt and taught by the Holy Spirit, overcome them. Many solemn warnings regarding the destructive heresies, the ungodly lives, and the fearful doom, of these apostate teachers are given in the New Testament.[38] 'Little children, let no man lead you astray', 3. 7 RV.

'A life of victory' is God's intention (plan) for His people, and an evidence of the new birth. 'Victory is of the Lord', Prov. 21. 31 RV. We 'are more than conquerors through him that loved us', Rom. 8. 37. 'Thanks be to God, which giveth us the victory through our Lord Jesus Christ', 1 Cor. 15. 57.

---

[37] See also: Heb. 2. 14; Rom. 16. 20.

[38] See Matt. 7. 15-19; Acts 20. 29, 30; 2 Tim. 3; 2 Pet. 2; Jude 3-19; 1 John 2. 18-28.

'The victory is ours!
For us in might came forth the Mighty One;
For us He fought the fight, the triumph won;
The victory is ours'.

H. BONAR

Happy are we if these five traits of a Spirit-born and Spirit-controlled life are seen in us. The walk and witness of such a life cannot but be a blessing to others, and glorifying to God.

Perfection - D. CLAPHAM

Perfection is a word which has been given an arbitrary meaning by some people. Perhaps it is because John Wesley is said to have been the first to have coined the expression 'Christian perfection' that, to so many since, perfection is still understood to mean 'sinlessness'. However, we hope to indicate that the subject of perfection is not to be restricted in this way.

In the King James Version of the New Testament the words perfection, perfect, perfecting, perfectly, perfectness, etc., occur sixty-six times in all. But what the King James Version does not indicate is that these many occurrences are not translations of one and the same root word in the original language of the New Testament. In fact they represent eleven different Greek words, and most of these are quite commonly translated by other words, such as, complete, exactness, fitted, framed, full, keep safe, mending, physical soundness, prepared, preserve, and restore. Therefore, we need to proceed with care, examining as far as possible the underlying words, and with the many helps available to us seek to discover the scriptural doctrine of perfection.
Now there is one word in the original language which, in its several grammatical forms, is translated perfection, etc., about forty times. It is the Greek word *teleios,* and it is this word which we must try clearly to understand. It derives from the verb *teleō,* which means, 'to set out for a definite point, or goal'. But the thought which is emphasized is the goal, or objective itself, as a point of termination, rather than the course taken to reach it. From this verb comes the noun *telos,* which means a terminus, an accomplished end, a completion, a fulfilment, an issue. So it is that the Greek adjective *teleios* has the meaning of completed,

entire, fulfilled, full-grown, and only in these modified senses does it mean perfect.[39]

A careful consideration of the references given below will serve to show that we all come short of perfection in its ultimate sense. Whatever others may fancy they have attained in this respect, the apostle Paul, for one, was not numbered among the 'perfectionists'. None could lay more claim to perfection in experience, and attainment in grace, than the apostle when he wrote, 'Not as though I had already attained, either were already perfect: but I follow after, if that I may apprehend that for which also I am apprehended of Christ Jesus. Brethren, I count not myself to have apprehended: but this one thing I do, forgetting those things which are behind, and reaching forth unto those things which are before, I press toward the mark for the prize of the high calling of God in Christ Jesus', Phil. 3. 12-14. This is realism and sober-mindedness which is exemplary. He continues, 'Let us therefore, as many as be perfect, be thus minded: and if in anything ye be otherwise minded, God shall reveal even this unto you', v. 15. Now there is no contradiction here, for the word which is translated perfect has the sense of full-grown, and is applicable to those who have developed in obedience to the word, through grace; who have grown up out of a spiritually immature condition into one of intelligence in divine things. They are become manly, as opposed to being babyish, Christians. And this is altogether consistent with the consciousness of much more still to be attained. Just how much more we never know but, to the mature Christian, there is bound to be an ever deepening awareness of what has to be gained of an infinite Christ. The further behind he leaves the start of the race, as he presses forward to the finish for the prize to be won, the greater will be his sense of its surpassing worth. Note that the apostle is not concerned at all about the things which are behind him. Neither is he proud of where he has reached, though he has been running well for many a year. For him, and others like-minded, **Christ is everything**; He is the Goal, He is the Objective, He is the Prize.

---

[39] For our present purpose, the following list of references will serve to illustrate the general teaching of the New Testament bearing upon human condition, or what is connected with human aspiration, namely: Matt. 5. 48; 19. 21; Acts 20. 24; 1 Cor. 2. 6; 14. 20; Phil. 3. 12, 15; Col. 1. 28; 4. 12; Heb. 6. 1; 12. 23; Jas. 1. 4; 2. 22; 3. 2; 1 Pet. 1. 13; 1 John 2. 5; 4. 12, 17, 18.

There are, of course, many other aspects to this doctrine of perfection, but we will only briefly allude to one or two more. All believers are called to walk before God, as Noah and Abram, Gen. 6. 9; 17. 1, in uprightness and sincerity, or singleness, of heart. This is to be perfect as to one's motives and purposes. In so doing believers are to manifest love and grace toward all, let their treatment of them be what it may. Only thus will they be seen to be perfect in impartiality, as is God the Father, Matt. 5. 48. All believers are now required to move up in the great school of divine revelation, that is, to 'go on unto perfection', Heb. 6. 1. All are expected to give diligent heed to the One who speaks from heaven of the fullness that there is in Christ, and of the finality of what is made known in Christianity. But none is perfect in the absolute sense of being free from sin; note, John 8. 7; 1 John 1. 8. He who can control his tongue, however, is perfect as to his ability to bridle every other passion, for there is no evil thing more wilful, and less controllable, than a man's tongue, Jas. 3. 1, 2.

Well might we, left to ourselves, despair of reaching the ultimate of God's will and purpose for us. But 'it is God which worketh in you [individually and collectively] both to will and to do of his good pleasure', Phil. 2. 13. And of this we are sure that 'he which hath begun a good work in you will perform it until the day of Jesus Christ', 1. 6. Therefore, with good reason, we hope one day to behold Him who is perfect in every spiritual quality, and moral attribute, when we shall be with Him where He is, and then like Him, forever perfected, beyond the reach of all that spoils our lives on earth, 1 John 3. 2.

The Peace of God* - S. Probert

On 30 September 1938, British Prime Minister, Neville Chamberlain, waved aloft one of the most famous pieces of paper in world history. He had just returned from the Munich Conference having signed an agreement with the German Chancellor that the two nations would never go to war with one another again.

This was when he uttered those famous words, 'I believe it is peace for our time'. This is the peace that the world gives. The following day

Germany invaded Sudetenland. The German leader derided the agreement as just a 'scrap of paper', and invaded Poland on 1 September 1939. Britain and France declared war on Germany two days later, and the Second World War began.

In stark contrast to this, stands the peace that God gives.

The peace of God is a real peace

This world has not truly known the peace of God since the day when Adam and Eve sinned. If we could imagine what life might have been like in the Garden of Eden before that fateful day, we would probably be imagining a world at peace with God, enjoying the blissful conditions associated with the peace of God. The entrance of sin changed that, and peace has been a distant prospect for most of creation ever since.

But the peace of God is still offered to men as individuals, even if the world cannot know it. Towards the end of His time with His disciples in the upper room, the Lord Jesus said to them, 'Peace I leave with you, my peace I give unto you: not as the world giveth, give I unto you. Let not your heart be troubled, neither let it be afraid', John 14. 27. This was only a few hours before the Lord Jesus was taken by wicked hands, and crucified and slain at Calvary. With all the anguish that must have been weighing down on Him at that time, His desire for His own was that they should have His peace – the peace of God. With the peace that comes only from God, the disciples would not be troubled in heart, and would not be afraid.

Then, a few hours after His resurrection, He is reunited with His disciples. Have you noticed the first words with which He greets them? 'Peace be unto you', John 20. 19.

Often, when we are apart from our loved ones, and our thoughts are occupied with them and their needs, the first thing that comes to our mind when we are reunited with them are the thoughts that we have been dwelling upon in relation to them while we were apart. How precious, then, the thought that our blessed Saviour, while going through the agonies of the cross and the dreadful isolation of death in Satan's domain, was thinking about those that the Father had given Him, and how much they were in need of His peace. What a Saviour! The disciples were shut behind closed doors 'for fear of the Jews', so He graciously repeats His greeting a second time – 'Peace be unto you'. The peace of God is, without doubt, divine treatment for a troubled heart.

Dictionaries commonly describe 'peace' in several ways, but they generally begin by defining it in relation to what it is not – i.e., the absence of war or other hostilities. Clearly, the absence of conflict is a necessary condition for a state of peace, but it is not a sufficient condition to appreciate the peace of God. The child of God who knows the peace of God within has something much deeper and much more comforting than anything found in the world. He, or she, will not be troubled in heart, and will not be afraid. For the peace of God is **real** peace.

Real peace comes from God

The world speaks of 'making peace'. Men and women set up organizations and societies dedicated to creating 'world peace'. But it is not within their power to bring about world peace. The truth is that peace comes from God. He makes it, and He has the power to take it away.[40]

In one of the great creatorial pronouncements in the prophecy of Isaiah, Jehovah – the covenant-keeping God – speaks of the creation of peace in the same breath as the creation of light, 'I am the Lord, and there is none else. I form the light, and create darkness: **I make peace**, and create evil: I the Lord do all these things', Isa. 45. 6, 7.

The word translated here as 'evil' is never used in the word of God to mean 'sin'. God did not create sin. Indeed, as the footnote to this verse in the *Scofield Study Bible* says, 'God created evil only in the sense that He made sorrow, wretchedness, etc., to be the sure fruits of sin'.

Because God is able to make peace, He has the right to 'speak peace unto his people, and to his saints', Ps. 85. 8. None other can speak so authoritatively about peace. As has been aptly observed, 'The world's peace always has war just around the corner. But the Lord's peace is

---

[40] 'And there went out another horse that was red: and power was given to him that sat thereon to take peace from the earth', Rev. 6. 4.

different; it is not how the world gives. Rather, it is heavenly, and independent of outward circumstances'.[41] This is because real peace comes from God.

The peace of God is an everlasting peace

We have seen that the peace the world gives is not real peace; it does not last. Have you ever wondered how far you would have to look backwards into the history of the world to find a period of time when there was not a war or conflict between two (or more) nations? The historians cannot agree on a precise answer to such a question, but the general thrust of their responses is a sad indictment of the hearts of men.

For example, one history book says, 'In the last 3,421 years of recorded history only 268 have seen no war'.[42] A search of the internet revealed the followed estimate, 'It has been calculated that between 3600 BC and today there have been only 292 years of peace; that there have been over 14,500 major wars in which close to 4 billion people have perished'.[43]

Whichever figure is right, one thing is clear – if ever there has been a period of time without war or hostility, it didn't last very long. The psalmist's lament has been the sad experience of many over the centuries, 'My soul hath long dwelt with him that hateth peace. I am for peace: but when I speak, they are for war', Ps. 120. 6, 7.

Yet this was not God's intention for the world that He created. In the valley of dry bones, the Lord told Ezekiel about His plans for the restoration of Israel.[44] The fulfilment of this plan is still future. The plan contains many promises that should be a source of encouragement to the Jew today; one of the greatest of them is the covenant of peace that the Lord discloses in verse 26, 'Moreover I will make a covenant of peace with them; it shall be an everlasting covenant with them'.

---

[41] JOHN HEADING, *What the Bible Teaches: The Gospel of John*, John Ritchie Ltd., 1988. Comments on John chapter 14 verse 27.

[42] WILL AND ARIEL DURANT *The Lessons of History*, Simon and Schuster, 2012, pg. 81.

[43] Source: Peace Pledge Union, London. www.ppu.org.uk.

[44] Ezek. 37.

The Jews have felt the bitterness, resentment, and outright persecution of the world, from the time that they became a people in the slave pit of Egypt to the present day. But when, eventually, the nation of Israel receives God's covenant of peace, they will never again suffer conflict or persecution . With God's sanctuary in their midst for evermore, and His dwelling place among them, they will appreciate that the peace of God is an everlasting peace.

The believer and the peace of God

So Israel will know the peace of God in a coming day, but what about the believer in Christ in this day of grace? Can we know the peace of God here and now? Assuredly yes! However, there is a difference between having peace **with** God, and having the peace **of** God. From the moment of salvation, the Christian has peace **with** God. This is the promise of Romans chapter 5 verse 1, and it is a permanent possession, 'Therefore being justified by faith, we have peace with God through our Lord Jesus Christ'.

However, the peace of God is not an automatic consequence of conversion; it isn't 'included in the box' of salvation. It is possible to be saved, and yet not experience the peace of God. Moreover, it is possible to lose touch with the peace of God even after we have enjoyed it for many years.

Writing to the Philippians, the apostle Paul said, 'Be careful for nothing; but in everything by prayer and supplication with thanksgiving let your requests be made known unto God. And the peace of God, which passeth all understanding, shall keep your hearts and minds through Christ Jesus', Phil. 4. 6, 7.

Here, then, is the secret: the blessing of knowing the peace of God is the result of taking everything to God in prayer. In the words of JOSEPH SCRIVEN's hymn:

> 'O what peace we often forfeit, O what needless pain we bear,
> All because we do not carry everything to God in prayer'.

Is the peace of God beyond our reach? No! The peace of God 'which passeth all understanding' is, literally, better than understanding. In other words, the peace of God (the result of taking our cares to God in prayer) is more effective than every (human) reason in its power to relieve anxiety.[45] Another paraphrase might be, 'the peace of God is better than knowing the reason why'.[46]

We cannot leave this verse without observing **how** the peace of God is such an effective cure for the troubled heart. Says Paul, it 'shall keep your hearts and minds through Jesus Christ'. The word 'keep' comes from the Greek word for a sentinel, or guard. It is a military word. There was a Roman garrison stationed at Philippi to guard the city. Drawing on this imagery, Paul tells the saints at Philippi that the peace of God will stand like a sentinel to guard their hearts and their thoughts. The believer who knows the reality of Philippians chapter 4 verse 7 has found the secret place of which the psalmist wrote, 'He that dwelleth in the secret place of the most High shall abide under the shadow of the Almighty. I will say of the Lord, he is my refuge and my fortress: my God; in him will I trust. Surely he shall deliver thee from the snare of the fowler, and from the noisome pestilence. He shall cover thee with his feathers, and under his wings shalt thou trust: his truth shall be thy shield and buckler. Thou shalt not be afraid for the terror by night; nor for the arrow that flieth by day; nor for the pestilence that walketh in darkness; nor for the destruction that wasteth at noonday. A thousand shall fall at thy side, and ten thousand at thy right hand; but it shall not come nigh thee', Ps. 91. 1-7.

When protected by the peace of God, the believer will not fall prey to the snare of the fowler, and will not fear any of the other forms of attack devised by the adversary. This is another reason why Paul uses a military word (sentinel, or guard) – i.e., because he is presenting the peace of God as defending the heart and mind of the believer against the assault of the enemy.

The peace of God and the local assembly

Other than the passage in Philippians, the only other place where the exact phrase 'peace of God' is found in the King James Version is

---

[45] M. R. VINCENT, *Word Studies in the New Testament.*

[46] Attributed to IAN JACKSON.

Colossians chapter 3 verse 15, 'And let the peace of God rule in your hearts, to the which also ye are called in one body; and be ye thankful'.

Here, the Revised Version (along with many other translations) has 'peace of Christ', but this is not a distinction that need concern us. The peace of Christ **is** the peace of God.

In the passage leading up to verse 15, the apostle is urging the saints in the assembly at Colossae to exhibit towards each other those qualities that will promote peace and harmony in the company. In verse 15 he reminds them of the oneness that should characterize the local assembly. We learn here that the peace of God not only guards the hearts and minds of individual believers, but it also has an important part to play in keeping peace in the local assembly.

In the previous section we found Paul using a military word, but here he uses an athletic word – 'rule'. The literal meaning of the word is 'umpire'. Paul is not here concerned with the assault of the enemy from without, so much as quarrels within; so the soldier's word gives way to the athlete's word. How often is the peace of the local assembly spoilt by a competitive spirit? We are not to follow the example of Diotrephes,[47] who loved to have the pre-eminence in the assembly. That place belongs to Christ alone.

Anticipating his visit to Corinth, Paul was concerned that he would find in the local assembly 'debates, envyings, wraths, strifes, backbitings, whisperings, swellings, tumults'. None of these things could have existed at Corinth if the peace of God had ruled in the hearts of the saints.

When disagreements arise, and the harmony of the local assembly could be disturbed, we are to allow the peace of God to 'be umpire'. If we can do this, we will have much cause to be thankful.

Assurance - J. Boyd

The present assurance that he is truly a child of God is of paramount

---

[47] 3 John 9.

importance to the believer. To make a mistake about such a matter is too awful to contemplate. Eternity would be too late for a man to learn that; though he had tasted the good word of God, he had never really believed in Christ to the saving of his soul. Many genuine believers have, at times, been beset by doubts as to their salvation. Not that they doubt God's promises, nor Christ's ability to save, but their great concern is to know if they have really trusted Christ, if they have truly believed. Such a condition of mind, often observed when the general health is impaired, causes great anxiety of soul. Satan's onslaught today takes the same form as his temptation of Eve in the beginning, to cast doubt in the mind of man. Happily we can know how to be sure we have eternal life. To give the believer confidence in his salvation is the concern of all three persons of the Godhead. The **word of God** to him settles it; the **work of Christ** for him secures it; the **witness of the Holy Spirit** within him seals it. Let us look, then, at some of the proofs of regeneration as set forth in these three propositions.

The word of God. In the word of God we find much to give us the assurance of salvation. John explicitly states that this was why he wrote his first Epistle, 1 John 5. 13. Note his recurring use of the words 'we know'. In a sevenfold use of these words he tells us how we can know.

1. *If we keep God's commandments* – desiring to do His will, 2. 3.
2. *If we keep His word* – having respect for the truth of God, 2. 5.
3. *If we do righteousness* – because God is righteous, and those begotten of Him do likewise, 2. 29.
4. *If we do not continually practise sin* – this is foreign to the new nature of a child of God, 3. 9.
5. *If we love our brethren* – if we do not love our brethren we have not yet passed from death unto life, 3. 14.
6. *If we heed the messengers of God* – if we are born again we know God's true servants, and we desire to hear them, 2. 6.
7. *If we overcome the world* – the ability to say 'no' to the blandishments of the world, 5. 4.

The believer often receives assurance through doing things God has enjoined upon him; for example, confessing Jesus as Lord, being baptized, and separating himself from the world. Thus, growth in grace assures him that his calling and election are sure, 2 Pet. 1. 10. Let us then rejoice in the assurance that God gives us from His word. We can know, even now, that we have eternal life. We should examine ourselves to see if we be in the faith, 2 Cor. 13. 5. Take the advice of SAMUEL RUTHERFORD; 'Search yourself with the candle of God, and try if the life of God be in you'. It is a healthy exercise.

The Work of Christ. The Lord Jesus Christ defined eternal life as knowing God, John 17. 3. He who is knowing more of God is assured that he possesses eternal life. The true believer has peace with God, having no fear of punishment, Rom. 5. 1; he has access to God in prayer, v. 2; he rejoices in the hope of the glory of God, v. 2; he is conscious of the unfailing love of God, 8. 39; he is comforted by God in affliction, 2 Cor. 1. 4; he accepts chastening as God's way of dealing with His true-born sons, Heb. 12. 7, 8.

Our salvation depends, however, not on what we are, nor on what we do, but on Christ. He gives His sheep eternal life, and they shall never perish, John 10. 28. We do not depend on our ability to believe, nor on our capacity to hold on, but on His strength to keep us. He is able to save to the uttermost, Heb. 7. 25. Through His death He has perfected for ever them that are sanctified, Heb. 10. 14. Thus Christian assurance is based on the work of the Lord Jesus Christ.

The Witness of the Holy Spirit. The presence of the indwelling Holy Spirit is a guarantee of the new birth. When Peter was reporting the conversion of Cornelius and his household, he informed his brethren at Jerusalem that God had given to them the Holy Spirit. Note the company's conclusions: 'Then hath God also to the Gentiles granted repentance unto life', Acts 11. 18.

How can I know that the Holy Spirit dwells within me? By appreciating His activity. He makes me think well of Christ, for the Spirit glorifies the Son. Through the Spirit I desire to speak to God, and call Him Father, Gal. 4. 6. He causes me to love as God loves, even to loving my enemies, Rom. 5. 5. He produces fruit, the nine-fold cluster of graces described in Galatians chapter 5 verses 22 to 23. If these are present in my life I am assured that the Holy Spirit lives within me, for these, like the fruit of a tree, are the outward manifestations of an indwelling power.

The presence of a conflict in my mind assures me of the Holy Spirit dwelling within me, v. 17. If I have an urge to keep separate from the world, it is the Holy Spirit working within me. The flesh delights in the things of the world, but the Spirit lusts against them. If I have a longing to go to a prayer meeting, it is from the Spirit, for the flesh has no love for prayer meetings. The unregenerate have none of these conflicts, for they have no indwelling Holy Spirit. Such evidence of the Holy Spirit's activity in my life gives me the grand assurance of eternal life.

The Christian's assurance, therefore, rests on the word of God to him, the work of Christ for him, and the witness of the Holy Spirit in him. Thus, assurance glorifies God. Redemption is based on God's ability. We ought, like Abraham, to be fully persuaded that what God has promised He is able also to perform, Rom. 4. 21. Assurance is a part of the gospel message, 1 Thess. 1. 5. God intended that joy, not doubt, should accompany salvation. The true believer can say with the apostle Paul, 'I know whom I have believed, and am persuaded that he is able to keep that which I have committed unto him against that day', 2 Tim. 1. 12.

'What from Christ the soul can sever,
Bound by everlasting bonds?
Once in Him, in Him for ever,
Thus the eternal covenant stands.
None shall pluck thee
From the Strength of Israel's hands'.

J. KENT

The Assurance of Salvation* - J. E. TODD

Those who deny that believers are now justified by the blood of Christ as a gift, are those who deny the grace of God. They also deny the assurance of salvation, for if one's own works, in any way or to any degree, contribute to our salvation, then we would be in a perpetual state of doubt. For if we should stand before the throne of God on the grounds of our merit, we could never know until the judgement day if we are good enough. But such a situation is disallowed by scripture. For scripture declares that we can all know, here and now, that we have failed the test of God's law. 'There is none righteous, no, not one . . . for there is no difference: for all have sinned, and come short of the glory of God', Rom. 3. 10, 23. Answering the question, 'Who then can be saved?', the Lord Jesus Christ replied, 'With men this is impossible; but with God all things are possible', Matt. 19. 25, 26. Salvation is by grace because it is impossible for it to be achieved by merit. 'Being justified freely by his grace through the redemption that is in Christ Jesus', Rom. 3. 24. 'I do not frustrate the grace of God: for if righteousness come by the law, then Christ is dead in vain', Gal. 2. 21. 'And if by grace, then it is no more of works: otherwise grace is no more grace', Rom. 11. 6.

A Completed Work

Very often the verbs used in scripture to speak of salvation are in the perfect tense, that is, speaking of a work that has been completed. These tenses are made clear in the Revised Standard Version. 'Since we are justified by faith', Rom. 5. 1. 'We are now justified by his blood', v. 9. 'By grace you have been saved', Eph. 2. 8. 'You have been born anew', 1 Pet. 1. 23.

The apostle John in his first letter lists those things which one can know, that is, one who has repented of sin and committed himself to Christ. The believer is the present possessor of sins forgiven, the Holy Spirit and eternal life.[48]

The apostle Paul also speaks of the salvation of true believers as an accomplished fact. We are already inside the kingdom of God 'who hath delivered us from the power of darkness, and hath translated us into the kingdom of his dear Son', Col. 1. 13. We are already guaranteed our heavenly inheritance by the seal of the Holy Spirit, 'ye were sealed with that holy Spirit of promise, which is the earnest (guarantee) of our inheritance until the redemption of the purchased possession', Eph. 1. 13, 14. We are already justified on grounds other than law keeping, 'by him all that believe are justified from all things, from which ye could not be justified by the law of Moses', Acts 13. 39.

The Sphere of Life

The Lord Jesus Christ Himself made it clear that those who exercise

---

[48] 'Ye know that he was manifested to take away our sins', 1 John 3. 5. 'We know that he abideth in us, by the Spirit which he hath given us', 3. 24. 'Ye may know that ye have eternal life', 5. 13.

faith in Him have already passed out of the sphere of death and judgement into the sphere of life, 'Verily, verily, I say unto you, he that heareth my word, and believeth on him that sent me, hath everlasting life, and shall not come into condemnation [judgement]; but is passed from death unto life', John 5. 24. The Good Shepherd has committed Himself as responsible for the final perseverance of His own sheep, 'I give unto them eternal life; and they shall never perish, neither shall any man pluck them out of my hand', 10. 28.

It is maintained by some religious people that to be assured of salvation is presumptuous and lacking in humility, indeed to be arrogant. But if God declares in His word that the believer in Christ is already saved, then to doubt one's salvation would be folly. Rather than being humble, it would be the supreme arrogance to contradict God and devalue the redeeming work of Christ.

With the divine declaration of an assured salvation, God is giving to the believer a solid foundation upon which to build a life of devotion to the Lord Jesus Christ.

In whatever measure people may look to themselves for their hope of salvation they are filled with doubts and fears. But the great purpose of scripture is to direct our attention to the person of the Son of God as the Saviour of the world, that we might place our trust in Him.

Let us trace the work of the Lord Jesus Christ as He enacts and fulfils the Father's plan of salvation. 'The Father sent the Son to be the Saviour of the world'; 'God sent his only begotten Son into the world, that we might live through him', 1 John 4. 14; 4. 9. The Son came into the world at the bidding of the Father, 'the word was made flesh, and dwelt among us', John 1. 14. He came for the express purpose of bringing salvation, 'thou shalt call his name Jesus [Saviour]: for he shall save his people from their sins', Matt. 1. 21.

The Lord lived His human life under the law, 'made under the law', Gal. 4. 4, but without sin or sinning, for 'in him is no sin', 1 John 3. 5. 'Who did no sin', 1 Pet. 2. 22. If He had sinned He must have borne His own sin and, therefore, could not have borne the sins of others. 'Ye know that ye were not redeemed with corruptible things . . . but with the precious blood of Christ . . . a lamb without blemish and without spot', 1. 18, 19. As the sinless One He could offer Himself to God as the atoning sacrifice for sins, 'Christ . . . offered himself without spot to God', Heb. 9. 14. The Lord Jesus Christ made a complete and actual atonement for the sins of the believer, 'who his own self bare our sins in his own body on the tree', 1 Pet. 2. 24. He made a sufficient and potential atonement for the sins of the whole world, 'he is the propitiation for our sins: and not for ours only, but also for the sins of the whole world', 1 John 2. 2. So perfect, complete and sufficient is His atoning death that the believer is now justified, 'being now justified by his blood', Rom. 5. 9. The believer has received God's final verdict, 'it is God that justifieth', 8. 33.

The Father raised Him from the dead, 'Christ was raised up from the dead by the glory of the Father', 6. 4. The resurrection of Christ fulfils two vital roles in God's plan of salvation. First, it declares the Father's complete satisfaction with, and acceptance of, the sacrifice of His Son for sin. 'Jesus our Lord . . . who was delivered for our offences, and was raised again for our justification', 4. 25. Second, the Lord Jesus Christ is alive and able to fulfil His promise to send from the Father the gift of the Holy Spirit into the life of each believer. 'I will pray the Father, and he shall give you another Comforter, that he may abide with you for ever', John 14. 16. Thus, the believer is justified by the blood of Christ and sanctified by the Spirit of Christ. In receiving the life of the risen Christ in the person of the Holy Spirit, the believer is born again and can now live in the power of this new life.

Although the purpose of the Christian life is that we should not sin, nevertheless we do sin. But the risen living Lord Jesus acts as our advocate in the very presence of the Father. 'My little children, these things write I unto you, that ye sin not. And if any man sin, we have an advocate with the Father, Jesus Christ the righteous', 1 John 2. 1. 'If we say that we have no sin, we deceive ourselves, and the truth is not in us. If we confess our sins, he is faithful and just to forgive us our sins, and to cleanse us from all unrighteousness', 1. 8, 9.

There is only one sense in which the saving work of the Lord Jesus Christ is incomplete. He has justified us by His blood, He is sanctifying us by His Spirit, but He is yet to glorify us by His coming again. 'So Christ was once offered to bear the sins of many; and unto them that look for him shall he appear the second time without sin unto salvation', Heb. 9. 28.

Thus, as we survey the completed work of Christ as set before us in holy scripture, we can readily see that He has provided for us a complete salvation. As we trust in Him and His redeeming work, we can enjoy the peace of knowing that we are saved. 'Which hope we have as an anchor of the soul, both sure and steadfast, and which entereth into that within the veil; whither the forerunner is for us entered, even Jesus', Heb. 6. 19, 20.

'For the gifts and the call of God are irrevocable', Rom. 11. 29 RSV. This means that God's decisions are unalterable. In the context of this remarkable statement we are told that, despite the weaknesses of the nation of Israel, God will fulfil for them every promise He made to Abraham. When God gives a gift He never takes it back. When God makes a call He never changes His mind. Thus, what God has given and promised to the believer, for the sake of His Son's redeeming work, will never be revoked or changed.

What God has already done in Christ for the believer shows that salvation is an accomplished fact. The scriptures record the many present possessions of the Christian.

The Christian's sins are forgiven, Eph. 1. 7. The sins are forgiven because Christ has paid the penalty for them by the shedding of His blood.

The Christian has peace with God, Rom. 5. 1. The problem of sin's guilt having been solved and the threat of its subsequent judgement having been removed, the Christian is now reconciled to God and is at peace with God.

The Christian has received the gift of the Holy Spirit, Eph. 1. 13. The life of God has been revealed in the person of God the Son, 'the only begotten Son, which is in the bosom of the Father, he hath declared him', John 1. 18. That same divine life has been imparted to the Christian by God the Holy Spirit, 'whereby are given unto us exceeding great and precious promises: that by these ye might be partakers of the divine nature', 2 Pet. 1. 4.

The Christian has been born again, 1 Pet. 1. 23. By the gift of the Holy Spirit the Christian has received new spiritual life, the life of the risen Christ; God has 'made us alive together with Christ', Eph. 2. 5 RSV.

The Christian is now a son of God, Gal. 4. 6. 'And I will be a Father unto you, and ye shall be my sons and daughters, saith the Lord Almighty', 2 Cor. 6. 18. We have not only been adopted into the family of God, Gal. 4. 5; Eph. 1. 5, but we have been born into God's family by the spiritual rebirth of the Spirit.

The Christian is a member of the church, the company of the redeemed. The word 'church' in the original means a 'calling out', 'for by one Spirit are we all baptized into one body', 1 Cor. 12. 13. Christians do not belong to the church, they are the church, the members of the body of Christ.

The Christian has eternal life as a present possession, 1 John 5. 13. Eternal life does not begin for the Christian at death, it began at conversion.

The Christian is enrolled as a citizen of heaven, Phil. 3. 20. The roll of the citizens of the heavenly Jerusalem, 'they which are written in the Lamb's book of life', Rev. 21. 27, was completed before the creation of the world in the foreknowledge of God, see 17. 8. We are to rejoice in this stupendous fact, 'Rejoice, because your names are written in heaven', Luke 10. 20.

These gifts of God's grace will never be taken back. 'For the gifts and the call of God are irrevocable', Rom. 11. 29 RSV. Our assurance of salvation is founded upon what our Lord has already given to us and no one can take it away from us.

Living a New Life

As with all other things, the reality of a person's experience of salvation is proved by its results. Does it work? 'Even so faith, if it hath not works, is dead, being alone', Jas. 2. 17. The Lord Himself spoke of many types of people who claimed to be saved but were not saved. The shallow, 'when they have heard the word, immediately receive it with gladness;

and have no root in themselves, and so endure but for a time', Mark 4. 16, 17. The religious, 'Lord, Lord, have we not prophesied in thy name? and in thy name have cast out devils? and in thy name done many wonderful works? . . . I never knew you: depart from me', Matt. 7. 22, 23. The moralist, 'Certain which trusted in themselves that they were righteous . . . God, I thank thee, that I am not as other men are, extortioners, unjust, adulterers, or even as this publican', Luke 18. 9-14.

The same argument against the gospel of grace is used today as it was 2,000 years ago. 'Let us do evil, that good may come . . . shall we continue in sin, that grace may abound? . . . shall we sin, because we are not under the law, but under grace?', Rom. 3. 8; 6. 1, 15. The answer to these questions is not that we would lose our salvation if we sin. The answer of scripture is, 'God forbid. How shall we, that are dead to sin, live any longer therein?' 6. 2. As portrayed in our baptism, the believer has died to the old life of sin and is now raised up to live a new life in the power of the Holy Spirit, vv. 3, 4. The Christian has been born again of the Spirit of God. And the fruit of that Spirit is love, joy and peace; patience, kindness and goodness; loyalty, gentleness and self-control, see Gal. 5. 22, 23. The practising of these spiritual virtues is the concrete evidence that assures us that we are saved, that we are born again of the Spirit of God. 'And these are they which are sown on good ground; such as hear the word, and receive it, and bring forth fruit, some thirtyfold, some sixty, and some an hundred', Mark 4. 20. 'We know that we have passed from death unto life, because we love the brethren', 1 John 3. 14.

Security

In John chapter 10 the Lord speaks of the security of His sheep, 'I give unto them eternal life; and they shall never perish', v. 28. In Matthew chapter 25 the Lord speaks of the conduct of His sheep, 'the Son of man . . . he shall set the sheep on his right hand . . . ye gave me meat . . . ye gave me drink . . . ye took me in . . . ye clothed me . . . ye visited me . . . ye came unto me . . . inasmuch as ye have done it unto one of the least of these my brethren, ye have done it unto me', vv. 31-40. The conduct of the Lord's sheep is the present evidence of their eternal security, Luke 6. 46.

The new birth is a spiritual experience, therefore invisible, but, like the invisible wind, its existence is known by the results it produces. 'Ye must be born again. The wind bloweth where it listeth, and thou hearest the sound thereof, but canst not tell whence it cometh, and whither it goeth: so is every one that is born of the Spirit', John 3. 7, 8. In the case of the invisible wind it is the sound of it that proves its reality. In the case of the new birth it is the new kind of living that proves its reality. The new birth is invisible because it consists of the inward attitudes of repentance and faith, also the invisible incoming of the Holy Spirit. It is the good works that are the visible and tangible proof of the inward spiritual experience. 'For we are his workmanship, created in Christ Jesus unto good works, which God hath before ordained that we should walk in them', Eph. 2. 10. As the Christian lives the new life, so he or she has the continual assurance of their salvation.

The Purpose of Salvation

As Christians we must always remember that the purpose of salvation is not only to save our souls from judgement but also to save our lives from sinning, and even more to conform our lives to the life of Christ. 'We know that, when he shall appear, we shall be like him; for we shall see him as he is. And every man that hath this hope in him purifieth himself, even as he is pure', 1 John 3. 2, 3. 'The great God and our Saviour Jesus Christ; who gave himself for us, that he might redeem us from all iniquity and purify unto himself a peculiar people, zealous of good works. These things speak, and exhort, and rebuke with all authority. Let no man despise thee', Titus 2. 13-15.

' It is a good thing to be saved and know it.
It is a better thing to be saved and show it'.

Paul's Seven Men - R. J. K. JEFFERY

In his writings, Paul makes frequent allusions to men of seven different classes. In the broad outlook, he distinguishes only two, namely 'saved' and 'lost', as in 1 Corinthians chapter 1 verse 18, where he speaks of 'them that perish' and those 'which are saved'. But when he wishes to speak of those of the old order 'in Adam', and those of the 'new creation', 2 Cor. 5. 17 JND, he uses varying prefixes to denote his seven men. Let us look at these, noticing how thoroughly the apostle by the Spirit of God has set forth these things for our instruction.

The First Man. Adam was the head and the first of the race; see Acts 17. 26. He was 'created', Gen. 1. 27; he was 'formed', 2. 7; he joined Eve in disobedience, 3. 6. The fruit of this is described in Genesis chapter 3 by the words 'afraid', v. 10; 'sorrow', v. 16; 'cursed is the ground', v. 17; 'sweat', v. 19. Guilt is implied in verses 12-13, and banishment in verse 24. The apostle writes 'The first man is of the earth, earthy', 1 Cor. 15. 47, and this man is confined within the limitations of all that is of the earth. Moreover, this is characteristic of the whole human race, 'As is the earthy (man of dust), such are they also that are earthy', v. 48. We see then that we derive our nature from this first man; sinners in the sight of God have the sentence of death, through sin, upon them, Rom. 5. 12; 6. 23.

The Natural Man. The natural man is another man often alluded to by Paul. He is the ordinary unconverted man, whether educated or illiterate, civilized or uncivilized, religious or not. He is governed by natural instincts, appetites and senses. In 1 Corinthians chapter 2 verse 14, Paul says of the natural man that he 'receiveth not the things of the Spirit of God: for they are foolishness unto him: neither can he know them, because they are spiritually discerned'. From this and other scriptures we see, then, that this natural man is unable to understand the things of God; like the pious and learned Nicodemus, he knew not 'these things', John 3. 10, for the things of God are only made known to man by the Spirit of God, 1 Cor. 2. 11. The Spirit indwells every born-again person, thus enabling them to receive the things of God.

The New Man. We now come to a brief consideration of the new man, who is born again and a Christian in the true sense. The proper rendering of 2 Corinthians chapter 5 verse 17 is, 'Therefore if any man be in Christ, he is a **new creation**'. Such a man has not mended his ways or taken up religion; rather he has been born again, having repented of his sins and having received the Lord Jesus Christ as Lord and Saviour. Thus, according to the promise of God, he has received the divine gift of everlasting life, John 5. 24. Indwelt by the Holy Spirit, such men are 'partakers of the divine nature', 2 Pet. 1. 4, having been 'born again . . . by the word of God', 1 Pet. 1. 23.

There should be no confusion between this 'new man' and the 'new man' in Ephesians chapter 2 verse 15, where the apostle writes of the

Jew and Gentile made one in Christ, the 'middle wall of partition' having been broken down by the cross.

The Old Man. This name is not, of course, a reference to some aged person as some might suppose; rather, it is the term that Paul uses to denote that old nature in the believer that is still present 'to tempt and annoy'. The great apostle was no less troubled by the old man than any of us. He is very emphatic about identifying him and his works, and gives us Spirit-taught advice as to how we are to deal with him. In Romans chapter 6 verse 6, for example, he writes, 'our old man is crucified with him'; this is the language of **faith**. Believing that Christ died for us, we reckon ourselves 'to be dead indeed unto sin', v. 11. The language of faith is supplemented by **works**. For example, 'put off concerning the former conversation [behaviour] the old man, which is corrupt according to the deceitful lusts', Eph. 4. 22; 'put on the new man . . . putting away' things characteristic of the old man, vv. 24-31.

The Carnal Man. This is Paul's description of a Christian who is not getting on very well in the life of faith. Carnal is another word for 'fleshly', denoting that behaviour which is similar to that of any unconverted person. It is the exact opposite of 'spiritual', Rom. 8. 5-9. In these verses the apostle points out the way in which the carnal mind is opposed to the spiritual mind. The carnal mind manifests itself in many ways; see, for example, 1 Cor. 3. 1-4. In this passage, Paul points out to the saints at Corinth the marks of their carnality, namely, envying, strife and divisions. Because of this, they were unable to take the meat of the word of God, and, as babes stunted in growth, they could only assimilate milk, or the elementary truths of the gospel. Paul's ministry amongst the Corinthians was thus a restricted ministry; he could not speak unto them as unto spiritual, v. 1.

Some of the Hebrews were also stunted through carnality, Heb. 5. 13. They were dull of hearing, so, instead of being teachers as they ought to have been, they had need to be taught again the rudiments of the word of God. Their sluggishness produced hardness of hearing, v. 11, and loss of memory, v. 12.

The Spiritual Man. Here is a man whom we should all seek to emulate. The spiritual man is one whom the Spirit not only indwells (as is true of every believer, Rom. 8. 9), but also controls. He has the ability to 'know the things . . . of God', 1 Cor. 2. 12, to speak words which the Holy Spirit teaches, v. 13, and to recognize and acknowledge 'the commandments of the Lord', 14. 37. One of his most useful spheres is in the practical realm, where his spirituality is such that it disproves the strange notion held by some that one can become so spiritually minded as to become of no earthly use. Nothing could be further from the truth.

To what sort of person does Paul appeal when he seeks spiritual first-aid for a believer who falls into sin? Does he appeal to the brother who has a persuasive manner, or the brother who is an employer and knows how to handle offenders? Does he suggest obtaining help from one who has rather an overbearing manner in the assembly and might scare the wrongdoer into getting things put right? No! the apostle has had a long experience helping those who have fallen by the way, and is well qualified to give his advice as led by the Spirit of God. Consider Galatians chapter 6 verse 1, for example, 'Brethren, if a man be overtaken in a fault [this may be called a mishap], ye which are **spiritual**, restore such an one in the spirit of meekness; considering thyself, lest thou also be tempted'. The spiritual man is called in to render first-aid to his fallen brother. His primary object is restoration, not remonstration. He will not assume the spirit of the Pharisee, and say in effect, 'I am not as other men are', Luke 18. 11, or 'this is not the way I should behave'. Rather, he will be as his Master, 'meek and lowly in heart', Matt. 11. 29, and in such a spirit he will be used by the Lord to effect the restoration of the one who has been overtaken. At the same time, he will consider himself liable to be tempted in the same way, and will remember the exhortation, 'let him that thinketh he standeth take heed lest he fall', 1 Cor. 10. 12.

The spiritual man (or woman) acts in the same manner as did the Samaritan in Luke chapter 10 verse 33. Seeing the unfortunate traveller fallen amongst thieves, he 'came where he was', and rendered loving help. Or, again, the prophet Jeremiah takes his place with the nation of Israel and confesses, 'The crown is fallen from our head: woe unto us, that we have sinned', Lam. 5. 16. He identifies himself with a fallen people, and cries to the Lord for their recovery.

7. The Second Man. Alternatively, the second Man is called 'the last

Adam', and clearly refers to our Lord Jesus Christ. He is the second Man in that He is head of the new creation; He is 'from heaven', as distinct from the first man who is 'of the earth, earthy', 1 Cor. 15. 47. In using the title 'the last Adam', v. 45, Paul indicates that there will not be another.

Just as we have borne the image of the earthy so 'we shall also bear the image of the heavenly', v. 49. What an incentive for the believer to seek to show those features of the heavenly Man now! As we read of the Lord Jesus in the Gospel records, we are given a glimpse of how very different He was from all other men. There was a complete absence of all those Adamic marks of failure which so mar even the best of Christians.

As we have briefly noted these seven men in Paul's writings, may the lessons that God would teach us become more clear, and by the help of His Holy Spirit may we be enabled to bear the image of the second Man, as did those early disciples, when the people 'took knowledge of them, that they had been with Jesus', Acts 4. 13.

Access, Prayer, and Worship - H. A. Barnes

We now consider what must surely be one of the Christian's greatest privileges while here on earth: access and prayer to, and worship of, our God and Father. It is a privilege we need to appreciate and appropriate more in our lives here below. We shall deal with these subjects separately, giving a general outline of each, and readers are encouraged to pursue the study of these subjects themselves from the scriptures.

Access. The literal meaning of the word translated 'access' in the New Testament is 'to bring near'. We might think that its meaning is just 'the way by which we enter', but this comes short of the true meaning. The way the Greek word is otherwise translated in other contexts in the New Testament, apart from having access to the Father, illustrates this point. The debtor was brought to the creditor, Matt. 18. 24; he did not want to come, but was 'brought near'. The father of the son needing healing was told to 'bring thy son hither', Luke 9. 41; the son could not come himself, so had to be 'brought near'; see also Acts 16. 20; 27. 27. The Christian's position was previously 'afar off', Eph. 2. 17, but he has been 'brought near'; access has been given to him. Previously he did not want to come near, being an enemy, Col. 1. 21, neither was he able to, being dead, 2 Cor. 5. 14. The moral order is: justification, for we were guilty; peace, for we were enemies; then access, Rom. 5. 2, 'through the Lord Jesus Christ' and 'by one Spirit to the Father', Eph. 2. 18. We now come near by the new and living way, Heb. 10. 20. We have been brought near forever in God's sight, 1 Pet. 3. 18, (that is positionally), but are called upon to use this access day by day, Heb. 10. 22 (that is practically).

In the Old Testament it is clear that 'the way into the holiest of all was not yet made manifest', Heb. 9. 8. Free continual access was not available into the 'holy of holies' of the tabernacle. Limited access was available to certain classes of people, namely the priests, to the outer parts of the tabernacle, but complete access was exclusively reserved for the high priest, and this was limited to a brief annual event.

The continual availability of access to God's very presence thus came as a wonderful surprise to the believer, in fact, as STIER says: 'no believer under the Old Testament dared or could, though under a dispensation of preparatory grace, approach God so freely and openly, so fearlessly and joyfully, so closely and intimately, as we now, who come to the Father by the blood of Jesus His Son'.

This privilege is to be secured by faith and used with boldness. Some Hebrew believers in New Testament times, although they knew that the blood of Christ had secured the right of entry, and that their faith in Him gave them the objective right, yet they lacked the subjective boldness to enter. Perhaps they were robbed of that privilege by listening to those still with us, who were deceived into thinking that access is the right of entry into a certain place on earth, and that worship is connected with a material form. Access is enjoyed with 'a true heart in full assurance of faith', Heb. 10. 20; Isa. 38. 3.

Access is claimed in the person of the Lord Jesus Christ, Eph. 3. 12; 'no man cometh unto the Father, but by me', John 14. 6, either for initial or continual access to God. Only our sin and unbelief hold us back from continual enjoyment of it.

Prayer. We may now consider the things that we wish to be occupied with in God's presence, after having been assured of entry. The first of these is prayer.

Prayer stems from the fact that we are still connected with earth; contrast worship, which originates in our connection with heaven. Prayer, we are told, 'is the Christian's vital breath', and, like the air we breathe, is made up of many components; included are:

- Intercession: for those who cannot or do not pray, Luke 23. 34;
- Meditation: a prayerful attitude over God's word, Ps. 27. 11;
- Petition: for our own and fellow believers' needs, 1 Thess. 5. 25;
- Adoration: concerning what He is; see later;
- Confession: of known sin, 1 John 1. 9;
- Thanksgiving: for His blessings, 1 Cor. 15. 57; 2 Cor. 8. 16.

Prayer, to be most effective, should be characterized by: persistence, 1 Thess. 5. 17; faith, Jas. 5. 15; knowledge, 1 Cor. 14. 15; acceptance, Matt. 6. 10; holy living, Jas. 5. 16, and reverence, Matt. 6. 9. It is generally addressed to the Father, should be in the Spirit, and is presented through the Son.[49] Public prayer, in a mixed congregation, is to be carried out by 'the **men**', 1 Tim. 2. 8 RV, JND, with the women's heads covered, 1 Cor. 11. 13. Public prayer is not more elevated, better, or more quickly answered, by being loud and longwinded. The shortest, quietest (though not public) prayers have often been the more quickly answered and more far reaching, Neh. 2. 4; Matt. 14. 30.

The Lord Jesus, as the pattern man, and as our true example, has left the record of a life of constant private and public prayer, before and during every event of His life; e.g. Luke 6. 12; 23. 34, even on the cross.
Continual prayer characterized the early church, Acts 2. 42; 4. 31, which 'advanced on its knees', and prayer is constantly commended by the apostle Paul, 1 Thess. 5. 17.

Prayer, although as natural to a Christian as a child speaking to his father, has, like natural speech, to be learned. The disciples

---

[49] Eph. 3. 14; Jude 20; John 14. 14.

acknowledged this in asking the Lord Jesus to teach them to pray, just as John the Baptist had taught his disciples, Luke 11. 1.

Prayer, when learned and practised, becomes the means of two-way communication between earth and heaven. We are able to speak to our Father in heaven, and He is able to send blessing to this earth by means of our prayers. Unbelievers have severed connections between a holy heaven and a sinful earth, but the Christian stands as the link, for, though on earth, he has audience in heaven.

The passage of prayer to heaven can be interfered with, just as radio waves can be interrupted by adverse conditions. Unconfessed sin in the life of the believer leads to our prayers not being heard, 'If my people, which are called by my name, shall humble themselves, and pray, and seek my face, and turn from their wicked ways; then will I hear from heaven', 2 Chr. 7. 14. A bad conscience is sure to wreck our prayer life, 1 Tim. 1. 19. Of vain repetitive prayers, Matt. 6. 7, we know:

> 'My words fly up, my thoughts remain below,
> Words without thoughts, never to heaven go'.

Scripturally approved subjects for prayer include: the Lord's servants and their work for Him, 1 Thess. 5. 25, for more of the Lord's servants, Matt. 9. 38; for one another, Jas. 5. 16; for all men; for kings; and for all that are in authority, 1 Tim. 2. 1, 2.

Prayer, like access, is to be associated with faith.[50] In particular let us notice Mark chapter 11 verse 24, 'What things soever ye desire, when ye pray, believe that ye receive them, and ye shall have them'. The Greek word here rendered 'receive' occurs 237 times in the New Testament; it is translated 133 times as 'receive' and 104 times as 'take'. It denotes the definite act of faith which receives or takes the thing asked for.

Of course, the prayer of faith grows. GEORGE MULLER, a man whose life was marked by remarkable answers to prayer, testified that through sixty years his faith had steadily grown. Shortly before his death he said, 'Today, if it were the will of God, I could as easily trust God for a million

---

[50] Matt. 8. 13; 21. 21, 22; Jas. 1. 6-8.

dollars as I could have trusted Him for a few rolls for breakfast in the early years of our orphanage work'. God asks us to believe Him for small things before He gives us the conviction concerning His will to pray the prayer of faith for a greater thing. Being in the will of God is the secret of successful prayer, 1 John 5. 14; Luke 11. 2. When this is so, something does take place as a result of our prayers, which otherwise would not take place, either **before**, Isa. 65. 24, **during**, Dan. 9. 23, or **after**, *2* Cor. 1. 11; Philem. 22, our prayers.

Lastly, when all is done, and we feel perhaps we have failed, we remember that the Spirit Himself 'maketh intercession for us', Rom. 8. 26.

Worship. 'Bowed down', 'bend the knee', 'fell down', 'fell at His feet' – such phrases characterize worship, because it is a complete diminishing of self, which sinks out of view as we become occupied in thought and word only with the worth and value of God the Father and the Son, through the Spirit. This is the highest occupation of redeemed man; it is spiritual (above material, above mental); it can be imitated but not substituted.

Worship is above prayer, although while we are still 'in the flesh', it usually follows it, for the unburdened heart becomes a liberated, worshipping heart.

Although the Father is seeking worshippers, He does not do so without reference to His eternal standards, for they that worship God must worship Him 'in spirit and in truth'. The Lord Jesus taught this to one who had a wrong idea of the location and condition for worship, John 4. 21. The Father is seeking true (*lit.* real, genuine) worshippers as opposed to those who were 'apparent, false or pseudo'.

Worship had always been characterized by specific locations, Gen. 22. 5 (first mention of worship), and conditions, 24. 26; Exod. 4. 31. But worship today is 'in spirit', not in a place or building, and 'in truth' as the correct condition.

The Old Testament ends its consideration of worship by mentioning the future worship of the divine King, Zech. 14. 16, 18, while the New

Testament opens with the magi seeking to worship One born King, Matt. 2. 2, but even there false worship is anticipated alongside the true, v. 8.

Matthew tells us that the Lord Jesus was the object of worship: of the leper, 8. 2; a ruler, 9. 18; the disciples, 14. 33; the Syro-Phoenician woman, 15. 25, and Zebedee's mother, 20. 20. Not all were allowed to worship Him on earth, John 12. 20, but all in heaven worship Him, Rev. 5. 13.

Knowing the Will of God - A. Rouse

Perhaps the most important question for a devoted Christian is 'How to know the will of God for my life?' And perhaps the most perplexing one is, 'How to discover that will, taking into account the complex life we live?' Further, when that will has been discovered, perhaps the most pressing question is, 'How to do that will, in view of the weakness of my flesh and the power of opposing influences from without?'

A Beautiful Experience. First of all, let us clear away a misconception which is all too common. The will of God is not hard, irksome and oppressive. To be in the pathway of the will of God is a beautiful experience, bringing us into an enjoyment of His actions of ineffable love, infinite wisdom and eternal righteousness, and making life on earth a harmony of happiness and holiness so that 'days of heaven on earth' may truly be enjoyed now. The highest joy, the greatest usefulness is found in living to the will of God and no longer to the desires of self or of others. His will, indeed, is 'good and acceptable and perfect'.

How to Know the Will of God. How, then, am I to know the will of God for, and in, my life? It would seem that there are three necessities: (1) a passion for; (2) the perception of; and (3) persistence in, His will. Passion for the will of God is seen in a pattern – a person; perception of that will is discovered in the principles of His word; persistence in His will is accomplished by the Holy Spirit's power.

No life has reached its fullness until the passion for the will of God has been gained. This passion is seen in the pattern: and the pattern in a person. God has made known His will as to human life once and for ever, in the principles and practice of life in a man, the perfect Man – Jesus Christ. He was the only one who could say to God, 'Lo, I come to do thy will'; 'I delight to do thy will'; 'My meat is to do the will of him that sent me'. A revelation of that will has been perfectly given in the Man of Nazareth – the holy Child, the perfect Servant, the devoted Son. The life, therefore, of that perfect One is a revelation of God's will for me. He had one motive only, and that was the secret of everything. All His actions, His words, His thoughts were motivated by a **passion** – 'I delight to do thy will, O my God', Ps. 40. 8.

Do I want, then, to know God's will for me? What am I to do? First and foremost, I should examine myself carefully as to motive. What is the deepest desire of my heart? What am I out for? What am I after?

If this examination is persisted in to its rightful depth, this alone should settle many things for me. As has been said, the will of God has been made known in a person, the Lord Jesus Christ. We shall do well if we hold up our lives to the mirror of His life. It will be found that the will of God is not necessarily the easiest path, but often the path of suffering. As we view our Lord in Gethsemane we hear His cry and see His agony; but His passion for the will of God triumphs, 'not my will, but thine, be done', Luke 22. 42. That same will of God may lead **us**, not to a Gethsemane or a Calvary – which, in all truth, were unique – but along a path of suffering, and through suffering to a renunciation of all that this world can offer: to sacrifice; to a denial of self, the renunciation of the self-life; to death **with** Him. Now only a passion for the will of God will lead us to such denial and give us the enabling for it.

Passion for His Will. First, then, how is this passion to be attained?

(a) *By a Vision.* That is how the apostle Paul came by it. With his greatness of character, his personality and his extreme devotedness, he was, after Christ, the greatest example set before the church. And it was the vision of the risen Christ of God, the Lord and His claims upon us, that set Paul on the road of the will of God, 'Lord, what wilt thou have me to do?' Acts 9. 6.

(b) *By a Surrender* – a surrender to God's will, with all its implications. 'I beseech you therefore, brethren, by the mercies of God, that ye present your bodies a living sacrifice, holy, acceptable unto God, which is your reasonable service. And be not conformed to this world: but be ye transformed by the renewing of your mind, that ye may prove what is that good, and acceptable, and perfect, will of God', Rom. 12. 1, 2.

We are called to present our bodies and to prove His will. Calvary alone is the place where this can be done. There our Lord presented His body for us: we are to present our body to Him. His sacrifice was to death: ours is a living sacrifice. Henceforth, our values of life must be estimated there. The same will of God which led our blessed Lord to Calvary will lead us to this consecration. The result will be a transformation of life, of outlook, of mind and of motive. As we prove that will in its outworking to be good, well-pleasing and perfect, we shall gain a passion for the will of God.

Perception of the Will of God. Secondly, how am I to obtain the perception of the will of God? By this we mean, How – in view of the complexity of life, the differing viewpoints, the many standards, the opposing opinions and the contrary advice offered – can I come to be assured beyond doubt that I am following a plan for my life in which I have the full approval of God, that I am doing that which is well-pleasing in His sight?

Now God guides by principles, not by rules. Some would like an elaborate set of rules. But God wishes for intelligent cooperation from us. And it seems that just as navigators bringing their ships up the Bristol Channel are assured that, if they steer so that the three main lights appear as one, they will have a safe passage, so God has given us three main lights by which to steer. These are:

1. the **knowledge** of His will, gained in the mind from the word, Col. 1. 9;
2. the **understanding** of His will, Eph. 5. 17, which is to be had by walking in the Spirit; and
3. the **full assurance** of His will, reached through God's gracious providential dealings. Of these,

(1) *The Knowledge of His Will* comes to the believer's mind through the scriptures. God gives no guidance where His word is not reverently and

worshipfully studied. It is not reverent to open a Bible at random in order to take as a hint from God the first words one's eyes light upon. We are to be intelligent students of His principles and of His mind. We should saturate our minds with His word in order to walk, not by 'snatch guidance' but in the spirit and intention of what He has communicated to us through prophets, seers and apostles in the scriptures.

(2) *The Understanding of His Will* must only be obtained through the Holy Spirit in my spirit. The implication is that God's will may be understood. Such understanding is spiritual, not intellectual. It is the fruit of walking in the Spirit – of communion with the Holy Spirit rather than consultation with others – elders, friends. The valued counsel and advice of elders and friends must be tested by the leading of the Holy Spirit in our spirit. In this communion, we test in the light of the scriptures the various impressions we may have, and the judgements received from others; we weigh up all the elements and contributory factors remembering that 'the **meek** will he guide in judgement' (or, 'in their mental processes', as it has been rendered); and leaning not to our **own** understanding, for that would not be meekness, we come to a judgement. In this way the Holy Spirit brings us not merely to an opinion but to a judgement involving a deeper understanding in our spirit.

(3) *The full Assurance of His Will.* As the apostle was forbidden to preach in Asia, not suffered to go to Bithynia, and given a vision in the midst of his uncertainty, Acts 16. 6-10, so may we be taught by the coming into line of circumstances with what we have learnt in the word and by communion with the Spirit, and thus arrive at full assurance. We must always wait for God to bring circumstances into line. A shut door should never be forced; a block in our plans should never be disregarded. The third light – the providential dealings of God in our circumstances – must be lined up with the other two lights, that is with our knowledge from the scriptures and our understanding gained through spiritual meditation. We thus have God's word and the Holy Spirit leading to a considered judgement and providential circumstances. And then, above all things, we need to bring these voices into the sanctuary where we can hear God's voice without the conflicting sounds of earth or the variance of human opinions.

'O the pure delight of a single hour
That before Thy throne I spend,
When I kneel in prayer and with Thee my God
I commune as friend with friend!'

F. J. CROSBY

The one who knows God's guidance from the secret place can afford to wait until he sees the Spirit's leading. God is willing to give clear guidance to all those who will wait for Him.

Persistence in the Will of God. 'Ye have need of patience, that, after ye have done the will of God, ye might receive the promise', Heb. 10. 36. 'That he no longer should live the rest of his time . . . to the lusts of men, but to the will of God', 1 Pet. 4. 2. Wherefore we make it our aim, whether at home or absent, to be well-pleasing unto Him, 2 Cor. 5. 9 RV.

Principles, not rules, are required whereby we may test what is and what is not God's will. As Mary instructed the servants at the wedding-feast at Cana, 'Whatsoever he saith unto you, do it', so we have four 'whatsoevers' clearly recorded as testing principles:

1. 'Whatsoever ye do, do all to the glory of God', 1 Cor. 10. 31;
2. 'Whatsoever ye do in word or deed, do all in the name of the Lord Jesus', Col. 3. 17;
3. 'Whatsoever ye do, do it heartily, as unto the Lord', Col. 3. 23;
4. 'Whatsoever is not of faith is sin', Rom. 14. 23.

These principles are to be considered and applied as tests universally ('whatsoever') and personally. What others do is **their** concern. There is another principle: doubtful things are sinful to a Christian. The greatest difficulty often is concerning things (a) harmless in themselves, or (b) engaged in or indulged in by others. We **must** decide these things for ourselves. We must not go by what others do or say. Equally, we must not bind our own personal decisions on others. Unless we exercise our personal and spiritual liberty in such respects we shall stultify our own personality and stunt our spiritual growth.
But remember that the exercise of liberty is restricted by three tests:

1. Not all things are expedient, though lawful, 1 Cor. 6. 12; 10. 23;
2. 'I will not be brought under the power of any', even lawful things, 6. 12;
3. Not all things edify, though lawful, 10. 23.

That which I do may be allowable, but does it help? Does it profit me in my life and service? Especially, does it stumble others? Until such questions are favourably answered, my liberty to do anything, however lawful, must be questioned. The apostle said, 'I will eat no flesh . . . lest I make my brother to offend [or stumble]', 8. 13. Then that which enslaves or masters me, as a habit, a fashion, an indulgence of appetite, prevents full loyalty to Christ's control. The last mentioned 'fruit of the Spirit', Gal. 5. 23, is temperance – better rendered self-control or self-mastery. It represents, perhaps what is most mature in me and what is most beneficent towards others. If we cannot give a habit up, we have come under its power, its mastery, and so we are not fully under that of Christ through the Spirit.

So by these tests we exercise our conscience that we may be void of offence toward God and toward men, Acts 24. 16. By so doing we shall come to be able to say,

> 'Thou sweet beloved will of God,
> With triumph now I make it mine;
> And faith shall cry a joyous, Yes!
> To every dear command of Thine'.
>
> G. TERSTEEGEN

'The trouble, very often, is not that we fail to comprehend the Lord's way for us, but that we fear to follow' (Anon). 'Obedience is the best expression of reverence' (Anon).

Glorification - J. MITCHELL

Scripture quotations are taken from the Revised Version

The certainty that believers in Christ will be glorified is not only dependent upon the many promises contained in the scriptures, but is assured through their union with the Lord Jesus, Rom. 8. 17. At His own future revelation, He comes to be glorified in His saints, 2 Thess. 1. 10, 12. The verbs used in these references are found only here in the New Testament, and are compounds of the more usual word for glorify, *doxazō*, found over fifty times in the New Testament. The associated noun, *doxa,* is used about 170 times. The words 'brightness, splendour, radiance' convey the basic meaning of *doxa.* It may also be rendered 'magnificence, fame or honour'. Everything in heaven is associated with radiance – heavenly bodies, 1 Cor. 15. 40, 41; cherubim, Ezek. 10. 4; Heb. 9. 5; angels, Luke 2. 9; and God Himself.[51] Christ is the Lord of glory, 1 Cor. 2. 8, and we read of the glory of: (1) His pre-existent state with the Father, John 17. 5; (2) His earthly life consummated in His death;[52] (3) His resurrection and ascension, 1 Pet. 1. 11; Luke 24. 26; (4) His present session at God's right hand, Heb. 2. 9; and (5) His future manifestation.[53] Glory is also used to describe the Christian's state in the life to come, 1 Cor. 15. 43; Col. 3. 4. What super-abounding grace, that those who had fallen short of God's glory, Rom. 3. 23, are ultimately to share in His glory! We, who at present rejoice in the hope of the glory of God, Rom. 5. 2; Col. 1. 27, are destined to behold Christ in His glory, John 17. 24, for He, our forerunner, is in heaven guaranteeing that we, too, will be brought to heaven. God is bringing many sons to glory, Heb. 2. 10, by and through the One who is crowned with glory and honour. In God's purpose we are viewed as glorified, for 'whom he justified, them he also glorified'. Paul uses the Greek aorist tense in the six verbs used in Romans chapter 8 verse 30 expressing completeness and decisiveness in each act. Glorification is already included in this full sweep of the divine plan, cp. 1 Cor. 2. 7.

The verb, *doxazō*, means 'to clothe in splendour or glorify'. This refers to the glory of the life to come, when the Lord Jesus will be glorified in His people, John 17. 10. (Paul uses a similar word of the church, glorious and brilliant in purity, being presented to the Saviour, Eph. 5. 27). Both Peter and Paul contrast the present temporal suffering of believers with the future eternal glory in which they will share.[54] 'Therefore', says Paul,

---

[51] Exod. 24. 17; 40. 34; Num. 14. 10; Rom. 1. 23; Acts 7. 2; Ps. 29. 3; 2 Thess. 1. 9.

[52] John 1. 14; 2. 11; 17. 4, 22.

[53] Matt. 25. 31; Luke 21. 27; 2 Thess. 1. 9.

[54] 1 Pet. 5. 10; cp. 1. 7, 8; Rom. 8. 18.

'I endure all things for the elect's sake, that they also may obtain the salvation which is in Christ Jesus with eternal glory', 2 Tim. 2. 10; see also, 2 Cor. 4. 16-18.

Glorification for the believer is the completion of the process which began, in our experience, with God's effectual call in the gospel. It is the goal of God's purpose, and is not associated with death, but rather with the second coming of Christ when the complete and final redemption of our whole person, spirit, soul and body, will take place, 1 Thess. 5. 23. Paul, in connection with the dead in Christ, speaks of the body being sown in corruption but raised in incorruption, sown in dishonour but raised in glory, sown in weakness but raised in power, 1 Cor. 15. 42, 43. However, in Romans chapter 8 verse 23 the apostle looks beyond present difficulties to what he calls 'our adoption', that is the redemption of our body. The apostle does not say the redemption **from** the body, but **of** the body, so we, the living, wait not for death but the return of Christ when our salvation will be fully realized, 1 Pet. 1. 5, 7. We are told of the instantaneous change that will affect both the dead in Christ, and living believers, when the Lord comes.[55] We will be given bodies conformed to the body of His glory, Phil. 3. 21, so that when we shall see Him we shall be like Him, 1 John 3. 2. The practical outcome of considering what is in store for us is that our lives are purified, and we become more like our Saviour in the present. Through the operation of the Spirit of God we are changed in the present, our 'unveiled' occupation with Christ leading us further on in the experience of being transformed into the same image from glory to glory, 2 Cor. 3. 18. However, on His return we shall be completely conformed to His image, and be made suitable to be His eternal companions. It is a part of His purpose to be manifested in glory, and when this takes place we are assured of being manifested in glory with Him, Col. 3. 4; 2 Thess. 1. 10. In that day grace will issue in glory, Titus 2. 13.

Another aspect of glorification is its close association with the renewal of creation, which at present is subject to the bondage of corruption. When we are revealed in our character as sons of God, then the groaning creation will be delivered from its bondage, and enter into the liberty of the glory of the children of God, Rom. 8. 18-22.

---

[55] 1 Thess. 4. 16, 17; 1 Cor. 15. 51, 52.

The nature of the believer's glorified body defies description. The scriptures give us indications of the superiority of our future state over the present. The body of glory will be a spiritual body, 1 Cor. 15. 44-46, suited altogether as a vehicle for the spirit, as our present 'body of humiliation' is for the soul, and sense-consciousness. The evil 'flesh' principle will be gone forever, and our redeemed bodies will know no inner conflicts or restrictions. Our present body, although enjoying a certain liberty of spirit, is very much bound by natural conditions, needing nourishment and rest, knowing the dangers of sickness and misfortune, not to mention death. The spiritual body, however, is completely superior to the restrictions of matter, space, and time. This is demonstrated in the appearances of the Lord Jesus after His resurrection, although at that time He was not yet glorified. We note:

1. He ate, but this was in no way essential, showing superiority over the material sphere, Luke 24. 41-43;
2. He appeared in a room where the doors were closed, showing freedom from the restrictions associated with space;[56]
3. In addition, Paul refers to that which is immortal, denoting freedom from all the limitations connected with time.[57] The body of glory truly bears the image of the heavenly, 1 Cor. 15. 49.

These concepts are difficult to grasp in our present state, but in the future our comprehension will be in keeping with our glorified state, 1 Cor. 13. 12. Again, our present body is subject to pain and sorrow, whereas in that day God 'shall wipe away every tear from their eyes; and death shall be no more; neither shall there be mourning, nor crying, nor pain, any more: the first things are passed away', Rev. 21. 4; see also 1 Cor. 15. 42, 43. God will not be satisfied until we bear the image of His Son, so that He may be the firstborn among many brethren, Rom. 8. 29; Col. 1. 18. J. N. DARBY'S hymn captures much of the truth we have been considering:

> And is it so! we shall be like Thy Son,
> Is this the grace which He for us has won?
> Father of glory! (thought beyond all thought)

[56] John 20. 19; Luke 24. 31, 36.
[57] 1 Cor. 15. 42, 54; 2 Tim. 2. 10; 1 Pet. 5. 10.

In glory to His own blest likeness brought.

As those who will be glorified in the future, should we not live to God's glory in the present?[58]

Tried and True, or The Trial of Our Faith* - M. Kolchin

It could hardly be said that any Christian enjoys going through a trial. It is one of those aspects of our faith that we would rather avoid. Depending upon its depth and length, it could shake us to the core, far more than we ever anticipated when we first began travelling down its winding (and perhaps harrowing) path. Yet after coming through it in dependence upon the Lord, we will undoubtedly admit that it had a significant part in the deepening of our faith, sharpening our once nebulous convictions, and conforming us more closely to the character of Christ, Rom. 8. 28, 29.

The Benefit of Trials

Scripture refers to the purifying and beneficial effect that trials can have in the life of a Christian. When Job was going through his great trial of affliction, he could hardly be thankful for the series of calamities that befell him. But through the eye of faith he uttered his deep confession of faith with unshakeable conviction, 'But he knoweth the way that I take: when he hath tried me, I shall come forth as gold', Job 23. 10. Job well understood the benefit of God's refining process, a process he would have rather sidestepped if he had the option, but one that proved invaluable in deepening his faith. It is not that Job was a blatant sinner, he was anything but that. Yet, it could never have been said of him that 'he feared God for nothing', that is, for no personal benefit, thus dismissing the arrogant charge of the devil, Job 1. 9. There are a lot of trials that many believers would also have preferred to sidestep, but, if they had, they would have forfeited their beneficial effect. It was a tough road for Job and it may be a tough road for many of God's own, but it can and often does, turn out to the glory of God and to be a shining example of how the Lord brings many sons to glory.

[58] 1 Cor. 6. 20; 10. 31; 1 Pet. 4. 11, 16.

The Necessity for Trials

Sometimes, however, there are gaps in the life of a Christian that necessitate the disciplining hand of God through trial. Peter stated, 'If need be ye are in heaviness through manifold temptations (or trials)', 1 Pet. 1. 6. There are at times those 'need be' situations in which certain sins have found entrance in a life and have been permitted to remain unjudged. Like Israel, who failed to cast out all of the Canaanites in the land, sins can be tolerated and the residue of our past life not sufficiently dealt with, Jas. 1. 21. This can only impede spiritual progress in the life of faith. Things objectionable to God are allowed to coexist without us realizing the damaging effect that they can have in the course of time. This is exactly why trials come into the life of the Christian to jar us out of our spiritual complacency and to realign our biblical priorities. Just as Samuel had to hack Agag to pieces, so we too are exhorted to take decisive action and mortify the deeds of our flesh in obedience to the Lord, Col. 3. 5. The psalmist confessed, 'Before I was afflicted, I went astray: but now have I kept thy word', Ps. 119. 67. David knew too well the disciplinary hand of God upon his life on more than a few occasions, only to express, later, the surpassing value of it. No wonder God would later call him 'a man after mine own heart', Acts 13. 22. In short, trials keep the believer on track, spiritually. Regarding this, CHARLES SPURGEON, the great 19th Century preacher, once related the account in his day of a rope bridge that collapsed unexpectedly, plunging many to their deaths in a ravine below. Upon investigation, it was determined why the catastrophe occurred: a little seedling which had taken root between the strands of rope and the wooden planks had been ignored, thus weakening the bridge. Trials from the Lord help us to do the necessary inspection in our lives so that we can identify and pull out the weeds of sin that could eventually weaken and mar our testimony.

Made into His Image

God wants all believers to reflect the character of Christ in their lives. To accomplish this, He may bring about certain trials to soften the heart, making the Christian more compassionate and sensitive to the needs of others. In so doing, he will be able to comfort others with the same comfort, 2 Cor. 1. 4. Becoming more like Christ, fulfils the principle of Colossians chapter 1 verse 27, 'Christ in you the hope of glory'. Just as it was with Daniel's friends, the believer entering the furnace of affliction will sense the Lord's nearness in a trial, perhaps more than at any other time in his experience. There will be a reality to the words of Isaiah chapter 43 verse 2, 'When thou walkest through the fire, thou shalt not be burned; neither shall the flame kindle upon thee'. Ironically, despite questioning God's ways, many often come to see through their difficulties that they actually are the object of His special affection and that their trial will ultimately serve a greater purpose. This is what Zechariah prophesied to Israel about the Man among the myrtle trees, the preincarnate Lord Jesus, who reassured the nation of a future glory though, at the time, they were at the 'bottom' and oppressed by the nations, Zech. 1. 8-11. Later, in Malachi's day, God had a similar lesson to teach them. During the future tribulation, God will effect a great national cleansing as a result of His refining work during that time. Described as sitting, like 'a refiner and purifier of silver', He will 'purify the sons of Levi and purge them as gold and silver that they may offer to the Lord an offering in righteousness', Mal. 3. 3. The work of any refiner and purifier of silver is to subject precious metal to intense heat in order to remove the impurities from it. The dross which rises to the top is then scooped away. As the refiner sits over the purified metal and looks down upon an even more valuable product, he is able to see his own image in the metal. And so it is with us: our Father in heaven, subjecting His own special people to the purifying process of trial and affliction, makes of us an even more valuable and precious commodity, as we are conformed to the image of His Son, Rom. 8. 28, 29.

Joseph's Example

Joseph also offers additional lessons about the trial of our faith. After going through many years of severe personal trial, he acknowledged the beneficial effect that it produced in his life. Rising to the rank of Prime Minister of Egypt, he was able to look back and acknowledge the hand of God at work in his life. The names of his two sons, Manasseh and Ephraim, outlined his response to trials. The first he named Manasseh saying, 'God hath made me forget all my toil, and all my father's house', Gen. 41. 51. The second he named Ephraim, stating, 'God hath caused me to be fruitful in the land of my affliction', v. 52. Despite the rejection and hurt caused by his brothers, the slander of Potiphar's wife, and being forgotten in prison by the chief butler, he was able to avoid the snare of bitterness and resentment, deliberately forgetting the plethora of personal slights against him. By so doing, he was able to attest to the fruitful result from such a course of action, and a right pattern and the right order: first, 'forgetting'; then fruit-bearing; always the inevitable consequence of committing our way to the Lord. In due time, God will honour those who honour Him.

Certainly, much more could be said about the work of trials in the life of the believer. There is Paul's request to have his thorn in the flesh removed, only to be denied by the Lord to keep him humbly dependent upon Him and cognizant of His all-sufficient grace, 2 Cor. 12. 9. There is Jacob's all-night wrestling episode at Peniel with the Angel of the Lord, ending in a limp, but also a changed life, as well as a changed name, a changed purpose and a changed direction as he crossed back over the river Jabbok to be reconciled to his brother Esau, Gen. 32. 24-32. What a picture and what a transformation! And then there is James' direct exhortation to adjust our attitude as we enter a trial to see the rounding-out of character that it produces, 'My brethren, count it all joy when ye fall into divers temptations; knowing this, that the trying of your faith worketh patience. But let patience have her perfect work, that ye may be perfect and entire, wanting nothing', Jas. 1. 2-4.

The apostle Paul reminds us, 'For our light affliction, which is but for a moment, worketh for us a far more exceeding and eternal weight of glory', 2 Cor. 4. 17. Peter stated it this way, 'The God of all grace . . . after that ye have suffered a while, make you perfect, stablish, strengthen, settle you', 1 Pet. 5. 10. Only as we look into the mirror of God's word, will we begin to understand more clearly the bigger picture and the wisdom of God in taking us through various trials and tribulations that He sends our way. As we do, we will be able to sing more convincingly the words of the hymnwriter,

> 'Every joy or trial falleth from above,
> Traced upon our dial by the Son of love.
> We may trust Him fully all for us to do,
> They who trust Him wholly, find Him wholly true',
>
> F. R. HAVERGAL.

THE DOCTRINE OF THE LAST THINGS

Hope - M. Horlock

In everyday experience the phrase 'to hope for' expresses a desire or a wish for the future. Almost invariably, there is implied in it the element of complete uncertainty. The hope of the believer, however, is of an altogether different kind. It is a confident and well-grounded expectation concerning the future which has its basis in the revealed will of God.

The Bible sometimes uses the word 'hope' in the more conventional sense. When planting the seed the farmer desires and expects a harvest, 1 Cor. 9. 10; the lender of money desires and expects a return, Luke 6. 34, 35; Paul wishes and plans to send Timothy to Philippi, Phil. 2. 19, 23. Even in common usage, however, the accent often falls strongly on expectation rather than desire. Consequently, desire can still remain after hope is lost, Acts 16. 19; 27. 20.

The Old Testament. Although the Old Testament is partly dominated by a longing for Israel's future golden age and Messiah's coming, the word 'hope' is not used to describe such matters. The object of 'hope' is not so much a future of good and blessing, as the person upon whom the realization of that good depends. Jeremiah speaks strikingly of the Lord as 'the hope of Israel', 14. 8; 17. 13.

The English word 'hope' translates several Hebrew words, ranging in meaning from 'trust' to 'expectation'. *Betach* signifies trust and confidence, and occurs in the familiar text, 'My flesh shall also rest in hope', Ps. 16. 9. *Machseh* carries the idea of refuge or shelter. When Jeremiah called God his hope, Jer. 17. 17, he employed the same word as is translated 'refuge' in Psalm 46 verse 1. *Sabar* means 'to await with eager anticipation and expectation'. It is rendered 'wait upon', Ps. 145. 15, 'The eyes of all wait upon thee; and thou givest them their meat in due season', and occurs as 'hope' in Psalm 119 verses 116, 166. *Yachal* signifies 'to tarry', 'to wait patiently', and occurs in Psalm 130 verses 7, 8, 'Let Israel hope in the Lord. . . And he shall redeem Israel'.

The hope of the godly man expressed itself variously in confident reliance upon God, in the patient bearing of trials in view of the divine promise of vindication, and in taking refuge with God as his rock and fortress.

The New Testament. Hope appears, often, as a member of the familiar triad 'faith, hope, and love',[1] although it generally attracts less attention than its companions. As a rule, hope has to do with the future, and with things not yet seen, Rom. 8. 24, 25; Heb. 11. 1. The word translated 'hope' bears a neutral meaning in the Greek classics, and is used to describe an expectation for the future, whether good or bad. It is often used, for example, to signify fear and anxiety. The Greek Old Testament (Septuagint) also used the word in both a good and a bad sense (see Isaiah chapter 28 verse 19 for an evil hope). In the New Testament, however, it is always employed of a favourable and pleasant expectation.

The word 'hope' is used in three distinct ways. First, it often describes an emotion: the happy anticipation of future good. This hope centres in the consummation of the work of God. This consummation is capable of flexible description, being referred to severally as salvation, 1 Thess. 5. 8; eternal life, Titus 1. 2; 3. 7; the glory of God, Rom. 5. 2; Col. 1. 27; righteousness, Gal. 5. 5; and the resurrection of the dead, Acts 24. 15. Second, it frequently describes the object of expectation: the thing hoped for, Col. 1. 5; Titus 2. 13; Heb. 6. 18. This use of the word is often termed its 'objective sense' in contrast to its use in describing an emotion, which is termed its 'subjective sense'. Christ is not only our peace, Eph. 2. 14, and our life, Col. 3. 4, but also our goal, future and hope, 1 Tim. 1. 1. Third, hope sometimes denotes the foundation upon which expectation is based, Col. 1. 27; 1 Thess. 2. 19.

The Grounds for Hope in the New Testament. These are stated to be:

1. *The Gospel*, Col. 1. 5, 23. Our hope is guaranteed by the gospel promises. It stands in sharp contrast to the pervading despair of the first century pagan world and of mankind in general today, Eph. 2. 12; 1 Thess. 4. 13. Christ has brought 'life and immortality to light through the gospel', 2 Tim. 1. 10.

---

[1] Rom. 5. 1-5; 1 Cor. 13. 13; Col. 1. 4, 5; 1 Thess. 1. 3; 5. 8.

2. *The Love of God, the Indwelling Spirit, and the Experience of the Believer*, Rom. 5. 1-8. Hope arises out of the sense of God's love to us as demonstrated in the death of His Son, and is deepened and intensified by the bracing of character that comes from tribulation. The Father and the Son join in graciously giving us our hope, 2 Thess. 2. 16. Here that hope is conveyed through the Holy Spirit that dwells in our hearts; cp. Rom. 15. 30; Gal. 5. 5. The triune God is therefore our source of hope, Rom. 15. 13.

3. *The Resurrection of Christ,* 1 Pet. 1. 3, 21. By Christ's resurrection we are begotten to a living hope, and through that resurrection our hope in God is established. The disciples' expectations had been shattered by the Lord's crucifixion, Luke 24. 21 RV, but their hope was reawakened when He subsequently arose. In Paul's preaching hope was often bound up with the resurrection. As an earnest of the fulfilment of the ancient promises it constituted the vindication of Israel's hope, Acts 23. 6; 26. 6-8; 28. 20. The rooting of hope in the resurrection may have contributed to the fact that the Gospels do not use 'hope' in its full theological sense. The noun *elpis* does not occur there at all, and the verb *elpizō* occurs only five times. On two occasions the verb carries the Old Testament sense of trust, Matt. 12. 21; John 5. 45 RV, and the other references are non-technical, Luke 6. 34; 23. 8; 24. 21 RV. Jesus' teachings, of course, helped lay the basis of our doctrine of hope, but no record exists of the Lord using the word hope of future expectation.

4. *The Scriptures*, Rom. 15. 4. The recorded works of God in the past, and His revealed purpose in the future, inspire the reader with hope.

The Practical Effects of Hope. Hope functions in the life of the believer in the following ways:

1. It is a spring of ceaseless rejoicing, Rom. 12. 12; Heb. 3. 6; Rom. 5. 2 (lit. exult with boasting in hope);
2. It finds expression in endurance and steadfastness under trial, 1 Thess. 1. 3; Rom. 12. 12; cp. Heb. 10. 36, 37;
3. It provides motivation for continuance in well-doing, Heb. 6. 11. It is the anchor by which the saint is moored, amidst life's storms, to the heavenly sanctuary, Heb. 6. 18;

4. It is a stimulus to holiness and purity of life, 1 John 3. 2, 3.

We are exhorted to abound in hope, Rom. 15. 13, to persevere in it, Heb. 3. 6; 10. 23 RV; 1 Pet. 1. 13, and to be ready to answer those who ask the reason for it, 3. 15.

Various descriptions are given of hope. It is presented as living, 1 Pet. 1. 3; blessed, Titus 2. 13; and good, 2 Thess. 2. 16.

The non-rational creation will share in the realization of our hope, Rom. 8. 19-23. Creation's present imperfections, and bondage to death and decay, has been brought about by the fall of man; see Gen. 3. 17, 18. As creation has partaken in the results of man's sin so, also, it will ultimately share in the emancipation of God's children. In common with the creation we groan for glory as we await our final redemption, 'the grace that is to be brought' to us 'at the revelation of Jesus Christ', 1 Pet. 1. 13.

An Introduction to the Study of Prophecy - P. J. POOLE

Prophecy is a vast subject, divisible into several categories. There are, for instance:

1. Prophecies of the coming of the Messiah, of which Genesis chapter 3 verse 15 is the earliest, and indeed the first prophecy of all, and contains, in a sense, the germ of all;
2. Prophecies of the rise and progress, downfall and reinstatement of Israel;
3. Prophecies of the progress of certain Gentile nations, and the appearance, development and fall of successive Gentile world-empires;
4. Prophecies of the kingdom, etc.

As to the first category, **all** the elements of the birth, life, death, and resurrection of the Lord Jesus were foretold in the Old Testament scriptures, Luke 24. 25-27, 44, as well as the Messianic elements.

On one great subject of the highest importance to the believer, namely, the church, the body of Christ, the Old Testament scriptures are completely silent. The reason is that it was a 'mystery' (what is known only to the initiated, *Young's Concordance*), something completely hidden until first mentioned by the Lord Jesus, Matt. 16. 18, but not even by Him elaborated or described at that time. The details were later committed by the Spirit to the apostles and (New Testament) prophets, John 16. 12-14; Eph. 3. 5; 5. 23, among whom Paul, by his writings, was chosen to communicate the truth to the readers of the New Testament.

Prophecy is contained not only in the prophets generally so called (Isaiah, Jeremiah, Daniel, Ezekiel, Zechariah, etc.), but some of the Psalms, and parts of many others are highly prophetic, Luke 24. 44, and really can only be understood rightly when this is borne in mind. The prophetic impulse was outside the control of the prophets, 2 Pet. 1. 19-21, who ardently longed to see the fulfilment and thus the elucidation to **them** of the prophecies they uttered by divine inspiration, Matt. 13. 17; 1 Pet. 1. 10. This will account for some of the striking utterances in the Psalms, e.g. Psalm 40 verses 6 to 8, which could not possibly be true of David who wrote the Psalm, which is in general an expression of matters that were true of him. Psalm 16 verse 10 is another case in point, as is clearly shown by the Spirit through Peter, Acts 2. 25-31, where the emphasis is on 'him' in verse 25 and on 'Christ . . . his . . . his' in verse 31.

The prophetic scriptures in the third category above deal in general with broad outlines, but omit the details. While, therefore, in some parts of our studies we may wish that more details were given, we must content ourselves with the assurance that time will make all clear, as the prophecies come to their fulfilment.

The 'action' of Old Testament prophecy revolves round Israel, the history, past and **future**, of Gentile nations as such being the setting or background; while the ultimate centre of prophetic action is the land of Israel. It is necessary to bear this in mind to avoid confusion. As before said, the church has no place in Old Testament prophecy, notwithstanding the man-inserted headings to some of our Bibles in some parts of Isaiah, for instance! The whole of this long 'church' period is an interval of undiscoverable duration. But while the church is not seen in prophecy as such, we must appreciate that she existed in the heart and counsels of God from ages past. Thus, she is no 'after-thought' with God. The Lord Jesus maintained silence on the subject until His rejection by Israel was clearly manifested after His presentation of Himself to that nation. This rejection was itself foretold in the Old Testament, but the **fact** of rejection could not be seen until the presentation had been made. The outcome and final issue of the rejection was the crucifixion, which was the very means whereby Christ gave expression to His love for the church, Eph. 5. 25, and the means by which He cleansed her and made her His own.

He made yet another appeal to Israel through the apostles, but this time on the basis of His death and the atonement thereby accomplished. That appeal was also rejected, the martyrdom of Stephen being the symbol or sign, as Christ had foretold, Luke 19. 14. That event was the occasion of bringing Saul to notice, albeit as an arch-persecutor and hater of Christ and His people. Later, by the direct intervention of Christ, this persecutor was transformed into perhaps the most zealous of all the servants of Christ and, as before remarked, the vehicle of much truth to us. But Israel rejected Paul's testimony too, Acts 13. 46 etc., which fact being clear he turned to the Gentiles. The Jews thus remained unbelievers, and have been since, and **are still**, in the opposition camp.

Now the appeal is to all, Jews and Gentiles alike, without distinction, on the ground of their individual need as sinners, both alike being received into the church, that is, the spiritual body of Christ, upon believing in Jesus, Eph. 2. 14; Col. 3. 11.

When, however, this church period is brought to an end by the coming of the Lord for His people, 1 Thess. 4, God will again turn to Israel, with a view to bringing in the kingdom foretold by the ancient prophets, with the hitherto rejected and scorned Jesus of Nazareth as King; see Psalm 2. Then the prophetic clock, so long still and silent, will begin to tick off the days, weeks, months, and years required for that fulfilment. Yet further centuries must elapse before the remainder of prophecy comes to its completion by the events prophesied in the later chapters of Revelation; e.g. Rev. 20. 7.

'**Rightly** dividing the word of truth' is essential to the proper understanding of all scripture, but nowhere more so than when dealing with prophecy. In the Table that accompanies this paper, I have described certain verses as 'key verses'. When these are noted it is clearly seen that the 'futurist' interpretation of prophecy is the only valid one. It is demonstrable that many of the major events foretold have never taken place, therefore they **must** be future. Daniel's 70th 'week', Dan. 9. 24-27, does still remain to run its course. This is provable by the fact that no such covenant with Israel as that scripture foretells has ever been made. Titus, who destroyed the then existing city and sanctuary in AD 70 was not 'the prince who shall come' of that prophecy, as he made no covenant with the Jews, nor has anyone since. The kingdom of Daniel chapter 2 verse 44 has never yet been set up, this being **not** the spiritual kingdom of God with which we are familiar, but the millennial kingdom of the Lord Jesus, when He shall rule in power and majesty and **might**, vv. 44, 45; therefore 'these kings' of the verse have not yet arisen in the sense of the verse. The 'little horn', Dan. 7. 8, is not yet manifested, because he is to be overthrown by the Lord Jesus. Matthew chapter 24 remains to be fulfilled, as the sign of 'the-Son-of-man-in-heaven', v. 30, that is, in the visible heavens, has not yet appeared. Yet other instances might be cited of the simple way in which we can prove the futurity of many of the great prophecies of scripture. It is no argument against their futurity to say that it is impossible that so many great events can be crowded into a few years. Quite apart from the fact that scripture says or implies that they **can**, the events of the past fifty years have taught this generation at least that, given the need, or suitable conditions, anything can happen in a period that would otherwise have been utterly inadequate.

Collate, compare, meditate, cogitate, and **pray**; by these means alone can light be obtained upon the prophetic scriptures. The mental effort involved will be considerable, which is probably why so few really **study** prophecy. Thus, the 'many' are at the mercy of whatever teaching they get, and, unless this is sound and scriptural, the resultant mental 'hotchpotch' is deplorable.

Collate, compare.[2] These cited stand up like Alpine giants in the Sierra Montana of prophetic revelation. A careful comparison of these scriptures shows them to have so many features in common as almost to warrant one in saying that they constitute one vast prophecy. Parts

---

[2] Among the great prophetic scriptures may be cited: Dan. 2, 7, 9, 11, 12; Matt. 24; 2 Thess. 2; Rev. 6, 13, 17, 19.

of Daniel chapters 2 and 7 have been fulfilled, that is, those parts that relate to the Babylonian, Medo-Persian and Greek Empires. Daniel chapter 8 seems to have been fulfilled in the person and acts of Antiochus IV Epiphanes (172-168 BC), who may, however, most certainly be regarded as a type of Antichrist.

The study and comparison of these great scriptures will be greatly facilitated by mounting them in parallel columns on suitable paper. The individual portions of prophecy, Daniel, etc., can be purchased quite cheaply, and the 'mount' can be folded like a road map and carried in the pocket for reference and study as occasion may offer. I have myself derived great help from this simple device.

The accompanying Table is designed so that the reader might go further into the study of prophecy and confirm for themselves the certainty concerning the things that they are being taught. We may use the remainder of our space to deal with one or two important and sometimes debated subjects.

Matthew 24. This chapter is of the utmost importance, but it is necessary first to be sure of the time or period of its fulfilment. Unless we get that right it matters little what else we get. This utterance of the Lord Jesus followed His declaration to the Jews at the end of chapter 23, which **see**, and was in response to the question of the disciples, 24. 3, which also **see**. If we contrast this discourse of the Lord with that spoken to these very men within a few days only of this time as recorded in John chapters 13 to 16, we cannot fail to be impressed with the enormous dissimilarity both of tone and matter between the two utterances. The explanation seems clear that in Matthew chapter 24 He was speaking to them as Jews in response to an enquiry that was altogether Jewish in its bearing and implications, while in the upper room He spoke to them as the nucleus of the church so soon to be formed. I believe that, in fact, no other view can logically be taken. Thus, John chapters 13 to 16 had to do with matters that would become immediately operative upon His departure and the coming of the Spirit, while Matthew chapter 24 overleaps the centuries and is applicable to a time that is even still future. We are thus enabled to see that the judgement of the living nations, spoken of in Matthew chapter 25 verse 31 will be quite distinct in character, location and time from the judgement seat of Christ,[3] though they will both precede the millennium. The one will be a punitive judgement on earth of people then living on earth, while the other will be not punitive, but for the apportioning of awards for faithfulness to Christ on the part of His people, who will have been taken to be with Him before they appear at His judgement seat. The judgement of the great white throne, Rev. 20. 11, will be distinct from and much later than both of these, being the final judgement of **all** unrepentant sinners, believers in Christ having no place there.

The conclusion thus reached as to the futurity of Matthew chapter 24 is strengthened by the numerous correspondences, shown in the Table, between this chapter and the other prophecies. Among these last is Revelation chapter 6, the chapter of the opening of the seals. The two chapters march **exactly** together, Revelation chapter 6 giving the outline and Matthew chapter 24 some of the details. We are thus enabled to determine the period of the fulfilment of Revelation chapter 6, namely, after the church has been taken away. This view is yet further strengthened by the setting of Revelation chapter 6. Revelation chapters 2 and 3 have obvious reference to the church and individual churches on earth. Revelation chapter 4 begins with the invitation to John to 'come up hither' into heaven, where he immediately was, in spirit. There he sees the glory of God, ch. 4, and hears the praises of the redeemed, ch. 5. Thus, in chapter 6 and onwards, figuratively speaking he is looking down from heaven on scenes being enacted on earth. What was vision to John will be reality to the church when the vision is fulfilled. She will be there with Christ, after He has called her to Himself, 1 Thess. 4. In chapter 6 therefore we see the Lord beginning to exercise that function of **judgement** that God has reserved to Him, John 5. 22, 27 RV. Yet further details of the judgements of Revelation chapter 6 are given in the following chapters, as chapter 6 seems to cover the whole period between the commencement of the judgements and the imminent appearance of the Lamb in His wrath, v. 17.

The little horn of Daniel chapter 7, the wilful king or vile person of Daniel chapter 11, the man of sin of 2 Thessalonians chapter 2, and the first beast of Revelation chapter 13. A careful comparison of the various

---

[3] Rom. 14. 10; 1 Cor. 3. 12; 2 Cor. 5. 10.

scriptures in the Table shows that these descriptions all relate to the **same man**. I have no doubt myself that he is Antichrist, **the** 'Anti'-Christ, Christ's personal opponent and 'opposite number', the very embodiment and incarnation of all that is anti, opposed to, the opposite of, Christ. The actual name or appellation Antichrist is found only in 1 John chapter 2 verse 18, in which Epistle the distinguishing characteristic of Antichrist is described, 2. 22; 2 John 7. Scripture speaks of two opposite and opposing Trinities, and their anti-positions may be shown thus:[4]

	Good	**Evil**
The source, spring, initiator, or originator.	The Father, God	The Dragon, Satan
The visible representative of that invisible or hidden originator	The Son, Christ	The Beast, Antichrist
The executive agent who causes men to receive and believe in the visible representative	The Holy Spirit	The False Prophet (the second beast, Rev. 13, see Rev. 19. 20)

The solemn lesson of unfulfilled prophecy is that man's opposition to God and to Christ will increase in intensity until, at last, it finds embodiment and expression in the man of sin, who will be an accepted and acknowledged leader of the nations of the world. Present world-movements are all in this direction, whether moral, mental or scientific, while the rapid deterioration in the religious sphere shows the same trend and tendencies. This last is going to culminate in the manifestation of the symbolic great whore of Revelation chapter 17, whose character, actions and **end** are in tremendous contrast to those of the bride, the Lamb's wife, the chaste virgin, 2 Cor. 11. 2. Today **all** standards are being lowered and debased, moral, mental, ecclesiastical. May we be ever and increasingly among those who wait for the Lord from heaven, and in so waiting walk in holiness, purity and faithfulness to Him.

[4] This is one point of view adopted by expositors.

A Table showing the Inter-relation of some of the Great Prophetic scriptures: Notes

A short dash '–' after a verse number indicates that the verse is the first of two or more on the subject. Read on.
References in brackets () are suggestive, but not necessarily true parallels (except item 32).

Item 8. In Revelation chapter 13 the first Beast is initially a symbol or representation of the nations, but in Revelation chapter 19 verses 19, 20 he is referred to as an individual, distinct from the kings and the armies of the nations, and **as such** is cast into the lake of fire. Hence it is correct to describe the king or head of the confederacy as 'the Beast'.

Item 21. The expression 'the saints', Dan. 7. 21, is to be understood of **Jewish** saints, **not** of the saints of the present dispensation, so often referred to as such in the Epistles. The use of the word in Revelation chapter 13 verse 7 is in the same sense as in Daniel chapter 7 verse 21. These will be the 'remnant', the future successors of the Old Testament faithful. As to the seals. It will be seen that in the Table they do not follow in consecutive order. The reason is that Seal 5 refers to events that have taken place prior to the opening of the seal. In the Table, I have endeavoured to place the actual martyrdoms in their time of occurrence.

Item 32. The resurrection of Daniel chapter 12 verse 2 is in two parts: (1) some to everlasting life; (2) some to shame and everlasting contempt. There is nothing in this verse to show that at least 1,000 years will elapse between these two events, but Revelation chapter 20 verse 5 makes it quite clear that it will be so.

	SUBJECT	
1	The Fourth World Empire (Rome)	
2	Out of Sea	
3	10 Horns	
	Its King or Head:	
4	Little Horn	
5	Prince that shall come	
6	Vile person	
7	Man of Sin: Son of Perdition	
8	First Beast of Revelation chapter 13	
9	Arises after Messiah cut off	
10	Energized by Satan	
11	Boastful, blasphemous	
12	Exalts himself above every god	
13	Hides real character for 3.5 years	
14	Sets up abomination of desolation	
	Conditions during that Period	
15	False Christs, false prophets, lying wonders, strong delusion	
16	One Arch-Deceiver, counterfeiting Christ	
17	Iniquity abounds, love grows cold	
18	Many Jews 'offended', betray one another	
19	The 'Remnant':	Faithful and wise servants
20		Preach gospel of kingdom
21		Afflicted, hated, some killed
22	This is the great tribulation	
23	City and sanctuary destroyed by 'the Prince'	
	Divine Judgements being poured out during Period	
24	Wars, nation against nation	
25	Famines, pestilences, earthquakes	
26	Sun and moon darkened, powers of heaven shaken	
27	THEN the end	
28	CHRIST appears in power and glory	
29	The Beast and the kings make war against Him	
30	They are overthrown by Christ	
31	This is the DAY of the LORD	
32	Tribulation martyrs raised	
33	Christ judges the living nations	
34	And sets up HIS KINGDOM	
35	Keys, to fix the **Periods**	

DANIEL				MATT	2 TH.	REVELATION					Other references or parallels
7	9	11	12	24	2	6	Seal	13	17	19	
23-											Dan. 2. 40-
3								1			
7								1	7-		
8-											
	26										
		21-									
					3						
								1-	3-		
22	26	35									
		(38-)			9			2			
8 25		36			4			5-	3		
		36-			4						
	27										
	(27)	31	11	15	4			(14)			
				11 23-	9-			13-			Rev. 16. 14; Isa. 66. 3, 4
						2	1				
				12							
		30-		10							John 5. 43
		33	3	45-							Isa. 1. 9; 10
				14							
21-		33-	(7)	9		9-	5	7			Ps. 44, Zech. 13.9
			1	21-							
	26										Zech. 14. 1-
				6		4	2				
				7		5-	3				
				29		12-	6				
22		35		14							Isa. 13. 9-
13			(1)	30		16-				11-	Zech. 14. 3-
									14	19-	Isa. 8. 9-
26		(45)			8					20-	Isa. 8. 9-; 1 Thess. 5. 2-
			2			9-	(5)				Rev. 20. 4
											Matt. 25. 31-
9-[5]	27	35	9	30	3						Rev. 20. 4; Ps. 46

[5] See also Dan. 2. 44.

As is well known, expositors differ depending on their attitude to the doctrine of miraculous foretelling, and whether they see the church merely as an earthly institution, or whether they see the church as a heavenly body entirely distinct from all other groupings of men brought about by academic theology and institutional religion. This difference largely centres around the thesis: 'The church is not the subject of Old Testament prophecy'. If it is thought otherwise, all we can remark is that to fuse is to confuse. When God made promises to the Jewish nation, He meant what He promised, and therefore such promises will be fulfilled. The spiritualization of all the Jewish promises in the Old Testament (to make them refer to the church) is the method of those who wish to obliterate the Jews as a nation, thereby preventing them from being the head and not the tail. Only in the age of church testimony on earth is there no difference between Jew and Gentile, whether in the matter of sin or in the matter of salvation, Rom. 3. 9; 1. 16; 3. 29. But outside this, the redemptive work of Christ provides different aspects of blessing on the Jews and on the nations.

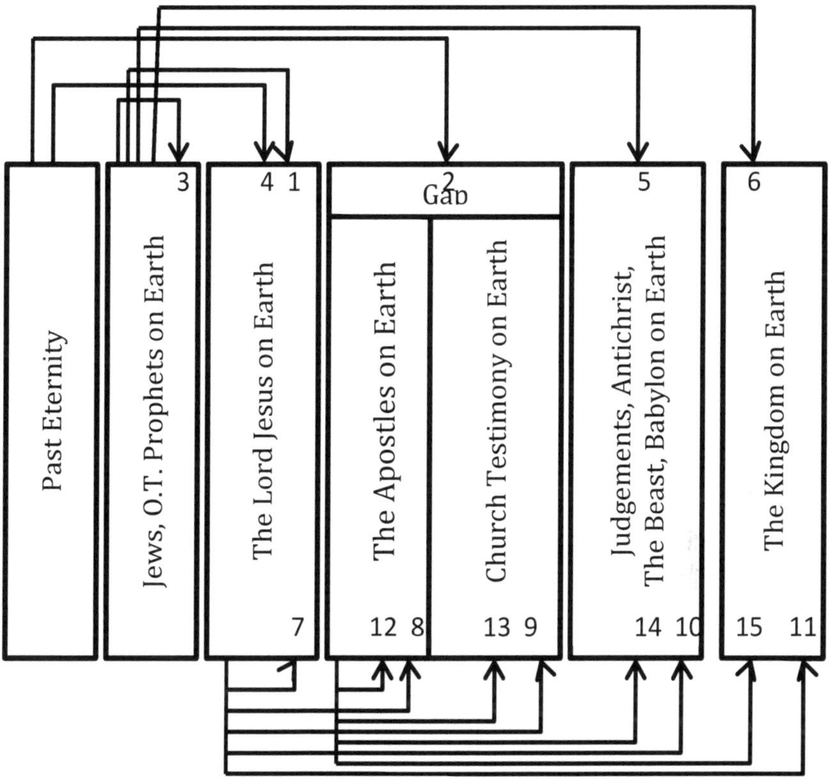

From Eternity		From the Lord Jesus	
1.	1 Pet. 1. 20	7.	Matt. 16. 21; Luke 18. 31-33
2.	Rom. 16. 25; Eph. 1. 4; 3. 5, 9	8.	John 14-16
		9.	Matt. 24. 2; John 14. 2, 3
		10.	Matt. 24. 3-41
		11.	Matt. 13. 43; 16. 27 to 17. 3
From the Old Testament		From the Apostles' Teaching	
3.	Jer. 25. 11; 29. 10; Ezra 1. 1	12.	Acts 11. 28; 21. 11
4.	Isa. 7. 14; Mic. 5. 2; Ps. 22. 1	13.	Acts 20. 29, 30; 2 Pet. 2. 1; Rev. 2-3
5.	Dan. 2. 40-43; 7. 8, 23-25	14.	2 Thess. 2. 3-12
6.	Isa. 40-66; Jer. 31-33; Ezek. 40-48	15.	Rev. 20. 1-6

The diagram shows the direction of the prophetic word. The various periods throughout the ages are named within the horizontal blocks in order from left to right. The various lines with arrows are lines of prophetic foreshadowing, showing the period in which the prophecy originates, and showing the period to which the prophecy applies (represented by arrows). The upper lines refer to those prophecies originating before the Lord's life on earth, mostly during the Old Testament period. The lower lines refer to those prophecies originating during the few years covered by the New Testament books, again being directed to those periods to which they looked forward prophetically. There are thus four periods in which there originated prophecy in its widest sense: eternity, the Old Testament prophets, the time when the Lord Jesus taught on earth, and the apostolic period during the early days of the church testimony. The trajectories are numbered, and underneath one or two scriptural references are given to illustrate each line of prophetic unfolding. In particular, the reader should note that no line reaches the period named 'church testimony on earth' from the Old Testament, in keeping with the thesis stated above. This fact enables us to assess the peculiar character of the church, Eph. 3. 5, 9. Justification by faith is an Old Testament doctrine foretelling Christ's redemptive work and our associated blessings by faith, but this is **not** a peculiarity of the church of which we speak – it is the common basis of salvation through all periods. Every verse of scripture containing a prophetic thought should fit into one of the arrowed lines in the diagram (bearing in mind that we have omitted what may be termed the 'future eternity'). Promises of **global** blessing, such as justification by faith promised before to Abraham, Rom. 4. 3, are excluded from our inquiry. We provide here a few comments upon the various prophetic trajectories as illustrated in the diagram.

The Diagram Described. The divine thought in eternity past looked forward to the time when the Lord Jesus would descend to the created earth to suffer and to die. He was the Lamb foreordained before the foundation of the world, 1 Pet. 1. 20, and His crucifixion was in keeping with the 'determinate counsel and foreknowledge of God', Acts 2. 23. The divine purpose also looked forward to the church and to the peculiar blessings of the Lord's people in this present age. This peculiar purpose was known as a 'mystery', hidden through Old Testament times, but made known by the Spirit through the apostolic ministry,

Rom. 16. 25; Eph. 3. 5, 9. Believers know that they were chosen in Christ 'before the foundation of the world', 1. 4.

In the Old Testament, there are many examples of what may be termed 'local prophecy', namely the foretelling of events that took place later in Old Testament history. Thus in Jeremiah chapter 25 verse 11, the Jewish nation would serve the king of Babylon for seventy years; when this period was complete, they would return to their own land, 29. 10. This took place, Ezra 1. 1, while in Isaiah chapter 44 verse 28 it is asserted that Cyrus would cause the temple to be rebuilt. Additionally, the whole life of the Lord Jesus is traced through the Old Testament prophetic word, Luke 24. 44-46. Thus Isaiah chapter 7 verse 14 and Micah chapter 5 verse 2 speak of His birth, Psalms 22, 69 and Isaiah chapter 53 speak of His death, while Psalm 16 speaks of His resurrection. As to the future, the Old Testament looks forward to the time after the church is taken to be with the Lord; Daniel chapter 2 verses 40 to 43 demonstrates in the legs and feet of the image the political system on earth at that future time, while further information is contained in Daniel chapter 7 dealing with the fourth nameless beast. But the ultimate vision of the Old Testament prophets was the kingdom age; the major prophets contain the great restoration sections: Isaiah chapters 40 to 66 show **Zion** restored; Jeremiah chapters 31 to 33 show **bridal affections** restored; Ezekiel chapters 40 to 48 show the **glory of the Lord** restored in His house. Daniel chapter 7 verses 9 to 14 show the **throne** restored.

Many parts of the Lord's teaching were prophetic. On many occasions He spoke of His death and resurrection, then but a short distance away, Matt. 16. 21; Luke 18. 31-33. Such prophecies always seemed to be unpalatable to His disciples. Moreover, the Lord prepared His disciples for His return to heaven by promising the Holy Spirit, so John chapters 14 to 16 presents His teaching that prepared the disciples for this new period. His teaching also looked forward to the testimony of the church on earth. The temple in Jerusalem would be destroyed, Matt. 24. 2, so that no rival religious attraction after the flesh should remain in Jerusalem. He also extended His teaching up to His coming again for the church, John 14. 2-3, 'I will come again, and receive you unto myself'. Beyond this church age, the Lord prophesied of the future apostasy that would overtake the earth, resulting in His return in glory, Matt. 24. 3-41. Finally, His teaching extended to the millennial reign, when the righteous would shine forth in the kingdom of His Father, Matt. 13. 43.

The gift of prophecy existed during the apostolic era after the ascension of the Lord Jesus.[6] Some examples are entirely local in character; Agabus spoke of a famine, Acts 11. 28, and showed that Paul would be bound, 21. 11. Many events were foreseen by the apostles; Paul could see the decline in eldership, through wolves entering in to spoil the flock, Acts 20. 29-30. The growth of false teachers was inevitable, 1 Tim. 4. 1; 2 Pet. 2. 1. The progress of church history is shown pictorially in Revelation chapters 2 and 3, while Paul traced out the hope of the church, the return of the Lord Jesus Christ, 1 Thess. 4. 13-18. After this, Paul spoke of terrible times to come, under, for example, the man of sin, the son of perdition, 2 Thess. 2. 3-12. Since the millennial age is spelt out in such detail in the Old Testament, not much more is added by the apostolic teaching; Revelation chapter 20 verses 4 to 6 shows the one thousand years and those who reign with Christ. Revelation chapter 21 verse 9 to chapter 22 verse 5 treats this subject from the heavenly point of view, the Old Testament treating it from the earthly aspect.

The reader should convince himself that every prophetic utterance fits into this plan.

The Jews, the Gentiles, and the Church of God - B. Osborne

When man's condition before God in relation to eternity is considered, two classes are seen – the saved and the lost. When God's government of the world, which is the subject of prophecy, is considered, there are three classes – Jews, Gentiles, and the church of God, 1 Cor. 10. 32. God's purposes regarding these three groups are referred to in Acts chapter 15 verses 13-18. In the present, He is taking out a people for His name and forming His church. After the accomplishment of this, Christ will return to rebuild the tabernacle of David, and fulfil the promises relative to the nation Israel. And this will be to the end that the residue of men and all Gentiles may seek the Lord. This threefold division, 1 Cor. 10. 32, must always be kept in mind when dealing with the subject of the Lord's coming. The scriptures make clear the distinctive relation of the coming of the Lord to each.

---

[6] Rom. 12. 6; 1 Cor. 12. 28; Eph. 4. 11.

The church of God. The church has a peculiar relation to God, and has received from Him specific promises. It has a beginning. It is not found in the Old Testament, where it was still a 'mystery', Eph. 3. 5-10; Col. 1. 26. It was still future when the Lord spoke of building His church, Matt. 16. 18. It could not have existed before the resurrection and ascension of the Lord Jesus. It consists of saints baptized into Christ's body by the Holy Spirit sent down from heaven, Acts 1. 5; 1 Cor. 12. 13. The Holy Spirit descended after the Lord Jesus was glorified. Before that He could not come, John 16. 7; 7. 39. But when He was sent at Pentecost, believers were baptized in the Spirit, whether Jew or Gentile, into one body, with Christ their glorified Head.

The church is not Israel, nor has it taken Israel's place. Israel has its own promises and hopes which are not to be confused with those of the church. Failure to distinguish the calling and position of the church from that of Israel only results in confusion. Today there are no distinctions of Jew and Gentile in the church of God, though they will be maintained when the church period is over. Note the phrase 'in time **past** Gentiles', Eph. 2. 11, cp. 1 Cor. 12. 2; they were **now** members of Christ's body, the church. The existence, calling, and glory of the church is 'the mystery', Eph. 3. 4, which in other ages was not made known to men, but from 'the beginning of the world hath been hid in God', v. 9. The mystery consists not in that Gentiles will be blessed, for the Old Testament promised them blessing in Messiah's kingdom, but that Jew and Gentile should be united in one body, all differences swallowed up in the pre-eminent grace that made both alike members of the body.

The present purpose of God will have its consummation in the rapture of the church, 1 Thess. 4. 13-17. The movements up to it are described in Ephesians chapter 5 verses 25 to 27. 'Christ also loved the church, and gave himself for it' refers to the past, when He died on the cross, v. 25. For the present, He is sanctifying His church, v. 26, until that future day when He will present it spotless unto Himself, v. 27. For that church He will come, John 14. 3, into the air, 1 Thess. 4. 17, to receive it to Himself. This is the church's hope.

The Jew. Israel has a very distinct place in the dealings and counsels of God. The Old Testament is a record of their history, and of God's promises to them, and their response. Israel is the nation of God's choice and calling, and 'the gifts and calling of God are without repentance', Rom. 11. 29. Whatever Israel may yet pass through, as to the purpose of God, Israel can never cease to be the nation of His choice.

The nation had a beginning when God called a man, Abram, Gen. 12. 1. He bound Himself to them by covenants,[7] which involved a land with definite territorial dimensions, prosperity and a kingdom. Those promises would be fulfilled in Abraham's seed,[8] and David's Son, Luke 1. 32, 33. But Christ came and was rejected, John 1. 11. He came in humiliation, and they did not want Him. He will come again in great glory to deliver Israel.[9] In the meanwhile Israel is 'blinded', Rom. 11. 7, 8, 25, but God is saving Jews on the same basis as Gentiles, that of grace, v. 5. But when the church is complete, Israel will once more be the centre of His purposes. There will be a remnant amongst those gathered back to the land which will be looking for the Messiah. Oppressed by the Gentile nations, Zech. 14. 2, the nation will be delivered from their oppressors by 'the Deliverer' who comes 'out of Zion', Rom. 11. 25, 26 RV. He will come to earth to deliver them, Zech. 14. 3, 4.

The Gentiles. This refers to all the nations of mankind except God's chosen nation, Israel. We only read of Gentiles in the Old Testament as being in some way or other connected with Israel. When Israel were obedient, the Gentiles were either friendly or subjected to their yoke; when Israel were rebellious, the Gentiles were used to chasten them for their sins. God directed their history, though they were not in the main line along which He carried forward His gracious purpose, Acts 17. 26, 30. Furthermore, God distributed the Gentile nations around Israel in such a way that they might have the opportunity of seeking the Lord by contact with His people, Deut. 32. 8.

When Judah was taken in captivity to Babylon, however, a new development took place. It signalized the commencement of 'the times of the Gentiles', Luke 21. 24, the period of Gentile world power. The 'times' started with Nebuchadnezzar, the rise of the Babylonian Empire,

---

[7] Gen. 12. 1-3; 13. 14-17; 15. 18-21; 22. 17, 18; Deut. 30. 1-10; 2 Sam. 7. 8-16; Luke 1. 32, 33.

[8] Gen. 15. 18; 22. 18; Gal. 3. 16.

[9] Isa. 60. 2, 3; 66. 19-24; Jer. 16. 14-16; 23. 2-8; Zech. 14. 1-21, etc.

and the fall of Judah. The course of these 'times' is found in visions in Daniel chapters 2 and 7, the former of an imposing, powerful figure, the latter of wild beasts. The first presents man's conception of world empires, the latter reveals God's estimate. In the vision of chapter 2 the head of gold was the Babylonian empire as seen in its ruler, v. 38. Its successor, the Medo-Persian Empire, was pictured in the breast of silver, v. 39; cp. 5. 30, 31. In turn, that was succeeded by the Grecian Empire as seen in the belly and thighs of brass, 2. 39; cp. 8. 20, 21. The legs of iron represented the Roman Empire, Luke 2. 1. What of the feet of iron and clay? What of the reference to ten kings, 2. 42, 44? The Roman Empire has not existed in this form before. This is, then, still future, Rev. 13. 1. The stone, cut out without hands, that is, its irruption is without human instrumentality, comes from above, pulverizes this last form of the vision, and sets up an eternal kingdom, Ps. 2. 9; 2 Thess. 1. 7-10. Gentile government will be terminated by a sudden catastrophe. That coming of Christ will be when He comes to deliver Israel from Gentile oppression. Christ is coming first for His church to the air, then with them to earth to judge the Gentile world, and conclude the times of the Gentiles, and at that time He will also deliver Israel.

Gathering Together All Things in Christ. The Lord's coming in glory will also involve blessing. There will be **blessing for the church**, which will reign with Him, 2 Tim. 2. 12; Rev. 20. 4-6. His glory will be our glory; His rule will be shared with us. We shall be a kingdom of priests with Him. There will be **blessing for Israel**, for whom it will mean regeneration, Matt. 19. 28; Ezek. 37; Isa. 55. 8; refreshment, Acts 3. 19; restitution, Acts 3. 21, and redemption, Luke 2. 38. And finally, there will be **blessing for the Gentiles** for whom there shall be rest, Isa. 11. 10; and righteousness, vv. 4-5.

The 'Days' of Scripture - J. H. Large

Scripture quotations are taken from the Revised Version

Prophecy is such a vast subject that many are regrettably deterred from its study by the feeling that they will never be able to unravel the mass of seemingly complicated scriptures. We think that such will find that a careful examination of three particular 'days' will provide a useful frame of reference into which the many and varied features of prophecy can be fitted.

These are: (1) The Day of the Lord; (2) The Day of Christ; and (3) The Day of God, understanding 'day' to mean a protracted period in each instance.

The Day of the Lord. This is principally an Old Testament theme, where the expression occurs some twenty times, but related expressions like 'the day', 'that day' and 'that great day' occur about seventy times. Perusal of the scriptures will show that the Day of the Lord has to do with God's active and open intervention in world affairs at the end of this age.[10] Even if space allowed for comments on these passages, it would rob the student of the pleasure and profit of satisfying himself that they speak plainly about events on earth, involving Israel and the nations, specifying many geographical locations, the land of Israel and other countries, sites like Zion (Jerusalem), the house of the Lord (the temple), God's holy mountain, and the mount of Olives. He should also notice how the Day is associated with judgement, wrath, destruction, and the terror produced by these momentous happenings. The effects on the fortunes of Israel and the nations, especially as a result of the Lord reigning as King over all the earth, should also be considered.

The few references to the Day of the Lord in the New Testament are consistent with the Old Testament picture.[11] It is very important to notice that in 2 Thessalonians chapter 2 verse 2 'the day of Christ' KJV should read 'the day of the Lord' RV**.** Verses 8 to 12, therefore, describe certain aspects of the Day of the Lord.

Features similar to those of the Day of the Lord have emerged in the course of history, but these events have not been fulfilments but foreshadowings. Peter connected the events on the day of Pentecost with Joel's prophecy, but he did **not** say that the prophecy had been fulfilled. Many years after Pentecost, Paul and Peter spoke of the day of the Lord being yet future, 2 Thess. 2. 3; 2 Pet. 3. 10. That it is still future

---

[10] Isa. 2. 12-19; 11. 9-12; 12. 1-6; 13. 6-11; 14. 1-3; Joel 1. 15; 2. 1-11; 31-32; Zech. 14. 1-11.

[11] For example, Acts 2. 20; 1 Thess. 5. 1-3; 2 Pet. 3. 10.

is clear from the fact that the signs indicated have not occurred; see, for example, the passage just quoted, 'for it will not be, except... the man of sin be revealed', 2 Thess. 2. 3.

2 Peter chapter 3 verse 10 is very interesting in that the first part of the verse speaks of the opening of that Day (unexpected – 'as a thief') and the remainder of the verse of the close of that Day, 'in the which the heavens shall pass away with a great noise, and the elements shall be dissolved with fervent heat'. From this passage we learn that the Day of the Lord, commencing with God's sudden and unexpected intervention, will extend through the Lord's reign on earth, and on to the end of earth's history. This ties up with Old Testament prophecies linking the Day of the Lord with the Lord's reign over all the earth, e.g. Zech. 14. 9. Did Peter have this in mind when speaking of a thousand years in 2 Peter chapter 3 verse 8?; cp. Rev. 20. 2-7.

The Day of Christ, also called the Day of our Lord Jesus Christ, of our Lord Jesus, of Jesus Christ, and of Christ.[12]

If confusion is to be avoided, a clear distinction must be drawn between the Day of the Lord, and the Day of Christ. The latter is exclusively a New Testament theme – it is not envisaged in the Old Testament. The Day of Christ covers the same ground as the 'coming' of Christ for His people, as we shall see later by comparing similar expressions in parallel scriptures.

Before we do that it should be noted that 'coming' is an inadequate translation of the well-known word *parousia,*[13] which signifies not merely the arrival of a visitor, but also his subsequent presence with

---

[12] 1 Cor. 1. 8; 2 Cor. 1. 14; Phil. 1. 6, 10; 2. 16.

[13] Confusion has been caused by the false idea that the word ***parousia*** applies ***only*** to Christ's coming for, and His presence with, the church. It is a word of more general application; e.g., 'I rejoice at the coming (***parousia***) of Stephanas', 1 Cor. 16. 17. So the word, of itself, is quite appropriate for the 'coming' of the Son of man 'with power and great glory' to judge all the tribes of the earth, Matt. 24. 30. Christ 'comes' to the air for His people, and He 'comes' to earth to judge. The fact that the same word is appropriate to describe both does not invalidate in any way the distinctions to be drawn between the Day of the Lord and the Day of Christ.

those whom he has visited (see the margins of KJV and RV, 'presence').

'Coming' expresses one side of the truth, 'presence' the other side.

DAY OF CHRIST	COMING OF CHRIST
'We are your **glorying**, even as ye also are ours, in the day of our Lord Jesus', 2 Cor. 1. 14; cp. Phil. 2. 16.	'For what is our . . . crown of **glorying**? Are not even ye, before our Lord Jesus at his coming', 1 Thess. 2. 19.
'Who shall also **confirm** you unto the end, that ye be **unreproveable** in the day of our Lord Jesus Christ', 1 Cor. 1. 8.	'To the end he may **stablish** your hearts **unblameable** . . . at the coming of our Lord Jesus', 1 Thess. 3. 13.
'He which began a good work in you will **perfect it** until the day of Jesus Christ', Phil. 1. 6.	'May your spirit and soul and body be **preserved entire**, without blame at the coming of our Lord Jesus Christ', 1 Thess. 5. 23.

So the Day of Christ, and the coming of Christ, refer to a protracted period. That the two periods are identical will be seen by the following comparisons:

We need, then, to combine scriptures from both the groups represented by the above selections, in order to form a composite picture of the Day of Christ. It will then become abundantly clear that the Day of Christ is a complete contrast to the Day of the Lord. We cannot stay to tabulate the many points of contrast, not only in regard to the people and the spheres involved, but in the general character of the two 'Days', the one being largely associated with wrath and terror, and the other with comfort and joy.

The Day of God. This expression is found only in 2 Peter chapter 3 verse 12. The word 'wherein' (KJV) gives the impression that the heavens will be dissolved, and the elements melt with fervent heat in the Day of God. This is so similar to the language of verse 10 with regard to the Day of the Lord, as to make it appear that the Day of the Lord and the Day of God are one and the same thing. But verse 12 RV substitutes 'by reason of which' for 'wherein', and makes the meaning clear. The dissolution of the present heavens and earth at the close of the Day of the Lord is in preparation for the ushering in of the Day of God, and, with it, the new heavens and the new earth wherein dwelleth righteousness, v. 13. The word 'dwelleth' suggests the idea of 'being at home'. During the Day of the Lord righteousness will reign – it will be active to deal with any opposition to God's perfect will. In the Day of God, in the new heavens and the new earth, all will be in such exquisite accord with God's eternal purpose, that righteousness will at last have found its congenial home.

Peter's words, 'we look for', remind us that the hope of Christians is really three-fold. They look first for **Christ's coming for them**. Then, they look beyond that to **Christ's reign over the earth**, and then, beyond that to the final triumph in **the eternal state** where God will be all and in all.

'Wherefore, beloved, seeing that ye look for these things, give diligence that ye may be found in peace, without spot and blameless in his sight', 2 Pet. 3. 14.

The Lord's Coming for the Church - I. Harris

Tradition records that the frequent greeting of Christians in the early church was 'Maranatha!'. Moreover, the word was often the triumphant cry of believers in ancient Rome when they were cast to wild beasts, nailed to crosses, burned – the victims of hatred and persecution unleashed by a pagan society. In our Bibles the word appears but once, 1 Cor. 16. 22, with the meaning, 'Our Lord is coming!'.

An examination of the New Testament shows that the coming of the Lord for the church was not something relegated to obscurity or infrequent reference – quite the reverse. It is a theme to which the writings repeatedly return, and we can see from random verses selected from the New Testament that the first Christians saw this as their great hope, and were encouraged so to do.

The **fact** of the Lord's coming for the church is the subject of such emphasis that we wonder how any sincere Christian could fail to be gripped by the certainty of it. Consider first that it was **promised** by the Lord Himself, John 14. 3, (and this must surely provide the highest claim for our attention), in words used to His own disciples as they were gathered around Him: 'if I go . . . I will come again, and receive you unto myself; that where I am, there ye may be also'. Can such clear phraseology be misconstrued? It was **endorsed** by heavenly messengers on the occasion of Christ's ascension, and here we note the emphatic nature of their reassuring words to those who had witnessed the departure of Jesus: 'this same Jesus, which is taken up from you into heaven, shall so come in like manner as ye have seen him go into heaven', Acts 1. 11. It was repeatedly **confirmed** in the Epistles, for example 'ye turned . . . to serve the living and true God; and to wait for his Son from heaven . . . even Jesus', 1 Thess. 1. 9-10. And it is surely not without significance that the closing words of holy writ include the Lord's personal reiteration (for the third time in the chapter!), Rev. 22. 20, and the seer's responsive, thankful prayer, 'Surely I come quickly, Amen. Even so, come, Lord Jesus'.

Turning again to the word of God to determine the **manner** of the Lord's coming for the church, we find it to be personal, literal, purposeful, and dramatic. How could we legitimately 'spiritualize' or render mythological such plain assertions as 'I will come again', or 'this same Jesus . . . shall so come in like manner as ye have seen him go'? To do so would be to destroy at a stroke our acceptance of scripture and, indeed, the teaching of our Lord; take them at their face value and the personal and literal return of Christ cannot be in doubt.

Other passages expand upon this great event, so that we learn something of the associated happenings. Notably, 1 Thessalonians chapter 4 verses 14-18 provides an authoritative and dramatic picture: 'For the Lord himself shall descend from heaven with a shout, with the voice of the archangel, and with the trump of God', and likewise 1 Corinthians chapter 15 verses 51-52: 'In a moment, in the twinkling of an eye, at the last trump'.

And the **purpose**? We are not left to speculate, for scripture is clear. To quote 1 Thessalonians chapter 4 again, 'the dead in Christ shall rise first: then we which are alive and remain shall be caught up together with them in the clouds, to meet the Lord in the air: and so shall we ever be with the Lord', vv. 16-17.

So the plan of God and the promises of the Saviour will be coming to fruition: the dead raised, the living changed, the church complete, gathered across the centuries from every tribe and people, tongue and nation.

We do well to note the precision of scripture. The passages in 1 Corinthians and 1 Thessalonians to which we have referred do not speak of Christ's coming to be with us, but rather of our being changed, and meeting Him in the air. Inherent in the teaching of the Lord's return for the church is that those who are 'Christ's at his coming', 1 Cor. 15. 23, (that is, the millions who have passed through death and those alive on that great day), will be caught away from earth – the literal meaning of the original word is 'snatched away'.

Two other facets merit our consideration; they are closely linked. The Lord's coming for the church is one of the Christian's motivations, and it is most certainly the church's hope. How unthinkable merely to assemble the facts, and master a head knowledge of this glorious theme! True acceptance of the doctrine must result in greater devotion, and a surer foundation as we face life's future days, 1 Cor. 15. 58. Paul left the Thessalonians in no doubt of the significance of it all. He reminded them particularly of the inevitable sorrow of bereavement which arises on the loss of a loved one, but concluding his summary he says, 'Wherefore comfort one another with these words', 1 Thess. 4. 18.

More than this, John presents the Lord's coming to us as that which should greatly influence our living, 1 John 2. 28: 'abide in him; that, when he shall appear, we may have confidence, and not be ashamed before him at his coming'. Likewise 'every man that hath this hope in him purifieth himself, even as he is pure', 3. 3. Indeed the Christian should be looking forward to his Lord's coming[14] and that, of necessity, means a daily life pleasing to God and right with others.

Can we forget the Lord's coming? Surely not. Each time we celebrate the Lord's Supper we are reminded that we do it 'till he come', 1 Cor. 11. 26. Yet the fact is that over the years this sublime theme has sometimes been a true hope, burning bright and clear; at others it has grown faint

---

[14] See Phil. 3. 20; Titus 2. 13.

and dim, many believers seemingly being indifferent to its significance. On occasion the truth has been distorted by misguided folk, and grossly perverted by false sects.

What of us today? Shall we not turn again to the book which, unchanged, still tells of the coming of the Lord for the church? As we do, let us note that it gives guidance as to the conditions we may expect to see as His coming draws near. Perilous times, described in detail in 2 Timothy chapter 3; days when cynics sneer at the promise of His coming, 2 Pet. 3. 3, 4. It would not only be unwise but positively wrong to join the ranks of those who attempt to predict when He will come, but we do observe a likeness in conditions around us to those and other features mentioned in the Bible; they encourage us to believe that His coming may be very near.

The Judgement Seat of Christ - J. Boyd

PART ONE – FOUR VIEW-POINTS OF THE JUDGEMENT SEAT

These are the four main accounts of the Judgement Seat of Christ, each giving a different viewpoint of the judgement, namely,

1. The **Individuality** of the Judgement – Rom. 14. 10-12 – each one for himself.
2. The **Nature** of the Judgement – 1 Cor. 3. 10-15 – a thorough testing of works.
3. The **Basis** of the Judgement – 1 Cor. 4. 1-5 – a manifestation of secrets.
4. The **Purpose** of the Judgement – 2 Cor. 5. 9, 10 – a display of character.

Romans 14. 10-12. The theme of this chapter is the regard of brethren one for the other. A brother strong in faith, one rejoicing in the liberty of the gospel, ought not to receive a weak brother merely with a view to settle points on which they differ. A weak brother does not fully appreciate his liberty, but tends to Judaism, with its scruples about foods and Sabbath keeping.

The strong brother must not set his weak brother at nought. This leads to pride. On the other hand the weak brother must not judge the strong. 'Judge' here includes passing sentence, and its execution.

God has received both, v. 3, and He is able to make each stand, v. 4. Thus neither should seek to criticize the other's way of thinking concerning matters not contrary to sound doctrine, nor affecting the moral conduct of believers. Each is free to hold his own opinions; each is answerable only to his Lord; each should be fully persuaded in his own mind about his beliefs. This difference of opinion must always be conformed to God's will, for to Him we live or die.

In verse 10 the apostle says why we should not judge nor despise our brethren. All, weak and strong, will stand before the Judgement Seat of Christ ('of God', RV).

This appearing is in keeping with Isaiah chapter 45 verse 23, which Paul cites, and from which he draws conclusions. Each one of us concerning himself shall give account to God. None will miss the testing of that day, nor escape the searching eyes of the Lord as he presents himself for judgement. The individuality of the judgement is stressed here, as the words 'each one of us' (RV) stand in the position of emphasis in the verse. Thus, we see why each should be fully persuaded in his own mind, v. 5, for each must stand in awful loneliness before the divine scrutiny. There will be none to prompt, and none upon whom to lay blame. Each will give his own account, not his brother's. He will explain his own attitude to the Judge. The word here translated 'account' is *logos*, lit., a word. It expresses the thought of the mind, the reason. Compare Acts chapter 19 verse 40. At the judgement seat each will explain to God the reasons for his attitude of mind towards things on earth. Finally, the account must be given to God; to none other are we obliged to answer; none other has a right to demand an explanation of the workings of our minds.

1 Corinthians 3. 10-15. Paul in 1 Corinthians chapter 3 deals with the tendency in the Corinthian church to form opinions concerning the relative merits of teachers. The various teachers are fellow-workers, all doing the work of God. God works through them, and He will reward the labourers. Then follows advice to would-be teachers, to labour keeping the judgement seat in view, vv. 10-15.

The picture Paul would set before his readers is this. A town surveyor wants houses built. He specifies the foundation, but leaves to the builders the choice of what the finished house should be like. To one is given the task of laying the foundation, but to different builders the erection of the superstructure.

Some build beautiful temple-like structures, with gold, silver and marble much in evidence. Others merely use the foundations upon which to place shacks, with wood, hay and stubble for building material. These look big, but cannot withstand adverse conditions. When the work is finished, it is inspected – the test applied being fire. What survives is shown to be of value, hence rewarded. What burns is lost; it has been wasted effort.

The key to the passage is verse 9, 'Ye are God's building', not in the sense of a finished house, but one in the course of erection. God is the surveyor. The building was commenced when the Corinthians were converted, the foundation being Jesus Christ, v. 11. Paul laid this foundation at Corinth.

Apollos and other teachers had built the superstructure, the spiritual and moral fruits produced in the believers by the teaching. There are many ways in which the superstructure may be added, and Paul warns the teachers to take heed how they build. Some build into it gold, silver and precious stones. They edify the church by their teaching, conversation and example, and succeed in developing in it a healthy spiritual life, abounding in sanctification and love. Others build wood, hay and stubble. These preach to attract the crowds; they tickle the ears with oratory; they produce only carnal Christians, characterized by jealousy and strife.

The Judgement Seat of Christ will be the testing time. The work will be tested by fire, figurative of the all-searching judgement of the eyes of the Lord, Rev. 1. 14, whose attributes are omniscience and consuming holiness. Each worker will receive his own reward, according to his own work, 1 Cor. 3. 8.

Verse 13 tells us when and how this judgement will take place. 'The day' is the day of Christ. It will be during the *parousia* of the Lord Jesus

Christ, 1 Thess. 3. 13. The results of the trial are seen in verses 14 and 15. What stands the test will be rewarded; what fails will be disapproved, and will receive no reward. He who had built with wood, hay and stubble will suffer loss, even though he himself will be saved. His eternal security will never be in doubt, for it was settled when he trusted Christ. The Judgement Seat of Christ has nothing to do with that. The apostle likens such a teacher to a builder who, while putting the finishing touches to his task, is overtaken by fire. He escapes with his life, but fails to save the building. He suffers the disappointment of seeing his work all go up in smoke. Had he put better materials into the building, the fire would have left it unscathed.

Paul would teach believers not to set too high an estimate upon their teachers. Those whose work brings them into the limelight now, may be shown to have nothing that will abide the fire in a coming day. Those whose work today is despised, may well be proved at the judgement seat to be worthy of reward, for their work is more solid, and will stand God's test. Let each of us who seek to build up God's people take heed how we build.

1 Corinthians 4. 1-5. Paul would have believers regard those who labour among them as ministers of Christ. The word translated 'minister' here is, lit., an under-rower, that is, a sailor serving under another's command. So teachers have the honour of serving under Christ. Paul also calls them stewards, lit., house-managers, administrators of something not their own. They teach deep things, even the way of salvation, not their own plan, but God's, 2. 7.

The steward, once he is commissioned by God, is required to be faithful to his trust. Whilst faithfulness is essential, it is not in man's province to assess it. This belongs to God. Though not despising the judgement of man, Paul considers it of little weight compared with God's. He places little value on the assembly's ('you', 4. 3), or on any human judgement (lit., man's day, that is, a human tribunal). Judgement in this verse means the critical examination of the qualities of a servant of God. Paul was not concerned about human criticism. He did not attach much value to his own evaluation of himself. Whilst his conscience did not upbraid him, yet he could not pronounce himself perfect. His conscience was not a safe guide. No human judge is competent. He who makes the only valid examination is the Lord, Rom. 14. 12.

Infallible judgement presupposes three things: (a) The proper time, when the acts of life are added up, and seen in all their fullness; (b) The bringing to light of things done secretly, both bad and good; (c) The manifestation of the motives that prompted service. The word here translated 'counsels' means the secret thoughts from which active volition proceeds. The Lord alone knows the motives and the secret things; He alone can make a true estimate of the work done.

Paul contrasts the Corinthians' criticism of their teachers with the results of God's investigation into their work. From God each man will have praise, each his own, and not what rightfully belongs to another.

As the Corinthians were placing too high a value on some teachers, Paul in chapter 3 mentions the severity of the test with which their works will be proved. But in chapter 4, when he is warning against the tendency to belittle the teacher, he indicates the praise that God will bestow on each one, despite what men think.

2 Corinthians 5. 1-11. In chapter 4 Paul mentions the affliction associated with his work of serving in the gospel. He calls it light affliction, and contrasts it with the abounding glory of the life to come. He goes on in chapter 5 to refer to the eternal state, when he will have left his earthly body, and will have gone to be with Christ. In view of this prospect, he is ambitious (RVmg) to be well-pleasing to his Lord. The word here translated 'ambitious' is that used of the Greek athlete striving for the laurel wreath.

In verse 10 Paul gives the reason why he wants to be well-pleasing to his Lord, namely, because, in company with all believers, he will be made manifest at the Judgement Seat of Christ. 'Manifest' suggests that the inmost soul will be displayed before all. The character will be seen; all false pretences will drop off; the believer will appear exactly as he is before God. The purpose of this manifestation is that each one may receive, not **for the things done**, but **the things done**, in the body. This is not his reward, but the display of his character, what he has done in his body here, whether good or bad. It is the handing back to a believer of his fully-developed character.

Paul regarded the Judgement Seat of Christ with fear. He had apparently been accused of handling the word of God deceitfully, 4. 2. This accusation he refutes, by reminding them that he kept the fear (RV) of the Lord always before him in his work of persuading men. This fear produced a great sense of accountability to God; it was manifest to God even then; Paul hoped that it would be manifest to their consciences also.

PART TWO – DEDUCTIONS CONCERNING THE JUDGEMENT SEAT

1. There will be Judgement for All Believers. 'God shall bring every work into judgment . . . whether good or evil', Eccles. 12. 14. The works of believers are not excluded. They too must stand before the Judge. Their eternal destiny is not in question; that was settled here on earth. But every 'born again' one must stand at the Judgement Seat of Christ for his investigation. None will miss it, Rom. 14. 10; 2 Cor. 5. 10.

2. There will be a Strictly Individual Investigation. 'Each man . . . concerning himself . . . to God', Rom. 14. 12. No intermediary, no priest, none to blame, none upon whom to rely for help. Alone before God each will speak for himself, and not for another. The ultimate responsibility for any action rests upon the individual, and for it he must give account personally.

In all the four accounts of the Judgement Seat of Christ the Revised Version stresses the strictly individual aspect of the judgement; **each** shall give account, Rom. 14. 12; **each** man's work shall be made manifest, 1 Cor. 3. 13; **each** man shall have his praise from God, 1 Cor. 4. 5; **each** one will receive the things done in the body, 2 Cor. 5. 10.

3. There will be a Rendering of Accounts, an Explanation of Reasons. Each shall give his own account, for out of his own mouth will God judge His servants, Luke 19. 22. He must give an account of his words, especially of his idle words, Matt. 12. 36; of his overseership, Heb. 13. 17; of his reasons for doing things, Rom. 14. 12. In that day God will show him his motives, and will ask, 'Why?' 1 Cor. 4. 5.

4. There will be Direct Dealing with God. The believer will give his account to none but God, the omniscient, impartial, and righteous Judge,

2 Tim. 4. 8. And from God direct shall he receive his praise, 1 Cor. 4. 5.

5. There will be an Evaluation of the Believer's Works. To His servants has God given the work of building up the saints, Eph. 4. 11, 12; Heb. 13. 17. How they have done this work will be investigated at the Judgement Seat of Christ.

Everyone who labours to build up the people of God should seek to produce in them likeness to Christ. This will abide the fire. He should not preach with his eye on the appreciation of his hearers. This causes believers to make distinctions between teachers, and produces strife and jealousy. Such will be burnt up.

6. There will be a Very Searching Judgement. So searching will be the judgement of our works that the Holy Spirit uses four different words to express the thoroughness of the testing, 1 Cor. 3. 13. Each man's work will be:

a) **Made manifest**, lit., become manifest, shine forth. It means that the work will be shown openly. Seven times this expression is used in the New Testament, and each time it means to show openly to all around. See especially Mark chapter 6 verse 14, where it is rendered 'spread abroad'.
b) **Declared**, lit., made evident. For the meaning of this word compare, 'Your speech betrays you', Matt. 26. 73 NKJV. No matter what Peter said about himself, his speech told what he was. So at the Judgement Seat of Christ the believer's works will be seen as they really are, not what he says about them.
c) **Revealed**, lit., uncovered, the veil removed by the fire. The believer's work will be seen with all its veneer removed.
d) These three words (in (a),(b), and (c) above) express a public manifestation of works, not merely a private insight into things.
e) **Tried** (RV 'prove'), lit., to test if fit to be received, as gold is tested and proved by fire before it is put into service, 1 Pet. 1. 7. So the believer's work is tested to see if it is worthy of a reward.

7. There will be a Recompense Following the Testing. After the testing of the believer's works there will be a righteous retribution. Each will receive a suitable return for work done. There will be a two-fold result, (a) Rewards for those whose work abides the fire, (b) Loss for those whose work is burnt up.

Rewards

a) A five-fold joy:
   1. Knowing that the Lord is satisfied with one's work;
   2. Seeing those whom one had led to Christ, 1 Thess. 2. 19;
   3. Seeing believers whose sanctification one's ministry had helped to accomplish, 2 Cor. 1. 14;
   4. Sharing the joy of the Lord, Matt. 25. 21;
   5. Knowing that one's work was not in vain, Phil 2. 16.

b) Praise from God, 1 Cor. 4. 5.

c) A glorious position in the new order established by the Lord at His *parousia*, Matt. 25. 21, 23.

d) Incorruptible crowns, 1 Cor. 9. 25:
   1. The shepherd's crown of unfading glory, 1 Pet. 5. 4;
   2. The crown of righteousness for faithful service, 2 Tim. 4. 8;
   3. The crown of life for enduring trials, Jas. 1. 12.

e) The bridal array of white linen, the righteous acts of saints, Rev. 19. 8 RV.

Losses

a) Missing a full reward, 2 John 8.

b) The possibility of another taking his crown, Rev. 3. 11.

c) Forfeiting an honourable position in the kingdom, Luke 19. 17-26.

d) Less joy, less praise from God.

e) Shame, 1 John 2. 28.

f) Reproof, 1 Cor. 1. 8.

g) Regret, as he sees his work burned up. No punishment, but loss.

8. There will be Judgement based on Two Things.

(a) **The Bringing to Light of all Secret Deeds**. This is necessary for the proper evaluation of work. Some things done in secret are worthy of praise, some of blame. None but the eye of God sees these; He alone can assess these; He alone is fit to judge the steward's services. None but God knows the little things done quietly that have helped believers in their trials. None but God can estimate the harm done to another's conscience by a word wrongly spoken. It will take the Judgement Seat of Christ to bring to light the things done in secret.

(b) **The Manifestation of the Believer's Motives**. What causes a man to form resolutions is unknown to his fellow. He may know of the other's will, but what prompts that will, what his motives are, mere man cannot determine. To God alone these are apparent. He, who judges the work by the motives whence the actions sprang, is alone fitted to estimate fully the value of work done. Motives that miscarried, or that were thwarted, must be taken into consideration before a true estimate of the Christian's service can be made.

These will be made manifest at the Judgement Seat of Christ. Not till then will any be able to understand fully the work of those who labour for the Lord.

9. There will be Praise for All. When all these secret deeds have been brought to light, and the motives of men's hearts have been made manifest, God will find something in each of us that He can praise.

Each believer will have his individual recognition by God. Each will get his own praise, and not another's. God is omniscient; He will make no mistakes; He will praise impartially where it is deserved.

Those who have been misunderstood here will be praised aright at the Judgement Seat of Christ; those who have worked unostentatiously will be praised openly; those who worked for praise here will find little in that day, Matt. 6. 2. Let us seek praise then, and not now. We can afford to wait, for then it will be sweeter, as it comes from the Master Himself.

10. There will be a Full Manifestation of All. We must all be made manifest before, lit., in front of, the Judgement Seat of Christ, 2 Cor. 5. 10 RV. For an illustration of this compare Acts chapter 18 verse 17. As we stand there we shall all be fully manifest, our inmost soul displayed. There will be a manifestation of the believer's **mind**, Rom. 14, of his **materials**, 1 Cor. 3, of his **motives**, 1 Cor. 4, of his **manners**, 2 Cor. 5.

11. There will be a Judgement to be Regarded with Fear. With Paul we should make it our ambition to be well-pleasing to God. We should fear the Lord, not with the slavish fear of punishment, but with the reverence and regard due to One who knows us so thoroughly, and who will one day manifest us fully. We should regard the day of Christ with awe. The Judgement Seat of Christ will be no mere prize-giving. It will be a time of solemn manifestation, a time of true estimation, and a time to be kept ever before our minds.

Let us be so conscious of this fear that it will mould our thoughts, and model our actions as we seek to do the little bit of service that God has for us down here.

OTHER CONSIDERATIONS IN CONNECTION WITH THE JUDGEMENT SEAT

1. The Time of its Occurrence. The time of rewards will be during the *parousia* of the Lord Jesus Christ, 1 Thess. 2. 19. It will be during that period called in scripture 'The day of Christ', Phil. 2. 16, 'The day of Jesus Christ', 1. 6, 'The day of the Lord Jesus', 1 Cor. 5. 5, 'The day of our Lord Jesus Christ', 1. 8.

The time of rewards will be **after** the rapture, but **before** the coming of the Lord in glory. Then shall the saints be manifested with Him, Col. 3. 4, and shall be arrayed in their righteous acts, Rev. 19. 8 RV, received at the Judgement Seat of Christ.

2. The Conditions under which the Believer will Appear. At the rapture the Lord will give to His people bodies of glory like unto His own. In glorified bodies they will appear before the judgement seat. In this condition they will fully appreciate and approve the decisions of the Judge on that day. Being in the likeness of Christ, there will be no jealousy, nor envy, nor questionings concerning the fairness of the awards. God will be vindicated in all His dealings.

3. The Mention of Sins at the Judgement Seat of Christ. The believer's sins are covered, Ps. 32. 1; they have been cast behind God's back, Isa. 38. 17; they are in the depths of the sea, Mic. 7. 19; they have been blotted out as a cloud, Isa. 44. 22; God has promised to remember them no more, Heb. 8. 12. Whilst this is all true, the believer's works will be manifested at the Judgement Seat of Christ, whether they be good or bad. Thus there will be mention of his evil deeds. This will not constitute a punishment. It will not call forth recriminations from fellow-believers.

All with one consent will fall down to praise the God who so dealt in mercy, despite the believer's delinquencies. The more he knows of his sins the more he will love the Lord Jesus Christ, Luke 7. 47.

When a sinner trusts Christ the penalty of his sins is remitted. But sins' results are not all manifest here on earth. They will be at the Judgement Seat of Christ. Then those who were wronged here will be vindicated. God is a righteous Judge, and He will deal in righteousness with each one.

Whilst God will not remember the believer's sins He will not forget them. They will not be remembered, in that God will not again demand satisfaction for them. This was done once for all at the cross, and God is satisfied with that sacrifice. But the believer's wrong deeds will not be forgotten; they will be mentioned at the judgement seat. Just as David's sin against Uriah, as Peter's sin of denying his Lord, and as the sins of other believers recorded in holy writ, though forgiven, will last as long as God's word lasts, so will remain the evil deeds of believers today. The results of a careless life will be under review, a life lived to self, and not to God.

4. The Comparison and Contrast with the Great White Throne. There is a similarity between the Judgement Seat of Christ and the great white throne. In each the verdict has nothing to do with the eternal destiny of those appearing. This was fixed beforehand, John 3. 16, 18. In each the subjects of the judgement must give their accounts, Rom. 14. 12; 1 Pet. 4. 5. In each there will be degrees of award, 1 Cor. 3. 8; Matt. 11. 22.

But there is a difference between the judgements in that one is for believers only, and the other for the unsaved only. One is before the Day of the Lord; the other is after it. In one there are awards of praise; in the other of punishment.

Conclusions. The Judgement Seat of Christ will take place during the presence of the church with the Lord in heaven, prior to its manifestation with Him over the earth. Believers, and believers only, will be judged there. The questions under consideration will be the believer's works, not his destiny. The judgement will be a thorough, individual investigation into the believer's actions, his motives and his beliefs. Then the omniscient One will show him the true value of his service. The result of the judgement will be, not **where** he will spend eternity, but **how** – in what position of honour. Each will receive praise from his Lord for services rendered.

It will be a time not to be regarded lightly, but seriously; a time to be feared, lest, after all the service he thought to have done for the Lord, he will be disapproved in that day.

May this consideration of the Judgement Seat of Christ cause us all to mould our lives, and examine our works, in view of the solemn issues of that day.

'Behold, I come quickly; and My reward is with Me, to render to each man according as his work is', Rev. 22. 12 RV.

The Mystery of the Jewish Nation* - C. GAHAN

'For I would not, brethren, that ye should be ignorant of this mystery, lest ye should be wise in your own conceits; that blindness in part is happened to Israel, until the fulness of the Gentiles be come in', Rom. 11. 25. Written large on the pages of scripture and history is the story of God's dealings with His people Israel, and, little as they may realize it, the ultimate destiny of the nations of the earth is most intimately connected with Palestine and the Jewish people. From of old God had a glorious purpose for them, but, because of their constant backsliding, He scattered them among the nations; nevertheless, they are still God's chosen people and His purpose for them remains unchanged. The Jews are the people of the promises, the people through whom Christ after the flesh should come; they had a unique mission in the world, they were set apart to make God known to the nations of the earth. Well might the apostle Paul say, 'What advantage then hath the Jew? ... Much every way: chiefly, because that unto them were committed the oracles of God', Rom. 3. 1, 2. Divine truth was communicated to them, that through them it might be made known to the world. The Bible, therefore, came to us through the Jews; and the very laws which govern human life today and upon which the vast fabric of civilization rests have much of their basis in the statutes of God preserved by the Jewish people.

Further, not only may the Jewish people be a more highly honoured people in the world today, they are the most ancient. They have witnessed the rise and fall of the world's mightiest empires, survived all the great nations of the past, and they will survive all the great nations of the future. Almost all nations have at some time or another sought to exterminate the Jew, but the Jew cannot be exterminated, nor can he be assimilated. Concerning Israel God had decreed, 'The people shall dwell alone, and shall not be reckoned among the nations', Num. 23. 9, and they are not so reckoned to this day. Other peoples when dispersed abroad have been absorbed into other nations, but it is not so with the Jew. The Jew always remains a Jew no matter what country gave him birth. No matter where the Jew lives or what he does, he still retains his identity, and God has so scattered them that one cannot go anywhere without finding a Jew.

The Jew is the miracle and mystery of the ages, but it is the mystery that requires our attention here, the mystery being 'that blindness in part is happened to Israel'. For the word 'blindness', the Revised Version gives the word 'hardening', but for the purpose we have before us we prefer the word 'blindness'. That the Jews were blind is a fact beyond question, and many scriptures specifically say so; they were deliberately blind to God's goodness, to God's purpose, and to their own best interests, and for their folly He gave them 'the spirit of slumber, eyes that they should not see, and ears that they should not hear', Rom. 11. 8. Elsewhere, in a Psalm of the rejected Messiah David says, 'Let their eyes be darkened, that they see not', Ps. 69. 23, and Paul, a distinguished Jewish convert of New Testament times, has this to say of his fellow countrymen: 'But their minds were blinded: for until this day remaineth the same vail untaken away in the reading of the old testament; which vail is done away in Christ', 2 Cor. 3. 14. Well might one of their own prophets say, 'They shall walk like blind men, because they have sinned against the Lord', Zeph. 1. 17. Now let us consider some of the implications of this blindness.

This Blindness was Judicial. It was a judgement sent from the hand of God. We have said that no other nation ever has been so highly honoured as the Jewish nation; on the other hand no other nation ever has been so deeply guilty as this one; no other nation has sinned so long, so stubbornly and so desperately against the light of God's offered mercy. At long last, when in the blindness and madness of their hearts they killed the Prince of life, the long-promised Messiah, God carried out His repeated warning and scattered them among the nations; and the very nations that they were raised up to save, now became so many rods to flay them. From that moment the whole world became their enemy and for nearly two thousand years they have been robbed, persecuted, maltreated, enslaved, outraged, and hounded to death, and it all began in their own beautiful land. One million, one hundred thousand Jews were slain, and ninety-seven thousand were taken prisoners, when the Romans desolated Palestine. Constantine the Great decided to befriend the Jews who had survived the slaughter, but later changed his mind, cut off their ears, and dispersed them as vagabonds. From time to time many a country on the face of the earth has witnessed and willingly aggravated their sufferings; even in so-called Christian England they have been murdered and pillaged. On more than one occasion in the history of these islands, every Jew was imprisoned and his wealth appropriated by the state. Once King John imprisoned every adult Jew he could find in order to discover their possessions; then, by cruel torture, he extorted from them vast sums of money. At the coronation of Richard the First, mobs killed every Jew they could find, plundered them and set fire to their homes, and Edward the First decreed that the Jews and all that they possessed belonged to the king, but later he relented to the extent of taking only half their possessions.

To come to modern times; in Russia during the revolution there were four million Jews and many of them perished by the sword; as for the remainder, their sufferings were indescribable. In Germany during the Second World War six million Jews perished in the Holocaust. These are some of the ways in which the Jews have suffered during the present dispensation, and will continue to do so until the rod of chastisement is withdrawn.[15] All too often it is forgotten that God deals with nations in the same way that He deals with individuals. Nations, like individuals,

[15] [Editor's Note] God's spiritual hardening of Israel in no way justifies Christendom's persistent maltreatment of the Jews through the centuries; the Gentile nations responsible will yet face a solemn day of reckoning, cp. Isa. 10. 5-19.

must reap what they sow, and having sown to the wind the nation of Israel must reap the whirlwind. It was not merely that they had failed, their failure was a **guilty** failure; they had not only sinned grievously and deliberately, they had sinned against light and knowledge.

Nor must it be forgotten that God is dealing with the nations of the earth today just as certainly as He dealt with the Jewish nation, and He is dealing with them with special reference to their treatment of Israel. Whilst Israel's sufferings have been a judgement sent from the hand of God, woe unto them by whom they came. Gentile world powers have aggravated those sufferings; they have always found a fiendish delight in persecuting and maltreating God's chosen people, but no nation ever persecuted the Jew and escaped national retribution. We have only to think of Babylon, Egypt, Assyria, Persia, Greece, and Rome for examples of this. How are the mighty fallen! These nations once ruled the world, but because they dared to tread down the nation of God's choice, they themselves have been trodden down. The same thing is true of the great Western powers; as we have seen, they have at some time or another exploited and oppressed the Jewish people and judgement will certainly come. When they have served God's purpose they will be set aside and nothing will save them; in the language that describes the great image in Daniel chapter 2, they shall be broken in pieces. Israel's blindness is the direct result of their own sin, but let the nations beware; the Jewish people are still the people of God and no one can meddle with them except at their peril. Despised and hated by this world they may now be, but in the new earth that is yet to be, no people will be so great and glorious as restored and converted Israel.

Israel's Blindness is only Partial. In Romans chapter 11 verse 25, the apostle says that 'blindness in part is happened to Israel'. While the great mass of the Jewish nation had come under the judgement of God, there were and are individual exceptions to this: 'there is a remnant according to the election of grace', Rom. 11. 5. For example, he mentions the case of Elijah; the kingdom of Israel under Ahab had fallen into an awful apostasy, and darkness covered the land. Yet unknown to the prophet, God had reserved for Himself 7,000 men who had not bowed the knee to Baal. Later, in the still darker days of Malachi, there was a godly remnant. Amid the deepening gloom we are told that there were those 'that feared the Lord . . . and that thought upon his name', Mal. 3.

16. Later still, when darkness covered the whole land of Palestine, we find a little band of men and women welcoming Israel's Messiah. Even in that dark day, there were godly Jews waiting for the coming of Him who was to be the consolation of His people Israel. So, too, in the apostles' day there were godly believing Jews. The greatest of all apostles, the apostle Paul, was a Jew; he was an Israelite of the purest blood, but his eyes had been opened by the Spirit of God and gladly he had accepted God's way of salvation by faith.

Broken off the Jewish nation may be, but that does not prevent individual Jews coming into the blessing of salvation. Indeed, 'to the Jew first' was the watchword of the first preachers of the gospel; our Lord commanded His disciples to 'go rather to the lost sheep of the house of Israel', Matt. 10. 6. To these lost Jewish sheep, therefore, they went, and many of them were brought into the Redeemer's flock. In the first New Testament churches, converted Jews predominated, and from then until now myriads of Jews have received the gospel of the grace of God. All of which underlines the apostle's words, 'that blindness in part is happened to Israel'. This blindness is only partial; while the great mass of the Jewish nation have departed from the living God, there always has been a faithful remnant who have received the salvation of God. In countless cases the gospel has been 'the power of God unto salvation' to believing Jews.

Third, in explaining the mystery of Israel's blindness the apostle intimates that

This Blindness was Providential. There was a wonderful and far-reaching aim in Israel's blindness; it was overruled for the enrichment of the Gentiles. To the Jew the Lord Jesus came to fulfil the promises made to their fathers; 'He came unto his own, and his own [His own people, the Jews] received him not', John 1. 11. In the divine programme this contingency had been foreseen, and provision had been made to meet it. The long-promised Messiah had come; the King had offered Himself to Israel, but they had rejected Him, and this opened the way for the coming in of the Gentiles. Jewish unbelief cannot frustrate the purpose of God; the Lord Jesus was then despised and rejected, so they were set aside and the Gentiles brought in that God might take out of them 'a people for his name', Acts 15. 14.

This is what God is doing in this age; He is calling out of the Gentiles a people for His name, and constituting that people the church. Israel's fall, therefore, not only opened the way for the coming in of the Gentiles, it prepared the way for the manifestation of God's purpose concerning the church. The King being rejected by His own nation the Jews, the kingdom in glory has been postponed and the church has been established. The church has superseded Israel, and the divine testimony committed to them has been taken from them and given to the church. The purpose of God now is the out-calling of the church, and what is the church's business in this age? Must she begin where Israel left off? Must she take up the work of the rejected King and establish His kingdom on earth? By no means! The King who was rejected is now in heaven, and the kingdom cannot be set up while the King is absent. Must and will the church convert the world? Again the answer is in the negative. If we wait for the church to convert the world, the world never will be converted. This does not mean the church has failed – the scriptures nowhere intimate that the church will convert the world; to the contrary, the Bible teaches that throughout the church's day the world will get further and further away from conversion. What then is the church's business in this dispensation? Her great business is not to convert the world, but to evangelize the nations, that from them God may take a people for His name. Men must be left without excuse; until our Lord returns the gospel must be preached for a witness to all nations.

Thus did Israel's blindness open a door of opportunity to the Gentiles, but this leaves no room for Gentile boasting. For in Romans chapter 11 verse 25 the apostle is addressing Gentiles, 'For I would not', he says, 'that ye should be ignorant of this mystery, lest ye should be wise in your own conceits'. That Gentiles have been brought into the scope of God's electing purpose is not due to any merit of their own. Gentiles have no reason for pride, but much reason for gratitude; of this we can be certain: God will not be less severe with Gentiles than He was with His own nation the Jews. At the present time it is severity towards the Jews and goodness towards Gentiles, but it is only goodness towards Gentiles so long as they make wise and proper use of this time of opportunity. If they fail, they will, like their Jewish predecessors, be cut off; thus Gentile privilege involves a corresponding responsibility.

Jewish blindness was the occasion, and not the cause, of mercy being extended to Gentiles. God overruled it, and made it the opportunity for gathering out of the Gentiles a people, His church; with the still further purpose that, when the church is completed and gathered in, Israel also shall be recovered and restored. This brings us to the conclusion of the whole matter; in explaining the mystery of Israel's blindness the apostle is most careful to remind us that

This Blindness is not Final. There is a definite time limit to Israel's blindness; it is not a permanent blindness, it is only 'until the fullness of the Gentiles be come in'. This expression, 'the fullness of the Gentiles', means the complete number God will take out of the Gentiles in this dispensation, in this age in which 'blindness in part is happened to Israel'. We have seen that with the setting aside of Israel, salvation came to the Gentiles. True to God's promise, the Messiah came to the Jewish people. Instead of receiving Him, they crucified Him; since they rejected the Lord Jesus, God rejected them and turned to the Gentiles. For Gentiles He inaugurated a dispensation of grace, a dispensation when 'whosoever shall call upon the name of the Lord shall be saved', Acts 2. 21. But a day is coming when Gentile blessing will have reached its fullness, and when that day comes Israel's blindness shall be removed. In the words of Romans chapter 11 verse 26, 'And so all Israel shall be saved; as it is written, There shall come out of Sion the Deliverer, and shall turn away ungodliness from Jacob'. Israel's extremity becomes God's opportunity; at the very moment when the armies of the Beast are about to destroy the last remnant of the Jewish nation, the Lord Jesus, the Deliverer, will intervene. Descending to Mount Olivet with His saints, He will not only destroy Israel's last and most terrible enemies, He will, at the same time, remove forever the veil of blindness from her eyes. Then it is that the Jewish nation will be born again; recognizing and receiving their Messiah, the whole nation will be reborn. In that day, a converted and restored Israel will become God's light in the world and nations will come to that light, and kings to the brightness of its shining. The church has a glorious destiny but her calling is heavenly, and this will distinguish the church's role from that of the converted Jews of a coming day. The church will reign over the nations in the heavenlies, and the converted Jews will reign over the nations of the earth. As far as the earth is concerned, Palestine and the Jewish people will be the centre of all God's interests, and the focus of all God's dealings in that day.

Daniel's Seventy Weeks - W. F. NAISMITH

SIR EDWARD DENNY, that eminent Bible teacher, once observed that Daniel's seventy weeks formed the backbone of prophecy. The book of Daniel, which was authenticated by our Lord Jesus Christ, Matt. 24. 15, is a remarkable prophecy, and deals specifically with the end times. Daniel had addressed God, confessing his sins and those of his people, and, while speaking in prayer, the man Gabriel came to him informing him that he had been sent to give Daniel skill and understanding, Dan. 9. 21, 22. Daniel was designated a man 'greatly beloved', and to him there was given an unfolding of divine purpose.

The Divisions of the Seventy Weeks. In Daniel chapter 9 verses 24 to 27 there is presented the outlined programme regarding God's people Israel. 'Seventy weeks [or seventy sevens] are determined upon thy people and upon the holy city'. The seventy weeks are divided thus: 'from the going forth of the commandment to restore and to build Jerusalem unto the Messiah the Prince shall be seven weeks [or seven sevens], and three score and two weeks'. The 'going forth of the commandment' was in the time of Artaxerxes, king of Persia, as recorded in Nehemiah chapter 2. This relates to the building of the wall and the city of Jerusalem in troubled times. A perusal of the book of Nehemiah will readily reveal the conditions obtaining when the work was accomplished. Seven weeks (or seven sevens) measure out a total of 49 years. From the completion of the building of the wall and city until the entry of Christ through its gates, riding upon an ass, and a colt the foal of an ass, Matt. 21. 5, 9, was a further sixty-two times seven years, or 434 years. It will be remembered that Daniel had been informed that seventy weeks were determined upon his people, and upon his holy city. There is, therefore, one week (or seven years) still to be fulfilled. When the sixty-nine weeks were fulfilled Messiah was cut off and had nothing, Dan. 9. 26 RV.

The Seventieth Week – Some Features. It is important to distinguish between the two princes referred to in Daniel chapter 9. The first is Messiah the Prince: the second is the 'prince that shall come'. It is 'the people of the prince that shall come' who shall destroy the city, v. 26.

There are two essential factors at the end times. First, the Jew must be back in the land of Immanuel; this was made possible through the Balfour Declaration and the ensuing developments. Second, the Roman Empire must be restored. It may be that this second factor is beginning to take shape at this very time. Each of these communities will have a leader, as can be ascertained from an examination of Revelation chapter 13. The first of these is seen coming out of the sea. Since the book of Revelation is a figurative book, we feel justified in using the divinely-given symbolism to determine the meaning of this picture. We read, 'The waters which thou sawest, where the whore sitteth, are peoples, and multitudes, and nations, and tongues', Rev. 17. 15. Out of the disturbed conditions of the nations, the head of the revived Roman Empire will arise. Compare carefully Daniel chapter 2 verses 31-49 with Daniel chapter 7. In the former passage, an outline of the history of Gentile imperialism is revealed in the image which Nebuchadnezzar saw. Note the deterioration in the metals in this image from gold to miry clay. The second beast of Revelation is seen coming out of the earth or 'land'. This is the anti-Christ of the coming day. The first beast has seven heads and ten horns. The seven heads, it is intimated, are the seven hills upon which Rome stands. The ten horns (horns denoting power) are the leaders of the ten kingdom confederacy of Western Europe, Rev. 17. 12. In the image of Daniel chapter 2 there are ten toes, part of iron and part of clay, which do not coalesce. The second beast has two horns like a lamb, but speaks like a dragon, 13. 11. The duplicity which characterizes this beast is detected whenever he opens his mouth. These two leaders, who are satanically inspired, will make a covenant for one week, or seven years. The apostate part of Jewry under the leadership of anti-Christ will, for political purposes, and protection against the northern threat, make a covenant with the head of the revived Roman Empire.

It is clear from Revelation chapter 17 verse 8 that the Roman Empire will be revived. We learn that, 'the beast which thou sawest was, and is not; and shall ascend out of the bottomless pit, and go into perdition', is only a symbol of Rome in its different phases. The Roman Empire existed when Christ was born, 'it was', for under Caesar Augustus a decree was issued that all the world should be taxed, Luke 2. 1. That Empire has long since ceased to exist, but it will be revived when God's prophetic clock begins again, and that will be consequent upon the coming of Christ to take out of this world His own.

The Seventieth Week – the Two Divisions. The 'week' is divided into two parts. During the first half of Daniel's seventieth and last week, the seven-sealed book will be opened, Rev. 6. In the opening of the first four seals there is the description of the four horsemen of the Apocalypse. First, there is a bloodless conquest, and a phase of peace though this is short-lived. This is followed by war, in the train of which comes famine, death, and hell. The fifth seal reveals the souls of them that were slain for the word of God, and for the testimony which they held, crying out for vengeance on those earth-dwellers of the Apocalypse. Under the sixth seal there is darkness, the sun refuses to shine, and the stars fall – that is, potentates of time are robbed of their prestige and position before men. Through the breaking of the seventh seal, judgement paves the way for the commencement of the seven trumpet judgements, and finally for the vial judgements.

The latter half of Daniel's seventieth week is that period which is designated 'the great tribulation'. In the midst of the week, that is, after the first three and a half years have run their course, the covenant is not broken, as suggested by some, but the sacrifice and oblation are commanded to cease, that is, idolatry is introduced and worship to God is ended, Rev. 13. 12-18. The covenant which is made is designated a covenant with death and an agreement with hell. This covenant with death shall be disannulled, and the agreement with hell shall not stand, Isa. 28. 15-18. The Lord has a mighty and strong one which, as a tempest of hail and a devouring storm, as a flood of mighty waters overflowing, shall cast down to the earth with a hand. The framers of this covenant thought to have made themselves safe from the overflowing scourge that would pass through, and, like the ostrich, they would bury their heads in the sand, and say 'it shall not come unto us: for we have made lies our refuge, and under falsehood have we hid ourselves', v. 15.

Numerous scriptures indicate the duration of this time of severe trouble for the people of God's choice, the Jews. In that parenthetical portion of Revelation, the time is limited to 'a time, and times, and half a time', 12. 14. It is alluded to as 'a time and times and the dividing of time', Dan. 7. 25. The same period is referred to as 'forty and two months', Rev. 11. 2; see also 13. 5. It is a period confined to 'a thousand two hundred and three-score days', 11. 3; 12. 6. This period of tribulation lasting for three and a half years, and referred to by our Lord, Matt. 24. 21, will have no equal in the history of the past, nor shall there ever be anything to compare with it in the years of the future. By restricting the days to one thousand two hundred and three-score the elect will be saved, otherwise 'there should no flesh be saved', v. 22.

Conditions and Events on Earth - J. Heading

The Old Testament often runs the subject of the distant prophetic future on to events that were then quite near at hand. This is because the existence of the church of Christ from Pentecost to the rapture was not revealed to the Old Testament prophets. Thus the fourth beast (what we shall call the Roman empire), Dan. 7. 7, following the leopard kingdom (the Grecian kingdom), v. 6, existed in the days of the Lord Jesus on earth, and stretches up to the time of the Lord's coming in judgement without any apparent break, vv. 7-27. New Testament teaching, however, is given in the light of the existence of the church. The rapture is clearly explained, with subsequent events on earth (taking up Daniel chapter 7 again) that must take place prior to the Lord's coming in glory and judgement.

There are many paragraphs in the scriptures dealing with these subsequent events, though the attentive reader will discover many further references in the Lord's and the apostolic teaching.[16] Without the present restraint laid upon men (through the Holy Spirit and the testimony of believers on earth), there will be factions amongst men seeking their own advantage, heading up in vast power struggles for ultimate dominion over the earth.

Revelation chapters 4 to 19 presents readers with scenes in heaven prior to scenes on earth. The scene in chapters 4 to 5 is not that of divine

---

[16] These are: Matt. 24. 3-51 (the experience of the Jews); Mark 13. 5-37 (similar to Matthew chapter 24); Luke 12. 36-48 (part of Matthew chapter 24); 17. 20-37 (part of Matthew chapter 24); 21. 7-38 (part of Matthew chapter 24); 2 Thess. 2. 3-12 (the man of sin and his activity); 2 Peter and Jude (the heading up of apostasy, though not exclusively dealing with this period); Revelation chapter 4 to 19 (the final growth of apostasy, and answering judgements from heaven).

activity in eternity; rather, these two chapters depict the throne on high prepared for judgement. Paul, when he had been caught up into the third heaven, was not allowed to describe what he had heard, Acts 14. 19; 2 Cor. 12. 2-4. Consequently, when he later wrote to the Thessalonians about the rapture, he could say nothing about what would take place immediately afterwards, 1 Thess. 4. 13-17. But John was caught up in the spirit, Rev. 4. 1, 2, answering to the rapture taking place when judgement on the house of God had first been completed among the seven churches, Rev. 2-3. John was allowed to publicize what he saw and heard in heaven, events taking place immediately after the rapture both in heaven and on earth.

The throne is seen as the pure and righteous centre in heaven, occupied by the supreme Godhead desiring pleasure from the creation of all things, 4. 11, and surrounded by worshipping companies, particularly the twenty-four elders which we believe denote the freshly raptured church in its priestly capacity of God-given approach to the throne. The executor of judgement is the Lamb, 5. 6, unique in His capacity to unloose the seals of the scroll, a capacity arising from His having been slain, and from the fact that redemption had been achieved thereby, thus to save the redeemed out of every nation from judgement, v. 9.

Revelation chapters 6 to 19 do not present a chronological picture of events on earth. Chapters 6 to 11 deal with matters essentially **moral and social**. The seven seals followed by the seven trumpets (the last three being called the three woes) end with the last trump when the Lord returns in glory, 'The kingdoms of this world are become the kingdoms of our Lord, and of his Christ', 11. 15. Chapters 12 to 14 deal with matters essentially **political**; we find a pictorial summary of the history of the Jews and their Messiah, together with the last of men's kingdoms on earth, ending with the Son of man reaping the harvest of the earth, and an angel gathering the vine of the earth for judgement, 14. 15, 19. Chapters 15 to 19 deal with matters essentially **religious**, here we read of the seven last plagues, ending with the fall of Babylon whose description is fully given. This section ends with the victorious coming of the 'King of kings, and Lord of lords', 19. 16. In these three sections, there are considerable overlaps, the last two sections both containing references to the 'beast' and to 'Babylon'. This is because the ultimate development of (what we shall call) imperial Rome and papal

Rome occurs side by side simultaneously.

In Daniel chapters 2, 7, and 8, four kingdoms are described under various symbols, stretching from the Babylonian kingdom under Nebuchadnezzar to the period we are considering in this study.

The Fourth Kingdom. In Nebuchadnezzar's dream-image, interpreted by Daniel, the legs were of iron, Dan. 2. 33, referring to strength, v. 40. In the vision of the four beasts later, the fourth beast is not named, 7. 7; it is called 'dreadful and terrible, and strong exceedingly; and it had great iron teeth: it devoured and brake in pieces . . . and it was diverse from all the beasts that were before it'. No animal pictorially could represent it. Since Greece as an empire collapsed sometime before the Lord's birth, evidently the fourth kingdom takes us to the New Testament, referring to imperial Rome. Daniel chapter 7 lists no further kingdom prior to the end of world empires on earth; the visions therefore lead up to the end times. Millennial conditions follow: 'the God of heaven (shall) set up a kingdom, which shall never be destroyed', 2. 44; the beast is slain, the kingdom being given to the Son of man, 7. 9, 13, 14. The Roman kingdom therefore stretches from the Lord's first advent to His second advent in glory, with the intervening gap of the church age.

In its early stages, this beast had been responsible legally for the crucifixion of the Lord Jesus; this beast had destroyed Jerusalem in AD 70 having slaughtered millions of Jews; this beast had persecuted the early Christians throughout the Empire – Paul had died at the hands of Nero. Later, when it tolerated the church, this was then polluted, leading to the dominion of papal Rome.

But prophetically, the feet of the dream-image were part of iron and part of clay, Dan. 2. 33, 42, 43. The ten toes were of this mixture, implying that the kingdom will be partly strong and partly broken. In any democracy of the last days, the authorities may be unable to govern properly because of rebellion by those governed; this would show the impossibility of stable government, unless drastic steps are taken to constrain the hearts of men to submit. For example, the masses will be kept in submission by the anti-Christ ensuring that men worship an image of the beast, and that none can buy or sell without possessing the mark of the beast, Rev. 13. 14-17. According to Daniel chapter 7 verse 20, the beast has ten horns. This represents the final development, an amalgamation of many nations for an objective to be explained later. But one little horn shall be in control, 'a mouth that spake very great things'; thus, 'the kings of the earth set themselves, and the rulers take counsel together, against the Lord', Ps. 2. 2. Daniel chapter 7 shows the general activity of this world emperor controlling large tracts of the world after the rapture. He 'shall speak great words against the most High', v. 25; he will prevail against the saints, who will be given into his hand for three and a half years, the great tribulation. Further details are provided in Daniel chapter 9 verses 23 to 27; see the chapter 'Daniel's Seventy Weeks'.

The First Beast of Revelation 13. We believe that this beast represents both an emperor and the Roman empire revived from the days when it was once at its height. (We must recognize that other expositors take a different point of view regarding the two beasts in chapter 13. They suggest that the first beast is the anti-Christ, and that the second beast is the anti-Spirit, forming with the dragon of chapter 12 the anti-Trinity of evil. This is very instructive, but from our point of view hardly fits in with the fourth beast of Daniel chapter 7 representing a kingdom and a political head. Here, we shall understand that the first beast in Revelation chapter 13 verses 1 to 10 represents the revival of imperial Rome and its head, while verses 11 to 17 give the second beast as the anti-Christ, called the 'false prophet' elsewhere.)

This first beast rises from the sea, standing for the nations appearing in the Old and New Testament history (called the 'great sea' or Mediterranean, Dan. 7. 3). This beast partakes of the character of the previous three beasts, Rev. 13. 2; the emperor copies what is suitable for his policy. Verse 3 presents the gap of the church age; one head was wounded to death, but is healed in these last times. It is presented as 'the beast that was, and is not, and yet is', 17. 8. This beast is worshipped by men, and he has power for 'forty and two months', called 'a time and times and the dividing of a time', Dan. 7. 25. The only men who will not worship the beast are those whose names are in the book of the slain Lamb, this writing having been there 'from the foundation of the world', Rev. 13. 8. (That this is the correct interpretation of this verse is seen from chapter 17 verse 8; the oft-suggested idea that the Lamb was slain from the foundation of the world has no support from scripture.)

The Second Beast of Revelation 13. This second beast arises from the earth, v. 11, and speaks of the anti-Christ of the future, though there have been many anti-Christs abroad in the world since John's day, 1 John 2. 18. The 'earth' would speak of the land of Israel, and one rising from it would be a religious Jew, engaging in apostate activity to eliminate the true Christ. 'Like a lamb' would be to mimic the Lord as Lamb. 'As a dragon' shows his character is copied from Satan. He is the 'man of sin' and the 'son of perdition', 2 Thess. 2. 3; that is, his destruction will be irreversible. He may be referred to as 'the wicked (one)', Isa. 11. 4; one who 'shall come in his own name', John 5. 43. In Acts chapter 12 verse 22, Herod is seen typically as the anti-Christ, 'it is the voice of a god'. The spirit of anti-Christ is seen – in lying and denying, 1 John 2. 22; 4. 3. Simon of Samaria is seen as 'the great power of God', Acts 8. 9-11, history telling us that he was a skilful magician seeking to pass for God. Anti-Christ's future sphere of influence will be the temple, where he will seek to show that he is God, 2 Thess. 2. 3, 4.

His main work will be to direct the attention and affection of men to the political beast, this being the outcome of the political aspirations of Christendom throughout the centuries. Outwardly, he may well appear respectable – he does not encourage men to worship the dragon, but the political system on earth. The first beast is not described in chapter 13 as being able to perform miracles, but the anti-Christ has the miraculous powers of darkness, 'whose coming is after the working of Satan with all power and signs and lying wonders', 2. 9. The headquarters of the first beast will be in Rome, so, to keep the interest of the people of the land directed to this beast far away, the anti-Christ arranges for an exceptional idol to be placed in the temple as a substitute for worship. It is made to speak, with power to kill the faithful. We do not believe that this is merely some technical device such as television, since this is not miraculous. Men are therefore constrained to worship the godless political system and its head, together with a replica as an idol.

The Lord had predicted that there would be false Christs and false prophets, to deceive, if possible, the very elect, Matt. 24. 24. However, this will not be possible, although the elect will be in an almost impossible position. For Revelation chapter 13 verse 16 shows that the whole spectrum of society will be satisfied, receiving an identity mark in their right hand or in their forehead, which seems to be an attempt to copy the marks sustained by the body of the Lord Jesus. The mark of the beast has solemn consequences, for such men 'shall drink of the wine of the wrath of God', 14. 10. Many will die, unable to purchase the necessities of life without the mark of the beast – these are seen coming out of the great tribulation through death, 7. 14. For safety, the Lord warned them to flee to the mountains, Matt. 24. 16.

Mystery Babylon – Religious Apostasy. Apart from the activity of these two beasts, there is a third feature that spreads its apostasy around the world. Babylon is described in chapters 17 to 18, the latter chapter giving details of its riches, with the former chapter showing how it is associated with the political beast, and how the system falls never to rise again. John sees this 'woman' in the wilderness, 17. 3, so distinct from the glowing account in chapter 18 verses 9 to 19. This latter account is seen through the eyes of men who prosper through her idolatry, but the idea of the 'wilderness' is seen through the eyes of heaven – a place of spiritual barrenness and unfruitfulness. The description of the woman, 17. 4, is one of priestly mimicry; the reader may care to compare this with the corresponding and similar items occurring in the priestly garments and activity in the Old Testament tabernacle and temple. The idolatrous religion being described is a travesty of ceremony originally introduced by God to foreshadow Christ typically. But the religion of the flesh uses it to displace Christ completely.

The interpretation of the woman is beyond doubt. The first beast carries the woman, 17. 3, who is also seen as seated on seven mountains, v. 9. The beast is imperial Rome, supporting, both now and in the future, papal Rome, the city being known as the city of the seven hills. This support has existed over the centuries, and will blossom out in absolute defiance against God in this future day. The whole subject is not academic; words of practical exhortation come to all believers, 'Come out of her, my people, that ye be not partakers of her sins', 18. 4.

The End of all Apostasy on Earth. The Romish system of religion will be worldwide in its embrace – she 'reigneth over the kings of the earth', 17. 18; she 'sitteth upon many waters', v. 1; 'the inhabitants of the earth have been made drunk', v. 2. The beast will be emperor over his empire, but this will not cover the whole earth. Originally, the beast supports mystery Babylon, since they both have a common aim, to eliminate Christ in the testimony of His elect on earth. But the time will come when the beast will seek complete world dominion, and this will mean a worldwide conflict undertaken between massive armies of the beast and of the nations, gathered for this purpose at 'a place called in the Hebrew tongue Armageddon', 16. 16, a valley in the Middle East. The ultimate motivation for this gathering of armies is the dragon, 16. 13-14, influencing 'the kings of the earth and of the whole world'. One prior difficulty in overcoming these other nations is the common bond connecting them all, namely the bond exerted by Babylon in its widespread religious network. Consequently, the beast will propose to eliminate Babylon first. To do this, the emperor will require outside help, and to this end gains the co-operation of ten kings, who become unified with the beast and of 'one mind', giving their power and strength to the beast, 17. 12, 13. For 'one hour' they present a common front, possessing sufficient strength to overcome the woman throughout the world. 'These shall hate the whore . . . and shall. . . burn her with fire'; thus will be fulfilled the cry, 'Babylon is fallen'.[17] In spite of the policies of men, the will of God for the fall of apostate Babylon is behind this activity of the beast; 'God hath put in their hearts to fulfil his will', 17. 17; 'strong is the Lord God who judgeth her', 18. 8. By this means, the religious structures throughout the world will be destroyed, and the mourning of men will be great.

With this success, the beast and the ten kings now embark on their set task of eliminating the armies of the nations at Armageddon; 'the kings of the earth and of the whole world' are brought in, 16. 14. In the heat of the battle, the Lord comes forth from heaven with power and great glory in order to eliminate from His kingdom all that offends.[18] The warring factions will see the Lord in glory, and, for the first time, will take to themselves the opportunity of fighting against Him directly, rather than with His people as previously. Their weapons (of a sophisticated, ultra-modern type) will be turned upon Him instead; 'these shall make war with the Lamb', 17. 14. Of course, the Lamb will

---

[17] See: Rev. 17. 16; 18. 2; 14. 8.
[18] Dan. 7. 13; Matt. 24. 30; Rev. 19. 11.

overcome them. The armies from heaven with the Lord will not take part in the battle. The beast and the false prophet are cast directly into the lake of fire, 19. 20, without passing through the usual channels of death and Hades. The rest of the armies are slain with the sword – the word of God – proceeding out of His mouth, v. 21, to await their final judgement at the great white throne. By this means, apostasy in its political and religious forms are clean swept from the earth, not through the preaching of the gospel, but through a swift eliminating judgement.

The Lord's Coming in Glory - J. HEADING

The movements of the Lord have been largely unknown to mankind in general. His birth was revealed only to a few, but then made known by the shepherds, Luke 2. 17, 18. His resurrection was manifest only to the few, 'openly, not to all the people, but unto witnesses chosen before of God', Acts 10. 41. The coming of the Spirit was appreciated only by those in the upper room, while the world outside accused the apostles of being drunk, 2. 13. At the rapture, when the Lord comes in the air for His own people forming the final testimony of the church on earth, He will only be seen by believers as they are caught up to be with Him, these constituting the 'few' that find life, Matt. 7. 14.

How this contrasts with the Lord's crucifixion, when the heathen, the people, the kings and the rulers took counsel against the Lord's anointed, Ps. 2. 1, 2. On the cross He was made to be the spectacle of the speakers of Hebrew, Greek, and Latin, the masses enjoying the cruelty and infamy of their leaders in crucifying the Lord of glory. And secondly, by way of contrast is the event when the Lord comes in power and great glory, when 'every eye shall see him', Rev. 1. 7.

The Lord's coming in glory will change the whole character of the world. The Lord's birth changed but little of the world's ways; neither did His death and resurrection. These provided the means of salvation and of escape from the moral pollutions of the world, but the world remained the same in darkness and unbelief. When the Lord comes for His church, the only change in world affairs will be brought about by the removal of both the salt of the earth, and the restraining One, 2 Thess. 2. 6, 7, thus allowing the apostasy of men to blossom forth in the fullness of unbelief. But when the Lord comes in glory, this will be the great moment of divine intervention into the affairs of the world; it will be impossible for men to remain in ignorance of the event, and it will be impossible for them to avoid the consequence, whether in judgement or in blessing.

The two great events the most referred to throughout the scriptures are (1) the Lord's death, and (2) His return in glory. The humiliation of the Lord in death will be reversed by His vindication in glory. No wonder, then, that these two events received so much attention from prophet and psalmist, from evangelist and apostle, from the lips of the Lord Himself and the inspiring power of the Holy Spirit in His servants. The looked-for utopia of the Old Testament was not the then- future preaching of the gospel, but the coming of Messiah in power and glory to establish His kingdom in righteousness. We shall now consider many of these references, so that readers can appreciate the widespread distribution of this aspect of prophecy throughout scripture.

'The Redeemer shall come to Zion', was God's promise through Isaiah, Isa. 59. 20. This will be accomplished when all nations are gathered together to battle, when the Lord shall go forth and fight against those nations; at that time 'his feet shall stand in that day upon the mount of Olives', Zech. 14. 1-4. This takes place at the destruction of the fourth beast of Daniel chapter 7; 'one like the Son of man came with the clouds of heaven . . . and there was given him dominion, and glory, and a kingdom', Dan. 7. 13. There will be more than a battle; 'the Lord, whom ye seek, shall suddenly come to his temple, even the messenger of the covenant', Mal. 3. 1, when the Sun of righteousness arises with healing in His wings, 4. 2. The pathway from Olivet to the temple is described in Ezekiel chapter 43 verse 4, 'the glory of the Lord came into the house by way of the gate whose prospect is toward the east'. The Lord is seated at present on the right hand of Jehovah, until this day of display and glory when His enemies will be made His footstool, when He shall rule in their midst, and when His people will be willing in the day of His power, Ps. 110. 1-3.

In the New Testament, references are abundant, both in the Lord's teaching and in the subsequent writings of the apostles. The Lord promised some of His apostles that they would not taste of death 'till they see the Son of man coming in his kingdom', Matt. 16. 28, having just spoken of the time when 'the Son of man shall come in the glory of his father with his angels', v. 27. It is 'the kingdom of God come with power', Mark 9. 1. Six days later, the Lord was transfigured before them. Some assert that the Lord's transfiguration was a preview of Pentecost, but since the Lord was in heaven then, the movement being that of the Spirit, Acts 2. 33, we cannot follow this argument. We believe that the apostles' gaze was taken into the future (as was John's in the book of Revelation), enabling them to see the Lord actually in glory in His kingdom. His face shone as the sun, and His raiment was white as the light, Matt. 17. 2; His raiment 'became shining, exceeding white as snow', Mark 9. 3. His face 'was altered, and his raiment was white and glistering', Luke 9. 29, a description evidently that almost defied description.

Later, with the temple forecast as desolate, the Lord would no longer engage in public work, which He concluded with the words, 'Ye shall not see me henceforth, till ye shall say, Blessed is he that cometh in the name of the Lord'.[19] In other words, the Lord entering into Jerusalem as King was but a foretaste of that future day when He shall take control of the city of the great King. In parabolic form, too, the Lord Jesus made mention of that time; the kingdom would not appear until the servants with the pounds had put them to use – 'it came to pass, that when he was returned, having received the kingdom', Luke 19. 15. The great apocalyptic sections of the Lord's teaching contain many references to His coming in glory. All tribes of the earth shall mourn when they see the sign of the Son of man in heaven; they 'shall see the Son of man coming in the clouds of heaven with power and great glory'; with the sound of a trumpet, the angels will gather the elect from one end of heaven to the other, Matt. 24. 30, 31. Mark chapter 13 verses 26 and 27 contains the same thoughts. In Luke, the discourse appears to be split into two portions. In the first, the shining of the lightning from one part of heaven to the other is likened to 'the Son of man . . . in his day', Luke 17. 24, but in chapter 21 verse 27 the Lord said, 'then shall they see the Son of man coming in a cloud with power and great glory'. The parable of the sheep and goats will be enacted in reality at that time, 'When the Son of man shall come in his glory, and all the holy angels with him, then shall he sit upon the throne of his glory', Matt. 25. 31. Perhaps the most remarkable reference to this event occurred when the Lord answered

[19] See: Matt. 23. 39; 21. 9; Mark 11. 9, 10; Luke 13. 35; 19. 38.

the high priest at His trial, 'Hereafter shall ye see the Son of man sitting on the right hand of power, and coming in the clouds of heaven', 26. 64; Mark 14. 62. His future vindication before men was in His mind as He entered upon the sufferings of the cross.
Before His ascension, the disciples were interested in the restored kingdom, but the two men from heaven relegated this to the unknown future, when the Lord 'shall so come in like manner', Acts 1. 6, 11. Paul often wrote of this event. The day of the Lord coming as a thief in the night would bring to the wicked sudden destruction instead of peace, 1 Thess. 5. 2, 3; at that time the man of sin will be in control, 'whom the Lord shall consume with the spirit of his mouth, and shall destroy with the brightness of his coming', 2 Thess. 2. 8. Then He shall be revealed from heaven 'in flaming fire taking vengeance on them that know not God', 1. 7, 8. Peter recalled the 'power and coming of our Lord Jesus Christ', 2 Pet. 1. 16, when He shall come with ten thousand of His saints 'to execute judgement upon all', Jude 14, 15.

The book of Revelation provides the greatest and final description. Every eye shall see Him when He comes with clouds, 1. 7; believers will then sit down with Him in His own throne, 3. 21, when they shall be given power over the nations, 2. 27. Events move towards this coming in glory in three distinct sections. Chapters 6 to 11, dealing essentially with moral and social apostasy, lead to His coming, 11. 15-18, where the One who is, was and is to come, takes His great power and reigns. Chapters 12 to 14, dealing with political apostasy, lead up to His coming, 14. 14-20; here He is seen as the Son of man upon a cloud, reaping the harvest of the earth which we judge to be His people on earth at that time, while an angel is seen as reaping the vine of the earth unto judgement. Finally, chapters 15 to 19, dealing with religious apostasy, show the beast eliminating religious Babylon with the help of his ten confederates, 17. 16. After that, the beast, seeking world dominion, becomes interlocked with all other nations at the battle of Armageddon, 16. 16. In the midst of the battle, the Lord comes in glory; the warring factions seek to fight against Him, 17. 14, but the triumph of the King of kings and Lord of lords is described in chapter 19 verses 11 to 21, when all opposition is put down, and the triumph and vindication of the Son of man and Son of God is complete. Further details are given in the previous chapter.

The Millennium - G. B. Fyfe

A broad survey of the field of human affairs makes it increasingly evident that the world of men is careering onwards out of control. Massive problems in the moral, political, social and ecological spheres, confront the statesmen and rulers of the nations, and are so varied and complex in nature that no adequate or lasting solution can be found for them. The pace of change has accelerated with such rapidity that society can scarcely cope with all the pressures imposed by modern life. 'Where will it all end?' the man in the street is constantly asking. To this question the Christian can give no hopeful answer – save, of course, that contained in the good news of God which enables us to get ready for the next world, 'the world to come', Heb. 2. 5. For, as far as this present world-system is concerned, things are bound to get worse and to deteriorate faster, until the flashpoint is reached, and the divine judgement explodes with unparalleled tribulation upon those who have turned their backs on the Almighty God and rejected His Son as Saviour.

The great need of the world today is for the emergence of a superman – a strong, wise and competent overlord – a king among kings, a lord of lords. But where can such be found among the ranks of men throughout the nations of earth? The Bible alone has the answer – the Man of Calvary, now glorified in heaven, but soon also to be glorified on earth where, at His first advent, He was thrust out, hated and rejected, by way of a Roman gibbet. But this same Jesus shall come again! Not, however, as a Saviour in lowly guise, but in all the panoply of kingly power and majesty. As such, He will set up His universal kingdom and usher in the golden age, the utopian era of which poets and philosophers have dreamed, but which men have abandoned as an unattainable ideal. Yet it is most surely coming! In fulfilment of the counsels of God, it will arrive, not according to the concepts of men. The divine decree runs, 'Yet have I set my king upon my holy hill of Zion', Ps. 2. 6. Nothing short of this apocalyptic event will bring stability, justice and peace to a distraught world. Thus man's chequered history on this present earth will be brought to a close by the righteous reign of God's King, the Son of man, who shall bring one thousand years of uninterrupted peace, based on righteousness, to every part of His great world kingdom.

'But why is there a need for a millennium?' some ask. Why does God not wind up man's evil history in catastrophic judgement – destroy the planet by a gigantic nuclear explosion, or the like, wiping out forever this scene of iniquity and corruption? There are at least three logical and scriptural reasons why the millennium is a 'must':

Reason 1. Having crowned the ascended Christ with glory and honour in heaven, God will also glorify Him on earth, the scene of His humiliation and rejection. The matter cannot rest where it does at present. Highest honours and universal acclaim will be afforded the King of kings when He appears physically and visibly in this world again.

Reason 2. Again, God must demonstrate that He has a Man competent to rule the world in righteousness, and to maintain peace throughout His realm for a period of one thousand years, a state of affairs never before achieved throughout human history. So far, every form of human government has failed hopelessly. Neither king David nor his successors could accomplish peace with righteousness. The imperial rulers of the Gentile empires were not equal to the task. In contrast, God's King, the Son of man, will be an unqualified success.

Reason 3. Then there are certain unconditional promises that God has given His earthly people Israel, and which are still outstanding. All those will be fully implemented during this closing period of mankind's history, the millennium, Gen. 12. 3; 13. 15; 15. 18.

And so it is both a moral and a political imperative that, before time is replaced by eternity, the final phase in God's ways with men on earth should be a golden age ensured by the righteous reign of His all-conquering Son.

Now, it is important to recognize that this 'utopia' will not be brought about by worldwide evangelism, as some Christians maintain. Nowhere does the scripture teach that the spread of the gospel of God's grace will eventually effect the universal conversion of the human race; for although it is the desire of God that all men should be saved, all men, alas, are not willing to accept His Son as Saviour. No, the kingdom will be ushered in by the direct and personal intervention in world affairs by Christ in power and judgement. The Bible, indeed, presents a triple type of Christ in His kingly activities. At His advent to Olivet, His first task will be to destroy the enemies of God and deliver the remnant members of His Jewish people. This He will do in the character of David, as the **warrior** king, foreshadowed in Psalm 45 verses 3-5. Then, in Solomonic role, as the **wise** king, He will establish His kingdom in righteousness, and peace will ensue, Ps. 72. Melchizedek, the priest-king, portrays a further aspect of Christ's millennial operations, envisaged in Psalm 110. As the **welfare** king He will spread, through Israel's nation, then back in Immanuel's land, blessing and joy to the world's inhabitants.

The Administration. As to the administration of the King of kings, it will be a two-tier system of government. In the upper heavenly tier the Christians of the church era, and the saints of Old Testament times, together with the martyred Jewish saints of the tribulation period, will all share with Christ the administration of His vast dominion.[20] Not that **we** shall ever take up residence again on earth. Our proper and eternal environment is in the third heaven where the Father dwells. But the heavenly saints will, no doubt, on special state occasions, visit the earth with Christ, as at His majestic appearing. Indeed, it is very questionable if Christ will Himself be continuously in occupation in the earthly capital of Jerusalem. It would appear from Ezekiel chapter 44 verses 1-3 and chapter 45 verses 7-25 that the great King will be represented on the earth level of His empire by a Prince in Israel during most of the millennium.

On the lower tier of this regime of righteousness a restored Israel will function, then a unified twelve-tribed nation under the sway of her Messiah-King. Israel's millennial portion is an earthly one. She shall fully inherit the land of Canaan to the limits of its divinely prescribed frontiers. Jeremiah chapter 32 verses 40-41 applies. All Israel will be saved in that day, Rom. 11. 26, and will become the foremost of the nations. Jerusalem, the chosen city of Jehovah, will then be not only the geographical centre of the world, but its political and religious centre too. The saved Gentile nations, composed of the Gentiles who survive the tribulation period, will experience the blessings of the kingdom age

---

[20] Rev. 6. 9-11; 15. 2-4; 20. 4; Dan. 7. 18.

mediated to them through Israel.[21] And to the city of Jerusalem the representatives of those nations will journey annually to pay court to the King of kings and to celebrate the feast of tabernacles, Zech. 14. 16; Isa. 56. 7. Moreover, to the church, the Lamb's wife, shall the homage of earth's kings be given – that is to us Christians from whom, under the symbol of the resplendent heavenly city, poised above the millennial earth, the policies of government and the light of wisdom will emanate, to regulate all their international relationships, Rev. 21. 24.

The Creation. As for creation in general, a manifest transformation will take place when the King comes. Man by God was constituted the centre of a system of things, having been made the Creator's visible representative on this earth, and the federal head of His earthly creation. A consequential effect of this is that the entire creation suffers or rejoices in association with its ordained head, Rom. 8. 19-22. Thus, the present groaning creation will rejoice and flourish again at the manifestation of the sons of God, when we appear with Christ in glory. The only exception to these congenial conditions will be the serpent, through whose original (and possibly most beautiful) form, the tempter seduced Eve in Eden. The curse pronounced upon it after the fall of man will not be revoked, Gen. 3. 14.

What of Satan himself, the arch-enemy of God and men, during the reign in righteousness? He will be placed under restraint, confined within the fathomless depth of the bottomless pit (the abyss) throughout the thousand years of the kingdom age. This will be the place of interim confinement for him and his satellites, Gehenna, the lake of fire, being their eternal portion and place of doom. During the millennium, therefore, Satan will not be free to roam at large in the realm of men. The expulsion from the earth of his malevolent influence will be a noteworthy feature of this ultimate 'utopia', Rev. 20. 1-3.

Hasten then the day, glorious Lord, when Thou shalt ride forth in majesty, the mighty Conqueror of a ruined and rebellious world – and claim the kingdom for Thine own!

---

[21] Isa. 40. 5; Joel 2. 28; Zech. 8. 20-23.

The Great White Throne - B. Osborne

Though accepted by many, the teaching of a general judgement for all is absent from the word of God. In fact, the scriptures refer to more than one judgement which differ one from another as to the place, time, subjects and result. There are judgements which concern the believer, a judgement of living nations, and the final assize of unregenerate dead at the Great White Throne.

The Judgement of the Believer. This is threefold:

As a Sinner – in the Past.[22] Sins have been judged at the cross, and the result was death for Christ and justification for the believer, 2 Cor. 5. 21. For the believer judgement in the penal sense is past. His judgement as a sinner fell on his spotless substitute, when He stood in the sinner's place, bearing his sins upon Calvary. The holy Victim 'led as a lamb to the slaughter' presented Himself to God as a willing sacrifice, accepted all the responsibilities of His people, and bowed His sacred head to the stroke of divine wrath which sinners deserved. In Christ's death God reckons the believer to have died. His judgement has been borne by his substitute, and he, seeing things as God sees them, can say 'I have been crucified with Christ', Gal. 2. 20 RV. He is therefore judicially dead already. Judgement has been executed; it cannot be repeated.

As a Son – in the Present.[23] The believer no longer stands before God as a sinner awaiting judgement; he is now a child in the Father's family, 1 John 3. 2. He is within the circle of the rule and discipline of the Father, Heb. 12. 6-9. If he sins, communion is broken with the Father, and he must confess and forsake his sin for communion to be restored, 1 John 1. 9. If, however, sin remains unconfessed, he is disciplined of God. All chastening has its purpose. Times of affliction lead to heart searching, and the believer becomes increasingly aware of sins of which he had hardly thought at all. Furthermore, special discipline is the evidence of special love. It is part of a father's training, and one of the marks of sonship, Heb. 12. 5, 6.

---

[22] See: Rom. 5. 8; 1 Pet. 2. 24; Gal. 2. 20; John 5. 24.
[23] See: Heb. 12. 6-9; Jas. 5. 11; 1 Cor. 11. 31, 32.

As a Servant – in the Future.[24] The judgement seat of Christ as to time takes place in the interval between the rapture and the appearing. As no reference is made in the scriptures concerned,[25] it would seem that the judgement seat is an event of which the world knows little, and in which it takes no part, but is entirely a dealing of the Lord with His people; cp. 2 Tim. 1. 12, 18; 4. 8. The question of the believer's guilt as a sinner, and his evil state of nature as a child of Adam, have been settled at the cross; the question here is one of the believer's faithfulness and work, cp. 1 Cor. 3. 11-15. Rewards given here will differ according to the measure of faithfulness; cp. Luke 19. 16-19. Some will suffer loss; cp. 1 Cor. 3. 15. Their work was abundant in quantity, but sadly deficient in quality; 'every man shall receive his own reward according to his own labour', 3. 8.

The Judgement of the Living Nations. This judgement is quite distinct from the judgement seat of Christ. It occurs at the appearing of Christ in glory.[26] It will be held, not at the end of the millennial kingdom, but at its beginning.[27] The place of judgement will be in the Valley of Jehoshaphat; cp. Joel 3. 1, 2, 12-14. None but the living nations will be judged, those surviving from the catastrophic judgements which follow the opening of the seals, Rev. 6. All of them are alive, and none has passed through death. During the great tribulation a Jewish remnant will turn to Christ as their Messiah, and they will preach the gospel of the kingdom; cp. Matt. 24. 14. Some Gentiles will receive the preachers with hospitality, believing and accepting the message. Others will persecute them and refuse it. So the judgement will be on the basis of reception or rejection of the message preached, and thus of the messengers themselves, those godly Jews, to whom the Lord refers as 'my brethren'. Had the Lord been in their place, they would have treated Him accordingly. The decision of the Judge on those now rejected by Him will be eternal punishment, and for those 'blessed of my Father', entry into the earthly kingdom of glory; contrast Matt. 25. 34, 46.

The Judgement of the Great White Throne. The final settlement of

---

[24] See: 2 Cor. 5. 9, 10; Rom. 14. 10.

[25] 1 Cor. 1. 8; 2 Cor. 1. 14; Phil. 2. 16; 1 Thess. 2. 19; 3. 13.

[26] Cp. Matt. 25. 31, 32; 13. 40, 41.

[27] Cp. Rev. 20. 7-11; Matt. 25. 31.

God's controversy with fallen man will be at the judgement of the Great White Throne; cp. Rev. 20. 11-15. The judgement described here forms the conclusion of all God's ways with man. The kingdom of Christ on earth has been brought to a close; all enemies have been put under His feet; the devil will have received his final doom, and there remain only the wicked and impenitent dead to be dealt with, before the introduction of the new heavens and the new earth. The millennium opens and closes with an act of sessional judgement, and in both the Lord in person is the Judge. It must be pointed out that the scene here is not the same as that found in Matthew chapter 25, though many confuse them. That scene is **before** the millennium, and has to do with living nations; this is **at the close of the** millennium, and has to do with the dead. No resurrection is mentioned in Matthew chapter 25, but a resurrection is mentioned here. Revelation chapter 20 verse 5 refers to the 'first resurrection' before the millennium, and what is seen in the section commencing with verse 11 are those who comprise the second resurrection, that of the unjust, **after** the millennium. The scene in Matthew concerned good and bad; here it concerns the wicked dead only. There they were treated according to their treatment of Christ's 'brethren'; here it is a solemn scrutiny of what is written in the books. There the scene is on the earth; here the heaven and earth have fled away. In Matthew there were no books; here there are books opened. There three classes appear – sheep, goats, brethren; here, but one, the dead.

John sees 'a great white throne', v. 11. It is 'great' because of the majesty of the Judge who sits on it, because of His infinite power, and because of the eternal issues involved in its decisions. It is 'white' on account of its purity and holiness, and of the perfect righteousness of its judgements. No mercy or grace will be shown here, but inflexible, invincible justice. The throne in chapter 4 had a rainbow about it to indicate the fulfilment of covenant blessings and promises, v. 3. This throne now is naked, for it has no hopes to offer, no covenant grace to fulfil. No altar is seen before it, as in Isaiah's vision of the throne, nor any blood-sprinkled mercy seat. Nothing is seen here save a naked throne of unsullied purity, the claims of which are to be now finally and eternally vindicated. There can be no appeal from this court; its verdict is final.

The Judge. There can be no doubt as to who sits upon the throne. He is the Son to whom the Father 'hath committed all judgement', and to whom He has given authority to execute it because 'he is the Son of man'; cp. John 5. 22, 27; Acts 17. 31. He is truly man, and truly God, and to Him the secrets of men's hearts are open. Once His face was marred more than any man's, but full of tender mercy and compassion. Now, so terrible is that face of infinite righteousness that 'the earth and the heaven fled away'. The earth has been polluted by the iniquity of man, Isa. 24. 5, and the heavens have been contaminated by the defection of fallen angels, and 'are not clean in his sight', Job 15. 15. The earth must flee on account of the sins of men, and its defilement with the blood of God's Son. The heavens must flee because of the sins of spirits, and the wickedness of the world rulers in heavenly places, Eph. 6. 12; 2. 2. In what manner the earth and the heaven disappear we learn elsewhere; cp. 2 Pet. 3. 11-12. In the presence, then, of Him who is 'of purer eyes than to behold evil, and canst not look on iniquity', Hab. 1. 13, they flee away.

The Accused who stand there are 'the dead', v. 12. Not one spiritually alive soul shall ever be judged there. No saved person will be before that throne. No trumpet will be sounded for the dead, as for the sleeping saints more than a thousand years earlier. The eternal power of God will assemble them. The graves of all the wicked dead of all the centuries will be opened. Death and Hades will give up their wretched inmates. Soul and body will reunite for the great judgement. In resurrection, death will deliver up the custody of bodies, and Hades the custody of souls. There the dead will stand before the merciless gaze of Him who sits upon the throne. They have spurned His offer of grace; now an accounting of sins must be made.

The Accusers will be the opened books. Heaven keeps a record of all the deeds of men, and of all the thoughts and feelings under which they act. Millions of men have lived and died of whom the world has known nothing, but the lives they lived, their deeds, their thoughts, their tempers, stand written irrevocably in the books. Every detail is held in the divine records. But man is also writing his record in his own memory, and that record will tally with God's. Every event recorded in the books is also recorded in memory. Memory will condemn even if there were no written record. But it will corroborate the written record and condemn.

The book of life is also opened, the roll book of the regenerate in Christ Jesus. This book must needs be opened for many have loved sin, and many have lived honest and good lives who die in the belief that they have fulfilled all the requirements of virtue, but who have never been born again, have never felt the need of salvation by the propitiation of a crucified Saviour, and who have disdained to receive Christ as Saviour. Exalted they might have been in their own godlessness or goodness and morality, but not having believed in Christ, they have not life, and are not found written in the book of life. Though God is not answerable to men, yet He is careful to vindicate, even in their eyes, the rightness of all His judicial acts. Thus, here, incontrovertible proofs of the guilt of those on trial are shown from the books or works, and then, as a conclusive demonstration of their having no title to be spared, it is added that their names were not found written in the book of life. Thus every mouth will be stopped, and all will have to confess that He who sits on the throne is justified when He speaks, and clear when He judges, Ps. 51. 4.

Judgement is given according as the works have been, the deeds of every soul while living on earth; 'according to their works' is the basis, Rev. 20. 12, 13. No flesh could be justified on such a principle, but justification is not in question here. They are 'condemned already'. The question is of the degree of doom. There is a just gradation in the sorrows of the lost, as well as in the rewards of the righteous. The measure of the punishment will be adjusted to their works. There are degrees of responsibility, and there are degrees in punishment.[28] Privilege will increase responsibility, and when neglected or abused, deepens guilt. Sodom and Gomorrah will have a more tolerable cup than the cities of Bethsaida and Capernaum. Penalty will be in proportion to guilt.

Death and Hades were cast into the lake of fire. Since sin would no longer mar creation, death would never again intervene and, in guarantee thereof, death and its companion, Hades, were cast into the place of eternal wrath.

---

[28] Cp. Luke 12. 44-48; Matt. 10. 15; 11. 20-24; 12. 41, 42.

When the saints are raised, death is swallowed up for them in victory, 1 Cor. 15. 51-54, but here there is no victory, for the hitherto prisoners of death receive the same sentence as death itself, both being condemned to the same final doom. The last enemy, death, is thus destroyed. In contrast to the first death, soul and body are no longer separated, because the lost soul and resurrected body stand before the throne. But there is a separation – the eternal separation from God. Physical death is not the final sentence on man, for 'it is appointed unto men once to die, but after this the judgment', Heb. 9. 27. The death pronounced as the penalty of Adam's transgression meant far more than the death of the body. The phrase 'dead in trespasses and sins', Eph. 2. 1, indicates its meaning as separation of the soul from God, together with the state of the soul as being without a single movement of life towards God.

In the second death, death will keep its meaning – the absolute separation of the soul from God, its total exclusion from the source of all light and life. That second death will consist in the unending judgement of the lake of fire, Rev. 20. 15, and this confirms the doctrine that the first, or temporal, death is not cessation of existence, or extinction of being. The beast and the false prophet are cast into the lake of fire at the commencement of the millennial reign of Christ, and they are still there a thousand years later when Satan is cast therein; cp. Rev. 19. 20; 20. 10.

Is a place or a condition intended by the term 'lake of fire'? Everything in the context seems to indicate a place. Finite beings, because they have bodies, are limited to a particular place. But is condition excluded? The fire is indicative of the holiness of God as applied in judgement. Here is a picture of God's eternal judgement, according to the standard of His own unchangeable holiness, as visited upon those who refused His grace, rebelled against His authority, and chose death rather than life.

Eternal Punishment - E. W. Rogers

In writing upon such a solemn theme as eternal punishment, one needs ever to bear in mind the necessity of adhering as closely as possible to the very words of scripture. The actual two words are found in Matthew chapter 25 verse 46 RV, though we are sometimes told that they do not mean what they seem to denote. But though space is not available to give detailed proof, it is beyond effective contradiction that the English word 'eternal' correctly conveys the thought of the Greek original. You can test this by examining all its usages in the scriptures, and note how any limited sense of the word is totally inappropriate when applied to God, life, and so on. Do not allow anyone to deceive you by beclouding your mind with such phrases as 'unto the age' or 'unto the age of the ages'. Be satisfied with the word '**eternal**' and rest assured that scholars who have no unworthy axe to grind support this sense.

As to the word '**punishment**' the actual word employed here denotes a process; man never ceases to be, even though physical death ensues.

The world abounds with errors, but if you will carefully consider the record of the rich man and Lazarus, Luke 16. 19-31, words uttered by the Lord Jesus, you will see how that He refutes many false ideas. He denies **annihilation**, for neither the rich man nor the beggar was annihilated. He denies **sleep of the soul**, for each was conscious and aware of his state immediately after death. He denies **universalism**, for one was saved and one was lost; not all will be saved. He denies a **second chance**, for the eternal issues of each were settled in life and the great gulf fixed precluded their being altered after death. He denies **spiritism**, for no one who has gone into death can come back and speak to the living on earth, not even Lazarus could go to the rich man's brethren. He denies **non-eternity** of punishment, for there is no indication whatever that the state of each ceases at any time. He denies **purgatory**, for the punitive condition after death is not remedial. Do not then be misled by deceivers, but allow the words of the Lord Jesus to be your sheet anchor.

It is remarkable that the most solemn passages of scripture touching this matter were uttered by the Lord Jesus. Turn to Mark chapter 9 verse 44, and observe 'Where their worm dieth not, and the fire is not quenched'. This was no rhetorical statement, it was the affirmation of solemn facts. The worm does not die – personality never ceases to be; 'the fire is not quenched' – the instrument of punishment never becomes inoperative.

We must not imagine God to be vindictive and to delight in torture. He is just, and having offered a way of escape, what can He do if that way be rejected? His judgement will be both according to truth and according to a person's works. For some it will be **more tolerable** than for others, Matt. 11. 22, 24. Some will be beaten with **few** stripes and some with **many**. Every factor will be taken into account, such as the times when one lived, the opportunities afforded, environment, parenthood, and all else, and the righteous Judge will apportion the punishment accordingly.

It has been thought by some that a few years' sin do not merit a whole eternity of punishment, but in the nature of the case it cannot be otherwise. Even in life, often a few moments of sin reap a lifetime harvest of disease, for as a man sows so must he also reap. Unlike the beast, man is an eternally existent creature. He must be somewhere for the whole eternity of his being. Added to which, sin is an offence against the infinitely holy God. Its gravity cannot be computed. The supreme dignity of the One against whom man has sinned makes his wrongdoing **infinite in gravity**.

Turn to Revelation chapter 20 and read from verse 11 to the end of the chapter. Here is recounted in symbolic language the last great assize when the human race (other than those who have been gathered in safely beforehand) appears before the Lord Jesus Christ as God's appointed Judge. None escapes whether they have died on land or sea; all will be raised and their souls will be re-united to their bodies, thus to be cast into *gehenna,* which corresponds to the 'lake of fire'.

They are not dealt with as a class but each one is personally brought to judgement. The great test then will be, is their name in the book of life? If not, there will be no escaping the eternally settled state of judgement which is what the phrase 'lake of fire' suggests.

The heartless way that this subject has often been referred to in preaching has resulted in its total omission by others; thereby a serious loss has been incurred. We are duty bound to declare the whole counsel of God, but it is well to follow the manner in which the early evangelists spoke of the subject. Their words were unmistakeable in their significance but were wisely chosen; we should do likewise.[29]

---

[29] Read Acts 10. 42; 13. 40; 17. 31.

The reader should open his Bible and ponder the given references. They will do far more in giving him the mind of God than any article can.[30] It is to be feared that oftentimes when articles such as this are read, the scriptures are never consulted. For the present subject it is all-important that this should not happen. You should seriously weigh every passage and if you desire to know how you can be assured of escaping that judgement refer also to other passages. For example, 'shall not come into judgment', John 5. 24; 'there is no judgment', Rom. 8. 1; 'boldness in the day of judgment, for as he is so are we in this world', 1 John 4. 17.

It is no marvel that the devil should seek to deceive the unsaved into believing there is no such thing as eternal punishment, and to attempt to unsettle those that are saved by implanting doubts as to their eternal security. The way to avoid each danger is by simple acceptance of the plain written word of God. If you allow one scripture to shed its light upon another you will be preserved from many an error. For example, the word 'destruction' does not mean annihilation; it is rather the utter ruination of the soul. Similarly, the word 'perish' means ruination, and utter failure to achieve the original intention. Indeed, we use this word when we speak of an article 'having perished'. It is there, but not fit for its intended use.

But space forbids more. Beware of false translations; be content with the King James Version or the Revised Version, and for the examination of Bible words you cannot have anything simpler, even if not comprehensive, than W. E. VINE'S *Expository Dictionary of New Testament Words.*

The Eternal State - G. B. FYFE

Whereas many precise details are given in scripture regarding millennial conditions, little of a definite nature is said about the eternal state. Only the general features of the new heavens and new earth are indicated in the word of God. This is probably because the conditions governing life on the new earth and, even more so, life in heaven itself,

---

[30] See: Matt. 25. 46; Heb. 6. 2; Matt. 18. 8; 2 Thess. 1. 9; Rev. 14. 11; Rev. 20. 11; Mark 9. 43-50; Matt. 10. 28.

will be so different from what is experienced now that our finite minds have not the capacity to comprehend them, nor has human language the power to describe in detail the wondrous things God has in store for His redeemed in the timeless state.

There are only some four direct references in the Bible to the eternal state.[31] A mention of the creation of the new heavens and new earth, Isa. 65. 17; 66. 22, appears to have reference to the millennial era, and not to the timeless state. Concerning this, it has been said that 'the regeneration of the earth in the millennium is to the renovation of the earth in the eternal state, what the regeneration of the sinner now is to the redemption of the body of the believer at the rapture'; and this would seem to express well the doctrinal equation. For the practice of sin, although kept in check, will not be eliminated from the earth during the millennium; but the principle of sin in all its forms of manifestation will be totally excluded from the new heavens and new earth in the eternal state. It must be borne in mind, however, that all the heavenly saints will have reached the perfect state, morally and physically, a thousand years before the earth dwellers arrive at this ideal condition. Everything then, universally, will be in eternal harmony with God's own nature. What a prospect for all those who shall enter the perfect conditions of the eternal state, whether in the zone of earth or in the sphere of heaven!

We thus learn that different companies of people will be the subjects of fundamental change to suit them for the eternal environments which, in accordance with the counsels of God, they are destined to occupy. And not only **people** but **places** also – various regions of the universe will undergo radical changes to fit them for the fixed conditions which will remain forever.

Peter in chapter 3 of his second Epistle alludes to the globe of this earth in three clearly defined periods of its history. He speaks of (1) the **primeval** or **prehistoric** earth, (2) of the **present** or **postdiluvian** earth, and (3) of the **prophetic** or **prospective** earth. The last of these will be the product of this readjustment for the eternal state. This preparation will not be effected by a gradual process, but by cataclysmic

---

[31] 2 Pet. 3. 13; 1 Cor. 15. 28; Rev. 21. 1-4; Eph. 3. 21.

change in which both the present heavens and earth will be involved. It is described as the 'dissolution' (lit. the loosing) of the heavens and the earth. The terms used by Peter suggest a terrific explosion and extreme heat – enveloping fire which will destroy the earth's surface and all the works that man has brought into being during the centuries of human existence on the planet. The matter of which the earth and stellar heavens is formed will not be annihilated, but it will be thoroughly purged by fire of every trace of sin and corruption. The word 'melt' in verse 12 means 'to liquefy', and that in verse 10 denotes 'to loose', a loosing from the servitude imposed by sin's vile influence. The 'passing away' of the heavens does not imply that they will cease to exist, but rather that their present form will be changed by their passing into a different form of existence.

This preparatory work having been accomplished by divine power, the new conditions of the heavens and the earth will be brought into being to subsist sinlessly and timelessly, their every feature in harmony with the moral nature of the Almighty God. A glimpse into eternity is given us in Revelation chapter 21 verses 1-8. There the never-ending conditions of both saved and lost are tersely and vividly described.

Now, John sees **three** new things after time and the present cosmos have ceased to be. These are: (1) the new **heavens**; (2) the new **earth**; and (3) the new **Jerusalem**, Rev. 21. 1-2. The term 'new' used here does not signify that these were different entities altogether, but indicates that the same heavens and earth will then be characterized by completely different conditions – fixed and fadeless forever!

We shall conclude by summarizing simply the features revealed in scripture which relate to the eternal state:

(a) **Righteousness** shall **dwell** in the new heavens and new earth. In this present era, **grace** reigns **through** righteousness. In the millennial world to come, **righteousness** will **reign**. But in the timeless state, the absolute will be achieved, for then righteousness will dwell in an undisturbed universe of bliss, 2 Pet. 3. 13.

(b) **God shall be 'all in all'**, 1 Cor. 15. 28. All things shall be **of** God, and God shall be **in** all things – 'God in all, and all in God'. This is a

profound expression of perfection. There is nothing beyond this. Here we reach the last horizon!

(c) **God will dwell with men and be their God**. Surely this concept takes us back to the divine original, a simple and vital relationship between a Creator-God and His creature man who shall inhabit the new earth. Does this imply the total abolition of the divisive system of nations in the eternal state? It would appear so. Even Israel as a nation will continue no longer than the end of the kingdom age, its members being thereafter merged with all men spiritually and physically suited to the conditions of the reformed earth, with separating seas and national frontiers all gone forever.

(d) But here is **a notable phenomenon**, indeed a thrilling truth – for us at least – the bright conclusion of the eternal plan. The church, the bride of Christ, shall never be divorced or disbanded. The Lamb's wife shall never lose her identity. The church is by no means a temporary expedient in the purposes of God. It has a glorious future and a wonderful destiny before it. That the church is the subject of God's eternal counsels of love is made plain in Ephesians chapter 3: unto Him be glory in the church 'in Christ Jesus unto all generations of the age of ages', Eph. 3. 21 JND. Therefore, throughout the eternal ages, the church, embracing every Christian from its birth at Pentecost until its translation at the rapture, will be the showpiece for the display of God's glory to an admiring universe.

In the physical realm the closest form of organic unity is probably that of the head (the brain) and the body; and the mystical body of Christ (the church) will be eternally the fullness, the complement of her glorious Head – **closest** to Christ in spiritual union of all created intelligences.

Furthermore, the church will be the **wife of the Lamb forever** – **dearest** to Him among all the families of men and companies of angels, whether they be in the new earth or in the new heavens.

Such is our glorious and eternal future, for this is the goal of God's infinite grace!

Index